Fry The Brain
The Art of Urban Sniping and its Role in Modern Guerrilla Warfare

When the Serbs failed in their attempt to overrun the neighborhood, they switched tactics to what they called "Fry the Brain," a terror campaign meant to drive residents out. The Serbs shelled the area day and night, ringing the neighborhood with snipers, who killed everything they saw, especially women and children. They thought that killing kids would make the women, and ultimately the men, take flight.

- John Falk, describing the Serbs' sniper campaign against the people of Sarajevo in *Hello to all That*

Fry The Brain: The Art of Urban Sniping and its Role in Modern Guerrilla Warfare

Dedicated to the American servicemen and women who fight their nation's wars.

Front and back cover photo by www.dragunov.net

Countryside, VA

Published in the United States of America

Author: John West

ISBN: 978-0-9714133-9-9 (10-digit: 0-9714133-9-8)

Foreword

The year was 2005. I was in Baghdad. The sun was high above and there was a slight breeze. The merciless Iraq summer had not yet arrived and the weather was still mild. Our team was approaching an Iraqi military checkpoint. We had our identification cards out and our hands exposed, showing we were not a threat. Several Iraqi soldiers stood behind a row of dirt-filled protective barriers as they inspected us. Suddenly, a small puff of earth erupted from a barrier, several inches from one of the soldiers.

"Sniper!" I called out.

"What are you talking about?" One of our teammates hadn't seen the impact of the bullet and didn't hear a thing.

"Naw, I saw it." At least our driver confirmed I wasn't crazy. Amazingly, the Iraqi soldiers remained oblivious to the danger, having missed the impact of the round, although the incoming bullet landed only inches from one of their men. Had the shooter calculated their shot just a fraction of an inch better, one of the soldiers would have been dead with a bullet in their chest.

We were in a slight dilemma. If we sped past the guards, they might open fire on us, thinking we were Al-Qaeda or a car bomb. We were trapped and had to act normal. So, we cautiously eased our vehicles through the checkpoint, hoping the sniper wouldn't take another shot. We quickly drove behind the cover of a nearby building. We got out of our cars and discretely surveyed the surrounding urban terrain. There were literally thousands of places the sniper could have fired from. And the shooter either used a sound suppressor or shot from within an enclosed space that muffled the gunshot. That's why we didn't hear anything. We had no chance of finding the sniper, who was probably gone by the time we parked. Was this the work of the infamous Baghdad Sniper called Juba? We'll never know.

We explained to the Iraqi soldiers that they were just shot at by a sniper, but they didn't believe us. We advised them to build a better checkpoint that screened them from potential snipers. They never did. They remained victims waiting to happen.

That was my introduction to the art of urban guerrilla sniping. The shooter displayed superior snipercraft and we had no hope of catching them in the act. I felt helpless. I also felt a little sick knowing that myself or my teammates could have had their heads blown off by an invisible marksman and we would have been powerless to stop it. That incident drove me to learn more about sniping and urban guerrilla warfare. It has taken me several years of work, but this book is my response to that day when a hidden guerrilla sniper had us in his cross hairs but missed.

From personal experience and research, it is obvious that despite the general consensus that guerrilla wars are the 'wars of the future', little is actually known about the specific methodology guerrilla organizations use to wage these wars. Experts in the field - and even the soldiers themselves – generally don't understand guerrilla warfare because they are trapped in a world dominated by conventional militaries and their conventionally minded leaders. In the arena of military thought, the mind has become a prison. Because modern armies have invested so dearly in traditional concepts of warfare, from costly aircraft carriers to the latest main battle tanks, when they encounter a situation that does not fit their inflexible paradigms, they fall short.

For example, Great Britain fought the Germans to a standstill in the trenches of World War I and then helped win World War II. While there is no questioning the prowess of the British Navy or the skill of the Royal Air Force, how did England's war machine fare in Northern Ireland against the Irish Republican Army? During The Troubles, England fought a thirty-year war against a microscopic guerrilla movement that relied on kidnappings, drive-by shootings, and ski-mask wearing snipers. This bitter war only ended in 1998 after the leader of the IRA, Gerry Adams, became a recognized, elected member of Parliament.

We can also look at the Soviet Union who wallowed in Afghanistan for a decade, from 1979 to 1989, unable to defeat a guerrilla movement of unsophisticated tribesman. Then, in 1994, Russia found itself stuck in the mean streets of Grozny, suffering severe losses from Chechen snipers. In another example, the U.S. military failed miserably after ten years of guerrilla warfare in the steaming jungles of Vietnam. Then, in 2003, almost thirty years after the last helicopter limped out of Saigon, the U.S. invaded Iraq, destroying Saddam Hussein's entire military in less than three weeks. But, as of the writing of this book, the U.S. military was still confronted by a resilient urban guerrilla movement, which displayed the most sophisticated urban sniping techniques to date.

In these examples, we see conventionally built armies fighting unconventional enemies who refuse to follow the rules. In an increasingly urbanized world, militaries must be prepared to fight in major cities occupied by millions of inhabitants. Modern armies must accept an age where limiting infrastructure damage and preventing civilian casualties is just as important as engaging the enemy in combat.

While conventional armies try to maneuver their massive forces within the tight confines of places like Belfast, Beirut, and Baghdad, the guerrilla takes a different tact. Successful guerrilla movements embrace the urban terrain, manipulating the infrastructure and population to their advantage, fighting their clumsy enemies with deception, cunning, and precision. The embodiment of this urban guerrilla warfare is the sniper, a lone individual who moves among the people. They are a fighter that uses the city to their advantage, takes their shot under the noses of their enemy, and disappears into the population. The

Sniped!

France/June 7, 1940: An assaulting German soldier falls to a knee, grabbing his leg in pain, after taking a bullet from a French sniper hidden in one of the nearby buildings.

sniper is a precision tool, a scalpel the guerrillas wield to surgically target specific individuals with absolutely no collateral damage - either structural or human.

Resistance movements of all shades and stripes have employed the guerrilla sniper, from black pajama-clad Viet Cong fighters to the ragtag Somali militias in war-torn Mogadishu. From the perspective of the guerrilla, it is only natural. What better way to bloody a superior force than with an elusive shooter who takes a single shot and then melts away as quickly as they appear? The lone shooter is the hallmark of modern urban guerrilla warfare. While the world's many resistance movements employ a variety of tactics like car bomb attacks, IED ambushes, and martyr operations, they all employ a universal weapon - the guerrilla sniper.

However, resistance movements have achieved different levels of sniping success. For instance, the German Werwolf resistance movement of World War II employed guerrilla snipers to harass allied occupation forces. However, these German guerrillas were unable to build a mass support base and therefore never successfully blended in with the civilian population. In contrast, other movements like the Irish Republican Army, The Palestinian Liberation Organization, and the Iraqi Insurgency developed effective sniper corps that survived the test of time and the scrutiny of enemy security forces.

Fry The Brain peers into this murky world of urban guerrilla sniping to understand this little known or appreciated discipline. In doing so, *Fry The Brain* strives to educate the reader on all aspects of urban guerrilla sniping,

5

from training and equipping the guerrilla sniper to actual employment in the world's recent urban battle zones. The trained urban guerrilla sniper can be a formidable foe that exacts a fearsome toll from the unprepared. Truly, one must understand their enemy in order to defeat them. Taken in that vein, one could say this work, ultimately, is a counter-sniper manual.

However, *Fry The Brain* is more than that. While *Fry The Brain* discusses in extreme detail how guerrilla snipers operate, the basic methodology they employ is the same as used by other elements of a guerrilla movement, like Improvised Explosive Device (IED) and suicide bomber cells. If one understands how a sniper cell works, one also understands how the other components of the guerrilla machinery work. Importantly, *Fry The Brain* is a study of modern urban guerrilla warfare. As the world becomes increasingly urbanized, so will the world's never ending cycle of conflicts that are exhibited in the form of insurgencies, terrorism, and guerrilla warfare.

There is something in *Fry The Brain* for a variety of readers, from sniping fanatics and guerrilla warfare experts to casual readers and military history buffs. I have tried to entertain while educating, which is always a difficult task. In the end, I am confident the reader will come away with a richer understanding of the subject when they turn the final page.

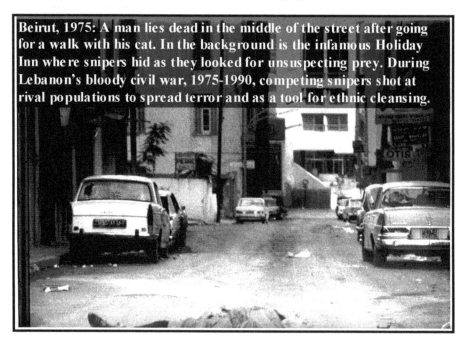

Beirut, 1975: A man lies dead in the middle of the street after going for a walk with his cat. In the background is the infamous Holiday Inn where snipers hid as they looked for unsuspecting prey. During Lebanon's bloody civil war, 1975-1990, competing snipers shot at rival populations to spread terror and as a tool for ethnic cleansing.

Table of Contents

Chapter 1

Belfast, Northern Ireland, Before the 1998 Good Friday Peace Agreement

Kill a British soldier or policeman. Gerry' instructions were clear. The orders originated from the senior leadership of the Provisional Irish Republican Army (PIRA) who felt the British government was not taking the current peace negotiations seriously. They intended to change this. Consequently, the PIRA leadership sent a message to the Belfast leadership: increase the pressure on the illegal occupation forces - now.

Until recently, the Belfast brigade had been lying low, recovering from a string of successful British raids based on intelligence from 'touts' - what the despised PIRA turncoats were called. The Belfast men had been focused on fixing their security problem and training new PIRA units. However, they were still ready to act as they had just finished training a new urban sniper cell. Gerry, the leader of this cell, got the order over a pint of Guinness in a smoke-filled pub. All it took was a single sentence uttered in between swigs of ale - the boss wants the Brits to feel some pain - and a death warrant was issued. That was it. No written orders. No drawn out moral discussions. Combat action had just been authorized, as if they were talking about organizing a late tackle in a rugby match. And Gerry's superiors didn't want to know the details; they just wanted to see results. That's what the word 'compartmentalization' meant. There would be no evidence linking the PIRA leadership to the trigger man. Gerry got paid to make it happen. It would take him several days to look over the intelligence reports and pick the right target, but in a week he would be ready.

Several years ago, Gerry had cut his teeth in the PIRA with the Goldfinger sniper crew that worked the rural South Armagh area. After serving the Republican cause faithfully since his initial membership and learning to keep his mouth shut, he had risen through the ranks. Gerry had his own crew now and he had new ideas of how to use them. Gerry wanted to bring his sniper war to the city. Even though his sniper cell was composed mostly of PIRA veterans, this would be their first operation as a team.

Eight Days later, Friday afternoon, 1:50 p.m.

Brrrrrrrrring! Brrrrrrrrrrring! Brrrrrrrring!

"Yeah, I'll be there already!" Mike said to himself as he hurried out of the garage and picked up the phone with his greasy hands, which was now all over the phone.

"Yeah?" Mike barked, unsuccessfully trying to hide his annoyance, wiping his hands on his jeans.

"Hello, is Mike there?"

"This is Mike."

"Are you free for a pint of ale, mate, down at Reilley's?" It took Mike a second to recognize the voice, a voice that sent a chill down his spine, as if a pitcher of ice-cold water had just been poured down his back.

"Just got done working on my car. Sounds good." He tried to sound like the conversation was absolutely meaningless to him, as if this was someone he talked to a thousand times before. But if the voice on the other end of the line could look into his stomach, it would see a bundle of knots caused by a cocktail of fear and adrenaline. It really didn't matter what Mike was doing. He'd have to cut short his project and get ready whether he wanted to or not. He could be in the middle of putting out a burning fire at his house and it wouldn't have mattered. The movement demanded dedication.

Minutes later, Shawn, Jimmy, and Tom all got the same phone call. An hour later, the group met at a pub, but it wasn't Reilley's. Reilley's was just the code word signaling they were meeting at a prearranged location. If the authorities were listening to their phone lines - which they always assumed - the police would have no idea where they were actually meeting. This was a standard security precaution for the cell.

3:00 p.m.

One after the other, Shawn, Mike, Tom, and Jimmy came in, saw Gerry sitting at a table in the back of the pub, and took a seat. They casually scanned the pub, taking stock of who was in it and what they were doing. Nothing unusual stuck out. The four men had never met each other before and the only familiar face was Gerry's. This was because the PIRA Active Service Units (ASUs) were designed in a compartmented manner so the risk of compromise was minimized. Often, different members of an ASU didn't know who the other members were until they met for an operation. After some small talk, Gerry got down to business.

"I'm glad everyone could make it. I assume you're all clean or you wouldn't be here."

Each member of the ASU had been trained months before in counter-surveillance measures at a PIRA safehouse in the northern city of Dundalk in the Irish Republic. They were taught to always take a route enabling them to determine if they were being followed, such as switching from taxicabs to walking on foot. If they did detect surveillance, they didn't go to the meeting. It was a real pain in the ass to keep switching their routes, to keep looking at who was behind them, and to switch meeting places time and time again. But, as their instructors had reminded them, *it's a bit better than being in Long Kesh, isn't it?* Long Kesh was the maximum security prison where PIRA members were sent to do time.

Gerry, running his hands through his jet-black hair, continued, "It's such a nice day out, maybe we should go for a drive, eh?" It was posed as a question, but it was really an order. Gerry was in charge and they knew it. Now it was time to get down to the business at hand.

3:20 p.m.

The four left the pub and followed Gerry to a cream colored van parked out front. With Gerry driving, they departed, taking an unpredictable series of side streets and unlikely turns. The van was stolen the day before from an airport long-term parking lot by a separate PIRA unit specializing in obtaining vehicles for combat operations. Their intent was the van would be stolen, used for the operation, and then returned before the owners knew their vehicle was gone. If anyone recognized the van during the operation and reported it to the authorities, the police would end up tracing it back to a completely innocent person. Since the PIRA had a contact working at the airport, it was easy to secure any vehicle they needed.

Once Gerry entered the specific western Belfast neighborhood he was looking for, the Ballymurphy Estate, he slowed down and pulled into an empty parking spot alongside the street. Stretched out on either side of them were long rows of two-story brick apartment buildings, all looking essentially the same. The neighborhood was poor, but clean. It was the same kind of urban dump they all either grew up in or still lived. They immediately grasped the key characteristics of the battlefield. Gerry kept the van running and began his brief.

"At the intersection in front of us, in two and a half hours, there will be a police patrol passing by. I'll make sure the patrol stops. See that apartment on the corner with the green door? The back door is unlocked and there is parking in the rear. It's been made available to us for the day."

The others looked at the various landmarks as Gerry briefed them. They were all vaguely familiar with the area. In fact, Jimmy had a cousin who lived a couple blocks away.

"Questions?" Gerry asked. He knew there had to be. This was the first time they were all working together and all he had done so far was sketch out the basics of the operation.

"What kind of patrol is it? How many? What direction are they coming from?" Shawn asked. These were normal questions since he was the trigger man. Shawn tried to sound confident, masking his true nervousness. This was the first combat operation for Shawn. He was still a 'virgin' – what the PIRA called a new member with a clean record with the British authorities. This was precisely the reason he was picked to be a shooter, because he was off the police's criminal radar and was still invisible. If he passed this first test, he would have a future with the organization. If he screwed up, he might be placed under suspicion and considered a possible infiltrator until proven otherwise. But that was the nature of the game he was now playing.

"From the south going north. That's their normal pattern. The patrol consists of two Land Rovers. They usually pass by about six, give or take a few minutes."

"Armored?" Mike wondered.

"Let's assume so, yes."

This meant a shot through the windshield or door was out. It would take a .50 caliber rifle to shoot through the armored glass and doors of the Land Rovers. It was too hard to hide and move such large sniper rifles in the city, so that option was out. They'd have to get the target out in the open.

"How good is the info?" Mike wanted to know.

"It's good." Gerry wasn't going say much more about it. In fact, Gerry had no idea where the information came from. The Belfast chain of command provided him with several target packages and he chose this one. It was standard practice in the PIRA to separate their intelligence collection activities from the ASUs who acted on it. However, it was likely the PIRA unit that ran the local 'neighborhood watch' obtained the information from a housewife or local kids who played in the area. Since the PIRA had strong support in this neighborhood, there were half a dozen people who may have volunteered the information.

The van only idled in place for two minutes when Gerry pulled back into the street, taking a different route back to the pub. He stopped a mile short at a small parking lot near several shops.

"Mike, do you have any more questions?" Gerry asked. Although Shawn was the shooter, Mike would lead the tactical execution of the operation.

"No problem. I'll figure it out," Mike quipped.

"Okay."

Gerry got out of the van and into a black, 500 series BMW and drove away. Gerry didn't want to know any more about their plans. This was another deliberate measure to protect the ASU. The rest of the ASU had no idea how Gerry was going to stop the Land Rovers and they didn't want to know. In turn, Gerry didn't want to know anything about the execution of the operation. That way, if any of them were captured and interrogated, they only had a partial understanding of the overall plan. Gerry had already done a stint in the infamous Long Kesh prison in the H-Blocks (you could still see where his nose was broken from his 'questioning') and he knew the importance of security. He didn't plan on going back anytime soon.

3:40 p.m.

Mike slid over into the driver's seat, lit a cigarette, and pulled into traffic.

"What kind of weapon do we have?" Mike said looking back at Shawn, blowing a thin column of smoke through his pursed lips and out the cracked window.

"AR-15 with scope and suppressor. I'm dialed in at two-hundred meters."

This civilian version of the standard M-16 assault rifle was imported from Boston through the PIRA's support network so no one could trace it to a domestic purchase in any one of Northern Ireland's six counties. It was a 'clean' gun.

"Who's shagging the rifle?" Mike asked.

"I am," Tom said, "It'll take me an hour to get it."

Only Tom knew where the gun was hidden – another ASU security precaution.

"Right. Jimmy, I take it you're from around here?"

Although the ASU members had all trained separately, they knew the standard sniper cell was composed of a team leader, a shooter, a quartermaster who provided the weapon and other materials, and a surveillance man. Process of elimination meant

Jimmy was the surveillance specialist.

"Something like that," Jimmy smirked. It was none of their business where he was from. He knew the area and that was good enough.

"Jimmy, I want you to case the area an hour out and in the corner flat thirty minutes before the hit. Give me a heads up on anything unusual. Here's your cell phone and here's my cell phone number. As soon as it's done, leave out the back. Make sure you take care of the phone as soon as possible." They were using cell phones 'procured' by another team, pilfered earlier from some tourists staying at a local hotel. After the operation, they would give the phones to a courier who would take them to a sup-porter who worked at a coal-burning power plant and would incinerate the phones in the blast furnace - no questions asked. A lot of things disappeared in that blast furnace over the years, some mechanical, some human.

"Got it."

Mike pulled into the pub parking lot. Jimmy got out and walked off to hail a taxi. Jimmy knew his part of the plan and didn't need to know anything else.

"Tom, we'll meet you in an hour and a half at the park in front of Hanrahan's."

"Right."

Tom walked off to his car, which was parked several blocks away. He had the rifle stashed in the boot of a car (hidden where the spare tire was supposed to go) in a parking garage. The car was registered to someone who worked in England. The owner was a family friend and supported the movement. However, the owner had no knowledge of the weapon in their car because they were overseas six months at a time, doing agricultural contract work. In case the car was compromised, the owner could legitimately claim ignorance because of their long absences out of the country.

Mike flicked his cigarette out the window and turned to Shawn, "Let's go in and have a pint. We have some time to kill." They could both be dead or in prison an hour from now. Might as well go out feeling good. Plus, Mike could smell the fear oozing out of Shawn. His body chemistry screamed, *I'm scared to death because I'm about to do something crazy.* A police dog would have smelled Shawn a mile away. Yep, a big brown pint of Guinness was just what the Doctor ordered. It would calm the nerves. It always did.

5:11 p.m.

Mike and Shawn pulled up to the small park across from Hanrahan's right on time. They were only sitting for about a minute when Tom pulled up. Tom got out of his car, opened the boot, and pulled out a bright, red cooler. Tom carried the plastic cooler to the van and heaved it through the side-door that Shawn had opened. The cooler creaked and moaned like an old woman as Tom set it down on the floor of the van. Once the gaudy cooler was in the van, Tom popped the top and pulled out an ice-cold Coke. He opened the can and took a long swig.

"Ahhhhhh!" Tom gave an exaggerated sigh after lowering the can. "Don't drink and drive!" he warned. Tom could afford to be a smart-ass since his part of the job was half over. "I'll service the drop off point fifteen minutes after the hit. Don't be late." Tom described where to drop off the rifle, a place located just a few short miles from where the operation would occur.

Tom got in his car and drove off, with Mike and Shawn a few seconds behind him.

Mike and Shawn had about thirty minutes before they needed to be in position, giving them enough time to make another series of turns and switchbacks to see if they were being followed. If they detected anything suspicious, they simply wouldn't show up. The absence of any member of the ASU meant the operation was terminated, no questions asked.

5:30 p.m.

"Shawn, we're ten minutes out. We'll park at the street corner north of the intersection. It'll be a hundred and fifty meter shot."

As Mike spoke, Shawn put on a pair of white, latex surgical gloves, reached into the cooler, under the top layer of ice and sodas, and secured a disassembled AR-15 wrapped in a heavy plastic bag with two metal grommets at the top. Shawn had trained on this exact rifle one month ago on an isolated farm in the PIRA dominated county of South Armagh. He hadn't seen the rifle since because Tom was responsible for hiding and maintaining it. After unwrapping the weapon, Shawn slid the upper receiver onto the lower receiver and snapped the well-oiled retaining pins shut. Then, he inspected the four-power scope that was attached directly to the Weaver rail on top of the receiver. The scope was still taped with foam to protect it. Shawn spied a small bottle of water in the cooler, next to one of the sodas. Tom had thought of everything. Shawn removed a suppressor from the plastic bag and poured the water into it. He slowly rotated the suppressor around by the ends, making sure the suppressor was completely soaked inside. He poured the remaining water from the suppressor back into the cooler and attached the suppressor to the end of the rifle's barrel. This suppressor, like many modern ones, was a 'wet' suppressor and was designed to have water poured in it to dampen the sound better.

Shawn kept the telescoping buttstock of the rifle as it was, all the way in, so he had more room to maneuver inside the restricted confines of the van. He pulled a twenty-round magazine from the bag, inserted it into the magazine well, and jacked a round into the chamber. He placed the rifle across the back seat and covered it with an old, green blanket with a pattern of pretty red roses sewn on it. It looked like something from a retirement home, like a blanket a grandmother would put over their old, cold legs. Shawn pulled the 'cleaner' bag from the cooler and took a quick accountability of its contents. He removed a light-weight, clear, plastic rain jacket, put it on over his black t-shirt, and zipped it up. It was one of those cheap ones you might buy at a concession stand at a football game.

Shawn picked up a black nylon balaclava and put it on over his head, covering up his curly blond hair, so just his blue eyes were visible. Then, over the balaclava went a woman's nylon. One couldn't do this job and be claustrophobic because the nylon smashed the balaclava into your face like someone was trying to smother you. The balaclava would hide his identity and the nylon served as a forensics barrier. His PIRA instructors in Dundalk hammered this into his head: *you can disguise yourself all day if you want, but if there's gunpowder all in your hair when you're done with the op, you're screwed aren't you?* There was also a small rag and several alcohol wipes in the bag. Shawn was just finishing as Mike pulled up to the curb. Shawn had talked himself through the procedures ten times already so there was no way he was going to miss anything. *If you get sloppy, you get yourself caught or get yourself dead.*

Shawn moved to the back of the van and slid open the rear window about two inches. The angle was perfect. Mike had eased the van into just the right position. Shawn just barely had a line of sight from the window to the intersection. A row of apartments blocked the rest of his vision and he knew the police patrol would only be able to see the rear of the van as they approached.

5:45 p.m.

Gerry' gleaming, black BMW – it looked like it had just been waxed and polished by hand - drove slowly through the intersection, stopped briefly, and then sped off. Mike's cell phone vibrated and he answered it.

"Hey, someone just dumped a body at the intersection. His legs are in the road."

It was Jimmy. He had a good view of the intersection as he peered through the drapes of the corner flat. The back door to the flat was unlocked just like Gerry said. It was obvious a family was living there, since there were a pile of dirty dishes in the sink. The owners were an Irish Republican family who supported the cause and were conveniently away for the day.

"Right," Mike confirmed. He put his head over his right shoulder and hissed to Shawn between clenched teeth, "Do you see the action at the intersection?"

"Yep. A black BMW stopped and took off. He dumped something."

They were running ahead of schedule. Mike's phone vibrated again.

"We've got two vehicles coming – Land Rovers. See ya'." Jimmy's job was done. He wanted to sprint to the car like madman, jumping down the brick stairs in a single leap like an Olympic hurdler, then tear open the driver side door, and burn rubber out of there like his life depended on it. But that's not how you do it. That's what idiots do who end up doing ten to life in Long Kesh. *You act like a chameleon, like everyone around you, like you're going to walk the friggin' dog.* Instead, Jimmy casually walked out the back door, down the stairs, and got into his car. He had given early warning of the arriving patrol like instructed. It was now up to the trigger man to do the rest. Jimmy was pulling away as the patrol arrived.

5:46 p.m.

The first Land Rover approached the intersection, slowed down, and came to a stop. The second vehicle stopped about fifty meters behind it. The occupants of the first vehicle were obviously looking at the body on the side of the road. A peeler got out of the passenger side of the lead vehicle, carefully scanning the area. A 'peeler' was slang for a policeman. He was wearing black body armor over his smartly pressed uniform and carried an MP-5 submachine gun, his finger gently massaging the trigger. In the distance, several teen-age kids walked down a side street, kicking a soccer ball. Maybe these were 'dickers' the policeman thought - kids used to scout operations for the PIRA. One could never really know.

One hundred meters up the main road a hand-painted mural was visible on the side of a building. White letters, a foot tall, screamed: COLLUSION! IT'S NOT AN ILLU-SION! The mural was in reference to the PIRA's long-held belief that the Royal Ulster Constabulary (the Northern Ireland police force) and the British military were working with Protestant paramilitary organizations, helping them to murder and terrorize innocent Catholics. Obviously, this wasn't a friendly Protestant Loyalist area. This was a hard-core Republican one. The policeman knew the PIRA frequently dumped the bodies of British informers so they could be easily found. This was done as a warning to others who might try and 'grass' (inform) on the PIRA. This was nothing to get excited about. However, since the PIRA often booby-trapped these bodies, it was standard practice for a patrol to secure the immediate area and call in the bomb squad. Better to let the experts deal with the body instead of getting blown up over someone who was already dead. It was probably some low-life any ways who deserved what he got, an informant who worked both sides of the fence and finally got nailed by the Nutting Squad - the PIRA's counterintelligence team who got rid of stool pigeons by putting a bullet in the back of their nut (their head).

5:47 p.m.

The muzzle of Shawn's dull-gray metal suppressor stuck out of the van's rear window by an inch. Shawn wanted to make sure he was clear of the window, but he didn't want to give his position away. He had to squat down awkwardly to get a good position, because his six foot frame wasn't meant to fit in the family passenger van while standing up. Shawn had the peeler in his sights as the man looked in his general direction. The peeler could see the rear of the van, but it didn't look any more suspicious than the scores of other vehicles parked on the same street. Shawn squeezed the trigger.

"*Pfft!*" The gas from the exploding gun powder rushed down the barrel, behind the rotating bullet, eventually getting caught in the internal baffles of the suppressor. By the time the gas exited the suppressor, it was muffled so much that the resulting gunshot sounded like a car door being shut. The policeman dropped to the ground, grabbing his lower stomach.

Shawn saw that the peeler was wearing body armor and had aimed for his pelvis. He could have taken a chest shot, hoping the body armor was only soft armor designed to defeat handgun rounds. But, what if it was hard ceramic armor, which would stop his 5.56 mm rifle round easily? A chest shot was out. What about a head shot? What if he missed? The head was a small target to hit at this distance, especially with sweat running down your forehead and into your eyes, like God himself was trying to create every challenge possible so you couldn't make a successful shot. Shawn only had a second to decide and he made the choice to go for the pelvis, hoping to hit an artery or at least the intestines. He knew this was the right answer. His instructors had been in the same situation before. *It's called a body armor drill, men. You have no idea what kind of armor they have on at a distance and at more than a hundred meters, the head is a difficult target. So, you go for the largest, unprotected area on the body – the abdomen. You shoot 'em in the bollocks.*

5:48 p.m.

"We're good!" Shawn called out, his heart pounding so loud in his ears he couldn't tell if he said it normally or screamed at the top of his lungs. All he wanted to do was get the hell out of there and begin the counter-forensics process. They didn't have much time. Mike started the van and pulled away, like a crocodile easing back into

the waters, its job on land done. Shawn immediately began wiping down the rifle with the rag, wiping clean any fingerprints and most of the gunshot residue. He dropped the magazine, jacked the live round out of the chamber, removed the suppressor, and broke down the AR-15 into the upper and lower receivers. Shawn put the rifle back into the plastic bag and re-padded the scope. He took a section from a metal coat hanger, ran it through the metal grommets at the top of the bag, and twisted the hangar so the bag wouldn't slide off.

Next, he took off the plastic rain jacket, the nylons, the balaclava - *you can disguise yourself all day if you want, but if there's gunpowder all in your hair when you're done with the op, you're screwed aren't you?* - then the gloves, and stuffed them in their plastic bag. He opened the alcohol wipes and cleaned his forehead, face, neck, and hands to get rid of the bulk of the gunshot residue. He knew this wouldn't pass close scrutiny, but it would remove enough residue to create doubt in the legal system. Maybe you got all the ingredients of gunpowder on your hands from painting your fence earlier today. After all, the key identifying elements found in gunpowder are also found in common house paint. Shawn even had some white paint on his fingernails from working with his paint brush that morning. For the last stage of the clean-up, Shawn took several cue-tips and cleaned out his ears and nostrils. Even in these hard to get places, incriminating gunshot residue could settle.

When Shawn went for his initial training at the PIRA safehouse in Dundalk, one of the first classes he received was how to remove incriminating evidence like gunpowder residue, fingerprints, and even fibers from his clothing. Since the British had such a strong forensic capability, every ASU incorporated a counter-forensic cleaning stage into their operations. After Shawn thought he was relatively clean, he put the wipes in the same bag as the jacket and gloves. Shawn then buried the plastic-wrapped rifle back under the ice and began looking for the expended shell. It took a few seconds, but he found it on the floor. Since Gerry continued to make unexpected turns in order to lose anyone who might try and follow them, Shawn lurched all over the back of the van like pinball until he finally secured the lone casing. He picked it up with his shirt and dropped it in the cleaner bag and put the bag under the sodas.

6:00 p.m.

Shawn had just completed the cleaning process when Mike turned a corner and pulled up next to a sidewalk. Adjacent to the sidewalk was a gray metal grate for rainwater to drain into. There were several plastic garbage cans lining the sidewalk, right in front of the grate. As soon as the van came to a halt, Shawn slid open the side door about a foot. The garbage cans provided an effective screen, blocking the view of anyone who might be watching. Shawn lowered the plastic bag and the rifle through the grate, hanging the bag on one of the metal bars with the coat hanger. Shawn slid the door shut and Mike pulled away.

The grate was the drop off point Tom directed them to go to after the operation. Tom didn't want them going directly back to him with the weapon. The goal after any operation was to immediately disassociate oneself from the physical evidence connecting one to the activity. This way, Tom could watch the drop-off point and make sure Mike and Shawn weren't followed. When all was clear and it was a little darker, Tom would drive up to the grate and retrieve the rifle. Once Tom secured the weapon, he would clean it and return it to its hiding place. After two or three more sniping operations, Tom would change out the upper receiver with a new one. The old upper receiver would then be taken to a machine-shop and the barrel drilled out, removing all the lands and grooves in the barrel. This way, the old incriminating barrel, which could be ballistically linked to the rifle and the shootings, would be removed from circulation and forensically sterilized. Then, Shawn would have to re-zero on the new receiver.

It was a warm summer evening and Shawn's shirt was soaked in sweat. If he had stepped into a shower for a full minute, he would have been drier. He had just seriously wounded a man, maybe even taken his life. A perfect stranger who was doing nothing more than his job was gunned down and Shawn pulled the trigger. While you're sighting in on a human for the first time its almost surreal, like it's not even you doing it. You're floating in the sky, looking down, watching someone else named Shawn pull the trigger. Taking the shot was easy. Thinking about it later was something different. *You just killed a man, Shawn. You're a killer. A wanted man. You'll be on death row someday when they catch you. If they catch you.* The operation drained him mentally. He was glad it was over. Mike dropped Shawn off halfway to the pub so he could take a cab home.

"Good job, mate. Really good. Gerry is gonna' like your work." Mike had been in Shawn's shoes before. He worked as a trigger man until he moved up the ranks. It didn't matter how tough you were, or how tough you thought you were, the first time always weighed on you. Every man you killed, you carried on your back for the rest of your life. After a few more shootings, Shawn would get calloused like the rest of them. In another year, shooting a peeler would be just like shooting an inanimate object, like shooting a scarecrow. It wouldn't mean a thing.

Shawn managed a weak smile and a shrug and walked off to hail a cab. As soon as he got home, Shawn would take a long shower, being sure to thoroughly clean any remaining gunshot residue from his body. He would also burn his clothes in the chimney, eliminating any forensic link connecting the shooting to him. Then, he would throw up, heaving until it seemed his guts would fall out.

6:12 p.m.

Mike pulled into the original pub parking lot, put the keys under the driver's seat, and walked off. Half an hour later, a PIRA 'cleaning crew' arrived and took the van directly to a nearby warehouse in the industrial district where rows of near-identical, pre-fab, rusted buildings dotted the landscape. In the warehouse, the cooler was removed and the clothing bag and its contents were burned later that day at the coal plant. The cleaning crew wiped down the entire vehicle to remove any fingerprints, even though everyone in the ASU had been instructed not to leave any. It was better to be safe than in prison and under interrogation. The cleaning crew also vacuumed the seats and floor carpet, sucking up any trace fibers. After the van was cleaned inside and out, which took about thirty minutes, the cleaners brought the van back to the airport parking lot where it was stolen. With any luck, the family wouldn't even know the vehicle was borrowed for the day.

Mike was home before the cleaning crew arrived. He took a long shower even though he never touched the weapon. There still might be some gunpowder particles that were transferred onto him. Stranger things had happened. They all wore blue jeans during the operation because blue denim fibers were was so common in Northern Ireland they were forensically useless. Also, all their t-shirts were nylon soccer shirts, which shed relatively few fibers. Gerry was dead serious about limiting fiber transfers during operations, even though it was a tedious chore for everyone involved. *Let 'em bitch about it all they want. I'm not going back to the H-Blocks.* The Maze Prison was referred to as the 'H' blocks because, from the sky, the layout of the buildings looked like a giant letter H.

Gerry would get in touch with him in a week or so. He just had to lay low until then. The entire ASU would know the results of their operation the following morning when the headlines inevitably screamed, "IRA TERRORISTS SUSPECTED IN SHOOTING OF POLICE." The article might even disclose the name of the officer, the unit he served with, what town he was from, and the exact nature of his injuries. If he was dead, the paper may even say where the funeral was being held. Maybe they could get more officers of the Royal Ulster Constabulary at the funeral with a drive-by. The newspapers usually provided the best post-operation review.

If this operation proved to be successful, Gerry would get another order to conduct another operation. The PIRA needed to step up the tempo in the cities. The British would be forced to the negotiating table - at gunpoint if necessary. If Gerry and his ASU could provide the steady stream of casualties the Republican movement demanded, there was plenty of work for them.

Chapter 2

Urban Guerrilla Sniping

Shooting and marksmanship are the urban guerrilla's water and air. His perfection of the art of shooting makes him a special type of urban guerrilla – that is, a sniper, a category of solitary combatant indispensable in isolated actions. The sniper knows how to shoot, at close range and at long range, and his arms are appropriate for either type of shooting.

> \- Carlos Marighella, author of 'Minimanual of the Urban Guerrilla'

Taking Aim at Conventional Sniping

The previous chapter demonstrates that urban guerrilla sniping is a drastic departure from traditional concepts of sniping. In fact, traditional sniper methodology falls flat in the arena of urban guerrilla warfare for a variety of reasons we will discuss. In spite of the very real limitations of traditional sniping, conventional concepts still dominate the field. As a result, very little is known about the discipline of urban guerrilla sniping, despite thousands of soldiers, policemen, and civilians shot by snipers during the course of the world's recent guerrilla wars.

If we are to understand the art of guerrilla sniping, we must first strip away the decades of misconceptions about what a sniper actually is. The Merriam-Webster dictionary defines the act of sniping as, "to shoot at exposed individuals from a usually concealed point of vantage." This bare-bones description is good because it is broad enough to incorporate various styles and methods of sniping. In contrast, many have

A conventional sniper in a Ghillie Suit.

Photo by CPL Storm

whittled down their definition of a sniper to such a narrow concept that only traditional styles of sniping are recognized. For these sniper purists, their claustrophobic definition of a sniper is a young, fit male, who is a school-trained professional, inevitably wears a camouflaged Ghillie Suit, has a high-powered rifle and an equally high-powered scope, and fires from extreme distances. This concept is a reflection of a conventional, rural-centric mindset that works in a specific kind of high-intensity warfare environment. The urban guerrilla sniping realities are something different.

The School-Trained Sniper Myth

A person formally educated in their field usually has an advantage over someone with no organized learning in this same field, but this is not always true. In fact, some of the world's best snipers are self-taught. Case in point: Vassili Zaitsev of Stalingrad fame started his career as a Navy payroll clerk, becoming a self-taught sniper as he fought the German Sixth Army on the banks of the Volga River in the fall of 1942. Sepp Allerberger, the second-most prolific German sniper of World War II, with hundreds of rigorously confirmed kills, learned to shoot on his own with a captured Russian rifle while convalescing at an aid station. Zaitsev and Allerberger were both excellent snipers because they understood the tactics of sniping, not because they were school-trained experts. In a similar vein, a guerrilla sniper's training methodology may be scoffed at by professional snipers, but just because their learning process is different does not make them any less deadly.

The Ghillie Suit Myth

The Ghillie Suit is a rural-centric camouflage method that constrains a sniper to a specific environment – it only works in the woods. A sniper in a Ghillie Suit stands out in an urban environment as opposed to blending into it. For example, Urban sniper/ mass murderer Charles Whitman calmly walked to the observation deck of the Texas Tower in Austin, Texas on August 1, 1966 wearing a pair of coveralls. To the surrounding people he looked like a janitor. Whitman certainly could not have driven on campus with his face painted green and wearing olive drab netting sewn to an old uniform. In the cities, camouflage may be a pair of jeans and a leather jacket.

The High-Powered Rifle Myth

A high-powered rifle is not required for effective sniping, especially in an urban environment where a long-barreled, bulky weapon is more of a liability than an asset. In Chechnya, guerrillas were successful at killing Russian soldiers with head shots fired from .22 caliber rifles. These .22 caliber rifles were light, quiet, maneuverable, easily concealed, and if a sniper hit a person in the head with a .22 caliber bullet, they were just as dead as if they were shot with a .50 caliber rifle. Also, Israeli soldiers found the .22 caliber rifle particularly useful for putting down select targets during riots and demonstrations. Others still, from common criminals to guerrillas fighting the Third Reich, employed pistols as a sniping tool.

The High-Powered Scope Myth

A high-powered scope is not a requirement for effective sniping. Simo Hayha, the most successful sniper of all times, was a Finnish soldier credited with killing 542 Russian soldiers over the course of only three months, during the Russo-Finish War in 1940. During this time, Simo killed six Russians a day until he was wounded by a bullet to the face. Simo did not use a scope on his Finnish M28, 7.62 mm, bolt-action rifle (this rifle was essentially a copy of the Russians' own Mosin-Nagant battle rifle) because he thought he created too great a silhouette when he raised his head to look through the scope. As a result, the world's most prolific sniper scored all of his kills over iron sights.

The Long Distance Myth

As mentioned already, urban combat ranges are frequently much less than those found in a rural setting. In many situations, soldiers are so close to their enemy they cannot take a long distance shot even if they wanted to. In Grozny, Chechen fighters clung so tightly to their vastly superior Russian foe that subsequent gun battles were fought entirely by shooting through the walls and ceilings of adjacent rooms. Also, to date, some Iraqi insurgent snipers have made many of their shots at two hundred meters or less - some as close as fifty meters.

The Male Sniper Myth

Because organized warfare is a male-dominated endeavor, snipers are expected to be men. However, one's gender has nothing to do with the ability to be an effective sniper. In World War II, the Russians employed entire sniper companies composed of women - not only because they were desperate for recruits, but because they were good snipers. In the world of guerrilla warfare, the sex of the sniper can be critical. Since being male makes up part of an expected sniper's profile, deviations from this profile help a guerrilla to remain free from security force scrutiny. Women all over the world receive less scrutiny from security forces and the general public than do men,

Simo Hayha

Finnish national hero, Simo Hayha, poses for the camera while holding an M28 rifle, a copy of the Russians' own Mosin-Nagant battle rifle. Hayha and other Finnish snipers used unconventional tactics to pick off the Russians' life essential field kitchens and to shoot the ill-clothed Russian soldiers as the huddled around their brightly burning campfires. Consequently, most Russians lived in fear of the Finnish 'White Death'. The Russians later said they captured just enough land in the war to bury their dead.

enabling them to move more easily in government controlled areas. To this end, the Bosnians in Sarajevo and the guerrillas in Chechnya both used female snipers to good effect.

How is Guerrilla Sniping Different from Conventional Sniping?

Now that we have broadened our definition of what a sniper is, how does the art of guerrilla sniping differ from conventional sniping? While both conventional and guerrilla snipers have the same job, their lifestyles are much different.

An Anonymous Life

Life for the conventional sniper is simpler. The conventional sniper does not have to conceal their profession since they live and work in the open. For instance, any person interested in learning about sniping can contact world-renowned sniping expert John Plaster and talk to him in person. It is no secret where he lives, where he works, or what his email address is. In contrast, the guerrilla sniper must live a life of secrecy, never allowing the public to know their true discipline. While one can look up John Plaster's contact information in the phone book, there are no listings for 'Guerrilla Snipers' in the Grozny, Belfast, or Fallujah yellow pages. For the guerrilla sniper, exposure means death or imprisonment.

Freedom of Movement

Because they operate in the open, conventional military snipers have considerable freedom of movement. A Russian sniper can hop on the back of an armored vehicle and drive to any place they need to go in Chechnya. On the other hand, a guerrilla sniper has a limited ability to move because some areas are closed off to the public. The guerrilla sniper has to deal with checkpoints, random searches, nighttime raids, and trained guard dogs trying to sniff them out. Therefore, a large part of a guerrilla sniper's life is spent developing methods to bypass a security force's population control measures in order to remain anonymous and retain an acceptable level of movement.

Making the Shot

Making a shot for a member of a military organization or a police force is usually an overt act. This kind of overt sniper, because they have nothing to hide and are defending the established government, can take their shot in the open with few repercussions. Think of a Royal Ulster Constabulary (RUC) sniper on duty at a police station in Northern Ireland. This sniper can openly look for IRA guerrillas with a pair of binoculars, and if they see an armed IRA gunman, they take a shot. After firing their weapon, the RUC sniper has a cup of tea, writes up an incident report, and maybe gets an award several months later.

In contrast, the guerrilla sniper cannot operate like this - everything they do must be done in absolute secrecy. The guerrilla has to hide the fact they are going to take a shot, they must hide the shot itself, and they must hide the fact they just took a shot. Not only must the guerrilla hide these details from their enemy, they must hide them from the public. The guerrilla may even have to hide these events from their guerrilla organization and even their own family in order to remain compartmentalized and thus secure. After the shot, the guerrilla does not have the luxury to pat themselves on the back or even stay around to make another shot. Instead, the guerrilla's primary goal is to immediately blend into the urban terrain, like a human chameleon, and disappear.

Physical Association Between the Sniper and their Weapon

A professional sniper in the military or law enforcement takes great pride in their weapon. They train with it for hours on the rifle range, they baby it with regular cleaning, and they keep it in a protective case. The conventional sniper not only takes pride in their weapon and their shooting skills, they make specific measures to associate themselves with their weapon. This association takes many forms like taking a picture of them holding their rifle, signing for their weapon by serial number on an official document, placing their name on their weapon (or placing a number on that weapon that is associated with their name), and keeping their weapon in an established arms room or in an elaborate gun case at their home.

In contrast, the guerrilla sniper pursues the complete opposite approach. In fact, they take extreme measures to disassociate themselves from their weapon. This disassociation is an integral part of the guerrilla's anonymous lifestyle. The disassociation measures the guerrilla may take include: wearing gloves so as not to leave incriminating fingerprints on the weapon, filing the serial number off their weapon, using a different weapon for each sniper attack, hiding the weapon in a public place, securing the weapon only moments before the attack and then discarding it just as quickly, and cleaning gunshot residue off the weapon and the guerrilla's own person and clothes

WW II French Resistance Sniper

A female guerrilla, with a captured German Mauser K98 sniper rifle slung over her shoulder, smiles for the camera. Women guerrillas receive less scrutiny all over the world because they do not fit our preconceived notion of what a soldier is. The French resistance, and other guerrilla movements worldwide, have all used women in some manner to advance their respective causes.

after making a shot.

Overall, the guerrilla sniper has a difficult task because they are burdened with conducting every aspect of their operation in complete secrecy. A guerrilla sniper who is an excellent shot at long distances, but is unable to effectively pass through government checkpoints, is useless. The guerrilla sniper must possess a variety of skills that go far beyond making a bullet hit its intended target, but that are as much a part of their job as squeezing the trigger. These skills include creating believable cover stories to deceive local authorities, blending in with the local population, conducting clandestine reconnaissance and surveillance of future targets while remaining undetected, moving to and from the guerrilla sniper's shooting platform while under direct observation by the enemy and the public yet arousing no suspicion, understanding the security forces' forensic methodology, and being educated in the loopholes of the government's legal system.

Understanding the Urban Environment

We know a guerrilla must operate differently than their government foe, but how exactly does the urban environment affect the sniper? To start, there are four distinct features of the urban environment one must appreciate: a large volume and variety of 1) people, 2) vehicles, 3) buildings, and 4) avenues of travel (roads, sidewalks, stairs, crosswalks, alleys). Unlike the relatively simple qualities of the rural world, the city is a complex place.

People

A large number of people living in confined spaces mean the sniper has to conduct their operations under the scrutiny of a diverse population that may or may not support the guerrilla's actions. As a result, in order to counter the scrutiny of so many people, the guerrilla sniper develops methods to conceal their weapon, to conceal their intentions, and to conceal the actual taking of their shot. Concealing all of these elements of their operation is difficult and requires a detailed methodology and strict discipline. On the other hand, the masses can also be exploited by the guerrilla sniper. This is because the sniper can move as one anonymous individual among many where the sheer volume of people makes it impossible for the human eye and brain to observe, pick out, and remember specific individuals.

Vehicles

Just as with mobs of people, the number and variety of vehicles in a city can be an asset for the sniper because they can hide in the sea of cars just as they disappear in an ocean of people. For example, a guerrilla sniper can be in a vehicle, surrounded by people, but at the same time be completely isolated from them. In this situation, the vehicle is its own microenvironment, providing complete concealment from the rest of the urban surroundings. Let us think of a sniper positioned in the back of a van, completely invisible to people standing even one foot from them. This relative isolation, provided by the completely enclosed space inside vehicle, allows the urban sniper to get close to enemy check-points, guard towers, and government facilities, and still remain undetected. A sniper has several options when using a vehicle. They can shoot from a parked vehicle, shoot from a temporarily halted vehicle, or even fire from a slow moving vehicle. As soon as the sniper takes their shot, the driver takes off and is miles away from the scene of the shooting in just minutes.

Buildings

The thousands of structures found in any large city offer the guerrilla sniper an endless choice of sniper platforms to shoot from. Buildings, which are their own completely enclosed microenvironments (just like vehicles), allow the guerrilla sniper to observe their target and make a shot completely isolated from the surrounding populace. The sniper can further manipulate the vast number of windows and doors in a specific area to confound enemy security forces. If the sniper fires from a complex urban area, security forces will have to search a thousand different windows, doors, and rooms in order to determine where the shot could have been made from – a difficult task indeed.

Avenues of Travel

The endless number of roads, exit and entrance ramps, bridges, crosswalks, stairs, crossroads, and intersections in a large city can be exploited by the guerrilla sniper in many ways. First, the sniper has many ways to approach a particular target. If a certain road is blocked off, the sniper can come in from another direction using any number of alternate roads. If cars are not allowed near the target, the sniper can approach their target on foot using sidewalks, back alleys, stairs, or other pedestrian means of travel.

The guerrilla sniper also has the opportunity to use the various avenues of movement in a city as obstacles to restrict their enemy and help their own getaway. For

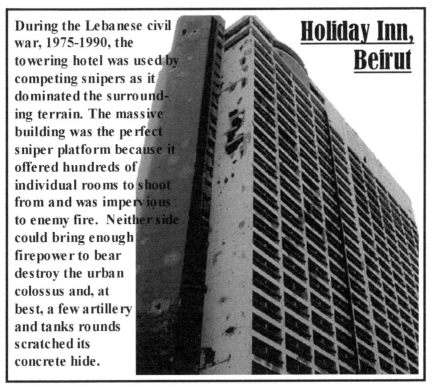

During the Lebanese civil war, 1975-1990, the towering hotel was used by competing snipers as it dominated the surrounding terrain. The massive building was the perfect sniper platform because it offered hundreds of individual rooms to shoot from and was impervious to enemy fire. Neither side could bring enough firepower to bear destroy the urban colossus and, at best, a few artillery and tanks rounds scratched its concrete hide.

Holiday Inn, Beirut

instance, a guerrilla sniper (like Charles McCoy, the infamous Ohio highway sniper who we will later discuss a little more in-depth) may shoot a target sitting in a car, who is stuck in traffic so they cannot drive away or even pursue the sniper after the attack. Or, the sniper might engage a target walking on a bridge who is trapped by the concrete terrain and cannot physically escape from the kill zone.

Importantly, the city presents the guerrilla sniper with an endless array of options for escape. The sniper can incorporate various means of travel to confound pursuing forces like moving through alleys and shopping malls, taking taxi cabs, and switching out vehicles under bridges and in parking garages. An experienced urban sniper exploits not just avenues of travel, but all the different elements of the complex urban terrain - people, cars, and buildings - to overwhelm enemy security forces, make a shot, and secure an effective getaway.

How else does this complex urban environment affect the sniper? For one, the urban world is one of obstacles and a shooter will most likely have to fire through a variety of urban mediums such as car doors and windshields, windows and doors of structures, and body armor and helmets. Since these mediums are everywhere in a city, the sniper may need a weapon that can penetrate them. Because space is compressed in the cities, urban snipers may have to shoot from confined areas, such as from inside a vehicle, like the D.C. snipers who made their shots from the trunk of a Caprice Classic, four-door sedan. Consequently, the sniper may need a small maneuverable weapon to take advantage of all the unusual firing positions found in the city. Additionally, the sniper's target in a city may be very small, like the head of a person driving an armored vehicle, looking through a window, or peering through a jagged hole blown out of a wall. Targets wearing ceramic body armor and protective helmets make for a much smaller target because the sniper has to aim for other body parts like the face, the neck, the pelvis, the lower back, and the armpits. The urban sniper's target could be very fleeting due to the avalanche of uncontrollable random elements and obstacles found in a city: a target could walk quickly past a window, stroll hurriedly through a doorway, stop briefly to buy a newspaper, run down a street, or a car could drive in between the sniper and the target, blocking their shot. As a result, the urban sniper must be able to rapidly acquire and engage their fleeting targets.

We must understand the urban sniper cannot hide in the woods or a clump of bushes to conceal themselves from the enemy and prepare for their shot. In the urban world, much different shooting platforms are required to be successful. In Northern Ireland, IRA snipers routinely conducted home invasions, taking over people's residences and holding the owners temporary hostage while they used the house as a sniper platform. In Bosnia, competing snipers cut holes in the walls of abandoned high-rises, firing from these man-made rifle ports to pick off opposing populations.

Blending in with the Populace, Blending in with the Enemy

Perhaps the most important aspect that makes the guerrilla sniper such a frustrating foe is they intentionally blend in with the population. They do this by appearing as a normal citizen, wearing civilian clothes, concealing their weapon, and then taking a shot at an unsuspecting soldier or policeman. By definition, when the guerrilla sniper does this, they are committing a war crime. Because, to be considered a lawful combatant, a guerrilla must wear a uniform visible at a distance, they must carry their weapons openly, they must have established leaders, and they must obey the laws of land warfare. But, conforming to the above laws makes the guerrilla just like their conventional enemies, that is, an easily identified target. Since the urban guerrilla cannot successfully fight their enemy using these rules, they choose to break them. However, a guerrilla sniper can work around the laws of land warfare in order to remain a legal combatant and still be successful.

Let us take a look at a hypothetical situation in Chechnya. An unarmed Chechen sniper in civilian clothes walks to a van and then get inside it. Could the sniper then take a colored cloth band out of their pocket, put it on their arm, pick up an SVD sniper rifle stashed inside the vehicle, shoot a Russian soldier, then stash their rifle and arm band, and get out of the van and walk away like nothing happened? Yes, they could - legally. It is legal because during the actual act of shooting they were wearing a recognized uniform, which (by law) can be nothing more than an arm band and at the time they were handling their weapon in the open. It is not the sniper's fault that the enemy cannot see their arm band or SVD while positioned inside the van. Sure, many countries, like Russia, would argue that such actions are illegal. However, ask them to show you where it is written in the Geneva and Hague Conventions that the guerrilla sniper, in this situation, is violating the laws of war.

While the guerrilla sniper benefits from blending into the civilian population, they also benefit by mimicking their enemy by wearing captured or stolen uniforms. For example, resistance movements who fought against Nazi Germany during World War II mimicked their enemy by dressing as German soldiers. The French, Polish, Rus-

Warsaw, Poland 1944

Colored arm band

A Polish insurgent takes aim with a captured German Mauser K98 rifle.

photo by Wieslau Chrzanowski, Museum of Warsaw Uprising

sian, and Yugoslav resistance movements all dressed as German soldiers to set up fake checkpoints, to move safely through enemy controlled areas, to execute ambushes, and to conduct surprise attacks. In later wars, Palestinian guerrillas mimicked their Israeli foes, Chechen guerrillas wore Russian uniforms, and Iraqi insurgents donned both government police and army uniforms. So, is a guerrilla sniper who wears their enemy's clothing a war criminal? Not necessarily.

According to the laws of land warfare, it is perfectly legal to impersonate the enemy as long as one does not fight while in the enemy's uniform. With this as a legal baseline, think of a Polish sniper fighting in Warsaw in 1944, walking openly down the street wearing a German uniform and carrying a Mauser K98 sniper rifle. Could this same guerrilla then walk into an abandoned building, go up the stairs to the top floor, put a colored arm band on their upper right arm and now be dressed in the proper uniform of their guerrilla army? Yes. Then, could the sniper take aim at a German soldier, blow their head off, put the colored arm band in their pocket, and walk back down the same street they came down? Yes, legally, they could do all of the above.

Traditional Sniping and the Law

While guerrilla snipers face a torrent of legal scrutiny from their conventional foes, let us examine traditional forms of sniping and see if they are themselves in compliance with international law. From at least the time of World War I, snipers in the world's major armies (British, French, American, German, Italian, Turkish, Russian) took extensive measures to disguise themselves, a process we know as camouflaging. However, by donning various camouflage outfits composed of anything from netting and cloth strips to real vegetation and hiding in fake trees, these snipers no longer wore a recognized uniform and they certainly could not be identified from a distance. In fact, the whole purpose of camouflaging was to be invisible to the enemy. Were these snipers violating the laws of land warfare? Defenders of camouflaging say it is not illegal to hide one's self as long as the sniper does not intentionally dress like a civilian. Others argue that as long as the sniper wears some sort of uniform under all this camouflage, they are abiding by international law. Another defense is that their camouflage outfit *is* their uniform.

In many cases, the world's leading nations even copied the guerrilla sniper's methods when it fits their needs. Just think of all the undercover police and military special operations units worldwide who wear civilian clothes, conceal their weapons, but still conduct offensive actions against their enemy. How are the British going to say IRA snipers violated the law of land warfare when the Royal Ulster Constabulary, the Special Air Service, and the 14th Military Intelligence Detachment all worked under cover in civilian clothes, concealed their weapons, and shot IRA guerrillas when they saw the opportunity?

Ultimately, international law, like morality, is flexible and varies from which perspective you look at it from. During the Warsaw Ghetto Uprising in 1943, Jewish snipers wore both civilian clothes and stolen German uniforms while shooting and killing German soldiers. In the course of the battle, the Jews broke every law under the sun. From the German perspective, the Jewish guerrillas broke the law by simply resisting. This was based on the German racial policy, formalized in 1935 under the Nuremburg Laws, which made persecution of Jews public policy. In early 1942, after the Wannsee Conference in Berlin, this discrimination against the Jews was transformed from 'mere' racial segregation into a process of systematic genocide which became the Holocaust. The mass murder of the Jews was 'legal' since the final arbiter of German law, the Fuhrer, ordered such gifted men as Reinhard Heydrich and organizational genius Adolf Eichmann to make it so.

What were the Ghetto Jews supposed to do, walk calmly to the gas chambers, poorly disguised as showers, and deeply inhale the Zyklon B? Should they have jumped right into the heated ovens and willingly burned themselves to death like the Germans wanted? Should the Jews have worn a common uniform, visible from a distance, and carried their weapons in the open so they could fight the Germans legally and fairly? I say 'no' as does the majority of the world. In this case, one should break the law as early and as often as possible when confronted with a genocidal regime. To date, we can safely say not a single Jewish sniper or guerrilla has been brought to trial for breaking the Geneva Convention while fighting the Nazis. Clearly, the Holocaust showed that urban guerrilla sniping, as a methodology, is neither illegal nor immoral. How this methodology is employed and to what ends it is used defines the righteousness of the act. Jewish guerrilla snipers, who desperately picked off their Nazi butchers from the sewers, attics, and alleys of the burning Warsaw Ghetto, could not have served a more noble cause.

But where do we draw the line? What about the Russian invasion of Afghanistan in 1979; was that a legal military intervention? The Russian government said it was. Then, the Soviet military proceeded to carpet bomb much of the rural Afghan population and dropped untold numbers of mines, some disguised as toys, in order to effect a policy the Afghanistan resistance described as limited genocide. In this situation, what do you think of a Mujahideen sniper in the capital of Kabul putting a single, full-metal jacket round into the skull of an off-duty Russian officer? Should this sniper be charged with a war crime because they were dressed like a sheep herder at the time of

British Snipers 1943

Are these legal uniforms?

the shooting? The United States, the Afghan resistance, and Pakistan – all with strategic interests in the country – would say this was a legal shooting because the Russians themselves had long ago discarded any pretense of fighting a legal war.

We can also look at the British occupation of Northern Ireland, the Israeli takeover of the West Bank and Gaza Strip in 1967, and the American invasion of Iraq in 2003. In these situations, the occupiers all claimed to be conducting lawful military operations in support of national security interests. In turn, each resistance movement (all have used guerrilla snipers that broke the laws of land warfare) argued that their oppressors broke international law first by invading and occupying them. On top of it, each resistance movement could point to numerous documented examples of their enemy violating the laws of land warfare by torturing captured guerrillas and repeatedly killing innocent civilians with their clumsy counter-insurgency measures. So who is right? The reader will have to make their own decision as the best answer I can come up with is 'it depends'.

Why Urban Guerrilla Sniping?

If urban sniping is such a difficult endeavor, requiring creative thought, rigid discipline, and receiving extreme legal scrutiny, why do guerrilla movements employ them? What is the advantage? In January 2000, a Chechen sniper shot a Russian major-general as he inspected his front lines in Grozny. In March 2006, Iraqi insurgents shot and killed the Iraqi military's most competent general as he drove in downtown Baghdad. This ability to remove specific, influential personalities underlines one of the sniper's best characteristics: the ability to discriminate. Because military actions in a guerrilla war are unavoidably linked to public perception and government legitimacy, the ability to limit structural damage and civilian casualties is crucial. When the guerrillas employ a lone sniper, they can be assured the sniper will destroy a specific target without harming bystanders.

The guerrilla sniper's ability to avoid collateral damage can be used to exploit the government's own inability to do the same. If government security forces are unable to detect and selectively eliminate the guerrilla sniper, these security forces often resort to massive, indiscriminate firepower to silence the shooter. As a result, if a guerrilla sniper fires from amongst the population, they can often bait security forces into butchering the population with a massive response. This overreaction in turn provides ammunition for the guerrillas' information war and undermines the legitimacy of the government.

Overreaction and clumsy massacres are one kind of reaction from enemy security forces, but so is organizational paralysis. A skilled guerrilla sniper, relentlessly working a specific geographic area, picking off targets regardless of government security measures, is a powerful tool. In this manner, the unseen sniper, selectively killing their prey and getting away with it every time, creates bone-gnawing fear and can freeze the targeted unit.

Guerrilla snipers are also a viable means for attrition warfare, steadily picking off security forces one by one, raising the body count to an intolerable political level. Chechen guerrillas fully embraced this form of attrition warfare through their widespread use of snipers, which was one of the number one killers of Russian soldiers in that war. In turn, Iraqi insurgents understood the political importance of attrition warfare, using their own snipers to raise the American body count. Both Chechen and Iraqi guerrillas calculated that a steady stream of casualties would eventually become politically unpalatable to the Russian and American publics.

At the tactical level, snipers perform a variety of functions, and for a guerrilla force, pinning down the enemy's superior forces is a vital task. The Chechens expertly used snipers to slow down vastly superior enemy forces, causing Russian forces to bog down in the streets of Grozny as the dead piled up. Serbian snipers, taking careful aim at surrounded Sarajevo, paralyzed entire sections of the city, forcing thousands of people to hide inside their homes and stay off the streets. A single sniper team in Fallujah, Iraq, rumored to be Chechen, was able to pin down an entire American infantry company all day during the November 2004 assault on the city. As these examples show, a single sniper enables the guerrillas to economize their force and expend only one man for disproportionate results.

Another use for the lone sniper is creating terror. German snipers on the Eastern Front, confronted with massive human wave attacks by the surging Russians, learned to inflict horrible wounds on the advancing Soviet soldiers by blasting gaping holes in their intestines with explosive bullets. These strategically placed shots reduced the Russians to screaming masses of bleeding flesh incapable of continuing the fight. This calculated use of battlefield terror enabled the Germans to repeatedly beat back human wave attacks, buying themselves much needed time.

While tactical terror on the battlefield is within the reach of the individual sniper, so is the application of widespread terror against the civilian populace. The ugly civil war in Bosnia during the 1990's introduced the widespread use of urban snipers to instill terror in competing populations. Every day, Serbian snipers butchered their opposites, preying on old men, women, and young children. In this war, snipers were used as an ethnic cleansing tool rather than a discriminating battlefield weapon. And

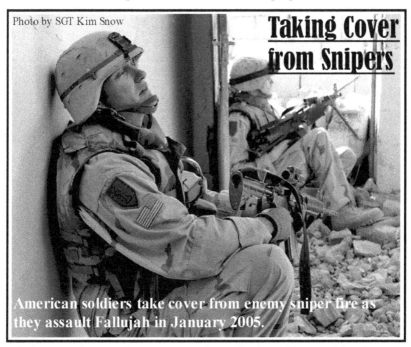

Photo by SGT Kim Snow

Taking Cover from Snipers

American soldiers take cover from enemy sniper fire as they assault Fallujah in January 2005.

long before Bosnia, American mass murderer Charles Whitman, firing from the lofty heights of the Texas Tower in 1966, showed the world that the lone sniper in a densely populated area was just as deadly as a homicide bomber.

For all these reasons, resistance movements employ the urban guerrilla sniper. While the guerrilla understands their own tactics, conventional security forces have either been slow to figure out their enemy's slippery methodology or simply never do. To connect the dots of the urban sniper one must first realize it is the guerrilla's unconventional tactics that make them effective, not their exceptional shooting ability. To focus on the guerrilla's technical shooting skill, as traditional snipers do, is to miss entirely the power of the urban guerrilla sniper.

Chapter 3

Shoot to Thrill
The Psychology of Sniping

Photo by Frank Capa, "Moment of Death", from the Spanish Civil War.

The best success for snipers did not reside in the number of hits, but in the psychological damage caused to the enemy by shooting commanders or other important men.
> - German sniper Matthais Hetzenaur, 345
> confirmed kills

The idea of filming the operations is very important, because the scene that shows the falling soldier when hit has more impact on the enemy than any other weapon.
> - Commander of Iraqi insurgent sniper brigade

More than half of this battle is taking place in the battlefield of the media.... We are in a media battle, in a race for the hearts and minds of our people.
> - In a letter from Al-Qaeda's Ayman
> al-Zawahiri to Abu Musab al-Zarqawi

The Psychology of Sniping

The psychology of sniping is the psychology of fear. John Falk, a journalist who worked in sniper infested Sarajevo, described it best: "Knowing a sniper is loose is like knowing a cobra is at large somewhere in your house. It makes you paranoid. It freezes you. You stop walking by beds, couches: you open drawers. One is left with the eerie sensation that instant death is always just a moment away. People who live under the fear of snipers lose track of everything in the world but their fear; it's a very

The IRA's Sniper At Work Sign

The marketing of modern guerrilla sniping has come a long way from when the IRA first put up their infamous signs during 'The Troubles'.

dark hold that these gunmen have on the regions they terrorize. That's why, if captured, snipers are almost always executed on the spot. It is also the reason why most armies disband their sniper units immediately after a war. Snipers are spooky even to the people they serve."[1]

There is something absolutely terrifying about knowing that a lone, skilled gunman is in the area, possibly placing their crosshairs on your head at any moment. This makes people think. And when people think, they think about saving themselves. Sniper-conscious people take less risks and play it safe. In a war zone, where soldiers and police officers are paid to do dangerous work, playing it safe means you no longer do your job. In 1993, British forces working in South Armagh, Northern Ireland were gripped with sniper-fear. During this time, an Irish Republican Army sniper team worked the area and in nine separate sniper attacks killed seven British soldiers. Some British units were so afraid of being the next victim they stopped doing their jobs.

In fact, one Royal Scots platoon was disciplined because instead of manning a vehicle checkpoint like they were supposed to, they stayed inside the safety of their

---

1 Falk, *Hello to all That*, p.84. (A great account of sniping & the war in Bosnia.)

base and falsified the registrations of the vehicles they were responsible for checking. In this case, the fear of being shot by a sniper overcame military discipline and, in effect, ceded the surrounding area to the IRA.[2] A subsequent summary of operations in Northern Ireland, written by the British army in 2006, admitted the effects of IRA snipers: "Republican information operations, such as the 'Sniper at Work' signs combined with media hype helped build the myth of the sniper. The attacks affected security force operations and had an impact on morale among some troops and police officers serving in South Armagh."

A guerrilla sniper can also have a significant impact on a larger civilian population. A perfect example of this was the murderous sniping spree committed by the DC Snipers – John Muhammad and Lee Boyd Malvo. During the fall of 2002, Muhammad and Malvo stalked the greater Washington, DC region, killing people at random over a geographically large area in order to spread a web of terror. No one was safe. Small children were targeted as were old men and women. Over the course of several weeks, the DC Snipers struck fear in the hearts of tens of thousands of people as entire towns changed their daily habits to avoid the random death lurking the streets. People stocked up on food, children remained at home, and unknown numbers of tourists stayed away. Persistent rumors even spread that Muslim gunmen, loyal to Al-Qaeda, were responsible for the slaughter.

The Sniper's Second Goal: Overreaction

While one goal of a sniper is to instill fear in the hearts of their enemies in order to paralyze and degrade their every move, a second objective is to manipulate this fear into an overreaction. As John Falk described, snipers are not only feared, they are hated. While fighting on the Eastern Front against the Russians in World War II, German sniper Sepp Allerberger was able to elicit a murderous reaction from the opposing Red Army.

On April 2, 1945, the night he won the Knights Cross, Sepp showed the kind of sniping that drove the Russians mad for revenge. On that night, Sepp was on patrol with an infantry squad. The sky was pitch black when a Russian flare suddenly turned the night into day, exposing Sepp and his patrol. Most of the patrol was quickly wiped out by Russian machine-gun fire, leaving Sepp alone to face a Russian infantry company. The Russians then attacked the decimated German patrol in two separate waves. However, the assaulting Russians did not realize Sepp was still alive until he opened fire, at a range of only eighty meters, striking the startled red Army soldiers with explosive bullets. Sepp intentionally aimed at a spot just above the Russian's hips, so his bullets exploded inside their stomachs and intestines.[3]

After Sepp mowed down the assaulting infantry with well-aimed fire, he turned his attention to the remaining Russians still in their trenches. He targeted the closest machine-gun nest located about one hundred meters away. By now, the Russian machine-gun team knew exactly where he was located, but the two bodies of Sepp's fallen comrades protected him from the incoming bullets. Despite the enemy fire, Sepp took careful aim and placed an exploding bullet in the machine-gunner's head and the head of his belt feeder. Every so often Russian soldier would expose himself

2 Harnden, *Bandit Country*, p.401.(A must read about the IRA's war in N. Ireland)
3 Wacker, *Sniper on the Eastern Front*, p. 126-7. (The definitive account of a German sniper who fought on the Eastern front.)

A Viet Cong sniper hangs upside down by his feet from a tree as Chinese Nung mercenaries working for U.S. Special Forces interrogate him. The sniper admitted to firing on a church housing refugees.

Worldwide, irregular snipers are both feared and despised and commonly tortured upon capture. However, a guerrilla movement can use this type of abuse to their advantage.

Picture from Bettman/CORBIS, Photographer: Sean Kelly

in the trench and Sepp would put a bullet in his brain. In the course of ten minutes, Sepp killed all eighteen of the Russian soldiers who once occupied the trench. There were another fifty dead sprawled out across the open field.[4]

With riflework like this, it was unsurprising that the Russians, already prone to brutality, were in less than a charitable mood when capturing a German sniper. Sepp described an instance when a young German sniper was captured by the Russians. This sniper went out to go hunting, but never returned. Four days later, a German patrol came across his body. Sepp believes the Russians captured the German sniper with his rifle, which had notches cut in the stock for all the kills he made. The Russians cut the sniper all over his body, cut his balls off and stuffed them in his mouth, and then stuck the barrel of the rifle up his rectum, all the way to the back sight.[5]

After encountering horrible incidents like this, Sepp became a guerrilla sniper hiding among the larger population of 'regular' German soldiers. Sepp stopped cutting notches in the stock of his rifle for every Russian he sent to the grave. He refused to wear the issued sniper badge depicting a raven's head and three oak leaves. And if

4 Wacker, *Sniper on the Eastern Front*, p. 127-8.
5 Wacker, *Sniper on the Eastern Front*, p. 96.

it appeared that capture was imminent, Sepp ditched his sniper rifle and carried the more innocuous MP-40 submachine-gun. Sepp strived to avoid any outward appearance of being a sniper to become anonymous. This way, he might actually live if captured by the Russians.

In a guerrilla war, the rage and anger a deadly sniper like Sepp Allerberger brings out in the enemy can be used to advance the guerrillas' cause. This is because the security forces being killed one at a time by an invisible shooter are just as likely to turn their pent up frustrations on the civilian population as they are at the actual shooter. The United States' field manual *Combined Arms Operations in Urban Terrain* recognizes this problem in their chapter on sniping: "Historically, units that suffered heavy and continual casualties from urban sniper fire and were frustrated by their inability to strike back effectively often have become enraged. Such units may overreact and violate the laws of land warfare concerning the treatment of captured snipers. This tendency is magnified if the unit has been under intense stress of urban combat for an extended time. It is vital that commanders and leaders at all levels understand the laws of land warfare and also understand the psychological pressures of urban warfare. It requires strong leadership and great moral strength to prevent soldiers from releasing their anger and frustration on captured snipers or civilians suspected of sniping at them."

Since a central part of any guerrilla war is winning the support of the population, government forces that indiscriminately kill, injure, or inconvenience the civilian population in order to get a sniper will only turn the people against them. The same is true for government forces that carelessly destroy the surrounding urban infrastructure and blow up buildings, destroy bridges, and tear up roads. Therefore, a guerrilla sniper that induces fear in their enemy and causes an overreaction that results in the mass detention of innocent people and costly damage to the urban landscape, advances their movement by creating the conditions that turn public opinion against the government.

The Francs-Tireurs and the Franco-German Wars

An example of the power of overreaction took place during the 1870-1871 Franco-Prussian War when Francs-Tireurs (French partisan forces) fought against the invading Prussian forces. The Francs-Tireurs, which grew from French civilian gun clubs created in the 1860's, were intended to provide the French government with a corps of trained marksmen in case of war. When Prussia invaded France in 1870, the Francs-Tireurs, fighting in civilian garb, fought a guerrilla war against the Prussian troops, relying heavily on guerrilla sniper tactics to pick off unsuspecting Prussian soldiers and to tie down large numbers of the invaders. The French guerrillas were such feared marksmen that the Spanish and Portuguese words for sharpshooter (*francotirador* in Spanish and *franco-atirador* in Portuguese) were derived from the word franc-tireur.

In response, the Prussian army considered the Francs-Tireurs dishonorable assassins and executed all captured snipers (and other guerrillas) on the spot. The Prussians argued that the Francs-Tireurs, by fighting in civilian clothes, violated the norms of warfare and could be killed just like one would kill a spy. But, the invading Prussians did more than just kill captured Francs-Tireurs, they also employed widespread reprisals against entire villages and towns suspected of harboring the guerrillas. These

German Sniper Sepp Allerberger

Around his neck is the Knights Cross, awarded for the night he single handedly wiped out a Russian infantry company

reprisals, which included mass detentions, pillaging, and the burning of private residences, bred a long-lasting hatred between the French people and the Prussians.

The Prussian military command, seriously frustrated by the Francs-Tireurs during the war, believed only through even stricter population control measures and mass punishment could the problem be solved. Consequently, when World War I arrived with a terrible thunder in 1914, the invading German army, who found themselves plagued once again with accurately shooting Francs-Tireurs, reverted to harsh pacification measures against the Belgian and French civilian populations. As before, these measures only served to alienate the Belgian and French people, turning them ever more resolutely against the German invader. The by-product of the escalating Francs-Tireurs/German pacification war was an increasingly entrenched hatred for the German invaders, who were derisively called 'the Boches' or 'the Hun' after the barbaric conquerors from the east.

Due in part to this hatred generated from German mistreatment of French civilians during the Great War, France and the other victorious nations enacted their own revenge on the German people with the Treaty of Versailles in 1919. The German army may have subjected large swaths of Western Europe to their repressive counter-guerrilla measures during the Great War, but a vengeful France imposed an even harsher post-war sentence on the entire German nation which included a humiliating de-militarization of the Fatherland, allied control of Germany's vital industrial Ruhr area, and absolutely crippling war reparation payments. These measures shattered the German state's self-esteem, destroyed the German economy, and created a chaotic environment that led to a low-grade civil war.

Out of this toxic, bubbling cauldron of fear, hate, and loathing came a most unlikely savior: Adolf Hitler. Through the Fuhrer, the resuscitated German people unflinchingly funneled their two decades of humiliation, disgrace, and misery. With a vengeance, the Nazi Phoenix righted past wrongs, steamrolling sacrificial Poland in

1939 and crushing hated France under the steel treads of German panzers in the summer of 1940. And yet again, Western Europe, and particularly France, responded with guerrilla warfare. Just as with the Franco-Prussian War and the Great War, German occupation forces responded with increasingly repressive counter-insurgency tactics.

This time the war was different, as Germany now had the Gestapo, which employed such brutal counter-insurgency experts like Klaus Barbie, who tried to beat, execute, and torture the French population into submission. Captured French resistors were also dumped into the German Todt Organization, where they were worked to the bone as forced labor. If digging ditches for the Reich failed to cure the will to resist, more permanent measures might work, like being thrown into the giant maw of the comprehensive system of concentration camps and slaughterhouses that devoured millions of resistors and enemies of the state - from suspected guerrillas and communists to Jews and the mentally retarded.

After the Third Reich's final defeat in 1945, the allies learned they made a serious mistake after World War I by punishing Germany, but leaving her people to their own devices. This time, with the horrors of the Holocaust firmly in mind, the allies decided to occupy and castrate Germany, ensuring a new, militant Germany did not rise from the ashes of the former Nazi state. As of the writing of this book, the allies' post-war strategy worked. In this example, the use of guerrilla snipers - begun in the Franco-Prussian War - contributed to an inseparable chain of events, fueled by spiraling hatreds, that contributed to the greatest bloodbath the world had ever seen.

Amplifying Fear, Amplifying Reaction

A sniper's effectiveness is multiplied tenfold when their enemy thinks they are a greater threat than they actually are. For example, we read earlier in this chapter about the British platoon in Northern Ireland that stopped doing their jobs because of sniper-fear. Most likely, the platoon had no specific information that an IRA sniper team was singling them out. However, because several other soldiers over the course of several months were hit, fear of attack was enough for them to give up on carrying out their duties. The IRA's campaign of sniper-intimidation was aided immensely by a publicity campaign involving road signs showing the silhouette of a sniper and the words *Sniper At Work* painted below. The Sniper at Work signs greeted British soldiers as they went on foot patrol and drove their vehicles in IRA dominated areas in Northern Ireland. These signs (some of which were booby-trapped to prevent their removal) reminded the British they were entering IRA sniper country. In reality, relatively few British soldiers were killed by IRA snipers. However, the British thought the threat was greater and this was enough to put an enormous drag on all their operations like a giant lead anchor, allowing the IRA a much greater freedom of movement than they deserved.

The Cult of Sniperism: The Myth of Vassili Zaitsev

Like the modern IRA, the Russians of World War II understood the power of promoting their sniping efforts and the single greatest feat of sniper propaganda is without doubt the myth surrounding Russian sniper Vassili Zaitsev and his supposed duel with the Germans' best sniper during the battle of Stalingrad. To understand the power of this myth, one must first understand the circumstances surrounding the battle. Up

This grainy still frame is from the documentary *La Liberation de Paris* showing French guerrilla snipers opening fire on the retreating German garrison.

until the Battle of Stalingrad, which ended in February 1943, the German Wehrmacht (armed forces) mauled the Soviet Union as a vicious wolverine would savage a giant, ponderous bear. During the course of this mauling, the Red Army and Soviet people suffered losses on a scale never been seen before in the history of warfare. By the time the German Sixth Army could see Stalingrad's skyline in the fall of 1942, millions of Russian soldiers had already been killed and seriously wounded in combat, millions more languished in Spartan POW camps, and millions of Russian civilians were executed, starved to death, or simply obliterated by the German war machine.

Taking into account this grim situation, the Soviet Union needed a psychological victory - they needed a hero. By sheer chance, young Vassili Zaitsev, a Navy payroll clerk who grew up hunting wild game in the Ural mountains to feed his family, became this hero. No one in the Russian army knew that Zaitsev was an excellent shot and nor that, one day, he would become an expert urban sniper. The Russian leadership literally stumbled across Zaitsev when stories about a short, tough, seaman who was picking off Germans finally reached their ears. General Chuikov, commander of the reeling Russian forces in Stalingrad, knew his hard pressed men needed inspiration, so he promoted and publicized Zaitsev's exploits.

Chuikov's decision to exploit Zaitsev's sniper successes led to the creation of what the Russians called 'The Cult of Sniperism.' Chuikov intentionally encouraged the development of a Russian sniper corps in Stalingrad and he wanted more snipers like Zaitsev fighting in his ranks. As a result of this guidance, Zaitsev started an urban sniper school in the ruins of Stalingrad and eventually trained scores of students that either equaled or surpassed his sniping skills and total enemy body count. By the height of the battle for Stalin's city, the Russians had a large, trained sniper corps inflicting significant, daily losses on the Germans.

While the Cult of Sniperism had real bite to it, Zaitsev and his sniper corps were larger than life in the Russian media. Moscow radio shows trumpeted Zaitsev's success to the Russian people, giving them faith in the fight against the Nazi invaders. Red Army newspapers gloated as Zaitsev's body count grew by leaps and bounds. Soviet propaganda units in Stalingrad cranked out crudely inked flyers glorifying Zaitsev's sniper prowess and distributed them by the arm loads to their front line troops (which found their way to the Germans who suffered under his crosshairs).

The Sniper Duel That Never Was

Zaitsev's popularity hit its zenith with the much publicized duel between him and a German sniper, who was supposedly sent to Stalingrad to take him out. According to the Russians, the German Wehrmacht, who were professionally and publicly humiliated by Zaitsev's sniper successes, sent their chief instructor from the sniper school at Zossen, located near Berlin, into the crumbling city of Stalingrad to settle the score. The story of this most famous duel was told by Zaitsev himself in his memoirs *Notes of a Sniper.*

In Vassili's tale, a team of the Russian scouts captured a German soldier for the explicit purpose of interrogating him for battlefield information (the Russians referred to these kind of prisoners as 'tongues' because their sole purpose was to talk). This frightened prisoner indeed talked to save his life and told his captors the German high command had flown in their best sniper – a Major Konings, head of the sniper school near Berlin - with the mission to take out Zaitsev.

Now that Zaitsev knew the German super-sniper was in the city, Zaitsev had to find him just as he assumed the German was looking for him. Zaitsev took his usual thorough approach, trying to detect a pattern from how his own Russian comrades were being shot and wounded in the city. After no luck, he finally had a breakthrough. In one day, two of the Russians' best snipers were targeted by a sniper. One sniper was shot and wounded and the other had his rifle scope shattered.

The next day, Zaitsev and his partner Kulikov went to the scene of the sniper attack to see if the German shooter was still around. While they surveyed the German lines, they saw a German helmet appear in a trench line and bob along the ditch. However, the movement of the helmet looked unnatural, as if it was placed on top of a stick. Zaitsev knew this was a trap. Konings must have had his assistant present the helmet to get Zaitsev to shoot at it, thus revealing Zaitsev's position and making him vulnerable to Konings' own shot. Instead, Zaitsev and Kulikov snuck off under the protection of darkness in order to think of a plan.

The two went back to the same location the second day, and after hours of careful surveillance, they still saw nothing. They assumed Konings was still lying in wait somewhere, conducting his own surveillance against them, hoping they would make a mistake and expose themselves.

On the third day of their stakeout, the two were accompanied by a political officer named Danilov. As they scanned the rubble, Danilov thought he spotted Konings and rose out of his trench to point him out to Zaitsev. As soon as he did, Konings shot Danilov, but only wounded him. Still, Zaitsev could not figure out where Konings was hiding. Zaitsev continued to study the urban terrain, taking notes as he looked for a

Russian Propaganda

БЕЙ ТАК:
ЧТО НИ ПАТРОН-
ТО НЕМЕЦ!

This Russian World War II - era poster says, "Shoot Like This: One Bullet - One German!" The sniper has seven shell casings in the palm of his hand and seven crosses, with a German helmet atop each one, are visible in the background. Posters like these were meant to restore morale on the home front and instill fear in the enemy.

clue of where he might be.

Zaitsev finally deduced where the shot came from – directly in front of their position. In front of them were only three possible sniper positions: a burned out tank, a pillbox, and a sheet of iron. Zaitsev guessed Konings was under the sheet of iron, in the shadows underneath it, completely invisible. To test his theory, Zaitsev raised his mitten on a piece of wood. A shot rang out, piercing the mitten and small board. Zaitsev inspected the wood, noticing the bullet entered it from straight on, where the iron sheet was. Zaitsev decide to stay in place for another night. He would try and get Konings the next day.

The next day, Zaitsev and Kulikov scoured the terrain again. Then, as the sun shone brightly above, they saw a glimmer of light reflecting off of something under the sheet of iron. Perhaps a rifle scope? Kulikov tried to lure out Konings by raising his own helmet carefully above his position. *Bang!* A shot rang out, striking the helmet. Kulikov, the consummate actor, screamed out in agony and collapsed to the ground in imaginary death. Zaitsev in turn fired under the iron sheet, striking Konings, killing him. Later that night, Zaitsev and Kulikov went to Koning's position and recovered his rifle and identification papers, turning them over to their command.[6]

This story has since become the most repeated tale in the history of sniping until it has been accepted as gospel by many historians and sniper enthusiasts. General Chuikov himself repeated this exact story in his 1959 book *The Battle for Stalingrad*. Since Chuikov's book is critical of the Russians' own failures and gives due credit to the German war machine, his citing of the Zaitsev story gave it considerable credence. William Craig's 1973 work *Enemy At The Gates* repeats this same story as if repeating some sort of religious doctrine. In 1999, David L. Robbins published his novel *War of the Rats*, a fictional account of the events leading up to the duel between

6 Zaitsev, *Notes of a Sniper.*, p. 233-245. (Written by Zaitsev himself and is a superb account of all aspects of urban sniping & the fight for Stalingrad.)

Zaitsev and Konings. Only two years later, in 2001, the movie *Enemy at the Gates* hit the theaters, billed as the 'true story' of the now famous sniper duel between Zaitsev and his German nemesis. To top it off, John Plaster repeats a shortened version of the same story in his 2006 book *The Ultimate Sniper.*

I have no doubt many people who read these books or saw the movie also believe the story Zaitsev himself printed in his book *Notes of a Sniper.* The only problem with this story is it never happened. Yes, Zaitsev did shoot it out with a German sniper – he shot it out with many German snipers. However, the supposed duel between Zaitsev and a German super-sniper is pure propaganda. There are many reasons why an investigator, looking at the tale with a critical eye, would find the story less than convincing. While we could write an entire chapter as to why this yarn does not hold any water, here are some of the most salient reasons:

• It is unlikely the German high command, fighting a costly war in North Africa, worried about an invasion of France, and taking astronomical losses all along the Eastern Front, would get so involved as to make the decision to send one man, their best sniper-instructor, to Stalingrad. And there is absolutely no official or personal documentation anywhere supporting this happened.

• No one, either Russian or German, has proven a 'Major Konings' ever existed. If he did die in combat, the German army would have issued a death notice and sent official documents to his family. This never happened.

• German officers were not snipers, enlisted men were.

• It is statistically improbable two individual snipers, fighting in a twenty-mile long city, caught in between two armies equaling more than 100,000 men, could find each other to duel.

• The German that Zaitsev supposedly shot was not a skilled sniper. He stayed in an isolated position for too long, he fell for Zaitsev's obvious ruses, and failed to detect Zaitsev's own predictable trap. In short, he did everything that Zaitsev said a good sniper would never do.

• Some researchers claim the Germans really sent SS Standartenfuehrer Heinz Thorwald to kill Zaitsev. Again, there is no proof of this anywhere, SS colonels were not snipers, and this additional name reveals yet another inconsistency in the story.

• The Russians say a German prisoner told them the Germans were sending a sniper to get Zaitsev. How did this soldier know? Did someone tell him personally? Was it common knowledge in the German ranks? There is no evidence of this ever happening except word of mouth…from the Russians.

• Zaitsev said he took the personal documents from the German sniper's body and gave them to his superiors. The Russians also say they have the scope from the German sniper in a museum, but where are these supposed documents?

The Russians' propaganda machine spun this story so aggressively and consistently that even today many people accept this account as fact. This is exactly what the Russians wanted. They wanted to create the image of a perfect sniper who was always victorious and triumphed over evil, no matter what the odds. In this sense, the story of the famous duel was an analogy for the larger battle of Stalingrad. Just as Zaitsev, the humble Siberian shepherd, was able to beat the best the Aryan race had to offer, the Russians' rag-tag army in Stalingrad soundly beat the mighty German Sixth Army. The story of Zaitsev's duel was really a story of the whole Russian Army, the entire Russian people. Zaitsev was Russia.

One must appreciate what the Russian propaganda machine accomplished. They made it seem, to both Russian and German troops alike, there was a Russian sniper under every roof, in every trench, behind every bush, patiently watching and waiting for each and every German soldier in the entire Wehrmacht. As a result, the Russians instilled fear in the average German soldier, making the German soldier sniper-conscious throughout the rest of the war. While we can admire the Russian success in the field of sniper psychology, one has to wonder at the German failure. Why did the Germans fail to promote their own sniper movement in order to instill fear in their enemies?

Germany and Sniping

There were many reasons why the Germans did not embrace 'The Cult of Sniperism' like the Red Army did. The primary reasons were institutional. The German Wehrmacht was a combined arms war machine and the lone sniper did not figure in their larger calculations. The panzer divisions and the Luftwaffe were the champions of the Wehrmacht, not the lowly *scharfschutze*. While the rifleman was given due respect, most were not national heroes. Many wartime Germans knew who Michael Whittmann was, the blond, handsome panzer commander credited with being the most successful tank commander in the history of war, destroying hundreds of enemy tanks, artillery pieces, and armored vehicles. Equally famous was unrepentant Nazi Hans Ulrich Rudel, a Stuka dive bomber pilot who destroyed over 2000 ground targets and won the diamonds to the Knights Cross. And the German people knew very well the name of Erich Hartmann, called the Black Devil of the Ukraine by his enemies, a dashing fighter pilot with 352 confirmed kills.

But who ever heard of Matthais Hetzenaur, a German sniper with the 3rd Gebirgsjaeger Division? Hetzenaur had at least 345 confirmed kills during the war and probably several hundred unconfirmed kills. Sepp Allerberger had 257 confirmed kills and most likely a total body count of 500. These men got a pat on the back from their fellow soldiers who appreciated their dirty work, they were eventually awarded a cheap, cloth sniper badge for their efforts in 1944, and some were recommended for a higher award if they pulled off a particularly spectacular feat like the night Allerberger wiped out an entire Russian infantry company to the last man. There were no front page headlines for these men who did the most dangerous of jobs. As a result, the German people were not inspired by the actions of these men and the Russians did not live in fear of them. German snipers were like a tree falling in the forest with no one to hear them.

An unlikely supporter for a more robust German sniper program was the Reichsfuhrer of the SS, Heinrich Himmler. Although the bookish Himmler had no experience in sniping himself, he saw its value. In a letter Himmler sent to Albert Speer, dated December 18, 1944, Himmler expressed some of his views about the overall German sniping effort: "Dear Party Member Speer: Perhaps you have already heard that I'm encouraging and accelerating sharpshooting training in the Grenadier Divisions. We have already attained outstanding results. I have initiated a contest between all divisions of the army and the SS that are under my command. With the 50th confirmed sharpshooter hit – that is, when he has virtually eliminated a Soviet Infantry Company – each man receives a wristwatch from me and reports to my Field Headquarters. With the 100th hit, he receives a hunting rifle and with the 150th he is invited by me to go hunting to shoot a stag or chamois buck.

The heavy requirement of sharpshooting underlies my following representation: Per experience, it is entirely possible that a division can effect at least 200 hits a month. I have several divisions which have attained 300 and 400 hits.

Suppose there were only one hundred divisions on the entire Eastern Front – there are significantly more – that would mean 20,000 dead foes in one month. It should be taken into consideration that these fallen foes belong to fighting infantry, not to the supply lines, the artillery or the rear support services. The Soviet rifle division today has 2 Infantry regiments of 12 Companies with 50 men each; in all about 1200 men.

20,000 dead foes per month by means of sharpshooter hits means the elimination of the infantry of almost 17 rifle divisions, a result we cannot obtain more effectively, and – if you prefer, more expensively – with the employment of the least amount of armament. For this, however, it is necessary that we obtain more sharpshooter rifles. I would be very grateful if you could step up the production of telescopic sights, rifles with telescopic sights and perhaps also machine carbines with telescopic sights as soon as possible. Signed Himmler."[7]

Any support for a more aggressive sniper program was a good thing for the Wehrmacht, but Himmler appreciated the sniper corps for statistical – not psychological – reasons. As 1945 approached the dying Reich, Himmler thought that killing 240,000 Russians in the final year would make a dent in the Red Army. He could not have been more wrong. The Russians buried 240,000 dead a month, for four months, in the murderous slag heap called Stalingrad and they still kept coming. The Russian nation as a whole, since the first horrible summer of 1941, lost five million dead a year for four years and endured. A statistical perspective on sniping, when facing the Red Army, was doomed to failure. The Red Army, as an institution, was designed to take gigantic, near-fatal losses but survive, like some teetering, grotesque Frankenstein, with its limbs hacked off and then crudely reattached.

Instead, Himmler should have written a letter – not to Albert Speer – but to Joseph Goebbels, Germany's Minister for Popular Enlightenment and Propaganda who had a white-knuckled stranglehold on the German media outlets. The German sniper movement would have been better served if Goebbels' propaganda machine ran regular radio broadcasts about its eagle-eyed Aryan sharpshooters and plastered running tallies of their kills on the front pages of the Reich's newspapers. Goebbels and the Wehrmacht should have copied the Soviet approach, since the spreading of fear was a more powerful tool for the severely outnumbered Reich. Ultimately, the Red Army understood the psychology of sniping far better than their German foes.

Marketing the Modern Sniper

Over the course of many decades and wars, no military – and certainly no guerrilla movement – equaled the Russian exploitation of sniping until the 2003 war in Iraq. While most Iraqi insurgent snipers were not exceptionally talented shooters, (not one has displayed the prowess of a Vassili Zaitsev or a Sepp Allerberger) the Iraqi resistance did understand the psychology of sniping. In Iraq, the insurgents gave a name and an identity to their guerrilla sniper campaign, creating a single super-sniper they

7 Senich, *The German Sniper 1914-1945*, p. 283.

Germany's Unsung Snipers

This highly unusual photo shows a late-war German sniper squad armed with Walther Gewehr 43 sniper rifles. It wasn't until mid-1944 that the German sniper corps matched the Russians in quality, when the war was already lost.

called 'Juba'. The insurgents cleverly attributed a variety of skillful sniper attacks to this single sniper entity who seemed to be everywhere. Importantly, the key to the insurgents' marketing success were their procedures for filming and then distributing their sniper attacks to an international audience.

The Iraqi insurgent snipers got their film coverage by assigning a cameraman to record the sniper's attack. Most often, the shooter and the cameraman were collocated side by side. When the sniper made their shot from their concealed position, the cameraman filmed from an angle almost in line with the shooter. The cameraman was so close to the shooter that, at times, it looked like the camera was attached to the rifle. On occasion, the snipers even filmed the shootings through the scope of their rifle. The end result was a 'you-are-there' perspective of the shooting.

Getting good sniper footage was just one step in the insurgents' marketing process. The next step was getting this film into a format the hungry consumer could devour. This was easy since the sniper attacks were filmed on digital cameras. After the cameraman filmed the attack and made their getaway, they went to a secure location, like a safehouse, and hooked their camera up to a computer. Using basic, commercially available software, they downloaded, edited, and burned their footage onto compact discs (CDs). Once the insurgents burned a couple of hundred CDs, they were ready for distribution. One way to get them into the hands of the Iraqi people was to simply stand on street corners and hand them out. Or, the CDs were distributed to the vast, thriving underground CD network in Iraq that sold CDs to the discriminating customer on anything from fiery IED attacks to gruesome beheadings.

The most important venue for insurgent sniper videos was the internet. The Iraqi insurgency was media-savvy enough to develop its own websites that promoted the insurgency and glorified their attacks on the government and American occupation forces. If the average Iraqi citizen was unwilling to risk being caught in possession of insurgent propaganda – which may get them a painful beating by the police or even jail time – it was safer just to log onto a guerrilla website and see the video online. If the consumer watched the video in the comfort of their own home, they could always delete the web history and the internet cookies after getting their insurgency fix. If they did not want to risk having incriminating electrons hidden away somewhere in the electronic guts of their computers, they could go to an internet café and log on there. In Iraq, watching insurgent propaganda was like watching porn. No one would publicly condone it, it was officially outlawed by the government, but everyone did it and the government could not stop it.

Because the insurgents placed their sniper footage on internet service providers (ISPs) in neutral countries like Syria and Jordan, the Iraqi and U.S. governments were unable to control it or shut it down. Even if an ISP was shut down, it was a temporary annoyance at best, as another ISP was just a few clicks and an anonymous credit card away from being up and running. With the internet's global reach, insurgent sniper propaganda found itself readily available across the world and in America's own living rooms. One just had to log onto *www.YouTube.com* or *www.ogreish.com* to see this footage. YouTube is a particularly potent media tool because 100 million people a day log onto the site and one Iraqi insurgent sniper video, which offered the interested viewer tips on how to shoot American soldiers, received 30,000 hits before it was taken down. Today, anyone in the world can do a Google or Dogpile search for 'propaganda + sniper' and find what they are looking for.

Another arrow in the Iraqi insurgents' media quiver was international television. Just think of the hundreds of millions of people a day who watch the world's major news channels like America's Cable News Network (CNN), the British Broadcasting Company (BBC), Germany's Der Spiegel news network, and Qatar's Al-Jazeera. CNN has a true global reach, and as of 2007, its news services were available to more than 1.5 billion people. If CNN was a giant in its field, then BBC was a colossus, bringing in even larger audiences through its radio shows, TV news, and internet sites. In 2007, the BBC was rated as single, largest media organization on the planet. Germany's Der Spiegel operated in the shadows of media giants like CNN and the BBC, but it was Germany's number one magazine with millions of readers and had its own internet site. And then there was Al-Jazeera, the most influential Arab media network in the Middle East. Although it was only created in 1996, Al-Jazeera already reached an estimated 50 million Arab homes and 80 million English speaking homes by 2007.

It is important to understand the reach and influence of these media giants because each one of them aired stories and/or videos of the Iraqi insurgents' sniper attacks against Iraqi government and American forces. On October 18, 2006, CNN's show *Anderson Cooper 360* aired a five minute piece about Iraqi insurgent sniping, including a sniper video produced by the Islamic Army in Iraq. While the show had a huge audience, even more attention was brought to the sniper piece when the American public debated if CNN should have showed the insurgents' sniper video or not. In fact, the controversy brought more coverage to the insurgents' sniper operations than if there was no controversy at all.

On their website, CNN explained why they showed the sniper footage. They admitted that there could be some benefit to the insurgents by airing the sniper piece and that some viewers would be upset by the graphic footage. However, CNN argued that the piece was newsworthy and important to show because of the rising casualties in Iraq, many of which were caused by snipers. Out of respect to the soldiers actually

Juba Sniper Video

In this grainy still frame taken from a video made by the Islamic Army in Iraq, an American soldier is seen fallen to the ground after being shot by Juba.

targeted in the film, CNN explained they faded the screen to black before actually showing the impact of the sniper's round. Some readers expressed outrage at CNN airing the sniper video while others praised CNN for showing the American people the 'unvarnished truth'.[8]

During the same period as the CNN piece, Der Spiegel's TV network aired a special on the Iraqi insurgent snipers that included Juba sniper footage, an interview with an American soldier wounded in that sniper attack, and then an insurgent sniper showing off his sniper equipment and explaining some of their new methods. For the German media giant, this was just another informational piece on the guerrilla war in Iraq that revealed some of the insurgents' latest tactics. Because Germany did not have any soldiers in Iraq getting shot by urban guerrilla snipers, there was no outcry from the German public and no resulting swirl of controversy.

In October 2006, Al-Jazeera ran a similar video showing insurgent snipers shooting U.S. soldiers. This piece included an interview with the commander of an insurgent sniper brigade who explained the impact of their sniping on the enemy. From the insurgents' perspective, it was important to get their sniper footage on a mainstream Arab news network in order to reach out to the millions of Arabs living adjacent to Iraq in Syria, Jordan, and Saudi Arabia (and the rest of the Middle East for that matter). Videos like this showed the insurgents' success against the occupiers, inspired new volunteers to come and fight in Iraq, and reassured existing supporters around the world that their moral and monetary backing was a good investment.

It is significant to note that the insurgent film airing on the October 2006 Al-Jazeera piece was an example of high quality media work. In the beginning of the guerrilla war in 2003-2004, the Iraqi insurgents' media efforts were often of poor quality, with grainy videos and pictures pasted together haphazardly, obviously made by amateurs. By the time of the sniper video in 2006, the insurgents' media process had improved drastically as they now employed professional media experts to create, edit, exploit,

8 *Anderson Cooper 360* Blog, October 17, 2006.

and distribute slick, well-packaged sniper propaganda worldwide. The Iraqi insurgents showed themselves to be a learning, adaptive organization that valued the art of sniping. They also understood that the impact of their attacks would be amplified exponentially if they put them in the hands of the world's media giants.

Once Juba became a hero to the insurgency, other independent supporters of the resistance capitalized on his popularity to spread the myth of Juba even further. A Brazilian named Carlos Latuff made a comic book about Juba, where the main character does battle with arrogant American forces and guns them down with his sniper rifle. While most writers try to protect their works, Latuff, who posts his Juba comic book on various websites, encourages his readers to copy, download, and distribute his Juba comic book as widely as possible.

Sniper-Media Technology

Ever since the creation of compact, portable still and motion picture cameras in the mid-1800's, man had the ability to photograph and film their sniper attacks. However, it was not until World War II and the battle for Stalingrad that snipers actually began employing cameras in combination with their sniping. The Red Army, for example, took staged photos of their much vaunted snipers gunning down supposed German soldiers in the streets of Stalingrad. In these staged photo sessions, the Russian photographer stood right over the sniper's shoulder, getting pictures of not only their falling victim, but also the shooter's rifle. From this perspective, the reader could almost believe they were holding the rifle themselves, staring down the cold barrel at a Nazi invader.

During his sniping in Stalingrad, Vassili Zaitsev noticed some German snipers were actually doing one better, they photographed their targets through the scopes on their rifles. Zaitsev mentioned this in his book, that a German sniper (who Zaitsev eventually shot) used some sort of photographic device to take pictures through his scope. Unfortunately, Zaitsev makes no mention of recovering this device and other historical accounts of German snipers never mention this practice. One can only assume the German sniper was using a personal camera, attached to his rifle scope, to take pictures of his targets, perhaps before and after he shot them. While any sniper anywhere in the world with a camera could do the same from World War II and on, the practice never caught on. Even Zaitsev and the Russians, who took sniper-media exploitation to new levels, failed to recognize the potential for capturing their actual sniper attacks on film.

Some guerrilla organizations have embraced the use of modern media technology – like the Chechen and Palestinian resistance movements – but they too failed to exploit their sniper operations to the fullest. Only with the guerrilla war in Iraq did one see an organization using 'you-are-there' video footage of their sniper operations. It was the Iraqi insurgent sniper teams who first filmed their sniper attacks on a large scale in an effort to distribute them worldwide. And it was easy. All they did was have a cameraman stand shoulder to shoulder with the shooter and film the entire attack from the sniper's perspective. Again, this was easy because all it took was someone placing an inexpensive, hand-held camcorder up to the scope while taking a shot.

Why it took 150 years for an organization to figure out how to exploit existing media technology and sniper operations is anyone's guess. It took an appreciation of the

An excerpt from the Juba comic book.

media, modern technology, sniper operations, and guerrilla warfare to produce the latest methodology of actually filming sniper operations from the shooter's perspective. It just happened to be the Iraqi insurgents, for whatever reason, who finally cracked the code and figured it out.

While all it takes is a person with a cheap, digital video camera to film a sniper attack from the shooter's perspective, modern technology has made this task easier and more efficient. For example, Bushmaster sells a pair of eight-power binoculars that have an integral camera with LCD (Liquid Crystal Display) screen and 32 megabytes of internal memory, which can capture 30 seconds of video or hundreds of still photos. With these binoculars, someone can zoom in on a target, record an attack, and then download the video/pictures with the USB cable, all for about $500.00. The advantage of using the binocular cam is that it is rugged, has good zooming ability, and does not look like a camera.

Another option is the helmet mounted camera (helmetcam) that has been used for years by law enforcement officers, skydivers, race car drivers, and other outdoor sport enthusiasts. The cameras are very small and the recording devices lightweight and concealable. It is easy for a shooter to attach the helmet cam to their head with a ball cap, bandana, wool cap, or even a piece of string. This way, as the shooter looks down the sights of their weapon, the camera is recording almost exactly what the shooter sees. Several companies make high-quality helmet cams for $300-$500.

Good propaganda can also be realized with a gun mounted camera. The Real Action Paintball company makes a gun mounted camera, for only $200, that can be used during paintball wars or the real thing. The RAP4 Land Warrior System, which can record up to an hour of video, comes with a standard 32 megabyte memory chip, although 1 gigabyte chips are available. This camera is a stand-alone, wireless system that can be connected directly to a TV set for viewing after the action or downloaded to a computer through a USB cable.

A significant leap in sniper-media technology is the new generation of rifle scopes with an integrated video camera so the optical device is a combined scope/camera. For example, SmartScope is a 3x10 variable power scope with an internal color camera that can either record video or still photos. SmartScope weighs 24 ounces, has 32 megabytes of memory, and can take excellent, detailed, color photos out to several hundred meters. With an integrated scope/camera the shooter does not require an additional cameraman and can film their own targets by themselves without the need for additional equipment like jury-rigged cameras. Currently, scope/cameras like the SmartScope cost about $1000.00 each.

Two Israeli arms companies, Eyerec Technologies Ltd/Elbit System, teamed up to produce the Sniper Control System that consists of an integrated scope/camera placed on up to six different sniper rifles, providing real-time feedback from the separate shooting positions to a central command and control station. In this manner, the sniper commander, positioned at a central location, can manage and order the simultaneous shooting of up to six separate targets. While this sniper control system allows the user to record their shots on video, the real innovation in this system is real-time imaging is relayed to a separate location.

The natural progression from here is to beam live, to millions of viewers, the real-time shooting of a sniper's target. A government like Israel, which must take into account international media exposure and political pressure, would surely suffer worldwide condemnation if they aired the real-time shooting of a Palestinian gunman. However, a guerrilla organization would have no such restriction.

But how could a guerrilla organization pull off such a media coup? The Israeli sniper control system is a restricted access item, sold only to Israeli/allied law enforcement and military communities. A guerrilla organization like Hezbollah, Hamas, or the PLO might get one through the black market, or even steal one, but do they have to go through all that effort? No, they do not. In 2004, Texas entrepreneur John Lockwood established an on-line hunting business where people could remotely log onto his website and hunt wild game over the internet. All it took was a webcam attached to a rifle, which was in turn connected to a nearby computer, so the end user could get real-time video streaming through the rifle's scope.

The technology is out there - it is cheap, easily assembled, and commercially available. And it has already been done by a small town businessman in Texas. Now it is up to a guerrilla organization to determine if they want to show real-time video streaming of their sniper attacks on the internet or not. Chances are, they will not want live sniper streaming because their guerrilla media cells need time to review and edit the sniper attacks to present them in the most favorable light. However, live video recording to a remote location would ensure the sniper coverage would be saved at a location independent of the shooter. This way, the shooter would not have incriminating video recordings on their person. Even if the sniper was captured or killed, the sniper attack has already been recorded and is safe elsewhere, perhaps hundreds of miles away or even in a different country.

Shoot to Thrill

The exploitation of the psychology of sniping has lurched forward unpredictably over the years. The first step in maximizing the effects of sniping is to understand its psychological impact: it is better to shoot to thrill than to shoot to kill. The sniper can cause enemy casualties, but the sniper's true power is the ability to instill gut-wrenching fear that paralyzes a military organization or a civilian population. Then, this fear and hatred of the sniper can be used to spark an overreaction from the enemy, helping to alienate the population and build widespread support for the resistance.

Once an organization appreciates what these deadly snipers can do, they can magnify their effects through skillful manipulation of the media. The Russians at Stalingrad

The Smart Scope

The Smartscope is truly an innovation, allowing the shooter to film their shots through their scope.

appreciated the psychological impact of snipers and the benefits of advertising their feats through their media outlets. More recently, with the Iraqi insurgents' melding of sniper psychology and media saturation, the guerrilla sniper has reached new heights. Today, the lone guerrilla sniper, combined with a savvy marketing machine, can produce strategic effects on the battlefield. Because of modern marketing technology, like the internet and other mass market media outlets, the ability to manipulate the psychology of sniping has never been greater.

Chapter 4

Tools of the Trade

Bundes Archive 1011-695-0403-30

When the Provisional Army Council came into being, the arms situation was chaotic. Before the reorganization, representatives of the local defense committees had been forced to seek equipment and supplies on their own from any sources willing to provide (or promise) them.

> - IRA leader Sean MacStiofain commenting on the poor state of the IRA's arms supply network in 1969

Long Guns as Sniper Weapons

While psychology is the most important aspect of sniping, the shooter's weapon is a close second. However, the urban guerrilla sniper chooses their weapon based on different considerations than conventional snipers. For example, an IRA sniper in Northern Ireland cannot go to their local gunshop in Belfast and ask the dealer for their best urban sniping rifle. Instead, the sniper may have to use an existing weapon system designed for something else and then use this dual-purpose weapon for their own requirements.

I heard the saying once, "Your mind is like a parachute...it only works when it's open." This is true when talking about the kind of weapons suitable for urban sniping. With that saying in mind, I was eager to bounce some ideas off a few friends to see if their minds were like a parachute. I started on friend number one, Tom, who is an avid shooter and hunter. I asked him what he thought about using a shotgun for sniping. He looked at me like I had been drinking too much and simply shook his head. I then explained to him exactly how a shotgun could be used as a sniper weapon and he had to concede, after I presented a solid argument, that it was possible. He conceded to my superior logic by saying, "I guess. Whatever." Even though a shotgun with a slug barrel and a scope is designed for killing deer at hundreds of yards, Tom did not want to shatter his preconceived notions.

Then, I decided to talk these ideas over with another friend, Jack, who is a school-trained Army sniper. Jack fought in many recent conflicts, to include Afghanistan and Iraq, and had a score of enemy kills to his credit as a sniper. I knew Jack, as an experienced sniper, would be open to new ideas. So, I tested the waters with a few questions about what he thought about using an AK-47 assault rifle as a sniper rifle. I described how I would accurize it with a scope and a bipod. This time, unlike Tom, Jack did not look at me like I was inebriated. Instead, he looked at me like I was an idiot: "Why would you ever want to use an AK-47 for a sniper rifle? It's a piece of junk."

I said, in an urban environment, at close range, it is good enough. But he insisted, "Why? There are so many better, accurate weapons out there." Yes, I knew that. But what if you had to? What if you had to make due to with a second-rate piece of equipment because you had no money, the government controlled all the guns, and you were in this less than perfect situation? So what if you didn't have a beautiful, gleaming sniper rifle to fight with? Would you give up? Or would you make due with what you had? I would make due with what I had.

The first thing one must understand is the urban sniper does not necessarily need a far-reaching gun. Something accurate to 300 meters will do. Many guns the average shooter classifies as a piece of junk will probably work. This includes semi-automatic weapons, short-barreled surplus carbines, submachine guns, and weapons firing underpowered cartridges like a .22 caliber LR or even a 9 mm round. When the reader surveys the following weapon systems presented as potential sniper weapons, they should look at these systems with the critical eye of an urban guerrilla sniper. They should try and understand what the guerrilla needs to be effective and what is good enough for the job. Also, the reader should consider how expensive is the weapon in question, how hard is it to get ammunition, are replacement parts readily available, and are there suppressors for the weapon?

A German soldier aims down range with a Stg 44, the first assault rifle to ever be used for sniping.

Mauser Karbiner 98 (Kar 98)

Production History: The Karbiner 98 was designed as a general-purpose infantry rifle for the German armed forces in World War II. It was produced in the millions from 1935-1945 and saw action in every theater of the war, from the frigid wastelands on the Eastern Front to the scorching sands of North Africa. Many people consider the Kar 98 to be the best, all-around, military standard, bolt-action infantry rifle to ever be mass produced.

Description: A bolt-action rifle, fires a 7.92 mm x 57 mm round (also called a Mauser 8 mm), fed by a 5-round stripper clip, is 40-inches long, with a 24-inch barrel, and weighs approximately eight pounds.

Range/accuracy: During factory testing in WW II, the most accurate rifles were pulled from the production line and designated as sniper rifles. These hand-selected rifles, when using a telescopic scope, were able to hit man-size targets at 800 meters. Some German snipers used the Luftwaffe's high-velocity, anti-aircraft ammunition, which used a faster burning, smokeless powder, allowing them to reach out to 1000 meters. While accuracy depends on many elements, modern day shooters using 198-grain, match-grade ammunition can shoot one-inch groups at one hundred meters, which meets the standard sniper norm of achieving one Minute of Arc (MOA) accuracy.

Strengths: Surplus models can be bought cheaply for $100-$200. The Kar 98 is a rugged, dependable weapon proven in all weather and environmental conditions. They were produced in such numbers and have exchanged so many hands after the end of World War II that they are essentially 'laundered' guns.

Weaknesses: The Kar 98 is not a purpose-built sniper rifle, it is an infantry rifle pressed into use as a sniper weapon with a few modifications (i.e. the addition of a scope). Some modifications must be made to make it a more suitable weapon, like adding a synthetic (collapsible) stock. With an overall length of 40 inches, it is not concealable. Sound suppressors are rare.

Sniper Use: German snipers used the Kar 98 extensively in World War II, to include the Battle of Stalingrad. The guerrilla Werwolf movement used Kar 98's to fight the occupying powers. Israeli snipers used Mausers as they fought for their independence. NVA/VC snipers used surplus Kar 98's in Indochina. Some of the assassins that killed JFK employed Kar 98's. Bosnian snipers used Yugoslavian copies of the Kar 98 (called the M48) throughout the Bosnian War. Kar 98's with sniper scopes, used by insurgents, have been found in the recent 2003 Iraq war.

Mosin-Nagant 1891/30

Production History: The original Mosin-Nagant 1891 was produced in that year to replace the Russian Empire's obsolete single-shot rifles. The 1891 model was further modified in 1930 (it was shortened and gained a modern receiver) and became the standard-issue infantry rifle for the Soviet Union from 1930-1945. Just like Germany's opposing Mauser Kar 98, the 91/30 was a general-purpose infantry rifle, produced in the millions, and saw action in every theater of the Russians' war.

Description: A bolt-action rifle, fires a 7.62 mm x 54 mm round, fed by a 5-round internal charger clip, is 52-inches long, with a 29-inch barrel, and weighs approximately nine and a half pounds. The 91/30 was most often used in conjunction with a 4 x power PE or 3.5 x power PU scope.

Range/accuracy: During production testing, exceptionally accurate 91/30's were hand selected as sniper rifles. Modern shooters can place five 168-grain, hand-loaded rounds in a one-inch circle at one hundred meters. A trained Russian sniper was expected to place ten rounds into a one and a half inch circle at 100 meters, into a three-inch circle at 200 meters, into a seven-inch circle at 400 meters, and into a fourteen-inch circle at 600m.

Strengths: This is an inexpensive rifle and surplus models can be bought legally for as low as $49.99. Ammo is plentiful and is also relatively cheap. The 91/30 is a rugged, dependable weapon proven in all weather and environmental conditions.

Weaknesses: The 91/30 is not a purpose-built sniper rifle, it is an infantry rifle pressed into use as a sniper weapon. Some modifications must be made to make it a more suitable weapon, like adding a synthetic (collapsible) stock. At 52 inches long, it is not a concealable weapon by any means. The 91/30 is a loud weapon with a large muzzle flash. Sound suppressors were not manufactured for the 91/30.

Sniper Use: Russian and German snipers used the 91/30 extensively in World War II, such as Vassili Zaitsev, who became famous during the Battle of Stalingrad. Many other Russian snipers scored hundreds of kills against the Germans using the 91/30. North Korean and Chinese snipers used the 91/30's during the Korean War. NVA/VC snipers used surplus 91/30's in Indochina against the French and Americans. The PLO used the venerable rifle in their sniper war against Israel. Any country having political/military relations with the former Soviet Union, like Afghanistan, is likely to have a supply of 91/30's on hand.

Varmint Rifle (Weatherby Vanguard Sub-MOA Rifle)

Production History: The Weatherby Vanguard Sub-MOA Varmint rifle is a modern weapon that comes in several calibers to include: .204 Ruger, .223 Remington, .22-250 Remington, and .308 Winchester. The Weatherby Vanguard Sub-MOA is marketed as an ultra-accurate varmint rifle capable of hitting the smallest game out to far distances. This rifle is more expensive than a standard deer rifle and sells for $900-$1000, depending on what options you select.

Description: A bolt-action, centerfire rifle, fires a .22-250 round (for the model shown), fed by a five-round internal magazine, is 41 and 1/2-inches long, with a 22-inch barrel, has a fiberglass-reinforced synthetic stock, and weighs approximately eight and one quarter pounds. This is a quality sniper rifle.

Range/accuracy: The .22-250 Remington was officially manufactured as a commercially available round in 1965, after being available as a hand-made 'wildcat' round for years before. The .22-250 is a .22 caliber bullet fitted into a necked-down Savage 250-3000 cartridge. This is truly a hyper-velocity round, traveling out of the muzzle at 3700 feet per second. The .22-250 is a popular round for shooting varmints because of its flat shooting trajectory and accuracy. Weatherby guarantees its rifle will shoot sub-MOA groups at one hundred meters and the company even delivers the target they shot at the factory, proving its accuracy.

Strengths: The primary strength of the Weatherby Vanguard Varminter is without a doubt its extreme accuracy. Also, the Weatherby Vanguard Varminter can be bought from the factory with a variety of camouflage patterns for the stock, recoil pads are standard, Accubrake muzzle brake is available (reduces felt recoil by fifty percent and reduces muzzle jump), and adjustable triggers are also available.

Weaknesses: The Weatherby Vanguard Varminter, like many higher end hunting rifles, does not come with iron sights, and is meant only to be used in conjunction with a scope. Also, as a civilian varmint rifle, it is not designed to be used covertly, so sound suppressors are not commercially available; a custom one would have to be made. Another potential weakness for varmint guns is they are designed to kill small animals like prairie dogs. While they fire a very accurate, high-velocity round, the round itself is lightweight so it is more easily deflected and lacks knock-down power.

Sniper Uses: Various resistance movements used civilian hunting rifles for sniping such as French Franc-Tireurs, Russian partisans, the IRA in Northern Ireland, and the Chechen rebels just to name a few.

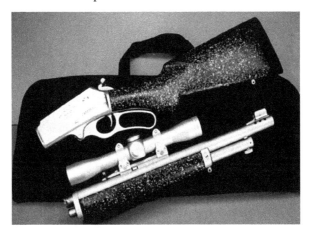

Takedown Rifle (The Alaskan CoPilot)

Production History: The Alaskan CoPilot is produced by Wild West Guns. They take a factory made Marlin 1895 rifle, cut the barrel to a shorter length, and machine it into a takedown rifle, where the barrel quickly and easily de-attaches and re-attaches to the receiver. This weapon is designed as an easily stowed, backwoods survival rifle, capable of taking down the biggest game like grizzly bears.

Description: A lever action rifle, fires a .457 Magnum, .45-.70, or .50 Alaskan round (depending on the model), fed by a tubular magazine, is 32-inches long (depending on the model – half that size when broken down), with a 16, 18, or 20-inch barrel, and has a synthetic stock.

Range/accuracy: This takedown rifle is available with a 3-pound trigger pull and a custom made mount for a variety of high-quality scopes. It fires a .50 caliber Alaskan round with a 450-grain bullet traveling at a velocity or 2050 feet per second. This is not an exceptionally accurate weapon, but four-inch groups at 100 meters are easily done. Lever action rifles are inherently more reliable than semi-automatic rifles.

Strengths: This rifle, like all takedown rifles, is designed to be concealed. When in takedown mode, it is only twenty inches long. A variety of stocks can be custommade by the manufacturer to include synthetic, non-warping stocks. Matching this weapon with a folding stock would make it very concealable even when assembled. This rifle is hard-hitting and if used with armor piercing ammunition, will penetrate helmets and soft body armor. Because this weapon is lever-action, the shooter controls how they eject the expended cartridge, as opposed to semi-automatic rifles that automatically send them flying after each shot.

Weaknesses: This is not a mass-produced weapon and is therefore easier to trace. Unique rifles like the CoPilot means there are fewer aftermarket products available for them. Ammunition, because it is less popular, is harder to find in battlefield conditions. Aftermarket suppressors are not readily available and must be custom-made. Most takedown rifles are expensive…as high as $5000.00 apiece.

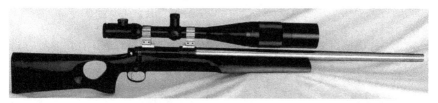

Benchrest Rifles

Production History: Benchrest weapons evolved from the modern benchrest competitions that grew in popularity in the 1940's. Benchrest is a type of shooting where the shooter sits at a bench and uses mechanical means (like specialized tripods) to stabilize their weapon; the shooter intentionally minimizes their interaction with the rifle since more human contact equals reduced accuracy.

Description: Dimensions vary depending on the model. Most benchrest guns are custom-made where a shooter selects a specific action, chooses a barrel, and then selects a stock and combines them. Benchrest guns are bolt-action, single-shot, centerfire weapons. These guns have heavy, free-floating, bull-barrels and the front forestock is extremely wide so the weapon can rest on it and remain stable.

Range/accuracy: Benchrest guns are known for their accuracy and are often referred to as 'nail drivers' since they are expected to fire multiple rounds into the same hole. 1/4-inch minute of arc accuracy is expected. Much of this accuracy comes from the high-velocity ammunition they fire; common calibers are the .204, .222, .223, and 6 mm rounds, which can reach velocities in excess of 4000 feet per second and only drop three feet at 500 yards. Benchrest guns have true hair-triggers, some having a pull of only two ounces.

Strengths: Benchrest rifles are without question the most accurate rifles in the world. Also, since there is such a large civilian market/industry that supports the sport of benchrest shooting, a large variety of benchrest rifles, accessories, and ammunition are available worldwide.

Weaknesses: Benchrest guns are designed for overt competition shooting, not tactical combat operations. These guns are heavy and can weigh up to fifteen pounds because of the wide stock and the super-heavy barrels. They are not manufactured with open sights or sound suppressors.

Sniper Use: In the 1950's, American snipers fighting in the Korean War used civilian benchrest target rifles (because they lacked a dedicated sniper system) with much success against their Chinese and Korean foes.

Air Rifle (Gamo Hunter Extreme)

Production History: Air rifles are popular in many countries for shooting small game, teaching youths the fundamentals of rifle marksmanship, and for competition sport shooting (including an event at the Olympics). Gamo, a Spanish company, started out making a variety of lead products, transitioned to making lead air gun pellets, and then started its own airgun company. Today, Gamo is the largest airgun manufacturer in Europe and its products are well known and sold worldwide.

Description: The above model is the Gamo Hunter Exterme. It is a break-barrel weapon, where breaking open the weapon compresses the air which is then used to fire the pellet. The weapon fires a .177 pellet, is single shot (must be manually loaded each time before firing), is 48 and 1/2-inches long, with a 24-inch barrel, and weighs approximately nine pounds. The stock is made of hardwood.

Range/accuracy: The Gamo Hunter Extreme fires a .177 pellet (4.5 mm) which travels 1600 feet per second at the muzzle. This means the weapon fires the pellet at well over the speed of sound - the pellet is a supersonic projectile that will break the sound barrier just like a rifle that fires a powder propelled bullet. The weapon has a jacketed steel, bull barrel. The scope is 3 x 9 power with an illuminated mil dot. It fires the Raptor Performance Ballistic Alloy (PBA) pellet, a non-lead alloy pellet that increases pellet velocity up to 25% while maintaining match grade accuracy. The PBA is specifically designed as a hunting load and can shoot one-inch groups at 30 yards.

Strengths: Make no mistake, this air rifle is a man-killer that fires a lethal, supersonic round. This weapon, like all airguns, is quiet, has no muzzle flash because it is air-powered, and is thus inherently hard to detect. Airguns do not leave incriminating shell casings behind like powder guns. Since most people do not think airguns are man-killers, few people expect a sniper to use this kind of weapon.

Weaknesses: This is an air rifle designed for overt target shooting and hunting. It is not concealable, suffers from firing a small pellet that has short range and lacks penetration power.

Sniper Use: A video clip by *Outdoor Guide* shows a hunter armed with a Gamo air rifle shooting a 200-pound wild boar at 25 meters. The shooter drops the boar with a single shot to the head, killing him in his tracks. Watching a man armed with a .177 caliber air rifle kill a tough, wild boar makes one appreciate more the capabilities of the common .22 caliber rifle.

Shotgun (Harrington & Richardson)

Production History: Shotguns have been around for several hundred years and have been used primarily for hunting small game like rabbits and birds. Hunters eventually transitioned to firing a single, large slug from the smoothbore barrel for larger game. Then, gun designers produced interchangeable chokes which could be inserted into the barrel of the shotgun which offered rifling for the last several inches of the barrel. Also, rifled slugs were developed where the rifling was on the slug itself. Eventually, designers created a shotgun barrel that was truly rifled, referred to as a 'slug' barrel.

Description: The above model is a Harrington and Richardson Ultra Slug Hunter. It is single-shot, fires a 12-gauge, 3-inch shell, is 40-inches long, with a 24-inch rifled heavy barrel, and weighs approximately nine pounds. Comes with a factory mounted 3 x 9 power scope.

Range/accuracy: Modern slug guns offer rifle-like accuracy. Many shooters get two-inch groups at 100 yards and six-inch groups at 200 yards. Some shotguns have a bull barrel, making them inherently more accurate, and others have break-open or pump actions, which are more accurate than semi-autoloaders. With the advent of modern sabot ammunition, slugs can reach velocities of 2000 feet per second (like the Hornady SST sabot).

Strengths: Shotguns are adaptable weapons and a large variety of aftermarket products are available for them like synthetic, collapsible and folding stocks, scopes of every kind, and a wide selection of ammunition and slugs. Shotguns can be bought legally worldwide, and are relatively cheap, going for around $200 for a good quality slug gun. They fire a large round that is absolutely devastating upon impact. Hunters have repeatedly proven the ability to take down large game, with a single shot, at distances as far as 250 yards. Modern slug guns can definitely be used as a sniper weapon.

Weaknesses: The shotgun has a large muzzle flash/blast and is extremely loud. It is not designed to be used in conjunction with a sound suppressor. The shotgun is not designed for long-range shooting and cannot reach far targets like surplus bolt-action rifles or modern assault rifles can.

Sniper Use: Protestant paramilitary contract killer Michael Stone used a shotgun to commit several of his murders in Northern Ireland because he knew authorities could not ballistically link the weapon to the killings.

Purpose-Built Sniper Rifle (M-24)

Production History: The M-24 Sniper Weapon System (SWS) is a purpose-built sniper rifle built on the Remington 700 action, first fielded by the U.S. Army in 1988. The acquisition of the M-24 represented a return to bolt-action rifles for sniping, as opposed to semi-automatic rifles like the previous use of the accurized M-14.

Description: A bolt-action rifle, fires a 7.62 mm x 51 mm NATO round (.300 caliber), fed by a 5-round internal magazine, is 43-inches long, with a 24-inch barrel, and weighs approximately twelve pounds empty. The adjustable stock is a composite made up of graphite, Kevlar, and fiberglass bound together with epoxy resins. A M3A 10 x power Leupold scope is standard issue.

Range/accuracy: The M-24 meets the Army's requirement of firing one MOA at 800 yards. While the M-24 can fire regular 7.62 NATO bullets in a pinch, it is specifically designed to fire the M118 bullet, a special ball bullet consisting of a gilding metal jacket and a lead slug. The M118 is a boat-tailed bullet weighing 173 grains. The M3A scope is wedded with the M118 as it has a bullet drop compensator designed specifically for that round. The M-24 comes issued with an adjustable stock and bipod to enhance shooter accuracy.

Strengths: This is a durable, rugged, accurate rifle, proven in combat. Ammunition is plentiful and cheap. Because the M-24 is a military version of the very popular Remington 700, there is a large variety of aftermarket accessories available for purchase.

Weaknesses: The M-24, like most conventional sniper rifles, is designed for overt military operations. The M-24 is thus long and heavy, not designed for concealment or covert operations. It was not designed to be used with a sound-suppressor.

Sniper Use: American snipers have successfully used this rifle for years in America's wars in Afghanistan since 2001 and in Iraq since 2003. Iraqi insurgent snipers have been known, on several different occasions, to kill American snipers and then steal their M-24 rifles and use them against other American forces. The original Remington 700, and other ruggedized versions of the sporting rifle, can be bought legally through gun dealers, so insurgents and their networks can purchase these rifles abroad and then funnel them into their respective organizations with relative ease.

Snayperskaya Vintovka Dragunova (SVD)

Production History: The famous SVD was designed by Evgeniy Fedorovich Dragunov in the Soviet Union over the course of several years between 1958 and 1963. The SVD is recognized as being the world's first purpose-built military precision marksman's rifle. The SVD came into general issue in 1963, replacing the venerable Mosin-Nagant 1891/30.

Description: A semi-automatic rifle, fires a 7.62 mm x 54 mm round, fed by a 10-round box magazine, is 49-inches long, with a 24 and 1/2-inch barrel, and weighs approximately ten pounds with the excellent, durable, standard issue 4 x power PSO-1 scope.

Range/accuracy: The SVD fires the 7N1 round, a steel-jacketed projectile with an air pocket, steel core, and a lead knocker in the base for maximum terminal effect. A newer, more accurate lead-core 7N14 round consists of a 151-grain projectile which travels at 2723 fps. The SVD is not an exceptionally accurate rifle and can reasonably expect to achieve two minutes of arc (MOA) at 600 meters. The SVD is not as accurate as competing bolt-action rifles due to its semi-automatic action and how this affects its barrel harmonics.

Strengths: The SVD, like all AK variants, is rugged, durable, and battle-tested in the harshest environmental conditions. SVD's are available throughout the Middle East and Eastern Europe and can be bought cheaply on the black market. Every SVD comes with a factory attached flash suppressor. Aftermarket accessories are plentiful.

Weaknesses: The SVD is a large, conventional sniper rifle and is not easily concealed However, a paratrooper version actually had a folding stock. It is a long, ungainly weapon in the tradition of the 1891/30 it replaced. The SVD is not nearly as accurate as bolt-action rifles like the M-24 and other such purpose-built sniper rifles.

Sniper Use: Since 1994, Chechen snipers used the SVD extensively against invading Russian forces. Iraqi guerrilla snipers used the SVD in large numbers against invading American forces since 2003. The SVD is used throughout the Middle East to include by all participants of the civil wars in Lebanon (1975-90) and for the past several decades by the PLO against Israel. Despite the fact that the SVD is too ungainly for covert, urban sniping, guerrillas use the weapon because it is available, and they modify their tactics to work with their weapon.

Vintovka Snayperskaya Spetsialnaya (VSS)

Production History: The VSS "Vintorez" was designed in the late 1980's specifically for Russian special operations forces like the Spetsnaz, MVD, and KGB. The VSS was intended to replace certain AKM/AK-47 weapon systems to give select forces a stealthy sniping capability.

Description: A semi-automatic rifle (is capable of fully-automatic fire), fires a 9 mm x 39 mm round, fed by either a 10 or 20-round box magazine, is 36-inches long, with an eight-inch barrel, and weighs approximately eight pounds with a full magazine and the excellent, durable, standard issue, 4 x power PSO-1 scope.

Range/accuracy: The VSS has a maximum effective range of 400 meters, with ranges of 200-300 meters offering the best chance for accurate hits. The VSS fires the SP-6 subsonic cartridge that is based on a 7.62 mm x 39 mm case which has been modified to fit a 9 mm bullet. However, the 9 mm bullets are long and unusually heavy. The SP-6 round has a steel penetrator core and can defeat most soft-body armor at ranges of 300-400 meters.

Strengths: The VSS is a purpose-built urban sniping weapon which is compact and relatively light. The VSS is rugged, proven in combat, is concealable, and has an effective sound-suppressor. Because the VSS fires a subsonic cartridge (meaning the bullet does not break the sound barrier), it is a stealthy weapon and cannot be detected by modern acoustic-based counter sniper systems. Because the VSS can be broken down into three separate parts (buttstock, receiver, integral suppressor/barrel), it is concealable and can be carried either in a briefcase or strapped to one's person, underneath a coat.

Weaknesses: The VSS is designed as a close-in urban weapon and therefore suffers from limited range. Since the VSS fires relatively unique ammunition, rounds are harder to come by than the more plentiful 7.62 mm rounds fired by the AK-47 and SVD family of rifles.

Sniper Use: The Russian military used the VSS in Afghanistan and extensively in Chechnya. Chechen guerrillas captured/purchased significant numbers of the VSS and have put them to good effect against their Russian enemy. Now-deceased Chechen warlord Shamil Basayev was often photographed carrying a VSS.

Colt M-4A1 Carbine

Production History: The M-4 is a weapon modified from the earlier M-16 series of assault rifles. The M-4 was first produced in 1994 when the U.S. military recognized a need for a more compact, maneuverable, lighter weapon. The M-4 is the standard weapon for U.S. special operations forces.

Description: A semi-automatic rifle, fires a 5.56 mm x 45 mm NATO round, fed by a 30-round box magazine (magazine capacity varies), is 30-inches long with the adjustable stock retracted, has a 14 and 1/2-inch barrel (different barrel lengths can be installed), and weighs approximately five and a half pounds empty.

Range/accuracy: The M-4 is a very accurate weapon firing a hyper-velocity bullet that reaches speeds of 3000 feet per second, depending on the ammunition used. The average rifleman can hit man-size targets at 300 meters with open sights, and at 500 meters with a scope. The M-4 comes equipped with the excellent, rugged 4 x power ACOG (Advanced Combat Optical Gunsight).

Strengths: The M-4 is a modular system meaning almost everything can be changed out or modified to suit the needs of the environment and the shooter. Different length barrels can be used, a large variety of sights and optics are available, and a large number of high-quality sound suppressors are available over-the-counter. Because the M-4 is so popular as a military weapon and for recreational shooting, ammunition and spare parts are plentiful worldwide.

Weaknesses: The M-4 carbine fires a .223 (5.56 mm) round which is small and lacks penetration power at a distance. The gas-operated system causes chamber fouling from the cartridges' gases and powder. In general, the M-4 action is finicky and jams when dirty. The M-4 requires regular cleaning and care must be taken to keep foreign elements, like dust and sand – which are permanent features of desert environments – out of the weapon's action.

Sniper Use: U.S. forces used the M-4 extensively in their wars in Iraq and Afghanistan. Other armed forces like that of Israel and Colombia also use the M-4, meaning the PLO and FARC have access to these same weapons. The DC snipers used an M-4 in 2002 when they went on their killing spree.

AK-47 (Avtomat Kalashnikova 1947)

Production History: The world's most famous assault rifle, the AK-47 was designed in 1947 by Mikhail Kalishnakov. Most gun enthusiasts agree the AK-47 was copied from the Sturmgeweher 44. Mikhail Kalishnakov argued the AK-47 was really a combination of different designs and may have been 'influenced' by the German assault rifle.

Description: A semi-automatic rifle, fires a 7.62 mm x 39 mm round, fed by a 30-round box magazine (the one in the picture has a 10-round magazine), is 35-inches long (depending on the stock), with a 16 and 1/2-inch barrel, and weighs approximately nine and a half pounds.

Range/accuracy: The AK-47 has terrible World War II-era iron sights which have never been changed to the more accurate peep sight systems. However, the excellent PSO-1 scope pictured here can be quickly fitted to a side mounting rail. The standard Russian round achieves a velocity of 2300 feet per second. Because the AK-47 is a relatively 'loose' weapon, not a finely engineered specimen, its accuracy is poorer than the 'tightly' made M-4. However, with a scope, man-size targets can be reliably engaged up to 300 meters.

Strengths: The 7.62 mm round has greater knock-down power than competing 5.56 mm rounds. Since the PSO-1 scope sits above the iron sights, a shooter can alternate between the two, depending on the distance. The AK-47 is the definition of reliability and ruggedness – it has been battle tested in the harshest environmental conditions from Afghanistan to El Salvador. Excellent sound suppressors are available. Spare parts, ammunition, and accessories are cheap & available worldwide.

Weaknesses: The AK, due to its inherent loose engineering, is not very accurate.

Sniper Use: Various accurized and modified AK-47s have been used in different conflicts to include the Vietnam War (1965-1975), Russo-Afghan War (1979-1989), Bosnian War (1992-1996), Russo-Chechen War (1994-2007), PLO-Israeli conflict (1947-Present), Lebanese Civil War (1975-1990), U.S.-Iraq War (2003-2008), U.S.-Afghan Wars (2001-2008), and any number of battles fought by Russia's allies and surrogates since the end of World War II.

Part II - Pistols

Handguns As Sniper Weapons

A handgun is a good sniper weapon for a variety of reasons. First, a pistol is concealable and can be hidden on one's person. A pistol can fit in the small of your back or under your armpit – a full-length, bull-barrel, bolt-action sniper rifle cannot. And depending on the situation, concealability may be the most important consideration. Second, a pistol is maneuverable in the restricted confines of the urban environment. A pistol can be fired from inside a car, from a closet, from a stairwell, from under a bed, and in any number of unpredictable places and positions a shooter may find themselves in while operating in a city. Perhaps the best reason for employing a handgun for sniping is that using one is unconventional and people do not expect a precision shooter to use a pistol.

When I first talked to people about using a handgun for sniping, most were skeptical. However, after I explained to them exactly how one could employ a handgun for sniping, I appeared a little less imbalanced, but just slightly so. When people think of a pistol cartridge, they think of some weak, low-velocity round that is accurate out to about 50 meters. But, with the production of new pistols and their accompanying cartridges, the old, weak, 50-meter pistol round is dead. If we consider that some big-game pistols actually fire a rifle cartridge, using a pistol for sniping becomes less comical. These specialized hunting pistols can actually bring down large game, like deer and elk, at hundreds of meters. A handgun suitable for sniping does not have to be an ungainly specialized weapon. For example, the Israeli Desert Eagle .50, which is a 'normal' style handgun, fires a hard-hitting round out to two hundred meters.

Truthfully, a shooter does not need an immensely powerful round for effective handgun sniping. One of the primary reasons why one cannot accurately fire a handgun at long distances is due to traditional, unmodified handgun stances and tactics. Since most people practice firing handguns from a standing position, it is the shooter's own inability to hold the gun steady enough to be accurate at long distances that limits them as a sniper. But, accurate long-distance handgun shooting can take place, even with normal handguns, if the shooter modifies their tactics and equipment.

To start, the shooter has to rest the weapon on a stable platform, like a windowsill or a car door. Pistols with a tactical rail system can be fitted with a bipod to allow a stable firing position no matter where the shooter is. Also, a pistol can be fitted with a shoulder stock, which is either commercially available (depending on the handgun) or can be fabricated easily by using an existing rifle stock and some sheet metal. This combination of using a stable shooting platform and a rigid stock allows for a much more accurate shot. Since a handgun's open sights have such a short sight radius, the firer can attach a scope using a commercially available mount. The shooter can even use a longer barrel for improved accuracy and then attach a sound suppressor. So, after modifying the pistol with a bipod, adding a shoulder stock, mounting a scope, and attaching a suppressor, the shooter has created a sniping weapon - more closely resembling a carbine - capable of accurate shots out to one hundred meters or more, depending on the ammunition used and the handgun itself.

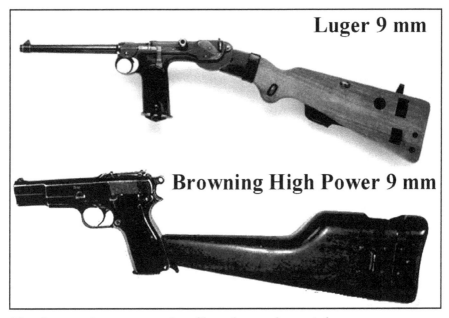

The above are just two examples of how shooters have tried to get more accuracy and range from their pistols. Adding a stock is one of the most common conversions when trying to improve on an existing handgun. Even as far back as the American Civil War, where soldiers attached custom made stocks to their Colt revolvers, gunmen tried to modify the basic handgun design. Eventually, gun manufacturers produced carbines, which fired a pistol round but had all the other characteristics of a rifle.

Thompson/Center Contender

Production History: In 1965, the Thompson/Center Arms Company was created and in 1967 they began selling their Contender high-performance hunting handgun. The Contender Pistol is the most popular hunting pistol today and its reputation for reliability and quality craftsmanship has led to over 400,000 sold. Unlike most other competing firearms, the Contender was designed for inter-changeable barrels and its break-open design does not require the barrels to be specially fitted to the individual action. Any barrel made for the Contender will fit onto any frame. Because the sights/ optics are mounted on the barrel, they remain zeroed during changes.

Description: A break-open action pistol, fires a variety of rounds to include: .17, .22LR, .223, .204 Ruger, 6.8 mm Remington, 7-30 Waters, 30/30, .357 Magnum, .35 Remington, .375 JDJ, .44 Magnum, .45 Colt/.410 Ga, and .45/.70 Gov cartridges, is 17-inches long (model dependent), with a variety of barrel lengths to include 10, 12, 14, 16, 21 inches, and weighs up to four pounds, depending on the type of barrel.

Range/accuracy: Depends on what caliber barrel used, its length, and what cartridge is fired. The .45-.70 Contender is capable of firing three-inch groups at 100 meters. Velocities vary from 1500-1900 feet per second.

Strengths: The Contender is a superb urban sniping weapon because of its flexibility. Many different stocks (collapsible ones as well) are available, as are aftermarket sound suppressors. The large variety of barrel lengths in different calibers allows the shooter to tailor the Contender to a specific tactical situation. While the Contender is single shot, this allows for improved accuracy and enables the shooter to maintain control of their expended cartridge since it is not automatically extracted. When used in conjunction with a good scope, the shooter can consistently engage targets, accurately, out to 200 meters. Because the Contender is so popular, a large aftermarket industry exists that can provide the shooter with any number of stocks, optics, scope mounts, cartridges, repair parts, and ammunition.

Weaknesses: The Contender is a single-shot weapon so it cannot put a large volume of fire down range or rapidly engage multiple targets.

Remington XP-100 Fireball

Production History: The Remington XP-100 was built in 1963 as a long-range target shooting and hunting pistol. The pistol was produced, in various forms, from 1963 until 1998. Different models, depending on the production year, cone in different calibers like .221 Remington, .22-250 Remington, .223 Remington, 6 mm & 7 mm BR Remington, and .308 Winchester. The Remington XP-100 helped create the sport of pistol varmint hunting and target shooting.

Description: A bolt-action pistol, fires a variety of rounds (the above example is chambered for the .221 Fireball), is single-shot (except for the XP-100R model made in 1998 that had a four-round internal magazine), has a 10 and 3/4 inch barrel (or up to 14 and 1/2 inches, model dependant).

Range/accuracy: Depends on what caliber is used, but the .221 caliber Fireball round, a shortened version of Remington's popular .222 caliber round, travels at up to 3000 feet per second and is capable of hitting man-size targets out to three hundred meters. The XP-100, which is intended to be used with a scope, is one of the most accurate, commercially produced handguns ever made.

Strengths: The Remington XP-100 is a superb urban sniping weapon because of its accuracy and concealability. The XP (from eXperimental Pistol) is popular enough that a variety of aftermarket accessories are available for it like various stocks, scope mounts, and scopes. Ammunition is cheap and readily available. The bolt-action on the pistol allows the shooter to control their expended brass. Since the XP-100 is intended for field use, it is sufficiently rugged.

Weaknesses: The XP-100 is a single-shot weapon so it cannot put a large volume of fire down range or rapidly engage multiple targets. The .221 Fireball, while a flat-shooting, high-velocity round, does not have good penetration power.

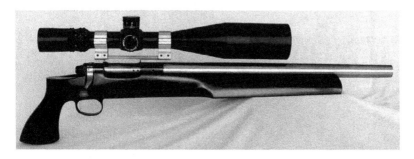

Benchrest Pistols

Production History: Benchrest pistols evolved from their bigger brothers, the benchrest rifles, and both are now used in modern benchrest competitions as well as for varmint hunting. Benchrest pistols are generally produced by custom manufacturers who specialize in benchrest weapons. These pistols are relatively expensive and uncommon as compared to traditional handguns.

Description: Dimensions vary depending on the model. Most benchrest pistols are custom-made where a shooter selects a specific action, chooses a barrel (with a specific length), and then selects a stock and combines them. Benchrest pistols are bolt-action, single-shot, and centerfire. These pistols have heavy, free-floating, bull-barrels and the front forestock is extremely wide so the weapon can rest on it and remain stable.

Range/accuracy: Benchrest pistols are designed from the ground up for superior accuracy and are still expected to fire multiple rounds into the same hole. A good benchrest pistol can easily achieve sub-MOA accuracy and are more accurate than even contemporary hunting rifles. Much of this accuracy comes from the high-velocity ammunition they fire; common calibers are the .204 (shown at right), .222, .223, and 6 mm rounds, which can reach velocities in excess of 4000 feet per second and only drop three feet at 500 yards. Benchrest pistols have true hair-triggers, some having a pull of only two ounces.

Strengths: Benchrest pistols are without question the most accurate handguns in the world. Also, since there is such a large civilian market/industry that supports the sport of bench shooting, a large variety of benchrest pistol accessories and ammunition are available. Even though benchrest pistols are large compared to other handguns, they are still much smaller than an assault rifle and are thus easily concealed.

Weaknesses: Benchrest pistols are designed for overt competition shooting, not tactical combat operations. Since they are bolt-action, single-shot weapons, they cannot be used to rapidly engage multiple targets.

Ruger .22 Caliber Charger

Production History: Ruger introduced this pistol in 2007. It is a shortened version of their popular 10/22 Rifle that has sold so well over the years. Ruger markets the Charger as perfect for long-range target shooting and small game hunting.

Description: A semi-automatic pistol, fires a .22LR round, uses Ruger's famous ten-round rotary magazine, is only 19-inches long, with a ten-inch barrel, has a laminated wood stock, weighs approximately three and a half pounds empty, and has a four-pound trigger pull.

Range/accuracy: The Charger is limited by the characteristics of the .22LR round it fires. At one hundred meters, the Charger is capable of consistently making head shots on a human. Most shooters would agree that 150 meters is the farthest the .22LR can be fired and maintain a reasonable accuracy based on drop of the bullet. Ammunition manufacturers like CCI make 32-grain bullets that travel at 1600 feet per second at the muzzle and over 1000 fps at 100 meters. The Charger comes with a scope base already attached to the receiver in order to easily mount a scope. A Harris bipod mounts readily on the forestock.

Strengths: The Charger is a precision shooting tool. Armed with a scope and bipod, the shooter is only limited by the .22 caliber round itself. The weapon is small, light, and eminently concealable. The shooter can rapidly engage multiple targets. The .22 caliber round is inherently quiet with little muzzle blast and is thus easy to suppress.

Weaknesses: The only weakness with the Charger is it fires a small, relatively under-powered .22 caliber round. This is not the weapon of choice when having to shoot through urban mediums like windshields and body armor.

Smith & Wesson .44 Magnum

Production History: Smith and Wesson's Model 29 .44 Magnum revolver, introduced in 1955, was used primarily by hunters for big game. However, after the Model 29 was used in the 1971 movie *Dirty Harry* with Clint Eastwood, its popularity exploded. A stainless steel version, the Model 629, was introduced in 1978.

Description: A double-action revolver, .44 Magnum, fed six rounds from a revolving cylinder, is 12-inches long (model dependent), with several barrel lengths available to include, 4, 6, 8, and 10-inch versions (model dependent), weighs up to four pounds empty (model dependent).

Range/accuracy: Overall, very accurate but depends on what barrel length is used. Because the .44 Magnum revolver was intended for big-game hunting, many companies produce excellent scopes and accompanying scope mounts for the weapon. Smaller frame revolvers generally do not have such a selection of optics and mounts to choose from. A .44 Magnum cartridge with a 180-grain soft-point bullet can reach velocities of 1600 feet per second. Big game like deer and bear can be killed out to 150 meters. Beyond 150 meters, it is hard to accurately gauge the drop of the bullet.

Strengths: Large-frame revolvers are good urban sniping weapons, although not as precise and adaptable as a weapon like the single-shot Contender. Since revolvers use a cylinder-type magazine, when a round is fired, it stays securely in the chamber so the shooter can maintain positive control of their expended cartridges. Also, some revolvers have non-fluted cylinders so they can fire 'hot', high-velocity rounds. A revolver is inherently more accurate than a semi-automatic pistol because the action on the revolver does not move when it is fired. Revolvers are more reliable than semi-automatic pistols because they are virtually immune to jamming.

Weaknesses: Most revolvers do not have a rail system for mounting accessories like bipods and vertical foregrips in order to enhance accuracy. Few companies manufacture suppressors for revolvers so they are hard to come by. Because revolvers have a revolving cylinder magazine, they are not as flat as automatic pistols and are a little harder to conceal. Different barrels cannot be rapidly interchanged like the Contender or most semi-automatic pistols.

Glock Pistol System

Production History: Glock is an Austrian company founded in 1963. Glock first introduced its 9 mm pistol in the 1980's for the Austrian Army. The Glock was unique in several ways, including its use of light-weight polymers, a high-capacity magazine (17 rounds), its hammerless design, and integral trigger safety. Today, Glock is one of the most popular handguns in the world because of its simplicity, reliability, and availability in 9 mm, 10 mm, .357, .380, .40, and .45 calibers.

Description: A semi-automatic pistol, fires a variety of calibers depending on the model, fed by a double-stack magazine, holding anywhere from 10 to 33 rounds (depending on the magazine capacity), up to nine inches long, 3 and 3/4 to 6 inch barrel lengths are available, and weighs less than two pounds empty.

Range/accuracy: A shooter firing a Glock in .40 caliber, with a six-inch barrel, using 180-grain jacketed hollow points and enough powder to produce a muzzle velocity of 1100 feet per second, and using accuracy enhancing modifications (i.e. scope, stock, vertical foregrip), can consistently hit man-size targets at 100 meters.

Strengths: Aftermarket companies provide products enabling the shooter to turn the Glock into a pistol/carbine that can realize its full accuracy potential. Aftermarket products include shoulder stocks, scope mounts, optics, bipods, and vertical foregrips. Spare parts and ammunition are readily available worldwide. Extended threaded barrels with matching sound suppressors are commercially available. Because the Glock has proven so popular, a large aftermarket industry has developed where these more exotic accessories are readily available, unlike other less popular handguns.

Weaknesses: Inherently less accurate than break-open pistols and revolvers due to its semi-auto action. Only fires traditional pistol rounds (i.e. 9 mm, .40, .45). Not intended for long-range shooting like the Thompson Contender.

FNH USA 5.7

Production History: Fabrique Nationale de Herstal (FNH), has been in business since the late 1800's and is a Belgian manufacturer of firearms. Currently, FNH produces several weapons for the U.S. military to include the M-16, Squad Automatic Weapon, and the M240 General Purpose Machine Gun. In 2000, FNH designed and produced the basic firearm that would become the FNH USA 5.7.

Description: A semi-automatic pistol, fires a 5.7 mm x 28 mm round, fed by a 20-round double-stacked box magazine (30-round magazines are available), is slightly over eight-inches long, with a 4.8-inch barrel, and weighs approximately a pound and a half loaded.

Range/accuracy: The FNH is being discussed here because of the round it fires, which is a hyper-velocity cartridge that is essentially a scaled-down rifle cartridge. When modified for accuracy (as discussed with the Glock pistol system) the FNH can accurately engage targets out to 200 meters, which is unheard of in a semi-automatic pistol, of such small size.

Strengths: The FNH is an extremely light pistol and its 5.7 mm cartridge weighs less than even a standard 9 mm round. When shooting a hyper-velocity, armor piercing round, it defeats most Kevlar helmets and soft body armor. The recoil on the FNH is light - less than that of 9 mm pistols. The FNH comes with a rail system to mount accessories like a bipod or vertical foregrip. Threaded barrels and suppressors are available. When using a 30-round magazine at 100 meters or less, it is equivalent in firepower to an M-4 carbine, except it fits in your hand.

Weaknesses: The 5.7 mm x 28 mm cartridge is not a popular round and is not widely available, especially in battlefield environments. The small-size, hyper-velocity round is good at penetrating its targets, but suffers from a lack of knock-down power.

H&K MP7 Personal Defense Weapon (PDW)

Production History: Heckler and Koch designed the MP7 in order to meet a 1989 NATO requirement for a new pistol round that could penetrate body armor. Tradition-al-size pistol rounds, like the venerable Luger 9 mm round, were recognized as lacking sufficient penetration power on the modern battlefield. The MP7 and its newly designed pistol round are competing with Fabrique Nationale's own 5.7 mm x 28 mm round as well as their new 5.7 pistol.

Description: A semi-automatic/automatic pistol, fires a 24.7 grain, 4.6 mm x 30 mm round, fed by a 20 or 40-round double-stacked box magazine, is only thirteen inches long, twenty-one inches long with the stock extended, has a seven-inch barrel, and weighs only four and a half pounds fully loaded with a 40-round magazine!

Range/accuracy: The MP7 is an accurate weapon out to 200 meters. It achieves this accuracy because it fires a high-velocity 4.6 mm x 30 mm round traveling at 2379 feet per second. Essentially, this round is a scaled down assault rifle cartridge. The MP7 fires a specially designed copper-plated, hardened steel penetrator, which has very low recoil and is designed to penetrate body armor and then tumble.

Strengths: In many ways, the MP7 is the perfect guerrilla sniping weapon. The MP7 is light and concealable; it can be hidden easily on one's body (like in the small of the back, under the armpits, or even inside the waistband) or in any number of urban concealment devises (shoulder bag, purse, grocery bag). The MP7 is designed to be fired from the shoulder and has an integral shoulder stock which quickly extends or slides back into place. Since it comes with a top-mounted Picatinny rail system, a variety of excellent optics can be fitted it to it. Also, the snap-down vertical foregrip allows the shooter to control and stabilize the weapon for greater accuracy. And to top it off, factory-made suppressors can be purchased. All of the accuracy enhancing accoutrements – shoulder stock, vertical foregrip, quality optics – enables the shooter to realize the full potential of the MP7's hyper-velocity round which can penetrate Kevlar helmets and level IIIA soft body armor.

Weaknesses: The 4.6 mm x 30 mm round lacks knock down power and is relatively rare on the modern battlefield, although as of the writing of this book, German NATO troops are using this weapon and ammunition in Afghanistan.

Case Study: The Ohio Highway Sniper

Deranged killer, Charles A. McCoy, Jr. understood the urban terrain and took advantage of it to terrorize the people of Columbus, Ohio from October 2003 until his capture in March 2004. Importantly, McCoy was able to spread this terror with nothing more than a 9 mm Beretta pistol. Over the course of five months, McCoy conducted a dozen separate shootings against highway drivers, residences, and even an elementary school. Many of the attacks involved McCoy standing on a highway overpass as he fired down at oncoming cars. Since McCoy was on an overpass with no available entrances or exits, he was able to fire a shot, walk to his nearby car, and quickly drive off without anyone being able to pursue him.

In response to the shootings, Ohio commuters stopped driving on Interstate 270 that circles the city of Columbus. Instead, they took back roads. After an attack on a school, some schools cancelled their classes while others remained opened but held their recesses indoors to protect the children from an easy, outside shot. In hopes of catching the shooter on film, the state of Ohio installed surveillance cameras at likely sniper locations along Interstate 270. Police also set up public hotlines (they received thousands of tips) and put a $60,000 bounty on the sniper's head. However, since there was no evidence to go on, the shooter could have been any one person out of several hundred thousand living in the surrounding areas. The shooter was literally swallowed up by the surrounding population.

Eventually, the police got a break when they received a call from a relative of McCoy who identified Charles, suffering from paranoid schizophrenia and off his medication, as the probable shooter. Then, McCoy's father turned over to police four of his son's guns, including two Beretta 9 mm pistols. After test firing these pistols, the police conclusively linked one of the Berettas to nine of the shootings, including the murder of Gail Knisley, a 62 year-old woman who was killed as a friend drove her to a doctor's appointment on I-270. Now that the police had a suspect, they involved the community by posting pictures and descriptions of McCoy in newspapers and on the internet.

This public exposure brought quick results. McCoy was captured thirty-six hours later in Las Vegas after an alert citizen, Conrad Malsom, recognized him from a picture in a copy of USA Today. Malsom immediately notified the sniper investigation task force in Columbus as well as the FBI. The police arrested McCoy, peacefully, when he returned to the Budget Suites where he was staying. While McCoy's identity was unknown, he was able to manipulate the urban and human terrain to his advantage and inflict terror throughout a large urban area, armed only with a handgun. Once McCoy's anonymity was stripped from him, this same urban and human terrain worked against him, leading to his exposure and arrest. In 2005, McCoy was sentenced to 27 years in prison with no chance of parole.

Case Study: The Warsaw Ghetto Liquidation

In the summer of 1943, the Jews trapped in the Warsaw Ghetto, armed primarily with pistols, prepared for battle against their German executioners. The Jews were so poorly armed due to the Germans' effective system of gun control. This gun control started in 1928 when Germany's Weimar Government enacted the Law on Firearms

Captured Jewish men and women guerrillas await their horrible fate as the Warsaw Ghetto burns behind them.

Photo from the Stroop Report

and Ammunition that required all German citizens to apply for a permit in order to buy a firearm, to purchase ammunition, or to go hunting. From then on, every firearm had to be stamped with a serial number and an identifying mark by the manufacturer so the government could track these weapons. As a result, when the Nazi regime came to power in 1933, they had a complete database listing the owners of all the legally-held firearms in the country. Armed with this knowledge, the Nazis were able to re-move any legally owned weapon from any strata of society appearing to be a threat to the Reich. Then, further gun control followed when the Nazis issued the Weapons Law of 1938 which stated, "Jews are prohibited from acquiring, possessing, and car-rying firearms and ammunition."

As matter of course, after Germany invaded and occupied Poland in 1939, the new occupying administration dutifully enforced all the racial laws previously instituted in the Reich. From that point on, Poland's Jews were outlawed from buying, own-ing, or possessing any handgun or rifle – period. Firearms possession was illegal and any violator would most likely be shot on the spot (why put Jewish violators in the court system when they were doomed to perish as a race anyways?) or they would be shipped off to work camps or crematoriums. Any one of these options was a death sentence. Even the Jewish police, who were responsible for maintaining law and or-der behind the walls of the Ghetto, were armed only with wooden sticks. As the War-saw Ghetto Jews prepared for an urban guerrilla war in the spring of 1943, they were confronted with the harsh fact there were almost no guns available for them. The only weapons the Jews could get through the black market and the Polish underground were a few dozen pistols.

Compounding the problem was the fact the Polish resistance was preparing for their own uprising, which finally came in the summer of 1944. However, as the Jews and Poles competed for weapons on the black market, the Polish underground secured the lion's share of these limited, valuable commodities. The Poles were unwilling to give up their precious few weapons – like rifles and submachine guns – to the Jews who, clearly, had no hope for victory or even survival. Even though the Jews did not want to rely on their absurdly low number of handguns for their survival, they had to.

When the German Army moved in to liquidate the remaining Jews of the Warsaw Ghetto in April of 1943, they encountered several guerrilla organizations armed almost exclusively with pistols. The most well-known of these resistance groups was the ZOB (Żydowska Organizacja Bojowa – Polish for the Jewish Fighting Organization). The ZOB was armed largely with handguns because it was next to impossible to buy larger weapons, like rifles or sub-machine guns, on the black market. Because the ZOB fought from the close confines of a dense, urban area, they were still effective using handguns.

Convicted war criminal SS-Brigadefuhrer Jurgen Stroop was the commander on the scene responsible for reducing the Warsaw Ghetto. Stroop's task was to clean out the Ghetto by forcibly transporting the Jews to Treblinka or slave labor camps. Any resisting Jews were killed outright. However, Stroop's 1,500 well-armed men encountered fierce resistance from Jewish guerrillas. During the initial fighting Stroop reported, "The Jews responded with grenades and automatic fire aimed at our gun crews. The snipers must have been low on ammunition because they made each shot count. They managed to kill two of our light artillery men [anti-aircraft gunners]."

Armed only with pistols, the Jewish guerrillas denied the Germans access to key areas in the Ghetto. Again, Stroop reported, "The second thing that struck me that Thursday was our inability to capture Jews and Poles who had fled to the sewers beneath the Ghetto. These 'catacombs' made excellent secret passages and ambush sites, and the Jews thwarted all our efforts to flood them. The few SS men who went underground were met with pistol fire. Smoke candles and the addition of creosote to the water also proved ineffectual. We never did gain control of those sewers."

Another Stroop report described the fierce resistance put up by the pistol-wielding Jews, "In most cases the Jews offered armed resistance before they left the bunkers. We had two men wounded. Some of the Jews and bandits fired pistols from both hands. Since we discovered today that on several occasions Jewesses had concealed pistols in their bloomers, every Jew and bandit will from now on be ordered to strip completely and be searched."

It took the Germans twenty-eight days to clear out and destroy the Warsaw Ghetto. In the end, the Germans captured only nine rifles, but secured fifty-nine pistols. Stroop was at a loss to explain how his men, armed with anti-aircraft guns, howitzers, armored cars, Mauser sniper rifles, and machine-guns, took so long to defeat such a lightly armed enemy composed of starving men, untrained women, and young teenagers. The Jewish guerrillas violated every traditional concept of sniping, but still stalled the Germans for an entire month. To put this feat in perspective, it took the Germans five-weeks to conquer all of Poland in 1939. It took them four weeks to destroy the Warsaw Ghetto, which covered only four square kilometers and was inhabited by some 60,000 wretched, terrorized Jews. The Jewish guerrillas were forced by necessity to use the weapons at their disposal, combining handguns with unconventional tactics to exploit the urban terrain to their advantage.

In the end, the Warsaw Ghetto Jews paid a horrific price. More than 56,000 Jews were forced out of the Ghetto by Stroop and his men. Of these, 7,000 were killed during the operation. Another 7,000 of those captured were sent to Treblinka where they were stripped, gassed, and cremated. Stroop estimated his men burned, blew up, and buried alive another 5,000 to 6,000 Jews during the course of their urban combat. This inexact estimate is understandable when one considers Stroop burned down entire city blocks filled with screaming Jews and blew up hundreds of underground bunkers occupied by unknown numbers of still more terrified victims.

Once the battle - or more aptly, the massacre – began, the Jews fought fiercely to secure more guns from the assaulting German soldiers. By dragging the rifles from the bodies of dead German soldiers, the Jews were able to get a few more rifles here and there. Because the Jews could not get guns, legally or illegally, they could not defend themselves from the German onslaught. The Nazi's bureaucratic war-machine so effectively kept guns out of Jewish hands that they were able to slaughter the disarmed Jewish citizenry with great success.

Guerrilla Gunsmithing

As we can see, a guerrilla organization may not have the luxury to pick and choose the weapons they will fight with. Most likely, the organization will have to modify or make their own custom-made weapon systems, which is relatively easy with a basic understanding of gunsmithing and access to a machine-shop or home workshop. Additionally, gunsmithing books and magazines are widely available as are CD and DVD's that show one how to do basic gun maintenance and repairs. Once one has a basic understanding of gunsmithing, welding, and metal-cutting, they can modify existing weapons at will. One can cut barrels to shorter lengths, make suppressors and flash-hiders, make scope mounts, and create stocks. One can also learn to mix and match different parts from different weapons systems to create a superior, hybrid weapon.

For example, the IRA had its own custom weapon shops where they designed everything from unconventional mortar systems to complex IEDs and car bombs. Snipers from a variety of wars mixed and matched scopes, rifle barrels, and stocks

Guerrilla Gunsmithed Rifle

A soldier in Iraq inspects a Mauser K98 fitted with a modern scope and a makeshift suppressor, which covers the entire barrel of the rifle.

Photo by GySgt Oliva

to try and create a better weapon. For instance, American gun designers, who created the first .50 caliber sniper rifles, put a .50 caliber machine-gun barrel on a German anti-tank gun frame to create a long-range sniper rifle. If a guerrilla organization is unable to produce or modify their own weapon systems, they can contract this out, on the black market, to someone who can. With enough money, they can pay someone, who is an expert in their field, to custom-smith a specific accessory to their weapon, or modify it to make it concealable or quiet.

The modifications the shooter requires for their weapon may not even involve any gunsmithing or shop work, but merely adding an accessory like a stock or a rail mounting system. Since there is a large, commercial, aftermarket industry that serves the needs of hunters and shooting enthusiasts worldwide, a shooter can get anything they want for their weapon, like folding stocks and compact scopes, from any number of places such as the internet (ebay, Amazon.com), and popular publications like Shotgun News and online stores like Cabellas and Brownells just to name a few. On the web, getting spare parts and exotic accessories is both easy and anonymous, requiring only a credit card and a postage box.

This cursory review of available sniper weapons was meant to open the reader's mind to the possible tools for effective sniping. There are many more tools available than just conventional, bolt-action, long guns that are commonly used by the world's militaries and police forces. The guerrilla sniper may not have the luxury to use the expected norm like their conventional enemy. They must adapt to their battlefield conditions, take what is available, and modify them to suit their needs.

Chapter 5

Snipercraft

The urban guerrilla sniper is the kind of fighter especially suited for ambush because he can hide easily in the irregularities of the terrain, on the roofs and tops of buildings and apartments under construction. From windows, dark places, he can take careful aim at his chosen target.

- Carlos Marighella, 'Minimanual of the Urban Guerrilla'

Guerrilla Snipercraft: Getting Weapons

A guerrilla's snipercraft involves areas the traditional sniper never thinks about, but which are just as critical as the camouflage they use, the hidesite they choose, and the weapon they shoot. The first challenge for the guerrilla sniper is getting a weapon in a secure manner. Because the guerrilla is an outlaw committing a crime against the state, government security forces will enforce strict gun control measures to keep weapons out of their hands. That is why it was important to discuss, as we did in the previous chapter, the different types of weapons suitable for sniping because the guerrilla has to make due with whatever they can get. Let us take a look at what measures a government may take to limit the distribution of weapons in a country and how this gun control affects the guerrilla.

One year after the Jewish guerrillas were crushed in the Warsaw Ghetto, the Polish Home Army in Warsaw ignited their own uprising. The Polish resistance hoped to seize and hold Warsaw in order to link up with the surging Red Army clawing its way forward to the Polish capital. From August 1 until October 2, 1944, the Polish insurgents fought a brutal urban guerrilla war against the occupying Germans. Because the Home Army had a wider support base and was larger in size than the Ghetto Jews, they secured more supplies and weapons for the fight. Even though the insurgents had relatively few weapons to start with, they were able to attack and capture enough surprised German garrisons to secure more arms. In this manner, the Home Army captured everything from Mauser K98 rifles and MP40 submachine guns to armored half-tracks and Panther heavy tanks. Also, the Home Army received some weapons through airdrops from British, American, and Russian aircraft, although these supply runs were costly to the allies and the results were sporadic at best.

The battlefield recovery of weapons, as Warsaw's insurgent were able to do, was beneficial from a security perspective because once the guerrillas had these guns, they were 'clean' - they could not be traced back to a specific person. The guns could be traced to the police station or the military unit that was issued the guns, but the link in the evidence chain stopped there once the insurgents took off with their loot. Now, the government had no idea who had their guns. They were effectively laundered.

While battlefield recovery of weapons can be a dangerous proposition, there are other less risky ways to get a firearm. One such method is to steal a firearm from a gun store, weapons depot, or a private residence. It is certainly less risky to break and enter into a store or someone's house than it is to go toe-to-toe in a gun battle with the police or army. Breaking and entering can be made easier, and involve no risk at all, if the guerrillas have someone on the inside helping them. For example, a secret supporter of the IRA could legally buy a deer rifle and then arrange for its 'theft'. When the IRA entered their supporter's house and took the weapon in the dead of night, complete with a broken window or other 'evidence' of a break in, the police had a hard time proving this was not a legitimate case of robbery. This way, the existing laws could be used to legally purchase a weapon and then illegally supply the guerrillas.

As mentioned previously, guerrillas often work with black market arms dealers to get the weapons they need. This has the advantage of reducing the guerrillas' risk in some ways because the arms dealer is also committing an illegal act against the state. With an arms dealer, the guerrillas do not have to kill anybody or steal anything, all they need is money. It is up to the arms dealer to get the weapons in a secure, anonymous manner if they want to stay out of prison. However, the guerrillas must accept the risk that the arms dealer may be setting them up.

If they are being set up, the guerrillas may be placed under surveillance by government security forces when they meet with the dealer. Security forces can then follow the guerrillas from their meeting place with the dealer and track them back to their homes, safehouses, or bases. Or, security forces may place hidden tracking devices inside the guns themselves. For instance, at various times during their struggle, the IRA's arms network was infiltrated by police informers both in the United States and Ireland itself. In these cases, American and British undercover police became adept at 'tagging' the IRA's weapons with miniature, hidden tracking devices so they could follow the weapons trail to the final end user – the guerrilla.

The guerrilla organization takes into consideration all of these potentially unpleas-

Battlefield Recovery Paris, France, August 1944

Two members of the French Resistance strip a rifle from the cold dead hands of a German soldier.

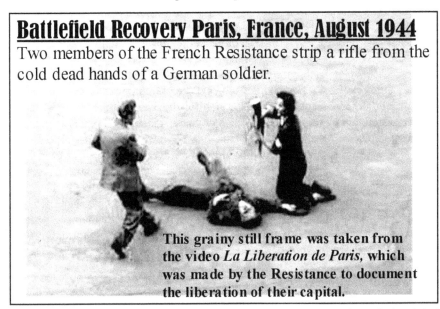

This grainy still frame was taken from the video *La Liberation de Paris,* which was made by the Resistance to document the liberation of their capital.

ant possibilities and determines what risks they want to accept. Ultimately, it might be safer for the guerrillas to attack and raid an unprotected police station, knowing they are not being set up, as opposed to dealing with an unknown element like an arms dealer.

Hiding the Weapon

Once a guerrilla has secured their weapon in such a way it cannot be traced to them, they have other hurdles to master. Now, the guerrilla must store their weapon so government security forces cannot find it, and if they do find it, they cannot connect the weapon to the sniper. There are an endless number of ways of hiding a weapon, but there a few things guerrillas avoid. First, the experienced guerrilla never stores their illegal weapon for long-term safekeeping in their own house or on their property. This is a rookie mistake a novice guerrilla might make because it is convenient, but this is the first place security forces check. No matter how clever a person thinks they are, if security forces want to make the effort, they can tear a building apart until they find what they are looking for. Especially with the advent of portable x-ray machines and ground penetrating radar devices, government forces, just like Superman, actually have the ability to see through walls and floors. And if an illegal weapon is found in a person's home or business, the property owner is now legally connected to the weapon.

The same can be said of a person's car. While it is understandable the guerrilla transports their weapon in a vehicle from time to time, experienced ones do not store it in their own car for the same reasons they do not keep it in their home. Mass murderers Lee Malvo and John Mohammad (the DC Snipers) made the mistake of being caught with their assault rifle in the trunk of their car, resulting in a life sentence for Malvo and the death penalty for Mohammad. Guerrilla snipers operating in a wartime environment also face the same prospects of life and death sentences.

The IRA understood hiding their weapons was a critical task so they appointed specialists who did nothing but hide and transport weapons in a secure manner. Why let an untrained novice expose the whole organization through sloppy tradecraft? The IRA's specialists often hid their weapons in public places owned by the government or public businesses (like inside an enclosed power relay box), so there was no incriminating link between the weapon and the sniper if the weapon was discovered. Disciplined guerrilla organizations like the IRA plan for the eventuality of their weapons being discovered, but by hiding them in an anonymous manner, the repercussions are minimal.

In Iraq, the insurgents became fond of hiding their weapons in the trunks of cars, something termed 'rolling caches'. Furthermore, the cars were stolen and could not be traced to a specific individual. The cars were parked in public places like parking lots or city streets, thus they were not on private property and could not be connected to a private citizen. These rolling caches allowed the insurgents to hide their weapons in an anonymous manner with no incriminating links to the guerrilla organization if the arms caches were discovered.

Guerrilla Sniper Training

Once the guerrilla secures and hides their weapon anonymously, they still must train with it before they can conduct an attack. The guerrilla shooter may have to zero their weapon and test their ammunition, as well as, practicing the fundamentals of effective shooting like: proper trigger squeeze, breath control, sight picture, target alignment, and body positioning. Because of the combination of the security forces' control measures and an intrusive populace, sniper training must take place in a clandestine manner. Because sniper training in the cities is difficult does not mean it is impossible. With a little creativity, good sniper training can be conducted even in a sprawling city with millions of people living in close proximity to each other.

One way guerrilla organizations get trained snipers into its ranks is through recruitment. If an organization can recruit someone who is already trained as a sniper in the police or military, they can bypass the lengthy and dangerous process of clandestine training. When the IRA stepped up its attacks in the late 1960's and early 1970's, they benefited from employing snipers who had already received training in the British military as British soldiers. Even Sean MacStiofain, a senior IRA commander, received weapons training from the British Royal Air Force before he returned to civilian life. He took a course teaching the fundamentals of marksmanship and weapons handling while still a member of the British military. Even though MacStiofain was not an active member of the IRA at the time, he knew this training would come in handy in the future.

If a guerrilla organization cannot recruit a trained sniper into the movement, then they can buy one. For years, the PLO greased the palms of foreign shooters who were imported into the occupied territories to bag unwary Israeli soldiers. Iraqi insurgents did the same, paying for the services of foreign snipers to work in Iraq as guns for hire, getting paid by the kill. The Chechen guerrilla movement also exploited the services of foreign snipers from the Baltics, the Ukraine, and from various Islamic groups throughout the Middle East who were paid good money to pick off Russian recruits.

Captured Sniper Rifle
These weapons were captured during a raid on an insurgent's home in Baghdad. As the war progressed, the guerrillas learned to hide their weapons in community areas or caches that could not be connected to them.

Open Source Training

If the guerrilla sniper cannot be hired or recruited, they can be taught the old-fashioned way. The first step in urban guerrilla sniper training is the same as a college student researching a term paper. An IRA member can go onto Amazon.com and buy Mark Lonsdale's *Sniper, Counter-Sniper* to study the subject. A guerrilla in Ramadi, Iraq can order Jack Coughlin's book *Shooter* from Barnes and Noble to learn exactly how American Marine snipers killed his fellow countrymen in the beginning of the war. A Chechen rebel can order Vassili Zaitsev's book *Notes of a Sniper* at *notesofasniper.com* and study urban sniper tactics from the great, Russian master himself.

To highlight the fact guerrilla snipers study available open sources, an Iraqi insurgent video released in late 2006 discussed some of their training methods. In the video, the insurgents revealed they copied passages from a book written by sniping expert and author John Plaster. According to them, the guerrillas bought Plaster's book *The Ultimate Sniper* and then took what they needed from his manual to train their own snipers. (In response, John Plaster offered to download his chapter on counter-sniping for free.) As we can see, the internet is a tool guerrillas use to learn about the sniper trade and it is both legal and anonymous. Besides ordering various sniper publications from internet book dealers, a guerrilla sniper can enter any number of internet chatrooms and discuss sniper tactics with other interested people and actual snipers.

Movies are another medium the guerrilla sniper can study to learn the trade. A guerrilla can go to any local DVD store and for a few dollars buy *Enemy at the Gates*, *Shot Through the Heart*, and *Sniper* to get new ideas. Or, they can watch the best urban guerrilla sniper training movie ever made, *Day of the Jackal* by Frederick Forsyth, which spins a fictional story of an English sniper hired by the French Secret Army Organization (OAS) to assassinate French President De Gaulle. *Day of the Jackal* shows how to conduct a textbook guerrilla urban sniping operation from start to finish, complete with methods of how to custom-smith and hide the perfect urban sniping weapon. Also, personal videos shot by actual guerrilla snipers are another source of knowledge. Iraqi insurgents in particular (as we discussed in chapter three) were unusually adept at merging their sniper operations with actual footage of their attacks and then distributing the footage through the internet and black market street corner sales. These 'how-to' videos are in fact the most realistic, current sniper training films made to date.

An often overlooked form of sniper training can be found in first-person shooter video games made for personal computers, Sony PlayStations, and Nintendos. Any game like *Rainbow Six, Ghost Recon, Urban Sniper 2*, and *Call of Duty* offers a person the chance to learn the basics of sniping like key-hole shots, manipulating angles, and the importance of cover and concealment. Hezbollah took it one step further when they designed and released their own video game in the summer of 2007 entitled *Special Forces II*. This computer game, selling for only $10 in the dusty markets of Hezbollah-controlled Lebanon, offered exciting battle scenes with professional, high-quality graphics. In the game, Hezbollah children (and adults) can aim at virtual Israeli soldiers with their sniper rifles and blow away their Zionist enemy on the safety of their computer screen. With *Special Forces II*, Hezbollah ingeniously found a way to integrate political indoctrination and battlefield training to gain revenue for the movement.

A guerrilla sniper does not need to buy a video game and download it on their computer to learn how to snipe in the cyber world. The interested gamer can enter any number of on-line internet service providers (ISPs) that organize real-time computer wars between competing teams. Today, a person can log onto a *Red Orchestra* ISP and fight among the ruins of Stalingrad as either a German or Russian sniper. Urban sniping is just a click away.

The advantage of using open sources to train is they are legal, dual purpose information. A guerrilla watching Antonio Banderas' sniper techniques in *Assassins* can claim they are merely relaxing on a Friday night – not training for combat. A guerrilla playing *Call of Duty* is not learning to take a long distance head shot – they are just playing a kid's game to pass the time. And a guerrilla reading about the assassination of JFK is just a history buff. Are security forces going to arrest and imprison someone for reading history?

On-Line Training Manuals

As part of a guerrilla organization's training efforts, a guerrilla movement may publish their own training manuals to professionalize the movement. The IRA produced their now infamous *Green Book*, Brazilian guerrilla Carlos Marighella published his *Minimanual of the Urban Guerrilla* and it makes sense guerrillas committed to better sniping would produce their own sniper training manuals. In May 2005, this is exactly what an Iraqi insurgent group did, publishing an on-line sniper training manual. Importantly, this publication revealed a level of professionalism rarely attained by a guerrilla organization and shows how difficult it is to stop sniper training if the guerrilla movement is committed to it. What are security forces going to do with an on-line site…locate and shut down the website, just to have another one pop up a day later on a different address, in a different country?

Safehouses

Screen Shot from a Sniper Video Game

Modern video games allow virtual rooftop snipers to estimate range and judge crosswinds as they take out enemy targets with surgical shots in the cyber world.

A common method of clandestine training is through one-on-one instruction in safehouses. In a safehouse, a sniper instructor can train several students at a time on the basics of the trade using lectures, dry erase boards, and videos. Students can practice the fundamentals of marksmanship all without firing a single shot. In any safehouse the students can put these fundamentals to the test with pellet guns, which are quiet, do not penetrate the surrounding walls, and allow the student to begin bridging the gap between theory and reality.

Bosniak soldiers trapped in Sarajevo learned to become snipers in part from foreign instructors who volunteered to come in and teach them. Because the Bosniak government did not want UN forces or potential Serbian collaborators to know about the training, the sessions were held in secret at local safehouses. The sniper students took advantage of private buildings with large, sturdy basements so they could actually shoot their rifles in homemade, indoor shooting ranges, all within close proximity to the populace. Even though the Serbians had the city surrounded and bombarded the Sarajevans daily, they did not stop the defenders from developing and training their own snipers in secret using a system of urban safehouses.

Public & Underground Ranges

Why should the guerrilla sniper student try to hide when they can train in plain sight in any number of civilian sniper schools? It is easy to attend one of a thousand marksmanship or sniper courses offered somewhere in the world. Beyond signing up for and attending recognized shooting courses, the guerrilla sniper can join a shooting club or go to a civilian rifle range to tune their skills in an open, legal manner. Think of the basic combat tactics to be learned at a hunting club: as the guerrilla shoots birds, hunts deer, and stalks wild boar, they are also maintaining their wartime skills.

If the guerrilla organization has trouble finding a suitable range or club, they can create their own with a little money and a piece of open land or a warehouse. The guerrilla organization then forms their own gun or hunting club in order train their members under the guise of a legitimate business. Honest civilians are encouraged to join these clubs to give the club a better cover, but guerrilla snipers go there and train free of charge. This is essentially what the French gun clubs in the late 1800's did; they provided a core of trained guerrilla snipers (Francs-Tireurs) to fight the neighboring Prussians' inevitable invasions. True, the French gun enthusiasts openly practiced the art of target shooting when their country was at peace. But, when their homeland was invaded, they used these same skills to pick off and harass the Prussians as they marched westward towards Paris. Although the Prussians surrounded, starved, and sacked the French capital in 1870-1871, they never did solve the problem of the guerrilla marksmen who were the product of local civilian gun clubs.

A different solution for live-fire shooting practice is going underground in sewer systems or basements. Shooting underground is a good idea because the surrounding earth absorbs the noise of the gunfire. Also, when underground, there is no chance of random security patrols or civilians coming by and stumbling upon the training. Essentially, the guerrilla organization creates their own range, mimicking the methods legitimate in-door ranges use to muffle the sound of gunfire. These ideas are not new as the IRA used underground rifle ranges to hide their training and Iraqi insurgents have used mattresses to absorb the sounds of their shooting. Guerrilla movements of all shades and stripes have taken advantage of the underworld to provide a secure living/training/travel space like the Warsaw Ghetto Jews in 1943, the Polish Underground during the Warsaw Uprising in 1944, and the Chechen guerrillas when defending Grozny in the 1990's.

Suppressed Weapons

The suppressor is an invaluable training tool for the guerrilla sniper because it enables them to train covertly. Since the biggest problem with target shooting in a secure manner is the sound of gunshots, suppressors alleviate this problem. If the guerrilla is shooting underground, in a basement, or in a remote area just outside of town, suppressors allow the sniper to train without fear of discovery due to the sound of gunfire that can normally be heard for a mile in all directions. (The tactical employment of suppressors is discussed in depth in the following chapter.)

Guerrilla Safehavens

The urban guerrilla can solve most of the problems associated with hiding from enemy security forces and civilian informants if they can secure an urban safehaven. For example, when Iraqi insurgents took control of Fallujah from April to November 2004, they secured one giant urban training facility. The insurgents were free to train when and where they wanted to. As long as the guerrillas took security precautions from aerial surveillance, they could run ranges and conduct practical shooting exercises anywhere in the city. More importantly, insurgent snipers could use their control of the city to combine their unhindered urban sniping training with preparation for future coalition attacks. This allowed an integration of sniping theory, training, and

A Polish Insurgent Takes Aim

Once the Polish Home Army took over large sections of the city, their guerrillas were able to train in the open in order to prepare for the German onslaught.

Photo by Jerzy Kokczynski courtesy of the Warsaw Museum

actual execution.

Out of Country Training

If the guerrilla organization cannot train in their own country because enemy security forces are just too oppressive, they may have to leave the country and get training elsewhere. If an Iraq guerrilla cannot train in Baghdad, they can go to Syria, Lebanon, or Iran and get in-depth training unmolested by American forces. If an IRA sniper was under constant watch in Northern Ireland, he could slip across the border into the Republic of Ireland and train there. A Chechen sniper-trainee may be harassed and harried in their own country, but there are plenty of places in neighboring Georgia, Dagestan, and Ingushetia where they can train at their leisure. For years, Afghanistan embodied the idea of a distant guerrilla training university, churning out future snipers, car bombers, and assassins. On the other hand, if a group cannot leave the country for whatever reason, they can bring in an outside expert to assist them. This importation is common in guerrilla circles since IRA members are known to train the FARC guerrillas in Columbia, Hezbollah is known to train the PLO, Iran trains Iraqi Shiite insurgents, and American forces have already encountered Chechen snipers in Fallujah and Najaf.

Advanced Training

Depending on the government's population control measures, advanced sniper training may be conducted right under the noses of enemy security forces with relative ease and little risk. For example, sniper teams can plan dry runs of future attacks by blending into the population and conducting rehearsals by walking through their actual plan. Observation and security teams can walk to where they would set up their positions and have a cup of coffee and talk to a friend. The actual sniper can walk to where they would take their shot and instead of having a rifle with them, they can carry a camera and take a picture from where they would shoot. For the dry run, pressing the shutter of the camera is equivalent to pulling the trigger of the rifle. The sniper teams that shot President Kennedy conducted this exact kind of pre-operation walk through which allowed them to successfully plan their ambush.

Training urban guerrilla snipers is not an easy task since they are members of an illegal, clandestine movement. The guerrilla organization does not enjoy the open training of conventional military forces. They are burdened with training its members in a secure manner, hidden from omnipresent security forces. However, just as the guerrilla conducts combat operations in an unconventional manner to succeed, so must they conduct training. The guerrilla movements in Northern Ireland, Iraq, Palestine, and Chechnya show us that urban guerrilla sniping skills can be taught in a clandestine, secure manner even while under constant pressure from enemy security forces.

Transporting the Weapon

Once the guerrilla sniper has trained with their weapon in a secure manner, they must transport their weapon to wherever they intend to conduct their sniper attack. Moving their weapon may be easy or difficult, depending on the environment they are operating in and the characteristics of their weapon system. Charles Whitman, drove onto the University of Texas (Austin) campus in his car. He then walked calmly, pushing a dolly with a footlocker on it, to the Texas Tower, and took an elevator to the top floor. Hidden inside the footlocker were the various weapons he would use to kill a dozen-plus people. Because Whitman looked like everyone else (he was wearing coveralls, like a janitor would), acted completely normal, and had his guns hidden in a wooden box, he appeared non-threatening to both security guards and students. Since he blended in with the environment, Whitman was able to move in the open, without suspicion, to his shooting platform - the Texas Tower.

In the cities, where cars are allowed to move freely about, any vehicle – a van, a pick-up truck, a car – is a means of concealment for both the shooter and their weapon. If civilian automobiles are allowed to travel freely in a war zone (like Baghdad or Belfast) then the guerrilla sniper can take advantage of this freedom of movement to travel, undetected, by car.

If a car is not an option and moving or carrying a large object, like a footlocker, is too suspicious, then the guerrilla sniper might have to conceal their weapon on their person. Again, we see why guerrilla snipers often choose concealable weapons. A guerrilla sniper wearing civilian clothes, walking down the street with a Barrett .50 caliber sniper rifle over their shoulder will not make it very far. However, a guerrilla sniper with a broken-down, short-barreled carbine concealed under their jacket can walk among the people, even by security forces, and raise no suspicion.

It is important to note a guerrilla sniper does not necessarily have to hide their movement to their place of attack, but they do have to conceal their weapon system. In fact, the guerrilla sniper is prepared to move among the people, and to be observed by security forces, but to do so in a manner that raises no suspicion. Even during combat operations, while being fired upon by the enemy, the guerrilla sniper conceals

Vehicle Checkpoint, Iraq

Photo by SPC Magby

American soldiers search a car at a checkpoint as they look for insurgents and contraband items like weapons.

their weapon. They do this because the sniper understands enemy security forces operate under certain rules of engagement and it is illegal for them to shoot unarmed civilians. However, if these security forces see someone in civilian clothes holding a rifle in their hands, they are dead. If these same security forces see someone with no visible weapon, even if they suspect the person is an enemy combatant, they will most likely not shoot, or at least delay their shot until they can get more information. Either way, the guerrilla buys a little more time.

Depending on the situation, a guerrilla sniper may choose not to conceal their weapon and may choose not to be in civilian clothes. In this manner, the guerrilla sniper chooses to operate in a completely legal manner in accordance with the laws of land warfare. However, the guerrilla organization can still take measures to ensure their security and ensure they are not detected as they move to their sniper platform. In Northern Ireland, Chechnya, and Lebanon, guerrilla forces employed a series of lookouts to help move their snipers into position. With this method, the guerrilla organization established a series of surveillance positions, all the way to the target area, to look for the enemy and warn the sniper of any threats. If the lookouts, who might be anyone from school children to taxi drivers, saw anything suspicious, they made a call and the attack was called off. If the lookouts gave the 'all clear', the sniper could move safely to their target.

Another successful method to get the weapon and the shooter safely to the target area is to move them separately. For example, if a Christian sniper in Beirut wanted to shoot at Hezbollah militiamen from a certain building, they could do so discretely. The Christian sniper's group could move the weapon to the building at night, several days before the actual attack, and hide the rifle inside the building. Then, the sniper could move to the building, weapons-free, in case they were searched at a checkpoint, and enter the building without any incriminating evidence on their person. Then, the sniper would recover the weapon, make the shot, put the weapon back in its hiding place, and leave the building, evidence-free.

Choosing a Shooting Platform

The guerrilla sniper chooses their platform based on what their target is and where it is. In most circumstances, the guerrilla sniper knows the specific characteristics of their target beforehand because security forces wear a uniform (so they are easily identified as a target) and they are predictable while manning their vehicle checkpoints, outposts, guard towers, and observation points, and conduct their regular security patrols.

Consequently, when a guerrilla sniper targets a static vehicle checkpoint, they had ample time to study their target, like a homework project. Some snipers spend days, weeks, or even months studying a particular checkpoint. Over the course of time the sniper studies the checkpoint's habits, patterns, security measures, level of alertness, rotation schedule, and the like. After the sniper identifies the checkpoint's weaknesses, they construct a plan to exploit these weaknesses. The sniper's plan takes into consideration the range of their weapon system and the shooter's own ability. There may be a great shooting platform located 500 meters away from a target, but the sniper, firing an AK-47, may only be able to hit their target at 300 meters. The sniper then selects the best shooting platform within this 300 meter radius from the target.

Once they are within their range, several more elements are weighed. One consideration is the need to maintain anonymity. If the shooter fires from an abandoned or unoccupied building (a favorite tactic of Chechen snipers in Grozny), they will be alone when they make their shot. Or, if the shooter can fire from a public facility, like a parking garage, then security forces will be unable to connect the firing platform to the shooter, since the government or a private company owns the parking garage. No matter what choice the shooter makes, they strive to achieve relative isolation when they make their shot. This means when the shooter pulls the trigger, they are isolated from any potential eyewitnesses. A shooter can achieve this isolation by firing, for example, from an apartment. There may be people all around the sniper in adjacent apartments, but as long as no one is physically with the sniper when they make their shot, they are anonymous.

The shooter also takes into consideration any urban obstacles near the target. If the sniper places an obstacle between them and their target, then the target will have a difficult time reacting effectively, thus aiding the sniper's escape. For instance, the Miljacka River runs east to west, down the center of Sarajevo, dividing the city into southern and northern halves. From the southern side of the city, Serbian Bosnian snipers fired across the river at Sarajevo's civilians, the Bosniak armed forces, and the UN's own troops, with little fear of retribution. While Sarajevo is just one example, any large city has a multitude of obstacles, like bridges, overpasses, elevated highways, and rows of buildings, that can be used as a physical barrier to prevent government security forces from getting to the sniper.

The sniper can make the security forces' job difficult, or even impossible, if they use 'position overload' and 'split the seams' when choosing a shooting platform. What is meant by 'position overload' is the sniper intentionally fires from an area with many

Positional Overload

1945: A Russian soldier studies the ruins of Berlin as his companion lies dead next to him. Where did the sniper fire from?

potential firing positions. So, firing from the top of a mosque tower, is not a good spot, because it is an obvious location with few actual firing positions. However, firing from a massive building, like the Holiday Inn Beirut, offers positional overload. Because, in the Holiday Inn, there are hundreds of individual loopholes and sniper ports from which a sniper could shoot from and reacting security forces will be unable to narrow down the exact location quickly, if at all.

'Splitting the seams' means a sniper fires from a position where security forces are unable to backtrack the sniper's firing azimuth. In order to split the seams, the sniper chooses a location, like a building, that is adjacent to, or in line with, another building. This technique works best when a sniper fires at angle, down a parallel street, towards a target. Since the street is lined with block after block of buildings and cars, it is hard to backtrack the shot to a specific location because a miscalculation of only a degree or two will send security forces to the wrong building, or even the wrong city block, depending on how faulty their calculations were. (This subject will be discussed more in subsequent chapters on counter-sniper techniques and sniper forensics.)

Urban Camouflage

Once the sniper chooses a suitable sniper platform, they camouflage themselves so they are invisible to their target and nearby civilians. However, the urban camouflage required to be successful is drastically different than that used in a rural setting. For the urban sniper, camouflaging oneself in an urban hidesite is much easier than camouflaging oneself in the woods, which can take hours of painstaking preparation to get the right look.

Depending on the structure a sniper is in, excellent camouflage may be already available. For instance, one can simply draw the curtains of a window close to be effectively concealed from outside eyes. Or, the windows may already be tinted or have reflecting material on the surface so the people inside the room are invisible to anyone looking in. The sniper can also use common furniture found in a building to construct a concealed position within a room - a hidesite within a hidesite. An overturned desk, couch, or bed makes for excellent visual screening when positioned properly inside a room. If furniture, curtains, and windows are unavailable (like in the bombed out ruins of Grozny) then other methods can be used. One thing the sniper can do is paint the room they will shoot from a different color so the shooter blends in with it. It would take two people, armed with paint cans and rollers, less than ten minutes to paint the interior of a room a more subdued color that matches the shooter's clothing. Or, the shooter can match their clothing with the room's interior to get a better color blend.

Another technique is for the shooter to hang a fine mesh net along the room, in front of their position, so the room has a mesh wall concealing the shooter. Since the shooter is up close to the mesh, they can see and shoot through the mesh. However, people that are far away cannot see past the mesh - it looks like a solid wall. This technique works well if the room is dark or in the shadows, for the darkness enhances the deception, making the mesh look like the back wall of the room.

Perhaps the easiest, and by far the most effective means of camouflage, is the use of a sniper shroud. With this method, the sniper takes a bed sheet or blanket that matches the color of the room they will shoot from (this method works the same inside a vehicle, as well). Usually, if the sniper has a light colored tan sheet or a dark gray sheet, they can cover most color/lighting scenarios. The sniper places the shroud over themselves and their weapon system so nothing is showing. Then, they make a small hole in the shroud for the scope, place matching color gauze over the scope itself to prevent reflections, and rubber band the shroud tightly to the scope. With this shroud, the sniper and their weapon are totally concealed. They are a shapeless, formless blob that blends in perfectly with their background. All it takes is a ten-dollar bed sheet and the shooter has achieved invisibility.

The Hidesite

There are many considerations when configuring a hidesite. If a sniper plans on staying in a hidesite for extended periods of time or intends to use the hidesite repeatedly, then they may have the luxury of preparing the place to meet their needs. First, the sniper must be able to enter and exit the hidesite without being seen or announcing they have arrived. A common mistake is to use a door when entering a room, which momentarily changes the light in the room as the door opens and closes. If the sniper uses a door, they need to cover the entrance with blankets so when they enter and exit through it, there are no light changes in the room.

Once in the hidesite, the sniper must ensure the enemy cannot see any movement in the room whatsoever. One thing the sniper can do to hide their movement in the room is to hang mesh netting or sheets along the walls to create 'corridors' the sniper moves through while in the room. Another good technique, used by snipers as far back as Stalingrad, is to brick up the window in a room so there is only a small port remaining that the sniper shoots out of. That way, the sniper can easily block off the small

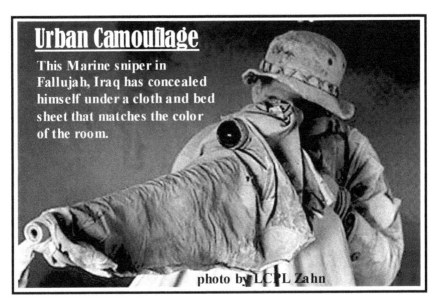

Urban Camouflage

This Marine sniper in Fallujah, Iraq has concealed himself under a cloth and bed sheet that matches the color of the room.

photo by LCPL Zahn

window opening and move freely throughout the room while remaining undetected. Or, instead of bricking up a window, a sniper can knock a small hole in the wall of a building so they have their own gun port to shoot from. This instant gun port method has been used all over, from Stalingrad to Sarajevo and Ireland to Israel.

If a sniper uses a building for their hidesite, they probably do not need to be uncomfortable or cold. Lying in the prone position, as most conventional snipers are taught to fire from, is fatiguing. A person's body is simply not designed to lay flat on their stomach, with their head raised up, for long periods of time. There is no reason why a sniper cannot sit comfortably in a chair as they observe the surrounding terrain through a small gun port or loophole. In fact, a good idea is to use the 'executive position' for prolonged periods of time. With this method, the sniper sets up their position with a desk and a chair. They place their weapon on the desk, pointing toward their target, and sit in their chair, facing the desk, as if they were a businessman writing a memo. This relaxed position enables the sniper to observe an area for hours on end with their weapon at the ready to make a quick shot.

If a sniper must lay on the floor of a building due to tactical reasons, they should think of the materials present to make themselves more comfortable and to insulate themselves from the heat-sapping qualities of a cold stone or concrete floor. It might be useful to line the sniper's position with a mattress, left-behind clothes, cushions from a couch, or blankets. The entire building should be thought of as a tool to help the sniper accomplish their mission.

An unconventional but effective means of acquiring a good hidesite is through a home invasion, which was a popular method used by the IRA, by both sides in Israel, and by the Iraqi insurgents. The home invasion has the advantage of providing a sniper team with a good shooting platform, regardless if people are in the home or not, and regardless if they support the guerrillas or not. With this method, a sniper team selects a private residence that they want to use as a shooting platform. Then, a security team conducts a forced entry of the house and holds the family hostage. The sniper

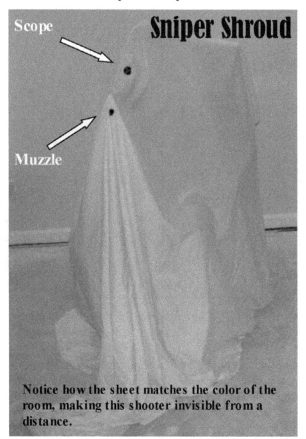

Sniper Shroud

Scope

Muzzle

Notice how the sheet matches the color of the room, making this shooter invisible from a distance.

arranges the temporary hidesite to meet their operational needs, takes their shot, and leaves the residence. Simple, right? Maybe not. This tactic has its challenges since it is only a short-term method (after all, how long can you hold a family hostage before someone knows there is something wrong…a few hours?) and the family are potential eye-witnesses who will later be questioned by enemy security forces. Just think of all the challenges: the guerrillas must conceal their own identities, herd the family into an isolated room so they can be controlled, blindfold the hostages, keep them quiet, block their hearing, rotate them to the bathroom, deal with phone calls and unexpected visitors, and keep the hostages calm, all while creating an appearance of normalcy in the house until the operation is over.

As mentioned before, a sniper may prefer to use a vehicle as a shooting platform, which is, in fact, a mobile hidesite. A vehicle, like a van, may be chosen for a hidesite because it conveniently hides the shooter and their activities. However, a van is a suspicious vehicle by nature and a regular vehicle like a large four-door sedan or an SUV may be more appropriate since they raise less suspicion. Regardless of what vehicle the sniper chooses, something must be done to conceal the sniper's activities inside the vehicle. This can be done by applying tinting to the vehicle's windows (like the DC snipers did), putting up sun shades or curtains (like the Iraqi insurgents do), slapping on bumper stickers and signs, or even temporarily screening the sniper by holding up a newspaper or a road map.

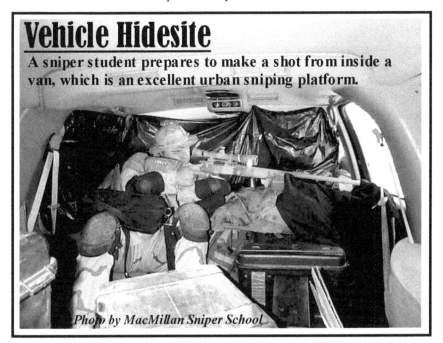

Vehicle Hidesite

A sniper student prepares to make a shot from inside a van, which is an excellent urban sniping platform.

Photo by MacMillan Sniper School

Experienced snipers will devise a method for shooting from the vehicle without raising eyebrows. This may be as simple as opening a tinted window a crack, sticking the barrel of a weapon out, and firing a shot. The sniper could make a gun port in the car, just as with a building, by drilling a hole in a side door and then firing through this hole as they lay down in the back of the vehicle. The same thing could be done if the shooter fires from the trunk of a car. When firing from the back of a vehicle, the shooter can remove one of the rear tail lights and shoot through it. Or, the shooter can make a gun port behind the rear bumper, rig the bumper so they can lower it when they are in sight of their target, make a shot, and raise the bumper again to cover up the gun port (Iraqi insurgent snipers have used all of these techniques to modify their vehicles). With the help of a metal shop, a sniper can modify their vehicle by armoring it to withstand counterfire from opposing security forces. The IRA Goldfinger sniper crew did this where they installed an armored shield in the back of their Mazda hatchback. (We will discuss this IRA sniper team in a subsequent chapter.)

Observation

Good observation is a fundamental skill for any successful sniper. This requirement is no different for the guerrilla sniper, except they go about in a covert manner. When one thinks of observation and sniping, we naturally think of a dedicated observer that works with the shooter. We also think of this observer sitting behind a high-powered spotting scope, surveying the terrain, looking for targets for the shooter to engage. The guerrilla sniper can use this method if they are in a hidesite for a prolonged period of time, but extra precautions should be taken. To begin, the sniper should think of their spotting scope just as they would think of their weapon. They must conceal themselves and their scope just like their weapon.

The most intelligent method of long-term observation I found was conducted by the Bosniaks' master counter-sniper in Sarajevo. This sniper established a series of observation ports in an apartment building by cutting holes in the concrete walls. He then placed his spotting scope into these ports so that he could observe the terrain. From a distance, since the spotting scope fit snugly into the hole, it did not look like there was a hole cut into the wall of the building at all. When the observation ports were not in use, he plugged the holes with foam balls, which had been painted black, to match the outside of the charred building. From these clandestine observation ports, the master sniper was able to secretly observe and record every aspect of the opposing Serbian lines until he knew every inch of the terrain.

But, the sniper or spotter does not even have to be present to observe the terrain, not with today's technology. The guerrilla sniper can use an observation port, but instead of inserting a spotting scope, they insert a digital camcorder. The sniper sets up the camera in the morning, the camera records a certain area of terrain all day long, and then the sniper recovers the camera at night and downloads the recorded film. When the sniper gets home, they watch the film on their television, fast forward through periods of inactivity, and pause on a single frame and study any detail of the terrain which may give a clue about enemy activity.

With the advent of reliable, inexpensive, remote tilt-pan camera mounts a sniper can set up a camera system, hidden behind a mesh net or sniper shroud, and actually view the urban terrain – real time - from a remote location. The sniper can move the camera from left and right, up and down, and observe any specific area they want to, all while sitting several hundred meters away in a vehicle or a building. This tactic has the advantage of allowing the sniper to be completely safe, at a separate location from the camera, so that they are invulnerable to enemy observation teams or counterfire.

Technical means of observation, while entirely feasible, are expensive and have drawbacks (all machines break down eventually). There are other means of covert observation just as effective as remote video cameras, but are easier to employ and with less risks. A tool for observation that should be in every sniper's collection is the periscope. With a periscope, a sniper (or observer) can look over a wall, around a car, or through a small hole cut in a building. The sniper periscope has been in use since at least World War I (a very valuable tool during the sniper war fought from competing trenches) and allows a sniper to observe the terrain without exposing themselves and getting shot for their troubles. Modern periscopes are lightweight, durable, reasonably priced, and available on the internet (like Ebay).

Depending on the the operational environment, the sniper may not have to sneak around to observe their enemy, they can do it in broad daylight. In Grozny, a Chechen sniper can peruse the local food markets, looking for the best deal on fresh vegetables as they size up a nearby Russian position. In the West Bank, a PLO sniper can sip tea at a Jerusalem café as they watch an IDF guard tower. As long as the guerrilla looks and acts like everyone else around them (and is free of incriminating physical evidence) they can go anywhere they please and openly case their next target.

If the sniper does not want to risk observing the target in person, they can have someone else conduct the surveillance for them. The IRA used 'dickers' - local school-age children - to watch British patrols and report on their activities so they could decide how to attack them. Hezbollah did the same thing in Lebanon where they set up 'neighborhood watch' groups that did nothing but look for and report on

Mesh Netting

Urban Sniper Hide

Improvised elevation so as to make an angled shot deep from the room.

Photo by MacMillan Sniper School

In this picture, a sniper student uses their uniform top to blend in with their background. Also, they have emplaced a mesh netting in front of them for visual screening and to hide their muzzle blast. This is excellent urban sniping technique.

the Israeli occupation forces. Hezbollah snipers did not have to sit for hours watching an Israeli outpost, a local citizen did, who then fed this information to the guerrillas. The important point to make is a guerrilla organization (or sniper) can observe a target without using any mechanical or technical means of observation whatsoever and still be successful. They can do it all with brains and eyeballs.

Determining Distance

Determining distance is a key element of sniping because knowing the distance to a target is integral to accurate shooting. If a shooter does not know the correct distance to their target, the may undershoot or overshoot it. Over the years, many methods have been developed to estimate range, but today most conventional snipers use a laser rangefinder to determine the distance to the target. Although a laser rangefinder works in all environments, it is more appropriate in a rural environment where featureless terrain and long distances make range determination difficult. Laser rangefinders today are inexpensive and one can buy a good one, which is small and lightweight, for only $150.00. Some manufacturers even make scopes with integral laser rangefinders so the shooter does not have to carry extra equipment.

However, in an urban environment there is no need for a laser rangefinder. First, any laser rangefinder is an active device that emits a light source that can be detected by night vision devices. Plus, manufacturers make several different types of counter-sniper systems that can 'see' in the infrared spectrum, so using a laser emitting device is not a good idea from a security perspective. Second, the guerrilla usually does not have the luxury of carrying and concealing superfluous equipment, it only makes their job harder. And if a guerrilla were to use a scope with an integrated laser, that scope would be expensive (around $800, give or take), and would be easier to trace if captured, because they are relatively uncommon.

Since a guerrilla knows the target they are going to attack and knows the location they plan to shoot from, they can walk from their target (like a checkpoint), then to their sniper platform, and calculate the distance by measuring their pace. Or, the sniper can measure the distance on a bicycle or in a car.

Another method, which determines distance with pinpoint accuracy, is using a Global Positioning System (GPS). Instead of counting paces, the guerrilla uses their GPS when they are near the target (or parallel to the target, several blocks away), gets a pinpoint grid coordinate, then moves to the location they will shoot from, gets another pinpoint grid coordinate, and measures the distance between the two points. The shooter can get the exact distance, within a meter or two, every time.

The sniper can also use the natural characteristics of the city to aid in calculating distance. For instance, if a city block measures a hundred meters in length, then a target three blocks away is three hundred meters away. Additionally, a good city street map is more valuable to the urban sniper than the best laser rangefinder. A sniper can take a commercially produced, highly detailed street map and measure the distance between major landmarks, like intersections, bridges, monuments, and the like, and establish their own map with the distances written down between various points. This way, the sniper figures out where their target is on the map and then measure the distance to their shooting platform.

A variation of his technique is to use overhead satellite imagery, which can be found on GoogleEarth. All a sniper does is go online, download current, overhead imagery and uses the computer program to accurately measure distances between the target and the proposed shooting platform. As with using a GPS, the sniper can determine the exact distance to within several meters. In fact, Iraqi insurgents have used commercially available satellite imagery to not only measure distances, but to show for propaganda purposes exactly where they have shot American soldiers.

Hiding the Shot

A critical skill for the guerrilla sniper is the ability to successfully hide the muzzle flash, muzzle blast, and sound of the gunshot. Most snipers can move undetected to their shooting platform, lie in wait and remain invisible, and hit their intended target. Far fewer can successfully conceal their weapon's visual and audio signature, even though this is the number one reason why snipers get killed.

The first issue we will discuss is muzzle flash, because the speed of light is much faster than the speed of sound and muzzle flash is the first signature that will be detected when a shot is fired. Let us define what 'muzzle flash' is. Muzzle flash is the visible flame caused by burning gunpowder exiting the barrel of a weapon after a shot is fired. Generally speaking, the larger the caliber of the weapon, the larger the muzzle flash.

The Loophole Shot

In this picture, an Iraqi insurgent sniper fires from a loophole cut into the wall of a building. A sniper can fire from a small hole which not only provides them with visual screening, but will hide their muzzle flash. (Photo by www.dragunov.com)

Muzzle blast, which accompanies muzzle flash, is the disturbance caused at the muzzle when the rapidly burning gunpowder explodes out of the end of the barrel. This exploding gas disturbs any dirt, dust, or debris located near the weapon's muzzle, raising a small cloud of matter. Even if the muzzle flash itself is not seen, the disturbed matter near the muzzle might be, giving away the sniper's exact location. The most effective way to conceal this muzzle flash and prevent muzzle blast is to use a sound suppressor. The suppressor will eliminate almost all visible muzzle flash and reduce muzzle disturbance to almost nothing. However, since we will discuss the characteristics, limitations, and advantages of suppressors in the following chapter, we will discuss other means of concealing the muzzle flash and blast. This is certainly a valid exercise since, in many parts of the world, factory manufactured suppressors are hard to come by.

A simple way to hide the muzzle flash and blast is to fire the weapon from a loophole, for instance from a hole in a wall, so the wall itself blocks the flash and blast. A variation of this method is to take a keyhole shot. In other words, to fire from deep in a structure, where there is a restricted, enclosed, elongated opening so only the target, which is directly in front of the keyhole, can see the flash and blast. A perfect example of a keyhole shot is firing down a hallway, through an opened door, and outside at the target. Unless a person is looking directly down the relatively narrow opening, no one will see where the shot came from.

Another way to eliminate muzzle blast (although it does nothing to stop muzzle flash) is to spread out a damp rag, about two feet by two feet in size, under the muzzle of the weapon so the cloth absorbs the muzzle blast and prevents dirt or debris from flying up after the shot. It's even easier to pour water over the surface of whatever area a sniper is going to shoot from, to eliminate the dust cloud after the shot. If the shooter cannot wet down their area to prevent muzzle disturbance, they may want to fire from an upright position, away from the ground.

A shooter can reduce their muzzle flash by firing in daylight hours, or from a well lit area to reduce an observer's ability to distinguish the muzzle flash from surrounding light sources. However, firing a weapon without a suppressor at night, or from a darkened area, produces a huge light flash readily identified for what it is - a muzzle flash from a weapon. The sniper use a flash suppressor to reduce the incriminating flash, but all a flash suppressor (not to be confused with a sound suppressor) does is prevent the shooter from being blinded from the blast, while doing nothing to hide the flash to enemy observers.

The sniper can use other concealment methods like shooting through a medium that acts as a visual screen without affecting the performance of the bullet. For example, the sniper can shoot from behind fine mesh netting that no one can see through at a distance, but the sniper can see and shoot out of without affecting bullet trajectory. The sniper can also shoot through plastic, cardboard, or cloth, as long as it does not affect the bullet's path.

If a sniper takes advantage of their optics, they can shoot from such a distance the target cannot see the muzzle flash and blast due to the limits of their eyesight. A sniper firing at a target from a thousand meters away from a concealed position can be sure their target cannot see the sniper even if they were looking directly at them. While any one of these improvised techniques may work, a sniper will most likely have to combine several of these techniques to conceal their muzzle flash and blast, depending on the situation and local conditions.

There are a few things, in regards to ammunition, the sniper should be aware of. To start, the sniper should never use tracer ammunition because it allows enemy forces to follow the tracer round back to the source. While this may sound like an obvious statement, there is an Iraqi insurgent video that shows a sniper shooting at an American checkpoint with a tracer round. One can be sure this was meant to create a more impressive visual effect, but it also exposed their position, more than their muzzle flash or blast did. Another reason why we mention this is that some people put tracer rounds in the bottom of their magazine so they know they are running out of ammunition and that it is time to change their magazine. It would be a mistake to accidentally fire off a tracer round when one was trying to be stealthy.

Another consideration is the type of powder used with the ammunition being fired. Most modern ammunition uses smokeless powder so hardly any smoke from the burning gunpowder is visible after a shot is made. But, if a sniper hand -loads their own ammunition, or they use ammunition someone else hand-loaded, they need to make sure they are using smokeless powder.

The Gunshot

Without doubt, the most compromising element for the sniper is the noise of the gunshot, which gives away the firer's location to the target and civilian bystanders. There are several methods to reduce this noise signature, but only one of them is truly effective. A sound suppressor, while it does an excellent job of hiding muzzle flash

Concealing the Gunshot

This Marine sniper in Iraq is not using a sound suppressor, but by firing from inside a building, the room will help to contain the sound of the gunshot as well as conceal the muzzle flash from the barrel of the rifle.

and muzzle blast, is purpose-built to reduce the noise signature of a weapon. A good sound suppressor reduces a gunshot to such a low level it is indistinguishable from the normal sounds of a busy city, like a car door shutting, and is not recognizable as a gunshot.

Other forms of sound suppression can be used such as shooting from a room lined with mattresses so when a rifle is fired within the room, the mattresses absorb the sound of the gunshot. This is what indoor rifle ranges do to absorb the sound of weapons being fired, except they use specially designed foam. This same sound absorption method can be used inside a vehicle. In this case, foam or mattresses are used to line the back of a vehicle so it becomes a mobile, silenced shooting range. Obviously, lining a room or building with padding to absorb sound takes a lot of preparation, creates a large signature, and remain as incriminating physical evidence after the attack.

If the sniper cannot use a sound dampening tactic, they can still use the inherent qualities of the city to confuse and deceive people listening for a gunshot by simply manipulating where and how they make their shot. One must first understand the hard, flat surfaces of a city, like walls and pavement, serve as sound deflectors and reflectors. When a gunshot is fired in the city, the sound waves hit and bounce off the surrounding surfaces. Consequently, it is difficult to determine exactly where a gunshot came from in a built-up area because of this echoing. To confuse their enemy, a sniper could fire a shot from the average city block, where there is a road down the middle and rows of buildings on either side. The sound of the gunshot will echo off the pavement and the surrounding buildings, and then bounce back and forth off each other, making the original source of the shot hard to determine.

Another way to hide the sniper's shot is to use cover noise. For instance, one group of guerrillas could open fire with a machine-gun from a location separate from the sniper. During the machine-gun burst, the sniper makes their shot (this was a common method used by both sides in Stalingrad). Or, the sniper calls in artillery fire and makes their shot as the explosive shells burst on target. Whatever cover noise method that is used – exploding hand grenades, mortar fire, etc. – it only has to be sufficiently loud enough to disguise the noise of the gunshot.

If the sniper cannot cover their gunshot, they can at least confuse their enemy as to the source of the shot through multiple shots fired simultaneously. With this technique, the sniper coordinates with other sniper teams and fire together, on command. That way, multiple shots and gunshot echoes are heard at the same time. Enemy forces hearing these simultaneous, overlapping shots will not know how many shots were fired or where they came from. (JFK's assassins used this method successfully in Dallas. We will discuss this assassination in depth in a subsequent chapter).

The Supersonic Crack

Hiding the sound of the gunshot does not eliminate the supersonic 'crack' the bullet makes as it breaks the sound barrier speeding towards its target. The supersonic crack is not as compromising as the gunshot itself, but it does indicate a shot was fired. Depending on how far one is away from the bullet, they will hear the crack before they hear the gunshot. This is because the bullet is traveling faster than the speed of sound. Once, when I was about 500 meters away from a sniper, I heard the supersonic crack first as the bullet zipped over my head and then heard the gunshot a second later.

One solution to the supersonic crack is to use sub-sonic ammunition which does not break the sound barrier. However, this creates its own problems since subsonic ammunition has a reduced velocity, has a decreased range, and lacks penetration power. The combination of a sound suppressor and sub-sonic ammunition makes an excellent team, but is best used for relatively close shots where a high-degree of bullet penetration is not required.

Another option to deal with the supersonic crack is to create cover noise such as revving the engine of a motorcycle, playing loud music, honking of car horns, or creating a distraction with gunfire from a different location so the crack is not heard. Even if the supersonic crack is not completely masked, as long as it is distorted enough by the other noise so it is not distinguishable as the crack of a bullet, that is good enough.

Post-Shooting Activities

Life can get difficult for the guerrilla sniper after they make their shot. First, civilian bystanders may report the shooting to the police. Consequently, the best thing a sniper can do is immediately disassociate themselves from the scene of the shooting. In layman's terms, they need to make a fast getaway. This need for immediate physical disassociation from the scene of the shooting is exactly the reason why more sophisticated urban guerrilla snipers have evolved into using a car as a shooting platform.

Imagine if an IRA sniper, hidden in a 500 series BMW, fires at a British soldier in an armored car. Even if the soldier sees the sniper drive off in the BMW, what are they going to do, give chase? The BMW can go 120 miles per hour, but the armored car is lucky to do sixty on a straightaway. Pitting the high-performance passenger car against an ungainly, lumbering conventional military machine, like an armored car, ensures the guerrillas will escape every time. This is an example of what some would call 'asymmetric warfare', where the guerrillas mix their unconventional tactics with the government's own predictable ones, enabling the guerrillas to have the edge, even

Beirut, Lebanon - 2006

If a sniper shot at you, would you know where they fired from? A good firing position means security forces will not be able to conduct an effective counter-sniper investigation.

though they are outgunned. The armored car could blow up the BMW, but it certainly cannot catch it.

If high-speed chases are not the sniper's style, they can use a ruse to escape, like dressing up as a government soldier or police officer. This mimicking allows the guerrilla to make a concealed shot from a building and then walk outside as if they are looking for the culprit. On a variation of this, the guerrillas could have a team dressed up as police 'capture' the sniper, drive off in a police car with the sirens wailing, and then drop the shooter off at a safehouse. These types of false-flag operations have been used successfully by many guerrilla organizations, from the French resistance in World War II, dressing up like Germans, to the Iraqi insurgents, dressing up like American soldiers.

Perhaps, if the sniper selected a good hidesite like a tall apartment building with hundreds of individual units, escape may be simple. The sniper makes their shot undetected, stash their weapon in a secure hiding spot, take the elevator to the street, and calmly walks away. Later, when the coast is clear, the sniper goes back to the apartment and resumes their normal life. Or, if security forces search the apartment and find the weapon, the sniper disappears and never comes back. In this case, the weapon is a throw away and the sniper is prepared to lose it during the course of the operation.

Here is another option. The sniper takes a shot from an apartment building, or a car, and immediately hands the weapon off to another guerrilla, whose sole job is to remove, transport, and hide the weapon. This way the shooter and the incriminating weapon are immediately separated from each other. Then, the shooter stays in place, sips a cold drink, or watches the news. When security forces arrive and ask the shooter if they saw anything, they shrug their shoulders, "I dunno." And if the security forces test the shooter for gunshot residue or put a dog on them, they have an answer for that too. "Oh, I was painting earlier today, that's why you're getting a false positive with your residue kits. You know, don't you, common house paint has all the same ingredients as gunshot residue?" Or, the shooter has some creosote on their boots from working in a wood shop. "Oh, you're tracking dog is going absolutely crazy because it smells the creosote on me. It happens all the time. Don't worry about it." Dogs can be tricked just like residue kits can be tricked, and the IRA used all of the above in their counter-forensics war against the British.

If the sniper is working alone, then they have to deal with escaping and hiding their weapon themselves. That is why the weapon they choose might have to be concealable. A shooter working for the FARC in Colombia will fail if they shoot a Colombian policeman in downtown Bogota and then try to run down a busy street, dragging a long, Russian SVD behind them. However, if this same FARC sniper took a shot, disassembled their takedown carbine into two separate pieces, secured them to their upper body under the armpits with an ace bandage, put on a loose Hawaiian shirt and a leather jacket, walked calmly down the street to a restroom, and dumped their weapon in the garbage can, they have a much better chance of pulling it off.

As always, after the shooting, the sniper has to take counter-forensics measures, of varying degrees, depending on the forensic threat they are facing (a subsequent chapter on sniper forensics discusses this subject in depth). As soon as the guerrilla takes their shot, they are thinking of many things: where did the ejected cartridge go, are the security forces going to be able to recover the bullet intact, did anyone see the muzzle flash, do I have enough time to wipe off the gunshot residue now or do I do it later, do I stash the weapon or hide it on me, how is my alibi, will my cover story work, can I beat the security cordon or will I get stuck inside it, and if I mimic 'normal' behavior and wear a ball cap, can I beat the public surveillance cameras?

This chapter in no way covers all the aspects of sniping tradecraft. It was intended to raise some of the salient elements a guerrilla sniper has to be mindful of - many which are different than what a conventional sniper thinks about - if they want to survive. In most cases, good urban sniping is good urban sniping, regardless of if it is a guerrilla or conventional sniper who is taking the shot.

Chapter 6

The Sound of Silence

How a Suppressor Works

The tactical employment of sound suppressors - also known as 'silencers' or simply 'cans' - is really an extension of the chapter on snipercraft. However, the subject is so important, and sufficiently technical, it deserves its own dedicated space. I cannot emphasize enough how important it is for the urban sniper, and even more so for the guerrilla sniper, to hide their muzzle flash, muzzle blast, and gunshot in combat. And there is nothing more effective at hiding all three of these potentially devastating signatures than the sound suppressor.

Suppressors were originally called 'silencers', but since they do not silence a weapon (they only quiet the weapon), the term 'suppressor' is more accurate. A suppressor is simple and has not changed much since American designer-genius Hiram Maxim started producing and selling the first commercially successful suppressors in the early 1900's. A suppressor is simply a muffler designed to trap the exploding gases after a gun is fired. When a cartridge is fired in a gun, a firing pin hits the primer, the primer explodes, setting off the more powerful gunpowder, which in turn explodes. Since expanding gases take the path of least resistance, the exploding gun powder rushes towards the opening of the barrel (the muzzle) as it pushes the bullet ahead of it. Once the rapidly expanding gases push the bullet out of the gun and exit the restricted confines of the barrel, they explode with great force and noise into the relatively unrestricted air.

What a muzzle mounted suppressor does is trap this rapidly expanding gas into a series of baffles, which creates turbulence and redirects the gas back against itself, thus slowing, cooling, and dissipating the gas. An integral suppressor is different in that it has a series of ports that gradually bleed off the expanding gas as it moves out towards the muzzle. So, by the time the bullet actually exits the barrel, so much gas has already been bled off there is no final explosion to contain. Fundamentally, both types of suppressors slow the expanding gases to muffle the explosion.

Manufacturers constantly try to create new suppressors with more efficient designs. In general terms, the larger a suppressor, the quieter it is. However, since weight and concealability are always a concern, manufacturers must balance noise reduction ability with the size of the can. Currently, a shooter should expect a detachable can to weigh around a pound and give anywhere from 30 to 40 decibels of noise reduction.

109

The caliber of the weapon being fired and the size of the cartridge are important when it comes to noise reduction because the bigger the cartridge, the louder the noise. Many .22LR rifles are inherently quiet because the .22LR cartridge is such a small round, with a relatively small powder charge, and therefore has a correspondingly reduced gunshot when the expanding gases exit the muzzle. Thus, small-bore rifles, like the .22LR, are easier to suppress than large-bore weapons, like a .50 caliber rifle, which has a huge round and a large powder charge.

Wet and Dry Suppressors

All suppressors are dry suppressors, meaning they are fired 'as is' with no liquid additions to the interior of the device. While dry cans are the norm, many suppressors are also capable of firing 'wet'. To make a can wet, all one has to do is pour a small amount of water into the suppressor, turn the can slowly to distribute the water inside the device, and then pour the excess water out. The water in the suppressor will help cool the expanding gases, thus making the gunshot quieter. This dampening effect from the water only lasts for about half a dozen rounds until the heat from the expanding gases causes the water to evaporate, then the can is dry and slightly louder again. Although water is the most common additive, other liquids like urine, engine coolant, and IV fluids like Ringer's Lactate and Normal Saline will also work.

Even though there are many different liquids that can be put in a can if the situation demands it, the shooter should be careful not to put anything corrosive or flammable inside. If the shooter does not want to improvise, they can purchase a suppressor coolant designed specifically for wet cans. Capital City Firearms markets a suppressor coolant that is superior to water and similar liquids in that it is heat and pressure resistant, absorbs heat better, clings more to the insides of the suppressor so it is not shot out of the can like water, does not burn, and will not smoke when the can gets hot. Some suppressors can be used with special grease, which is longer lasting than water because it will not evaporate. Some gun oils and lubricants can also be used, but they are not usually recommended because when the can gets super-hot, the oil can smoke or even catch fire.

The Supersonic Crack

As mentioned in the previous chapter, when a bullet has such a high velocity it breaks the sound barrier, people can hear a *'crack'* as the speeding bullet whizzes by. Contrary to popular myth, a detachable sound suppressor does not reduce the velocity of a bullet below the sound barrier, in fact, depending on the suppressor model, a can may actually increase bullet velocity. As we know, there are weapons with integral sound suppressors that bleed off the expanding gases as the bullet travels down the barrel towards the muzzle. Some weapons, like the MP5SD, do bleed enough of the gases off that they reduce bullet velocity to the point the round is no longer supersonic. In this case, the integral suppressor reduces both the muzzle noise and the supersonic crack.

Suppressor Maintenance

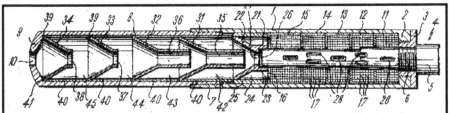

This is a patent drawing of the MP5SD sound suppressor. Notice the internal openings in the barrel that bleed off the bullet's gases and the baffles at the end of the suppressor that actually muffle the gunshot.

A suppressor is a mechanical device made out of lightweight steel or aircraft-grade aluminums and alloys. As a mechanical device, all suppressors require maintenance and are prone to eventual failure. Over time, the constant super-heating and cooling of the metal suppressor, combined with the corrosive property of the weapon's gases, will erode the suppressor's effectiveness. Suppressor life depends on how well it is maintained and on the inherent quality of the can. Some suppressors may outlast the life of the gun barrel as Surefire claims their cans have a service life of up to 30,000 rounds.

Recommended suppressor maintenance depends on the manufacturer. Canadian Tactical says this about Reflex Suppressors: "Remove the suppressor or leave the action of the rifle open after use to avoid corrosion by letting condensation evaporate away. A small amount of light gun oil sprayed into the suppressor will help prevent corrosion. Roll the suppressor around to spread the oil over all interior surfaces. Normal fouling from powder and primers does not effect the suppressor's functioning. Loose solid impurities like powder grains and carbon chips are easily removed by shaking the suppressor, while keeping it vertical, front end down. Washing with liquids or solvents is unadvisable. Store weapons muzzle down with the action open to promote air circulation and prevent oil and fouling from entering the action."

Knight's Armament Company says this about their M4QD suppressor: "Mount and dismount the suppressor to/from the weapon several times using a twisting motion to enable the compensator's carbon cutting grooves to dislodge carbon and metal fouling buildup. Dry brush loosened residue from parts using the general purpose toothbrush from the weapon cleaning kit. Take care to orient the parts so carbon does not fall down into the weapon bore, or down into the suppressor body. Copper remover should be used to remove copper fouling from both the QD compensator and the corresponding internal QD suppressor surfaces which contact the compensator if obvious. Remounting and dismounting the suppressor (with the muzzle and suppressor held horizontal), once it is wet with copper remover, may also help remove residue. The user should final clean and dry the copper remover affected parts with an absorbent cloth. Do not oil the QD suppressor body; wipe it dry with a clean cloth. Apply only a light oil coat of CLP to the QD compensator to prevent corrosion each time the weapon is cleaned. A very light coat of CLP should be applied to the suppressor latch plate legs to smooth their operation."

A final word on suppressor maintenance is to ensure the suppressor is aligned properly to the weapon. Once aligned properly and securely, the shooter should check the suppressor regularly to make sure it is in the proper position. If the suppressor is not perfectly aligned, an outgoing bullet can strike the suppressor, damaging the can and throwing off the bullet. Furthermore, even if a suppressor remains in proper alignment, the shooter should check the suppressor periodically after shooting. When a bullet leaves the barrel of a weapon it may yaw, meaning the bullet deviates from its intended rotational axis. I have seen a bullet, which was fired from a perfectly mounted suppressor, yaw upon exiting the barrel and clip the end of the suppressor, tearing off a small piece of the can. The suppressor had to be removed and sent back to the manufacturer for replacement.

Resistance to Sound Suppressors

Even as far back as World War II, some professionals appreciated the capabilities of a sound suppressor. Colonel Mason-McFarlane, who was the British Military Attaché in Berlin in the 1930's and lived within view of where Hitler observed the big parades in Berlin, wanted to kill Hitler using a suppressed weapon. By the spring of 1939, Mason-McFarlane correctly judged that Hitler intended to start a war and warned the British government to either kill Hitler now, or start a preemptive war, because with every passing month, the likelihood of either prospect dimmed. Mason-MacFarlane later related his plan: "In London…I had strongly urged that Hitler should be assassinated. My residence in Berlin was barely 100 yards from the saluting base of all the big Fuhrer reviews. All that was necessary was a good shot and a high-velocity rifle with telescopic sight and silencer. It could have been fired through my open bathroom window from a spot on the landing some 30 feet back from the window."[1]

True, Hitler could have been shot with a suppressed weapon as the loud sounds of marching soldiers, cheering crowds, and ceremonious bands would have provided so much covering noise that the shot would have been undetected. However, the subsequent dragnet conducted by Hitler's SS bodyguards would have found the likely shooting platform and the Gestapo would have used their persuasive questioning techniques to get some answers. It would have been a suicide mission, but millions of lives would have been saved. The sniping plan was rejected by London and World War II erupted later that year.

Surprisingly, almost seventy years after Mason-MacFarlane's plan, most people in military and policing communities are ignorant as to the capabilities and advantages of the sound suppressor. Even in professional sniping circles, with men who have experienced combat, many do not appreciate and thus do not use a suppressor. Today, there is no excuse for modern military and police sniper not to use a suppressor. They are readily available by a score of professional manufactures who turn out quiet, durable, lightweight, inexpensive suppressors for any weapon out there. And if a company does not have an existing model to choose from, they can custom-make one.

Why is it so many people, despite being in the shooting profession, know virtually nothing about the characteristics, advantages, and disadvantages of using a suppressor? I think that the main reason is obvious - conventional tactics dominate the field of sniping and this conventional mindset has become a mental prison, confining security professionals to what they know. Even career military sniper Mark Spicer writes in his book about sniping: "The suppressed sniper rifle is a strange weapon and requires a lot of practice to master…" Simply put, most of the world expects that when a gun is

---

1 Hoffman, *Hitler's Personal Security*, p.99. (This is a detailed work that studies the security measures used to protect Hitler.)

CZ452 .22 Caliber Rimfire Rifle

This rifle is equipped with a lightweight, detachable Tactical Innovations Quest suppressor. Notice how short the suppressor is, adding only several inches to the overall length of the weapon.

fired, flames belch out of the end of the barrel along with an ear-splitting explosion. Instead of solving this problem, the sniping world has grown used to the gunshot and has adapted their tactics to deal with it instead of getting rid of the gunshot itself.

Because of this conventional mindset, I have heard officers, who were leading men in combat, scoff at the idea of using suppressors. They discounted suppressors as 'something Special Forces might use' as opposed to thinking of suppressors as being an every day tool that every soldier and sniper needs to succeed and survive in close urban combat. I have spoken to Special Operations soldiers, who were combat veterans, who also scoffed at the idea of using suppressors simply because they too were untrained in the tactical employment of suppressors.

The civilian community, who has very little knowledge or experience with suppressors, only see suppressors used in James Bond movies and think of suppressors as an assassination tool. The logic follows, why would you need to use a suppressor unless you were going to assassinate someone? As a result, in the United States, suppressors are highly regulated and a person must get a special permit to own one. Because this assassination-suppressor link is so strong in peoples' minds, possession of an unlicensed suppressor, even a homemade one, is a felony offense.

If someone is a professional urban sniper and does not fully understand the capabilities and limitations of a sound suppressor, then they are not a well-rounded sniper. If a sniper fully understands the characteristics of a suppressor – both good and bad – has trained regularly with a suppressor, has tested the suppressor in realistic training and combat, and then decides consciously not to use a suppressor due to tactical reasons, then that is another story. In that situation, the sniper is making an informed, as opposed to an uninformed, decision.

Ambush in Iraq

Let me tell a short story about John, an acquaintance of mine, who recently served in combat in Iraq. One afternoon in Iraq, John and his team were ambushed as they drove down a road to investigate reports of an insurgent attack on an Iraqi army checkpoint. As the enemy opened fire, John and his men quickly got off the road and fought their way into a nearby row of houses that lined the ambush zone. John, a trained and experienced sniper, was armed with an SPR Mk12 5.56 mm suppressed sniper rifle. John, and his spotter Mike, moved to an elevated position in one of the buildings so they could have a commanding view of the surrounding terrain.

From this perch, John and Mike had an excellent view of the immediate battle-field and could see several insurgent positions. Soon, Apache gunships arrived to support them. As the Apaches circled overhead like giant, angry insects, the helicopters took fire from the insurgents. John searched for targets and saw an insurgent aiming an RPG at the Apaches floating slowly overhead. John aimed at the RPG gunner's head and put a single bullet into the side of his skull, blowing brain matter out the other side. John soon found other targets. An insurgent armed with an AK-47 stepped around a corner and then took a round from John in the chest, knocking him off his feet. Another insurgent stepped around the corner and looked around, trying to find the source of the gunfire. *Pffffft!* John hit him too, killing him just like the first one.

In the space of about five minutes, John located, engaged, and killed thirteen insurgents in an enclosed urban area where the longest shot taken was about 200 meters and most of the shots were half that distance or less. The only reason why John made so many kills in such a short space of time at such close distances was because he used a suppressed weapon. He killed one enemy, and then another, and then another because they had no idea where the deadly shots were coming from. They could not hear the shots and they could not see a muzzle flash. What prevented John from making more kills was that his spotter, Mike, started firing at the enemy too, but his weapon was not suppressed. As soon as the insurgents heard and saw Mike's gunfire, they knew where to hide from.

It was no surprise to John that a suppressed weapon helped him fight off a much larger, heavier armed foe. He knew suppressed weapons could give his small team an advantage in an urban environment because he trained with suppressors before deploying to combat. In fact, every man on John's team carried a suppressor on their kit. It was a mandatory piece of equipment just like their radios and night vision goggles. They knew the advantages of the suppressors (there are many) and they knew the disadvantages (there are a few). In short, they were trained and skilled in the tactical employment of suppressors for combat operations.

Advantages of Using a Suppressor

If there are so many advantages of using a suppressor, what are they? First, a suppressor, because it totally encases the muzzle of the weapon, almost completely hides the muzzle flash of the weapon. In fact, from a distance, even at night, it's almost impossible to even know a weapon is being fired. One might be able to see a small flash of light inside the suppressor itself, but this small signature is easily lost among the much brighter, more noticeable lights of a city's background like streetlights, car head lights, and normal house lamps. Also, one must understand, a weapon emits some flash/fire from any space that is not totally enclosed. For example, when firing a semi-automatic weapon, some flash can be seen as the action works, ejects, and chambers another round. Even with a revolver, some flash can be seen where the cylinder meets the barrel. While these flashes are small compared to the enormous flash from the barrel, the shooter still needs to take this signature into account and employ good concealment techniques to compensate for it.

As the suppressor conceals a weapon's muzzle flash, it also eliminates muzzle blast and any resulting muzzle disturbance. Anyone who has fired a weapon in a dry climate – like the Middle East – can attest as to how much signature is created by

Mk 12 SPR 5.56 mm Sniper Rifle

John takes aim with his SPR equipped with a very quiet Ops, Inc, detachable sound suppressor. This photo was taken a month after John fought off an insurgent ambush with this same weapon.

muzzle blast. After firing a high-powered rifle, a small cloud of dust erupts in front of the shooter, giving their position away. In daylight hours, this muzzle disturbance is more incriminating and revealing than the muzzle flash, which, in contrast, can hardly be seen. When a shooter uses a suppressor their tactical options multiply because they do not have to worry about hiding their muzzle blast. A shooter can lie on the ground, or put their muzzle near a dirty, dusty window frame and fire a shot without fear of giving their position away.

Just as a suppressor nearly eliminates muzzle flash and blast, a can does an excellent job of what it was designed for - reducing the audible noise heard when a shot is fired. Most modern suppressors on the manufacturer, will reduce the sound of a weapon until it is no louder than a car door being shut. With this level of noise reduction, a shooter can easily combine their muffled gunshot with urban cover noise like music, a motorcycle revving, and even a honking car horn to conceal the gunshot from the target and the surrounding population. Ultimately, a sound suppressor is the best form of urban camouflage. If a sniper allows their muzzle blast and flash to be seen and their gunshot to be heard, it is the equivalent of the sniper jumping up and down, waving a big red flag, and yelling to the entire city, "Hey everyone, look at me, I'm a sniper, and I just fired a shot from a hidden position!" Of course, it does not make any tactical sense to jump up and down and scream and wave a red flag and it does not make any sense to fire a rifle without a suppressor.

Another advantage of a suppressor is it allows for better weapons control by eliminating what is called 'muzzle flip' or 'muzzle climb'. There is a whole industry designed to increase muzzle control through such attachments like muzzle brakes and muzzle compensators. Why use these devices when one can use a suppressor that works even better? The fact is, a suppressor eliminates muzzle climb and works much better than any muzzle brake or compensator. On top of this, a suppressor reduces weapon recoil, improving the shooter's control of the weapon. All I ask the reader to do is take a simple test. Take your weapon and fire an entire magazine as fast as you can at a 25-meter target and see what kind of control you have. Then, attach a suppressor and take the same test. Tell me which one offers better control. The truth is, a suppressor enables a shooter to rapidly and accurately engage multiple targets because their barrel will stay on target the entire time.

While muzzle control is a big concern when firing a semi-automatic weapon, does the shooter really care about muzzle control when firing a bolt-action, lever-action, revolving action, or break-open weapon? Yes, the experienced shooter does care about muzzle control, even with non-automatic weapons. This is because a sniper wants to stay on their target throughout the engagement process. Even a sniper firing a bolt-action rifle wants to maintain the same sight picture until they are done servicing the target. Especially when a sniper fires a large-bore rifle like a 7.62 mm or a .50 caliber weapon, muzzle control is difficult and it takes a second for the shooter to compose themselves and get back on target after making a shot. A suppressor, which is also the world's best muzzle brake, speeds up the entire engagement process.

Because a suppressor eliminates muzzle flash and muzzle blast, one can use a suppressed weapon in ways and in environments that would otherwise be off limits. For example, if a person is sitting in the front passenger seat of a car, armed with a suppressed MP5SD submachine-gun, they can shoot in close proximity to the driver, or anyone else in the car, without fear of injuring them. Specifically, they can aim their weapon across the front of the driver, with the suppressor only inches from their face, and fire out the driver-side window at their target, all without fear of blowing out the driver's eardrum or blinding him with the muzzle flash or burning his face with the muzzle blast. If one used a suppressed weapon, they can work in confined spaces and in close proximity (within inches) of other people and do so in a completely safe manner.

The use of a suppressor also allows one to work in a potentially hazardous environment with reduced risk of injury. For instance, police officers who regularly raid methadone labs use suppressed weapons because if they fire an unsuppressed weapon in an enclosed space like a drug lab, they can cause an explosion due to the volatile gases given off by the methadone-making process. A suppressed weapon enables a shooter to operate in close proximity to explosive or flammable gases with much less chance of igniting them.

There are a whole variety of tactical tasks that can be accomplished quietly when using a suppressed weapon. For instance, one can quietly shoot out a street light with a suppressed weapon in order to hide in the darkness. One can shoot a barking dog with a suppressed weapon and quietly remove this potentially mission compromising threat. A sentry or guard can be discretely removed with a single, quiet shot from a suppressed .22 caliber pistol. A car's tires can be shot out in near silence or a window can be shattered with a few well-aimed, quiet shots. An electrical junction or phone relay box can also be quietly put out of action with a suppressed weapon, prior to conducting an assault. These are just several examples from a whole list of things that can be accomplished with a suppressed weapon.

From a command and control aspect, suppressors bring a lot to the table. The single biggest obstacle to effective communication during a gunfight is the inability to hear or to be heard over the roar of gunshots. Regularly, in combat, soldiers have been unable to communicate effectively on a radio or even give or receive simple directions from fellow teammates because somebody is on the machine-gun pounding away at

Colt M4 5.56 mm Carbine

This soldier takes aim with an M4 equipped with a Knights Armament Co. detachable wet/dry sound suppressor.

a target.

Another problem presented in combat is the use of earplugs. Whenever someone is on a combat patrol, and contact is likely, most people put a hearing plug in one ear and have the other one in their pocket. This way they can cut their hearing losses, because while they are moving, they can still at least hear out of one ear. But, if they suddenly have enemy contact and have to fire unsuppressed weapons, they would not destroy the hearing in both of their ears – they would damage only one of them - until they get the other earplug in. The use of suppressors eliminates this potential for temporary and permanent hearing damage, one does not have to worry about juggling earplugs, and one does not have to yell at anybody to be heard.

Suppressing a weapon is useful for more than just combat operations, they are also useful in training. It is far easier to train a new shooter using a suppressed weapon because the shooter will not suffer from flinching, bracing, eye-closing, and anticipating the shot like they would if the weapon was unsuppressed and had the normal muzzle flash, blast, gunshot, recoil, and muzzle climb. With a suppressor, a new shooter can focus on the fundamentals of marksmanship as opposed to weathering the blast of an unsuppressed weapon. In short, a suppressor makes a weapon more pleasant to shoot, reduces gun-shyness, and instills confidence in beginners.

Disadvantages of Using a Suppressor

There are several disadvantages to using a suppressor, all of which can be compensated for in some way and, in my opinion, are far outweighed by the advantages. The biggest problem with using a suppressor is it extends the overall length of a weapon, making it less concealable. But this all depends on the weapon and the type of suppressor used. Some pistols, like the famed Ruger MkII, have integral suppressors, meaning that the suppressor is not detachable and is actually part of the weapon. Weapons like these are usually shorter in length than a pistol with a suppressor attached to the end of it.

Also, modern rifle suppressors are so compact and fit over the first several inches of the muzzle, they may only extend the length of the rifle by an inch or two. In some situations one may actually want a suppressor to lengthen the weapon. For example, if a person is firing an M-4 assault rifle with a shortened 7 and 1/2-inch barrel, they will suffer from an enormous muzzle blast and flash, which makes the weapon almost impractical. In this case, the shooter must have a suppressor on the weapon to make it manageable. And an M-4 with a 7 and 1/2-inch barrel and a suppressor is still far shorter than the regular M-4 with a 14-inch barrel.

Another option for the shooter is to carry their weapon without the suppressor attached, as it may be easier to conceal them both if carried separately. Then, once the shooter gets to their shooting platform and they have some privacy, they pull out their suppressor and attach it to their weapon to take the shot. This is an easy task depending on the weapon and the suppressor. Some suppressors are screw-on models, so they have to be threaded carefully onto the barrel to ensure alignment. A suppressor like this may take a minute to secure to the weapon. Other suppressors simply slide over the muzzle and snap on to the barrel, taking mere seconds to either attach or detach.

Weight is another consideration when using a suppressor, although modern suppressors are very light - most weigh around a pound - and some rifle suppressors are as light as seven ounces! The overall weight is not a serious problem. The real problem is this weight is at the end of the barrel, making the weapon barrel-heavy and harder to maneuver. One way to solve this problem is to use a weapon with an integral suppressor so there is no imbalance in the weapon from the start. Another option is to choose a suppressor that is short and overlaps the front of the barrel as much as possible, thus moving the suppressor's weight towards the center of the weapon. Weapon imbalance may not be an issue if one plans on taking a slow, deliberate shot and fires from a stable platform like a bipod.

Perhaps the most serious consideration when using a suppressor is it affects the barrel harmonics and performance of the weapon. Again, it all depends on the suppressor and the weapon used. If a weapon has an integral suppressor and a free-floating barrel, then the weapon will not suffer from any adverse affects. However, if one places a quick-attach suppressor to the end of a barrel, this will affect the barrel harmonics enough to affect bullet placement. So, if a shooter is zeroed with their weapon without a suppressor and then places a muzzle-hanging suppressor on their weapon, they will get different shot placement. A solution to this is to zero the weapon with the suppressor attached to it.

Importantly, a shooter should want to fire their weapon with a suppressor attached because the suppressor positively impacts barrel harmonics, meaning it reduces muzzle whip and increases accuracy. Surefire Inc., which makes several kinds of high-quality sound suppressors, says their suppressors not only act as a harmonics dampener, but increase bullet velocity by as much as fifty feet per second. Obviously, before using a suppressor on an actual operation, the shooter must train with their weapon, and measure how bullet placement is affected by the suppressor, to determine how the suppressor affects their overall shooting.

Considerations for the Guerrilla

H&K MP5SD Submachine Gun

Here is Heckler & Koch's famous MP5SD with its integral suppressor that bleeds off the weapon's gases as the bullet travels down the barrel. A very quiet, accurate weapon.

A guerrilla sniper using a suppressor has other considerations above and beyond these tactical issues. Only conventional military and law enforcement snipers have the luxury of focusing strictly on tactical concerns. To start, the guerrilla must be concerned with how they acquire the suppressor. Because suppressors are viewed by most as an exotic accessory, they may be hard to come by on the battlefield and this scarcity will drive up prices. Consequently, suppressors are generally an expensive item compared to more mundane items like ammunition, scopes, and collapsible stocks. This rarity may raise eyebrows from whoever is selling the suppressor. If the seller is a black marketer, there may be no problem. But if the seller is legitimate, it will be hard to explain why you need a sound suppressor – so you do not disturb your neighbors while you target shoot?

In almost every country, a sound suppressor has to be acquired illegally, through the black market, battlefield recovery, theft, or other means. This is because a suppressor, which is instantly tied to assassinations, cannot be bought casually or anonymously. In the United States, the government requires a person to get a license to possess a suppressor. This means the buyer must show redundant forms of identification, state the reason for wanting to own one, have no criminal record that would disqualify them from ownership, and state the address where the suppressor will be maintained. In other words, you cannot get a suppressor anonymously. In the Russian territories, specifically Chechnya, suppressors are just not allowed for civilian use. This is not surprising considering Russia has strict gun laws preventing widespread ownership of handguns, outlaw night-vision scopes, and requires every weapon sold to fire a bullet into a soft target for a ballistics comparison in case the weapon is ever suspected of being used in a future crime.

One should note that the use of a suppressor in combat is legal according to the laws of land warfare. An irregular combatant, like a guerrilla sniper, can use a suppressor during combat operations and be in full compliance with international law. While international law does not forbid the use of suppressors, it is the individual countries that restrict their sale and impose national laws on their use. This puts the guerrilla sniper in such a position that they are not committing a war crime, but may violate a state's internal laws.

119

The Gamo Whisper .177 Air Rifle

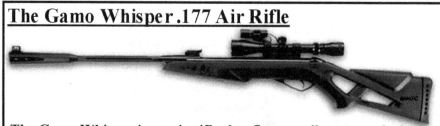

The Gamo Whisper is an air rifle that fires a pellet at speeds that break the sound barrier. The Whisper is unique in that it has a patented 'sound dampener' designed into the rifle barrel, which further quiets an already stealthy weapon.

Since a guerrilla has to violate national law to get a suppressor, they understand they must hide this incriminating evidence from the authorities just like they hide their illegal firearms. For, if a person is found with a suppressor, but not a gun, what possible reason do they have for possessing this proscribed item? A suppressor cannot be used for anything but to muffle the sound of a gunshot. It has no 'dual purpose' that can be explained away. What is the guerrilla going to say when caught red-handed during a raid or stopped at a checkpoint, "Oh, I found this by the side of the road and I thought it would make a really cool paperweight." That will not hold up in a court of law or even a battlefield interrogation.

All of these legal ramifications are exactly what the guerrilla organization must keep in mind and prepare for upon compromise, because the government fighting the guerrilla will use the full weight of their legal system as a counter-insurgency tool to put pressure on illegal combatants. In the United States, possession of an unregistered suppressor is a felony offense, regardless if it is attached to a weapon or not. In Northern Ireland, if an IRA sniper is captured with a sniper rifle and a suppressor, they just doubled their jail time.

Possession of a suppressor also brings to bear the issue of intent. If a guerrilla is caught with a folding-stock Armalite carbine under their car seat, it is hard to prove what their intent was. Maybe they were going to go target shooting. Maybe they were going to go hunting. Maybe they were going to turn it in to the police. Maybe they were going to sell it to somebody. Maybe they were dropping it off to someone else. Maybe they were going to kill somebody. If we add the suppressor to the equation, it is harder for the guerrilla to explain their intent as something less than lethal. In contrast, government prosecutors will have a much easier time convincing a judge or jury of criminal or terrorist intent, which will then add years of prison time, as opposed to a lighter sentence for mere weapons possession.

Improvised Suppressors

Since a government will go to extra lengths to keep commercially manufactured suppressors out of the guerrillas' hands, a few words on improvised sound suppressors is warranted. First, it is not difficult to make an effective, improvised suppressor that is nearly as effective as a manufactured one. The best improvised sound suppressors are those copied and reverse engineered in a workshop by someone who has experi-

Improvised Suppressor

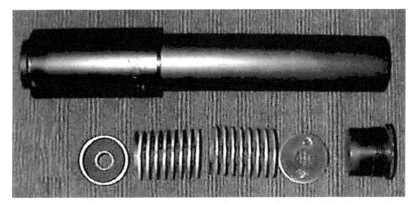

A homemade suppressor can be made relatively easily with a few basic items readily available at most hardware stores like: a metal/plastic cylinder, metal washers, soldering gun, glue, and a rod or dowel for aligning the finished product.

ence in metal fabricating. Guerrilla organizations like the FARC in Colombia have the manpower, resources, and technical know-how to take a commercially manufactured suppressor and then recreate their own in FARC-run metal shops. Although World War II resistance movements did not fully appreciate suppressed weapons, some groups, like the Polish Underground, had the ability to fabricate their own suppressors if they wanted to as they did make their own sub-machine guns, explosives, hand-grenades, and other weapons.

There are several detailed books and videos on the market today that show the interested reader how to make improvised suppressors in their own garage using materials that are easily and legally purchased at the local hardware store. This is not reverse engineering, this is making a suppressor out of commercially available items like a metal pipe and washers that require simple tools like a hack saw, a file, and a soldering gun. Some weapons are easier to fit with an improvised suppressor than others. The M4 assault rifle in particular uses a suppressor that snaps on. Other weapons like purpose-built sniper rifles, with nothing for a suppressor to snap onto, require the suppressor to be secured to the barrel using a tightening device like ones that can be found on a bicycle seat. With the help of an inexpensive manual off of Amazon.com, or a 'how-to' video available as cheaply as $2.00, and some practice, a person can make a homemade suppressor for almost nothing. It may be a little bulkier than a commercially made one, but it will still work. However, it is hard to find anyone who will admit to having fired and tested a homemade suppressor since (in the United States at least) it must be registered with the Bureau of Alcohol, Tobacco, and Firearms, which costs several hundred dollars. If not, it is a felony offense.

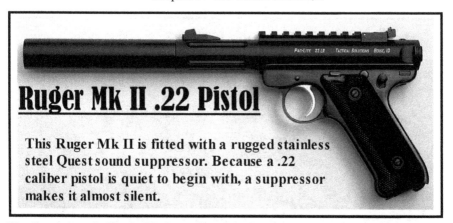

Ruger Mk II .22 Pistol

This Ruger Mk II is fitted with a rugged stainless steel Quest sound suppressor. Because a .22 caliber pistol is quiet to begin with, a suppressor makes it almost silent.

The Suppressor's Use in Modern Guerrilla Warfare

Since we have established that a suppressor is crucial for successful urban sniping (even more so for the guerrilla), then guerrilla movements all over the world must be using them, right? Wrong. Most guerrilla organizations are as ignorant of the benefits of a modern suppressor as are conventional snipers, perhaps even more so. Guerrilla snipers, like their conventional opponents, have spent most of their efforts adapting their sniping tactics to deal with the gunshot, instead of spending the time and resources on getting a suppressor by hook or crook. Some resistance movements, by sheer chance, have stumbled upon the benefits of suppressed weapons, but most have not.

The French resistance in World War II used suppressed weapons on occasions, but they never developed a strong sniper movement against the invading Germans. Some Palestinian snipers used suppressed rifles against the Israelis, but these incidents were so rare, such an occurrence created quite a commotion on the Israeli side. The Iraqi insurgents eventually used suppressed sniper rifles, but not on a large scale. Although this may change since an Iraqi insurgent website recently posted a video of a guerrilla cell fabricating homemade suppressors by the hundreds. The resistance movement that used suppressors the most were the Chechens. This was due to operational mimicking because the Russians themselves used suppressed weapons on such a relatively large scale. The Chechens, in turn, saw their effectiveness and then stole, captured, or bought suppressors on the black market to copy the Russian tactics.

While we can name a few movements that have employed suppressors, we can name far more that never did. What about Carlos Marighella, the Brazilian revolutionary who fought in the 1960's, whose ideas on urban guerrilla warfare are studied today? He mentions the importance of the urban sniper in his much-cited work *Minimanual of the Urban Guerrilla*, but he never makes the tactical leap to suppressed sniping. What was the IRA doing - who many consider to have displayed some of the most sophisticated urban guerrilla warfare methodology to date - from 1969 until 1998? Where was their suppressed sniping campaign? And what about the siege of Sarajevo, from 1992 to 1996, where the most concentrated, prolonged urban sniping in history took place? Again, suppressed sniping was a rarity.

Of course, guerrilla movements suffer from the same lack of foresight, leadership, and innovation that their conventional opponents do. Just because a resistance movement grasps the fundamentals of urban sniping does not mean they are experts in their discipline and understand all aspects of their field. However, a lack of understanding of the tools of their trade might make a guerrilla sniper an endangered species. This is because the threat to the unsuppressed shooter is very real as every human being is their own gunshot detection device, armed with two ears and two eyes that can accurately and instantly determine the general location of a gunshot. As modern warfare becomes more technically oriented and acoustic counter-sniper devices grow in popularity, the importance of the sound suppressor becomes apparent. Fortunately, for the government security forces with the job of fighting a resistance movement, few urban guerrilla snipers have taken their profession to a higher level, which the use of a suppressed weapon would certainly indicate.

Chapter 7

Invisible Death

Sniping in Stalingrad

The snipers went out 'hunting' early in the morning to previously selected and pre-pared places, carefully camouflaged themselves and waited patiently for targets to appear. They knew that the slightest negligence or haste would lead to certain death: the enemy kept a careful watch for our snipers.

- Marshal Chuikov, Commander Soviet 62nd
  Army, Stalingrad

Into the Slaughterhouse

Any discussion of modern urban sniping starts with Stalingrad, located on the banks of the Volga River, where Europe ends and Asia begins. The battle of Stalingrad, fought from September 1942 until February 1943, was the bloodiest urban conflict in the history of human warfare. Over the course of this brutal contest between the invading German armed forces (the *Wehrmacht*) and the defending Soviet Red Army, more than two million soldiers and civilians were killed, wounded, or captured. Estimates of German casualties and their allies hover at 800,000, while the Russians suffered well over one million in losses. One will never know the Russians' exact casualty numbers because Stalin made the official figures a state secret, calculating his battered people would think the cost too high.

To the men who bled in Stalingrad's streets, these enormous casualties meant the life expectancy of the average Russian soldier was less than twenty-four hours. The fighting in the city was so fierce German soldiers intentionally shot themselves, often

A German artillery piece pounds the city.

In the background towers the massive grain elevator, an urban fortress the Russians defended, holding up the entire German advance for a week.

firing through a loaf of bread in order to hide any incriminating powder burns on their skin, hoping their 'home wound' would get them sent out of the terrible city and to a rear area hospital. Battlefield desertions were so serious for the Russians that Stalin's secret police, the NKVD, executed almost 15,000 soldiers for cowardice – an entire division's worth of men. The men on both sides were pushed past the normal limits of human endurance and suffered ghastly emotional, mental, and physical wounds.

Russian soldiers approaching the city saw from afar what looked like Dante's inferno, as Viktor Kartashev, a cadet in the 193rd Rifle Division, noted, "On the horizon ahead of us, there was a continuous glow. It was Stalingrad burning. By day it smoldered and smoked, and by night it blazed brightly."[1] And what was awesome from afar was horrifying up close. Russian soldier Nikolai Maznista of the 95th Rifle Division described his experience in the center of Stalingrad: "The slopes of the Kurgan were completely covered in corpses. In some places you had to move two or three bodies aside to lie down. They quickly began to decompose, and the stench was appalling, but you just had to lie down and pay no attention."[2] For the German soldiers the situation was equally bleak as a Panzer crewmember described: "It was a ghastly, wearisome battle both on the ground and below the ground, amid the ruins and in the basements of that large city, in its industrial quarter. The tanks tottered over mountains of rubble and broken bricks, they screeched as they picked their way through the factory workshops, shooting at short range down blocked streets and in crowded factory yards."[3]

One element contributing to the astronomical casualty rates and the brain-numb-

1 Archive of the Muzei-Panorama Stalingradskoi Bitvy, Volgograd, p. 424/1309.
2 Popov, Petr (ed.), Perelom, Izdatel 2000.
3 Yakovlev, Nikolai, 19 Noyabrya 1942, Molodaya Gvardiya 1979.

ing battlefield stress was the urban sniper. During the first weeks of the battle, the Red Army - pulverized by the Luftwaffe's planes, pounded by German artillery, and pressed by assaulting panzers – was slaughtered at a fearsome rate. In a desperate bid to turn the tide of a losing battle, Russian commanders found an improbable answer to German firepower: the lone rifleman. Through sheer necessity and chance, the Red Army discovered the urban sniper, hidden amidst Stalingrad's bombed out buildings and smoking ruins, could exact a serious toll on their German foe.

From early on, Russian snipers forced the Germans to take extreme caution in the city, lest they fall victim to a carefully placed bullet to the head. As a result, the constant menace of invisible snipers forced the Germans underground for protection. This sub-surface existence gave rise to a miserable *Rattenkrieg* or a 'war of the rats'. Meanwhile, Russian propaganda companies reminded the Germans of what lurked above, announcing through their cold metal loudspeakers, "every seven seconds a German soldier dies in Russia." Even though both sides employed snipers in the tortured city, it was the Red Army who embraced their widespread employment to even the odds and stave off annihilation.

The Red Army: The Right Men, The Right Time

Under the cloak of darkness, on the night of September 19th, 1942, the Red Army ferried most of Lieutenant-Colonel Batyuk's 284th Infantry Division across the Volga and into the city. The fighting in the city itself raged for a week, ever since the German Sixth Army made its first push into central and southern Stalingrad on September 13th. The 284th Division, composed mostly of Siberians, came in the dead of night because the Luftwaffe made daylight crossings suicidal. Any boat caught out on the open water while the sun was still up was sure to be gutted by the Luftwaffe's dive bombers - the dreaded Stukas. Once the men of the 284th made it to the relative 'safety' of the far shore, they dug into the ruins for cover.

One of these soldiers was a short, stout young man who was drafted into the Soviet navy as a payroll clerk. His name was Vassili Zaitsev. Zaitsev had no formal sniper training, but he hunted wild game in the dark, thick forests of the Ural Mountains where he grew up. Zaitsev, just one soldier in a 10,000-man division, was thrown into the Russian lines as just another expendable rifleman with a predictably short life expectancy. However, Zaitsev, the natural hunter, excelled in the Stalingrad inferno and managed to shoot forty Germans in a ten-day period. Zaitsev and his 7.62 mm Mosin-Nagant 1890/31 bolt-action rifle made a deadly pair.

While Zaitsev zeroed in on the Germans, General Vasili I. Chuikov, commander of the Soviet 62nd Army, was busy organizing the city's defense. Chuikov, a plain-speaking, strong-willed man, intended to hold the city at all costs. This unwavering determination ultimately kept the Russians' defenses from falling apart under a frightful onslaught. Importantly, Chuikov understood the Red Army's methods on the Eastern Front, up to that point, ensured repeated failures. In an effort to reverse these costly defeats, Chuikov studied the Germans' tactics during their summer drive across the Ukraine towards Stalingrad. Chuikov was determined to find a way to limit the Germans' strengths and exploit their weaknesses. Consequently, as Zaitsev was making a name for himself as a sniper, Chuikov took notice as he was eager to try new methods that could hold off the surging Germans. Without any prompting, Chuikov

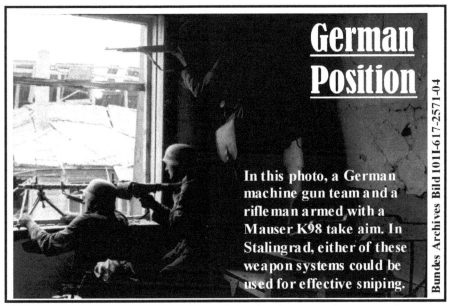

German Position

In this photo, a German machine gun team and a rifleman armed with a Mauser K98 take aim. In Stalingrad, either of these weapon systems could be used for effective sniping.

Bundes Archives Bild 101L-617-2571-04

seized on Zaitsev's success and supported the development of an aggressive sniper program. The combination of Zaitsev's skill and Chuikov's innovative mind proved to be the perfect union leading to the Russians' widespread use of snipers in Stalingrad.

Once Zaitsev proved his mettle as a marksman, he was directed to establish a sniper school so more Russian shooters could learn his tactics. Zaitsev set up this sniper school at the Lazur Chemical Factory located in the central part of the city. The Lazur, although bombed into a lunar landscape by the Luftwaffe, was one of the few areas of Stalingrad still in Russian hands. In one of the long industrial buildings of the Lazur, Zaitsev created a rifle range. Pictures of soldiers, helmets, and bunker slits were painted on the wall, giving Zaitsev's initial thirty students targets to shoot at. As the students shot at their make-believe enemy, Zaitsev instructed them on their form. After their brief introduction to marksmanship amidst the rubble of the Lazur, Zaitsev took his students out on live missions for the second phase of their sniping education - on the job training.[4]

This training of new snipers meshed with Chuikov's guidance to make every German soldier feel like, "they were living under the muzzle of a gun". The Germans definitely lived under the muzzle of Zaitsev's gun, as he managed to shoot some 242 of the enemy in Stalingrad. Several of Zaitsev's students achieved even more success, like Viktor Medvedev and Anatoli Chekov, who were each credited with killing hundreds of Germans apiece. Zaitsev also trained women snipers who proved to be as effective as their male counterparts. One of these female snipers, Tania Chernova, who fell in love with Zaitsev, went on to kill eighty Germans after receiving her training in the Lazur.[5] For the Germans, Zaitsev was a virus, growing in the Stalingrad Petri dish, infecting other Russians with his deadly skills. Zaitsev, and the snipers he personally trained, eventually accounted for over 3000 German deaths during the course of the war.

---

4 Craig, *Enemy at the Gates*, p. 121.
5 Craig, *Enemy at the Gates*, p. 122.

The Russians also seized on what they called the 'Sniper Movement' to shore up the Red Army's morale. The Red Army's daily newspaper *In Our Country's Defense* trumpeted their snipers' successes, published daily tallies of their kills, and proudly displayed their pictures. The Soviets' political organizations also became actively involved in supporting and promoting the Sniper Movement in Stalingrad. Officials as high ranking as Stalingrad Front Commander Colonel-General Andrei Yeremenko and famed commissar Nikita Krushchev took personal interest in promoting the Sniper Movement. As a result, the Russian snipers received direct support from the highest levels of their military and political command.[6]

What did this trained group of snipers amount to on the battlefield? How did they affect the Germans fighting and scraping their way forward through the ruins? German First Lieutenant Herbert Rauchhaupt, whose battalion was attacking the Red October factory, wrote an account of the deadly effects the Red Army snipers had on the exhausted, bleeding, German Sixth Army: "Suddenly two shots whiz by us from the left and hit the wall of Hall 5 some paces to our right. Luckily there is a deep bomb crater right at the foot of the factory hall. Into it – cover! Damn, where are those shots coming from? Here it is again, this eerie, horrid war, as it is being waged in Stalingrad for weeks. Not openly and honestly, but invisibly, sneakily, furtively and hidden. We crawl up to the other edge of the four meters deep crater and carefully peek over the edge. Twenty meters in front of us the soldier stands behind the wall that is jutting out. "Which way to the fight?" we shout at him. "Straight down the works road!" So we're in the right place! Then he comes from behind the corner of the wall for our crater. At the same moment it whizzes over our steel helmets and hits an iron beam that has fallen to our right. We pull our heads in. The soldier appears over us, one moment he waits at the edge of the crater to jump in – patsch – again a shot! Head first the soldier tumbles down to us in the crater. Hit! Headshot! Dead! In the invisible battle for Stalingrad there are nearly only headshots. We are cornered in a trap."[7]

German Sniping

While we know from accounts like that of Lieutenant Rauchhaupt that the Red Army's sniping efforts in the city were effective, what was the Germans' sniping program like? For a variety of reasons there is little literature on the subject. Peter Senich's book *The German Sniper 1914-1945* does not mention one word about the German Sixth Army and their struggle in Stalin's city. Breaker McCoy's *Death by Precision Fire: The World War II German Sniper* is equally silent. Even Jason Mark's definitive works on the battle, *Death of the Leaping Horsemen* and *Island of Fire*, only offer fleeting glimpses of the German marksmen. Ironically, some of the most detailed accounts of German snipers are from the Russians themselves who suffered from their carefully placed shots. Some historians argue this lack of information is because all of the German snipers were captured or killed when the Russians surrounded and captured what was left of the Sixth Army in February 1943. Upsetting this theory is the tens of thousands of Germans who were evacuated from Stalingrad during the battle and the very detailed unit histories of the organizations who actually fought in

---

6 Chuikov, *The Battle for Stalingrad*, p. 155. (A very detailed book written by the commander of Russian 62nd Army himself.)
7 Wijers, Hans J., *The Battle for Stalingrad: The Battle for the Factories.*

Red October Tractor Factory

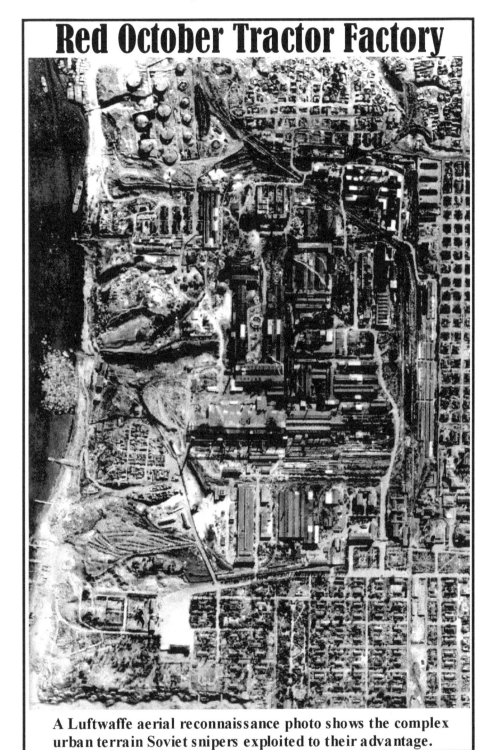

A Luftwaffe aerial reconnaissance photo shows the complex urban terrain Soviet snipers exploited to their advantage.

Stalingrad, which survived the war. Perhaps we must accept the fact, as discussed in chapter three, the Germans' sniping efforts in Stalingrad simply did not achieve the same level of importance.

While the German senior leadership did not appreciate the full potential of the urban sniper, their usefulness was recognized by the combat units fighting and dying inside the city. The staff of the 24th Panzer Division wrote a report entitled *Experiences Fighting in Stalingrad*, noting snipers should be used to support infantry assaults and units suffered much lower casualties when snipers actively supported their operations.[8] Other units employed snipers not just to support their assaults, but for attrition warfare. For instance, during the early fighting in September, the Germans managed to work snipers far enough forward to target the Russian rear lines in the northern factory district, allowing them to observe Russian movements between the Barrikady and Krasny Oktyabr factories. These snipers killed so many Russians trying to cross a washout between the factories, the Russians referred to this crossing as 'the gully of death'. Only after the Russians built a stone wall for protection could they move back and forth with a reasonable chance of survival.[9]

Other Russian soldiers found themselves under German crosshairs as well. Vasily Sokolov, a lieutenant in the Soviet naval infantry, recounted a particularly close call with a hidden German sniper that missed him, but killed some of his comrades. "It was the 26th or 27th (September 1942) and three of us had to go from the command post of the 62nd Army back to our own 92nd Brigade. There was me, Lieutenant Zhurba who was the adjutant of the brigade commander, and one soldier who was accompanying us. Before we reached the sector of the 13th Guards, we caught sight of a sergeant sitting on the ground some distance away. He was wounded. We asked him: where are you hit and what is your unit? He made a gesture with his hand and said: 'I was crossing this open patch of ground about half an hour ago when I was hit in the leg by a German sniper.'

The sergeant told us that he was from the 92nd Brigade. A short time ago, he had seen the German sniper kill two of our men, even though the sergeant had shouted to them not to come over as there was a sniper in the building near by. Sure enough, there were a couple of bodies lying not far from us.

As for us, we still had to get across the area controlled by the sniper, as we could not go back without having carried out our orders. I decided to make a run for it first. I hunched up, thought to myself 'what will be will be', and dashed across the square and down the steep bank.

The German didn't shoot. Lieutenant Zhurba made his run next, and then the soldier who was with us. Again the sniper didn't shoot. Either he was taking a nap, or he didn't get us in his sights quickly enough.

We found ourselves lying in the midst of fifteen or so corpses, our people. There was one woman among them – most likely a medic. Only the torso was there: her head, arms, and legs had been torn off, probably by the blast of a bomb or a shell. Three of the bodies were in a sitting position, leaning against the high bank, almost as if they were asleep.

Two signalers now came our way. They were dragging a drum of cable with them.

8 Mark, *Death of the Leaping Horsemen*, p. 326.(This is one of the definitive works on the Battle of Stalingrad.)
9 Chuikov, *The Battle for Stalingrad*, p. 130.

A German sniper takes aim at a target. The Germans were unprepared for the intense urban sniping they experienced in the city.

I advised them to run across the sniper's field as quickly as they possibly could ('Fly like a bullet!' I said). I thought they had got my meaning, but they didn't seem to go any faster for it. Maybe the drum of cable slowed them down. While they were on their way across the square, two or three shots rang out. They were dum-dum bullets – I knew because you always get a puff of smoke with an explosive bullet. Both soldiers went down. They looked to be dead, but we didn't go near them because we would certainly have killed ourselves. We went on our way to Brigade HQ."[10]

In another case, during an assault on the Barrikady Gun Factory in October, German radio specialist Heinz Neist and his squad secured the bottom floor of an industrial building, while the Russians occupied the top floor. The two groups fought for days over the lone stairwell in the building, with neither side daring to venture up or down the deadly stairs. Neist, trapped in the building with his men, called in reinforcements. Help came in the form of friendly snipers who took roost in a building opposite their own. These German snipers had perfect view of the Russian squad barricaded in the upper floor. After observing their prey, the snipers opened fire, picking off the Russians one at a time. By the time Neist and his squad snuck up the stairs to search the upper floor, they found seven Russian soldiers lying on the floor, all dead from the snipers' well-aimed bullets.[11]

In the northern factory district near the Barrikady Gun factory, snipers were crucial for interdicting Russian reinforcements and their accompanying supplies coming across the now-frozen Volga River. As groups of much needed Russian replacements

10 Archive of the Muzei-Panorama Stalingradskoi Bitvy, Volgograd, p. 862/7294.
11 Craig, *Enemy at the Gates*, p. 139-40.

tried to cross the Volga in early December and shore up the beleaguered Soviet 138th Rifle division, German snipers picked off scores of victims who were caught out on the open ice. One of these snipers who gave the Russian command fits was Oberleutnant Hans Wegener, a junior leader of Pazerjager-Abteilung 389 who said, "We had the possibility of shooting over the Volga with our telescopic-equipped carbines. We German snipers were at least as good as the Russians!"[12]

After the Germans became encircled in Stalingrad, the sniper grew in importance because of the dire supply situation. Since all ammunition was flown into the city on the Luftwaffe's dwindling numbers of aircraft, the Germans were forced use their ammunition sparingly. The supply situation was so bad some German battalion commanders became the only ones who could authorize their men to open fire. Taking this logistical starvation into account, the sniper became the most economical weapon in the arsenal. While the use of mortars was cut back and machine-gunners began rationing their ammo, the snipers continued their deadly work, one bullet at a time.

On November 13, a Russian soldier noted, "After a few hours, a German sniper – within the span of about 5-6 minutes – killed four of our men, three of them were sergeants and one officer. I spotted the German sniper sitting between a brick chimney and some metal on the roof, not far from us (60-70 meters)."[13] Two days later Russian Senior-Sergeant Gorbatenko was defending his regimental command post, "At midday I was standing at the ready with soldiers on the second floor. We fired two cartridges toward the Germans. When the third jammed, snipers hit the soldiers at the embrasures."[14] On December 19th, when two Russians soldiers were taking a German soldier prisoner they came under accurate fire. "They had just approached the first trench positions of the 650th Regiment when machine-gun fire suddenly erupted from the basement of the corner house. Snipers also opened fire from the same building. Grigoriev managed to quickly jump into the trench, dragging the 'tongue' behind him. Petukhov was hit by a sniper's bullet. He released the rope and fell near the trench. The German sniper shot him two more times."[15]

A Target Rich Environment

As these accounts indicate, the urban war in Stalingrad, with tens of thousands of soldiers crammed into a geographically small area, offered snipers many potential targets. Russian sniper Anatoli Chekov regularly targeted German soldiers bringing rations up to the front lines.[16] These soldiers, carrying heavy food containers in both hands, preoccupied with getting food to their comrades, were slow moving targets. As soon as one of these men was shot, they became bait for other soldiers trying to rescue them. In this manner, a sniper could get two or three kills in the space of a few minutes. Other tempting targets were German soldiers on water detail, where a soldier carrying an armful of empty bottles became another prized kill. Not only did the sniper kill the targeted soldier, but the soldier's comrades now had to endure unbearable thirst.

12 Mark, *Island of Fire*, p.309. (There is no better book recounting the battle for the factory district.)
13 Mark, *Island of Fire*, p.165.
14 Mark, *Island of Fire*, p.197.
15 Mark, *Island of Fire*, p.304.
16 Beevor, *Stalingrad: The Fateful Siege*, 205.

Above, General Chuikov inspects Vassili Zaitsev's Mosin-Nagant rifle for the Red Army's cameramen.

Key members of both armies were intentionally targeted like artillery observers, radio operators, machine-gunners, other snipers, and officers. If a sniper could remove these critical personnel, the enemy's unit would cease to function as a cohesive organization. Surprisingly, prime targets for Russian snipers were German panzers. Because panzer crews suffered from such poor situational awareness in the claustrophobic confines of the city, they often stuck their heads outside of their steel hatches to communicate with adjacent infantry units and to get a better view of their surroundings. As soon as the panzer crews exposed themselves, hidden snipers picked off these now vulnerable targets. With a single shot to the head of a panzer commander, a sniper could shut down an entire crew. Also, Russian snipers were instructed to shoot out the glass vision ports on the panzers, blinding the crews. With their vision ports shattered, panzer crews became more vulnerable to other threats like anti-tank guns and dug-in T-34 tanks.

The Russians were so aggressive in their use of snipers, they tried to kill the commander of the German Sixth Army himself, General Friedrich Paulus. On December 13th, Russian intelligence units thought they had pinpointed Paulus' command bunker inside the city. A four-person sniper team was dispatched to kill him. One of the snipers was Tania Chernova and another was her teacher, Zaitsev. While the team picked its way through the rubble and snow, ever weary of German sentries, the lead girl in the team stepped on an unseen land mine. Tania was seriously wounded by the resulting blast and Zaitsev had to carry her back to a field hospital for immediate surgery. The attempt to eliminate Paulus with a single well-aimed shot was over. Unknown to them, their intelligence was faulty and Paulus was miles away, outside of the city at Gumrak airfield.[17]

Urban Snipercraft

Tania and Zaitsev's attempt to kill Paulus revealed that movement in the city was serious business. Death could come from anywhere: another sniper, an artillery observer, a minefield, a pilot looking earthward, or any number of enemy machine-gun positions, trenches, pillboxes, bunkers, and strongpoints. Since foot movement could be a death warrant, snipers made use of the available cover, which included moving through basements, trenches, and the shells of bombed out structures. The ideal way to travel was over a route providing all around protection from observation. Although this was not usually available, Zaitsev was able to move undetected at various times using a building's air duct, another time by crawling through a heating duct, and still other times moving through the empty pipes of a petrol storage yard. In Stalingrad, to be seen was to be killed.

After a sniper made it safely to a specific area, the city's complex urban terrain, made even more chaotic by its destruction, offered the sniper an endless number of positions to shoot from. Russian snipers, for example, found excellent positions atop the towering smokestacks of the Barrikady gun factory. Because the Barrikady's giant Martin furnaces were located underground, the Russians were able to get inside them and climb to the tops of the smokestacks unseen by the Germans. Once in these lofty perches, the snipers held a dominating view of the surrounding city. For weeks on end, Russian snipers picked off their enemy from the tops of these chimneys, impervious to German counterfire. Finally, in early November, the Germans brought up newly commissioned SIG33B assault guns and emplaced them in front of the Barrikady. Once in position, the SIG33Bs pumped round after round of 150 mm high-explosive shells straight into the massive smokestacks. Even these huge chimneys could not withstand such firepower and they collapsed in an avalanche of rubble.[18]

As the dead men in the smokestacks could attest to, once in position, the sniper had to be able to observe the terrain and still remain undetected. Zaitsev remained invisible from the Germans through the use of a trench periscope he carried with him. Once Zaitsev was in position, he never showed more than the unobtrusive tip of his periscope to assess his surroundings. While enemy soldiers exposed their positions with sunlight reflecting off their binoculars and rifle scopes, they never saw Zaitsev. Zaitsev understood the slightest movement or exposure before, or even after a shot, could give his position away. In an example of this, a German sniper once exposed himself to Zaitsev by reaching out to collect his expended brass after he made a shot.[19]

To increase the chance for survival, both sides used deception, like raising helmets above trench lines and window sills to make it look like a soldier was exposing themselves. The goal was to get the enemy to shoot in order to expose their position. When Zaitsev employed these methods, he always examined the bullet hole in the helmet he had raised to determine from what angle the bullet came from. If the enemy sniper

17 Craig, *Enemy at the Gates*, p. 235-36.
18 Mark, *Island of Fire*, p. 50-51.
19 Zaitsev, *Notes Of A Sniper,* p.154.

A German soldier stands guard in the cellar of a demolished factory in the southern part of the city. This was part of the underworld where both sides lived like rats.

did not fall for the helmet trick, then Zaitsev used a full-sized dummy to try and coax a shot from them. Dummies were also good for making the enemy think a sniper was still in a certain position even though he had moved to another. Germans and Russians alike built dummy positions to include fake pillboxes, foxholes, and bunkers that were unoccupied, except for a dummy. Snipers then mixed the fake positions with real, camouflaged sniper hides. These multiple positions gave a sniper the ability to make a shot from one location and then move quickly to another position to observe their enemy.

Hiding the Shot

While moving undetected to a camouflaged position was critical, so was making the actual shot in an inconspicuous manner. For example, machine-gunners firing tracer rounds were easily spotted and had a low survival rate. Soldiers who fired their rifles and allowed their muzzle flashes to be seen were also vulnerable to enemy observation. Soldiers who fired repeated shots from the same position were susceptible to detection from the sound of their gunshots alone. Zaitsev observed one German sniper who killed four Russians in a few hours because the sniper worked in conjunction with several submachine gunners. When the submachine gunners fired, the sniper fired his shot. In this manner, the firing of the submachine gunners masked the sound of the German sniper's own gunshot.[20]

Zaitsev used the sounds of the battlefield to hide his gunshots and he fired in daylight to hide his muzzle flash. Russian sniper Anatoli Chekov fabricated his own flash hider that he affixed to the end of his sniper rifle to help hide the muzzle blast of his

20 Zaitsev, *Notes Of A Sniper*, p.179-80.

weapon. Even after taking precautions to conceal his shot, Zaitsev found that those measures were not always enough to save him. Many times Zaitsev took a shot and then immediately left the area to avoid German reprisals like mortar barrages, artillery bombardment, and air strikes. Zaitsev knew to shoot and move after one or two shots to avoid getting pinned down or obliterated. Chekov, like Zaitsev, was careful to never fire in bad light where his muzzle flash could be easily seen. When he could, Chekov fired in front of white colored walls so his muzzle flash would be washed out to the casual observer.[21] Exposure in Stalingrad, either from muzzle flashes or the sound of gunshots, meant death.

Tania Chernov and a team of fellow snipers learned the importance of concealing their shots when they worked the Krasny Oktyabr area of the northern factory district sometime in October. During this particular mission, Tania and her group surveyed the terrain and established a sniper hide in the upper story of a building, behind a pile of bricks. From their perch, they watched the German front lines for hours. Then, a German assault group came into the open, completely exposed. Tania and the other snipers, unable to resist such a lucrative target, opened fire and gunned down seventeen Germans. However, the snipers' shots exposed their position, enabling the Germans to pinpoint them. Minutes later, artillery shells screamed in and collapsed the entire structure. Tania managed to escape, but the rest were killed from the hot shrapnel of the bursting shells and the massive weight of the collapsing building.[22]

Sniping Innovation

Because the fighting in Stalingrad often took place up close, unconventional sniping methods could be used. At a hundred meters, the average rifleman, with no sniper training or scope, could accurately hit a target. What made this soldier a sniper was their understanding of urban warfare tactics, not their extremely accurate rifle. Adelbert Holl, a member of the German 94th Infantry Division, found himself in the roll of sniper even though he was armed only with the standard-issue 7.92 mm Mauser Karbiner 98. One day, as Holl and his unit fought their way through southern Stalingrad, he spied some Russian soldiers 150 meters away in a building. The Russians were going up and down some stairs, but were exposed by a hole in the wall of their building. Holl took aim over the iron sights of his rifle from his concealed position and shot four Russians through the hole in the wall. An hour later, Holl shot a Russian messenger as he ran across an open square to where his comrades were just killed. At these short distances, Holl was just as effective as a sniper with formal training and a specialized rifle.[23]

The intense urban combat of Stalingrad also spurred sniper innovation in other ways, like employing anti-tank rifles for sniping. In fact, both sides employed bolt-action, anti-tank rifles for sniping. Zaitsev himself tested the Russian-made PTRD-1 14.5 mm anti-tank rifle as a sniper's tool. The PTRD-1 was not often employed as a sniper rifle because of its weight (over 35 pounds), its enormous muzzle blast/flash, and its inaccuracy as compared to purpose-built sniper rifles. (These men did not know it at the time, but they were pioneering the first heavy-caliber sniper rifles, which

---

21 Beevor, *Stalingrad: The Fateful Siege*, 205.
22 Craig, *Enemy at the Gates*, p. 145-6.
23 Holl, *An Infantryman in Stalingrad*, p.61-63.

Soviet Snipers

In this staged photo, a two-man Russian sniper team take up positions in the rubble on the outskirts of Stalingrad.

would only come into popularity fifty years later in the 1990's.) However, Adelbert Holl employed a captured PTRD-1 for sniping when the situation demanded it. One such situation arose as Holl and his unit attacked through the Barrikady workers settlement. During the assault, Holl encountered a Russian team firing a machine-gun through a hole in a wall. After pinpointing the position, Holl brought forward the bulky PRTD-1 and fired a single round into the machine-gun position, silencing it.[24] Although pinpoint accuracy was not possible with the inherently inaccurate PRTD-1, relatively large targets located close to the shooter were sitting ducks.

A good sniper also had to be a good counter-sniper. Zaitsev, for one, consistently located enemy snipers through an established process combining battlefield questioning, forensic investigation, ballistic analysis, and his own understanding of sniping. By analyzing the way his fellow soldiers were shot by German snipers, Zaitsev reverse engineered the circumstances of the shooting. In this manner, Zaitsev turned every sniper victim into a potential counter-sniper operation. Zaitsev described such a situation where German snipers gunned down a Russian artillery observation team concealed in some factory smokestacks.

His investigation started by interviewing fellow Russian soldiers who saw their comrades hit by the German snipers. Zaitsev asked these eyewitnesses to draw maps showing exactly where the dead spotters were located and how they were killed. From studying these drawings and listening to the after action reports of the shootings, Zaitsev made an educated guess as to the angle the German bullets were fired from. After backtracking the trajectory of the bullets from the smokestacks, Zaitsev determined the position the German sharpshooters most likely shot from. Aiding in

---

24 Holl, *An Infantryman in Stalingrad*, p.113.

the investigation were the deceased spotters' own periscope, which had bullet holes in it, and allowed for further analysis of the bullets' trajectory.

Zaitsev partitioned his disciplined investigation into two parts. The first part, as described by his questioning about the artillery observer shooting, was to study the circumstances of the shooting. An especially valuable tool in this first stage were the field medics who became expert at recognizing different kinds of battlefield injuries and were intimately familiar with gunshot wounds. Once Zaitsev completed his homework, he knew where to search for his foe. This ended the first investigative stage and signaled the beginning of the second stage of his counter-sniper operation.

The next stage was the actual physical search for the enemy shooter. Zaitsev would carefully move to an observation point where he could analyze the suspected enemy sniper hide. He conducted this methodical study of the enemy lines undetected because of his trusty trench periscope, which enabled him to remain invisible while he glassed the German lines. Zaitsev was aware some Russian snipers liked to use binoculars or their own rifle scopes to scan the enemy positions. Zaitsev thought this offered too much exposure and was much too risky since he knew thousands of German eyes were doing the same thing, scanning the Russian positions looking for someone one to make a mistake. Zaitsev summarized his detailed approach with the old adage, "measure seven times, cut once." Zaitsev felt only a sniper who did their homework and conducted a thorough analysis of the situation had any business trying to take out an enemy sniper.[25]

While understanding the technical aspects of an enemy's shot was important, so was reading the enemy's patterns and behavior. Just as modern police forces conduct pattern analysis of violent criminals, Zaitsev too studied the behavior of his German foes. Zaitsev, after his experience in the Stalingrad cauldron, could 'read' certain enemy snipers from the way they operated: the kind of camouflage they used, the firing positions they chose, and the targets they selected. Zaitsev could quickly discern who were the more experienced, cunning snipers and who were novices.[26] As Zaitsev's observations show, snipers from both sides became adept at judging each other's relative sniping ability as well us identifying their enemy's habits. No sniper could afford to become predictable or they would be studied, located, and then hunted down.

Since the Germans did not have the same number and quality of snipers as the Russians, discriminate counter-sniper operations, like the ones conducted by Zaitsev, were infrequent. Instead, the Germans responded with massive force to include the use of infantry assaults, mortars, artillery, air strikes, anti-tank guns, and tanks. When countering Russian snipers, the word 'restraint' did not enter the German vocabulary; they were simply unconcerned with civilian casualties or infrastructure damage. The Russian population unfortunate enough to remain in the city was stuck between the German hammer and Stalin's anvil and was pounded. The Germans did not care about winning Russian popular support, did not care about minimizing infrastructure damage, and did not care about their image in the international community. Therefore, craftily hiding a Russian sniper amongst the populace failed to beget moderation. Before the fighting started in August 1942, the industrial city of Stalingrad had a civilian population of 850,000 people. At the end of the war, just 1,500 remained.[27]

---

25 Zaitsev, *Notes Of A Sniper, p.236-7.*
26 Zaitsev, *Notes Of A Sniper, p. 234.*
27 news.bbc.co.uk, 1943, *Germans Surrender at Stalingrad*

Winter 1942/1943: Russian women and children hide out in an underground bunker, somewhere on the northwestern outskirts of Stalingrad, waiting for the end of the brutal fighting.

However, as the Germans punished the city, obliterating hundreds of thousands of Russian civilians and soldiers in the process, they created problems. First, turning the city's buildings into rubble did not stop Russian snipers from their deadly craft – the snipers merely burrowed into the mounds of debris like moles. Also, rubbling the city limited German mobility as they could not drive their panzers through the cluttered streets and their assaulting infantry units found fewer buildings to take cover in. Forward artillery observers had a harder time calling in accurate fire since their most prominent reference points were already flattened into the ground. In sum, as Germany's blitzkrieg machine bogged down in Stalingrad's ruins, the high intensity warfare tools that initially worked for countering the Russian snipers became less relevant. As a result, the Germans' unrestrained and massive use of firepower actually made them more vulnerable to Russian snipers as opposed to less so.

The Soviet and German armies were both unprepared for the high-intensity urban warfare they experienced in Stalingrad. However, it was the Soviet 62nd Army that adapted more readily to their new concrete battlefield, as shown by their creation of the Sniper Movement. The Russians' widespread use of urban snipers enabled them to exact a steady toll of casualties despite being outnumbered and outgunned. Importantly, there was no other battle in World War II, before or after Stalingrad, where urban sniping was practiced by both sides on such a large scale. Thus, the journey of any student of sniping will inevitably lead them to the bloody streets of Stalingrad, where desperate marksmen from the Red Army and the Wehrmacht dueled to the death amidst the scarred ruins of the city of steel.

Chapter 8

The Werewolves

We Werewolves consider it our supreme duty to kill, to kill and to kill, employing every cunning and wile in the darkness of the night, crawling, groping through towns and villages, like wolves, noiselessly, mysteriously.

> - Joseph Goebbels, German Minister of
> Public Enlightenment & Propaganda

The End of the Third Reich & the Birth of the Werewolves

By 1943 even the most ardent Nazi supporter could see the end was near. In February, the German Sixth Army, long-suffering in the frozen hell of Stalingrad, finally collapsed under the massive weight of the Red Army. Only four months later, in the scorching sands of Tunisia, the German Afrika Korps and its Italian Allies were crushed by a combined British and American force. And then that July any glimmer of hope went up in smoke at the Battle of Kursk, along with the shot-up hulls of a hundred burning panzers. While the conventional war was most certainly lost, some leaders in the German war machine looked for other means to continue German resistance. Thus did impending defeat give birth to a fledgling Nazi guerrilla movement.

The resistance movement was called 'Werwolf' after the book by Hermann Lons entitled *Der Wehrwolf*. Lon's novel spun a tale of German communities waging a

A German boy in the Hitler Youth receives marksmanship training on the Mauser K98.

Bundes Archives Bild 146-1981-053-35A

guerrilla war against invading armies during the Thirty Years War, a conflict that devastated German society. Also, a werewolf is a mythical creature that is human by day, but turns into a fearsome, bloodthirsty creature at night. What better code name for the German resistance than one drawing on a historic guerrilla movement and a terrifying myth that inspired fear at the same time? While the idea to create a guerrilla movement was born in 1943, the Werwolf movement was not officially organized until the fall of 1944 under the leadership of Reichsfuhrer-SS Heinrich Himmler's Higher SS and Police Leaders (HSSPF).

Himmler picked SS Lieutenant General Hans Prutzmann as his personal representative to oversee the Werwolf program. While the handsome Prutzmann, with a severe dueling scar on his face, was an exceedingly competent officer, he also accumulated enemies within the Third Reich bureaucracy because of his arrogance. Regardless of his abrasive personality, as a leader of the HSSPF, Prutzmann certainly possessed the resume for the job since he spent several years on the Eastern Front conducting counter-insurgency operations in the Ukraine. With this background, Prutzmann was well versed in the discipline of guerrilla warfare such as methods of infiltration, the interrogation and exploitation of prisoners, the use of propaganda, and the 'pacification' of populated areas with techniques ranging from police checkpoints and curfews to mass executions and scorched earth policies.

However, from the very beginning, Prutzmann's Werwolf organization suffered from a lack of bureaucratic support and was forced to draw recruits and supplies from several different sources. True, Prutzmann could get weapons, equipment, and recruits from the Waffen SS (the Field SS), the RHSA (Reich Security Central Office), the Gestapo, and the Hitler Youth as ordered by Himmler. But, as the situation became increasingly more desperate for the collapsing Reich, these organizations were less willing to part with their limited resources to help a rival group. Also, support from

Germany's armed forces outside of SS channels – like the Wehrmacht – felt no obligation to help the Werwolf program. Some army commanders saw the usefulness of the Werwolf movement and helped accordingly, while others did not.

The Werwolf program, by being placed under the SS and specifically the HSSPF, ensured it was never fully supported by the key personalities of Germany's various bureaucratic fiefdoms. This situation forced Perry Biddiscome, the leading expert on the Werwolf, to surmise, "It is thus impossible not to conclude that the Werwolf was poorly organized, that it suffered from a terminal case of bureaucratization, and that most of the limited successes in German guerrilla warfare were gained despite the organization rather than because of it."[1] In the end, the Werwolf program was only able to recruit an estimated 6,000 men and women. This paltry number was like sticking a single, feeble finger in a massive dyke that would burst forth with the combined fury of the Soviet and Western armies.

Werwolf Training

The Werwolf recruits, who were culled largely from the ranks of the Hitler Youth, received training in a variety of skills like basic weapons familiarization, sabotage and the use of demolitions, orienteering, field survival, camouflage, basic infantry tactics, and wireless radio operations. Not every Werwolf received the same training since instruction varied from region to region, depending on the time and resources available. Some courses were several weeks long and others only a few days. Overall, the quality and duration of the instruction was not even close to what was required to accomplish such a monumental task. It was clear the Germans only had a rudimentary understanding of guerrilla warfare even though they repressed various resistance movements across the breadth of Europe for several years. Fighting a guerrilla movement was one thing, but actually building a successful underground organization was far harder than they anticipated.

An indication of the Germans' lack of preparation for unconventional warfare was the fact the first guerrilla warfare manuals the Werwolf students were issued were captured from the Russians and then translated into German! It was only at the start of 1945 when an original guerrilla warfare manual was drafted and issued specifically for the Werwolf movement. This manual, while at least written by the Germans themselves, was rudimentary at best and revealed nothing new, innovative, or particularly effective for waging a guerrilla war. The manual would have been better marketed as an outdoor survival guide. As this manual indicates, the Germans saw the Werwolf as a rural movement living in the countryside, away from the cities, and only have minimal contact with the population when it was necessary. Essentially, the Germans copied what the Russian partisan movement did in their own guerrilla campaign against them on the Eastern Front.

The Werwolf movement was thus only prepared to conduct operations in a rural – not an urban – environment. This created severe problems for the Werwolf organization as a whole. While the Werewolves received rudimentary training in field craft and traditional small-unit combat operations, this was the exact area their enemies excelled in. The Russian, British, French, and American forces who occupied Ger-

---

1 Biddiscome, *Werwolf!*, p.55. (This is a must read for anyone interested in learning about the Werwolf resistance movement - Biddiscome's research is superb.)

Aachen, Germany, October 1944

photo by National Archives

An American infantryman with the 1st Infantry Division returns fire against a German sniper hidden in the city. Several months later, the newly appointed mayor of Aachen, Franz Oppenhoff, would be assassinated by a Werwolf hit team.

many in 1945 were well prepared for such kinds of rural counter-guerrilla operations. In fact, they preferred to fight such a war in the woods and hinterland, away from the real sources of power such as major population, economic, and industrial centers. By focusing on a rural existence, the Werewolves isolated themselves from the people and their own potential sources of support. They incorrectly judged the physical terrain – like inaccessible mountains and forests – was more important than the human terrain for their success.

As the surging Allied forces relentlessly ground forward into Germany, and then occupied the Fatherland outright, the Werewolves found themselves drawn to the cities like a magnet. They could not help it. Enemy collaborators and traitors who no longer supported the defunct Nazi government - and thus were targeted for assassination or intimidation by the Werewolves - lived in the cities. Occupation forces had their barracks, supply depots, headquarters, radio stations, chow halls, hospitals, and checkpoints established in the major urban areas. The battle for the hearts and minds of the conquered German people took place in built-up areas like Munich, Bremen, and Hamburg. The capital of Berlin alone had a pre-war population of 4 million people. Consequently, when the Werwolf guerrillas found themselves forced to conduct their operations in the urban areas, they were unprepared and outmatched.

Guerrilla Warfare

The Werewolves conducted the full spectrum of operations in their guerrilla war against the occupation forces. Explosives were placed on parked military vehicles, blowing them up in place. Gas tanks were filled with sugar. Telephone lines were cut. Wires were affixed to trees at head height to decapitate soldiers riding on motorcycles or in open jeeps. Tanks, lined up in motor pools, were shot up with anti-armor weapons like the portable Panzerfaust. Concealed land mines were hidden on dirt roads used by enemy forces. While the Germans certainly had the technology and equipment to electronically detonate explosives and land mines - what today we would call an Improvised Explosive Device (IED) – the Werewolves were untrained in this art in an urban setting.

Small units of Werewolves also ambushed vulnerable allied patrols when possible. The guerrillas could draw on supplies of the excellent Panzerfaust and Panzerschreck anti-tank weapons to blow up careless supply convoys or military police vehicles. The tried and tested MG34 and MG42 general purpose machine guns were also perfect for ambushing Allied foot patrols or unarmored vehicles like motorcycles, jeeps, and trucks. However, these were large weapons, not easily concealed, and difficult to employ clandestinely in a populated area.

Acts of sabotage and intimidation were better suited to the Werewolves because it was less risky and required less training, something the guerrillas sorely lacked. It was much safer to derail supply trains, booby-trap industrial buildings, set fire to fuel dumps, and distribute anti-occupation literature. In one storied example, a Werwolf hit team was sent to the Western German town of Aachen and assassinated the mayor, an attorney by the name of Franz Oppenhoff. In another heralded incident, two members of Field Marshal Montgomery's personal staff were ambushed by the Hitler Youth in April 1945. Major Peter Earle was wounded and Major John Poston was killed.

Despite these few successes, exhausting research by the leading expert on the United States' post-war occupation of Europe, Earl Ziemke, shows the Werwolf movement produced few concrete results. Ziemke found, "Except for black marketeering, some thefts of food and firewood, and petty violations of military government ordinances, the German civilian crime rate was low, sometimes almost disconcertingly low for the Army agencies charged with ferreting out and suppressing resistance.

Patrols occasionally found decapitation wires stretched across roads, ineptly it would seem, since no deaths or injuries resulted from them. Military government public safety officers from scattered locations reported various anti-occupation leaflets and posters, some threats against German girls who associated with US soldiers, and isolated attacks on soldiers."[2] Aside from the murder of Oppenhoff and the ambush of Montgomery's staff, the Werwolf movement was unable to change the tide of the losing war or construct an underground movement with any sort of longevity.

Guerrilla Sniping Potential

When it came to sniping, the Werwolf movement certainly had the potential for a deadly campaign. For one, there was an abundance of anonymous weapons available for sniping use. The most likely candidate was the reliable, accurate Mauser Karbiner

---

2 Ziemke, *The U.S. Army In The Occupation Of Germany*, p.354-5. (Ziemke's research is a must for those interested in U.S.counter-insurgency policies in Germany.)

Werwolf Sniper Weapons

Mauser K98 bolt-action rifle.

Walther Gewehr 43 semi-automatic rifle.

FG42 semi-automatic paratrooper rifle.

98 battle rifle, chambered for the 7.92 mm round, produced by the millions, and used by conventional German snipers in every theater of the war. Most German soldiers were at least familiar with the K98 and many civilians received basic marksmanship training on it to include the Volkssturm (home defense militia forces), the Hitler Youth, and even the League of German Women. While the K98 could be paired with factory made sound suppressors (the suppressors were little understood and rarely used), the K98 was still a large, conventional rifle that was hard to conceal.

The resistance also had access to the Gewehr 41/43, a 7.92 mm semi-automatic battle rifle which was produced in much smaller quantities than the K98, but was still used by the Reich's snipers. Some sound suppressors were manufactured and tested on the Gewehr 43, but there is no evidence they were ever fielded for combat. Perhaps better suited for urban sniping was the FG42, a compact (36 inches in length), semi-automatic rifle fed by a 20-round box magazine. The FG42 was designed for Germany's Fallschirmjagers (paratroopers), could be fitted with a scope, and with its large-capacity magazine, was ideal for rapidly engaging multiple targets in an urban setting. Also, since it fired single shot from a closed bolt, it was fairly accurate.

A late addition to the sniping arsenal was the Sturmgewehr 44 assault rifle, which was shorter in length than the K98 and Gewehr 41/43, could be fitted with a scope, and was fed by a thirty round box magazine. A sister assault rifle was the semi-automatic Volkssturmgewehr 1-5 which was designed as part of a 'primitive weapons program' and produced for the civilian Volkssturm. This weapon was not very accurate, was designed to be produced cheaply en mass, and was first produced in January 1945. Enterprising shooters could even use pistols for sniping like the semi-automatic Mauser C96 'Broom handle' which fired a 9 mm round and came with a detachable shoulder stock that doubled as a holster. The Mauser C96 had the advantage of being concealable and exhibited the stable characteristics of a carbine when fitted with the stock. In one incident, a Hitler Youth Werwolf was captured with a Mauser pistol with several notches cut into the handle, presumably for the number of kills made.[3]

All of these weapons suffered from the fact they were conventional weapons intended for use in overt warfare. None of them had collapsible stocks so they could not be concealed on one's person or hidden in an easily accessible cache (accept for pistols). These weapons were never intended to be used with a sound suppressor and, except for the K98, factory-made suppressors were not available. While suppressors were produced for the K98, there is no evidence German snipers, conventional or otherwise, were instructed and skilled in their use. The Germans did use suppressed weapons on rare occasions during special operations (the Werwolf hit team that assassinated the Mayor of Aachen used a suppressed pistol), but there is no evidence Werwolf snipers were ever taught the necessary art of suppressed sniping.

The Werwolf Sniping Campaign

There is very little recorded about the Werewolves' actual sniper campaign and there are no published personal accounts from Werwolf snipers. However, from studying post-war records, we know sniping was a widespread tactic, both while the German armed forces were retreating back into the Reich and when the Fatherland was occupied by the Allied armies.

For example, in late August 1944, as the Allied forces and the French Resistance liberated the capital of Paris, hidden German snipers opened fire on the celebrating Parisians, sending people scattering in all directions. This was a fitting end to the occupation of the city since French guerrilla snipers recently helped kick out most of the German garrison by picking off careless Wehrmacht troopers. The guerrilla sniping continued as the Americans moved east and captured the quaint town of Saarguemines on the German border in December 1944. Even though Saarguemines was under American control for several weeks, SS guerrilla snipers continued to target soldiers of the 35th Infantry Division who occupied the town.[4]

As the Allied armies continued to pound the collapsing Reich and entered German soil proper, more guerrilla snipers were encountered. In March 1945, guerrilla riflemen targeted surging American forces when they entered the western German town of Bad Kreuznach, which before the war was known for producing quality Riesling wines.[5] In April 1945, the American 42nd Infantry Division entered the city of Wurzburg, located in central Bavaria. Wurzburg was considerably larger than Saarguemines in population and had a much bigger urban area with taller buildings. This meant Wurzburg was better suited for urban sniping and the invading Americans found themselves plagued by guerrilla marksmen even though the city was officially 'secured' and no uniformed German soldiers were present.[6] That same month, American troops rolled into Nuremburg, the site of the Third Reich's famous Nazi Party rallies. Here, the invading forces encountered teen-age guerrilla snipers, as young as fourteen, who hid in spider holes, allowing the American forces to advance past them. Once the Americans cleared an area, the guerrilla snipers, dressed in civilian clothes, would appear from their hide

3 (Ziemke, *The U.S. Army In The Occupation Of Germany*, p.254.
4 Biddiscome, *Werwolf!*
5 Biddiscome, *Werwolf!*
6 Biddiscome, *Werwolf!*

German Soldiers Round Up Russian Snipers

Even though Germany waged a bitter, widespread, counter-insurgency war against various occupied countries from 1939 to 1944, they were unable to translate this experience into a successful resistance movement of their own.

sites and open fire. Because of these stay-behind tactics and the more densely populated urban terrain of Nuremburg, U.S. soldiers spent considerable time searching again and again areas of the city which by all accounts had been secured.[7]

On the Eastern front, the Russians too encountered German guerrilla snipers who placed them in their cross-hairs. The eastern guerrillas used the same stay-behind tactics as their western brothers, with the goal of shooting the advancing Russians in the back or to kill unsuspecting rear-echelon troops who thought they were in the safety of 'pacified' areas. Marshal Chuikov, famed General of the Russian 62nd Army at Stalingrad, noted the German guerrillas, "They hid in the basements and in ruins and they allowed the forward units of our advancing forces to pass, and sometimes the rearward units as well, and then opened fire, with the object of sowing panic in the rear and slowing down or paralyzing action along the front line."[8]

In another incident, Werwolf snipers targeted Red Army support troops in the town of Stegliz, a suburb of Berlin. The Russians suspected the fire came from a nearby apartment complex and diverted troops to clear out the buildings.[9] On May 15, 1945, a week after Germany officially surrendered, three Red Army soldiers were shot and found dead on the grounds of the beautiful botanical gardens located in southwestern Berlin. Just two days later, a Soviet officer was shot from the ruins along the Berlinstrasse. Then, in late July, two Soviet railway guards were shot at night - one soldier was wounded and the other killed.[10] Werwolf snipers even managed to stay underground long enough to target Soviet occupation forces into the New Year as a Red Army guard unit in Merseburg found out on January 1, 1946, when hidden snipers opened fire, wounding a man.[11]

7 Biddiscome, *Werwolf!*, p.29.
8 Chuikov, *The End of the Third Reich*.
9 Biddiscome, *Werwolf!*, p.21.
10 Biddiscome, *Werwolf!*, p.21.
11 Biddiscome, *Werwolf!*, p.76.

The Problem With Werwolf Snipers

While the Werwolf guerrilla snipers experienced minor successes, sowing fear behind the front lines by picking off scores of careless soldiers, their overall effect was limited. In most cases, Werwolf snipers made some close shots or scored a few kills and then were taken out. For example, the American 42nd Infantry Division in Wurzburg suffered from guerrilla sniping, but during a search of the town they found and captured five civilian snipers, both men and women, who were hiding in a cellar.[12] Obviously, this group pursued the standard stay-behind sniper cell tactic, which could only result in a short-term success. This cell did not have a credible long-term cover story for being in the area, they could not find a practical safehouse to hide in, and thus were unable to blend into the civilian population, which is an absolute necessity for any guerrilla movement.

In other cases, Werwolf snipers displayed poor snipercraft, firing from easily identified positions. In the medieval German town of Tangermunde, under-age Werwolf snipers opened fire on the oncoming American soldiers who were in turn able to identify the source of incoming fire. Thus, it was a relatively easy task to call in supporting artillery units to destroy the buildings the snipers were hiding in. These inexperienced shooters never stood a chance.[13] Other Werwolf snipers would simply lay on the ground as if dead, allow their enemy to pass by them, and then open fire. While this kind of tactic might allow for a single successful shot, the shooter was sure to be captured or killed soon after. In short, these tactics offered no prospect for long-term success.

Part of the reason for the Werwolf sniping failure were the snipers themselves. Notably, the Germans were the first nation to use large numbers of under-aged boys in an organized manner to conduct guerrilla sniping. While these young boys, most of them products of the Hitler Youth indoctrination program, were easily manipulated and at times fearless, they also suffered from poor tactical judgment and the inability to comprehend the complexities and nuances of modern urban guerrilla sniping. These pre-teen shooters, some who were as young as eight, certainly did not have the mental maturity to understand counter-forensics, interrogation/counter-interrogation methodology, or even the basic physics of concealing a gunshot. The best these boys could do was don civilian clothes, drag their heavy rifle to a window, fire a shot, and then wait to get captured or blown away - hardly a prescription for a successful guerrilla sniping campaign.

It would be easy to blame the sniping failure on impressionable pre-pubescent boys who were brainwashed into fighting Hitler's disastrous world war. But this is just part of the answer. The historical record shows adult Werwolf snipers, both men and women, also failed in their efforts to conduct an effective guerrilla sniper campaign. This lack of effective snipercraft can be attributed directly to their poor training in the art of both sniping and guerrilla warfare. For instance, the Werewolves' issued guerrilla training manual spent much of its space on how to block mountain roads, how to camouflage one's self, and how to construct survival shelters. This is what the manual said about guerrilla sniping: "It is very advantageous to use a silenced weapon and to have a sniper weapon. Also, some of the weapons should be equipped with luminous

---

12 Biddiscome, *Werwolf!*
13 Biddiscome, *Werwolf!* p.64.

German Prisoner, 1945

This underage Hitler Youth soldier is only thirteen years old! Fortunately for him, he was captured by American forces when they invaded Germany. While these children were easily manipulated into fighting for their country, they did not have enough maturity or judgement to wage an effective guerrilla war. When captured by Allied forces, the majority of Werwolf children broke quickly under interrogation and revealed damning intelligence about the rest of their organization.

photo by National Archives

sights." And there you have it. The manual spends more time on showing how to navigate wooded terrain with the help of a pocket watch than it does teaching the art of sniping.

We do know some Werwolf units received dedicated sniper instruction from various units, like the SS and Wehrmacht, but the quality of this training varied in both length and quality, depending on the local wartime circumstances. Judging from the ultimate results on the battlefield, this training was unsatisfactory at best. We know German sniper schools used pre-war Russians sniper films to train their own marksmen, because they did not value the art of sniping enough to make their own films until the war was already lost. We also know German-made sniper training films, when they were finally produced, concentrated on rural tactics. The only urban snipercraft these films taught was for the shooter to fire from a building with multiple open windows. That was it. Combine these substandard sniper training efforts with the Germans' belated guerrilla warfare program, which was again based on the Russians' own manuals, and you have an under-trained guerrilla sniper corps completely unprepared for the rigors of sniping in an urban guerrilla warfare environment.

Allied Counter-Insurgency Operations

Guerrilla sniper cells do not function in a vacuum; they are just one part of a larger resistance movement. As soon as the Werwolf snipers began pulling their triggers, it became obvious they were working for an organization enjoying little popular support. Part of this antipathy came from the fact the majority of Germans did not support the Nazi Party (the most Hitler ever won in open elections was 36% of the votes cast in 1932), and they certainly did not support a resistance movement seeking to bring back rule of the Party. After all, who wanted to reinstate the concentration camps, Gestapo torture, and slave labor?

Perhaps of even more importance, the German people were physically and psychologically exhausted from more than six years of constant warfare. The Germans lost well over 5.5 million uniformed men and women and 1.5 million civilians during the course of the war – 10% of their pre-war population. Many of their cities – like Dresden, Cologne, and Berlin - were bombed into rubble or destroyed during devastating street fighting. Most Germans wanted a normal life, free of never ending, morale-sapping warfare. All the Werwolf movement promised was more of the same.

Hence, the Werwolf movement was susceptible to the Allied forces' counter-insurgency measures. One thing the occupation forces promised were harsh reprisals and mass punishment for supporting the resistance. The Russians in particular had little tolerance for guerrilla snipers wearing civilian clothes and shooting their soldiers in the back after hostilities ended. The Russians lost an estimated 20 million casualties during the war and were not in a charitable mood. Stalin promised to unleash his secret police, the NKVD, on any population supporting the guerrillas and this meant the mass rape of German women, the imprisonment of large numbers of people in deadly slave labor camps, and the summary execution of captured guerrillas. The German population was so fearful of the Red menace, an American war correspondent reporting from Berlin in the Spring of 1945 noted snipers were operating behind the Russian lines and the people lived in absolute terror because, "the least suspicion of sniping means death."[14]

While the American occupation forces in the west practiced a more humane form of counter-insurgency, the consequences of supporting the guerrillas were still unpleasant. Nobody wanted to adhere to nightly curfews, or have to show their identification cards at menacing checkpoints, or have their homes searched in the middle of the night. Also, the Americans executed Werewolves who were captured wearing civilian clothes. Plus, the U.S. government actually seemed interested in rebuilding Germany and the American soldiers proved to be exceedingly friendly with the German people.

Consequently, when a Werwolf sniper cell opened fire on American soldiers in Bad Kreuznach in March 1945, it did not take long to penetrate the resistance and find the culprits. Only several weeks after the shooting, the Werwolf cell was penetrated and seventeen suspected guerrillas arrested.[15] The American Counter Intelligence Corps (CIC) found many captured Werwolf members turned quickly against their fellow insurgents, which made it easier to penetrate the German resistance.

In another case, British occupation forces captured two Werewolves who quickly rolled over on the rest of their cell despite little pressure to do so. "Their attitude was typical, at first openly defiant, then as hunger and fatigue began to work, more and more malleable. The amusing thing about these youths and the Nazis we subsequently questioned was their complete willingness to betray one another once they were convinced a friend tattled, and it required very little persuasion to convince them that they had been betrayed. To the disappointment of some of our men, it was quite unnecessary to become physical in the interrogation. As a result we organized a raiding party

14 St Louis Dispatch, May 9, 1945.
15 Biddiscome, *Werwolf!* p.24.

April 2, 1945: Soldiers of General Patton's Third Army frisk a German sniper who was wounded in a gunfight just prior to his capture. *(ACME photo)*

of four officers and six enlisted men. We picked up three Nazis in possession of illegal arms. All of them lied like troopers to start with, but invariably would lead us to where the weapons were hidden-generally under the eaves of an outbuilding.[16]

In fact, it was so easy to penetrate the Werwolf movement, one joint British-American counter-insurgency operation in December 1945 managed to round up and jail 2500 suspected insurgents.[17] The allied forces were so successful in rooting out the resistance using informers and double agents, they estimated by January 1946 the Werwolf movement was crushed with no hope of recovering. In total, the Americans and British detained 80,000 suspected resistance members while the Russians imprisoned almost a quarter of million people - of which one-third died in captivity.[18]

16 Ziemke, *The U.S. Army In The Occupation Of Germany*, p.245-6.
17 Biddiscome, *Werwolf!*, p. 82.
18 Biddiscome, *Werwolf!*, p. 51-2.

Another important element of why the Allied forces were so successful in their relatively harsh counter-sniper/counter-insurgency efforts was Germany's isolation on the world stage. No country in Europe was going to intervene on Germany's behalf to protest the rough treatment of the German people. Who had any sympathy for the creators of the Holocaust? Importantly, the German resistance movement did not have a single bordering foreign sanctuary to operate from. Germany was surrounded by its former victims and current enemies – like France, Poland, and Czechoslovakia to name just a few – who wanted revenge and certainly supported the stern counter-guerrilla operations of the victors. Hence, the Allied forces got away with using indiscriminate firepower to silence Werwolf gunmen like when the American army fought its way into Aschaffenburg, Germany and called in fighter-bombers to blow up buildings housing guerrilla snipers. [19]

The German Werwolf: A Failed Movement

The Werwolf sniper program was a reflection of the overall German understanding of guerrilla warfare, which was limited at best. While the German people were able to create the greatest conventional military war machine known to man up until that time, they spent little effort improving the art of sniping and certainly spent no time perfecting its use by guerrillas. To be fair, the Germans achieved the same level of guerrilla sniping expertise as their peers - which is not saying much. At that point in history, few countries put much thought in how to wage a successful guerrilla campaign and the idea of waging a successful urban guerrilla war was an even more alien concept. The art of urban guerrilla sniping suffered accordingly, falling under this shadow of general apathy. Even urban guerrilla movements that fought during the war, like the Polish Home Army and the French Resistance, displayed little innovation in the field of guerrilla sniping.

From the perspective of the student of urban guerrilla sniping, the Werwolf movement is good to use as a baseline. The Werewolves displayed the same level of urban sniping competence that could be reasonably expected from any other resistance movement of that period. During World War II, the art of urban guerrilla sniping was still in its infancy. It would be several more decades before urban guerrilla snipers learned to shoot from vehicles, to use sound suppressors, to construct remote sniping systems, to practice strict counter-forensic measures, to use human bait, and to film and market their sniping exploits to a global audience. The art of urban guerrilla sniping would become progressively more deadly and effective, but it would take several more wars to evolve.

---

19 Biddiscome, *Werwolf!*, p.28.

Chapter 9

The Dealey Plaza Snipers

Public figures or guarded officials may be killed with great reliability and some safety if a firing point can be established prior to an official occasion.
  – 'A Study of Assassination', a 'how-to' manual
  allegedly written by the CIA

The committee believes, on the basis of the evidence available to it, that President John F. Kennedy was probably assassinated as a result of a conspiracy.
  - From the U. S. House Select Committee on
  Assassinations (HSCA) 1979 report

The shot from the grassy knoll is not only supported by the acoustics, which is a tape that we found of a police motorcycle broadcast back to the district station. It is corroborated by eyewitness testimony in the plaza. There were 20 people, at least, who heard a shot from the grassy knoll.
  - G. Robert Blakey attorney for the HSCA

Balancing Operational Success with Deception

The Dealey Plaza snipers had two critical tasks: kill the President of the United States and make it look like Lee Harvey Oswald committed the murder. The assassins accomplished their first goal, but failed at the second. The crux of their problem was in order to accomplish the first goal, they were unable to achieve the second. While the killers required redundant sniper teams to ensure the death of the President, by increasing the number of sniper teams, they multiplied the difficulties of concealing the evidence of the operation. In order for the snipers to effectively frame Oswald, they needed to conduct the assassination in a manner consistent with the 'evidence' left behind for public consumption. However, this is precisely where they went wrong because the incriminating physical evidence meant to convict Oswald did not match the actual events of the shooting.

What complicated the killers' efforts was the need to insulate the actual planners of the assassination from the operation itself. The most important aspect of this insulation was using contracted shooters, teams of snipers with deniable connections to the planners. These shooters took the form of hired guns from the Corsican mob, the American mob, Cuban exiles, and domestic trigger men. It was necessary to even insulate the individual sniper teams from one another, making the operation truly compartmented. This compartmentalization, while good from a security perspective, meant the separate sniper teams were forensically out of synch with each other. The resulting sloppiness compromised the overall operation.

Preparing for the Assassination

The Kennedy killers had every opportunity to study their proposed kill zone in detail before the operation took place. This was because the President's plan to visit Dallas, Texas on November 22, 1963 was published two months prior to the actual trip. Lee Harvey Oswald then secured a job at the Texas School Book Depository (TSBD) six weeks before the assassination. This makes Oswald's employment at the depository less like a random job to make ends meet and more like a long-term, pre-operation reconnaissance of the kill zone.

While Oswald had six weeks to pick out potential sniper platforms and study the terrain of Dealey Plaza, so did Dallas mobster Jack Ruby. Ruby (real name Jacob Rubenstein, a Polish-Jewish immigrant, and former employee of Al Capone), gained notoriety for killing Oswald on November 24, 1963 in front of a police escort of seventy armed officers. Ruby ran a sleazy nightclub and dealt illegal arms to both Castro and the anti-Castro Cuban opposition based in the United States. Ruby was the perfect front man to supply Mafia shooters with a local support network including safehouses, guns, and information about the area and the kill zone.

Author Craig Roberts' investigation into the assassination revealed one group of snipers from the Corsican mob infiltrated Texas through the Mexican-American border and set up at a local safehouse in Dallas, avoiding incriminating hotel receipts. This contracted team of Frenchmen entered the country only with the help of the American mob, which got them across the border. After their arrival, the Corsican shooters took detailed photographs of the kill zone and studied them in-depth at their safehouse. One of these shooters, Lucien Sarti, is believed by many researches to be the man in the police uniform who hit President Kennedy with the final, fatal head shot from the northern grassy knoll position.

Because the United States was not under martial law, anyone could walk freely wherever they wanted with absolutely no interference from the military or local law enforcement. In any open society, criminals can case potential targets with ease. The situation was no different in Dallas in November 1963. The various sniper teams

Texas School Book Depository

The Infamous
Window Position
on the Sixth Floor

walked freely in Dealey Plaza itself before the operation to personally inspect their future sniper positions. This aspect of the operation was the easiest, because the shooters could go where they wanted to collect the information they needed for their part of the operation.

The Problem of Compartmentalization

Most likely, the separate sniper teams planned their individual pieces of the operation in isolation from one another. This isolation would be intentional to ensure there was no incriminating link between the separate shooters and organizations. Since the separate teams had no physical contact with one another, their ability to communicate with one another was difficult. Meeting in person would not be advisable, nor would discussing the plans on the phone. While there were many ways to communicate with one another once they were all in Dallas, they probably communicated through the means of cutouts.

These cutouts were responsible for communicating the overall plan to the sniper teams and ensuring they were all in synch, operationally. The cutouts would be skilled in counter-surveillance and their sole job would be passing information to the various groups in a secure manner so no connection could be made either between the separate sniper teams or the planners themselves.

While the need for operational security is understandable, a compartmented operation is vulnerable to problems like miscommunications and a lack of coordination. Compartmentalization means the separate sniper teams never got a chance to rehearse their plan together. Rehearsals are crucial for shaking out a plan and identifying problems that may arise in the actual operation. Because the different groups never rehearsed together, they made serious errors during the execution of the assassination. A realistic rehearsal, while physically connecting the separate sniper teams to one another, would have resulted in a more forensically sound operation. Clearly, the planners balanced the need for security with hiding the evidence of the operation and ultimately failed in their balancing act.

Dealey Plaza Kill Zone

No final plan to kill the President could be made until a proposed kill zone was chosen. The place was Dealey Plaza. Dealey Plaza was a good location because it was an open area and allowed observation of the Presidential motorcade from all directions. When observed from above, the plaza is symmetrical, a mirror image with Main Street dividing it down the middle, running east to west. With Main Street as the central dividing line, Elm Street to the north and Commerce Street to the south form the Dealey Plaza boundaries. This near symmetry means while there is a grassy knoll on the north side of the plaza adjacent to Elm Street, there is also a grassy knoll on the south side of the Plaza adjacent to Commerce Street.

While the road layout in the Plaza is symmetrical, the surrounding building layout is not. The intersection of Houston and Elm Street in the northern half of the plaza is surrounded by tall buildings: the Dal-Tex (Dallas Textile) Building, the Dallas County Records Building, the County Courthouse Building, and the Texas School Book Depository (TSBD). The southern intersection of Houston and Commerce Street does not have this same dominating layout of buildings. For instance, the Old Red Courthouse across Main Street from the County Courthouse building is several stories shorter and has few windows on the west side facing the Plaza. Also, the Old Red Courthouse has a steep-sloped ornate roof, not a flat one that could be used by a shooter. In general, the Houston-Commerce Street intersection is more open with fewer quality sniper positions to choose from. If a team of snipers had to make a choice, they would choose the Houston-Elm Street intersection because it gives them more options.

At the Houston-Elm Street intersection sits the Texas School Book Depository (TSBD), seven stories high with seven sets of windows per floor on the Elm Street side, giving 42 separate positions to fire a weapon from, if one counts the second through seventh floors. Also, there was an enormous Hertz billboard on the roof of the depository that could break up the outline of a person, so they would not be silhouetted from below. A gunman could make a shot from the roof, step behind the billboard and be screened from Elm Street. Further helping a rooftop sniper was the low safety wall surrounding the roof perimeter. A sniper could crouch down behind the wall and take aim with nothing but the barrel of their rifle and the top of their head exposed.

The Dal-Tex Building is of equal height to the depository with three sets of windows per floor for a total of eighteen windows from the second to seventh floor on the Houston Street side of the building. Also, in front of the windows on the Houston Street side was a series of fire escape stairs. These stairs could provide an excellent perch for a sniper (although they would be exposed) or the stairs could provide effective visual screening for a sniper firing from a window, with the stairs obstructing the view of anyone looking in.

The Dallas County Records building, at seven stories tall, also provides an excellent view of the presidential motorcade, and has a score of windows facing the Houston-Elm Street intersection. A sniper could be positioned on the roof or at anyone one of

A view of Elm Street from the Sniper's Perch in the TSBD

From the Warren Commission

the western windows overlooking Dealey Plaza and have an excellent, unobstructed view of their target.

However, some of the best firing positions are not located in buildings at all, but at the two grassy knolls located at the northern and southern ends of the triple underpass. The northern grassy knoll offers the best location because it is an elevated position with a fence and foliage providing effective cover and concealment for a sniper. More importantly, the motorcade would drive almost directly at the northern knoll, allowing a shooter to make a head-on shot, as if the target in the vehicle was not even moving. The shooter at the southern grassy knoll would have an equally good vantage point, with excellent screening. Importantly, because this southern point is further away than the northern one, people would not expect a shot from there.

Numerous alternate positions were available for back-up shooters. Anywhere a car, van, or pick-up truck could be parked alongside Dealey Plaza, another potential sniper could be positioned. In these cases, a shooter could fire from inside a vehicle, underneath the vehicle, or simply behind the vehicle, using it for visual screening. In fact, vehicles parked alongside Commerce Street to the South of Dealey Plaza provided excellent sniper positions for back-up shooters. The variety of suitable positions meant separate sniper teams could hit a moving target from a variety of locations, from almost any direction. The elevated stature of the surrounding buildings would allow snipers to shoot down, over the surrounding populace. Less elevated positions, like from the two knolls and the second floor of various buildings, would allow someone to get a shot at a target in a vehicle moving either directly away from them or towards them, giving them a constant sight picture as if the target was stationary.

The Plan

After the assassins walked the actual kill zone and thoroughly studied the terrain, a plan was developed. In this plan, redundancy was emphasized. First, numerous sniper teams would be established in a circular pattern around the kill zone so regardless of the spectators lining the way, several of the teams would always have a clear shot. A central kill zone enabled the snipers to take simultaneous shots and expect to hit their target. As the motorcade progressed down its route, some teams would have shots and others would not. However, it was intended at some time during the period the motorcade traveled through kill zone, every shooter would have a chance for a viable shot.

In order to make identification of the target easier in the crowded confines of the Plaza, different vehicle colors would be used. So, when motorcade organizers picked up the rental vehicles before the event, none of the rental vehicles were the same color as the President's limousine.

As mentioned before, some shooters would be in elevated positions. This was a critical component of the overall plan because an elevated position was necessary to secure a bird's eye view of the President. This top-down position enabled an elevated shooter to fire over obstacles near the President like spectators, secret service men, and would help avoid shooting through the body of the limousine or accidentally hitting a passenger like the President's wife.

Each sniper team would have at least one shooter and one radio man to receive and relay commands. The non-shooter would pick up any incriminating shell casings ejected to hide their presence.

When given the command, the sniper teams would fire in unison so the sounds of each others' shots would be masked. This meant several shots fired together would only sound like one. Also, suppressed rifles would be fired along with non-suppressed ones so the regular gunshots would mask the noise of the suppressed ones, thus concealing the total number of shots fired. The snipers firing from the west and south side of the plaza (which was in front of the President) would have suppressors to conceal the fact some shots would be fired from the front. The overall layout of the plaza helped to mask the gunshots, because the buildings caused echoes, confusing spectators as to the real source of the firing.

The shooters would only fire as many volleys as required to ensure the president was dead. Unnecessary shots were not desired because of the three shot limit already planned in the incrimination of Oswald. More specifically:

- A sniper team would be placed in the second floor of the Dal-Tex Building.
- A sniper team would be placed on the roof of the TSBD.
- A sniper team would be placed on the sixth floor of the TSBD.
- A sniper team would be placed on the roof of the County Records building.
- A sniper team would be placed on the northern grassy knoll.
- A sniper team would be placed on the southern grassy knoll.
- A sniper team would be placed behind the pergola, between the TSBD and the northern grassy knoll.
- A back-up sniper team would be placed in a pick-up truck on Commerce Street.
- A two-man signal team, one with a radio and one with an umbrella, would signal some of the shooters as a back-up.
- Another person would signal other shooters by waiving a handkerchief.

The Northern Grassy Knoll

The killing head shot was made from the northern grassy knoll by a shooter firing from behind this picket fence.

- A man, Jim Hicks, would be assigned as the radio man to coordinate the overall assassination.
- A mobile command and control vehicle would be stationed at the scene.
- At each sniper position there would be two or three plainclothes security personnel responsible for keeping unwanted spectators away from the snipers preparing for their shots. After the shooting, these same security personnel would sweep the immediate crowd and confiscate any cameras with incriminating evidence.
- Most personnel would either dress like police officers (perhaps because some really were officers) or carry official government credentials from either the secret service, the FBI, or the CIA.
- Personnel not involved in the actual shooting, security, or evidence confiscation would dress and act like spectators and maintain a plausible, consistent cover story explaining their presence at the plaza.
- Personnel not involved in planting or confiscating evidence would immediately leave the area in the confusion.
- Lee Harvey Oswald would be the fall guy.
- A Mannlicher-Carcano 6.5 mm rifle would be left behind as evidence.
- Three shell casings would be left behind on the 6th floor of the TSBD.
- At least twenty-five people would be required to execute the actual operation.

This was a complicated plan with many moving parts. Half a dozen sniper teams had to scout and secure their positions, undetected by the public, and be in position at the time of the arrival of the President's motorcade. A lot of potential evidence would have to be covered up and there was a lot of room for miscommunication and other unforeseen problems. Because the different elements of the operation were compartmentalized to some degree, no group rehearsal could be conducted. And without rehearsals, mistakes would be made.

Setting Up In Dealey Plaza

All the players in the operation were in position approximately 10-15 minutes prior to the arrival of the President's motorcade. They arrived as close to the actual execution time as possible in order to minimize their exposure to the populace and legitimate security personnel. Their key to infiltrating was simply masquerading as law-enforcement officers and flashing credentials from various government agencies. This deception worked surprisingly well.

In fact, dozens of eyewitnesses saw the multiple sniper teams setting up in their positions, but they wrote these men off as counter-sniper teams as opposed to being assassins. For example, rail yard employee Lee Bowers saw the snipers on the northern grassy knoll get in their positions ten minutes prior to the hit (Mr. Bowers died in a car accident three years later in 1966 - many believe he was murdered). Several witnesses saw the two separate snipers (neither of whom were Oswald) waiting in the upper floors of the depository, well before the motorcade arrived. All these witnesses later stated they assumed these riflemen were secret service agents.

The conspirators helped the snipers infiltrate Dealey Plaza by staging a medical emergency at the corner of Elm and Houston Street. At approximately 12:19 p.m., eleven minutes before the Presidential motorcade was scheduled to arrive, a man suffered an apparent 'seizure', drawing the attention of bystanders in the immediate area. This drawing of attention facilitated the deployment of the various cogs of the assassination machine into their appropriate positions. While every one watched the poor 'victim' driven off in a wailing ambulance, the signalers, snipers, and security/evidence suppression teams moved into position, unnoticed by most people. (Note: Nearby Parkland Hospital never recorded the arrival of a 'seizure' victim.)[1]

Into The Kill Zone

As the Presidential motorcade traveled west on Main Street, towards Dealey Plaza, the snipers were probably warned by radio well ahead of time. Jim Hicks' job as communications coordinator for the operation was to make sure all the shooters had this kind of updated, real-time information on the Presidential motorcade. When the motorcade approached the Main Street-Houston Street intersection and then turned right and north onto Houston Street, most of the shooters could see their target approaching. When the President's limousine approached the intersection of Houston and Elm Street, the shooters must have been nervous as they took the safeties of their rifles and prepared to receive the order to open fire. Even if an individual sniper already had a good picture of the target, they were to hold their fire until given the go ahead. An operation of this magnitude required discipline.

At 12:30 p.m., the President's vehicle slowly turned left and west onto Elm Street, cruising past the Texas School Book Depository, the front of which was marked as the kill zone. It rained earlier in the day and it was warm out. The killers must have been

---

1 Fetzer, *Murder In Dealey Plaza*, p. 28-29.9 (Easily the most detailed accounting of the events before, during, and after the assassination. A must read on the subject.)

The President in his Limousine

Library of Congress

Because of the other people in the car, sittting so close to the President, the snipers had a very difficult task.

sweating, watching their target roll into the kill zone. They saw secret service agent William Greer driving the limousine and agent Roy Kellerman sitting next to him. Seated behind Greer was the wife of Texas Governor Connally and on the passenger-side, behind Kellerman, was the Governor himself. Sitting in the driver-side back seat was Jackie Kennedy and to her right, sitting behind Governor Connally, was President Kennedy. A total of five people were in the lead vehicle with the President. They all smiled at the gathered crowd as the sun shined brightly from above on a beautiful November afternoon with gusting winds. Mrs. Connally even said, "Mr. President, you can't say Dallas doesn't love you."

Conspicuously absent from the President's vehicle were any secret service agents. Agents were standing up, lining the sides of the following vehicle, but not the President's. This absence of secret service agents allowed the carefully positioned snipers to get a clear view of their target and then take multiple shots free from obstruction by the agents.

As the President's motorcade approaches the entrance of the kill zone, an unidentified woman walks away from Elm Street and onto the grass of the plaza, near the Elm and Houston Street intersection, waiving a white handkerchief above her head. The command to open fire is given and the first volley is fired. A gunshot is heard from behind the limousine, causing people to look in that direction. A bullet strikes the pavement on Elm Street, near the President's vehicle. Also, James Tague, standing near the triple underpass, hundreds of feet in front of the motorcade, is hit in the face with a bullet fragment. Of the initial shots fired simultaneously, the shot wounding Tague probably came from the sniper position on the second floor of the Dal-Tex building. The umbrella man, a signaler, is located on the north side of Elm Street only a few feet from the President. He opens and closes his umbrella several times, signaling to the others the President is still alive.

A second volley is fired moments later. A bullet passes through the front windshield and into the President's throat. Governor Connally is shot through the chest from the rear, most likely from a rifleman in the depository. A bullet strikes the president in his upper right back. Several other bullets are fired that miss their target altogether. Witnesses are unable to determine exactly how many bullets are fired because of the echoing and some are still unsure where the gunfire originated from.

Agent Greer slows the vehicle, pulls over slightly towards the left/south side of Elm Street, and halts the vehicle, making the President a stationary target. Another volley of fire erupts, with a shot made from the northern grassy knoll hitting the President in the front right side of his head. The bullet explodes on impact, spraying brain matter, blood, and bits of skull backwards, towards the rear of the car. Only now, after the President has received a fatal head wound, does agent Greer decide to speed up and drive out of the kill zone.

A Detailed Look at the Assassins' Plan

Now that we understand something of the preparation and execution of the overall assassination, let us look more in depth at the individual mechanisms of the larger killing machine. A closer look reveals a plan executed by men and women skilled in deception, weapons concealment, and the use of cover stories. The sniper positions themselves were well chosen – a work of professionals with specific training. Some of the snipers probably did this kind of work before. (Note: see the picture entitled 'The Killer's Plan' to match up the following positions with the actual locations at Dealey Plaza.)

Sniper position #1, TSBD: There was a 3-4 man team in the TSBD on the sixth floor. Numerous eyewitnesses observed three different men, two of them holding rifles, but the witnesses assumed the gunmen were secret service agents. There is no question there were armed snipers in the TSBD, it is just a matter of determining their identities. The weapons fired from the TSBD did not have suppressors in order to later incriminate Oswald and 'prove' the shots came from the TSBD. According to all the evidence, none of the several shots fired from the TSBD ever hit the President. This was because the TSBD was such a poor position. The trees at times blocked a sniper's view of the President and their target moved laterally across their field of view, from left to right, making a shot difficult. These snipers most likely hit Texas Governor John Connally, missing their intended target by several feet. The TSBD snipers most likely hit the Stemmons Freeway sign and also fired a round that ricocheted off of the sidewalk, adjacent to the TSBD. Overall, their poor shooting increased the number of incriminating bullets found later without even hitting their target.

Author Claudia Furiati in her book *ZR Rifle* interviewed a Cuban intelligence officer who identified the two TSBD shooters as being most likely Yito del Valle and Herminio Diaz, who were both Cubans with bald patches on their heads. Several eyewitnesses observed two men with rifles in the TSBD before the shooting who

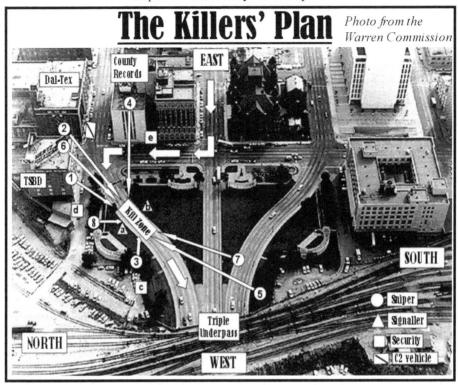

The Killers' Plan *Photo from the Warren Commission*

matched the physical description of these two Cubans. Conveniently, Herminio soon died in Cuba, shot by Cuban forces while on a suspected assassination attempt of Castro. Yito was murdered in 1967.[2]

Because the team was already in the TSBD, they should have planted Oswald's rifle and the three shell casings. However, this team was not assigned roles in the post-shooting process, although in an ideal position to do so. Perhaps due to the compartmentalized nature of the operation, the evidence team was kept separate from these shooters. Whatever the reason, gross errors were made concerning the rifle used, the shell casings left behind, and even contradictory photos of Oswald's sniper position, where different pictures showed different arrangements of boxes.

Sniper position #2, Dal-Tex: There was a sniper team on the second floor of the Dal-Tex building. The shooter fired from a darkened broom closet window with a metal fire-escape stairs in front of the window, helping to visually screen their position. This position offered the shooter excellent cover and concealment and if they used a suppressor, no one would see them pulling the trigger. This slightly elevated position allowed the shooter to fire at the President as the limousine drove away, which is a relatively easy shot when compared to the challenge the firers had in the TSBD. However, since this position was only elevated 10-12 feet, the firer had a difficult time clearing the second follow-on vehicle and its accompanying secret service men. Because of this, they most likely missed several of their shots, hitting the curb

2 Furiati, *ZR Rifle*, p.140. (Another good work that looks into, specifically, the shooters who are believed to have taken the actual shots from the TSBD.)

near the triple underpass that wounded Tague and lodging a bullet into the windshield frame of the presidential limousine. Overall, this sniper did a poor job of shooting and most likely never hit the President.

Sniper position #3, Northern Grassy Knoll: The northern grassy knoll position, with its trees, picket fence, and concrete retaining wall, offered the two shooters who fired from here excellent cover and concealment from the front. This elevated position also allowed a direct shot into the presidential limousine. While this position offered good concealment from the front, it was exposed to the rear and several eye-witnesses saw a man in a police uniform fire a rifle and another shooter dressed in civilian clothes. One man was observed, after the shooting, throwing his weapon to a 'rail yard worker' who broke the rifle down, placing it in a tool box.

Some investigators believe Corsican contract killer Lucien Sarti pulled the trigger that inflicted the fatal head wound on the President. French heroin trafficker Christian David told a reporter Sarti admitted shooting the President. David also said Sarti, when working overseas, liked to wear a military or police uniform and he used explosive bullets. Seeing as how the President died from a head shot with an exploding bullet by a man in a police uniform, the connection to Sarti is established.

Other researches, including author Craig Roberts, have suggested Roscoe White was the second shooter at the northern grassy knoll position. White was on the Dallas Police Department at the time. White's own son was later to say his father admitted he was one of the shooters on the northern grassy knoll.

Sniper position #4, Dallas County Records: This position had a top-down view of the target, seven stories high, and offered the best overall view of Dealey Plaza and the kill zone. A small parapet encircles the roof's perimeter, offering visual screening from people below. Without a doubt, there was a sniper on the roof of the Dallas County Records building. We know this because Sheriff James Decker ordered police sniper Harry Weatherford onto the roof as a 'counter-sniper' before the motorcade arrived. Interestingly enough, three weeks before the President's motorcade drove through Dealey Plaza, Weatherford ordered a custom-built sound suppressor for a rifle. Additionally, a missed shot near a manhole cover on the south side of Elm Street lined up exactly with the Country Records building Weatherford was on.[3]

To reinforce this, in 1976, a worker discovered a .30-06 shell casing lying under some tar paper on the roof of the Country Records building, which is more physical evidence at least one shot was fired from this location. When a reporter asked Weatherford if he shot the President on November 22, Weatherford did not answer with a "no". Instead, Weatherford said, "You little son of a bitch, I shoot lots of people."[4] Many investigators believe the shot striking the President in the back was fired from this position.

And since the shell found on the roof in 1976 had an unusually crimped neck, like a sabot round, this shell could have been used to fire a 6.5 mm bullet (like the one corresponding to the Mannlicher-Carcano) into the President. This evidence has led investigators to guess Weatherford had a suppressed rifle, firing a sabot round into the President's back to introduce 'evidence' that Oswald shot the President. The sniper

3 Fetzer, *Murder In Dealey Plaza*, p.94.
4 Fetzer, *Murder In Dealey Plaza*, p.94.

Photo by Ike Altgens/
Warren Commission

A view of the President's car after the first shot had just been fired, which is believed to have come from the open window by the fire escape stairs in the background.

from this position also missed a shot, hitting the sidewalk near the manhole cover, just like the other snipers who, all combined, missed more shots than they made.

Sniper position #5, Southern Grassy Knoll: The southern grassy knoll position had all the same attributes of cover and concealment from the front as did the northern one. Many investigators believe the bullet penetrating the front windshield of the limousine, hitting the president in the throat, was fired from here. Many eyewitnesses thought a shot originated from the southern knoll and one person stated they smelled gunpowder in that area after the shootings. A study of the angle from the hole in the windshield to the President's throat leads one to trace the trajectory back to the southern knoll.

Other investigators suggest a shot may have been fired from a storm sewer located near the southern knoll. This would have allowed a shooter to fire from a completely concealed position, invisible to spectators. Of interest, the tunnels from that storm sewer connect to the basement of the Dallas county jail, located in Dealey Plaza, adjacent to the county records building. These tunnels would allow a shooter to make a shot and then move underground and escape undetected. This shot was either an extremely lucky one, or an incredibly skilled one, or a little bit of both. When a bullet hits glass, its initial trajectory becomes altered, causing the bullet to deflect, veering off its intended course. A shooter can minimize this deflection when shooting through glass by using a high-velocity, jacketed bullet that resists fragmentation and has the speed and weight to punch cleanly through the obstacle.

Imagine the shooter on the southern knoll as he made this shot. The sniper was two hundred feet away, sighting in on the President's head as the limousine drove towards him. The shooter had to look through a windshield that distorted the view of the target. The shooter also has to shoot past the two secret service agents sitting in the front seat and shoot between Governor Connally and his wife sitting in front of the President. This was an extremely difficult shot. The sniper probably intended to shoot the President in the head, but the glass deflected his shot down eight inches, making the bullet strike off target into the President's throat, which was a non-fatal shot.

Sniper position #6, Roof TSBD: There may have been a team on the roof of the TSBD, but this has never been confirmed. However, one police officer stated when he heard the first shot and looked towards the TSBD, he saw pigeons flying away from the roof. Also, several investigators reported that a rifle was initially found on the roof of the TSBD; this report was subsequently changed. After examining the problems the conspirators had concealing all the rifles they left behind, this extra weapon becomes part of a pattern. Another advantage of a roof shot from here is the increased elevation would help a shooter clear the trees below.

Sniper position #7, Pick-Up Truck on Commerce Street: There is no confirmation a sniper was established at this position, but there are several things to consider. First, in a picture taken by Frank Cancellare of *Life* magazine, a pick-up truck is clearly seen parked on the left-hand (north) shoulder of Commerce Street. In the back of this pick-up truck there is man seated in the bed, with his left arm reaching down, grasping an object that cannot be seen. The man, despite the numerous shots fired, remains sitting in the truck facing the motorcade. This truck would have made a good urban sniper hide because shooter could raise their weapon, fire a shot, and then quickly lower the rifle again.

The reader should also consider that after the Abraham Zapruder film (which recorded the entire assassination) was tampered with, the picture of this man in the bed of the pick-up truck was altered. In the tampered film, the man was erased and a flat bed cover was inserted into the picture, covering up the back of the truck. If this man was not a back-up sniper, then why was he erased from the tampered film? Other tampered film also blacked out the shooter on the northern grassy knoll, hiding a man numerous eyewitnesses saw. Since the conspirators erased the sniper on the grassy knoll, it makes sense they also erased the back-up sniper in the pick-up truck on Commerce Street.

Sniper Position 8, Pergola: Incarcerated criminal James Files stated he was one of the shooters in the northern grassy knoll area. He stated after he fired his round he bit into the shell casing, leaving indentations of his teeth as a personal 'signature' of his actions. Years after the assassination, John Rademacher found two .222 caliber shell casings, one behind the grassy knoll and another closer to the TSBD behind the pergola. The one on the grassy knoll had human teeth marks in the shell casings, corroborating Files' story.

Also, eyewitness Malcom Summers stated immediately after the shooting, he encountered a man adjacent to the pergola with a jacket over his arm, holding a weapon. This unidentified man told Summers he would be shot if he went any further towards the pergola. Summers later identified the man's weapon as a Remington XP-100 Fireball. The XP-100 is an ideal urban sniper weapon as it fires a .222 caliber rifle round, is extremely accurate, powerful, and concealable. Additionally, other witnesses stated at least one shot was fired from besides the President, which corroborates a sniper at

The President is Dead

Ike Altgens/Library of Congress

The limousine drives away, towards the triple underpass, as Jacqueline Kennedy climbs away from her bloodied husband.

the pergola position.[5]

Signaler a: There appeared to be two separate signalers, standing side by side, on the north side of Elm Street as the presidential motorcade approached. The most infamous of these signalers was the 'Umbrella Man', a man who was dressed in a dark jacket holding an umbrella. After the President weathered the first volley of fire, this man raised his umbrella high, and opened and closed it several times. Why this man had an umbrella out when it was warm and sunny is the first give away. Then opening and closing the umbrella while under fire is inexplicable, unless he was there to signal a shooter. (Author's note: Many investigators believe this umbrella was a modified device capable of firing a poison dart - in other words it was a concealment device for an assassination weapon. The reader should research this claim on their own as there is considerable public material on it.)

A second man was standing in front of Umbrella Man, wearing a long-sleeve white shirt, and was seen raising his hand high, looking past the motorcade and across Dealey Plaza as if signaling to someone. This man's white shirt is easily seen from a distance and would be the color of choice if one had to give someone a visual signal. Both of these men showed no reaction to the multiple shots fired and were later seen sitting down next to each other on the grass after the assassination. Both then walked off.

Signaler b: As puzzling as these two men was the woman observed on the south side of Elm Street, located closer to the intersection of Elm and Houston Streets. As the President's limousine approached the front of the depository (i.e. the kill zone) she pulled out a white handkerchief and waved it high in the air. Why she did this other than to signal the entrance of the limousine into the kill zone is unknown, but her ac-

5 Vernon, *John Rademacher And The .222 Casing,* www.jfkmurdersolved.com.

tions did not fit in.

It is possible redundant signalers were established just as redundant sniper teams were put in place. These signalers were used as visual back-ups in case there was a problem with the radio communications. While the props the signalers used (an umbrella, a handkerchief, and a man in a white shirt with an outstretched arm) all fit into the urban environment, it was their actions and body language exposing them. There is nothing unusual about an umbrella unless you have it on a sunny afternoon and then open and closed it vigorously several times while the President of the United States got his head blown off several feet from you. A handkerchief in itself is nothing to be concerned with unless you wave it over your head several times just before the President is riddled with bullets. While their props fit in, their actions did not.

Jim Hicks, who was caught on film walking towards the northern grassy knoll after the shooting with what appeared to be a radio in his back pocket, later admitted to New Orleans District Attorney Jim Garrison he was the radio coordinator for the assassination (Jim Garrison was subsequently admitted to an insane asylum and then murdered after his release). Analysis of other photographs revealed more 'civilians' caught talking into radios at the time of the killing. There is no question there was a system of communications established and it makes sense there would be redundant measures in this system.

Command and Control: Also of note, a white laundry van with a large silver trailer van parked behind it was positioned conspicuously on Houston Street, adjacent to the Dal-Tex building and facing the Elm and Houston Street intersection. The laundry van had an excellent view of the adjacent intersection and the entire kill zone. While no one knows the true purpose of these vehicles, they do appear out of place. However, either one would have served very well as an on-the-scene, command and control vehicle. Personnel could have been hidden in the back of either vehicle, passing reports, giving commands, and reporting on events as they unfolded, unseen by the bystanders around them. Why either vehicle was allowed to be parked so close to the Presidential route is unknown. However, this is just one more piece in an overall pattern of relaxed security allowing the conspirators to position themselves anywhere they wanted to prior to and after the assassination. Researchers have found that in the post-shooting tampered film the silver trailer was removed.

Security c: A two or three man security team worked this position by the northern grassy knoll, keeping random bystanders away by flashing government badges. After the shooting, a man dressed in a police uniform, with dirty hands, confiscated a video-camera at gunpoint from eyewitness Gordon Arnold so this evidence could not be viewed at a later date. Numerous eyewitnesses reported seeing several men on the northern grassy knoll who left immediately after the shooting.

Security d: Eyewitness met several men near the TSBD who were armed and stated they were with the secret service. The secret service said they never placed any agents in the area before or after the shooting.

Security e: Several suspicious men were 'arrested' in this area and were either released or never reported as being detained.

The Backyard Pose

A supposed picture of Oswald holding his Carcano rifle.

Photo from National Archives

The Rifle Problem

The assassins had a problem with their rifles. Several rifles were discovered and reported as opposed to the single Mannlicher-Carcano 6.5 mm rifle supposed to be left behind by Oswald. A closer look may reveal why these problems occurred.

1st Weapon: Mannlicher-Carcano 6.5 mm rifle. This was the weapon that was eventually 'found' on the 6th floor of the depository, hidden under some boxes on the far side of the building, away from the alleged 'sniper nest', and reportedly stashed there by Lee Harvey Oswald. However, this rifle was initially reported as being found on the fourth floor and specifically not on the same floor as the three spent shell casings. Many researches believe the rifle found was not the rifle shown in the infamous 'backyard photo' - (which many researchers agree is a poorly doctored image), nor the rifle shown as evidence during the subsequent Warren Commission proceedings. There were no fingerprints initially found on the rifle after dusting for them, until several days later, when Oswald's palm print was reportedly found on the rifle under the stock. When Oswald was given a paraffin test to see if there was gunshot residue on his body, the test came back positive for his hands (which could have been caused by handling paint during the day), but negative for his face. A person firing a rifle would have their head and face covered in a cloud of residue as well.

2nd Weapon: Mauser 7.92 mm rifle. Initially, the first rifle discovered in the TSBD and reported to the media by the Dallas police was a bolt-action 7.92 mm Mauser rifle with no scope. The officer who found the rifle even read to reporters the name of the weapon stamped into the receiver of the rifle letter by letter... M-A-U-S-E-R.[6] Authorities later said they mistook the Mauser rifle with no scope for the Mannlicher-Carcano rifle with a scope!

3rd Weapon: Lee-Enfield .303 rifle. Several witnesses recounted police officers finding a rifle on the roof of the TSBD. In fact, police officers were captured on film by the Dallas Cinema Associates standing on the east-side fire escape of the TSBD holding up this weapon.[7] Those who saw the rifle stated it looked like a Lee-Enfield rifle, not a Mannlicher-Carcano.

4th Weapon: Johnson semi-automatic .30-06 rifle. Another rifle reportedly found by police was a .30-06 rifle used previously in U.S. government sponsored anti-Castro operations in Cuba.[8] Further supporting this report was the fact a .30-06 rifle casing was found on the roof of the Country Records Building in 1976.

Why the assassins had such a difficult time planting the appropriate weapon in the right location is a mystery. It is likely one of the shooters in the TSBD, who used a Mauser rifle, left it behind by mistake. The plan may have been for the plant team to be in the TSBD before the police arrived on the scene, allowing them to plant the Mannlicher-Carcano and remove the Mauser. Since the shooters in the TSBD left without their weapons, they had to stash them somewhere. Due to poor planning on the conspirators' part, they did not get into the TSBD in time to make the switch. Consequently, when the plant team arrived late, they belatedly planted the Mannlicher-Carcano and had to deal with the now-embarrassing Mauser, which had to be covered up.

A similar pattern seems apparent with the other rifles. The snipers most likely left them behind after the shooting so they could escape the immediate area undetected. The plan was for follow on teams to secure these rifles discretely and spirit them away unknown to the general public. However, since there were so many people in the area after the shooting, various people saw the rifles. If the shooters concealed the rifles at their sniper positions (and recovered them later) or concealed them as they left, these embarrassing incidents would have been avoided. Instead, there were several 'rifle sightings' to cover up.

The Bullet Problem

While the conspirators failed to make it look like a single weapon was found and was in fact fired by Oswald, this part of their deception plan went better than the ef-

6 Fetzer, *Murder In Dealey Plaza*, p. 80,97.
7 Fetzer, *Murder In Dealey Plaza*, p. 94.
8 Griffith, *Extra Bullets and Missed Shots in Dealey Plaza*, karws.gso.uri.edu/JFK/ the_critics/griffith

The Mannlicher-Carcano (91/38)

Photo from the National Archives

Production history: The Model 91 was designed by Salvatore Carcano at the Turin Army Arsenal in Italy in 1890. A carbine version was introduced in 1938. The Model 91 was mass-produced and issued in large numbers to Italy's soldiers in both World Wars. The above 91/38 carbine, serial # C2766 is the one supposedly fired by Lee Harvey Oswald. It's alleged to have been received through a mail order company and shipped to a post office box in Dallas, to Alex J. Hidell, an alias Oswald used. It only cost $19.95.

Description: The carbine is a bolt-action rifle, fires a 6.5 mm x 52 mm cartridge (shown here, from the National Archives) fed by a 6-round stripper clip, is 49.5-inches long, with a 31-inch barrel, weighs approximately eight pounds nine ounces.

Accuracy: Accurate sniper versions of the M91/38 were never produced, but Italian forces did mount a scope to these carbines just the same. The M91/38 fires a 160-grain round traveling at 2300 feet per seconde. Although the M91/38 isn't known for being an exceptionally accurate weapon, tests have shown that the model is capable of shooting 2-3 MOA accuracy. While this is substandard for a dedicated sniper rifle, it means that a marksman can reliably hit someone in the head at 200 meters, but not any further. The assassination rifle had a side-mounted Ordnance Optics 4 x 18 telescopic sight attached.

Strengths: When Oswald supposedly purchased this weapon, the M91/38 was just another cheap, easily gotten, World War II-era surplus rifle with plenty of surplus ammunition available.

Weaknesses: However, the M91/38 isn't a very reliable weapon and is prone to jamming. It's a large, heavy, ungainly weapon (like the Mosin-Nagant) so it isn't easily concealed. Commercial sound suppressors aren't available. Like any bolt-action weapon, it isn't meant to engage multiple targets in rapid succession.

Sniper use: Oswald allegedly fired three shots from the depository: the first fired at 175 feet, the second at 240 feet, and the third at 275 feet. According to the Warren Commission, Oswald made the shots in the span of 4.8 to 5.6 seconds. While subsequent tests have shown that two hits, out of three shots, in six seconds is physically possible, these same tests showed that it's highly unlikely that a person working a bolt-action rifle, aiming through a scope, at a moving target could accomplish such a feat. The reader should set up their own test and see for themselves.

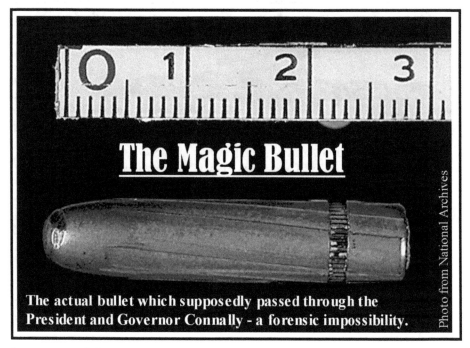

The Magic Bullet

The actual bullet which supposedly passed through the President and Governor Connally - a forensic impossibility.

Photo from National Archives

forts to conceal the actual number of shots fired. Since the conspirators planted only three shell casings in the depository, they were forced to explain the entire shooting with just three bullets. But, more than just an errant bullet or two had to be explained, they had to cover up evidence revealing a dozen or more shots fired but not planned for.

#1 Bullet: One of the first shots fired missed the target, striking the pavement on Elm Street near the President's limousine, seen by numerous eyewitnesses. This bullet distracted many people in the motorcade, causing them to look back, over their shoulders, for the source of the shot. This first missed shot drew most peoples' attention away from a subsequent frontal shot striking the President in the throat. This first shot may have been fired from one of the shooters in the TSBD and it is a mystery as how a shooter could have missed the target by such a wide margin. It may simply be because the President's limousine was a moving target and thus very difficult to hit on the first try.

#2 Bullet: Another early shot fired from the west/front of the Presidential limousine and went through the front windshield, hitting the President in the throat. Since the entry wound was relatively small, a smaller bullet of a .222 caliber size may have been used. The supposed windshield itself was provided to the Warren Commission as evidence but witnesses say it was a fake, because it now had a crack in it as opposed to the original bullet hole. Some investigators believe the position of the original bullet hole, on the left hand side of the windshield, indicates a shot that could have only come from the southern grassy knoll, not the northern one.

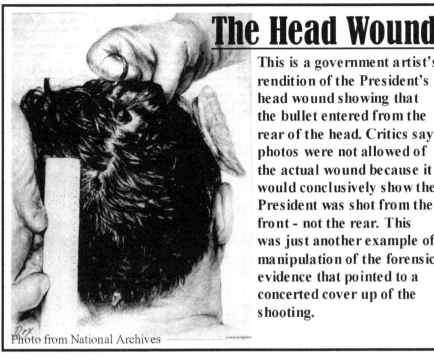

The Head Wound

This is a government artist's rendition of the President's head wound showing that the bullet entered from the rear of the head. Critics say photos were not allowed of the actual wound because it would conclusively show the President was shot from the front - not the rear. This was just another example of manipulation of the forensic evidence that pointed to a concerted cover up of the shooting.

Photo from National Archives

#3 Bullet: Another early shot missing the President and hitting a curb near the triple underpass, wounding bystander James Tague in the cheek with a fragment. The actual piece of curb was cut up and removed as evidence. This evidence has been accepted universally as proof of one of the bullets fired that missed the President. This shot was most likely fired from the Dal-Tex building sniper position.

#4 Bullet: The bullet hitting the President in his upper right back. Investigators theorize a shooter positioned behind the President on the roof of the Dallas County Records building made this shot. These same investigators say, due to the angle of the shot striking the President in the back, the bullet could not have possibly come out through the center of his throat as an exit wound.

#5 Bullet: Another near miss lodging into the top inside windshield frame of the Presidential limousine. This was most likely another shot fired from the Dal-Tex building due to the relatively flat angle of trajectory.

#6 Bullet: This is the bullet striking Texas Governor Connally in the chest. One should note that a bullet hitting flesh, muscle, and bone, like a bullet hitting Governor Connally, would show visible signs of deformation. Even a bullet with a full-metal jacket would deform on impact, unlike the 'magic' bullet found later.

#7 Bullet: This is the bullet hitting Texas Governor Connally in the wrist. Again, any bullet that hit flesh, muscle, and bone like this would have deformed upon impact.

#8 Bullet: There is some evidence to indicate the wound to Texas Governor Connally's left thigh was from a separate bullet. And regardless if the bullet was a separate shot or not, again, it would show definite signs of deformation after striking a large muscle like the thigh.

#9 Bullet: The bullet striking the President in the front, right side of his head. Some investigators believe a second bullet hit the President in the back of the head, almost simultaneously as the front shot, but since the conspirators 'lost' the President's brain during the subsequent autopsy, we will never know until the brain is 'found'. The known right, front head shot was from a frangible (or exploding) bullet. This type of fragmenting bullet is hard to identify in a post-shooting forensic investigation because the remaining fragments are so small and damaged they do not retain enough of the rifling marks from the gun's barrel, meaning they cannot be matched with the rifle they were fired from.

#10 Bullet: A missed shot hitting the Stemmons Freeway sign, causing the conspirators to remove this sign and replace it with a new and noticeably larger one after the assassination.

#11 Bullet: Another miss ricocheting off the sidewalk running along the TSBD, later altered to look like it was an old, weathered mark. This shot is generally believed to have been fired from a western window from the TSBD.

#12 Bullet: Another miss bouncing off of the concrete near a manhole cover next to Elm Street. Near this location were two furrows in the grass, which a police officer on the scene said looked like marks made from bullets. The woman who initially pointed out these furrows noted they led back to the northern grassy knoll.

#13 Bullet: A spent bullet later found in the grass of Dealey Plaza by a witness and then picked up by an unknown person assumed to be a government officer. The bullet and the 'officer' were never seen again.

#14 Bullet: In 1966, a bullet was extracted from a building located ¼ mile from and in line with the TSBD and was determined by the FBI to be a Full Metal Jacket .30 caliber M-1 carbine bullet.[9] In other words, it was not fired from Oswald's supposed rifle and must have been fired by another shooter with a different weapon.

#15 Bullet: In 1967, another bullet was found on top of a building located eight blocks from the TSBD. This bullet was a jacketed, .30 caliber, soft-point, weighing 149 grains, and was not from Lee Harvey Oswald's gun.[10] Again, another shooter with a different weapon must have fired this bullet.

#16 Bullet: In 1974, a bullet fragment was found in Dealey Plaza, 500 yards from the TSBD. The FBI reported it was from a metal jacketed, soft-point, (or hollow

9 Fetzer, *Murder In Dealey Plaza*, p.76.
10 Fetzer, *Murder In Dealey Plaza*, p.77.

Jack Ruby Shoots Oswald

Photo from National Archives

Jack Ruby's shooting of Lee Harvey Oswald got rid of the most important piece of evidence in the assassination - the shooter himself. With Oswald dead, he could not refute any of the 'evidence' arrayed against him.

point), sporting bullet. It was not fired from Lee Harvey Oswald's gun.[11] Another shooter with a different weapon must have fired this bullet.

#17 Bullet: There is some evidence the snipers may have accidentally shot one of their own men in the crossfire. Several times after the shooting, a report was issued about a secret service agent who was shot during the assassination. Also, Jerry Coley and Charlie Mulkey, two reporters for the Dallas Morning News, discovered a fresh pool of red blood on some steps leading to Elm Street near the depository. Mulkey actually tasted the red liquid and noted it was blood.[12] Both men returned later with their cameras and took pictures of the pool of blood. Other witnesses also confirmed the presence of blood stains found near the scene of the shooting, either in a similar spot or other areas. It is possible one of the bogus secret service agents was wounded by accident in the crossfire and initial reports of a wounded secret service agent referred to this conspirator.

11 Fetzer, *Murder In Dealey Plaza*, p.76.
12 Fetzer, *Murder In Dealey Plaza*, p.48.

In addition to this evidence showing more than three shots were allegedly fired that day, most of the eyewitnesses at Dealey Plaza stated anywhere from six to eight shots were heard. Other eyewitnesses to the shooting stated they thought the President was struck with six or more shots. All these bullets indicate the snipers fired several volleys of shots, with different snipers firing during each volley. These bullets also reveal the majority of the shots missed their targets. This is understandable as there is nothing more difficult than trying to shoot a small, moving target, from within a large crowd of people, without being seen. Since there was a mix of different snipers, some were more skilled than others. The skilled shot, fired through the front windshield, in between several people, and hitting the President in the throat, was impressive. In contrast, the shots fired from the TSBD, striking Governor Connally and missing President Kennedy by several feet, reveal a poor shooter who had not practiced hitting a moving target before the assassination.

(Author's Note: This list is not intended to be in the order the bullets were fired, as that is impossible to discern. However, the suspected order of the shots was taken into account to make it easier to follow. Several of the 'bullets' listed may not be hard evidence of a bullet, but the reader can decide on their own if more than the standard 'three' bullets were fired during the assassination.)

Conclusion

The Dealey Plaza snipers had a difficult job, which ultimately proved impossible. Anyone can kill the President, but killing the President and framing a single person is something entirely different. The assassins did develop an urban sniping operation which displayed sophisticated, unconventional urban sniping methodology. While they did kill President Kennedy, they failed to cover up the assassination. The most salient reason for this failing was the assassins spent more effort on killing the President than ensuring the forensic and physical evidence meshed with the actual execution. Notably, the assassins failed to match the number of rifles and bullets discovered after the operation with the evidence meant to link Lee Harvey Oswald to the shooting.

Chapter 10

Terror In Texas

I don't really understand myself these days. I am supposed to be an average reasonable and intelligent young man. However, lately (I can't recall when it started) I have been a victim of many unusual and irrational thoughts.

-Charles Whitman

Terror in Texas

On August 1, 1966, Charles Joseph Whitman gunned down forty-six people from the University of Texas Tower in Austin. In essence, Whitman was a guerrilla sniper. Just as a guerrilla commits a crime against the state by attempting to overthrow the government, a mass murderer also commits a crime. In Whitman's case, he was a mentally ill individual who moved among the sane world, masquerading as a normal person. Whitman's mental camouflage was to act like everyone else: to pay the bills, to come home to his wife, to go to school. If he let his guard down and his true thoughts oozed out, he would no longer be invisible, he would be identified for what he gradually became: a homicidal sociopath.

Whitman's case is instructive for a variety of other tactical reasons such as understanding noise in an urban environment and how people react to it. Whitman's shootings teaches us about the importance of elevation for an urban sniper, the advantage of shooting from a covered position, and what counter-sniper measures a security force may take against a shooter. Perhaps most important of all, the Charles Whitman case shows what a sniper can accomplish when they are unconcerned with saving their own life. When Whitman began his shooting spree, he did not care about surviving the event. His sole desire was to kill as many people as possible until he was killed himself. If Whitman wanted to live, he would have made a shot or two and then fled the scene. At most, a person or two would have their precious lives stolen from them. Because life ceased to have any meaning for him, Whitman's sniper attack became a gruesome bloodbath. Taken in this light, Charles Whitman could be described as a sniper-martyr.

Whitman's Sniper Training

Whitman's marksmanship training began at an early age because his father was an avid shooter, indeed a fanatical gun lover. As early as two-years of age, Whitman was seen posing with two of his father's rifles. By the time Whitman was a teenager, he was an excellent shot. Whitman received additional, professional shooting instruction as a member of the United States Marine Corps where he earned high scores in rapid long-range fire and was best at shooting moving targets. After Whitman left the Marine Corps and attended college in Austin, he regularly fired his personal weapons at local rifle ranges, continually honing his shooting skills.

It is important to note Whitman became a skilled and proficient shooter in a completely legal manner. All over the world it is perfectly legal to play with toy guns, hunt squirrels, and have your father take you shooting. It is equally acceptable to join a nations' military, receive extensive marksmanship training, and then be discharged from military service. In most of the world, it is possible to fire sniper rifles on public firearms ranges without raising an eyebrow from anyone. As long as the shooter maintains an outward appearance of normalcy, they can train as often as they want.

Planning and Reconnaissance

Just as a guerrilla sniper carefully plans for their operations, so did Whitman. Whitman picked the perfect structure to shoot from - the University of Texas at Austin's tower - and then conducted a thorough reconnaissance of it. As early as April of 1966, four months before his killing spree, Whitman was seen by the tower receptionist visiting the tower's observation deck. This did not raise any suspicions because many students visited the observation deck to enjoy the view, to engage in idle chatter, or just to relax. Because Whitman was just one of many students who regularly visited the tower, he fit in and visited the tower whenever he pleased.

Once he was in the tower mingling with the other campus' students, Whitman analyzed his future sniper platform in detail. He saw he had clear fields of fire in all directions and there were rain spouts on all sides he could shoot from while remaining hidden from view. Whitman also knew the layout of the observation deck, what security measures were in place (there were none), and what route to take to get from the bottom floor of the tower all the way to the 28th floor at the top. Because Whitman

The Texas Tower

The Texas Tower, at 307 feet, provided a dominating view of the surrounding terrain. There was no other structure on the campus that allowed a shooter such an excellent bird's eye view of the university. When Whitman fired from the rain spouts on the observation deck, he was completely hidden from view, invisible to his victims below. Also, people firing back at Whitman had little chance of hitting him because of the extreme angle they had to fire at. Most rounds went harmlessly over his head or bounced ineffectively off the concrete parapet of the observation deck.

Whitman fired from these rainspouts on the observation deck.

Photo by Larry D. Moore

was a student enrolled at the University, he had free reign to walk all over campus to observe security measures, student patterns, and the local terrain.

In this manner, Whitman used the same methods a guerrilla sniper uses to scout out a firing platform and the surrounding areas. As long as a guerrilla blends into the local population, has an effective cover story, and has no incriminating evidence on their person (like a weapon) they can go anywhere they please to conduct a reconnaissance for their sniper attacks. Consequently, the guerrilla sniper can plan their attack to the tiniest detail, in an overt manner, without raising any suspicion, just like Whitman did.

Preparation for the Attack

Once Whitman conducted his detailed reconnaissance of his sniper platform and the surrounding area, he equipped himself for the attack. Whitman planned a long siege and assembled a variety of goods to support his killing, packing them into a military-style footlocker. In this footlocker Whitman placed a portable radio, water, food, weapons cleaning gear, a variety of weapons, plenty of ammunition, and earplugs to name a few. In fact, just a day prior to his attack, Whitman purchased a Bowie knife, binoculars, and canned goods. Since these were normal items with a variety of purposes and uses, no one thought anything of it.

On the day of the attack, Whitman bought a rifle, a shotgun, and several hundred rounds of ammunition. Whitman purchased all of these items over the counter from a hardware store, a Sears store, and a local gun shop. Because Whitman had a believable cover story (he said he was going hunting for hogs in Florida), had good credit, and a reliable history of purchasing weapons on lay-a-way plans, he bought everything he needed with ease. Whitman even rented a dolly to transport his heavy footlocker, realizing he could not carry it all by hand. Whitman was ready for a sniping operation that could easily last all day, maybe longer.

The important thing to understand with these purchases is they were all completely legal. Whitman did not break any laws and was well within his rights to have everything he purchased. A guerrilla sniper can obtain weapons and ammunition in the same manner. Wherever it is legal to purchase firearms for sporting use, a guerrilla can get a weapon with ease. Whitman's ability to purchase weapons, legally, is not an isolated case as weapons are readily acquired anywhere in the world either over the counter or through thousands of black market dealers.

The only way the ensuing massacre could have been stopped was if Whitman's school psychologist, who knew Whitman was suffering from some degree of mental illness, reported Whitman's conditions to the authorities. The government could then have placed Whitman's name on a national 'do not sell' list, so Whitman could not buy a weapon from a legally recognized gun dealer in the country. However, at the time, Whitman's mental illness was far from being an established fact, a national 'do not sell to' database did not exist, and thus there was no mechanism in place to weed Whitman out from the rest of the population. He was invisible.

Choosing the Right Weapons for the Job

Whitman had a variety of weapons to choose from, not just from his own collection, but from whatever he could buy over the counter. Whitman ended up taking several different types of weapons to suit a variety of needs. First, he took a .357 magnum Smith and Wesson revolver, a Galesi-Brescia pistol, and a 9mm Luger pistol for personal protection. He also took a 12-gauge shotgun he modified the day of the attack, sawing off the barrel and the buttstock for close-in work. Whitman also took a .35 caliber Remington semi-automatic rifle and a .30 caliber M-1 carbine, both of which could maintain an accurate, high rate of fire out to several hundred meters. However, Whitman's real work horse was a 6 mm Remington bolt-action rifle with a four power scope. Since the Remington 6 mm is a flat shooting rifle and Whitman practiced shooting it so often, he could consistently hit man-size targets at 500 meters or more. Married up to the 6 mm rifle were soft-point 6 mm bullets designed to flatten and expand upon hitting a target, causing enormous soft-tissue damage.

It is important to note Whitman's most effective weapon was a common deer rifle. This rifle was not particularly sophisticated and did not have features common to modern sniper rifles like bipod legs and a high-power scope. Compared to today's powerhouse sniper rifles like the .338 caliber, .410 caliber, and .50 caliber variants, a 6 mm round is relatively small and lacks knock-down power. Despite the limitations of his weapon system, Whitman managed to inflict significant damage from accurate fire developed through constant practice.

Weapons Whitman Bought Legally

MURDER
4. ORIGINALLY CLASSIFIED AS

5. VICTIM'S NAME
SPEED, BILLY PAUL

6. VICTIM'S ADDRESS
1403 Payne Street

7. DATE REPORTED
8-1-66

8. NARRATIVE.

On 8-2-66 this Investigator went to CHARLES P. DAVIS HARDWARE, No. 2, 49th and Burnet Highway, and interviewed TED BEARD, employee in the Sporting Good Department. MR. BEARD stated that at approximately 9:00 A. M., 8-1-66, a white male, whom he identified as CHARLES WHITMAN, came into the store and made the following purchases:

1 - .30 caliber carbine, Serial No. 69799
2 - extra clips

the following ammunition:

3 - boxes six millimeter
2 - boxes .30 caliber carbine
2 - boxes 35 REM
1 - box 9 millimeter luger

MR. BEARD stated that at the time of the purchases WHITMAN told him that he was going to FLORIDA to shoot wild hogs. Further stated that there was no hesitancy on the part of WHITMAN when he purchased any of the foregoing items. He knew exactly what he wanted.

WHITMAN at this time was dressed in blue jeans and a plaid red shirt.

WHITMAN paid for the above purchases by cash.

From The Center for American History, The University of Texas at Austin.

Infiltrating the Tower

After Whitman packed up the necessary supplies in his footlocker, he had to get to his shooting platform, the University of Texas Tower, all while hiding his true intentions. Because Whitman was a registered student at the University of Texas, he knew what security measures the University had and he knew how to beat them. Part of his plan to infiltrate the University was to hide all of his supplies and weapons in the footlocker. The footlocker was in fact a concealment device, allowing Whitman to transfer his weapons in it without raising suspicion.

In addition to this, Whitman put on a pair of blue nylon coveralls over his red plaid shirt and jeans so he looked like a janitor or repairman. The real genius of this is Whitman matched his clothing to compliment his concealment device. Whitman's plan was to look like a person in the service industry who could move in the open, unquestioned by the general public. Whitman did not sneak onto the campus like a thief in the night, he did not cleverly bypass any sophisticated security measures, nor did he create an elaborate plan. Whitman put his guns in a footlocker, placed the footlocker on a dolly, put on a pair of coveralls, and walked right by the people he would later kill. Deception was Whitman's greatest tool.

When Whitman showed up at the University of Texas at Austin security gate, he was dressed in his coveralls with his footlocker in the back of his car and the dolly in the trunk. Because Whitman was a student at the University and a lab assistant, he was been issued a Carrier Identification Card for students who needed to transport heavy or bulky materials onto campus. The security guard noticed the footlocker in the car, but thought nothing of it and issued Charles a loading zone permit for 40 minutes.[1] Because Whitman used a believable cover story - he needed to unload equipment at one of the campus buildings - there was nothing out of the ordinary to arouse the guard's suspicion.

Once getting past the security guard, the rest was even easier for Whitman. He parked his car near the Tower, took the dolly out of the trunk, and placed his footlocker on it. Then, Whitman wheeled his footlocker into the Tower, onto the elevator and up to the 27th floor. Many people saw Whitman walking calmly to the Tower, but no one had any reason to stop or question him because he looked exactly as he intended to look - as a serviceman working for the University. Anything could have been in the footlocker: cleaning supplies, repair parts, or construction material.

Once Whitman got up to the 27th floor and dragged his dolly up three small flights of stairs to the 28th floor of the observation deck, he still had to get past the receptionist and other people who might be on the deck. Once Whitman discovered the Tower receptionist was alone, he bashed in her skull and hid her body. Whitman killed the receptionist so quietly and quickly, several minutes later visitors leaving the observation deck actually walked by Whitman and said, "hello". They saw stains on the floor, but they did not realize it was from blood.

Unfortunately, another group of people ascended the final few stairs to the receptionist's area and were confronted by Whitman, who was now armed with his sawed-off shotgun. Whitman shot this family at close range, killing a boy and a girl, and seriously wounding two others. Whitman then barricaded the doorway to the receptionist area with a table and chairs and blocked the door opening onto the observation deck with the dolly.

It is important to note the several shotgun blasts Whitman fired at the visitors were never heard by people outside the building. While the blasts must have been deafening in the enclosed, concrete hallways, this same sturdy construction effectively contained the sounds of the shotgun. The dynamics of sound and how sound functions in an urban environment with thousands of walls, sidewalks, patios, buildings were to play a key role in the carnage to come. Whitman's shooting would start at 11:48 a.m. and end 96 minutes later with his death. In between these times, Whitman brought death and agony to scores of people from atop his new shooting platform, the Texas Tower.

Tactical Significance of the University of Texas Tower

At 231 feet above the ground, the observation deck of the 307-foot tall University of Texas Tower dominated the surrounding terrain. From the Tower, Whitman had good observation and clear fields of fire in all directions. Because the Tower allowed Whitman to fire in a 360-degree circle, he could access the scores of microenvironments, insulated from one another, making up any urban area. That meant Whitman could shoot someone 500 meters east of the Tower, walk to the other side of the Tower, and then shoot someone 500 meters to the west of the Tower. Since the two different victims were a kilometer from each other, they never saw each other as they were separated not only by distance, but by numerous intervening buildings. As a

---

1 Lavergne, *A Sniper in the Tower*, p. 125-6. (A comprehensive work on Whitman's life and the events in the Tower.)

Whitman's view of the campus from atop the tower.

result, one victim could be shot and killed while the second one had no idea what just happened until they were themselves shot and killed.

Gunshots and Sound in an Urban Environment

Whitman's shooting spree is important to analyze as a case study due in part to the dynamics of sound and how the noise of gunshots work in an urban environment. For instance, people who were near the tower when Whitman started shooting said they heard a 'popping' sound. They did not recognize the sounds as gunshots. The first victim, Claire Wilson, had no idea she was shot. Thomas Eckman, who was standing next to Claire, asked her what was wrong (he too had no idea she was shot) and was then shot himself, dying instantly.[2] Thomas Ashton saw the bodies falling to the pavement and looked towards the tower to see what was going on. As he did so, he was shot in the chest and killed. He never realized someone was shooting at the other people or himself.[3]

People in nearby buildings, with the windows and doors shut, because the air conditioning was on, could not hear the shooting outside and if they did hear something, they did not recognize the sounds as gunshots. Consequently, people on campus left the relative safety of indoors, ran outside to see what was happening, and then were shot themselves. Other people heard the gunshots, but thought the sounds were coming from inside a building. These same curious people then walked outside, in plain view of hundreds of other people, and were shot.

The microenvironments preventing outside sounds from entering them, like vehicles, meant people could take a bus or drive their car into range of the tower and not know there was any shooting until they got off the bus or exited their vehicle. When these people heard a shot after entering their new environment, they had little chance

2 Lavergne, *A Sniper in the Tower*, p. 142-3.
3 Lavergne, *A Sniper in the Tower*, p. 145.

to recognize it for what it was or where it came from. Even people walking down the street could walk around a corner and enter Whitman's field of view, oblivious to anything going on until the shooting resumed.

One of the fundamental features of shooting in an urban environment is the sound of a gunshot echoes off of the surrounding buildings, pavement, sidewalks, and cars. This echoing means a person may hear and recognize the gunshot, but not know where it came from. Some people on campus heard and recognized the gunshots, but assumed they came from a building several hundred meters from the Tower. This misjudgment resulted in people hiding from where they erroneously thought the gunfire originated from. Consequently, these people hid from the wrong building, putting themselves into plain view of Whitman and the Tower. They thought they were safe from the source of gunfire when in fact their reactions made them the next victim.

One man heard the gunshots, but thought it was the backfiring of a car. This same man then looked towards the tower, stated he could see the shooter, and was then shot through the mouth, killing him instantly.[4] Other people thought the gunshots were actually sounds from nail-driving guns used in construction. Still others thought the sounds were wooden planks slapping on concrete, or even the school's Reserve Officer Training Course members shooting blanks.[5]

Whitman's Tactics

Whitman conducted an aggressive assault from his perch above the University. He moved constantly on the deck, taking a single shot and then moving to another position. He repeatedly popped-up over the railing of the observation deck, aimed, shot, crouched back down, and then moved to another position. When moving crouched down, the concrete parapet surrounding the observation deck blocked any view of Whitman so he could not be seen by the people below him. Several people saw puffs of smoke coming from the tower after Whitman's shots, some people saw a gun barrel poking over the concrete parapet, others saw the sun shining off his scope or binoculars, and some saw him pop his head up. Because Whitman fired from every side of the Tower and no one could actually see him, the people below did not know how many shooters there actually were. Many assumed there were several snipers instead of a lone, suicidal shooter.

Whitman made an effort to maintain his situational awareness by tuning his portable transistor radio to KTBC, a local radio station, allowing him to listen to a reporter describe what was going on at the University of Texas. In this manner, Whitman knew what the people below him knew and used this inside knowledge to better target his victims. The press became Whitman's personal damage assessment tool, enabling Whitman to realize the extent and effects of his shooting. Ironically, the radio eventually contributed to Whitman's demise since he turned it up so loud he did not hear the local police dismantle his makeshift barricade or loudly remove the dolly jamming shut the door to the observatory deck. While Whitman was kept up to date on what reporters on the ground saw hundreds of meters away, he lost awareness of what was happening on the observation deck, enabling policemen to gun him down, point blank.

---

4 Lavergne, *A Sniper in the Tower*, p. 170.
5 Lavergne, *A Sniper in the Tower*, p. 188.

Whitman's Guns

Remington .35 semi-automatic rifle

Remington 6 mm bolt-action rifle

12-gauge sawed-off shotgun

M-1 .30 caliber semi-automatic carbine

Any Chance of Escape?

Even up until the very end of the shoot out, Whitman could have escaped. And it would not have taken an elaborate plan to successfully get away. Whitman could have simply walked down the stairs of the tower and pretended to be just another scared campus student. Because no one below him knew what he looked like, never mind who was actually doing the shooting, Whitman could have easily intermingled among the surrounding people, blended in with the crowd, and escaped among the confusion. Obviously, Whitman did not plan on getting away – he conducted the entire attack in a manner that would eventually get himself killed. After all, Whitman killed his wife and mother before his massacre and left handwritten notes admitting to his guilt. On top of this, Whitman's footlocker holding his arsenal and supplies actually had his full name spray painted on it, leaving little doubt as to his identity once he was killed or apprehended. While he could have escaped, Whitman intended all along to die in the tower.

Counter-Sniper Tactics

While Whitman's killing spree is instructive on the dynamics of conducting an urban sniping attack, it is equally educational on how to counter an urban sniper. While Whitman shot at the local, unarmed citizens, many of the people departed and returned with their own hunting rifles. These armed citizens then opened fire on Whitman in an attempt to kill him, forcing Whitman to keep his head down and restricting his movement on the observation deck.

However, the observation deck's concrete parapet, combined with the fact the armed citizens were firing upwards at an extreme angle, protected Whitman. Nevertheless, Whitman was forced to shoot through the rain spouts located on each side of the observation deck's four parapets just to stay alive. Unfortunately, by firing through the rain spouts, Whitman was absolutely invisible from below and invulnerable from return rifle fire. Even though dozens of armed citizens fired hundreds of rounds back at Whitman with high-powered, scoped hunting rifles, he was never wounded by them. Not even a scratch.

The local law enforcement agency, the Austin Police Department (APD), was unprepared to deal with a suicidal sniper firing from a fortress. The APD did not have a SWAT team and the best they could do at the time was arm individual police officers with civilian deer rifles. In one location, several law-enforcement personnel were positioned at an adjacent building, armed with high-powered rifles, scopes, and binoculars, returning fire each time they saw Whitman. This prevented Whitman from sticking his head over the parapet, but he continued to shoot from the rain spouts, impervious to their fire. Because Whitman had such a good vantage point from which to observe his targets, he was able to pin down hundreds of people, to include police officers. Moving across any open area was dangerous, especially after Whitman successfully shot so many moving targets.

Because Whitman pinned down so many people, the APD considered using a helicopter as a shooting platform to get to him, but the APD also thought it was too vulnerable to gunfire. One armed police officer and a pilot did fly a small, cloth-skinned airplane by the tower in an attempt to get a shot at Whitman. However, the plane vibrated so much the officer quickly discovered he could not get off an accurate shot. Compounding the problem was the thermal lift from hot air rising off the pavement causing the airplane to bounce. Whitman did take notice of this new threat and fired two rounds through the plane's cloth fabric, forcing the vulnerable plane to back off and keep its distance.[6]

While most police officers were pinned down or returning ineffective fire, a few made it to an underground tunnel housing the school's telephone, power, and water lines connecting the campus buildings. These police officers recognized only underground movement, providing 360-degree protection, could get them into the tower both safely and undetected. Since airplanes and long-range counter-sniper fire had no effect on Whitman in his fortress, the officers realized only a close-in assault would solve the problem.

After these officers infiltrated the tower through the tunnel, they worked their way upstairs. Between the 27th floor and the observation deck they found the surviving family members of Whitman's initial, close quarters, shotgun blasts. These terrified survivors provided the police with critical intelligence that there was only one sniper and he was up on the observation deck.[7]

The cumulative effect of everything going on around Whitman meant he lost situational awareness of what was happening on the observation deck and the reception area. Because he was focused on shooting targets hundreds of meters away, because people were shooting back at him and planes were flying overhead, and because his portable radio was turned up full volume, Whitman was unaware people were closing

---

6 Lavergne, *A Sniper in the Tower*, p. 207-8.
7 Lavergne, *A Sniper in the Tower*, p. 204.

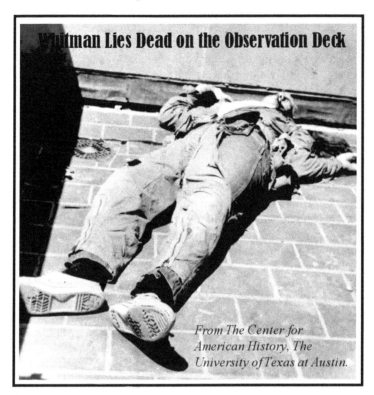

Whitman Lies Dead on the Observation Deck

*From The Center for
American History, The
University of Texas at Austin.*

in on him.

The police who entered the Tower were able to move upstairs, get into the reception area, and push out onto the observation deck oblivious to Whitman. Once they secured a foothold on the deck, it was not long before Whitman was shot at close range, dying of wounds sustained from a shotgun and a pistol. Whitman was well-prepared for a long-distance shoot out, but was a sitting duck to aggressive police officers willing to do close-in work and risk it all to stop the killing.

Lessons Learned from the Texas Tower Tragedy

While the University of Texas at Austin is an urban area, it was not a densely packed area like New York City, Chicago, or Los Angeles. Imagine if Whitman was shooting in an area packed with high-rise buildings, with thousands of pedestrians drowning in a honking sea of car horns. In a heavily urbanized area, Whitman could have shot a hundred people before they realized what was going on, instead of the forty-six victims he ended up shooting on campus. What if Whitman used a sound suppressor on his rifle? If people had problems identifying the gunfire on a bright sunny day in a relatively open campus area, think of the problems people would have locating a gunshot sounding no louder than a car door being shut.

The reader must keep in mind all this death and chaos was caused by a lone gunman with no security element. What if Whitman had one or two other people providing security for him as he fired? What if this security element booby trapped the 27th floor of the tower and the stairs and elevator leading up to the observation deck with high-explosives and detonated these explosives as the police entered? What if the 27th floor was so damaged from the explosives the responding police officers could not physically get to the observation deck? Then, the local police would not have gotten Whitman in the way they did. In fact, no one could have gotten to him in a close assault. The police would have to evacuate the general area to remove Whitman's targets - but hundreds were already pinned down and could not move (at least during daylight hours). The police could try and starve Whitman out, which would take days because of his supplies, or the police could try and talk him down, which did not seem likely. The only option would be to call in the military for an all out assault.

The Sniper Martyr

Whitman was effective for many reasons, but mainly because he had an unusual mindset: he was on a suicide mission and the only way to stop him was to kill him. As a result, Whitman did not care that he quickly gave away his position by firing scores of shots from the same location. As Charles Whitman so grimly proved, the urban sniper can be employed as a terror tool. In a crowded, urban area, from an ideal firing position, scores of people can be shot and killed by a lone gunman. However, employment of a sniper as a terror tool means the gunman is on a suicide mission. Repeated shots from the same position, as Charles Whitman showed, are a death sentence.

Chapter 11

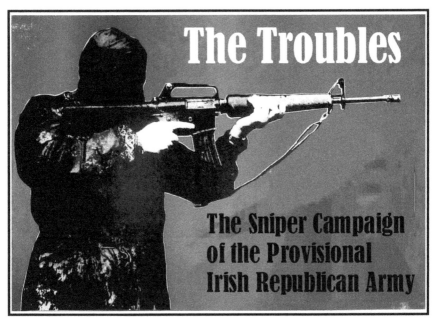

The Troubles

The Sniper Campaign of the Provisional Irish Republican Army

It seemed to me that prolonged sniping from a static position had no more in common with guerrilla theory than mass confrontations. One-shot sniping was in fact the theory of the guerrilla rifle. It turned up, struck once and vanished, presenting no target in return.

- Sean MacStiofain, originator of the 'One-Shot Sniping' method

The Troubles, 1969-1998

The conflict in Northern Ireland can trace its more modern roots to England's colonization of the island, starting with the founding of the Plantation of Ulster in 1609. After arriving in Ulster, the Protestant English and Scottish settlers, with the backing of London, systematically confiscated the surrounding property from the local Catholic Irish inhabitants. Here lies the heart of the existing English-Irish conflict. From 1609 onwards, Protestant England remained determined to hold onto one of its earliest colonies, while Irish resistance groups have tried to get their land back. Today, one can claim England won this centuries-old conflict because Ireland is divided and Northern Ireland is still under sway from London. However, England's 17th Century Ulster Plantation has proved to be a bleeding ulcer the English body has suffered from ever since.

The bleeding soon began with the Irish Confederate Wars, fought from 1641-1653, fueled by the massacres of Protestants and Catholics by both sides. These wars eventually cost hundreds of thousands of Irish lives, not to gunshot wounds or flying shrapnel, but to disease and famine. Next came the Williamite War, fought from 1688-1691, resulting in solidified English control of Ireland for the next hundred years until the failed Irish Rebellion of 1798. More than a century would past until the famed Easter Rising of 1916, which was followed quickly by the Irish War of Independence, 1919-1921. Upon conclusion of this war, Ireland was able to wrest away twenty-six counties from an England bled deathly white from four years of slaughter in the trenches during the Great War. Despite this Irish victory, England and its Protestant colony maintained a death grip on the remaining six counties that became Northern Ireland and are still under English rule to this very day.

The creation of an independent Ireland, less the six Northern counties, satisfied most Irish since they believed that was the best deal they could get. But, remnants of the original Irish Republican Army (IRA) were unwilling to write off the northern counties so quickly. Seeking to take advantage of England's weakened state during World War II, the IRA waged their unsuccessful Northern Campaign from 1942-1944. In this campaign, the IRA intended to take control of Northern Ireland if and when Hitler defeated England, but with Germany's unconditional surrender in 1945, this dream never materialized. Ten years later, the IRA was ready again to try to overthrow the government of Northern Ireland and create a united Ireland. Now, their enemy was post-war England, an England already recovered from the previous world war and now intent on keeping a hold on their shrinking colonial empire. The IRA's uninspiring 1956-1962 Border Campaign failed to garner any widespread support and the effort collapsed. At this stage of their existence the IRA was severely weakened as an organization - almost extinct. But, the IRA would unexpectedly rebound from this latest defeat, and by the end of the decade, the IRA would be resurrected and stronger than ever.

The Troubles Ignite

Many argue The Troubles began in 1968 when widespread rioting and public disorder broke out during the marches of the Northern Ireland Civil Rights Association (NICRA). The NICRA used the marches to bring attention to political and social discrimination by the Protestant government against the Irish Catholics living in Northern Ireland. Extremist elements of the Protestant population saw these marches as a threat to their political power and established way of life, resulting in violent clashes between mobs of Protestant 'loyalists' and Catholic 'nationalists.' The Protestants weathered many a storm over the past centuries and this was just one more opportunity to put the Irish back in their place.

In 1969, as the clashes between Protestants and Catholics escalated, the Northern Ireland police (the Royal Ulster Constabulary - RUC) and the British Army deployed large numbers of officers and soldiers to the six counties in an attempt to quell the violence. Instead of normalizing the situation, this show of force was the equivalent of dumping gasoline on a smoldering flame. The Catholics did not view the police and military as enforcing law and order, they saw them as advancing the Protestants' political interests. Subsequent attacks by Protestant loyalist paramilitaries like the Ulster Defense Association, the Ulster Volunteer Force, the Ulster Freedom Fighters, and the Shankill Butchers, who committed horrible acts of terror against Catholic communities, demanded a response. Who was going to right these wrongs and protect Northern Ireland's Catholic communities from British oppression and loyalist murderers? The IRA would.

Members of the Continuity IRA, a splinter group of the Provisional IRA, train with their weapons.

It was the Catholic community's perceived (and real) need for some one to protect their interests that breathed new life into a listless organization. In 1969, the IRA was ill-prepared to protect its communities. Some hardliners wanted an instant armed response against the established government, while others were unsure. Because of these diverging interests, the IRA split into the Official IRA and the Provisional IRA (PIRA). The PIRA was determined to take armed action to overthrow the existing government of Northern Ireland. With the PIRA leadership ready to act and Britain's own heavy handed tactics alienating the Catholic population, the ranks of the PIRA swelled. For every house the Protestants burned and for every Irishman the RUC beat up, the PIRA's ranks grew. According to early PIRA leader Sean MacStiofain, the Belfast branch of the PIRA alone skyrocketed from only fifty members in 1969 to over 1200 in 1971. While the British often get credit for their counter-insurgency efforts against the PIRA, one should take into account the fact they helped create the problem by alienating the Catholic population.

The Sniping Begins

Despite the increased support for their organization, the PIRA leadership understood they could not defeat the combined might of the British Army, the RUC, and the Protestant paramilitaries in a conventional test of strength. Instead, they would have to rely on a protracted guerrilla war where guile, cunning, and superior intelligence would accomplish their political objectives. One of the elements of this long war that would enable the PIRA to inflict casualties on their much stronger enemies and get away with it was the sniper.

One of the early leaders of the PIRA, Sean MacStiofain, is credited with establishing the PIRA's first organized sniper campaign to include the new 'one-shot sniper' tactic for the resurgent PIRA. At the beginning of The Troubles, MacStiofain was thoroughly unimpressed with the way PIRA snipers conducted their operations in the cities. These snipers fired multiple shots from a single location, thus exposing them to effective enemy counter-fire. Not only did MacStiofain find this lack of urban sniper-craft to be ineffective, he correctly saw it as a violation of the fundamental principles of guerrilla warfare theory. MacStiofain himself commented, "When a sniper did that he was breaking the guiding principle, giving away his location and presenting himself as a target to a counter-sniper or machine-gun fire from armored cars. But what gave away his location was his rifle itself every time he used it. One-shot sniping was in fact the theory of the guerrilla rifle. It turned up, struck once and vanished, presenting no target in return." [1]

MacStiofain's new method was simple. A PIRA sniper would take a single shot from a concealed hidesite and then disappear. They would not take a second shot, no matter what. If they missed their target on the first shot or had a lucrative second target, they still only took a single shot. MacStiofain understood it would take a systematic effort by the PIRA leadership to train their snipers in this new methodology. Conse-quently, the PIRA established new sniper courses where they hammered the principles of successful urban sniping into the shooters' heads. The PIRA trained their snipers to work in pairs where the best shooter was the trigger man and the second-best shot was the observer. MacStiofain explained, "The principle was to fire only one shot, after which, hit or miss – and this was drummed in until they practically screamed – the team went immediately to ground. It was impossible to locate their position provided they fired only one round."[2]

With this new training program in place, PIRA snipers began to have better suc-cess against the British security forces. Fewer PIRA snipers were getting caught or wounded and most were able to make their shot and get away if they followed the discipline of one-shot sniping. In the summer of 1972, the PIRA expanded their sniper operations as MacStiofain notes, "One-shot sniping was introduced on a wide scale in Derry, Belfast, Armagh and some rural areas. Crossmaglen developed an exception-ally good unit which exploited the terrain and used the sympathy of the local people to the utmost. Experience gained in engagements there taught the value of ensuring that each position had a good exit ready before the team went into action."[3]

This effective use of PIRA snipers, which inflicted increasing British casualties, gave the Irish communities a much needed morale boost while, at the same time, showed the British government they had a long struggle ahead of them. The effect of the PIRA's sniping campaign was such that rumors started to spread about a new threat. MacStiofain explains, "After the casualties in west Belfast, a story was fed to one of the more sensational tabloids that the PIRA were employing a crack mercenary sniper from Germany on contract. This phantom figure had a great run, and I believe he was referred to in Continental and other papers as well. He was supposed to be paid a bonus of five hundred pounds for each British soldier he killed. In between times, he lived under heavy guard in a house in the Falls, wearing dark glasses and eating car-rots to protect his night vision. Nobody, of course, ever interviewed him, for the simple reason he never existed. But that didn't affect the reputation he achieved. It seemed that if the British said the casualties were caused by a sniper from Mars, it would have

1 MacStiofain, Sean, *Memoirs of a Revolutionary*, p. 301. (An excellent personal ac-count by one of the founding members of the PIRA.)
2 MacStiofain, Sean, *Memoirs of a Revolutionary*, p. 302.
3 MacStiofain, Sean, *Memoirs of a Revolutionary*, p. 302.

been printed as fact."[4]

Even Gerry Adams himself, the current president of the Republican political party *Sinn Fein* and also an elected Minister of Parliament for West Belfast, was accused of being involved in sniping at British soldiers in that wild summer of 1972. Former British paratrooper Nigel Mumford witnessed the shooting of his fellow soldier, Francis Bell, who was killed by a hidden sniper while they were on patrol in the Ballymurphy Estate, Belfast. After the shooting, Mumford and his fellow soldiers searched a nearby apartment complex where they thought the shot came from. During the raid, Mumford said he saw Adams. While another PIRA member was ultimately convicted of the shooting, rumors abounded Adams either organized the sniper attack or at least knew of it ahead of time.[5]

It is interesting to note before MacStiofain's efforts in 1972, the PIRA lacked a basic understanding of urban guerrilla sniping. Up until that point, the PIRA was primarily a rural-centric organization. They were still unused to the extreme scrutiny any sniper would be placed under while working in cities like Derry and Belfast. Fortunately, for the PIRA, MacStiofain was the right man at the right time to bring the PIRA out of the dark ages. MacStiofain possessed an unusually agile mind and he always looked for new ways to modernize the movement. When MacStiofain started off with the IRA in the 1950s, he operated in an urban cell in England. He recognized the IRA at that time was not prepared for urban guerrilla warfare and did not have the equipment, training, or mindset to successfully work in the cities. However, MacStiofain tried everything he could to change this like securing modern communications equipment in order for the IRA to monitor and listen in on British police and military radio traffic.

Consequently, when the newly independent PIRA began its guerrilla campaign in 1970 and started its sniper attacks, MacStiofain was there to modernize the PIRA's

4 MacStiofain, Sean, *Memoirs of a Revolutionary*, p. 302-3.
5 *Times On-Line*, April 4, 2004.

outdated tactics. MacStiofain understood the single most incriminating element of a sniper attack was the gunshot. And since the PIRA had not yet evolved into understanding the tactical importance of using sound suppressors, the one-shot sniping rule was the next best thing. Any experienced military sniper would see the one-shot sniping approach as common sense and part of their standard operating procedure. But, to the inexperienced gunmen fighting for the PIRA in the streets of Belfast, this was a new methodology minimizing their operational signature and allowed them to shoot hundreds of British soldiers and RUC officers without getting caught.

Getting Weapons

The PIRA's new sniping tactics were a much needed change in the way they conducted their sniping business, but they still needed rifles to shoot. Getting good sniper weapons was always a logistical challenge for the PIRA because the British and Northern Ireland authorities did everything they could to keep weapons out of the hands of potential snipers. As we will see later in this chapter, the government of Northern Ireland eventually instituted some of the most restrictive gun control laws in the world just for this reason.

One of the ways the PIRA got its weapons in the early years was from breaking into poorly secured British military bases and then stealing and driving off with their weapons. In this way, the PIRA was able to procure hundreds of weapons to include issued British Army rifles like the accurate, bolt-action Lee-Enfield .303. The PIRA also used other methods like stealing rifles off the docks as they were shipped in from mainland England, buying guns and ammunition from British soldiers who were looking to supplement their low army salaries, and by going through established black market arms dealers who had no problem selling weapons to the PIRA to make a profit.

While getting good sniper rifles here and there provided a trickle of much needed weapons, what the growing PIRA really needed was an established weapons supply system that could secretly and securely provide reliable weapons to support a guerrilla war that might last decades. As the PIRA's campaign took off in 1969, Sean MacStiofain applied his guerrilla mind and organizational ability towards creating such a system. MacStiofain realized when the newly appointed Provisional Army Council was created, the PIRA's weapon situation was in poor shape. Local Republican defense committees were forced to acquire a motley collection of second-rate weapons by hook or crook, from anyone who was willing to supply them. Interestingly enough, even some Protestant Loyalist arms merchants were willing to deal with the fledgling PIRA in order to make a dollar. However, these arms dealers knew the PIRA was desperate for guns and charged them ridiculously high prices. [6]

In response, MacStiofain and the leadership of the PIRA created a supply department that employed procurement specialists who did nothing but acquire weapons through the black market. Now, a single PIRA entity purchased the weapons for the entire movement, as opposed to different local buyers competing for the same arms. In this manner, the PIRA brought down the prices of the black market arms dealers so they could buy more weapons for the movement. The PIRA's quartermaster section did more than just acquire guns, they also took responsibility for ensuring they

---

6 MacStiofain, Sean, *Memoirs of a Revolutionary*, p. 147.

An IRA honor guard fires their G3 assault rifles in memory of the 'Gibraltar Three' killed by the British SAS.

were serviceable and ready for combat. The quartermasters inspected the weapons and repaired them if required. This type of close-in professional inspection was necessary because something as simple as a failed firing pin could result in the untimely death of the volunteer whose life depended on a perfectly functioning weapon.[7]

By taking an organized systematic approach, the PIRA created a covert logistical system that could provide the weapons the movement demanded. This system proved to be critical because there was a constant requirement for weapons as the guerrilla war devoured guns just like it consumed men and money. Weapons caches would be discovered by informants and turned over to the police, rifles broke down through constant use, and sometimes guns had to be unceremoniously ditched after a shooting in order to protect the user from being caught in the possession of incriminating physical evidence. Since the weapon supply system the PIRA set up in the early part of their movement relied mainly on firearms procured domestically, the British were able to slowly put a squeeze on these efforts through stricter gun laws, tighter border controls, and an increasingly intense counter-insurgency campaign. However, the PIRA's movement still demanded firepower. But, where would a new supply of modern, effective weapons come from? Perhaps the PIRA's brothers across the sea, in the New World, could provide some help.

Friends in the United States

One of these Irish brothers was George Harrison, who moved from Ireland, across the Atlantic to New York City in 1938, and helped set up the PIRA's North American gunrunning network. Harrison was primarily a deal maker - he took money that was supplied to him and then made the actual transactions with a variety of gun merchants both in the United States and overseas, like the Corsican mob. Harrison was eventually caught and tried in the U.S. in 1981, but was acquitted. By then, it was too late. It is estimated over the course of twenty-five years, Harrison successfully infiltrated 2500 weapons and more than a million rounds of ammunition into Ireland. The work of

7 MacStiofain, Sean, *Memoirs of a Revolutionary*, p. 148.

Harrison alone was enough to sustain the PIRA movement for years and to keep PIRA snipers plying their deadly trade indefinitely.

Harrison was able to buy these weapons only because of the financial muscle provided by the Irish Northern Aid Committee (NORAID). NORAID was created in 1969 as a legitimate fund raising organization to provide financial help for the people of Northern Ireland, like families of PIRA political prisoners who suffered under the jackboot of British rule. NORAID's mission statement says, "Irish Northern Aid is an American based membership organization that supports through peaceful means, the establishment of a democratic 32-county Ireland. Our Strategy: To develop a broad coalition of supporters for Irish Unity through organizing and educating the public, our members, political leaders, and the media. To support the current Peace Process, including the full implementation of the Good Friday Agreement which was endorsed by the vast majority of the Irish people. To support a process of National reconciliation and equality for all the citizens of Ireland. Membership: In keeping with the principles of the 1916 Proclamation, Irish Northern Aid is open to anyone who shares these values."

While NORAID insisted they did not support the PIRA, the American courts won a decision in 1981 forcing NORAID to list the PIRA as a 'foreign principal'. However, after legal wrangling by NORAID's lawyers, this ruling was reversed in 1984 and the money continued to flow to help the, "poor people of Northern Ireland suffering under British occupation." Critics of NORAID, both in Britain and America, argued as soon as the money faucet was turned back on in 1984, the PIRA's weapons also started to flow again.

One would be oversimplifying the PIRA's North American gunrunning system if they said it consisted of just Harrison, his accomplices, and NORAID. If this was so, then weapons coming into Northern Ireland from the United States would have been shut off with the cases made against Harrison and NORAID. Truth be told, the PIRA had numerous contacts in America, like private citizens of Irish descent and the Irish mob operating out of New York and Boston, that funneled weapons into PIRA supply depots. It has even been said an employee at Barrett Firearms in Tennessee was a PIRA sympathizer and was responsible for getting several Barrett .50 caliber sniper rifles into the hands of PIRA snipers. Whatever the means employed, the PIRA and their North American supporters were able to purchase thousands of weapons for the PIRA to include Armalite AR-18s, Colt M-16s, Heckler and Koch G3 assault rifles, and various models of civilian sniper and hunting rifles.

The Libyan Connection

The PIRA was an organization that did not put all their eggs in one basket, so they looked to others arm suppliers in the international community like Libya. Libya's leader, Kadafi, established connections with the PIRA as early as 1972, which resulted in subsequent transfers of money and weapons to Northern Ireland over the next several decades. Unlike some arms transfers with other countries that could take the form of a dozen weapons here and there, Libya shipped the PIRA quantities of weapons in bulk. Over the course of several arms transfers by the Libyans using commercial shipping vessels, the PIRA smuggled in at least one hundred tons of weapons, explosives, and ammunition.

Copyright Eamon Melaugh/Guildhall Press www.ghpress.com

Through the Libyan connection, the PIRA received hundreds of AK-47 assault rifles, AKM machine guns, DSHK heavy machine guns, SAM-7 anti-aircraft missiles, huge amounts of Semtex plastic explosives, and at least one million rounds of ammunition. PIRA leaders jumped for joy over the size of the successful Libyan arms shipments because they received enough hardware now to sustain their guerrilla movement indefinitely. The PIRA sniper who waited patiently in a building somewhere in Belfast now had a variety of weapons to choose from to conduct their attacks. While the average PIRA sniper might not be getting world class sniper rifles to shoot their enemies with, the various assault rifles they did get, did the job just fine in the close confines of Northern Ireland's cities.

While North America and Libya were the PIRA's biggest suppliers, the PIRA system was more diversified than that. Any country or arms dealer that either needed money or PIRA training or held a grudge against Britain could be a potential source of supply. We know the PIRA was able to receive weapons from several continental European countries like Czechoslovakia, Croatia, and Serbia. Also, with the disintegration of the Soviet Union in 1991, a whole new Russian criminal class was available and willing to sell off former Soviet weapons tot he PIRA. And those are just the countries that are known. There were many more transactions which British intelligence never learned about. The bottom line was, if the PIRA worked hard enough, they could get weapons into Northern Ireland covertly, despite England's best counter-insurgency efforts. This in itself was a significant logistical feat considering all of the military, intelligence, and law enforcement assets Britain employed in an attempt to strangle the PIRA's weapons lifeline.

Gun Control in Northern Ireland

An important question to ask is why did the PIRA go to America and Libya to get guns? Was it really that hard to get them in Northern Ireland itself? The answer is 'yes'. From early on, the British mainland authorities and the Northern Ireland government understood tight gun control was needed to keep firearms from falling into PIRA hands. Subsequently, several gun control laws were passed in Northern Ireland reflecting the government's desire to tightly regulate firearms. The one gun control law in specific we will focus on is the 65-page Firearms (Northern Ireland) Order 1981 (No. 155 (N.I.2)). This gun control law, one of the most restrictive in all of Europe, must be seen for what it was - a reaction to the PIRA's guerrilla war that had been burning hot for more than a decade. The government wanted to be tough on the PIRA and gun control was one way to keep the pressure on them.

Order 1981 stated anyone who owned, purchased, or possessed a firearm or ammunition had to have a firearm certificate or they would be breaking the law. Additionally, anyone who owned, purchased, or possessed, "any accessory to any such weapon designed or adapted to diminish the noise or flash caused by firing the weapon" - in other words a flash or sound suppressor - must also have a certificate for that device or they would be breaking the law. Both shotguns and high-velocity air rifles were recognized as requiring a firearms certificate. Only recognized, licensed firearms dealers could buy, sell, trade, and repair firearms. Sales or transfers between two private citizens were illegal. Fully automatic firearms were illegal as were any semi-automatic or pump-action firearms other than .22 caliber rimfire weapons. Any exceptions must be approved by the Secretary of State. The Secretary of State also reserved the right to prohibit the transfer of firearms or ammunition from one place to another in Northern Ireland, to prohibit a transfer of these items from Great Britain to Northern Ireland, and to prohibit these items from being exported out of Northern Ireland itself.

Firearms dealers could sell legal weapons to private citizens, but the dealers had to report these transactions to the police and the dealers had to show they had taken the appropriate measures to ensure the true identity of the purchaser. The dealer also had to keep a record of all their transactions for the last ten years so police could check their records. Also, any gunsmithing done to a weapon, like alterations or repairs, had to be reported to the police within 48 hours. If a dealer failed to abide by these regulations, they were committing a crime.

There were some loopholes in the firearms certificate process, but they were microscopic. For instance, a citizen with no firearms certificate could possess a firearm licensed in someone else's name, but only if they were transporting the weapon for that person and it was for sporting purposes only. A citizen could have in their possession an unlicensed firearm if they were the member of a recognized shooting club and they were involved in target practice. And, a citizen could possess an unlicensed low-velocity air gun if they were shooting at an established range.

If a citizen did legally purchase and possess a firearm, they still had to use it in a lawful manner. Legally carrying a weapon, but with the intent to commit a criminal action, was a crime. As intended by the government, the various legal offences started to stack up if one was in possession of an illegal firearm. For example, trespassing with a weapon was illegal (such as PIRA members conducting home invasions), firing weapons in a public place or road was illegal (like PIRA snipers firing in urban environments), and anyone who spent three years in prison (like the hundreds of PIRA members who cycled through the legal system) could not legally own a firearm.

When applying for a firearms certificate, the government ensured they knew

IRA Firing Line

Masked IRA shooters practice firing a hodgepodge of weapons, including submachine guns, carbines, and WW II-era rifles.

Copyright Eamon Melaugh/Guildhall Press www.ghpress.com

exactly who they were giving a weapon to. The applicant had to provide up to four pictures of themselves and providing false information on the certificate (like PIRA members using fake identification cards) was a crime. Plus, the person applying for the firearms certificate had to prove to the police they had a good reason for wanting to possess a firearm. Once a citizen had a firearm certificate, which was valid for three years, it could be revoked at anytime by the police if that person was deemed a threat to public safety. So, if a citizen acquired a legal, licensed weapon and then joined the PIRA, their firearm certificate would be revoked as soon as the police found out about their affiliation with that illegal organization.

The police had wide authority to enforce Order 1981 and judges could issue warrants authorizing police to enter and search any private residence or premise to search for and seize firearms. The police could also conduct these searches in order to inspect the records of gun dealers. On the streets, the police had the authority under 'reasonable cause' to question and search any person who was suspected of carrying a firearm. As a result, any PIRA member looking suspicious or unnatural during an operation was inviting themselves to be searched and questioned. Since the authorities placed such a strong emphasis on forensic science, citizens, when asked in writing by the police, had to submit their firearms for ballistics testing. This allowed the police to compare the ballistics of any given firearm with that of incriminating bullets found at a crime scene fired by a PIRA gunman.

Punishments for violating these gun laws varied. If a PIRA member was caught in possession of unregistered ammunition, they could receive a five-year prison sentence. If a PIRA member was caught in possession of an unregistered handgun, they faced a ten-year prison sentence. For example, Irish National Liberation Army member Christopher McWilliams - who would later gain notoriety as the trigger man who killed Protestant paramilitary leader Billy Wright - was once arrested for illegal possession of a handgun with intent to cause injury and was given a fourteen-year jail sentence. And if, let us say, a PIRA sniper was caught in possession of a rifle and was determined to be using said rifle for criminal intent, such as shooting a British soldier, the sniper could face life in prison. Violations of many of these gun laws demanded a minimum, automatic five-year prison sentence to deter anyone from breaking the law in the first place. The authorities did not want some slick-talking lawyer in the pay of the PIRA's political arm, Sinn Fein, to come in and get a PIRA gunman off the hook through tricky legalese (although this still happened). The government wanted PIRA members to do hard time before seeing the light of day.

Even with these strict gun laws, many citizens did apply for and receive firearm certificates. This was possible since a person could state 'personal protection' as a legitimate reason for requesting legal ownership of a firearm. This opened the door for Protestants to argue they felt threatened by the PIRA so they could get a gun. One statistic for 1996 showed 10,867 firearms certificates were issued in Northern Ireland for the purpose of personal protection. Another record said approximately 90,000 firearm certificates, for all reasons, not just personal protection, were issued in Northern Ireland.[8]

True, a person could legally get a hunting rifle that could be used for sniping, but the authorities would know who sold it, who bought it, when the transaction took place, and where the present owner lived. Furthermore, the police could order the owner to provide a ballistic test of their weapon at any time. While a rifle could be legally purchased, the laws made it extremely difficult for it to be used in an illegal manner and have the owner get away with it. The laws were so restrictive with such strict penalties the PIRA was forced to go overseas for their weapons. In this respect, the government's gun laws inside Northern Ireland were effective. However, by going outside the country, the PIRA bypassed the British authorities' entire system of gun control.

IRA Sniper Tactics

As the war progressed from 1969 onwards, the PIRA modified its sniper tactics to meet the changing situation on the ground. Initially, PIRA snipers could get away with relatively unsophisticated tactics since the British and RUC were inexperienced in modern urban guerrilla warfare. Any British soldier or RUC officer wearing a uniform was a target waiting to get hit since they did not blend in with the local populace and openly patrolled the streets and neighborhoods to enforce law and order. These soldiers and officers walking patrols on the streets became favorite targets. Since walking a beat set a pattern, PIRA snipers studied their habits and ambushed them as they made their rounds. Even soldiers and officers driving in the back of open vehicles were targeted, as were those riding inside armored vehicles with open hatches and doors.

Whenever possible, PIRA snipers targeted these patrols as they passed through an intersection. While in an intersection, a shot could be made from all four directions. Consequently, the patrol had a lot of possible sniper positions to look for and they could not cover them all. As the patrol moved through the intersection, the PIRA shooters preferred to target the last person in the patrol. This way, the rest of the patrol

---

8 www.cybershooters.org

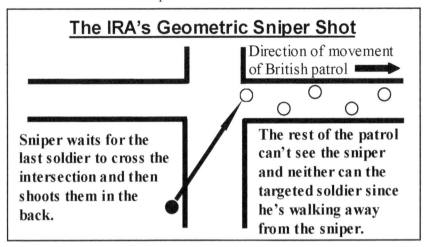

The IRA's Geometric Sniper Shot

Direction of movement of British patrol

Sniper waits for the last soldier to cross the intersection and then shoots them in the back.

The rest of the patrol can't see the sniper and neither can the targeted soldier since he's walking away from the sniper.

was already past the open area and moving down the street. When the last man in the patrol was shot, the other members could not see the sniper and thus could not respond effectively. All they could do was grab their wounded comrade and drag them to cover while the sniper made their getaway.

The urban areas the PIRA snipers worked in allowed them to manipulate the streets and buildings in other ways. For instance, as a British patrol passed an intersection, a PIRA sniper would fire from down a street, from a door opened slightly. Since the sniper was firing at an angle, from a row of connected residences, the targeted patrol had no idea which specific residence the shot came from. As the patrol tried to figure out where the shot came from, the sniper would close the door, lock it, stash the weapon, and then walk out the back of the building free of incriminating evidence. To the soldiers looking for the sniper, the row of buildings used by the sniper formed a visual and physical barrier allowing the shooter to make a getaway.

Soldiers and officers providing security at checkpoints and installations were also inviting targets. This meant any soldier or officer checking licenses at a roadside checkpoint, directing traffic at a busy intersection, or inspecting purses at the entrance to a court house were targets. To target these stationary men, PIRA snipers had to maneuver within shooting distance to take a shot, while remaining undetected. This required more skill and gave British counter-sniper measures a better chance to work. But, the complex urban environment still gave the prepared sniper the upper hand.

The PIRA resorted to all sorts of tricks or 'come-ons' to get a British soldier or RUC officer in their sights. Police officers trying to control groups of rioting people made a good target for a PIRA sniper hidden somewhere in the city. Soldiers providing security for bomb disposal specialists checking out a reported car bomb (called in by the sniper's crew) were targets. Any soldier or officer responding to any sort of incident like a robbery, IED, or car bomb did so with the realization they might be walking into an intentional trap meant to place them under the crosshairs of a waiting PIRA sniper.

In the cities, PIRA snipers had a variety of shooting platforms to choose from. A favorite choice was anything that was community property to include churches, apartment buildings, and businesses. Community property was preferable because no individual owned it and thus no one could be charged with a crime for letting the PIRA snipers use it. Another good choice for a PIRA sniper was an abandoned house or building. Again, no individual owned these buildings and because they were unoccupied, there was no one present to identify the PIRA snipers and give sworn testimony to the police after a shooting. Many a soldier and officer would have preferred these abandoned buildings be razed to the grown to prevent their use by PIRA shootists, but because of the environment they operated in, this was politically unacceptable.

The PIRA also made use of home invasions when it was required to take a shot at the enemy. For example, in early 1993, a PIRA hit team tried to assassinate Johnny 'Mad Dog' Adair - the ruthless leader of the Protestant Loyalist Ulster Freedom Fighters (UFF) - by means of a home invasion. The team knew where Adair lived so they planned to gun him down as he left his residence. The team hijacked a car and entered a home across the street from where Adair lived. A two-man security team stayed on the bottom floor while the shooter went upstairs and took aim out of a window with a rifle. The sniper team stayed in position for several hours, hoping to put a bullet into Adair but, he never showed up and they called the operation off.[9]

The home invasion had some complications because it required a small team to break into the house and possibly control a family. The sniper team, once in the home, had to be well trained in order not to leave behind any incriminating evidence like fingerprints or trace fibers. Plus, since they were in close proximity to the family, the family may be able to identify them at a later date from their voices, accents, or mannerisms. To complicate matters further, what about random phone calls, bathroom breaks, friends and family coming over unannounced to visit, or nosy neighbors?

As far as one can tell, the PIRA pioneered the method of conducting sniper attacks in an urban environment while hidden inside a vehicle. One PIRA sniper crew first used this method in the late 1970's while working in Belfast. For some reason, this method was not picked up by the rest of the PIRA and it was not until the 1990's that it was used again by a PIRA sniper crew working in South Armagh.

The Goldfinger Sniper Crew, South Armagh

Without doubt, the most notorious PIRA sniper team was the Goldfinger crew working out of the PIRA stronghold of South Armagh. The Goldfinger crew (Goldfinger was their code name) brought back the earlier PIRA tactic of shooting from inside a car. Shooting from a car gave them good concealment for their attack, provided them a mobile platform that was also their means of escape, and allowed them to put miles between them and the place of the attack in minutes.

The Goldfinger sniper crew were a seasoned lot and developed a successful guerrilla sniping methodology. They used a Mazda 626 hatchback as a shooting platform and installed a bulletproof metal shield in the back. A one-foot by one-foot shooting port was cut in the middle of the armor. The idea was the shooter, later identified as Michael Caraher, would fire through the port in the armor, then release a sliding armored door that covered the opening. So, as the Goldfinger crew drove off, any incoming enemy fire would strike the metal plate, protecting them until they escaped. The Goldfinger crew consisted of a driver, the shooter, and a man riding shotgun in the passenger seat, armed with an assault rifle. They all wore balaclavas to protect their identity and the shooter wore hearing protection so he would not be deafened

---

9 Dillon, Martin, *The Trigger Men*, p. 210.

IRA Snipers

Two hooded IRA shooters hold their hunting rifles at the ready.

Copyright Eamon Melaugh/Guildhall Press www.ghpress.com

from the blast of the Barrett .50 caliber sniper rifle he was firing.

On February 12, 1997, the Goldfinger crew targeted a vehicle checkpoint in Bessbrook Mill on Green Road for attack. They studied the terrain, the checkpoint itself, and came up with a plan of attack. On that morning, the three-man sniper team approached the checkpoint and parked the Mazda 626 near a concrete bus shelter about 120 yards away. The rear of the Mazda faced the checkpoint. The passenger riding shotgun lifted the rear hatch of the car and propped it open with a piece of wood so the shooter, Michael Caraher, had a clear shot through the armored firing port. Caraher got into position behind the big Barrett rifle and took aim at the checkpoint. But, he could not get a good bead on a target because the British soldiers were hidden behind the corrugated steel of the guard shack. What the Goldfinger crew needed was some sort of bait so a soldier would expose themselves.

This live bait took the form of Mrs. Lorrain McElroy as she approached the checkpoint in her car. When she got close to the guard shack, British soldier Lance Bombardier Stephen Restorick asked her to stop so he could check her identification. However, the young soldier had to step out from the protection of the guard shack and into the open to check Mrs. McElroy's driver license. This was all Caraher needed. He took aim through his scope, sighted in on Restorick, and squeezed the trigger. The massive .50 caliber bullet left the Barrett's muzzle traveling 2800 feet per second and struck Restorick's bullpup assault rifle. The fast-moving bullet fragmented upon impact, sending a piece of metal through Restorick's buttocks and out the side of his body. A piece of the gunsight unpredictably careened into the car, gashing Mrs. McElroy in the forehead.

As Restorick crumpled to the ground, Caraher pulled on a cord attached to the block of wood propping the rear hatch open. The hatch dropped shut and the driver took off at a high rate of speed. As Caraher and crew sped away from the checkpoint, another PIRA car scouted the way ahead, ensuring the sniper team would not drive blindly into a British quick reaction force or a hasty checkpoint. The PIRA scout car led them to a rock quarry where other PIRA members were already waiting. The sniper team dropped off their weapons and car, which were in turn spirited away to a hiding place. Caraher's team was taken to a safehouse where they immediately began their counter-forensics procedures, showering to wash off any gunpowder residue and placing their clothes in a bag to burned.[10]

Unfortunately for Stephen Restorick, he was the last British soldier to be killed before the 1997 cease fire agreement and the ninth victim of Caraher and his crew. Only two months after this deadly attack, the Goldfinger sniper crew, to include Michael Caraher, were arrested and their Barrett .50 caliber rifle seized. Caraher was later tried and convicted, receiving multiple life sentences and a 105-year prison term. The dismantling of the deadly Goldfinger sniper crew brought a sigh of relief to the soldiers and officers who continued working in South Armagh. While the capture and imprisonment of Caraher and his crew should have been heralded as a counter-insurgency victory, some troubling rumors began to surface.

But what kind of rumors could sour such a clear success? After all, a skilled sniper and hardened killer was brought to justice and would rot to death in a cold British prison. The evidence against Caraher was overwhelming and he had no hope of beating the system. The British authorities conducted a thorough investigation, resulting in an overwhelming mountain of incriminating physical and forensic evidence. Case closed. However, the case seemed too solid, almost like there was someone on the inside who already knew about the Goldfinger crew and their activities and tipped off the authorities.

These rumors appeared to be confirmed when the *Sunday Times* ran an article about Restorick on June 20, 2004 entitled, 'Last British soldier murdered by IRA 'sacrificed' for a spy.' The Restorick family, who suffered the painful loss of their son, wanted some answers. Were the rumors true? Did the British have an informant on the inside who knew about the sniper attacks? Is it true the authorities knew the Goldfinger crew was planning an attack, but did nothing to warn the troops on the ground because the military did not want to 'burn' their source? Was, in fact, Restorick sacrificed, used as live bait, to build a bigger case against the Goldfinger crew and to learn more about the PIRA structure in South Armagh?

After reading the article, the Restorick family made an official complaint against the Northern Ireland government and demanded answers about their son's death. In their official complaint, they cited damning statements from the article in the *Sunday Times*. The disturbing evidence of a cover up by British authorities included the following taken from the Police Ombudsman for Northern Ireland December 13, 2006 report:

- The murder of Stephen Restorick was preventable, since a special army surveillance unit bugged the PIRA sniper team and readied a SAS 'hit team' to arrest them.
- The police were monitoring the movements of the Mazda on the day of Restorick's murder and an interception team was ready for deployment. The *Sunday Times* quoted a source who stated, "The surveillance group and the SAS hit team went on standby ready to intercept the IRA. They picked up their weapons and got into their vehicles,

---

10 Harnden, Toby, *Bandit Country*, p.387-9. (Without question, the best book available concerning the PIRA in South Armagh.)

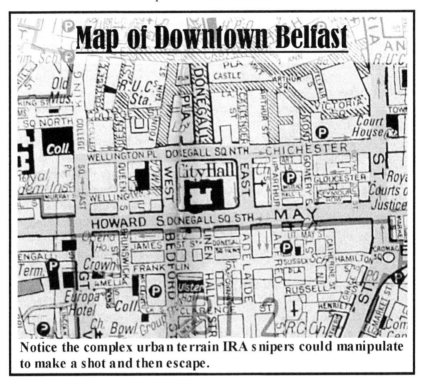

Map of Downtown Belfast

Notice the complex urban terrain IRA snipers could manipulate to make a shot and then escape.

ready to move. At that point the TCG came on the radio to order them to stand down and remain in the camp. They couldn't believe it. They protested and again told the TCG that the sniper was on his way to Bessbrook. Again our blokes were told not to move."

- The arrest team was prevented from intervening on the orders of a senior RUC police officer, just forty minutes before the attack.

- A Special Forces soldier using the pseudonym Tony Buchanan, who worked under cover in Northern Ireland for nine years, was the source of the claims.

- The article suggests that sources believe the order to stand down was made to protect an informant.

- Senior police commanders are believed to have wanted to avoid a gun battle so as not to damage fragile peace negotiations.

- Security sources suggest the AK-47 weapon being carried by Bernard McGinn, who was riding shotgun in the sniper attack, contained a tracker beacon, which provided the police with knowledge of its location.

- A possibility exists McGinn or someone else connected to the sniper team was cooperating with the security forces and their identity was protected.

- During the lull in sniper attacks before the shooting of Stephen Restorick, intelligence analysts instigated the planting of listening and tracking devices to create a better picture of the sniper suspects.

- The 14th Intelligence and Security Regiment were tasked by a Special Branch led Tasking and Coordination Group (TCG) to plant bugging devices on the sniper team.

- The police were fully aware of the movements of the sniper team for a tracking and listening device was installed in a Mazda motor vehicle used by the sniper team.

In spite of these strong allegations and after more than two years of investigation by the police ombudsman, there was insufficient evidence to substantiate the Restorick family's accusations. Disturbingly, there was a lack of evidence because the British authorities destroyed unknown quantities of documents relating to the case. If there was evidence supporting the Restoricks' claim, it was intentionally destroyed after the Goldfinger crew's last operation. The unsatisfying end to the investigation removed the last shred of hope the Restorick family had for justice being served in the killing of their son.

However, the main blow to justice came years before with the signing of the Good Friday Peace Agreement in 1998. An integral part of the agreement was imprisoned members on both sides would be released as part of the general reconciliation process. Even as Caraher was sentenced to a century in prison after the shooting, he laughed at the court because he knew he would be out after the signing of the peace agreement. And he was right. In 2000, Michael Caraher was released from prison, along with hundreds of other convicted PIRA members, and allowed to return to his home. One of the PIRA's most notorious snipers was back on the streets in the name of national healing.

In 2006, the British army wrote a summary report about its efforts in Northern Ireland entitled *Operation Banner,* which said this about the Goldfinger sniper crew: "In 1990 PIRA deployed a new weapon – a Barrett .50" heavy calibre rifle – to South Armagh and for a while this grabbed headlines. It was first used at Crossmaglen on 16 March 1990. The round struck a soldier's helmet, but he was not seriously injured. Thereafter PIRA snipers killed seven soldiers in South Armagh before effective counter-measures were found. Although tragic, this episode was a relatively small blip in the statistics of the campaign."

IRA Sniper Statistics

Fortunately, for the sake of research, the CAIN (Conflict Archive on the INternet) has extensive resources for studying the conflict in Northern Ireland to include Malcolm Sutton's *An Index of Deaths from the Conflict in Northern Ireland.* Sutton's detailed research describes the circumstances of every death during The Troubles to include killings by IRA snipers. According to Sutton's research, 218 people were killed by IRA snipers (to include shootings by the Real IRA, the Official IRA, the Provisional IRA, and the few sniper attacks made by the Irish National Liberation Army – INLA). The majority of the victims were soldiers in the British Army, officers of the RUC, and then members of various hated Protestant paramilitary organizations.

Over the course of the guerrilla war from 1969 to 2001, the PIRA and other Republican paramilitary groups killed 2,054 people with approximately 11% of these deaths caused by snipers. The following is a breakdown of those sniper attacks by year:

- 1969: No recorded sniper deaths of 3 total deaths. Start of the PIRA campaign.
- 1970: No recorded sniper deaths of 17 total deaths.
- 1971: 24 sniper deaths of 98 total deaths. 24% of total.
- 1972: 50 sniper deaths of 267 total deaths. 19% of total.
- 1973: 28 sniper deaths of 132 total deaths. 21% of total.
- 1974: 21 sniper deaths of 148 total deaths. 14% of total.

Goldfinger's Sniper Platform

photo by Toby Harden

Here is a picture of the Goldfinger crew's captured Mazda sniping vehicle. Notice the armored plate and the hole cut out from the middle where the sniper fired from.

- 1975: 7 sniper deaths of 125 total deaths. 6% of total.
- 1976: 12 sniper deaths of 154 total deaths. 8% of total.
- 1977: 14 sniper deaths of 75 total deaths. 19% of total.
- 1978: 7 sniper deaths of 61 total deaths. 11% of total.
- 1979: 11 sniper deaths of 102 total deaths. 11% of total.
- 1980: 5 sniper deaths of 51 total deaths. 10% of total.
- 1981: 7 sniper deaths of 70 total deaths. 10% of total.
- 1982: 5 sniper deaths of 83 total deaths. 6% of total.
- 1983: No recorded sniper deaths of 61 total deaths.
- 1984: 4 sniper deaths of 48 total deaths. 8% of total.
- 1985: 1 sniper death of 48 total deaths. 2% of total.
- 1986: No recorded sniper deaths of 40 total deaths.
- 1987: 2 sniper deaths of 71 total deaths. 3% of total.
- 1988: 5 sniper deaths of 70 total deaths. 7% of total.
- 1989: 1 sniper death of 54 total deaths. 2% of total.
- 1990: 2 sniper deaths of 52 total deaths. 4% of total.
- 1991: No recorded sniper deaths of 50 total deaths.
- 1992: 4 sniper deaths of 40 total deaths. 10% of total.
- 1993: 7 sniper deaths of 38 total deaths. 18% of total.
- 1994: No recorded sniper deaths of 25 total deaths. Temporary cease fire in effect.
- 1995: 1 sniper death of 7 total deaths. 14% of total.
- 1996: No recorded sniper deaths of 13 total deaths.
- 1997: 1 sniper death out of 5 total deaths. 20% of total.
- 1998: No recorded sniper deaths of 36 total deaths. Good Friday Peace Accords.
- 1999-2001: No recorded sniper deaths of 12 total deaths.

These statistics reveal the PIRA used sniping as just one part of a larger guerrilla campaign. Most killings were accomplished through IEDs (Improvised Explosive Devices), car bombs, drive-bys, and close-in assassinations. These statistics also reflect the fact, over time, sniping became less feasible for the PIRA because of the government's counter-sniper measures. From 1971-1974, the PIRA conducted more than half of their lethal sniper attacks, killing 124 people. Over the next twenty-five years, the PIRA killed less than 100 people in sniper attacks. The British military and RUC learned from their early years and changed their tactics. British soldiers stopped standing at unprotected checkpoints and began observing the terrain in sniper-proof guard towers. Soldiers stopped walking from one point to another and started traveling in armored cars. Or, patrols were ferried from one point to another in helicopters. Soldiers began wearing modern body armor and using more effective tactics when on foot patrol. Also, the government's forensic onslaught made sniper attacks more difficult from a counter-forensics viewpoint. As a result, it was easier for the PIRA to blow up an enemy patrol by a remote control bomb than it was to shoot them in person.

Another reason for the decrease in PIRA sniper attacks was the government's own increasingly aggressive use of snipers. As British patrols moved in Northern Ireland's cities, they were regularly covered by static sniper teams on the look out for PIRA snipers. During large rallies and rioting, counter-sniper teams provided overwatch for their fellow soldiers and police who were actually down at street level battling it out with the brick throwing crowds. While the PIRA snipers employed many clever tactics, some times their enemy's counter-sniper tactics were better. When this was the case, the PIRA paid the price. Sutton's research reveals at least seven PIRA sniper team members were killed during their operations:

- On September 29, 1972, James Quigley of the PIRA was killed by the British Army. He was shot during an attempted sniper attack on a British Army foot patrol on Albert Street, Lower Falls, Belfast.
- On December 27, 1972, Eugene Devlin of the PIRA was killed by the British Army. He was shot during an attempted sniper attack on a British Army patrol on Townsend Street, Strabane, County Tyrone
- On May 18, 1973, Sean McKee, of the PIRA was killed by the British Army. He was shot during an attempted sniper attack on a British Army foot patrol on Fairfield Street, Ardoyne, Belfast.
- On April 17, 1977, Trevor McKibben of the PIRA was killed by the British Army. He was shot while carrying a rifle on Flax Street, Ardoyne, Belfast.
- On February 22, 1986, Anthony Gough, of the PIRA was killed by the British Army. He was shot after being involved in a sniper attack on the Fort George British Army base, Derry.
- On September 14, 1986, James McKernan of the PIRA was killed by the British Army. He was shot after being involved in a sniper attack on a British Army foot patrol on Andersonstown Road, Belfast
- On March 14, 1988, Kevin McCracken of the PIRA was killed by the British Army. He was shot during an attempted sniper attack on a British Army foot patrol on Norglen Crescent, Turf Lodge, Belfast.

Armalite AR-18 Assault Rifle

This is the infamous Armalite, the first modern assault rifle the IRA received in large quantities. The folding stock enabled the AR-18 to be easily hidden and its supersonic 5.56 mm round was very accurate. The AR-18 was referred to in the IRA's notorious "The Armalite and The Ballot Box" slogan, meaning the IRA would simultaneously pursue a military and a political campaign.

PIRA Sniping and the Troubles

While the sniper deaths inflicted by the PIRA are revealing, they do not tell the whole story. Far more people than the 218 deaths listed in Sutton's study were wounded in sniper attacks but survived. An estimated five times the number of dead were also wounded by PIRA snipers for an additional 1090 casualties. Some victims were shot in the legs or arms and survived. Others were saved by body armor and helmets. Some received grievous wounds, but were saved by battlefield medics and emergency room teams who became trauma wizards after decades of treating gunshot wounds. No one knows exactly how many people were shot by PIRA snipers, as these statistics were never recorded, drowned out somewhere in the more than 37,000 separate shooting incidents that took place over the course of The Troubles. Additionally, more than 2000 killings out of a total of 3700 deaths have gone unsolved. A number of these victims may have been shot by snipers, but we will never know. This is a testament to the counter-forensic prowess of the Loyalist and Republican paramilitaries who became experts at getting away with murder.

The PIRA's sniping campaign showed real tactical innovation as far as the art of urban guerrilla sniping is concerned. The PIRA was the first guerrilla movement on record to employ a vehicle as a sniper platform. They were the first movement to successfully employ heavy caliber rifles in a sustained sniper campaign. They were the first movement to recognize the threat of forensic investigation and then employ disciplined counter-forensic methods during their sniper operations. Also, the PIRA was able to continually supply its snipers with weapons despite some of the most restrictive gun laws in the world and despite being physically isolated by virtue of Northern Ireland being part of an island. Fortunately, for the soldiers, police, and citizens of Northern Ireland, the 1998 Good Friday Peace Accords have taken root and have silenced the PIRA's sniper campaign for the foreseeable future.

Chapter 12

The Palestinian-Israeli Sniper War

photo by www.dragunov.net

We know only one word: Jihad, Jihad, Jihad. When we stopped the intifada, we did not stop the jihad for the establishment of a Palestinian state whose capital is Jerusalem.
-Yasser Arafat, Chairman of the PLO, 1996

When our enemies usurp some Islamic lands, Jihad becomes a duty binding on all Muslims. In order to face the usurpation of Palestine by the Jews, we have no escape from raising the banner of Jihad.
– Article 15, Hamas Charter

The Road to War

While the history of conflict between Jews and Muslims extends back to the creation of Islam in the Seventh Century A.D., the beginning of modern hostilities finds its roots in the Balfour Declaration of 1917, which outlined Britain's new policy towards the Palestine Territory - the acceptance of a Jewish homeland in Palestine. From then on, a flood of Jewish émigrés poured into the Territory, creating rising political and social pressures that eventually led to rupture. In 1948, Palestine's Jews declared independence from Britain. The Jewish state of Israel was formally created. Immedi-

210

Yassir Arafat, wearing sunglasses at a press conference in Amman, Jordan, 1970, believed Israel could only be successfully pressured through guerrilla warfare.

ately, the surrounding Arab states pounced on the new nation, trying to annihilate it at its birth. Troops from Syria, Jordan, Egypt, Iraq, and Lebanon, along with armed groups of Palestinian Arabs, all marched against Israel. However, with a ferocity born from desperation, Israel defeated all comers. An ensuing peace treaty brokered by the United Nations resulted in a greatly expanded Israel, with the Gaza Strip falling under control of Egypt, and the West Bank being occupied by Jordan.

This first war set the stage for an unbroken string of continuing violence, engulfing Israel for the next sixty years. In 1956, Egypt nationalized the Suez Canal and refused to allow Israeli shipping to pass through it. With British and French support, Israel launched a punishing attack and occupied the Gaza Strip and the entire Sinai Peninsula. In 1967, Israel launched a preemptive strike which ignited the Six-Day War. At the end of this fighting, Israel soundly trounced Syria, Jordan, Egypt, and Iraq and wrested control of the Gaza Strip and the Sinai Peninsula from Egypt, snatched the Golan Heights from Syria, and seized the West Bank from Jordan.

From 1969 to 1970, Egypt fought a war of attrition against Israel on the Sinai border, hoping to wear out Israel's military resources over time. Then, in 1973, Egypt and Syria launched a surprise attack which met with initial success and then ended with another humiliating defeat for both Arab nations. Fighting erupted again in 1982 when Israel, provoked by a steady stream of rocket attacks, invaded Lebanon and pummeled Syrian forces and various Arab and Palestinian militias. While Israel occupied southern Lebanon for the next eighteen years until 2000, it was engaged in a continuous guerrilla war with Hezbollah (The Party of God), which was created to resist the Israeli occupiers. Hezbollah and Israeli went at each other's throats again when Israel conducted a limited but destructive invasion of Lebanon for a second time in 2006.

A New Threat: Guerrilla Warfare

One of Israel's enemies understood they could not defeat Israel using conventional means of warfare. His name was Yasser Arafat. In 1959, Arafat formed the Palestinian National Liberation Movement, better known by the acronym FATAH. In 1964, as Arafat expanded his organization, the Arab League created the Palestinian Liberation Organization (PLO) whose goal was the destruction of Israel. Unlike his conventionally minded peers in the Arab League, Yasser Arafat offered a non-traditional solution to the problem posed by Israel. Arafat believed the only way to fight Israel was through a protracted guerrilla campaign. By 1969, Arafat and his Fatah movement gained enough support that Fatah became the dominant member within the PLO and Arafat was elected chairman.

From 1969 onwards, the PLO, under the stewardship of Arafat, waged a protracted insurgency to overthrow the Jewish state. This unconventional war was not fought with planes, tanks, and artillery, but with suicide bombers, ambushes, car bombs, snipers, kidnappings, drive by shootings, mass murder, and terror, all directed at the Jewish state. Other forms of pressure were used against Israel as well, as shown during the first Intifada (uprising) of 1987 where riots, stone throwing, boycotts, strikes and other forms of civil disobedience were used to pressure Israel and turn world opinion against the Jews. While the Intifada raged in Israel's backyard, in the Gaza Strip and the West Bank, new threats were forming. Out of the 1987 Intifada grew a new, more radical Islamic group known by its acronym, HAMAS. Hamas was more hardline than the PLO, rejected any sort of reconciliation with Israel, and its sole purpose was the destruction of the Jewish state. Consequently, as Israel ventured into the new millennium, it found itself less threatened by other Arab states, but mired in the sticky, bottomless pit of a vicious, complex, widespread guerrilla war.

The Urban Terrain

Israel's effort to fight the Palestinian insurgency was difficult in part because Israel rapidly grew into an urban nation where the vast majority of the people lived in the cities. For example, by 2007, Jerusalem and Tel Aviv alone housed over a million people. These large, modern, urban areas with concentrated populations and towering structures gave the Palestinian guerrillas excellent terrain to move, hide, and fight in. Complicating the situation even more was the fact many of the urban populations were mixed between Jews and Arabs. This mixing of people was a direct result of Jewish immigrants gradually moving in and forcing out the existing Arab populations, from the capture and occupation of the largely Arab Gaza Strip and West Bank, and the subsequent creation of Jewish settlements in these areas.

The different Arab guerrilla organizations fighting in the occupied territories discovered the familiar surroundings, filled with a supportive population, and combined with favorable urban terrain, allowed them to wage a guerrilla war indefinitely. In the 1.5 million person Gaza Strip (Gaza City itself had a population of 400,000 people in 2007), the Palestinians fought a sustained urban guerrilla war against the Israeli occupation government from 1967 until 2005 when the last Israeli troops pulled out.

The situation was even more complicated in the captured West Bank where the majority of the people were Palestinian Arabs (estimated at 2.5 million people) who

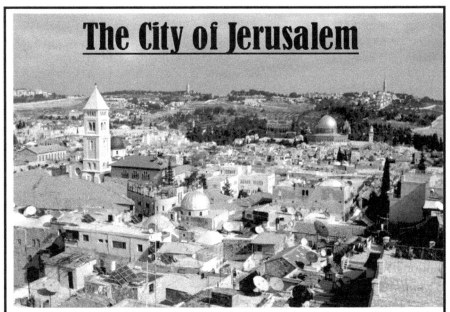

The City of Jerusalem

Many of Israel's cities are modern built up areas that can be exploited by urban guerrillas such as snipers and car bomb and IED cells.

lived in urban areas like East Jerusalem (which was annexed into Israel proper), Jenin, Hebron, Bethlehem, and Nablus. Among this sea of Arabs lived small, isolated settlements of Jews, numbering about 250,000 settlers. As a result, Israel soldiers and settlers in the occupied West Bank found themselves confronted by an entrenched urban insurgency enjoying widespread popular support. The inherent nature of the Palestinian-Israeli conflict, with its dense urban terrain, mixed populations, and lopsided military balance, ensured there would be some level of urban guerrilla sniping by the Arab insurgency. Only time would reveal its scope and intensity.

The Palestinians' Guerrilla Sniping System

From the beginning of the Palestinians' organized resistance against the Jewish state, they employed guerrilla snipers. This was a natural choice since the Palestinian resistance historically lacked heavy weapons such as tanks, artillery or modern anti-tank and anti-aircraft missiles. However, the lowly rifle was always available. Over the years, the Palestinian resistance established means for supplying themselves with weapons to include sniper rifles. To start, weapons were shipped across the Mediterranean Sea and into the Gaza Strip from Lebanon and other foreign donors through privately owned vessels. Also, gunrunners smuggled weapons in from Jordan and then across the border and into the West Bank. Down along the coast, tunnels were dug under the border between the Gaza Strip and Egypt where guns were brought in by the crate loads at night and then distributed to the PLO, Fatah, and Hamas through a covert supply system designed to defeat Israeli scrutiny. For certain, getting assault and sniper rifles was not a problem. The Gaza Strip and West bank were awash in weapons.

213

Over time, the Palestinian resistance developed a clandestine system of training to include sniper instruction. It was relatively easy for unarmed sniper students to cross the border into neighboring Jordan or Egypt, receive sniper training in complete freedom in the safety of the shadow of their Arab big brothers, and then return to the occupied territories, pick up a rifle, and begin their sniping. Also, Palestinian snipers could train in the comfort of their hometowns by attending underground guerrilla training camps run out of a series of safehouses. Since the guerillas had thousands of homes, businesses, and other structures to operate from, the Israelis could not account for even a fraction of them. Therefore, sniper training took place inside the occupied territories, under the noses of their enemies.

Perhaps the biggest strength of the Palestinians' sniper effort was its redundancy as exhibited by the confusing array of Palestinian resistance groups opposing Israel. Let us look at the PLO, which itself was an umbrella organization consisting of: Fatah (which had subgroups like Force 17, Tanzim, and the Al-Aqsa Martyrs' Brigades), the Popular Front for the Liberation of Palestine (PFLP), the Democratic Front for the Liberation of Palestine (DFLP), the Palestinian People's Party (PPP), the Palestine Liberation Front (PLF, Abu Abbas faction), the Arab Liberation Front (ALF), As-Sa'iqa, the Palestine Democratic Union (Fida), the Palestinian Popular Struggle Front (PPSF, Samir Ghawsha faction), the Palestinian Arab Front (PAF), and former members like the Popular Front for the Liberation of Palestine - General Command (PFLP-GC), and Fatah Uprising/Abu Musa Faction. While these groups fell under the PLO umbrella, they may or may not support specific PLO policies.

The end result was the Palestinian resistance became a redundant, covert movement able to conduct sustained guerrilla warfare over space and time in the face of fierce opposition by the best military in the Middle East. In spite of Israel's uncontested superiority in infantry, tanks, artillery, planes, helicopters, and ships, Palestinian snipers continued to plague the Israel Goliath for decades. The Palestinian sniper effort focused on two main goals: the gradual attrition of Israel's military and the infliction of terror on Israeli society. Either one is acceptable - shooting an Israeli soldier in the head helps weaken the Zionist military and shooting down an Israeli woman with a well-aimed bullet strikes terror in the heart of the enemy. In both cases, Palestinian snipers have intentionally fired from urban areas populated by Palestinian civilians to provoke an Israeli reaction resulting in the death of innocent people and the destruction of private property. Taking this into account, Palestinian sniper operations were intended to polarize Palestinian society and alienate the population against Israel by sacrificing their own people.

The Palestinians' Sniper Campaign on the Streets

A central element of the Palestinian sniper campaign was the attrition of Israel's military. Constant pressure against the Israeli military through effective sniping was meant to put the Israelis on the defensive, to raise their body count to an unacceptably high level, to wear them down mentally, and provoke them into an overreaction against the Palestinian people. A favorite target for Palestinian snipers was the Israeli outpost. Since these outposts were static (and therefore could be studied) and often located in predominantly Arab areas, they were a convenient and ever-present source of victims. For example, on April 1, 2001, a hidden sniper took aim at reserve Israeli

Palestinian Snipers - 1969

photo by Getty Images

These well-camouflaged, two-man sniper teams are armed with Mosin-Nagant rifles. These men have obviously received professional instruction and are properly equipped.

Sergeant Yaakov Krenchel as he was on guard duty at an outpost near the West Bank village of Salim. This sniper was accurate, firing a single bullet that struck the young twenty-three year old soldier in the head. Fatefully, before the shooting, soldiers at the outpost complained to their chain of command that the outpost was exposed and adding a camouflaged net could screen the soldiers from enemy snipers. However, the Israeli military had an enormous task in trying to make every single one of its hundreds of outposts sniper-proof. The reality was, if the Palestinian snipers analyzed a large enough sampling of outposts, they were bound to find one more exposed than the others.[1]

Any Israeli soldier on guard duty also makes an inviting target because they can be stalked by a methodical sniper. On April 2, 2001, Israeli Sergeant Danny Darai, a twenty year-old Israeli soldier, was shot and killed by a Palestinian sniper while on guard duty at Rachel's Tomb at the entrance to Bethlehem. In response to the attack, Israeli tanks opened fire on the hotel from which the sniper fired from. The hotel was an ideal sniper platform because of the multitude of windows/doors/openings to fire from, the sturdy construction of the building protected the shooter, and any attack on the hotel by Israel would inflict further infrastructure damage in another urban area in the West Bank. This was precisely the kind of reaction the Palestinians wanted. They wanted a tank to try and kill a lone sniper with a single rifle.[2]

The Palestinian resistance, like the IRA, was also skilled in using 'come alongs' to draw Israeli forces out of their protected combat outposts and into a less secure ambush site. For instance, in February 2003, an Israeli armored patrol investigated a

1 arutzsheva.org.
2 *Terrorist Attacks Causing Israeli Fatalities in the West Bank and Gaza Since the Oslo Agreements*, Gamla Intelligence Newsletter, 13 September 1993.

car suspected of being rigged with explosives, which was parked near the Church of the Nativity in Bethlehem. The Israeli forces responded appropriately, securing the surrounding area until explosive ordnance personnel could be brought in to detonate the car in a controlled manner. However, an Israeli company commander on the scene, Captain Shahar Shmul, was shot and killed by a sniper who opened fire at short range from a nearby alley. Even though Captain Shmul was wearing body armor, it did not matter, since he was shot in the neck. In this case, the car bomb proved to be an effective way to draw out Israeli forces, which in turn opened them up to attack by a hidden sniper who anticipated the Israelis' moves. The Popular Front for the Liberation of Palestine later claimed responsibility for the attack.[3]

The Ofra Checkpoint Shooting

The single most infamous and devastating sniper attack made against the Israelis was on a Sunday, March 3, 2002, near the small town of Ofra, north of the West Bank town of Ramallah. On this day, the Israeli military manned a vehicle checkpoint. As the soldiers stood at their roadblock, most of whom were army reservists, an unseen sniper opened fire, killing one of the soldiers. However, the other members of the checkpoint could not find the sniper and as they looked desperately in all directions they were in turn shot themselves. When the commander of the roadblock stepped out of an old British prison, located near the roadblock, to see what was going on, he was shot and killed. Then, a medic arrived on the scene to treat his fallen comrades and he too was shot and killed. Three other Jewish civilians were shot and killed as they approached the roadblock in their vehicles. In total, ten Israelis were shot and killed by the sniper: seven soldiers and three civilians. Another six were wounded. The soldiers wore flak jackets and helmets, but the sniper managed to shoot around these protective items to get a killing shot. Then the sniper vanished. An investigation of the scene of the shooting later determined a total of twenty-five bullets were fired by the sniper over the span of twenty-five minutes from a distance of seventy-five yards.

After the shooting, criticism of Israel and her military hit the media outlets like an avalanche. Senior members of the Israeli Defense Forces commented publicly it was disgraceful that a lone shooter could kill so many people and get away with it. Aerial Sharon and his government faced severe criticism for blundering time and again and the latest sniper attack was just one more example of his administration's military ineptitude. Military observers wondered if the PLO had finally developed a competent sniper corps and how long it would be until Israel admitted failure in its long-running counter-guerrilla campaign against the PLO and Hamas. In the hypersensitive situation inside Israel, the attack was interpreted as a foreshadowing of half a dozen different doomsday trends. In a knee-jerk reaction to the wave of criticism from all corners, the Israeli military immediately dismantled its most exposed roadblocks and beefed up security at others. Perhaps the Palestinians were waging a new war against the checkpoints and intended to bleed the Israelis by picking off a roadblock at a time while providing freedom of movement for their own guerrilla units?

What happened? How did an alert roadblock come under fire in the morning hours and get decimated by a lone gunman? To many, the horrific results were not surpris-

3 Stahl, Julie, *Israeli Tanks Enforce Bethlehem Curfew After Sniper Shooting*, CNSNews.com Jerusalem Bureau Chief, February 12, 2003.

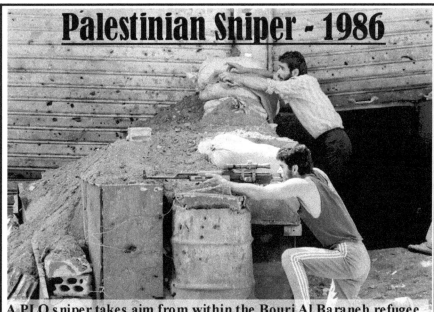

Palestinian Sniper - 1986

A PLO sniper takes aim from within the Bourj Al Baraneh refugee camp against the Christian Amal militia. While displaying no urban sniping skills, all this shooter has to do to avoid arrest is stash his rifle after taking the shot. *photo by Getty Images*

ing. In fact, the soldiers who manned the checkpoint previously told their leaders the roadblock was in a poor position and essentially indefensible as it was located in a valley below adjacent, wooded hills. However, their chain of command failed to provide any additional security measures such as placing an observation post in the hills above the checkpoint in order to forestall just such an attack. Investigators later disclosed they found a single, antiquated, World War II-era, bolt-action carbine on a hill near the checkpoint. The barrel had ruptured and was left behind after the sniper fled the scene. Was that the answer? Did a lone gunman climb on top of a nearby hill with an outdated rifle and pick off ten victims, only stopping after the gun blew up in their hands? Investigators calculated the walls of the valley caused the sounds of the gunshots to echo, making it impossible for the people at the bloody roadblock to determine from what direction the shots came from.

As soon as the gunfire died down, a gaggle of military analysts and experts created possible explanations as to what happened at the checkpoint. Some saw the hand of the IRA behind the shootings. After all, the IRA collaborated with the FARC in Colombia and with Hezbollah in Lebanon, so it made sense they could have trained the PLO. Also, reported tactic among IRA snipers was to leave a gun at the scene of a shooting so British investigators would focus on the wrong weapon and spend their limited forensic assets on a red herring. Other experts with purported access to official investigative findings said the lone gunman theory was all wrong and there was a shooter on one of the hilltops, but there was also another team set up in another location, armed with a machine-gun. In this scenario the sniper was used to distract and expose the soldiers at the checkpoint while the machine-gun team did the real work, mowing down the Israeli soldiers and civilians. Other experts said there were several sniper teams, using modern semi-automatic sniper rifles. Still others surmised no Palestinian sniper was so skilled as to conduct such an effective attack – foreign snipers from Chechnya or Bosnia, or even Arab veterans from Al-Qaeda, must have done the shooting. Some media articles were even floated stating the CIA trained a certain number of Palestinian Authority policemen in sniper tactics and one of these policemen had gone rogue and killed those at Ofra. The rumors were endless.

In October 2004, some light was finally shed on the Ofra checkpoint shootings when the Israelis captured twenty-eight year old Ka'ad Hamad, a member of Yassir Arafat's Fatah movement. Hamad was arrested in his hometown, near Ramallah, not far from Ofra. Under questioning, Hamad confessed to being the shooter who killed the ten people at the Ofra checkpoint more than two years earlier. Hamad stated he trained with an old Mauser 7.92 mm rifle in the wadis around his home until he became a proficient shooter. Hamad also described in full detail the events of the shooting, matching exactly the events pieced together by eyewitnesses and forensic evidence at the crime scene. According to Hamad's testimony, the shooting took place exactly how the 'experts' said it did not. Hamad was not a foreign mercenary or a trained sniper who was blooded in the wars of the Balkans and Caucasus. He was a local man who trained himself to shoot in true guerrilla fashion. He opened fire on the checkpoint at Ofra using a World War II-era Mauser K98. Hamad shot six Israeli soldiers with his bolt-action rifle, reloaded, and continued to shoot more. He kept shooting - and would have shot many more - until the old Mauser blew up in his hands as he was firing it. After that, he left the rifle where it was and fled back to the nearby territory controlled by the Palestinian Authority. Even though the Israeli military and government did not want to admit a lone, untrained man could shoot sixteen people with impunity and then simply walk away, that is exactly what happened.

Suppressed Sniping in Gaza

While the Israeli military was generally unimpressed with the professional ability of most Palestinian snipers (the Ofra checkpoint shooting caused such a stir because it shattered the established pattern), some snipers do not fit this established profile. Howard Linett, an independent journalist, experienced first hand one of the better trained Palestinian snipers in February 2007 as he reported on Israeli military operations in the Gaza Strip. Linett and his escort had just pulled over to offer a group of Israeli soldiers a ride when a small explosion of concrete erupted against the nearby wall, showering Linett and the adjacent soldiers with shards of concrete and bullet fragments. Everyone was stunned for a second, their minds moved in slow motion as they tried to comprehend what just happened. After all, there was no gunshot, just the sound of a metal object slamming into the concrete wall. Linett eventually yelled, "Get Down! Take Cover! Sniper!" As the exposed soldiers frantically took cover inside the building, Linett and his driver took off out of the kill zone. A subsequent inspection of their jeep showed the bullet ricocheted off the wall and struck the vehicle's rear bumper.

Everyone momentarily froze because the sniper used a suppressed weapon. Linett was not sure if the sound they heard was the supersonic *crack!* of the bullet or the sound of the round hitting the concrete wall. Either way, they never heard a gunshot. Linett assumed the sniper did not have a good shot of them so they intentionally tar-

Palestinian Sniper - 2001

photo by Reuters/Corbis

A PLO sniper takes aim during fighting in Bethlehem. The shooter is in the open and has rigged a scope to this bolt-action carbine. One can assume he has little training in the art of urban guerrilla sniping.

geted the building, hoping the soldiers' curiosity would draw someone into the open where the second shot would be dead on. Linett tried to reverse engineer the shooting and guessed if the noise he heard was the sound of the bullet striking concrete, then the sniper must have used a suppressed weapon as well as sub-sonic ammunition. Any weapon could have made the shot, like an SVD with hand-loaded sub-sonic ammunition. A sub-sonic shot would have to be made relatively close – 400 hundred meters or less since we know some sub-sonic ammunition with particularly heavy bullets, like the Russian Vintorez VSS suppressed sniper rifle, is lethal at that range. If the sound Linnet heard was really the supersonic crack of the bullet, then the shooter could be as far out as a thousand meters.[4]

Regardless of the actual sniper equipment used (suppressor and/or sub-sonic ammunition), clearly, some Palestinian snipers learned to exploit the capability of suppressed weapons in an urban environment. In this case, the sniper was able to make a shot in broad daylight, in the presence of alert armed soldiers, and remain undetected. Since the Israeli soldiers had no idea where the sniper shot from, they could not respond to the threat. All they could do was hide while the shooter made a stealthy getaway. If all Palestinian snipers understood the advantage silent sniping gave them, the Gaza Strip and West Bank would be a much more dangerous place for Israeli soldiers and settlers. In spite of successful experiences with suppressed sniping, most

---

4 Linnet, Howard, *Hunting the Terrorist Tunnels of the Gaza Strip*, Feb 17, 2007.

Palestinian snipers have not learned this lesson and still conduct unsuppressed sniping operations where the shooter suffers from a large muzzle flash and gunshot.

Mercenary Snipers

Whenever an unusually skilled sniper is involved in a shooting (like at the Ofra Checkpoint Shootings and the above suppressed sniper attack) the Israelis immediately suspected a foreign sniper was involved. This suspicion is due mainly to the long track record of the Palestinians' relatively poor sniping ability. As a result, when a sniper somewhere in the West Bank or elsewhere began picking of Israeli soldiers with difficult shots, eyebrows were raised.

While Linett was on his tour in Gaza, the Israeli officer escorting him told him there was at least one skilled sniper team working the Gaza Strip. This team, apparently, went to great lengths to plan their operations and only fired from ideal shooting platforms where it was difficult for the Israelis to determine where they fired from. Also, after the shootings, Israeli soldiers never found any incriminating physical evidence like expended brass. This sniper team had recently picked off several Israeli soldiers in the area. One victim was a high-ranking Israeli officer who was riding in a vehicle when he was killed with a single shot. Another soldier was on guard duty when they heard a burst of gunfire. The soldier opened the vision slot of their guard post to see where the gunfire came from. As soon as the observation slot opened, a bullet flew in, killing the soldier. Obviously, the snipers who shot a moving target and fired through a narrow vision port were not just tactically savvy; they were technically proficient shooters.

The word on the street was this particular sniper team, "learned Russian tactics and fieldcraft at one of the private, free enterprise schools run by retired Spetznatz snipers in a former Soviet Republic." This same team was also suspected of receiving sniper training in the United States by CIA subcontractors (another recycling of the CIA-trained PLO sniper squad story). Rumors even circulated the team had practical experience in Chechnya fighting the Russians. As with skilled snipers all over the world, the rumor mill went into overdrive as the shooters' reputation grew. If one were to believe all these rumors, this team was the hardest working snipers around, traveling the globe in search of better sniper schools and fighting all over the world, all without getting arrested, detained, questioned, or shot. Now they were back in Palestine, putting their years of experience and training to use to kill Israelis in the Gaza Strip.

Others, besides Linett and the Israeli unit he worked with, noted the same phenomena. Years earlier, in 2004, a soldier manning an Israeli Defense Force (IDF) rooftop guard post noticed a pair of men walking in the Gaza strip, about five hundred meters away. The two men were talking to each other and then disappeared from view behind some houses. An hour and a half later, this same Israeli soldier got up from where he was sitting in order to move to a different part of the roof. While he stood up, the soldier exposed himself for a few brief seconds, hardly anytime at all, really. Suddenly, he was knocked off his feet as an incoming bullet nailed him in the shoulder. Another soldier on the rooftop returned fire, but did not hit the sniper.

After the bullet was surgically removed from his shoulder, forensic analysis showed the bullet was a 5.56 mm round fired from an M-16. Further investigation revealed the round was fired from five-hundred meters away, in the same area the soldier saw the

Hamas guerrillas pose with an RPG

Hamas has built a guerrilla movement skilled in a variety of tactics from sniping and sabotage to kidnappings and martyr operations.

two men walking and talking. Apparently, these two men created the appearance of normal behavior while they scouted for Israeli victims. Since the men did not have any visible weapons and were not doing anything threatening, the Israeli soldiers could only report what they saw. In the ensuing ninety minutes between the scouting mission and the actual shooting, the sniper team observed the terrain and made a hasty plan. Ultimately, the sniper was able to move into position undetected, rapidly fire off a single shot into a slightly exposed, moving target and then safely leave the area without being caught. Overall, this was a pretty impressive piece of urban guerrilla sniping.

After the shooting on the roof, the Israeli soldier who returned fire at the sniper and caught a brief glimpse of him swore the man looked European. This was not an isolated incident as several other Israel units who worked the Gaza area said they too encountered extremely proficient snipers who they suspected of being foreigners. All these encounters were similar: a sniper took a quick shot at an exposed target and then immediately disappeared. The sniper never stuck around to be caught or to make another shot. These foreign snipers were suspected of staying in the Gaza Strip for only brief periods of time – maybe a couple days - and then they took their money and ran. This brief time period, combined with rotating the snipers, meant the shooters-for-hire did not set a distinct, identifiable pattern and were therefore very difficult, if not impossible, to track or anticipate. And since the snipers were not in-country for long, local Israeli intelligence assets failed to get any concrete information on them. Criminal profiling methods or other pattern analysis tools were thus rendered ineffective.[5]

A Complex Web: Combining Civil Disobedience & Urban Guerrilla Sniping

---

5 *European Marksmen-for-Hire in Gaza*, DEBKA file Exclusive Report, Sep 8, 2004.

Over the course of decades of resistance to the Israeli occupation, the Palestinians developed sophisticated urban guerrilla warfare techniques in which the urban sniper played an important role. For example, an attack on an Israeli outpost located in the West Bank town of Ramallah in October 2000 showcased the Palestinians' skills. The attack started off with a mob of several hundred young men, armed only with Molotov cocktails and rocks, approaching the outpost. The mob used the Molotov cocktails to set cars on fire and the rocks to harass and injure unprotected soldiers, but they did not use what the international community would consider 'lethal force'. This put the Israeli soldiers in a difficult situation because they knew the world would not approve of them shooting and killing teenagers for throwing rocks. However, the Palestinian resistance wanted to provoke an unjustified killing if they could.

Without doubt, an unjustified killing would quickly be splashed all over the world in the newspapers and on the internet because accompanying the legion of stone throwers were Palestinian media crews. The media crews set up their cameras, as if they were setting up crew-served machine guns, in strategically selected positions so they could get good coverage of the angry mob and anyone who happened to get shot by the Israelis. Accordingly, if the mob threw enough stones and maybe pelted a soldier in the head with a good sized rock, then the Israelis were sure to respond with increasing force. The Israelies would start off with tear gas canisters and stun grenades, escalating all the way to rubber coated bullets and .22 caliber sniper rifles to wound and put down specific members of the mob who were causing the most trouble. Of course, the camera crew would get all of this brutality on film.

On this day, as the groups of stone throwers crowded the Israeli soldiers, several stone throwers went down to Israeli bullets, which were usually aimed below the waist and specifically at the knees. Palestinian sirens soon wailed as fast moving ambulances careened into the swirling mob to extract the wounded. Just as intended, the rescue of Palestinian youths with gunshot wounds provided great media for the Palestinian camera crews who feasted on the bloodshed. While the ambulances picked up their cargo, they made sure to drop off more buckets of stones and crates of Molotov cocktails to sustain the mob's attack.

While columns of black smoke curled skyward from the burning cars and tires and clouds of tear gas swirled around the masses of irate demonstrators, unseen Palestinian snipers used the pandemonium as a screen and slipped into the surrounding buildings, several blocks back from the action. These silent partners of the choreographed mob searched for targets, looking for that one Israeli soldier who exposed themselves for a second too long or got too careless shooting off a tear gas canister. The Palestinian camera crews never saw these shooters and either did the hard pressed Israeli soldiers until the snipers' unseen bullets streaked in above the heads of the mob towards their targets.

One of the Palestinian snipers was successful and hit an Israeli soldier in the hip, causing the mob of Palestinians to erupt in a standing ovation, as if their home team just scored a goal at a football game. However, the shooting of an Israeli soldier signaled to the outpost they were now facing more than just civil disobedience. In response, the Israeli's own counter-sniper teams positioned on nearby rooftops began looking in earnest for a target. Plus, the Israelis had their own camera crews in place on the roofs so they too could film the attacking mob to later provide video evidence to refute the Palestinians' claims of excessive force and unjustified killings. But, as

The Intifada: Palestinians confront the Israelis

more Palestinian snipers took position in multiple buildings, firing at the Israeli outposts from different directions, the soldiers were put in the position of either abandoning their posts due to the intense level of sustained and accurate gunfire or raising the force level. Since a retreat was not an option, the decision to increase the force had to be measured as one Israeli veteran on the scene described it, "Since the first day, every time we shoot a person, it is because they deserved it, because they shot at us first. You don't want to shoot civilians and kids. On the other hand, you don't want your soldiers on the front lines to be killed. If I could, I'd shoot the kids with the Molotov cocktails. I'd give my soldiers a 'shoot-to-kill' order. But instead, we hit them in the knee."

The Israeli outpost asked their higher headquarters for permission to use a tank to open fire on an abandoned apartment building the Palestinian snipers were using as a shooting platform. The request was approved and a Merkava main battle tank opened fie on the concrete sniper nest. The heavy fire of the Merkava had the desired effect as the mob of teenagers took off for cover and the snipers in the building had to reposition or get blown up. In the end, this was a media victory for the Palestinian resistance because they could show film of the Israelis using main battle tanks to 'kill unarmed civilian youths.'

The Palestinians coordinated their sniper attack so well with the crowds, cameramen, and ambulances because they used an improvised communication system – they had cell phones with ear attachments so the shooters could receive orders and report back on what they saw over the phone without taking their hands off their rifles or their eyes off their targets. As luck would have it at this particular Israeli outpost, there was an official Palestinian Authority building located nearby which gave the Palestinian snipers a shooting platform. This way, the snipers knew the layout of the building, could prepare firing positions, and if the Israelis tried to blast out the snipers with tank fire, the Palestinians would get good media coverage of the Israelis using excessive force against the Palestinian Authority police who were 'only restoring order'.

During this attack, some of the Palestinian snipers were identified as members of the Palestinian police. In this instance, the Palestinian Authority became the infrastructure to facilitate a guerrilla sniping campaign - the Palestinian Authority provided the rifles, the ammunition, the trained shooters, and the buildings to shoot from. Since the Palestinian Authority was a recognized governing body, receiving tens of millions of dollars in aid from a variety of countries including the United States, the money needed to develop this urban guerrilla sniping infrastructure was provided by international donors who contributed money to promote peace and stability. While they may have intended to fund stability, they also funded Palestinian snipers intent on forcing Israel out of Gaza and the West Bank one bullet at a time.

This attack on the Israeli combat outpost, a scenario repeated over and over during the 2000 Intifada, revealed the complexities of modern urban guerrilla warfare in Israel. The Palestinian put the Israelis in a tough, lose-lose situation by integrating many clever tactics. First, the Palestinians used the teenage mob as a media tool. The use of teenagers was a calculated ploy to engender international sympathy, after all, who could blame these poor kids who were just being manipulated by their political leaders? Who would condone the Israelis shooting and killing young kids? The use of unarmed kids made the Israelis use less-than-lethal force, forcing the soldiers to be just as skilled in crowd control as they were in war fighting, a difficult balance for professional soldiers trained for high-intensity combat.

The use of ambulances to resupply the stone throwers, to move snipers into position, and to evacuate the wounded was masterful. Again, this put the Israelis in a lose-lose situation. If the Israelis actually fired on the ambulances (like the resistance wanted them to) then the Palestinians would claim Israel was committing war crimes by violating the Geneva Conventions, which protects Red Cross and Red Crescent vehicles and personnel from being targeted by military combatants. Even though the Palestinian resistance was already violating the laws of land warfare by using the ambulances for other than humanitarian reasons, there was no doubt the Palestinians would win this media battle. Consequently, the Israelis had to exert extreme professionalism to not fire on the ambulances, even though they knew they were being used to facilitate the attack against them.

The use of Palestinian Authority buildings as a sniper platform was a good technique for the resistance because it enticed the Israelis, just as with the ambulances, to open fire on an ostensibly neutral organization. If the Israelis happened to kill a Palestinian sniper in a Palestinian Authority police uniform, then the resistance would charge Israel with murdering a police officer who was only trying to stop the violence and restore the peace.

All of these potential traps - the stone throwing youths, the ambulances, and the use of Palestinian Authority property - were meaningless if they were not caught on film and broadcasted to the world. That is why the key element of the entire operation was the Palestinian media crews who were there to film the Israelis killing children, shooting up ambulances, murdering police officers, and destroying the surrounding city with main battle tanks. The street battle itself was an act of pure political theater to vilify the Israeli government and gain international support for the Palestinian cause.[6]

---

6 Kelley, Jack, *Street Clashes Now Deliberate Warfare*, USA Today Oct. 23, 2000. (An excellent article and study of modern urban guerrilla sniping.)

Israeli soldiers patrol the streets of Hebron

The Politics of Murder, The Politics of Hate

On April 1, 2001, a funeral was held for a ten month-old baby girl named Shalhevet Pass who lived her short time on earth in the West Bank town of Hebron. Shalhevet did not die from an irregular heartbeat, dehydration, malnutrition, or any number of afflictions that may take an infant's life. A week earlier, on March 26, Shalhevet was shot in the head by a Palestinian sniper while being pushed in a stroller by her father, Ytizhak Pass, who was also wounded after the bullet passed through his daughter's fragile skull and plowed into his legs. This murder begs the question - why? The shooter could not claim ignorance since sniping is a very personal act and every sniper knows exactly who they shoot. Sniping is surgical. The sniper knew they were shooting a baby, or, at the very least, knew they were shooting at a man pushing a baby in a stroller. But what did the Palestinians have to gain from this?

The Palestinians may have killed Shalhevet to get a reaction. To understand how killing a Jewish baby might work to the Palestinians' advantage we must understand the situation in modern Hebron. Hebron, located in the southern part of the West Bank, is the second holiest city for Jews after Jerusalem. But, Hebron's population is overwhelmingly Arab, with some 120,000 Palestinians and only about 700 Jewish settlers living there. The Palestinians did not (and do not) like having Jewish settlers living in Hebron because the Jews tend to multiply and take over whatever area they move to, creating a new demographic reality. Consequently, Palestinians see Jewish settlement in Hebron as the beginning foothold to a larger Jewish population invasion. This is because wherever there is a Jewish settlement, there is inevitably a nearby Israeli Defense Force base whose job is to protect the Jewish settlers. Thus, the Palestinians view the Jewish beachhead in Hebron as not only a demographic shift, but a military, cultural, religious, and political invasion of a historically Arab city.

One must also understand a central element of the Palestinian resistance's strategy

225

was the polarization of cities like Hebron so Israel's Arabs support the Palestinian resistance and oppose Israel. The resistance could not afford any Arabs living in the political middle ground, where they accepted the presence of Jewish settlers in a predominately Arab city. The killing of Shalhevet was a step towards removing people from the middle ground because it polarized the Jews by enraging not only the settlers of Hebron, but all of Israel. The Palestinian resistance wanted the Israeli people to hate and lash out at the average Arab, even though they were personally innocent of the murder of a baby girl. If the resistance could get the average Israeli to hate and persecute the average Arab, then it would be a relatively easy step to get the average Arab to hate and persecute the average Israeli in return. In short, the killing of a baby girl created polarization through a spiraling cycle of violent reprisals and growing hatred. This Arab hatred could then be manipulated by the resistance to build their organization, expand their power base, and accomplish their political goals.

The immediate reaction of the Israeli Defense Forces to the killing of Shalhevet was predictable - they opened fire with a tank on the building the sniper fired from. That was not enough for the Pass family or the Jews of Hebron. They wanted the Israeli army to occupy the entire Arab 'Abu Sneneh' district the sniper fired from. In fact, the Pass family initially refused to bury their daughter (Jewish law says the dead must be buried immediately) until the district was placed under Israeli military control. This insistence placed immense pressure on the Sharon government to take action. The Pass family's demand for an occupation of Abu Sneneh was not a new one since the Jewish enclave in Hebron received regular sniper fire from the district for the previous seven months, ever since the district passed from Israeli military control to administration by the Palestinian Authority.

The Jews of Hebron may have wanted a military solution to the troublesome district, but the Sharon government knew an occupation of Palestinian Authority land might escalate into an all out war between the Palestinian Authority and the Israeli Defense Forces, so Sharon refused. But, Sharon could not afford to do nothing. Less drastic measures would be taken. The Israel Defense Forces quickly set up checkpoints around Hebron to block the flow of traffic in and out of the city and a curfew was instated in the Jewish part of the city. This was not good enough for some of the Jews living in Hebron as they blockaded several roads on their own and even attacked some Arab citizens. Other Hebron Jews went so far as to threaten to occupy the Abu Sneneh district themselves, regardless of the political and military price. This was the reaction the Palestinian extremists wanted. They wanted a civil war to erupt between Jewish and Arab citizens. They wanted polarization. They wanted both sides committed to killing each other as opposed to living peacefully, side by side. This was the motivation behind the killing of Shalhevet. This was the politics of murder.

The Palestinian resistance may have lessened the outrage of the sniper attack if they produced a plausible explanation for the killing. For instance, if they said a rogue murderer committed the crime, who would then be hunted down like an animal and brought to justice, then, public opinion might have been more forgiving. However, the Palestinian Authority failed to present a plausible story. Instead, Palestinian Authority Minister Yasser Abed Rabbo refuted the very evidence of the shooting, stating, "We believe that the atrocities of the occupation are responsible for all crimes that have claimed the lives of Palestinians and Israelis." Then, the Voice of Palestine radio commentator Youssef al-Kazaz, broadcast on the Palestinian Authority radio station on

Foreign Training Sanctuaries

Above, members of the Popular Front for the Liberation of Palestine (PFLP) in Jordan pose for the camera. The majority of Arab nations in the Middle East oppose Israel in some way and many offer up their countries as training bases for the PLO and Hamas.

April 2, 2001, "On the matter of the baby settler who was killed in Hebron a few days ago, we already said that her death was a fishy action, and there is information according to which this baby was retarded and it was her mother who killed her in order to get rid of her."

The murder of one's infant daughter will affect any father and the murder of Shalhevet strapped Yitzhak Pass firmly to the wheel of continuing violence. Two years after the death of his daughter, in July 2003, Yitzhak Pass and his brother-in-law were arrested by the Israeli police with ten pounds of high explosives in their car. The police long suspected Pass and his brother-in-law were members of a clandestine Jewish terror cell conducting attacks against Arab citizens. For possessing explosives, Yitzhak Pass and his brother-in-law received a two-year jail sentence. Despite police suspicions, there was not enough evidence to connect the two to any specific murders. They were released in the summer of 2005. Ultimately, the Palestinian sniper got their wish as the murder of Shalhevet drove her father to commit unknown numbers of crimes against equally innocent Arabs.

Politicians in the Crosshairs

As can be seen from the targeting of unarmed civilians and the murder of children, sniping can be a political act. A sniper can instigate violence, cause public outrage, and create political dilemmas. Along with influencing regional and international politics,

227

snipers can also be used to actually kill politicians themselves. Therefore, it was to little surprise in March 2001, as newly appointed Israeli Defense Minister Binyamin Ben-Eliezer toured Israeli military bases in the Gaza Strip, he came under fire from a Palestinian sniper. As the Defense Minister walked down from the roof of an Israeli outpost, a shooter took two aimed shots, causing Eliezer's bodyguards to shield him with their bodies. It is doubtful the sniper actually knew who they were targeting and it is more likely a sniper working the area saw a target of opportunity. The shooter probably knew their target was someone of importance due to the added security and tried to make the shot. Either way, it would have been a coup for the Palestinian resistance to knock off Israel's Minister of Defense.[7]

Two years later the Palestinian resistance showed that killing Israeli politicians was more than just a case of opportunity. On November 1, 2003, Jamal Akal, a 23-year old Palestinian from the town of Nuseirat in the Gaza Strip was detained by the Israel Security Agency (ISA). Akal lived in Canada since 1999 and in fact was a Canadian citizen. He only recently returned to Gaza to visit his family. An investigation by the ISA revealed Akal met with Hamas representatives and agreed to assassinate a senior Israeli official when they traveled to the United States in an upcoming trip. Akal's plan was to observe and study the Israeli official's movement in the U.S. and then kill him in a sniper attack. Akal intended to purchase an M16 either in Canada or the United States and even received training (to include target practice) from Hamas on the use of the M16 while still in Gaza. Even with a dose of good luck, there was only a remote chance this far reaching operation would ever succeed. But, it does show Hamas' intent to export its guerrilla sniper methods overseas to assassinate Israeli officials.[8]

Israeli Counter-Sniper Tactics

True, the Palestinian sniper threat remained a constant element of the ongoing guerrilla war, but the Israelis used aggressive tactics to minimize it. First, the Israelis believed in physical barriers to prevent enemy snipers from targeting Israeli soldiers or citizens. Wherever possible, the IDF built sniper-proof surveillance towers, complete with concrete walls and bullet proof vision ports so Israeli guards could observe the surrounding terrain without being vulnerable. Around many Jewish settlements and communities the Israelis constructed towering twenty-foot walls, like some medieval fortress, so guerrilla snipers could not even see the Jewish settlers they were dying to shoot. In other situations, the Israelis used ethnic relocation where Israeli settlers moved into an Arab area and pressured the Palestinians to move somewhere else. It was difficult for an Arab Muslim guerrilla sniper to operate in an area populated only by Easter European Jews. In this sense, Israeli communities were a barrier in themselves to Palestinian gunmen. Only in a town with a mixed population or closely entangled communities could an urban sniper thrive.

If the IDF identified a favorite sniper position their enemy repeatedly set up in, they frequently employed 'structural denial' operations to remove this threat. In these instances, the Israelis used huge, armored bulldozers to raze these troublesome struc-

---

7 BBC News Online, *Sniper Targets Israeli Defense Minister*, Friday, 9 March, 2001.
8 Israel Ministry of Foreign Affairs, *Hamas-Trained Terrorist, Canadian National, Arrested by ISA,* Jerusalem, December 8, 2003.

Israeli Sniper Post

Israeli snipers take aim with their full arsenal of weapons: a Barrett .50 caliber rifle, an M-24 7.62 mm bolt-action rifle, and an M-16A2 5.56 mm assault rifle fitted with a scope.

tures. Since the bulldozers were fitted with bulletproof windows and solid steel armor, the Palestinians were unable to stop these armored behemoths from plowing under their buildings even if they tried. No building = no sniper nest. Problem solved. Plus, crushing a building with a bulldozer was a lot less dramatic and more controlled than dropping a bomb on a building. It seemed more humane when a building imploded on itself from the dull blade of a lumbering Caterpillar machine as opposed to erupting in a volcano of concrete and steel from high-explosives.

Perhaps the IDF's most preferred response to the threat of Palestinian snipers was their own sniper teams. If the IDF determined the location of an enemy sniper, they moved in several of their own teams to pin the shooter down, cut off their escape routes, and take the shot if they could locate their target. The IDF not only hunted down enemy snipers with their own sniper teams, they used large numbers of counter-snipers as a defensive measure. In these roles, the IDF routinely deployed rooftop snipers during public events, offensive operations, and to protect checkpoints. The IDF was successful in employing snipers as a counter-sniper tool in part because they developed a professional sniper corps that received both formal training and practical experience in the mean streets of Gaza and the West Bank.

The Israeli Defense Force's Sniping Architecture

Initially, the IDF placed little emphasis on sniping. Instead, the IDF focused on fighting large, conventional battles with its neighbors as the wars of 1948, 1956, 1967, and 1973 underlined. After these wars, the equation changed when Israel's domestic

Palestinian population realized their Arab neighbors could not free them or destroy Israel. As a result, groups like the PLO focused on waging guerilla warfare as a vehicle for victory. Only after fighting a sustained counter-insurgency campaign since the 1970's did the IDF appreciate the value of the sniper. Once the IDF learned precision rifle fire in urban, populated areas was preferable to their more blunt weapons of war, official support for sniping grew. Today, the IDF has several dedicated sniper training programs, which produce snipers with varying degrees of proficiency in urban warfare.

Israel's Sniper Tools of the Trade

The newly created IDF had limited time to research and develop the perfect sniper system. From the 1940's until the 1970's Israel fought for its very existence. What Israel's snipers needed was a simple weapon that was economical, easy to get, and utterly reliable. What the IDF ended up choosing - ironically- was the German Mauser K98. Some of these rifles even came complete with inscribed swastikas, but they were accurate, ammunition was plentiful, and the rifle was proven in combat. While the K98 was the official sniper weapon system of the IDF, many shooters used Britain's Lee-Enfield No 4 Mk I bolt-action rifle. The Mk I had all the same qualities of the K98 and performed reliably in the deserts of the Middle East. From 1948 to 1974, Israel's official sniper weapon remained the World War II-era K98.

In 1973, during the Yom Kippur War, Israel received large numbers of M-14 rifles from the United States. The M-14 was reliable and accurate and could fire twenty rounds from its box magazine. After battlefield testing the weapon against the Egyptians and Syrians, Israel made the M-14 the foundation for their sniper corps. But the M-14 was not ready for sniper service until the most accurate rifles were hand selected, fitted with a stock cheekpiece, a scope, and a bipod. After these changes the M-14 served as the IDF's official sniper weapon system until 1997.

In the 1990's, the IDF looked critically at its sniper corps and decided to modernize its arsenal based on American sniper rifles. In 1997, Israel chose the bolt-action Remington M-24 as its primary sniper weapon system. While the M-24 performed admirably for the IDF since 1997, counter-terror forces wanted a weapon with rapid fire capability. A search for an appropriate system resulted in the 2001 adoption of the SR25, an extremely accurate 7.62 mm, semi-automatic rifle that comes with a bipod, Leupold scope, and a detachable suppressor. Along with the SR25, the IDF adopted another American semi-automatic sniper rifle, the M82A1 Barrett .50 caliber rifle. The Barrett initially piqued the IDF's interest in the mid-1990's as an Explosive Ordnance (EOD) tool for destroying improvised explosive devices (IEDs). As the popularity of the Barrett grew in professional sniping circles, the IDF decided to buy the rifle en masse and employ it on a large scale, using it for hard target interdiction (HTI) missions like shooting targets through cars and behind walls. The hard hitting Barrett impressed the Israelis so much they refered to it as 'God's Gun.'

Rounding out the Israeli sniper arsenal is the Mauser 86SR, a bolt-action rifle. During the years the IDF used the M-14 as its primary sniper rifle, the IDF counter-terror forces required an extremely accurate rifle for close-in urban sniping work. The weapon they selected, the 7.62 mm Mauser 66SP with heavy barrel and thumb-hole stock, was a military version of a civilian competition sporting rifle. The Mauser 66SP

Israeli Sniper Team

An Israeli marksman takes aim with a suppressed Ruger 10/22 rifle.

served the Israeli Special Forces for years until it was replaced by an updated version in 1986, the Mauser 86SR.

An Unlikely Urban Sniping Weapon: The Ruger 10/22

Another weapon Israel employed in their urban guerrilla battles with the PLO and Hamas was the Ruger 10/22. However, these rifles were not used with the intent to kill. The small .22 caliber round is unreliable as a man-killer and certainly will not penetrate common urban mediums like walls, cars, and body armor. But, these limitations are fine with the Israelis since they used it primarily as a tool for crowd control. During the Palestinians' two intifadas, the first from 1987 to 1993 and the second from 2000 to 2008, the Palestinians used civil disobedience like riots, looting, and unruly mobs to harass, intimidate, and provoke Israeli security forces.

In many situations, Israeli soldiers were confronted with stone and brick throwing youths who could cause harm to the soldiers, but whom the Israelis could not justify killing outright. The IDF soldiers were in a lose-lose situation because they were armed only with lethal 5.56 mm and 7.62 mm assault and sniper rifles. What they needed was a weapon that could wound a specific target without actually killing them. Enter the Ruger 10/22, which was considered an ideal weapon because it was semi-automatic, had a 10-round rotary magazine, was lightweight, and accurate to a hundred meters. Because the weapons were suppressed and fired such a small round, a sniper could shoot from a concealed position and make a silent shot. A well-hidden shooter was impossible to detect. When an Israeli outpost or unit was confronted with an unruly mob, the Ruger 10/22 armed marksmen aimed for the leader of the mob or a particularly threatening rioter and shot them in the leg. This dropped the target to the ground, removed them as a threat, but left them alive, denying the Palestinians a

Suppressed Ruger 10/22 Urban Sniper Rifle

media victory.

Over time, Israeli soldiers became comfortable using the Ruger 10/22s and used them with less discrimination. Because the suppressed rifle seemed almost harmless - they were so quiet and fired such a small round - Israeli soldiers began shooting protestors above the waistline, hitting some people in the chest, and killing them. After several Palestinians were shot and killed in this manner, they protested the Israelis' use of the weapon. The Palestinians argued the .22 caliber round was indeed lethal at short ranges of one hundred meters or less and the Israelis knew this and intentionally killed their victims under the guise of ignorance. The Palestinians made such a stink about the whole matter the Israeli authorities tightly restricted the use of the Ruger 10/22s to prevent any more accidental killings and to deny the Palestinians another media victory.

This was a good decision as the Palestinians were already exploiting the more-than-lethal Ruger 10/22 used by the Israelis. After Palestinians started receiving serious lower extremity wounds, like shattered pelvises, some theorized the Israelis were using covert sniper tactics to intentionally and permanently cripple Palestinian protestors. The theory was Israeli forces took a .50 caliber shell case and necked it down so it would fit the much smaller .22 caliber bullet. Then, the Israelis used these custom-made rifles to fire the hyper-velocity .22 caliber bullets at the Palestinians. During riots, these snipers were hidden more than five hundred meters away so they could open fire and remain unseen by the crowds. The Israelis would claim the grievous wounds made from these hyper-velocity .22 caliber rounds were just freak accidents caused by their standard low-velocity Ruger 10/22s.

The Palestinians never proved the Israelis actually used necked down .50 caliber shells to create .22 caliber wounds that were difficult to forensically differentiate from one another. However, this idea should not be relegated to the world of fantasy. After all, many 'wildcat' cartridges used by competition benchrest shooters are necked down versions of some larger cartridge. In the 1930's, the Germans used a necked down .50 caliber cartridge to fit their standard 7.92 mm rifle round that was then fired from their Panzerbusche anti-tank rifle. The result was a hyper-velocity bullet traveling at 3500 feet per second and capable of penetrating an inch-of steel at a hundred meters!

The Church of the Nativity Siege: A Study of Urban Sniping

On March 29, 2002, Israel began Operation Defensive Shield, a multi-pronged invasion of several West Bank towns to destroy the Palestinians' insurgent network in those areas. On April 2, before the sun had even risen across the morning sky, Operation Defensive Shield arrived on the doorsteps of the ancient town of Bethlehem. Israeli tanks, armored personnel carriers, and infantry poured into the city limits. Around two hundred Palestinians, to include members of Yassir Arafat's Fatah move-

Nativity Church Siege

photo by Ofer Yizhar

Israeli snipers in Bethlehem zero in on Palestinian guerrillas near the Church of the Nativity.

ment and the Palestinian Authority police, fled the Israeli juggernaut, taking refuge in one of the holiest places in all of Christendom – the Church of the Nativity.

The Palestinians could not have chosen a more religiously and politically sensitive spot for refuge. The Church of the Nativity, built on the very spot Jesus was believed to have been born, was just one of a number of other important religious structures surrounding the adjacent Manger Square, like the Mosque of Omar, the Armenian Convent, the Greek Orthodox Convent, the Coptic Orthodox Convent, the Franciscan Convent, and the Church of St. Catherine. Because the Palestinians were holed up in such a religiously delicate location, the Israelis were limited from using their conventional tools of war to get them out. There would be no tanks firing high-explosive shells or Apache gunships launching hellfire missiles though the Door of Humility and into Jesus' place of birth.

What made the situation more complicated was not everyone in the Church was a confirmed insurgent. Some of the people in the Church were Franciscan monks who chose to remain inside to help prevent damage to one of Christianity's most sacred sites and to assist with an eventual negotiated settlement between the Palestinians and the surrounding Israeli forces. Even among the Palestinians, some were insurgents, some were police, and some were civilians with no prior criminal record. Plus, the ornate layout of the church, combined with its construction material - stone and marble – made it an urban fortress that favored the defenders. Consequently, if Israeli assault forces stormed the Church, there would be a bloodbath with the civilians caught helplessly in the crossfire.

The Israelis knew an all out assault or bombardment was out of the question so they took the only option left to them, which was to surround the Church and set siege to it. The siege lasted thirty-nine days, from April 2 to May 10, until negotiations between the Vatican, the United States, Israel, the Palestinian Authority, and the European Union finally bore fruit. In the end, twenty-six of the wanted men were sent in exile to Gaza and another thirteen were deported abroad to Europe. However, this negotiated settlement was only possible after the Israeli forces squeezed the Palestinians long and hard enough.

Because every aspect of the siege was conducted under the unblinking gaze of the international media to include film crews, freelance journalists and eye-witnesses, the Israelis had to apply pressure both humanely and surgically. To start with, the Israelis made life uncomfortable for those in the church by limiting the amount of food sent in. If the holdouts wanted to eat, they must surrender first. Also, since there were not any bathrooms inside the holy church, the holdouts had to sit in the stench of their own urine and excrement unless they wanted to give themselves up. On top of all this, day and night, the surrounding forces played loud noises from speakers elevated over the church by huge, yellow cranes, so the occupants could not sleep or think straight.

While these measures made life unpleasant, the Israelis ringed the church with snipers so they could put any exposed gunmen out of their misery with a carefully placed shot. This was difficult since the urban terrain, with its inconveniently placed buildings, was such that the surrounding snipers could not always get a good shot at their enemy. To overcome these urban obstacles the Israelis trucked in a mobile shooting platform (a large, rectangular, yellow steel and glass container) that was then raised a hundred feet up in the air by a big industrial crane. Once the shooters in the containers were dangling high above the surrounding terrain, they had a bird's eye view of the church and Manger Square and could make accurate shots at any enemy leaving the safety of the church.

To avoid any potential casualties among their snipers elevated by the crane, the IDF made innovative use of their Trap 2 remote firing weapon system, which they attached to their crane. The end result was the Israelis were able to raise a sniper rifle, secured to a Trap 2 remote firing system and secured to the end of a crane, high above the church. In this manner the Israelis could get a good vantage point and then remotely fire on the Palestinian holdouts without fear of Israeli soldiers being harmed with return fire.

Over the course of the siege, the Israeli snipers took their toll. On April 4, Samir Ibrahim Salman was seen running across Manger Square and was shot dead by an Israeli sniper. This killing turned out to be a serious blunder since Samir was not a Muslim-extremist terrorist, but the Christian bell ringer for the church. The IDF later said Samir ignored orders to halt and was suspected of being a suicide bomber. In this situation, the Israeli snipers failed to positively identify their target and shot an unarmed, innocent man. On April 10, Israeli snipers blundered again, shooting and wounding Armen Sinanian, a twenty-two year-old Christian Armenian monk who was looking out a window while inside the church. The IDF said they mistook the unarmed man for a Palestinian gunman. Another twenty year-old man was shot and wounded after he made the mistake of venturing into a church garden to try and find something to eat. Both men were later taken to a hospital to recuperate from their wounds.

Danish peace activist Allan Lindgaard, who managed to maneuver his way inside the church during the siege, correctly observed, "The Israelis are shooting at anything which moves in here. They shoot through the windows and at anyone going out to get

Nativity Church Siege

A crane lifts a container, filled with Israeli snipers, high above the Bethlehem sky-line. From this birds-eye perch, the snipers will zero in on Palestinian guerillas below them.

food." On April 13, the killing continued when an Israeli sniper positioned in a nearby building, armed with a suppressed rifle, took aim at Hassan Abdullah al-Nusman, a twenty-six year-old blacksmith from Bethlehem who was in the church. The sniper was dead on, striking Hassan twice in the chest. The Palestinians later charged Israel with refusing to let ambulances come and rescue Hassan who later bled to death from the gunshot wounds. Eleven days later, on April 24, Israeli snipers fired on two Palestinian men in the church compound, killing one and wounding the other. On April 26, two more Palestinians were shot by snipers and then evacuated by ambulance for further treatment.

Five days passed when, on April 29, Nidal Isma'il Abayat, one of the Palestinians holed up inside, got sloppy and exposed himself by going into the church courtyard. Nidal took a bullet in the chest from an Israeli sniper positioned in a nearby building. In this case, this was a 'good kill' since Nidal was a member of the Al-Aqsa Martyrs Brigades of Yasser Arafat's Fatah Movement. Several days went by and on May 2 an Israeli sniper shot and killed 21-year-old Ahmed Mohammed Abu Aabed, a member of the Palestinian Authority's Military Intelligence who was hiding out inside the church. Ahmed was struck in quick succession by two bullets, one hitting him in his chest and one plowing into his stomach. On May 4, Khalaf Ahmed al-Najajra, also made the mistake of venturing into a church courtyard. An Israeli sniper promptly placed a bullet directly into his chest, killing him.

When the siege finally concluded on May 10, the Israeli soldiers participating in the operation should have taken pause to carefully record the lessons they should have learned. One important lesson was the deliberate use of snipers, even on a large scale, minimized the damage to the urban infrastructure. After all, the Church of the Nativity suffered only superficial wounds to include a slightly damaged 12th century mosaic and a single bullet wound to the Virgin Mary located in the birth grotto. Another important lesson was just because one is firing a sniper rifle does not mean the operation will be surgical. A soldier with a precision firearm still has to identify their target to make sure they are shooting the enemy. In this operation, poorly disciplined Israeli snipers shot and killed numerous unarmed innocent people. This poor showing undermined Israel's credibility, gave the Palestinians ammunition for their media war, and actually encouraged the innocent civilians in the church to remain inside with the gunmen, less they be shot by Israeli snipers bent on shooting anything that moved.

Israel's Targeted Killings

As the Nativity church Siege showed, killing a specific target by a sniper can be a better alternative than many other options. A sniper is discriminating and could place a bullet into a specific target without causing collateral damage. With the surgical placement of a single bullet, there was no spectacular destruction and no gruesome collateral damage. There was nothing eye-catching for the media - maybe a bloodstained shirt or a hole in a person's head. Just as the Palestinian resistance groups judged their own sniper attacks would not garner too much international outrage, the Israeli military knew their sniper operations did not register high on the international community's radar. For all these reasons, the sniper rifle was perfect for the elimination of a specific target, or in other words, for assassinations.

Abdel Rahman Hamad, as a senior member of Hamas' Ezzedin Al-Qassam Brigade, must have known Israel would make the effort to kill him if they had the chance. Not only was Hamad arrested and imprisoned numerous times for terrorist related activities, he was involved in the planning of the June 1, 2001 discotheque attack where a suicide bomber blew themselves up while waiting in a line to get inside a night club. The resulting blast killed 22 young men and women and wounded another 120. A man who helped such slaughter should have been a very careful man, especially a man living in the West Bank. Hamad got sloppy. At seven a.m., on the morning of October 14, 2001, Hamad made a journey out onto the roof of his house, which was located in the town of Qalqilya. Hamad did not know it at the time, but a team of Israeli snipers had his house under surveillance and were waiting for him to expose himself. As Hamad stepped out onto his roof, he signed his death warrant. Immediately, two bullets ripped into his chest, killing him.

The assassination of Hamad, as with all significant killings, resulted in political fallout. The Israel government felt justified in killing Hamad since they labeled him a mass murderer. A government spokesman clarified their view on the assassination saying, "We're going to take all the necessary steps to secure our citizens because we don't have any other choice. If we won't do that we will face terrible terror attacks inside our cities, in our streets". The Israeli people may have agreed with this statement, but the United States was unhappy with the killing since it undermined the ongoing efforts to negotiate a settlement with the Palestinian Authority.

As could be expected, after learning of the killing of Hamad, Hamas vowed to take revenge. The Information Minister for the Palestinian Authority used the assassination as an opportunity to lash out at Israel: "The assassination today is a clear indicator that all the Israeli claims that they want to achieve peace and uphold the cease fire are just lies". The most serious problem was if Hamas did retaliate against the shooting, it could derail Israel's plans to withdraw that same day from Arab areas in the town Hebron. Ironically, the Israeli army occupied these neighborhoods just two weeks before to silence Palestinian snipers who targeted adjacent Jewish settlements.[9]

A Polarized Society

In many ways, Israel society is polarized. One either supports the Palestinian in-surgency or the government of Israel. Without doubt, elements on both sides of the ethnic, ideological, and religious trenches have found this polarization useful. Radical Palestinian elements insisting on the destruction of Israel cannot tolerate Palestinians sitting in the political middle ground. An Arab who accepts a two-state solution must be blasted out of the middle ground with suicide bombings and Israel's own heavy-handed reactions. In turn, Jewish radicals who insist on annexing and populating the Gaza Strip and the West Bank are equally fearful of moderate Jews who appreciate the Palestinian point of view. These moderates too must be removed so God's people can occupy Hebron and East Jerusalem.

For both sides, the most effective way to influence the population and create polar-ization is to wage a media war through TV shows, newspapers, articles in journals and magazines, books, and in cyberspace with web sites and blogs. On any given event like a sniper shooting, both sides spin the story to suit their political agendas. When a foreign journalist writes an article about a shooting and tries to maintain their impar-tiality, whatever side feels slighted by what is written, they viciously attack the author as being either a fascist, Neo-Nazi, Jew-hater, or a Zionist, American boot-licking, infidel.

The spin doctors on both sides created such a polarized environment, with the help of their respective media machines, that finding the truth was next to impossible – it was up for grabs, depending on if you were an Arab or a Jew, a Palestinian or an Is-raeli, the insurgent or the occupier. This was exactly how the extremists on both sides wanted it. In the meantime, the sniper war in Israel continues with Palestinian snipers stalking new prey and Israel snipers responding in kind, creating new tragedies, new media sensations, and new reasons for revenge.

---

9 ARABS-ISRAEL - Oct. 14, 2001-Sniper Attack, APS Diplomat Reporter.

Chapter 13

A Sarajevan woman runs for her life.

If you run, you hit the bullet. If you walk, the bullet hits you.
- A popular saying during the siege of Sarajevo

The Descent Into Madness

Sarajevo is a beautiful city, built centuries ago by the once powerful Ottoman Empire. Even after the Ottomans collapsed, the city remained and thrived with a vibrant, tolerant, multi-ethnic, multi-religious population that included Muslims, Jews, Croats, and Serbs. Sarajevo, located in the heart of Bosnia, was a true cultural kaleidoscope where East met West and merged into something that was a little bit of both. In 1984, when the Winter Olympics were held in Sarajevo, the world saw first hand the city's beauty – its hand crafted churches and mosques, the colorful orange roofs of its quaint residences, and the beautiful snow-capped mountains. If, during these splendid Olympics, you approached a resident of Sarajevo and said eight years later they would wake every morning to the echo of gunshots they would have called you crazy.

Even fewer people in 1986 would have predicted Mikhail Gorbachev's policies of glasnost (political openness) and perestroika (economic restructuring) would lead to genocide in the ethnic and religious patchwork called Yugoslavia. However, Gorbachev's attempt to make the Soviet Union stronger economically, and less threatening politically, led to an explosion of nationalism that burst across Eastern Europe like a hand grenade. Only three years later, in 1989, the Kremlin rejected the Brezhnev Doctrine, meaning Russia would no longer interfere in the internal political affairs of

Sarajevo's parliament building burns after being hit by Serbian tank shells.
By Mikhail Evstafiev

its Warsaw Pact satellites. This begged a most serious question: if the regimes of the old Iron Curtain no longer had Moscow's support, what was to stop the local populations from throwing their repressive communist governments into the dustbin of history? The powder keg was lit.

Soon, an irresistible revolutionary wave crashed down on the Soviet Union's former allies, bringing down government after government, in country after country, like dominoes: East Germany, Poland, and Czechoslovakia all rejected their communist systems. Yugoslavia, too, was hit by this wave as its own states vied for independence from the Serb-dominated, Belgrade-centered government. On June 25, 1991, Yugoslavia's western-most territory, Slovenia, rolled the military and political dice and declared its independence from Belgrade. After a brief ten-day war, with very few casualties, Slovenia was free. This quick road to nationhood was due mostly to the fact few Serbs lived in Slovenia. Serbia's leader, Slobodon Milosevic, calculated he could not muster the support to fight a civil war where there were no Serbs to 'protect'. To Slovenia's neighbor, Croatia, the road to independence appeared easy, almost costless. A dangerous precedent had been set because Croatia too thirsted for independence.

On June 25, Croatia also declared its independence. However, unlike Slovenia, Croatia agreed to defer their independence. It would be several months before Serbs and Croats started killing each other with gusto. But, by the end of 1991, the war was in full swing as Croatia found itself locked in brutal fighting against its minority Serb population, which was backed by Belgrade and its army, the JNA. The fighting between Croatia and the Serbs echoed loudly throughout the rest of former Yugoslavia and into neighboring Bosnia-Herzegovina. Bosnia-Herzegovina, a mish-mash of

Catholic Croats, Orthodox Serbs, and Muslim Bosnians, quickly disintegrated when its Croatian and Serbian minorities declared their own sub-states. Full blown war finally came to Bosnia-Herzegovina after it declared independence from Belgrade in March 1992. The stage for the Siege of Sarajevo was set.

The Serbian Siege of Sarajevo

The Bosnian government tried to navigate the perilous road to independence while avoiding a crippling war and failed. Because, as the Bosnian government performed their delicate political balancing act, the Bosnian Serbs were moving in weapons, heavy artillery, and supplies. When Bosnia-Herzegovina declared its independence, the Bosnian Serb Army (BSA) was ready, attacking along a broad front, gobbling up vast tracts of territory as they 'cleansed' the country of Muslims. The capital of Bosnia-Herzegovina, Sarajevo, was caught up in this cyclone of war when the BSA tried to overrun it in a tank-led assault. The Sarajevans found themselves unprepared, caught in a war they did not want, with few supplies, few heavy weapons, and nothing more than undisciplined gaggles of hastily raised militia for protection. But, this proved to be enough, because Sarajevo's complex urban terrain lent itself to the defense. The Serbian assault was stopped cold. What began as a lightning attack to steamroll the capital of Bosnia-Herzegovina ground to a sudden standstill and was transformed into the longest siege in modern military history.

While the surrounding BSA forces were well armed with heavy artillery, mortars, and tanks, they had relatively weak infantry forces – they only had 13,000 troops committed to the siege. In contrast, the Bosnian forces trapped in the city, while suffering from a lack of heavy weapons, had 30,000 soldiers, militiamen, and volunteers under arms. It was this superiority in foot soldiers that proved to be the trump card. Both sides eventually realized infantry was the key factor in their urban combat and the Bosnians, with more boots on the ground, were able to hold off the firepower-dependent Serbs in spite of their own dearth of weapons. Since the Serbs could not storm Sarajevo by force, they settled for surrounding the city, where the entrapped population would be brought to its collective knees the old fashioned way: through starvation, hardship, and terror. This was a strategy the Serbs referred to as 'Fry the Brain' where the people of Sarajevo would be hammered incessantly with such a stupefying stream of endless terror and random death they would stop thinking rationally, stop defending their city, and just give in to the Serbs' demands.

From April 1992 until February 1996 (the Dayton Peace Accords were signed in December 1995, but the Serbs only pulled out several months later) the people of Sarajevo suffered from a murderous barrage of high-explosive shells fired from Serbian artillery, rockets, mortars, and tanks. Almost every building in the city suffered some degree of damage and thousands of structures were completely destroyed. By the end of the siege, almost forty percent of Sarajevo's pre-war population of half a million people were killed, 'ethnically-cleansed', or fled in terror. As in other urban wars, the Serbian forces found the sniper could play a vital role in their plans.

The Serbian Sniper Campaign

Saying the Serbs valued the urban sniper is a gross understatement and does not do

1992: A Serbian commander playfully points a gun at the head of his own son as they wait to exchange prisoners outside Sarajevo.
By Mikhail Evstafiev

the Serbian sniper effort justice. A more accurate statement would be from 1992 to 1996, Serbian forces embarked on the longest, sustained, urban sniping campaign in the history of warfare. For 1,395 days Serbian forces directed a deliberate campaign of terror against the Sarajevans of all walks of life. Serbian sniper policy dictated their snipers shoot anything that moved – military or civilian, men or women, children or adults. To be a Sarajevan was to be marked for death.

The Serbs' sniper campaign served several purposes. First, the random killing of everyone and anyone sought to disrupt daily life in Sarajevo. No one was safe from the Serbian shooters and anyone could find themselves under fire from an unseen gunman hidden skillfully in one of the surrounding picturesque neighborhoods. The Serbian snipers hoped to cause utter chaos in the city, making the Bosnian government's attempts to defend the city impossible. Governing Sarajevo was indeed difficult since public employees were often the first ones to take a bullet. Policemen could not openly walk the streets, public transportation was paralyzed, and firemen were shot as they tried to put out fires. The garbage piled up because the sanitation workers were picked off. Serbian snipers even gunned down Sarajevo's zoo keepers.

The Serbs goal was to instill widespread public terror, i.e., to fry the brain. Since the majority of Sarajevans trapped in the city were non-Serbs, the attacking Serbs also used their sniper campaign as an ethnic-cleansing tool. The Serbs calculated large numbers of fearful, non-Serbian refugees would be inclined to evacuate the city rather than stay and be shot or blown up. Even though Sarajevo was besieged, people still managed to smuggle or bribe themselves out of the Serbian ring or get flown out by the United Nation forces securing Sarajevo's airport. As an added bonus, any non-Serb killed from the barrel of a Serbian rifle served to reduce the population of rival ethnic groups. Either way, a reduction of the non-Serb populace through death or forced migration was a step in the right direction for the attacking Serbs. Judging by the 100,000-plus civilians that fled Sarajevo, the Serbs' calculations were partially correct.

Furthermore, the Serbs used their sniper campaign as a means to pressure the government of Bosnia-Herzegovina into meeting their political demands. In this sense, the tortured city of Sarajevo was held hostage by the encircling Serbs. Every day the Serbs picked off more and more of the hard pressed Sarajevans, the Bosnian government could blame themselves for the carnage. If the Bosnian government wanted to stop the butchery, all they had to do was surrender and the killing would stop. Additionally, if the Sarajevans wanted to come to their senses and save themselves from further bloodshed, all they had to do was pressure their own government into giving up. The Serbs were saying *see, it's not our fault we are shooting you; it's your fault we are shooting you.*

Sniper's Alley

One of the city's prime killing fields and where one's brain may get fried was the east-west running main boulevard in downtown Sarajevo, dubbed 'Sniper's Alley' by its residents. This boulevard had wide, two-way streets and connected the newer industrial portion of the city with the older historic section. The southern edge of the boulevard was widened further by the tram tracks used before the siege for public transportation. Sniper's Alley became even more exposed after Sarajevans, who were desperate for firewood in the cold winter months, cut down the surrounding trees. Another open area - the ancient waters of the Miljacka River - bordered Sniper's Alley to the south, just a pistol shot away. It was from the far side of the Miljacka that the Serbian snipers had scores of excellent urban sniper positions to shoot from, including towering, concrete, multi-story apartment buildings.

Although Sarajevans quickly learned to avoid unnecessary movement along Sniper's Alley, risks still had to be taken to get food, water, and wood. For example, during most of the siege, one of the few sources of potable water was located near Sniper's Alley. People had to drink water to live and to get this life sustaining liquid they had to run a gauntlet under the gaze of waiting Serbian snipers. Also, people and soldiers had to regularly cross Sniper's Alley to get to the southern parts of the city still under Bosnian control. Even though north-south movement in the city was possible, the Serbian snipers tried hard to cut the city into northern and southern halves by focusing their efforts on Sniper's Alley.

Appropriately, the battle for Sarajevo began with a sniper attack along Sniper's Alley. The day was April 6, 1992 and thousands of Sarajevans gathered on the main boulevard, outside the Parliament building, to demonstrate for peace. Across the street (i.e. Sniper's Alley), just north of Parliament, was the Holiday Inn, a bright yellow building that became a famous landmark and reference point to all Sarajevans during the siege. In early April, the Holiday Inn was controlled by Serbs as it was the headquarters of the Serbian Democratic Party. While the crowd congregated on the streets in front of Parliament, hidden Serb snipers opened fire from the yellow Holiday Inn, wounding at least a dozen people. In response, the enraged crowd rushed the Holiday Inn, swarmed inside, and captured three people. One of those arrested was

reported to be a bodyguard for a Serbian official. The bodyguard was found hiding in the cellar of the Holiday Inn, armed with a sniper rifle. From that day on, the Holiday Inn was controlled by the Bosnian security forces and ceased to be a roost for Serbian snipers.[1]

As the war progressed, award winning war correspondent Peter Maass saw that the yellow Holiday Inn became a favorite target for Serbian snipers almost as if to say, *if you want the hotel, you can have it, and you can die in it.* The Serbs no longer occupied the hotel, but they still shot at it. One day, in March 1993, a Serbian sniper, positioned west of the city, fired an anti-aircraft gun at the people passing by the hotel. At the same time, other Serbian snipers fired from the eastern end of the city, targeting the hotel. Maass estimated the sniper with the anti-aircraft weapon fired fifty shots a day. At the time of his report, the snipers, altogether, were firing a shot every thirty seconds. Eventually, one of the snipers hit a man caught in the open. As the victim screamed in pain, nearby bystanders sprinted from cover and dragged the wounded man to safety. Then, a car drove up and took the bleeding man to the nearby hospital, which was only a few blocks away. Soon after the stricken man was hauled away, two unsuspecting girls were also targeted as they walked by the hotel. After hearing a bullet whiz by them, they dove to the ground and crawled through the mud to safety before they took off running zig-zag to a safer location.[2]

Not everyone was so lucky as to be merely wounded or to have to crawl through the mud to get away. Dienana Sokolovic lived with her family in Sarajevo where they were virtual prisoners in their own home because anyone who went outside was tar-

1 United Nations Report, *Study of the Battle and Siege of Sarajevo*, S/1994/674/ Add.2 (Vol. II), 27 May 1994).
2 Maass, *Love Thy Neighbor*, p. 146-148. (A superb account of the Siege of Sarajevo.)

geted by Serbian snipers. However, on November 18, 1994, a temporary cease fire was in effect and United Nations forces were present to enforce it. On that cold November day, Dienana and her seven year-old son, Nermin, took advantage of the lull in the shooting to go outside and find some firewood to heat their frigid home. As the two walked by a UN vehicle on their way home, a Serbian sniper picked them up in their scope. A single shot rang out and a bullet blew through Dienana's stomach and plowed into Nermin's head. The young boy died face down on the icy pavement, in a pool of his own spreading blood, in front of a UN armored personnel carrier. This was the reality of the Serbs' sniper policy.[3] This was the policy of Fry The Brain.

The Anonymous Killers

The men who blew the brains out of seven year-old boys did so from the security of the Serbian lines. These faceless killers lived in homes confiscated from non-Serbs and led relatively comfortable lives. Their homes had food, water, firewood, and electricity. While the Sarajevans sprinted for their lives, the Serbian snipers, who surrounded Sarajevo day and night, silently scanned the neighborhoods for their next prey. Since the Serbian snipers operated in relative safety, they could operate overtly. True, the Serbs had to be aware of the Bosnian's own snipers, but the Serbs still wore their uniforms openly as they went about their deadly work.

Sarajevans had little hope of finding out by name who the Serbian snipers that killed and maimed them. The Serbian military leadership certainly would not reveal who their snipers were and what areas of the city they targeted. Since numerous Serbian snipers overlapped one another, covering the same area of the city, only the individual sniper knew who they shot. For example, if three different snipers in three different locations targeted a man walking through the park behind the yellow Holiday Inn, only the man pulling the trigger knew who made the shot. The sniper who actually shot the unarmed civilian could always deny their role in the shooting since one of the other snipers could have done it as well. Multiple hidden snipers, firing at the same area of the city, provided the shooters with plausible deniability, making subsequent prosecution almost impossible.

While the majority of the Serbian snipers remained anonymous, some of the Sarajevans saw these killers up close. This close contact with their executioners happened whenever the Bosnian Serb Army recruited into their ranks other Bosnian Serbs who were from Sarajevo. These local recruits were a windfall to the BSA because they knew the city and the urban terrain like the back of their hands and, most importantly, they knew the people. But, the Sarajevan snipers working on the Serbian side were not killing strangers; they were killing their own neighbors. For this reason, a Serbian sniper, who was from Sarajevo and still lived in their own neighborhood, had to be careful. In fact, they had to operate like a guerrilla if they were to successfully conceal their crimes.

Journalist Michael Montgomery wrote about such an instance where his Serbian friend, Predrag Bundalo, worked as a sniper during the day, but lived in his Sarajevo neighborhood of Grbavica at night. Grbavica, strategically located in South-central Sarajevo, bordered the southern edge of the Miljacka River. Unlike the rest of Sara-

---

3 The Associated Press, *Bosnian Serb General Goes on Trial at Yugoslav War Crimes Tribunal for Sarajevo Siege*, Published: January 11, 2007.

A Sarajevan family mourns the loss of a loved one at a funeral...a product of the Serbs' terror campaign. by Mikhail Evstafiev

jevo, Grbavica was captured by surging Serbian forces in early 1992 at the beginning of the siege. What followed in the wake of the Serbian occupation of Grbavica was a particularly distasteful example of ethnic cleansing. In Grbavica, all the non-Serbs, to include old men, women, and children, were evicted from their homes, held as hostages, arbitrarily beaten, robbed, humiliated in every way possible, and executed at will. According to Human Rights Watch, the population of pre-war Grbavica was 31,000. After the brutal occupation by various Serb paramilitary groups, the post-war population was only 2,000.[4]

Predrag was truly a product of the new, cleansed Grbavica. He initially scoffed at fighting his fellow Sarajevans, but when a Serbian soldier stuck a gun in his face and ordered him to fight or die, he made the obvious choice to fight. The people of Grbavica, just like Predrag, became polarized in the ethnic-religious war forced on them. There were no gray areas. Either you fought for the Serbs or you were an enemy of the Serbs. There was no in between. Rumor said Predrag took up arms as ordered and manned the front lines in Grbavica in an apartment building hovering high over the Miljacka River. From this tall, drab, concrete apartment building, across from the yellow Holiday Inn, Predrag and his fellow Serbs had an excellent view of Sniper's Alley.

However, Predrag did more than just man an outpost with his AK-47; he volunteered to become a sniper. Predrag's motivation for his new trade came after a Bosnian sniper shot and killed his close friend (who was a fellow Serb soldier) right in front of him. Afterwards, Predrag secured an old M-48 rifle, which is a Yugoslavian copy of the famous German Mauser K98, and mounted a scope on it. Predrag the reluctant soldier died alongside his friend. The new Predrag, armed with his accurate sniper

4 Human Rights Watch, October 1994, Vol. 6, No. 15, Bosnia-Herzegovina Sarajevo.

rifle, began shooting across the Miljacka River with precision, killing his fellow Sarajevans. Along with this killing came a heavy drinking habit. The repeated, up-close killing of innocent people weighed so heavily on Predrag's mind he could only ease the burden through a painkiller - alcohol. Predrag was frying his own brain. After Predrag spent some time targeting Sarajevans across the Miljicka, he bragged to his own brother he already killed fifty people. A post-war investigation revealed Predrag was probably telling the truth since his favorite sniper position was across from a neighborhood where scores of innocent people were killed by sniper fire during the siege.

When the ugly siege of Sarajevo finally ended, the Bosnian War Crimes Commission investigated Predrag as a suspected war criminal. As fate would have it, the head of the war crimes commission was a Muslim lawyer who used to live in Predrag's own apartment building. But, Predrag would never be sentenced for his crimes. In May 1993, as Predrag sat in a friend's apartment, he was shot point blank in the head, execution-style. Predrag's death was ruled a suicide as no witnesses or potential suspects were ever named. The truth was, many people wanted Predrag dead. Ironically, some of Predrag's fellow Serbs thought he helped his Muslim neighbors too much. The local Muslims, who suffered under the Serbian jackboot and witnessed Predrag's own violent outbursts against them, also wanted him dead. In Sarajevo's new polarized society, Predrag was caught in the middle – and the middle was a dangerous place to be.

Even the Serbian military may have wanted Predrag dead. As a freelance sniper, killing unarmed civilians, Predrag was certainly carrying out an explicit Serbian policy of terror. However, since Predrag still lived among the remnants of the Grbavica populace and ran his mouth in bouts of drinking, his neighbors knew what he was doing. Predrag had lost his anonymity. Many people on both sides knew Predrag was a mass murderer. As a result, the Serb paramilitaries may have killed Predrag themselves just to shut his mouth. After all, the Serbs wanted to get away with their atrocities; they did not want to announce them publicly. The hard-drinking, violent, uncontrollable Predrag was a walking billboard for war crimes. With a bullet in Predrag's head, the Serbs' crimes were buried a little deeper. But not too deep.[5]

Sport Sniping: An Urban Myth?

The intense sniper campaign, involving shooters from both sides, provided perfect fodder for a growing sniper cult. The good shooters quickly acquired a reputation and became larger than life. Rumors about these deadly, incredibly accurate shootists spread like hot shrapnel throughout the city. The image of these feared snipers, seared into the mind's eye of the tortured public and fed by a constant supply of bone gnawing terror and morbid curiosity, created new urban myths. One story said a woman, who was a former marksman on the Romanian Olympic team, was now a bounty hunter, killing Muslim children in Sarajevo for 500 deutschemarks apiece. Another story circulated about a lone Bosnian Serb hunter. This old bearded man, who lived deep in the woods of middle Bosnia, had lost his son in the war. To avenge his son's death, the old man trudged to Sarajevo once a month to kill Sarajevans at random. A third tale said a young Bosnian girl, called the Raven, was forced out of her home at

5 Montgomery, *Face of Mercy, Face of Hate,* Minnesota Public Radio. (The information about Predrag came from Montgomery's article about his former friend who was transformed, and ultimately destroyed, by the Bosnian war.)

A member of the infamous Arkan Tigers holds a Heckler & Koch G3A3 sniper rifle. With its bipod, scope, and accuracy out to 500 meters, the G3A3 is a perfectly suitable urban sniping weapon.

gunpoint, along with her family, by Serb paramilitaries. The Serbs proceeded to rape her, shoot her, and left her for dead. However, she lived and woke up in a ditch as a raven pecked at the eyes of her dead father. From that day on, the Raven began her own merciless sniper crusade, shooting as many Serbs as she could.[6]

Along with these stories, another persistent rumor kept popping up concerning a new hobby for the outdoor-loving, adventurous type: the sport-sniping of Sarajevo's citizens. The first people to bring this practice to light were journalists who interviewed Bosnian Serbs on the front lines. One such journalist was Peter Maass who toured the Serbian lines and visited a Serbian heavy-machine gun position, pointing directly at the yellow Holiday Inn. During his conversations with the Serbs manning the machine-gun, the soldiers asked Maass if he wanted to fire off a few rounds at the hotel. Maass declined the invitation. But was this offer an isolated incident? Would other people get an invitation to kill Sarajevans? Would the next person, free from any legal repercussions whatsoever, decline the same tempting offer to kill? Or would they feel the adrenaline course through their body and make the decision to play god and take a life just because they could?

Maass was not alone in his experience. Another reporter recounted a similar story where a journalist visited a Bosnian Serb sniper position one night on the front lines to get a story. While the journalist was at the position, the Serbian sniper spotted two unsuspecting people down below, in the city, and asked the journalist who he should shoot…the one on the left or the one on the right? The journalist responded, with admirable moral strength, it was not his decision to make. This journalist was not going

6 Falk, *Hello to all That*, p.84-85.

to play god. The sniper then proceeded to shoot both people. Afterwards, the sniper counseled the journalist if he chose one of the victims, he would have let the other one live. This is an interesting story because it puts the impartial journalist in a moral dilemma. The journalist is pressured into actually participating in the war – rather than just observing it – in order to save lives.

In an even more disturbing report, a UN soldier, who served in Sarajevo during the siege, said he knew of a German 'businessman' who took the idea of shooting Sarajevans - just for fun - a step further. This businessman is alleged to have organized actual tours to the front lines around Sarajevo, in collusion with the Bosnian Serbs, so his clients could snipe at the city's people for sheer sport. While there is no hard evidence Europeans actually paid private businessmen to kill other humans for fun, many close observers of the siege of Sarajevo agree other Bosnian Serbs, who were not in the military and were not actively surrounding the city, did visit the Serbian lines and sniped at the people scurrying down below them in the city. These weekend warriors came to the front lines when their work schedules allowed them so they could bond with their Serbian brothers and help wipe out the Catholic Croatians and Bosnian Muslims infesting Sarajevo. In fact, the weekends were particularly deadly for Sarajevans because of the influx of these volunteer snipers who had some free time and an itchy trigger finger on their days off.[7]

The most damning evidence of sport-sniping involved an incident with Eduard Limonov, a well known Russian author and extreme left-wing nationalist who supported the Serbs and their policies of ethnic-cleansing, indiscriminate terror, and system of concentration camps. During the war, Limonov traveled to Bosnia to meet with and publicly show his support for Bosnian Serb leader Radovan Karadzic. While Limonov was in Bosnia, he traveled with Karadzic to Sarajevo so they could get a personal look at how the siege was going. While in the trenches, Karadzic invited Limonov to fire off a few rounds from a sniper rifle at the Sarajevans. Limonov was more than happy to comply. What better way to show one's solidarity for the poor Bosnian Serbs than to help them kill their inhuman enemy, hunkered down in the ruins of Sarajevo? We know this incident is not mere rumor because a BBC news crew filmed the entire sniping incident on tape and aired it to the world.

To what extent sport-sniping went on during the siege is unknown. To the Serbs, sport-sniping was no more repulsive than their system of organized rape camps and, as such, was a reflection of the Bosnian Serb mentality. The Serbs saw the Sarajevans as animals, who anyone had the right to kill. You did not have to wear a uniform or even be a lawful combatant to kill. All you needed was a rifle, a bullet (and those items could be supplied free of charge for your convenience), and the desire to kill someone. The Serbs were glad to get more people involved in the killing because it made their hands appear less bloody and made their consciences a little clearer. After all, if journalists, European businessmen, famous authors, and average working class slobs were all sniping at and killing Sarajevans, it must be okay. It was to the Serbs' advantage to dirty the hands of others, to include them in their own criminal campaign of indiscriminate terror, because it weakened the world's ability to stop the Serbs or to punish them after the fact. If the whole world was sniping at the people of Sarajevo, what was the big deal?

---

7 Maass, *Love Thy Neighbor*, p.110.

Grbavica

It was from these apartments in Grbavica where the Serbs directed most of their sniper campaign. The Holiday Inn and Snipers Alley was only a short several hundred meters away from these perfect sniper roosts.

Serbian War Crimes and the Sniper Campaign

There were many Serbian men like Predrag Bundalo and Eduard Limonov who killed innocent men, women, and children from the safety of their hidden sniper hides, separated by hundreds of meters of urban terrain. Most of these men never took a bullet to the head like Predrag or were caught on film like Limonov. Most escaped justice and blended back into Serbian and Bosnian society once the Dayton Peace Accords were signed. Dejan Anastasijevic interviewed one such former Serbian sniper who actually 'worked' in Grbavica during the siege. Of course, the former sniper, now a waiter in a Belgrade cafe, says he never did anything wrong, he never targeted innocents.[8] Who could prove he was lying? These anonymous killers could easily deny their wartime actions and claim to be common soldiers or even admit to being a sniper, but one that only engaged legitimate military targets. This denial of reality worked for the faceless men pulling the triggers, but not for their leaders who ordered the deliberate, coordinated sniper campaign against Sarajevo's population.

After the war ended and Sarajevans once again walked their streets without fear of absorbing a full-metal jacketed bullet, the UN war crimes tribunal pursued the architects of the siege of Sarajevo. One of the commanders who fell under UN scrutiny was Major General Stanislav Galic, commander of the Sarajevo Romanija Corps besieging Sarajevo from September 1992 until August 1994. Another war criminal was the subsequent commander of the Romanija Corps, Dragomir Milosevic, who commanded from August 1994 until the end of the war in late 1995. Even though Galic and Milosevic never pulled a trigger or killed an unarmed civilian with a sniper rifle, many of the men under their command did. According to the law of armed conflict, if they ordered their men to target civilians through a sniper campaign, they also committed a war crime. Furthermore, if they knew the men under their command were committing war crimes and then failed to stop them, they were again in breach of the law of armed

---

8 Anastasijevic, Dejan, *The End of The Sniper War, Death In The Eye.*

conflict.

While Galic and Milosevic denied any direct knowledge of the crimes committed under their command, Louise Arbour, the prosecutor for the international criminal tribunal for the former Yugoslavia, had more than enough evidence to the contrary. The tribunal charged Galic and Milosevic both with crimes against humanity. The specific charges concerning the sniper campaign were explicit: "Between 10 September 1992 and 10 August 1994, Stanislav Galic, as Commander of Bosnian Serb forces comprising or attached to the Sarajevo Romanija Corps, conducted a coordinated and protracted campaign of sniper attacks upon the civilian population of Sarajevo, killing and wounding a large number of civilians of all ages and both sexes, such attacks by their nature involving the deliberate targeting of civilians with direct fire weapons."[9]

In 1999, Galic was arrested and put on trial at The Hague. While Galic maintained his innocence, he was hit with an avalanche of thoroughly documented examples of terror and murder. For example, on October 24, 1994, Adnan Kasapovic, a 16 year-old boy, was shot in the chest and killed while walking in an alley adjoining Dzordze Andrijevica Kuna Street. On December 8, 1994, Lejla Bajramovic, a woman aged 24 years, was sitting in a friend's apartment in Franca Lehara Street, near the center of Sarajevo, when she was shot in the head and killed. The shot came through the apartment window. On May 3, 1995, Semsa Covrk a woman aged 27 years, was shot and wounded in the abdomen while walking in Josipa Krasa Street, Novi Grad, holding her young son's hand at the time. The list went on and on and on.[10]

After being swamped with case after horrible case, to include eyewitness testimony, the lawyers defending Galic could not deny the sniper killings took place. Instead, the defense argued the civilians who were killed and wounded during the sniper campaign were 'accidental victims' and 'collateral damage' of the overall conflict. The judge presiding over the trial did not agree with the defense and Galic was sentenced to twenty years in prison (a sentence that was subsequently raised to life in prison.) General Milosevic finally surrendered to authorities in 2004 and his case went to trial in The Hague in January 2007. Later that year, Milosevic was found guilty of war crimes and crimes against humanity and was sentenced to thirty-three years in prison. Just like the Nazis who were convicted of genocide against the Jews, the Serbian leadership was charged with their own war crimes, based largely on their sniper campaign. The judgments handed down at The Hague were intended to signal to the world that such crimes, directed against innocent people, were unacceptable. Maybe, just maybe, these rulings against the slaughter of innocent civilians at the hands of willing snipers would prevent similar crimes in the future.

The Bosnian Sniper Effort

The Bosnians trapped in Sarajevo, suffering a steady stream of losses under the Serbs' concerted sniper campaign, needed more than an eventual ruling at some distant UN court to stop the hemorrhaging. They too needed snipers to take out the Serbs' precision riflemen that ringed the city. Since the defending Bosnians did not have any professional snipers or an established sniper school to send new students

9 International Criminal Tribunal Indictment, The Prosecutor of the Tribunal against Stanislav Galic, Dragomir Milosevic Case IT-98-29-I.
10 International Criminal Tribunal Indictment, The Prosecutor of the Tribunal against Stanislav Galic, Dragomir Milosevic Case IT-98-29-I.

Yugoslavian M48 Mauser

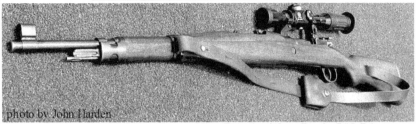

photo by John Harden

Above is an actual M48 sniper rifle, fitted with a Zrak ON-76 scope, used by Bosniak snipers to defend Sarajevo. The M48 was made at the Preduzece 44 arms factory, which was part of Zastava Arms. Before the war, Yugoslavian competition shooters frequently used the M48 for their target matches. When war came to Sarajevo, both Serbian and Bosniak snipers employed these same weapons on the front lines.

through, they had to make do with what they had. As a result, the Bosnian sniper corps consisted of a hodgepodge of volunteers, both men and women, with varying skills and experience (if any), and an accompanying collage of sniper weapons. Bosnian government officials were quick to state they only had anti-sniper teams needed to fight the Serbs' own snipers. Truth be told, the Bosnians used snipers to pick off careless Serbian soldiers, to silence Serbian sniper teams, and even to spread terror amongst civilians living behind the Serbian lines.

One of the early sniper volunteers was a Serbian woman who went by the nom de guerre Arrow. The daughter of a policeman, Arrow grew up around guns, eventually took up the sport of target shooting, and even had plans to try out for the Yugoslav national shooting team. After the war engulfed Sarajevo, Arrow was no longer shooting paper targets, she was on a dedicated Bosnian sniper team, hunting down Serbian snipers and eliminating enemy machine-gun crews. For Arrow, her target shooting skills transferred easily to the urban battlefield, enabling her to rack up a long list of kills with her scope-mounted, bolt-action hunting rifle.[11] According to other rumors, the Bosnians employed another female sniper who was previously on the Yugoslav Olympic rifle team. The UN commander of Sarajevo, General MacKenzie, seemed to confirm these rumors by telling reporters he, too, heard of a woman Olympic shooter who already scored sixty-five kills early on in the siege.[12]

Sniper Documentary

While stories of female Olympic shooters grabbed the imagination of Sarajevans and foreign journalists alike, the reality was often something different. Fortunately, a look into the daily life of Bosnia's real-life snipers was provided by French journalist Phillippe Buffon who made a 25-minute documentary about a group of Bosnian government snipers fighting in Sarajevo. The snipers in the documentary are not fiercely

11 Associated Press, Canberra Times, July 1992.
12 Maass, *Love Thy Neighbor*, p.29.

beautiful women, looking down the barrel of their expensive target rifles with eagle eyes; they are a group of average Bosnian Joes doing a dirty and dangerous job. Appropriately enough, Buffon begins the film with himself dodging Serbian sniper fire as he runs from cover to cover until he safely reaches the thirty-story Parliament building housing a group of Bosnian snipers. It is interesting to note the Bosnian militia members that guide Buffon to the building carry weapons, but are not wearing uniforms. If now-convicted General Galic had this movie in his hands during his trial, he would, without a doubt, have screamed, "Look how they carry weapons illegally with no uniform! Every person that our snipers shot was like this! As soon as we shoot an armed Bosnian, they hide the weapon and claim they are an innocent civilian!"

Inside the bowels of the towering building is a sniper group of about twenty men. The snipers are armed with Yugoslavian M76 sniper rifles, which they captured from the Serbs during previous fighting. The Bosnians have sniper teams positioned in the upper floors of the building and rotate them out every twenty-four hours. Buffon arrives in time to go with one of the shift changes, which consists of a two-man sniper team. One sniper is in a camouflaged uniform and carries an M76, with a scope, and a suppressor. The other shooter, a young man named Goran, also has an M76 with a scope, but no suppressor. Goran is wearing a blue, one-piece coverall, like what a mechanic might wear.

The two men take the still-working elevator to the upper floors to find a room to shoot from, like two businessmen going to their office to sell life insurance. From their sniper's perch, they have a commanding view of the Miljacka River and the Serb-held neighborhood of Grbavica. Goran is from Grbavica. Most likely, he knows who Predrag Bundalo is – the Sarajevan Serb turned sniper. Unknowingly, Predrag and Goran have dueled against each other for the past several months. Both grew up in the same neighborhood, one a Serb and one a Muslim, and both are snipers trying to kill each other - another sad story in a city torn apart by polarized factions.

From the room overlooking Grbavica, Goran takes aim and fires two shots. After the last bullet flies downrange, Goran and his partner quickly leave the room and go down the nearby stairs and change levels to escape any possible Serbian counter-attack. Goran is smart to vacate the immediate area because his sniper tradecraft is almost non-existent. All Goran does is walk in a room with a good view, aims his rifle for several seconds, fires a few shots out of a shattered window, and then moves to another position. Goran makes no effort to hide his muzzle blast and flash and any alert Serbian counter-sniper team could have seen and heard Goran's gunshots with ease.

Two things probably save Goran as a sniper. First, the Parliament building they operate in has dozens of floors and hundreds of rooms and windows to shoot from. Any one of these places in the enormous building could be used as a sniper hide. This sheer volume of possible firing locations alone makes it difficult for the Serbs to locate Goran's team because they are constantly changing positions. Goran's team shoots, moves, and then they are gone, lurking somewhere else inside the hulking building. Second, the Serbian counter-sniper teams are probably as unskilled as the Bosnian snipers. The Serbs know the Bosnians have been using the Parliament building ever since the start of the war as a sniper post. However, Goran and his partners are able to fire multiple shots, in broad daylight, and get away with it. Goran may not be a very skilled sniper, but he does not have to be. He is on par with his Serbian foe.

After this first episode, Goran and his partner go to another location. This time,

Yugoslavian M59/66 SKS

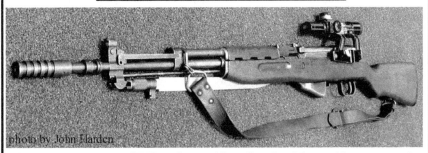

photo by John Harden

Above is an actual SKS sniper rifle, fitted with a side-mounted M89 scope, used by Bosniak snipers to defend Sarajevo. The SKS semi-automatic rifle isn't a weapon inherently capable of long distance precision shooting because of its sloppy design, but during the war, Bosniak soldiers were hard pressed and were forced to use anything they could get their hands on.

Goran's partner with the suppressed rifle takes aim and fires several shots. However, Goran's partner positions himself deep in the room so he is hidden by the shadows, behind the office's desks and window blinds. When Goran's partner makes his shots, even an alert Serbian counter-sniper team would be unable to determine his location. After this operation, Buffon films one more scene of other Bosnian snipers shooting from a bombed-out apartment building in the western suburb of Dobrinja, near the airport. These shooters also show very little knowledge of sniper tradecraft. Clearly they are untrained men and women who have been given a sniper rifle and told to go kill Serbs. In their minds, all you have to do is poke a rifle out through a hole in a wall, pull the trigger, then move to a new location somewhere in the ruins of the huge building and do it again.

Overall, the Bosnian snipers in the film are untrained in even the most rudimentary urban sniping tradecraft. They know enough to shoot and move because their comrades before them have been shot up by the Serbs before by not moving after shooting. Their understanding of sniper warfare is based entirely on personal experience. The reason why the Bosnian shooters can get away with their limited skill level is because the complex urban terrain allows them to. This documentary clearly shows what an equalizer the urban terrain is and how it protects the Bosnians from the more professional, organized Serb attackers.[13]

Shot Through the Heart

One of the true tragedies of the Bosnian war was friend often fought friend. After the war broke out, people who knew each other all their lives now found themselves committed to killing each other. This was the case of two long-time friends, Slavko Simic and Vlado Sarzinsky, who, before the war, competed on the same Yugoslav national marksmanship team. With Sarajevo at war, Slavko, a Serb, was called up to

13 Buffon, *Sarajevo: Sniper, The Fight*. (This is an excellent documentary any interested student of the Sarajevan sniper war should watch.)

fight in the new Bosnian Serb Army. Vlado, a Croat with a Muslim wife, choose to stay and defend Sarajevo. The war, like a giant bloody axe, effectively cleaved their relationship in half now that a Serb was expected to kill a Croat or Muslim and a Croat or Muslim was expected to return the favor.

Slavko's expertise as a long-distance rifle marksman inevitably led him to become a sniper for the Bosnian Serb Army where his extreme skill enabled him to train other Serbian snipers to become better shooters. For the Serbs and their sniper campaign, Slavko was a gift from heaven because he enabled the Serbs to spread their terror more accurately and from longer ranges. However, Slavko did not just train other snipers to spread terror, he personally participated in the slaughter, skillfully picking off unsuspecting men, women, and children with a single head shot, at extreme distances, from his customized target rifle.

On the opposite side of the battlefield, amidst the partially destroyed buildings and pockmarked streets, Vlado also served as a sniper. While sharing the same vocation as Slavko, Vlado's job was to stop the killing of Sarajevans by taking out the Serbs' own sniper teams. Vlado and the anti-sniper teams he trained proved successful, taking out twenty Serb snipers in the first three months of the war alone. Ironically, both men, due to their shooting skills and the importance of sniping in Sarajevo's urban setting, ended up training and leading competing sniper teams. Eventually, Vlado's and Slavko's paths crossed.

The collision course began in July 1992 when a particularly skilled Serbian sniper began working Vlado's neighborhood. Vlado described the new presence, "This one was different from the others. He shot from extremely far away, an expert shooter. Must be. Four, five hundred meter. And from that distance he never missed, always hitting his target in the head. Consistent. Always in head."[14] Vlado spent the following days studying this new threat, talking to people, and observing the urban terrain as he conducted an investigation in order to glean anything that might betray the enemy sniper. Finally, after a thorough detective effort, Vlado spoke to a medic who extracted a bullet from one of the victims. It was a 7.92 mm bullet, what is often referred to as a German 8 mm round. Then, a week after talking to the medic, the deadly Serb sniper took another shot, and Vlado heard an unmistakable sound - that of a 7.92 mm rifle.

Vlado recognized the sound of the 7.92 mm rifle as a Mauser K98. He knew the sound because he shot the Mauser K98 for years on the national rifle team with Slavko. The distinctive sound of the Mauser was much different from the sounds of the 7.62 mm M-76 sniper rifle most of the Serb snipers used. In fact, no one used a 7.92 mm rifle anymore. The 7.92 mm round was used by the Germans during WW II, but since was replaced by the standard 7.62 mm NATO round. Vlado calculated at the start of the war there were sixteen Mauser 98's in Sarajevo and he could account for fourteen of them. One of the missing two rifles belonged to Slavko.

In late July, the Serb sniper made a mistake. He was seen by one of Vlado's spotters as he entered a building, only two hundred meters away from the front lines. Vlado then moved into an opposing position, so he had a good view of the sniper when he exited his hide. Hours later, Vlado heard the distinctive report of the Mauser K98 and then saw a sniper running from the building. Vlado took aim, fired, and knocked the running sniper to the ground. Weeks later, Vlado talked to a former prisoner who was

---

14 Falk, *Hello to all That*, p. 201.

Bosniak Sniper Team

A Bosniak sniper, showing poor urban sniping tradecraft, takes aim with an M76 sniper rifle.

photo by Igor Beres

exchanged for other Serb prisoners. The ex-prisoner told Vlado what he already suspected, but did not want to hear: the sniper he shot was his best friend, Slavko.[15]

Freelance journalist John Falk, while he worked in Sarajevo, had a chance to talk to a Serbian defector named Slobo who was stationed in the front lines across from Vlado's sniper positions. Slobo told Falk, "Everyone out there knows of Vlado. The Chetniks call him the Ustashe, and he is the devil to them. Anyone here long enough fears the Ustashe. The new guys come on the line, but they don't know. I would try to tell them: Be careful, the Ustashe is out there. This man will kill you if you are not careful. Young guys, stupid, don't believe."[16] The Serbs called Vlado the 'Ustashe' because they knew Vlado was Croatian. During World War II, the fascist Croatian government, called the 'Ustashe', collaborated with Hitler's Germany and practiced their own bloody ethnic-cleansing campaign against the Serbs.

Falk, who spent many long hours with Vlado on sniper duty, noted Vlado was such a good urban sniper because he was a good observer. Vlado spent most of his time doing nothing more than watching and recording the urban terrain on the Serbian side. Vlado valued observation so much he organized teams of spotters who did nothing but watch the Serb lines. These observers recorded everything in their notebooks. Everything. They watched the Serbian people. They watched windows. They watched bunkers. They watched holes in the walls of buildings. They looked for the smallest detail that might reveal an enemy sniper's position. Then they wrote it down so all the other snipers could read and study the history of the neighborhood they were stalking. It was this steady, methodical approach that enabled Vlado to out-duel Slavko, to shoot scores of

15 Falk, *Hello to all That*, p.201-3.
16 Falk, *Hello to all That*, p.165.

Serbian snipers and soldiers, and to make it through four years of war alive.

Guerrilla Sniper Operations

While the initial stages of the war demanded any person with better than average shooting skills become a sniper, the defending Bosniak forces eventually developed a more sophisticated, deliberate sniper effort. This advanced sniping was developed covertly in a Bosnian paramilitary unit called 'Seve' (seva means "lark") which answered only to the senior Bosniak political leadership, to include the head of the Bosniak government itself: Alija Izetbegovic.

One of the specially trained snipers from the Seve, Nedzad Herenda, when being interrogated by the Bosniak intelligence service, described some of their training. Herenda, and other snipers who worked with him, to include foreign fighters, attended sniper instruction at various camps located in territory still under Bosnian government control. After receiving training in the fundamentals of marksmanship, the Seve snipers honed their skills by sniping at civilians living in the Serb-occupied suburb of Grbavica. Herenda and the other snipers found any civilian to be suitable as a target, like old women. When shooting old women, they made sure the victims were wearing all black, which was a common practice by elderly Christian women. The Seve shooters wanted to make sure they gunned down Christian, not Muslim, women.

Besides terrorizing the civilian populace through illegal killings, Seve was assigned even more politically sensitive operations, like the shooting of UN peacekeepers. In one particular incident, the Seve allegedly shot and killed a French soldier in downtown Sarajevo so it looked like the Serbs did the sniping. But, after a battlefield investigation, the UN determined the bullet could not have been fired from Serb-held territory in Grbavica as first claimed. Even though investigators determined the French peacekeeper was not fired on from Serbian lines, they could not prove who actually pulled the trigger. After this botched attempt to incriminate the Serbs in order to bring increasing UN political and military pressure against the Serbs, the Bosnian government used their political leverage to protect the Seve and prevent any further investigation into the matter. This was relatively easy to do because of the lack of forensic evidence and because the general public already knew Serb snipers targeted UN forces in the past. As a result of the Serbs' dismal sniping track record, which made it possible to frame them in the first place, it was hard for any investigation to build momentum.[17]

Sarajevo's Counter-Sniper Response

Dedicated anti-sniper teams, like the ones trained by Vlado, were just one way the Bosnians tried to lessen the effects of the Serbs' own sniper campaign. But, clearly, this was not enough to ensure the safety of Saraejvo's population. Just as the Bosnian snipers learned through trial and error, the hundreds of thousands of Sarajevans who suffered under the longest sniper campaign in history, became well versed in counter-sniper methodology through experience. It did not take long before everyone, from little children to old women, knew what it took to avoid getting hit by a Serbian sniper. Soon, warning signs emblazoned with *"Pazi! Snajper!"* sprung up across

---

17 Suljak, *Seve Practiced by Shooting Civilians in Sarajevo.*

photo by Tom Stoddart

Counter-Sniper

A Bosniak soldier replaces the head on a dummy in Sarajevo. The intent was for the Serbian snipers to shoot at the dummy, thus revealing their position. Then, the Bosniak snipers, who were hiding in the city nearby, would spot the Serbian muzzle blasts and then zero in on the now-exposed Serbian shooter. Counter-sniper ruses like this had been used at least since WW I and were still effective in the Siege of Sarajevo.

the city, cautioning people about particularly dangerous areas. Eventually, every technique known to man was used to stay alive, including new ones the world never saw before.

One of the easiest things to do to stay alive was to not give the Serbian snipers an easy target. People who lived in buildings located in the line of fire walled off the side of their buildings facing the enemy. Windows were boarded up, bricked up, or covered with blankets. Doors were nailed shut. People then altered their movement to and from their buildings so they always left through the back to avoid the more dangerous exposed ones. If the distance from one building to another was reasonable, the neighborhood got together and dug trenches between them so they could travel back and forth, out of sight of wary Serbian snipers.

Traveling in the open on the streets and sidewalks always involved an element of danger. Consequently, Sarajevans driving in cars sped down exposed routes like madmen, with tires squealing and brakes screeching, as they dodged potholes made by incoming mortar rounds, to make themselves a harder target. Pedestrians – old men, teenagers, little children or anyone else who wanted to live - sprinted from cover to cover. If they were in the open for long periods of time, they ran zig-zag patterns to throw off Serbian marksmen. Although it had nothing to do with fitness, Sarajevo became a city of avid runners. Walking and driving slowly increased your chances of catching a bullet. If you wanted to live, you went everywhere fast and in an erratic manner.

Whenever possible, additional measures were taken to protect the citizens of Sarajevo. For example, Kulovica Street ran North-South through downtown Sarajevo, offering Serbian snipers an open, linear kill zone. To block the Serbian view of the Sarajevans passing by Kulovica Street, the Bosnians emplaced a giant concrete block in front of it. This block eventually became a well known landmark after someone spray-painted the words 'Pink Floyd' across it. The block was removed during a temporary 1994 cease-fire, but the sniping soon renewed. This time, Kulovica Street was blocked off with an enormous piece of blue cloth that once hung at the Zetra sports hall, where the 1984 winter Olympics were officially closed. This blue shield, that once provided a royal backdrop to competing Olympians, now hid Sarajevans from Serbian snipers.

Sometimes nature helped protect the city of Sarajevo from accurately fired bullets. Whenever it rained, snipers had a difficult time acquiring potential targets. The same could be said during periods of fog and snow. The winter months provided much needed relief from the snipers because the days were shorter and the nights longer. While the Serbians did have some night vision equipment for their rifles, it was much harder to make a night shot as one stared through the grainy, greenish hue of a night-scope. Sarajevans were probably never safer from the sniper threat than at night and in bad weather. Then, they could be safe with a slow jog or by simply moving while concealed in the darkness.

The Airfield Problem

From the early stages of the siege, both attacking Serbs and defending Bosnians agreed to let the United Nations (UN) administer Sarajevo International Airport. Control of the airport was a critical issue because it enabled the UN to fly in humanitarian aid like medical supplies and food to the besieged Sarajevans. For sure, Sarajevans benefited from the UN aid because city officials were able to provide a higher level of care for their trapped citizens. Thousands of more Sarajevans would have undoubtedly perished through starvation, dehydration, and lack of medical care if the airport was not run by the UN. However, the attacking Serbs benefited too. By allowing the UN to run the airport and provide humanitarian aid, the Serbs showed to the world they were not fighting a war against the citizens of Sarajevo.

The UN control of the airport did help the Sarajevans, but the airport's location caused problems for the Bosnian government because it was located in an exposed suburb, several kilometers southwest of downtown Sarajevo. In order for Sarajevans to make it to or from the airport, they had to run a gauntlet of fire from wary Serbian snipers. The UN forces running the airport were themselves in a precarious situation because the airport was the only place on the Sarajevo perimeter not controlled by the Serbs. While the Serbs physically controlled the northern and southern ends of the airport, Bosnian government forces controlled the eastern and western sides of the airport. Consequently, UN forces were caught quite literally in between the warring sides, sandwiched in between two separate groups trying to kill one another.

The Serbs agreed to let the UN run the airport, but at a price. The Serbs would only let the UN control the airport if they prevented the Bosnians from crossing from the east, over the airfield itself, and into the western Bosnian held side. Consequently, the UN was placed in a position of helping to enforce the Serbian stranglehold on the city while providing aid to the very citizens the Serbs targeted with snipers and artillery. Still, many Sarajevans defied the UN and tried to sprint across the open tarmac to the

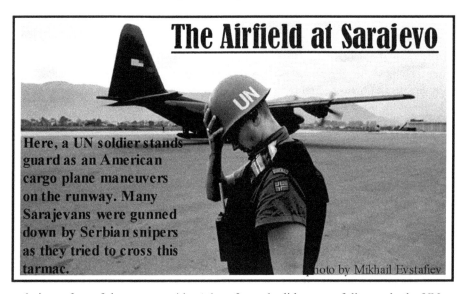

The Airfield at Sarajevo

Here, a UN soldier stands guard as an American cargo plane maneuvers on the runway. Many Sarajevans were gunned down by Serbian snipers as they tried to cross this tarmac.

Photo by Mikhail Evstafiev

relative safety of the western side. A lot of people did successfully evade the UN security guards and dodge the Serbian snipers as they ran for dear life across the asphalt pavement to the west.

But, crossing the windswept tarmac under the scopes of Serbian shooters was expensive. Hundreds of people are estimated to have been gunned down as they ran frantically in the open, completely exposed to the Serbs. Ironically, the UN forces helped the Serb shooters do their dirty work. Often times, UN security forces exposed groups of Sarajevans with floodlights as they made a mad nighttime dash to freedom. Once the people were lit up under the UN lights, the Serbian shooters had perfect targets. Men, women, and children of all descriptions met their end on the exposed airfield as they tried to make it past the UN guards aiming their bright spotlights and the hidden Serb marksmen aiming their sniper rifles.

By the end of 1992, it was clear the UN controlled airport was a major obstacle to the Bosniak government that had to be overcome. True, pockets of desperate civilians made it across the airfield on occasion, but, loads of weapons, ammunition, and fuel certainly could not make it through the gauntlet. Consequently, the Bosnian government made the decision (a decision that was a closely guarded secret) to dig a tunnel underneath the airport to connect the two Bosnian sides separated by the airport. Work started in early 1993 from both sides. It took months of back-breaking work, but after workers toiled night and day in eight-hour shifts, the two sides met together in July of 1993. The physical encirclement of the city was broken.

From that point on, weapons and people flowed underneath the airport. Sometimes it took up to two hours to travel the eight hundred meters, through the claustrophobic confines of the hastily excavated tunnel. While the journey could be drawn out and exhausting, it was infinitely preferable to running helter-skelter across the runway under the crosshairs of a Serbian sniper. The Serbian shooters could not see through tons of earth nor could they shoot through the paved runway. For the Sarajevans, the best counter-sniper method at the airport was to go underground like human moles.

The United Nations' Counter-Sniper Efforts

The UN first became involved in Yugoslavia's war in September 1991 when the Security Council adopted a resolution calling on all states to enforce a 'general and complete embargo on all deliveries of weapons and military equipment to Yugoslavia'. While this resolution appeared to be a fair and balanced way to limit an increase in the scope of the war, it hurt the Bosnian government more than the Serbs. This was because the Bosnian Serbs were supplied from the arsenals of the former JNA while the Bosnian government had to smuggle in arms from the international black market. This also meant while Bosnian Serbs targeted Sarajevans with state of the art .50 caliber Black Arrow sniper rifles manufactured by the Zastava Arms Factory, the Bosnian defenders resorted to using World War II-era rifles or sniper rifles captured from the Serbs.

From the initial stages of fighting in Sarajevo, the UN had a presence in the city. Their biggest impact, as mentioned, was the impartial management of Sarajevo Airport starting in July 1992. Besides the airport, the UN also had several outposts located throughout the city where they could monitor the fighting and better carry out their mission, which was to make the siege more humane by providing food supplies and medical care to the people, to evacuate people by air, to facilitate Red Cross operations, and to influence the way both sides fought the war. One of the ways the UN attempted to make the war more humane for Sarajevans was to protect them from the Serbian snipers ringing the city.

One thing UN forces could do to protect the people was to transport them from one place in the city to another inside the armored hulls of the UN's distinctive, white-washed armored personnel carriers. Thus, the UN, at times, became an armored taxi service. But, traveling in an armored car was no guarantee of safety as one could get shot as they entered and exited the vehicle. In fact, acting Bosnian Prime Minister Hakija Turajlic was shot in 1993 while riding in the back of a UN armored car as a French patrol escorted him from the airport. The French soldiers made the mistake of opening the rear of the vehicle at a checkpoint and then left it open as they drove off.

The UN did more than provide transportation in the city; they also provided a presence in civilian areas. This UN presence was meant to deter Serbian snipers by saying, in effect, *hey, we're the UN, we can see what is going on, so you better not shoot at the surrounding civilians because we will know who did it.* Again, being near a UN checkpoint or patrol did not automatically extend an invisible force field of protection around Sarajevans as many a person was shot within a stone's throw of UN soldiers on 'anti-sniper' duty. It also did not help the Sarajevans' confidence much when the UN soldiers themselves were targeted by Serbian snipers, as they frequently were.

Another counter-sniper measure the UN tried at various times during the siege was the arrangement of anti-sniping agreements between the warring sides. Often, such agreements were not worth the paper they were written on. In Sarajevo, such anti-sniping agreements lasted, maybe, for a few weeks or only days before a sniper decided, at least for him, the truce was over. During the trial of General Galic, an eyewitness for the prosecution, Mensur Jusic, described in detail one such incident where an anti-sniper truce only led to more carnage. It was September 1993 and an anti-sniper truce was in effect. Sarajevans felt a little more relaxed, walked a little more slowly, and even rode on the city's trams. Then, as one tram trundled along its tracks,

UN Peacekeepers

photo by Mikhail Evstafiev

The UN used these armored trucks to ferry civilians and soldiers across the city in order to protect them from Serbian snipers.

a Serbian sniper could not resist such a fat target - a tram packed with unsuspecting civilians. At an intersection, the sniper opened fire, hitting the tram with a bursting bullet, wounding four people to include the prosecution's witness, Mensur Jusic, and another witness's eight-year-old son. After the bullet impacted, the people dove to the floor for protection, lying in the blood that was now everywhere, until the tram driver accelerated out of the kill zone.[18]

The UN's Anti-Sniper Challenges

The UN also established dedicated anti-sniper teams whose job was to enforce the anti-sniper truces. However, these teams did not operate in the classic anti-sniper role and were largely ineffective. During a sniper truce agreed to on August 14, 1994, French peacekeeping soldiers were assigned the job of anti-sniping duties. What this equated to was the peacekeepers would observe the surrounding terrain and whenever a sniper made a shot, they would record the events, such as the date and time of the shot, from what location the shot came from, and which side they thought fired the shot. That was it. The UN anti-sniper teams had no teeth and were incapable of enforcing the truce. The teams only had the authority to arrest confirmed snipers who violated the truce and they could only use deadly force to defend themselves if they came under fire.

Since the UN was the only force in the city considered a higher authority, with the ability to influence the actions of the warring parties by arresting violators of a sniper truce, both sides found it to their advantage to conceal their sniper operations. For this reason, both Bosnian government snipers and Serbian snipers acted like guerrillas when the situation demanded it. It was easy for these guerrilla snipers to conceal their actions when they sniped at 'off-limit' people during the truces (like civilians, journalists and UN soldiers) due to the disposition of UN forces in the city.

Because the UN forces were positioned at various compounds at the airport and in

---

18 International Criminal Tribunal Indictment, The Prosecutor of the Tribunal against Stanislav Galic, Dragomir Milosevic, Case IT-98-29-I.

the city itself, they were located relatively far from the Serbian front lines and their sniper positions. So, if a Serbian sniper fired on an unarmed civilian during a sniper truce, what was the UN going to do? A UN anti-sniper team would have to determine the location of the shot, and then drive for ten minutes across open terrain, in their white armored personnel vehicles, until they reached the Serbian lines. Once they reached the Serbian lines, the Serbs may or may not agree to let the UN patrol enter their lines, or they may delay the patrol, giving the sniper time to get away. When the UN patrol finally reached the suspected location of the shot, the Serbian sniper was long gone, hiding safely as a regular soldier somewhere else in the Serbian lines.

Even if a UN patrol found the person who they thought fired the shot, how were they going to prove it? The patrol would have to, first, find the weapon fired in the incident and then seize it as evidence. Then, the patrol would have to go back to the scene of the shooting, find the bullet fired from that rifle, and then compare that bullet to a sample bullet fired from the captured weapon, all in a forensic lab. If it could be proven the captured rifle fired the bullet that hit an innocent victim, then the UN still had to prove a particular Serbian soldier fired that rifle. And where were the anti-sniper teams' fingerprint kits? Where were their gunshot residue test kits? Were these anti-sniper teams trained to dust a rifle for fingerprints and to test a person for residue in order to irrefutably link a suspected shooter with a specific weapon? Hardly. The UN was ill-prepared to conduct anything beyond basic battlefield investigations and had little chance to capture a Serbian sniper after the act.

In comparison, the UN had a better chance to capture Bosnian snipers who violated the sniper truces because the UN could move freely in the city, among the people. The UN did not have to cross a Bosnian trench line or get permission to pass through a Bosnian checkpoint because UN forces lived in the city, behind the Bosnian lines, and in many ways aided the Bosnians in their defense of the city. Therefore, the Bosnian snipers had to be more skilled at hiding their sniping activities than the Serbs who were separated by distance and the real barrier of a front line.

One day, at the end of August 1994, just two weeks into a UN enforced sniper-truce, several uniformed Bosnian men were seen in front of a downtown café, armed with sniper rifles. Then, they got in a beat-up, bullet-ridden Volkswagen Golf, drove off down the street, and snuck into the Parliament building. After firing several shots at the Serbians' own snipers positioned in the opposing Jewish cemetery, the snipers hastily departed the Parliament building and returned to the café, minus their weapons. French soldiers of the UN force heard the shooting and knew it came from the Parliament building. In response, the French soldiers contacted the Sarajevo police in order to get them to investigate the shooting and arrest the violators of the truce.

Of course, the police had no interest in investigating anything that involved their own snipers. By the time the French forces, along with a contingent of Sarajevan police, actually reached and surrounded the Parliament building to search for the snipers, the shooters were long gone. Fortunately for the shooters, the police stalled the UN forces long enough for the Bosnian snipers to escape the scene of the shooting, ditch their weapons, and resume their lounging at the café. In this case, even though the UN had better access and freedom of movement in the city, the Sarajevan police used their authority to hinder the UN investigation in order to keep the Bosnian snipers on the streets.[19]

---

19 Vasic, *The Spiritual State of Siege.*

The Muslim Brigade

Foreign Muslim volunteers fought an increasingly merciless war that included beheadings, torture, and executions.

Even if the UN forces captured this particular group of shooters, it would not have solved the underlying problem, which was the fact these Bosnian snipers were responding to the Serbians' snipers who were also violating the sniper truce by continuing to fire on Sarajevans from their positions in the old Jewish cemetery. If the UN silenced these Serbian sniper positions from the start, the Bosnians would not have felt compelled to respond in kind. At least in the incident described above, the Bosnians were targeting legitimate enemy combatants. It was this lack of real power to react to the sniper threat that ultimately made the UN's anti-sniper efforts ineffective. The Serbians, the originators of the sniper terror campaign, understood only one thing – force. To the Serbs, truces meant nothing and the UN's weak attempts at arresting their snipers just underlined UN impotence.

For example, UN forces once caught a Serbian sniper firing on a Red Cross vehicle and went to the house where the shot was fired from. After knocking on the front door, the patrol talked to the sniper's mother and told her to warn her son not to do it again because, next time, they would do something about it. One would guess the UN forces thought a really stern scolding would stop the Serbian sniper campaign. This lack of a resolute response to the indiscriminate killing of innocent people only emboldened the Serb snipers.

The NATO Response

After the Dayton Peace Accords of December 1995, NATO became involved in maintaining the peace in Sarajevo and elsewhere as SFOR (Stabilization FORce).

Because of the UN's previous weak responses to Serbian snipers, the Serbians were emboldened to challenge and intimidate the new NATO forces just like they did to the UN forces for the last three and a half years. In the last week of January 1996 alone, NATO catalogued a sniper attack a day in Sarajevo, including two that wounded both an American and a British soldier. On February 1, French forces under NATO command also came under sniper attack, except this time, they responded with deadly force and actually killed the sniper. A French patrol subsequently found the bodies of two gunmen in a so called 'zone of separation' between the Serb-controlled suburbs and the Bosnian-held city. NATO officers concluded the two men who comitted the shooting were Serbian snipers.

Apparently, NATO forces thought a tougher approach was needed to stop the Serbian snipers because the authority to arrest or to act merely in self-defense was insufficient. Instead, NATO adopted a shoot-on-sight policy to send the Serbs, who only understood words backed up by the barrel of a gun, a message NATO was not going to be intimidated or publicly humiliated like the UN was. In fact, the French killing of the two Serbian snipers was accompanied with a statement by the commander of NATO forces in Bosnia, U.S. Admiral Leighton Smith, who pledged his forces would retaliate swiftly, with force, against snipers targeting NATO troops.

Admiral Smith made the comment, "We've got some jerk up there pulling a trigger and he's got a nightscope. That makes it tough. But, boy, let me tell you, if we do see him he had better be fast and be clad in bullet-proof stuff because we will attack without warning." According to a Bosnian Serb television broadcast, NATO ground forces commander Lieutenant General Michael Walker even called up Bosnian Serb parliamentary speaker Momcilo Krajisnik and told him to stop the sniping incidents. In true Serbian fashion, Krajisnik condemned the incidents. What else was he going to do? Admit to the sniping attacks against NATO soldiers?[20]

Fallout from the Sniper Campaign: Spiraling Brutality

NATO's tougher stance came four years too late for the citizens of Sarajevo who suffered for forty-four months under the longest sniper siege in the history of urban warfare. NATO intervention came only after 1030 people were wounded, 225 people were killed, and 60 children were murdered by Serbian snipers. Importantly, killing these unarmed men, women, and children by rifle was a conscious act. If one were to fire a mortar round into the city, at least they were not targeting a specific person. A mortar round was too inaccurate to reliably hit an individual. A mortar round was more often than not delivered to, 'Whom it may concern.'

In contrast, the act of killing a person with a sniper rifle is a personal event. The sniper, with their enhanced optics in the form of a telescopic scope, sees exactly who they are killing. It is not a random act. Consequently, when a Serbian sniper blew the brains out of a seven-year old boy with a precisely placed bullet, they knew what they were doing. Just as another Serbian sniper who shot a young woman in the stomach, blowing out her guts, he too knew exactly what he was doing.

It was this specific campaign of mass murder by the Serbian snipers that prompted Goran, the young Bosnian man in Philippe Buffon's sniper documentary, to refer to the Serbians as 'animals'. Goran may not have known it at the time, but he, just like

20 CNN, *NATO forces kill Sarajevo sniper..*

the Serbian snipers who killed innocent people with glee, became polarized. Because the Serbs and their snipers treated the Bosnians and Sarajevans like so many wild boar to be shot at one's leisure, the Bosnians' hearts, in response, grew hard. After several years of massacre in Sarajevo, Bosnian snipers returned the favor and began to target Serbian civilians.

Without doubt, the Serbs' sniper campaign was instrumental in creating the upward spiral of violence that gripped Sarajevo. With every pull of the trigger, with every woman that fell screaming to the pavement in Sniper's Alley, the Serbs killed more than just people - they killed tolerance, they killed moderation. Maybe that is why the Bosnians began to turn to militant, Muslim extremist groups for support. Maybe that is why, during a mutual exchange of bodies in the winter of 1993 in Sarajevo, the Serbs received twenty-six decapitated bodies - their heads hacked clean off.[21] Maybe that is why, when NATO forces raided a ski chalet twenty miles west of Sarajevo in February 1996, they captured three Iranian intelligence officers. The raiding forces also found RPGs, suppressed sniper rifles, pictures of Iran's late Ayatollah Khomeini, and quantities of detonators, blasting caps, and high explosives. Most disturbing of all, the French found bombs built into children's toys, including a red plastic toy car, a helicopter, and an ice cream cone.[22]

The Serbs began their siege of Sarajevo, and their war against Bosnia, under the pretext the Bosnian Muslims were extremists who hated the Serbs because they were Orthodox Christians. The Serb leadership sold a bill of goods to the Serbian people saying Bosnian Muslims always had, and always would, oppress the Serbs living in Bosnia. These lies, spoken from the lips of virulent Serb nationalists like Slobodon Milosevic and Radovan Karadzic, built the foundation of hatred that enabled the Serbs' bloody sniper campaign in Sarajevo. Unfortunately, to some degree, the Serbs twisted Sarajevo's mixed, tolerant society into the very image they lied about to justify the war in the first place.

21 Committee for the Collection of Data on Crimes Committed against Humanity and International Law, *Decapitation as a Means of Genocide Over the Serbs in the Former Bosnia and Herzegovina.*
22 AP, *NATO Forces Seize Terrorist Training Camp in Bosnia*, February 17, 1996.

Chapter 14

The Chechen Wolves

Every nation has the right to their fate. Russia has taken away this right from the Chechens and today we want to reclaim these rights, which Allah has given us, in the same way he has given it to other nations. Allah has given us the right of freedom and the right to choose our destiny. And the Russian occupiers have flooded our land with our children's blood.

– Unknown Chechen, Moscow Theater Siege, October 2002

Chechnya and Russia: A Bloody History

The Chechens and Russians began spilling each others blood as far back as the 18th Century when an expanding Russian state clawed its way southward, into the Caucasus region on Russia's southern border. Russia's Tsars desperately wanted a warm water port, needed a land buffer against the still powerful Ottoman and Persian Empires, and always looked to fill Russia's coffers by subjugating its neighbors. However, the warlike people of the Caucasus, like the Chechens, Dagestanis, and Circassians, refused to lay down for the invaders and fought a series of fierce wars against the Russian Empire for the next century and a half, from 1718 until 1864.

The Chechen people may have been defeated by the vastly superior Russian forces in 1864, but whenever the opportunity presented itself, they rebelled against the hated occupiers and slaughtered the local Russian garrisons. Consequently, when the Russo-Turkish War broke out in 1877, the Chechens rebelled. They did so again during the Russian Revolutions of 1905 and 1917, during the subsequent Russian Civil War, and

266

Shot Down Soviet Helicopter

Chechen rebels inspect a Soviet attack
helicopter which they shot down near Grozny.

by Mikhail Evstafiev

then fought back against Stalin and his forced collectivization in the 1930's. Then, a sustained insurgency was fought from 1940-1944, which peaked during the time the Germans absolutely ravaged Western Russia. But, as soon as the German threat to Mother Russia was over, and Hitler's legions were blasted back into Poland and the Balkans, Stalin immediately went to work on the Chechen problem. Uncle Joe felt no pity for the Chechen guerrillas, or the Chechen people for that matter, and reasoned there could only be an insurgency in Chechnya if the Chechens still lived there. Starting in 1944, Stalin proceeded to cram the Chechens – all of them – into filthy cattle cars and shipped them out, across the frozen mountain expanses and tundra, to Kazakhstan and Siberia. No people, no insurgency.

Stalin thought he solved the Chechen problem, but he only put it on ice for a few years. In 1953, Stalin was dead and his successor, Nikita Khrushchev – who was present at Stalingrad and helped promote the Red Army's successful sniperism campaign – charted a new course of de-Stalinization. In 1956, as part of this new period of thawing internal politics, the Chechens were allowed to return to their homeland and rebuild their lives, culture, and society. For the next forty years the Chechens were integrated into Russian society (Chechen children learned to speak Russian, Chechen men served in the Russian military) and lived in peace. However, one could also say the Chechens needed the four decades to recover as a people and to prepare for their next grasp at freedom.

This chance came in 1991 when the Soviet system came crumbling to the ground like a terminally unstable brick wall. As Russia peered out from the rubble, they saw the demise of the Soviet Union was a dangerous event that could lead to political instability in the region. The Russians were correct because Chechnya immediately wanted to secede. Moscow was unwilling to sit idly by while Chechnya became an independent Republic because it would set a dangerous precedent and threaten Russia's national oil infrastructure in the Caucasus. Both sides, unyielding in their diametrically opposed goals, careened towards each other like runaway trains. They were on a collision course for another war.

War came in 1994 when Russia tried, through force of arms, to prevent Chechnya from becoming independent. The fighting raged from 1994 to 1996 until Russian President Boris Yeltsin declared a cease fire and signed a peace treaty in 1997. This war was a particularly brutal one where captured Russian soldiers were decapitated and their lifeless heads propped up on wooden stakes as a warning to their comrades. Other prisoners taken by the Chechens were killed on video, their throats sliced open, their last desperate seconds of life splashed all over the internet, and the film sent to their parents' homes. A new chapter in modern warfare was written as the seriously outnumbered Chechen rebels took a page out of the Stalingrad book and used the urban terrain of the nation's capital, Grozny (which, ironically, is Russian for the word 'foreboding'), to inflict huge numbers of casualties on the poorly led, poorly organized, unmotivated Russian conscript army. In some cases, entire Russian columns were ambushed and wiped out to the last man, blown up with volleys of RPGs and gunned down by Chechen snipers who seemed to be everywhere.

The 1997 peace treaty was short-lived as Chechen forces invaded neighboring Dagestan in 1999 and were then accused of setting off several massive explosions in Russia, which destroyed a series of apartment buildings, slaughtering hundreds. With these events providing ample pretext for a second invasion, Russian forces fought their way into Chechnya again in 1999. This time, Russia was better organized and prepared for an all out war. In a relatively short period of time, the Russian forces cleared out most of the country of organized resistance by using massive doses of aerial bombs and artillery barrages, intermixed with a liberal sprinkling of fuel air explosives and cruise missiles. By 2005, the invading Russian troops steamrolled large scale Chechen resistance, but were now stuck in a low-grade guerrilla war with no end in sight. Overall, these recent Chechen Wars were costly with an estimated 15,000 Russian soldiers and up to 100,000 Chechens killed either through direct combat, exposure, starvation, or disease. Considering Chechnya had an estimated pre-war population of only 1.1 million people, these losses were enormous.

Training and Equipping the Chechen Sniper

Despite their inevitable defeat, the Chechen fighters made combat operations in their breakaway republic dangerous for Russian soldiers as can be attested by the deluge of casualties filling the Russian morgues and hospitals. This high casualty rate was due in part to the Chechen snipers who were employed on a large scale, integrated at the lowest unit levels, and used in all their operations. In fact, one would be hard pressed to find any other guerrilla movement that employed snipers to such great effect and in such large numbers.

One reason for the Chechen guerrillas' affinity for sniping was their embedded gun culture. Chechen men admired guns and saw them as symbols of power and prosperity. Because Chechen men loved their weapons, they were skilled in both their use and maintenance at an early age and everyone had them. This cultural affinity was further reinforced by the training so many Chechen men received when they served in the Russian military. This combination of a skilled manpower pool and the widespread availability of sniper rifles resulted in a guerrilla movement with a high concentration

Grozny: An unfortunate Russian soldier lies dead after being shot in the head by a Chechen sniper.

AP Photo

of competent snipers.

Also, the Chechens were a military-savvy culture because most Chechen males served in the Russian military due to universal conscription. For example, deceased Chechen President Dudayev was a general in the Russian army and subsequent (and also deceased) Chechen President Aslan Maskhadov was a colonel. Guerrilla leader extraordinaire, Shamil Basayev (deceased), served two years in the Soviet military before waging his personal, decade-long jihad against the Russian invaders. Chechnya was not unique in this aspect as other republics of the former Soviet Union, like the Ukraine, Kazakhstan, and Belarus, had similar demographics with many of their own citizens trained in Soviet weapons and tactics.

Training in the former Soviet army was just one way for the Chechen guerrillas to get a trained sniper; there were other ways as well. Since Chechnya was an Islamic country and many guerrilla organizations in Chechnya were explicitly Islamic in nature, Chechens were welcomed in foreign training camps like the Amir Muawia training camp in Afghanistan.[1] Once out of the country, Chechen guerrillas trained freely in all the art of guerrilla warfare, to include the discipline of sniping. The Russian military may have been able to hamper the Chechens' ability to train in their own country, but the Russian government certainly could not stop Chechens from training in foreign sanctuaries like Afghanistan, Lebanon, and Iraq.

The Chechens did not always have to leave their country to get good training, they could import this training from abroad. Shamil Basayev did just this when he 'hired' Saudi-born Amir Khattab (a.k.a. the "Black Arab") and his crew of Afghani veterans to come to Chechnya as 'consultants' in February 1995 to train the Chechen

---

1 Murphy, *The Wolves of Islam*, p. 16. (Excellent coverage of the war in Chechnya.)

guerrillas.[2] Once in Chechnya, Khattab built his own training camps, to include one called the 'Training Center of the Armed Forces of the Chechen Republic of Ichkeria', which opened in September 1996. Ironically, the Russians unknowingly helped set up this training camp years before when it was created as a Soviet youth pioneer camp. Now, this former youth camp was transformed into a guerrilla university that churned out guerrilla fighters, many trained in sniping, who were bent on killing Russian soldiers.[3]

While training a Chechen guerrilla sniper could be an inconvenience, securing good sniper rifles to kill Russians with was much easier. When the Russian military pulled out of Chechnya in 1992, they left behind some 533 SVD sniper rifles for their future enemies.[4] These same Russian-made, Russian serial-numbered sniper rifles, after being turned over to the Chechen military, were subsequently used to kill and wound thousands of Russian soldiers from 1994 until the present. In this respect, the Russians must look to themselves as to why and how Chechen snipers were able to cull their ranks at such a fearsome rate.

Beyond these sniper rifles left behind, battlefield recovery was another means for Chechen guerrillas to secure the most current Russian sniper rifles. Throughout the Chechen wars, Chechen guerrillas regularly captured Russian soldiers and their accompanying equipment in combat. If the Russians they captured and killed had modern sniper rifles, the Chechen guerrillas now had these same sniper weapons.

But why should the Chechen guerrillas take the risk of getting killed or captured just to secure the latest Russian sniper rifles? It was easier to buy them on the black market, either in Chechnya or from the gun runners profiting from the war in the relative safety and comfort of neighboring Dagestan, Ingushetia, and Georgia. If the Chechens had a few thousand dollars (they had millions) they could buy the latest and greatest Russian sniper rifles in any quantity they desired. If nuclear waste and other radioactive materials could be bought on the black market in Grozny (as documented in 1992), purchasing a sniper rifle was like buying a loaf of bread.[5]

Often, the Chechen guerrillas cut out the middle man and bought the weapons they needed directly from the source: from the Russians themselves. Since the Russian military was so thoroughly corrupt, there were opportunities to buy all kinds of weapons from the Russian officers and soldiers they were actually fighting. Some Russians had no problem making a profit to help their families, enrich themselves, or to support a drug habit at the expense of other Russian soldiers' lives. Even former Soviet republics like Belarus contributed to the guerrillas' war chest, selling the Chechens the latest in weaponry. For the independent states of the defunct Soviet Union, selling weapons to Chechnya was a double bonus: the seller not only made a tidy profit, but the buyer promised to kill their former masters as quickly and ruthlessly as possible.

Chechen Sniper Tactics

Unlike some guerrilla movements, the Chechens believed the sniper was a key building block for a successful war against the Russian occupation forces. In fact, the basic Chechen eight-man squad had a sniper assigned to it. This organization was

2 Murphy, *The Wolves of Islam*, p. 19.
3 Murphy, *The Wolves of Islam*, p. 39.
4 Grau & Cutshaw, *Russian Snipers in the Mountains and Cities of Chechnya.*
5 Murphy, *The Wolves of Islam*, p. 139.

Grozny: A young Chechen rebel prepares for another round of combat in the capital.

by Mikhail Evstafiev

much different from conventional military forces, like those of America, Russia, and Britain, which do not assign snipers at the squad level, but prefer to keep them consolidated at higher levels, such as in a battalion sniper element. Because the Chechens viewed snipers as a basic asset - not a specialized tool used for high value targets or special operations - they were everywhere.

While most squads had a sniper, the Chechens were flexible in their tactics, employing the sniper at even lower levels like four-man cells organized with a sniper, a machine-gunner, an RPG gunner, and an AK-47-armed rifleman. These teams used the sniper and machine-gunner to pin down Russian soldiers while the RPG gunner took out the Russians' armor. Additionally, any number of these cells could work together as needed to engage larger Russian forces with their combined firepower. Another Chechen tactic was to employ a single sniper with a supporting four-man element. After the sniper fired, the support element distracted the targeted Russian soldiers, allowing the sniper to displace. This same support element then pinned down any Russian counterattacks whether they were armored or dismounted. The goal here was for the sniper to survive to make another kill another day.[6]

While Chechen snipers worked as part of squads and cells, they also routinely worked in two-man teams or even independently. Working in such small elements reduced the snipers' operational signature, allowing them to slip in between Russian units and behind Russian front lines. Once a Chechen sniper infiltrated in between two separate Russian units, they could pick off Russian soldiers from different groups, enticing them to fight each other, resulting in fratricide. These small elements also benefited in other ways from operating in close proximity to Russian positions because of the Russians' own tactics. Since the Russian military was dependent on massive, indiscriminate firepower to kill these snipers, they had to kill themselves. Although it seemed counter-intuitive, the more closely Chechen snipers intermixed with the Rus-

6 Grau & Cutshaw, *Russian Snipers in the Mountains and Cities of Chechnya.*

sian forces, the safer they were.

Decapitation Tactics

In their war with the Russians, the Chechens made every shot count. Consequently, Chechen snipers were savvy as to whom they targeted. When the Chechen snipers took their shot, they concentrated on high value targets like Russian officers, opposing snipers, machine-gunners, and drivers. This specific targeting was designed to eliminate the key components enabling the Russian military machine to function in combat. The Chechens reasoned if the serpent's head was cut off, the rest of the body would flounder aimlessly.

This theory was sound since the Chechen snipers' intentional targeting of the Russian command structure had significant effects on the Russian forces at the tactical level. Some Russian soldiers noted during the 1994-1995 battle for Grozny, there were very few platoon leaders and company commanders left to lead them.[7] This high loss of lower ranking officers meant Russian combat operations were disrupted from the bottom up. After all, who was going to lead a platoon and company attack for the leaderless Russian forces…conscripts and junior non-commissioned officers? The decapitation of the Russian leadership resulted in the headless Russian giant becoming paralyzed in the Grozny meat grinder, leading to even higher casualties.

This targeting of key personnel led to the January 18, 2000 death of Russian Major General Mikhal Malofeyev as he inspected his forces' front line positions in the northwestern section of Grozny. Unofficial sources from the Russian joint command group in Chechnya reported the general was shot and killed by a Chechen sniper as he made his rounds. Then, due to the continued intensity of Chechen sniper fire in that sector, Russian troops were unable to get to him for days.[8] It was not until January 23rd that Russian forces were able to recover General Malofeyev's bloated, bullet riddled body and give him a decent burial.[9]

Chechen Sniper-Martyrs

Chechen snipers always manipulated the urban terrain to give them an advantage over the numerically superior Russian forces. One favorite Chechen sniper tactic was to position themselves in high-rise buildings dominating the approaches into the city. These snipers positioned themselves deep in a room, when they took their shot they were invisible. The targeted Russian soldiers never saw the muzzle flash of the sniper killing them. These methods allowed a few Chechen snipers to pin down entire Russian units while extracting a rising toll from the Russian infantry. Because of the extreme angle the Chechen snipers fired from, the Russians' return fire could not reach them. In addition, many of these Chechen snipers were sniper-martyrs, on a suicide mission, where they picked off Russian soldiers until the building the snipers occupied was obliterated by Russian tanks and helicopter gunships. These sniper-martyrs could not be outmaneuvered or flushed out. They had to be killed or they would continue killing.

7 Novichkov, Snegovskiy, Sokolov & Shvarev, *Russian Armed Forces in the Chechen Conflict: Analysis, Results, Conclusions*, Moscow 1995, pg. 42.
8 *War in Chechnya - 1999*, News Archive, www.aeronautics.ru
9 *Russian General's Body Found*, BBC News.

Minutka Square - March 2000

An aerial photo of downtown Grozny reveals widespread devastation after continued Russian bombing.

In January and February 2000, Russian forces fought for weeks just to take Minutka Square located in the center of Grozny. Chechen snipers pinned down Russian assault groups near the square for days on end, stalling the entire Russian attack to clear the city's center. Again, Chechen sniper-martyrs barricaded in the upper stories of tall buildings had excellent view of Russian troop movements while the snipers remained invisible. Even after Russian forces called in a steady stream of air strikes on their positions, the shooters remained holed up in their sniper hides. If the snipers were located in the floors several stories down from the actual roof of the building, it took several direct hits from Russian aerial bombs to blast through the upper levels and get them.

The Chechen Sniper: A Technical Shooter

Chechen snipers in general were very good shots as one Russian soldier found out as he recuperated in a Russian Interior Ministry hospital. This soldier, with shattered leg bones, was walking at night when a Chechen sniper shot him. As any experienced shooter can tell you, making an accurate shot in the dark against a moving target is no easy feat. Also, Chechen snipers habitually made successful head shots against Russian soldiers - another difficult prospect requiring some technical ability.[10] In fact, head shots were a preferred tactic for Chechen snipers. At night, Russian soldiers sometimes gave their positions away by lighting a cigarette. Alert Chechen snipers would see the flame from the lighter or cigarette embers and aim in on this light source, hitting the Russian soldiers in the head or neck - most often resulting in instant death or a mortal wound.[11]

Since many front line Russian soldiers wore body armor for protection, Chechen snipers learned to work around the problem. Russian soldier Nikolay Aldakov experienced this first hand as he tried to save a wounded comrade during a gun battle. As he dragged away the wounded soldier, a Chechen sniper saw him and shot him twice in the back, in his body armor. The sniper readjusted his aim and then shot Nikolay in the legs.[12] In another incident, as Private Kuzin was on guard duty, wearing his assigned body armor, a Chechen sniper also aimed for his legs. Since Kuzin was standing with his arms by his sides, the bullet struck his hand instead.[13]

Intentionally shooting Russian soldiers in the legs does several things. First, it solves the problem of avoiding protective body armor. Second, it drops a soldier to the ground, forcing other soldiers to come to their rescue who then become targets themselves. In other words, a soldier shot in the legs becomes human bait. And third, because a soldier with a leg injury cannot walk off the battlefield, it stresses the Russian's medical/support capabilities because it takes several men to carry a wounded man long distances and will eventually require a vehicle for transport. (This is an identical philosophy to the Russians' own sport of Sambo, where combatants focus on leg, knee, and ankle attacks in order to disable their opponent. The theory is, a man who cannot walk is an even bigger burden to his comrades)

To the Russians' dismay, Chechen snipers proved capable of making long-distance shots. In one instance, a Russian OMON soldier serving in Grozny was eating an afternoon meal with his comrades when a hidden Chechen sniper shot him. The sniper was an estimated 1000 meters away when he pulled the trigger, striking the OMON soldier in the back. He died ten minutes later. At this distance, the bullet ripped through the soldier's body before anyone even heard the gunshot. The stricken soldier's comrades had no idea where the shot came from and they ended up trying to destroy every building in a one kilometer radius just to get the sniper. They did not know if they got the shooter or not.[14]

Guerrilla Tactics

While some Chechen snipers operated as members of organized units openly warring with Russian forces, others lived among the population. Chechen guerrilla leader Shamil Basayev noted in early 2000 he and his men were taking too many casualties fighting the Russians one-on-one, so he ordered his men to disband and take to the

---

10 Traynor, *Fighting Phantoms: The Toll Mounts, Russian Hospitals Bear Witness to the Price Moscow's Army is Paying in Chechnya.*
11 Koopman, *Traveling Through the Lunar Landscape - Poor People Line the Road Asking for a Handout.*
12 *Russian Troops' Tales of War*, BBC News.
13 Gordan, *Bold Chechen Rebels Fight the Russian Army on Two Fronts*, New York Times.
14 Vladmirov, *Valor Medal for Dead OMON Sergeant.*

A Chechen sniper waits in a hidesite in Grozny

AP Photo

villages.[15] In the villages the guerrillas blended in with the Chechen people so effectively, Russian units had no idea of the true number of guerrillas they were facing. Fighting this way meant many things for the Chechen snipers who previously slugged it out with superior Russian forces. Now, the Chechen snipers had to hide their sniper rifles in or near their villages so Russian soldiers could not find them. This also meant the guerrillas could no longer openly wear the mix of Russian field uniforms they had been fighting in. Now they had to dress and lead lives like the other civilians. More importantly, the Chechen guerrillas also had to defeat the investigative measures the Russian forces used to separate them from the real civilians. A successful investigation by Russian forces was no joking matter as the resulting arrest was sure to be followed with brutal interrogations, a starvation diet, exposure to the elements, and a strong likelihood of death.

Russian investigative measures did not have to be sophisticated and included soldiers looking for bruises on suspected Chechens' shoulders. This is because people repeatedly shooting high-powered rifles (or RPGs for that matter) may get bruising from the recoil that slams the butt of the weapon into the pocket of the firer's shoulder. The Russians also used specially trained dogs to sniff suspected guerrillas for anything from gunpowder residue to traces of high-explosives. Another constant threat for the guerrilla-civilian were informants who provided information for either the Russians or the despised pro-Moscow Chechen government. These informants were motivated for a variety reasons: money, clan or 'blood' feuds, personal advancement, religious animosity, and everything in between.

A Strategy of Long-Term Attrition through Sniping

The Chechen rebel leadership firmly believed if they inflicted a steady stream

---

15 Murphy, *The Wolves of Islam*, p. 113.

of casualties against the Russian armed forces, the Russian domestic public would eventually tire of the war. One observer of the war noted, "While the Russians concentrated on securing territory, the Chechens aimed to inflict Russian casualties and extend the conflict. Chechen leadership sought to cause one hundred Russian casualties daily; the Chechens believed if they could continue the war and inflict high Russian casualties, Russia would eventually pull out."[16]

For the Chechens, the widespread employment of snipers was a tool to generate this steady stream of Russian casualties. One could argue this sniper-attrition strategy was effective to a degree because a study covering the period from July 1995 to April 1996 revealed the Russians suffered up to five killed and another dozen wounded every day.[17] At this rate, the Russians were losing 1,825 killed and 4,380 wounded a year. However, it was believed by many close observers of the war these casualty rates were absurdly low, intentionally deflated by a Russian government desperate to keep a positive spin on the war.

A reporter interviewing wounded Russian soldiers in a hospital during the Russian drive for Grozny in 2000 found the truth about casualties to be different from the government's official statements. One wounded Russian soldier, shot by a Chechen sniper as he tried to rescue a comrade, said it succinctly, "The snipers are good. We lost many casualties." Another soldier in the same hospital said, "It's a guerrilla war now. The Chechens know the territory very well, even in territory that we've liberated. The Chechens are civilians by day but fighters by night. We suffered hundreds of casualties but then on TV they say we only lost four or five."[18]

Author Arthur L. Speyer III noted Chechen snipers were the second largest producer of Russian casualties overall and when Chechen guerrillas faced pure Russian infantry units, Chechen snipers were the number one casualty producer.[19] The Chechen sniper campaign not only chipped away at Russian troop strength, it caused fear, uncertainty, and terror. Russian soldiers patrolling Grozny's churned up streets or the dirt roads in the local villages had no idea where the next anonymous bullet would come from. No matter what you did, nobody was safe. More importantly, the Chechen guerrillas' widespread and effective employment of snipers had significant psychological effects on their Russian enemies, far beyond the immediate effects of Russian soldiers shipped home to Moscow in body bags.

The Unseen Casualties: Chechen Snipers and Russian Combat Stress

The brutal fighting in Chechen cities, like Grozny, where guerrilla snipers operated on a large scale, was the ideal environment for producing combat stress related disorders in Russian soldiers. In fact, V.S. Novikov, a Major General in the Russian medical services, researched Russian combat stress in Chechnya and published the results in his article "Psycho-physiological Support of Combat Activities of Military Personnel." Novikov's research was based on a sample of 1,312 Russian soldiers who

---

16 Glenn, Russell W. (editor), *Capital Preservation: Preparing for Urban Operations in the Twenty-First Century: Proceedings of the RAND Arroyo-TRAQDOC-MCWL-OSD Urban Operations Conference*, p. 66.
17 Blandy, *Chechnya: Two Federal Interventions An Interim Comparison and Assessment*, p.20.
18 Mottram, *Russian Casualties Under-Reported*.
19 Glenn, Russell W. (editor), Capital Preservation, p. 93.

A chechen guerrilla watches over the bomb blasted Presidential Palace in Grozny.

by Mikhail Evstafiev

previously served in Chechnya. Novikov found a large proportion of these soldiers, 72% to be exact, showed some type of psychological disorder symptom to include insomnia, depression, deterioration of moral values, and "focusing intently on self-interests and the lack of the capacity to care about others physical, moral or emotional sense, with a marked disregard for standard social values".[20] In other words, the war was producing sociopaths.

Novikov is not alone in his assessment as another estimate of Russian Chechen war veterans for the period March 1997 to March 1998 found that 10,000 Russian soldiers required psychological help. Aleksander Kucher, a Russian military psychologist published Life After Military Service, a study that found nearly 35,000 Russian veterans of Chechnya and their families received psychological counseling since 1996. The psychological trauma of fighting in Chechnya was so prevalent other Russian authors labeled returning Russian soldiers as murderers, rapists, marauders, sex perverts and abnormal people who could not re-enter the work force until they were 'fixed'.[21]

The Russian veterans' advocacy group, Union of Committees of Mothers of Russian Soldiers, said as many as 50% of Chechen veterans returning from the war plague Russian society with violent crimes like rape, murder and armed robbery. One soldier interviewed for a documentary about Chechen war veterans was captured by Chechen guerrillas and held captive in a hole for six months until he escaped. This soldier was since arrested in Russia and was serving a 15-year sentence in a work camp after raping a ten-year old girl. When this soldier was initially arrested and held in jail, of the other 19 inmates in his cell, five were Chechen war veterans and one an Afghanistan war veteran.[22]

---

20 Thomas & O'Hara, *Combat Stress in Chechnya.*
21 Thomas & O'Hara, *Combat Stress in Chechnya.*
22 Quilty, *'White Ravens': Speaking Through the Silence.*

Female and Mercenary Snipers

A common belief among the Russian military was the Chechen guerrillas employed female snipers to kill them, such as the persistent rumor that female Lithuanian snipers traveled to Chechnya as mercenaries to hunt Russian soldiers. For example, Mr. Timothy L. Thomas' and Major Charles P. O'Hara's article on combat stress in Chechnya alluded to beautiful women with Lithuanian accents operating in Chechnya, contributing to the uncertainty of the battlefield. The Russian soldiers even gave these Baltic snipers' a name - the 'White Pantyhose' or the 'White Stockings'. In the Chechen War documentary *White Ravens*, one Russian veteran of the Chechen war stated members of their unit captured a Chechen sniper that was a Baltic woman and a former Olympic shooter. When other Russian soldiers were interviewed in the documentary and asked about two Chechen women they captured, they responded they were probably snipers, despite giving no supporting evidence.[23]

Since Russia made itself many historic and recent enemies, the Chechens had many sources of potential outside support. During the 2000 fighting in Grozny for example, Russian forces discovered they were not only fighting Chechens, but also Ukrainians, fighters from the Baltics, and even volunteers from Russia itself. One Russian soldier recounted how his unit captured a female sniper from Saint Petersburg and another sniper who was a former biathlete - both who were guns for hire.[24] In response, Chechen supporters say these allegations of foreign female snipers are just a convenient excuse for Russian soldiers to rape, abuse, and kill Chechen women.

Employing women as snipers is hardly a new phenomenon in the annals of warfare as the Russians themselves employed women snipers in World War II on a large scale. Women, even in Chechnya, face less scrutiny from security forces than do their male counterparts since security forces all over the world are more reluctant to physically search women and females are frequently allowed access to government controlled areas that are denied to men. Therefore, the employment of women as guerrilla snipers in Chechnya makes sense. Chechen women can identify sloppy Russian troop positions during daytime trips to the local market, then, at night, these same women can recover a hidden rifle and pick off their carefully scouted prey.

The Murder of Elza Kungayeva

If there is any question that Chechen guerrilla snipers are a source of Russian combat stress casualties, the case of Yuri Budanov removes this doubt. Colonel Yuri Budanov was the commander of a Russian tank regiment during the second Chechen war who found himself positioned near Grozny, close to the village of Tangi. On the night of March 26, 2000, Budanov and several of his soldiers broke into the house of an 18-year-old Chechen girl, Elza Kungayeva.[25] Budanov kidnapped Elza, dragging her back to his personal quarters where he brutally beat and strangled her to death.

While Budanov denied raping Elza, a witness saw Elza's clothes piled on the floor and an autopsy report stated Elza's hymen was ruptured and her rectum was torn. Budanov did not deny killing Elza, but he claimed she was a guerrilla sniper and killed

23 Quilty, *'White Ravens': Speaking Through the Silence.*
24 Gordon, *Chechen Rebels Fiercely Attack Russian Forces.*
25 Wines, Michael, *Colonel's Trial Puts Russian Justice to Test.*

Portrait of a Chechen Sniper.

by Sergey Bratkov

several of his men two months prior. Budanov's defense lawyer argued Budanov only killed Elza because he was in a temporary state of sickness, in fact, he was suffering from combat fatigue.[26] Budanov's defense was not only a landmark case because a senior Russian commander finally faced punishment for a war crime, but because the defense explicitly linked the psychological trauma caused by Chechen guerrilla snipers with Budanov's act of murder. (Authors Note: The aforementioned Amir Khattab a.k.a. The Black Arab, later captured and filmed the execution of nine Russian OMON special forces policemen in retaliation for Budanov's murder of Elza. Then, another eight OMON soldiers were captured and beheaded as further retribution).[27]

Clearly, the Chechens' widespread employment of guerrilla snipers, moving among the people in the day and picking off Russian soldiers at night, took a psychological toll on the Russian soldiers. While in Chechnya, the Budanovs of the Russian army targeted the Chechen people, but when they returned to their homes in Moscow, Volgograd, and Saint Petersburg, they directed their violent urges at their own people. The Chechen snipers' greatest effect may not be on the battlefield, but in Russian society

26 Wines, Michael, *Colonel's Trial Puts Russian Justice to Test.*
27 Murphy, *The Wolves of Islam*, p. 33-4.

itself where maladjusted Russian veterans, after being placed in the pressure cooker of Grozny and elsewhere, decompress through violent crime, brutalizing their fellow Russians for years to come.

Brutality as a Russian Counter-Sniper Policy

Torturing and murdering suspected or confirmed snipers, as Colonel Budonev did, was at its core a central element of Russia's counter-sniper methodology. Through these brutal methods, the Russians hoped to instill such fear in Chechen snipers the snipers would think the price of getting caught outweighed the benefits of being a sniper. The Russians' counter-sniper terror policy in Chechnya was not a new one and was really a continuation of their policies employed during World War II. This same policy of terror was used against German snipers captured on the Eastern Front where captured sharpshooters were systematically tortured, mutilated, and killed by Russian soldiers to intimidate other snipers from employing their deadly tradecraft.

One can clearly see this policy of elimination with Yuri Budanov's strangulation-rape-murder of 'suspected' female sniper Elza Kungayeva. However, Budanov's murder was no isolated incident. One Russian soldier stated, "I remember a Chechen female sniper. We just tore her apart with two armored personnel carriers, having tied her ankles with steel cables. There was a lot of blood but the boys needed it." This policy of torturing and executing Chechen snipers was easy to do when this was the prevailing mindset of the Russian military as a whole. Killing a Chechen was easy as killing a stray dog. Another Russian soldier said, "I would kill all the men I met during mopping-up operations. I didn't feel sorry for them one bit." Another soldier said, "It's much easier to kill them all. It takes less time for them to die than to grow". The policy of limited genocide practiced by the Russians in Chechnya meant executing a captured Chechen sniper was easy to do because it did not even raise an eyebrow by the Russian military leadership, which supported such practices.[28]

Russia's Fire-Dependent Counter-Sniper Tactics

In many ways, the Russian experience in Grozny and other Chechen cities was similar to the Germans' experience in Stalingrad. In World War II, the German Wehrmacht was a fire-dependent force, poorly trained for close-in, urban warfare. Then, in Chechnya, the wheel came full circle where the Russian military was a fire-dependent army with its own conscript soldiers poorly prepared for street fighting. In Stalingrad, the Soviet Union depended on a skilled sniper corps and street savvy infantrymen to deal with German snipers. In Grozny, these same men were all but non-existent. Just like the Germans in Stalingrad, the modern Russian army responded to Chechen snipers, not with their own skilled counter-snipers, but with massive force.

When Russian forces confronted a sniper barricaded in a high-rise in Grozny, they attempted to destroy the entire building along with the sniper in it. There were several favorite counter-sniper tools in the Russian inventory that could be used to bring a building down. One tool was the Grad (BM-21) Multiple Rocket Launcher. The Grad had forty separate nine-foot long ,122 mm, high-explosive rockets with a range of over twenty kilometers. Once Russian forces encountered a sniper, they pulled back

---

28 Reynolds, *Russian Atrocities in Chechnya.*

WW II: A Russian sniper shows how many kills she has.

Ironically, while Russia demonizes the Chechens for using female snipers, Russia was the first to use women snipers on a large scale.

and called in the Grads, devastating everything around the sniper and hopefully the sniper too. Since the Grad was an area weapon, surgical precision was not possible, but that only mattered if you cared about limiting collateral damage. The Russians did not.

The Russians also used the RPO-A Shmel shoulder launched weapon and the TOS-1 rocket launcher, both which used a thermo-baric warhead (also known as a fuel-air explosive or a vacuum bomb) designed to kill people fighting from inside a building. When a thermo-baric weapon detonates within an enclosed space like a building, it causes extreme overpressure, killing everyone inside it. The flames, heat, and overpressure from the thermo-baric round fills the entire space inside a building, penetrating all non-airtight enclosures, meaning intervening walls and cover will not protect the people inside. The people are either incinerated or die from internal injuries caused by the overpressure. The vacuum created by the burning fuel ruptures lungs and internal organs, bursts eardrums, and causes blindness. Unreinforced structures hit with these devices are likely to collapse from the blast wave, which multiplies in intensity when detonated inside a building.

Anti-aircraft weapons like the Russian 2S6 also proved effective. The 2S6 was an ideal counter-sniper weapon because it was an armored vehicle that protected its occupants from small arms fire from snipers. Importantly, the 2S6 guns had a range of several kilometers - well out of the range of any sniper. At several thousand rounds a minute, the 30 mm guns could chew through concrete structures, reducing Chechen sniper positions to dust in mere seconds. Because the 2S6 was an anti-aircraft weapon, it was designed to fire towards the sky, meaning it could elevate high enough to hit Chechen snipers hidden in high-rise structures.

If the Russians could not blast the Chechen snipers with thermo-baric warheads of precision 30 mm fire, they were quick to employ close air support, to include high-speed fighters with large aerial bombs and helicopter gunships armed with explosive rockets. Another favorite was self-propelled artillery because these big guns, just like the 2S6, were armored and could destroy an entire building with a few well-aimed shots of high-explosive artillery. The Russians would rather expend ammunition than their own soldiers' lives when it came to dealing with Chechen snipers. (This same philosophy did not extend towards preserving Chechen civilian lives.)

Exporting the Sniper-Martyr

The Russians' fire-dependent solutions might have been acceptable within the borders of Chechnya, but they could not be used inside Russia itself. The Chechens recognized this and tried to turn this mentality of force against the Russians by bringing the war to the Russian Motherland:

- In June 1995, Chechen rebels led by Shamil Basayev infiltrated Stavropol and took over a hospital in the southern town of Buddyonnovsk, taking 1500 people and patients hostage. The hostages were then used by the Chechens as human shields, ensuring any Russian attack would result in the slaughter of innocents. After several botched rescue attempts, resulting in the deaths of hundreds of hostages, Basayev and his fighters were allowed to return to Chechnya as part of a larger peace plan.

- In October 2002, Chechen guerrilla Movsar Barayev and a group of fighters, to include women, crossed the border into Russia and headed for the capital. Once in Moscow, Barayev took over the House of Culture, a theater in the Dubrovka district, taking more than 800 men, women and children hostage. Many of the Chechen women had explosives strapped to their bodies, ensuring any government raid would be a bloody one. Barayev demanded Russia withdraw from Chechnya. After several days, Russian forces pumped an anesthesia gas into the theater, killing the Chechens and over a hundred hostages.

- In September 2004, Chechens infiltrated the southern territory of North Ossetia, taking over a children's school in Beslan, demanding Russia's withdrawal from Chechnya. Over 1000 hostages were taken and one terrorist was filmed standing on a deadman's switch, so if he was gassed or shot, nearby explosives would be detonated as soon as his weight came off the switch. Russian forces stormed the school any ways, resulting in the deaths of hundreds of children.

As these acts of terror show, Chechen rebels may export their sniper-martyr tactics as well. Sniper-martyrs would be more cost effective, as a three or four-man team could easily infiltrate the border with Russia and then move into any major city in Russia. This team could then set up in a populated, well-constructed, high-rise building in a densely populated area like Moscow. A small security team could rig the floors below and above the sniper with explosives, ensuring no assault team could get to the shooter. The shooter could then start their game of terror, targeting innocent people in the streets.

Government security troops would be forced to respond, but regular SWAT-style tactics would be rendered ineffective by the explosives. Escalating force would have to be used, Chechnya-style, forcing the government to destroy the surrounding infrastructure and population to get the sniper-martyrs. The Chechens could multiply the government's problem immensely by employing several mutually supporting sniper-martyr teams located within range of each other in the heart of the city. These tactics would be nothing new to the Chechens; they would merely be the exportation of the

A Russian sniper team takes aim with their suppressed 9 mm Vintorez sniper rifles.

tactics they already used in Grozny and elsewhere.

Bringing a Charles Whitman-esque shooting spree to Russian cities, modified with Chechen tactics, would introduce high-intensity warfare methods to a peaceful, urban, civilian setting. The resulting carnage – wreaked by thermo-baric weapons and heli-copter gunships - would bring the Chechens their desired publicity, terrorize the Russian public through a horrific body count, and force the Russian military to partially destroy its own cities.

A Discriminating Solution? Russian Sniper/Counter-Sniper Development

One solution to the above scenario is a more discriminating approach. In fact, the Russian military community learned in part from their losses to Chechen snipers during the first 1994-1996 war and took corrective actions. A problem the Russians identified in Chechnya was their snipers were used to SWAT tactics, not to the high-intensity warfare environment they found themselves in, where the enemy employed their own counter-snipers. In the summer of 1999, the Russians re-established a dedicated, professional sniper school. The Russian snipers also started to mimic Chechen guerrilla tactics, operating in small independent teams as opposed to strictly supporting a large attacking force. These Russian snipers also came from more professional ranks, not two-year conscripts.[29]

Overall, the quality of the Russian snipers/counter-snipers improved greatly during the Chechen Wars, giving Russian military forces an option to use a precision counter-sniper asset. It will still take years for the Russian military to train a large, skilled, professional sniper force that can affect the tide of battle. The first Russian sniper class in 1999 had only twelve students (three were later killed in Chechnya) - hardly a significant number.[30] However, as Russian counter-sniper competence and ability grew, Chechen snipers found that they had to improve their own snipercraft as sniper versus sniper battles became more frequent.

---

29 Grau & Cutshaw, *Russian Snipers in the Mountains and Cities of Chechnya.*
30 Grau & Cutshaw, *Russian Snipers in the Mountains and Cities of Chechnya.*

Chechen Exploitation of Russian Counter-Sniper Tactics

The central drawback with Russian counter-sniper tactics was their indiscriminate nature, wedded to a mentality that knew no restraint. As a result, Russian forces were unable to locate and kill single Chechen snipers without destroying the entire building the sniper was in. The Russians inevitably ended up destroying any surrounding structures and killed the surrounding population. This meant Russian military operations necessarily resulted in enormous infrastructure damage to include a large number of civilian casualties. This near-random devastation alienated the Chechen population and made Chechnya an economic wasteland. To date, Russia has already spent billions to repair the damage they caused and will have to live with a hostile Chechen population on their border for generations.

In turn, Chechen sniper operations were designed to cause this alienation and destruction so Russian armed forces wallowed in their self-produced devastation and lived among an angry, violence-prone population. Russia's heavy handed tactics were in themselves part of the Chechen guerrilla recruiting program where every Russian atrocity gave rise to another guerrilla fighter. Taken in this light, the Russians' counter-sniper policy of systematic murder and overwhelming response only served to create more Chechen snipers.

In the future, Russia may reduce its heavy losses to Chechen snipers if it develops an intelligent counter-insurgency and counter-sniper policy that gets off the perpetually spinning wheel of indiscriminate destruction. Until they do this, there will always be one more Chechen sniper, hidden carefully in a bombed out building, waiting to put a bullet in a Russian conscript's head.

Chapter 15

Urban Terror Perfected

The DC Snipers

We are going to go to the Washington DC area and we are going to terrorize these people.

- Alleged statement made by John Muhammad

Urban Sniping Hits its Stride

As Dean Meyers pumped gas into his black Mazda Protégé on October 9, 2002, he probably shivered as it was cold, wet, and a little after eight o'clock at night. The Sunoco gas station on Sudley Road in Manassas, Virginia was located in a busy commercial area, a thousand meters from Route 66. People, cars, and businesses surrounded the Sunoco and a police officer was nearby. Suddenly, a muffled *boom!* was heard, a split-second before a .223 caliber rifle bullet hit Dean behind his left ear, killing him instantly. Amazingly, no one saw anything suspicious and the police officer, who was briefly in the killer's sights himself, never saw a thing. Even when the shooter was pulled over just minutes later and briefly questioned by police, they were soon let go.[1]

How was this possible, a gunman could fire a high-powered rifle, with dozens of potential witnesses nearby, and escape undetected? How was it a police officer could be only yards away from the shooting, and then the shooter himself be questioned, but then escape? This was possible because Dean Meyers was John Muhammad and Lee Malvo's nineteenth victim and the two snipers had hit their killing stride. Muhammad and Malvo were planning and training for their sniper operation for months and

---

1 Horwitz & Ruane, *Sniper: Inside the Hunt for the Killers Who Terrorized the Nation*, p. 137-9.

they were now putting their sniper theories into practice. During the course of their previous eighteen killings they had perfected their tactics, allowing them to evade a massive police dragnet for weeks. A closer look at their deadly methodology shows exactly how Muhammad and Malvo managed to shoot twenty-three people over a span of eight months, from one end of the United States to the other, manipulating the urban terrain, until they were ultimately captured - not because of a sophisticated law-enforcement counter-sniper strategy, but because of the shooters' own mistakes.

The Snipers' Goals

John Muhammad, born in 1960, was a deeply disturbed, violent man who was emotionally and mentally unstable. Muhammad was a Desert Storm veteran, a converted Muslim, a habitual liar, obsessed with fitness, a studied con-man, lost custody of his children to an ex-wife he hated, and, for a while, earned money smuggling illegal immigrants from Antigua into the United States. In 2000, Muhammad met a troubled young man by the name of Lee Boyd Malvo in Antigua and unofficially adopted him as a second son. Malvo, the product of an absentee father and an irresponsible mother, quickly fell under Muhammad's strong personality, soon calling Muhammad 'Dad'. Out of this unusual relationship of two troubled men, a sniper team was created.

There is no telling when Muhammad actually sprung his idea for a murder campaign on the young Malvo. Regardless, the killings were Muhammad's idea and Malvo was a willing tool to accomplish them. Most likely, the shootings were part of a larger plan to kill Muhammad's ex-wife, Mildred, who lived with her sister in Clinton, Maryland. Muhammad threatened to kill Mildred previously when she and Muhammad lived in Tacoma, Washington. She since had a spousal protection order issued against Muhammad. In fact, Muhammad and Malvo went to Mildred's house in Tacoma to kill her, but she already moved away to Maryland. Instead, they shot and killed the unlucky young woman who opened the front door.

In Muhammad's plan, Mildred would have been just one of a score of victims who were shot at random by an unknown serial murderer. Mildred would have been the main target all along and the other murders were just a smoke screen to cover up this fact. Ominously, Mildred actually saw Muhammad's car parked near her house in Maryland after the killings started. Local residents also saw the same car parked several houses down from where Mildred lived. If Muhammad did not plan to kill Mildred, why did he and Malvo travel all the way from Tacoma, Washington to kill multiple persons within a mile of Mildred's house in Maryland?[2]

Another theory is Muhammad planned the killings to extort money from the U.S. Government since he did eventually demand $10 million from authorities if they wanted the killings to stop. An integral part of this extortion plan was creating terror among the local residents. After being captured, Malvo said the victims were chosen at random to cause maximum shock in order to spread fear. They wanted people to think anyone could be next.[3] Hence, old men, women, and even school children were targeted for execution. Muhammad said he wanted to terrorize so much of the populace as to affect the local economy. If the local economy started to decline, he was sure the authorities would pay his ransom.

Another theory blends several motives to answer the 'why' of these systematic

2 Horwitz & Ruane, p. 107-9.
3 Horwitz & Ruane, p. 105.

A Home Depot parking lot where the DC snipers shot one of their victims.

killings. Perhaps these killings were partially an outlet for Muhammad's and Malvo's seething rage for their unhappy childhoods and their going-nowhere lives. Muhammad probably did plan to kill his ex-wife, but never got the opportunity during their killing spree. Muhammad probably did want to extort money from the authorities - if he could get it. It also appeared Muhammad had a subconscious desire to be caught, but was determined to kill as many people and humiliate as many law enforcement agencies as he could along the way until the murderous ride was over.

Other possible reasons for the murders came to surface during Muhammad's trial in 2006, when Malvo publicly confessed what their motives were. First, Malvo heaped most of the blame on Muhammad, telling him, in front of the court, "You took me into your house and made me a monster. You fed me, you clothed me and you made me your child." Malvo said Mohammad hated America in part for being a slave state, he in fact hated all whites, and he planned to kill six whites a day for thirty days straight once their killing spree got underway. More specifically, Muhammad wanted to target pregnant white women and at one time, according to Malvo, Malvo had a pregnant white woman in his sights but could not bring himself to pull the trigger. This mass killing of whites would just be the first stage of a multi-phased terror campaign.

In the second stage, the two snipers would drive up Route 95 to Baltimore, Maryland and gun down a policeman. When friends and family went to the officer's funeral, Muhammad would have a surprise waiting. As the grief stricken mourners crowded around the deceased's grave, Muhammad planned to detonate an Improvised Explosive Device (IED) in order to blow to smithereens those who came to pay their respects. Muhammad knew ambulances would quickly respond to this horrific attack and he intended to compound the slaughter by blowing up the arriving ambulances with more IEDs. Malvo even admitted they planned to massacre a bus load of school children, but Malvo fell asleep while on the lookout for an appropriate target at a gas station and missed the opportunity.

Mohammad was far more ambitious and his dreams went beyond merely executing white pregnant women, shooting up bus loads of school children, and blowing up ambulances and crowds of grieving people. Once Mohammad conducted the first crop of killings, he intended to cross the border into Canada, escaping the United States' law enforcement dragnet. Inside America's northern neighbor, he planned on recruiting and indoctrinating up to 140 young homeless men at a remote compound. There, Mohammad would instruct his new legion in the dark art of urban sniper-terror just like he had successfully done with the impressionable Malvo. With these 140 trained killers, Muhammad would send them across the border into America where they would wreak havoc all across America's cities. Even though Muhammad wanted to bleed the United States and get some payback for unspecified injustices committed against him, he would grant America a reprieve if the Bush Administration paid him ten million dollars in ransom.

This grandiose plan, if it worked, could have inflicted hundreds of deaths on unsuspecting Americans far and wide, from Boston to Los Angeles, Saint Petersburg to Portland. Men, women, and children would be picked off everywhere, dying from precisely placed headshots while they strolled on sidewalks, shopped in supermarkets, and lounged on their front porches. This plan also sounded like pure fantasy - the demented ranting of a delusional megalomaniac. Who was going to pay for the rent, electricity, and food at the compound? Assuming these urban guerrilla snipers would work in teams of two, who was going to buy the seventy cars for them to drive around in? Where were the seventy sniper rifles going to come from? How was Muhammad going to communicate with these seventy separate teams? Where were these seventy teams going to get the money and credit cards from to pay for hotels, gas, and food? What happened when one of the teams got cold feet, went to the police, or were caught and interrogated, and confessed, exposing the whole plan?

Regardless of what their underlying logic was for the killings, at the time, it was impossible to discern their true motives, making it difficult to identify and locate the shooters. After all, if the two simply drove to Mohammad's wife's house and shot her as she walked outside to her car, it would be obvious who the police would investigate first. Muhammad would have been placed under suspicion immediately and arrested in a matter of days, if not hours. Importantly, the extreme distance between where the killings took place and where Muhammad and Malvo lived disguised their motives. If the killings took place in Seattle or Antigua, Muhammad may have been looked at a lot earlier. Who would have guessed Muhammad and Malvo would drive across the entire country to kill people at random in Maryland? Actually, only one person guessed this, an acquaintance of Muhammad's who suspected him only after the victims started to stack up. Ultimately, the extreme distance between the shootings and the snipers' home acted as a giant investigative barrier, helping to disassociate the shooters from their crimes.

Training for Their Mission

The way in which the two trained for their sniper campaign was a veritable 'how-to' lesson for urban guerrilla snipers. Muhammad and Malvo trained in the open and

AR-15 Bushmaster

The snipers used a 5.56 mm semi-automatic assault rifle for their attacks. Due to the close ranges they were firing at, the small, light, accurate weapon was perfect for their mission.

without suspicion. The two often shot, quite legally, at the Tacoma Sportsmen's Club, where they practiced marksmanship for hours upon hours with Muhammad instructing the younger Malvo. The two also played the Xbox game *Halo*, a first-person shooter game that allows a person to practice tactics as well as the finer points of sniping. Video games were just another legal, inexpensive way to practice military tactics under the cover of just 'playing games'. Muhammad also educated Malvo in sniper skills from a Navy SEAL sniper video he owned, receiving pre-recorded instruction from the special operations experts themselves. Another teaching method used was watching educational films like the movie *Savior*, which is about a mercenary sniper fighting in Bosnia.[4]

While the two future killers practiced the tactical aspects of shooting, they also led a healthy lifestyle. They worked out consistently and ate healthy. Muhammad, who benefited from seventeen years in the Army National Guard and the active duty Army, was an avid shooter, often going to gun shows. Importantly, the sniper operation was not a fly-by-night event. No, Muhammad planned the killings at least several months beforehand and looked into a variety of ways to better kill people in an urban environment. For example, Muhammad tried to build his own sound suppressor for a rifle, but it did not work. By law, any person manufacturing a sound suppressor must register this device with the federal government. This law only works if the people building the silencer consent to follow it. Muhammad also asked a local gunsmith if he could modify a rifle with a barrel that could be screwed/unscrewed in the middle. This request revealed Muhammad did not know much about gunsmithing as the barrel is the one place on a weapon you do not want to modify to make it shorter. The barrel may blow up at the point of connection and it would adversely affect weapon accuracy. Regardless of Muhammad's gunsmithing skills, he knew what he wanted: a weapon which was quiet and could be broken down into something concealable. In short, he was looking for a weapon designed for urban sniping.

Weapon of Choice: The Bushmaster

Muhammad eventually selected a weapon that was, in many ways, ideal for their

4 Horwitz & Ruane, p. 46.

planned killings - a Bushmaster XM-15 rifle, .223 caliber (5.56 mm), with a 16-inch barrel. The .223 Bushmaster, a near clone of the U.S. military's M-4 rifle, fires an extremely flat shooting round, capable of making accurate shots at man-size targets out to three hundred meters. The shots Muhammad and Malvo would be making were at much closer ranges, some less than fifty meters.

Their Bushmaster had a Bushnell holographic sight mounted on the top. This sight was not telescopic and was not intended for long distance shooting. It was designed for quickly acquiring close-in targets moving in low-light conditions. This description fitted many of their eventual targets. A telescopic scope was also found in the car, but was probably not used often since most shots were at night and the distances from the shooters to their targets were so close. At these distances and under these conditions, a high-powered telescopic scope was irrelevant. Their particular Bushmaster came equipped with a collapsible stock. This adjustable stock allowed the shooter to extend the stock to fit the shooter's shoulder when firing. When the shooting was over, the ability to adjust the stock's length made the weapon easier to conceal, both before and after the shot, or when transporting the weapon in a duffel bag.

The final feature on their Bushmaster was a detachable Harris bipod. The bipod is often used by snipers because it allows the shooter to fire from a stable platform. The legs of the bipod are adjustable in length so they can be adjusted to fit the shooter and their environment. When not in use, the legs fold up against the forward handguard of the weapon, out of the way, allowing the weapon to be more easily concealed. Overall, this particular model of Bushmaster with the corresponding additional features made it an ideal urban sniping weapon.

The manner in which Muhammad secured the weapon helped the two in their killings. They 'acquired' the weapon when they stole it from a local gun shop: Bulls Eye Shooter Supply in Tacoma. The owner never realized the weapon was stolen and never connected the missing Bushmaster to Muhammad and Malvo until they were captured by police and the serial number on the gun was investigated. Because the rifle was stolen, there were no financial records or written documents connecting Muhammad to the rifle. Until Muhammad and Malvo were captured in physical possession of the weapon, there was no way to connect the missing Bushmaster with them.

Constructing the Perfect Shooting Platform

For quite some time, Muhammad planned to use a car as a sniper platform for the killings. More specifically, Muhammad planned to shoot from the trunk of a car as a concealed sniper hide. When looking for a car to use for their operations, Muhammad looked at several cars, but discounted them because the trunk was too small. Muhammad eventually focused on a Blue, 1990, 4-door, Chevrolet Caprice Classic, which he bought for only $250 from a dealership in New Jersey. From that day on, the Caprice with New Jersey tags NDA-217 became a mobile killing platform.[5]

In many ways, the Caprice Muhammad purchased was perfect for facilitating their killings. The car's color, a dark blue, did not stand out or attract undue attention. At night, this dark color could look like several colors like a brown, gray, green, or red. In fact, one witness who saw the Caprice at the scene of a shooting stated the car's color was burgundy in color. From that point on, police were looking for a burgundy

5 Horwitz & Ruane, p. 16.

1990 Chevy Caprice Classic

The snipers took a used Caprice Classic and converted it into an urban sniping platform, firing from the large trunk.

Caprice, not the blue one that was pulled over multiple times during the course of the killings.

Since the Caprice was a big car with four doors and big seats, it was comfortable, which was important because Muhammad and Malvo essentially lived out of the car for six weeks. The big seats allowed one person to sleep in the back while the other person drove or kept a look out. The car was also big enough to hold supplies like food, water, and duffle bags without getting in the way. Once Muhammad bought the Caprice, they modified it to suit their particular needs. First, they tinted all of the windows except the windshield. This tinting was an effective form of urban camouflage, concealing the people inside from anyone looking in. This meant people seeing the car near a shooting could not identify anyone inside the vehicle, spectators did not know how many people were in the car, and they did not know what the people in the car were doing. This urban screening kept the occupants of the car anonymous and helped to conceal their activities inside the vehicle.

Another important modification the two made was placing the rear seat on a hinge at the top of the seat. This was done so the person in the back seat could swing the back seat rest up and then they could slide into the trunk. Since the back seat rest swung out, away from the trunk, the person in the trunk could then come back out of the trunk, swing the seat up, and go into the back seat again. With the car's tinted windows, a person could transition from the back seat, to the trunk, and back again without anyone noticing them doing this. The hinged rear seat also meant a person could hide in the trunk so when they were pulled over by police, the officer only saw a single person in the car, oblivious to the shooter hiding in the trunk.

As stated before, the Caprice was a big car with a big trunk, a trunk big enough someone could lay down and shoot from inside it. Since Muhammad planned to shoot from the trunk, he cut a small hole in trunk above the license plate. This hole was just big enough to shoot through, but small enough it did not arouse suspicion. When the firing port was not in use, the two stuffed it up with a cloth.[6]

Shooting from the trunk, through a small hole, did several things: it hid the muzzle flash, hid any muzzle blast, and muffled the sound of the gunshot. Many people heard the gunshot, but thought it was a car's backfire, a tire exploding, or something being dropped on the pavement. No one ever saw the muzzle flash from the weapon, making

---

6 Horwitz & Ruane, p. 107.

it almost impossible to associate the car with the shooting from visual clues alone. From a counter-forensic perspective, shooting from inside the car kept the immediate evidence from the shot in the confines of the trunk. The cartridges ejected from the Bushmaster bounced harmlessly off the inside walls of the trunk and stayed inside. Gunsmoke did not escape the trunk and neither did the smell of gunpowder. Only the tiny hole used as a gun port connected the forensic evidence inside the trunk of the Caprice to the outside world. Due to this forensic isolation, no evidence was transferred from the trunk of the Caprice to the immediate area near the crime scene, helping Muhammad and Malvo remain anonymous.

While the slightly beat up Caprice was nondescript in almost every way, there were certain giveaways to the trained eye. In fact, some police referred to the Caprice as a 'felony car' because it looked suspicious. Their Caprice was a former police car, which criminals were known to use because it gave them the illusion of authority. Also, the tinted windows made the car look like someone was trying to hide something, such as shooting someone with a sniper rifle. The car had an overall seedy quality to it, allowing it blend into the low-rent surroundings but, it caught the eye of law enforcement personnel on many occasions. However, looking suspicious and being connected to a string of killings are two separate and distinct things.

Financial Backing & Planning

Muhammad and Malvo could only conduct their killings if they had at least some income. While most people work at a job for their money, Muhammad and Malvo shot and robbed people to secure their finances. Their biggest coup came on September 5, 2002, when they shot and robbed the owner of a local store, stealing $3500 in cash and a $1400 laptop. This $3500 went a long way, helping them to purchase their $250 Caprice, it bought them food and supplies, and also paid for gas and phone calls. The two also tried using stolen credit cards, but all of the cards were quickly closed out so they never got more than a couple dollars worth of fraudulent credit card purchases.[7] Because Muhammad and Malvo were dependent on stealing money to finance their killings, they increased their exposure to law enforcement. The two got away with several robberies, but committing these crimes alerted the police and risked the chance of capture during the act. During one armed robbery, police arrived on the seen and chased one person (probably Malvo) who was standing above the wounded victims, going through a purse. The gunman got away, but dropped their pistol during the pursuit, which later became incriminating evidence used against them.

Sniper Tactics

Muhammad and Malvo used a variety of successful tactics to confuse the police and continue their killing spree. One of their tactics was to spread their killings out over a large, geographic area. This separation in distance made it difficult for police to connect one crime to another. For example, the police had no idea the people killing victims in the D.C. area were the same ones who killed in Tacoma, Washington, in Tucson, Arizona, in Atlanta, Georgia, in Montgomery, Alabama, and in Baton Rouge, Louisiana. There was no common thread between the victims, no obvious motives,

---

7 Horwitz & Ruane, p. 61.

The Trunk

AP Photo

NDA·21Z
· Garden State ·

Firing Port

Here is a view of the actual trunk that the snipers fired from. Note the firing port made just above the license plate.

and no way to link one single person to these different crimes. This geographic separation became a very real forensic gulf, helping keep the crimes unconnected.

Also, the initial variety between different crimes kept Muhammad and Malvo from being connected to the separate murders. For example, Malvo shot their first victim with a Sig Sauer .45 caliber pistol in Tacoma. A month later and a thousand miles away, a man was shot with a rifle in Tucson. Five and a half months later, across the country in Maryland, their third victim was shot up close with a pistol and then robbed. Victim number four was shot nine days later with a rifle. Victim number five was shot a day later with a pistol and was robbed. A week later and hundreds of miles away, victim number six was shot with a pistol and robbed in Atlanta. This variety in time, in weapons, in locations, and in apparent motives (sometimes money was stolen, sometimes it was not) made connecting the different killings impossible in the absence of physical evidence and eye witnesses. It was only after Muhammad and Malvo stopped varying their tactics to intentionally spread terror in the D.C. area that they set a pattern and the different killings became tied together.

When Muhammad and Malvo planned to kill a victim they were usually thorough. They would drive by the place of their intended attack a day prior and see if it met their needs. They would then conduct surveillance of their target area for a period of time - several hours if they were in a rush, or all night if they had more time. Regardless of how much time they had, they made sure they were aware of their surroundings and understood their immediate environment.

It was easy for the two to stay abreast of police progress against them by simply watching local television, reading newspapers, and listening to the radio. Muhammad and Malvo then combined this knowledge of the situation with maps of the area, downloaded on their stolen laptop computer, to plan their next killing. If they knew the police were focused on a specific area, they could plan a route to a less vigilant location and find a good target with close access to local highways for an immediate

293

escape. Even though they were not from the eastern seaboard and had no previous knowledge of the greater D.C. area, their map software made up for these deficiencies.[8]

When shooting from their car, Muhammad and Malvo faced their car away from their intended victim with the trunk of the car facing the target. After they made their shot, they slowly drove away in order to avoid suspicion. They intentionally appeared to look calm as the screeching of tires or erratic driving would surely catch a witness' attention and stick in their memory. This calm, cool demeanor worked for Muhammad and Malvo many times. Their Caprice was observed by numerous witnesses at different crime scenes, but investigators never thought there was a connection.

Muhammad and Malvo did not always fire their rifle from inside the trunk of their car. On at least four separate occasions, they shot their victims from adjacent woods. In these cases, they used walkie-talkies where one person with the car kept watch and called in situational updates to the shooter concealed in the woods. As these incidents revealed, the two could operate away from their car and use whatever surrounding terrain was available to facilitate their killings. This departure from shooting from the vehicle made the police's job more difficult because it broke the expected pattern. What good was it looking for a specific vehicle if the snipers were shooting from the woods or from a building?

Importantly, when Muhammad and Malvo's motives changed from killing for revenge (or money, or testing their tactics) to intentionally spreading terror, they no longer benefited from the variety in time, distance, and weapons to hide their motives and to hide the connections between their killings. Spreading terror meant they had to kill numerous people in a restricted geographic area to show they could not be stopped by the authorities.

While most of their killings were under the cover of darkness at night or in the early morning, some were committed in broad daylight in the presence of scores of potential witnesses. At least three of the shootings were done within eyesight, hearing, or close proximity to a police officer or a police station. At least one police officer was in Malvo's sights, but Malvo chose to shoot someone else nearby. Part of their methodology of spreading terror was intentionally making shots in proximity to law enforcement personnel, showing the communities the police were powerless to save them.

It was impossible for the police to protect everyone because there was a never ending array of targets for the two snipers to choose from, with millions of people living within a thirty minute drive in every direction of Washington, D.C. In this dense urban environment, Muhammad and Malvo ensured a steady opportunity of victims by concentrating on public places like gas stations, store parking lots, restaurants, schools, and liquor stores. People needed gas, had to eat food, and wanted liquor. All the two had to do was stake out one of a thousand different gas stations and they knew they would have an endless number of human targets to shoot. Liquor stores and gas stations were the equivalent of salt licks for deer hunters.

An integral part of their terror campaign in the D.C. area was how they killed their victims. They intended to kill, not wound, their victims and they usually tried to kill their victims with a head shot. Four of the victims shot with the Bushmaster rifle were shot in the head while others were not because Muhammad or Malvo could

---

8 Horwitz & Ruane, p. 147.

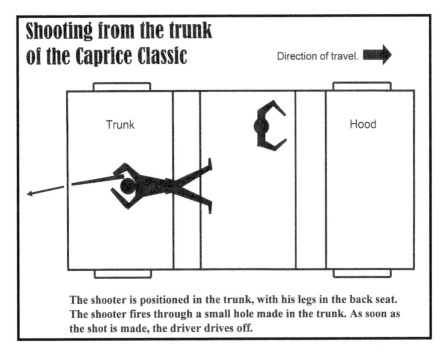

Shooting from the trunk of the Caprice Classic

Direction of travel.

Trunk

Hood

The shooter is positioned in the trunk, with his legs in the back seat. The shooter fires through a small hole made in the trunk. As soon as the shot is made, the driver drives off.

not acquire the target and had to settle for a different part of the body. If they had to shoot to the body, they tried to get a killing shot. Five victims received fatal wounds to their vital organs (heart, ascending aorta, pulmonary vein), two had their spinal cords severed, and one was shot in the neck. Others were shot in the lower back and some in the abdomen or stomach (more of these victims lived because of these less-than-fatal locations).

A reason why Muhammad and Malvo were able to kill for as long as they did under intense scrutiny by the police was their effective cover stories backed up by their demeanor. When questioned by local residents as they were parked somewhere, Muhammad would say he was traveling with his son from New Jersey and just wanted to get some rest. Since Muhammad was always polite and calm, people believed him. Even when questioned by police on several different occasions, the snipers remained calm, presenting a plausible story as to why they were in the area. Since the police had to deal with millions of potential suspects, as long as Muhammad and Malvo's stories seemed credible, backed up by a relaxed behavior, there were no red flags to single them out.

An additional piece of Muhammad and Malvo's strategy was overloading local law enforcement officials. For instance, on October 3, 2002, they killed five different people in a fourteen-hour period in Montgomery County, Maryland. Malvo later said these killings in Montgomery County were intentional, knowing the police could not handle this volume of activity.[9] With these killings, the police were forced to isolate and investigate five separate crime scenes, each one devouring scores of investigators, police, and security personnel. From a command and control perspective, Muhammad and Malvo hoped to overwhelm the authorities' ability to coordinate so

9 Horwitz & Ruane, p. 109-10.

many different investigative operations simultaneously. This part of their plan was effective because after those five killings, they managed to shoot another seven people over the next three weeks.

The Urban Snapshot

Muhammad and Malvo escaped detection by nearby witnesses on a dozen different occasions due to the nature of the urban environment they operated in. First, they drove a non-descript car, just one of hundreds of thousands in the area. Even at the crime scenes, there were scores of cars in the immediate area and the slightly beat-up Caprice was just one of many possible shooting platforms. When a shot was made, the nearby people had a second or two to observe the surrounding urban terrain before Muhammad and Malvo calmly drove off.

At the time of the shot, witnesses had a momentary urban snapshot of their surroundings. The more people, buildings, and cars that were around the crime scene, the harder it was for witnesses to narrow it down to a possible suspect. There were scores of possibilities at every shooting scene and if the witnesses happened to focus on the wrong object of interest, they missed the true culprits. Since much of the urban environment was made up of cars, the urban terrain was in a state of constant change and there was no way to freeze everyone at the scene of a shooting. Either a person picked out the Caprice instantly, or that part of the momentary urban snapshot was lost forever when it drove off.

The Forensics Battlefield

In order to catch the two snipers, thousands of law enforcement personnel were employed in some capacity. The Montgomery County police took the lead in trying to catch Muhammad and Malvo, accompanied by a host of other agencies like the FBI, DEA, ATF, and the Maryland and Virginia state police. While there were plenty of people on hand to help track down the shooters, it was a monumental task trying to coordinate between the separate agencies, all with different jurisdictions and capabilities. One thing authorities did was establish a hotline for tips in order to get the community involved and have the people on the streets act as the eyes and ears of law enforcement. However, the dense urban area the snipers worked in created complications. Once the hot lines were open, authorities were deluged with a flood of calls, overwhelming the authorities' ability to effectively process every citizen with something to contribute.

Eventually, authorities set up at least 82 lines to handle the thousands of tips they got every day.[10] In one case, the authorities found themselves swamped with 30,000 tips in a single day.[11] One lady working the FBI tip line received 500 calls on a single shift and actually interrupted Malvo when he called, redirecting him to another number.[12] Malvo later said they personally called the FBI hot line four times to discuss their demands, but could never get through to someone in charge![13] Ironically, just as Muhammad and Malvo hid among the sea of cars on the streets as they killed people,

10 Horwitz & Ruane, p.143.
11 Horwitz & Ruane, p.143.
12 Horwitz & Ruane, p. 172.
13 Horwitz & Ruane, p.177.

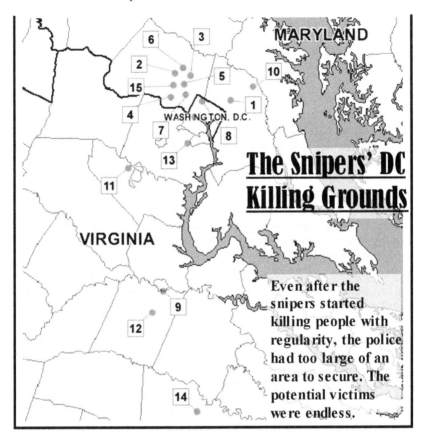

The Snipers' DC Killing Grounds

Even after the snipers started killing people with regularity, the police had too large of an area to secure. The potential victims were endless.

they got lost among the flood of phone calls swamping the various hot lines. Fueling this human crush of 'helpful' tips was a $50,000 reward Montgomery County offered, leading to the arrest of the two snipers. As the bodies continued to pile up, another $50,000 was added to the pot, and then another $100,000. A total of $200,000 dangled before the nose of any citizen who could bring the killings to an end by turning in Muhammad and Malvo. The more money offered, the more calls the police received.

While they had no hope of following up every call, the police followed up hundreds of the most promising leads. Police staked out and followed suspects, confiscated guns, fired the guns to compare their ballistics, and then gave the guns back when they did not match. The police's job was at times hindered due to a variety of false leads reported through law enforcement channels. For example, on more than one occasion, a white box truck was seen near the scene of a shooting and precious manpower was spent stopping and searching hundreds of these vehicles. In fact, there were over 70,000 white box trucks and white vans in Maryland alone.[14] Since people became focused on searching for a particular type of vehicle that was not the shooters', Muhammad and Malvo continued to cruise the streets in their modified, dark blue Caprice killing machine, invisible to the public and law enforcement.

Another problem went beyond mistaken identities - intentionally misleading reports. In one instance, a supposed eyewitness stated they saw a man with an AK-47

14 Horwitz & Ruane, p. 184.

getting into a cream colored Chevy Astro van near the scene of a shooting. This report further confirmed authorities should focus on a white truck or van instead of the blue Caprice repeatedly seen or stopped near the crime scenes. This report about the man with an AK-47 later proved to be completely fabricated and the eyewitness admitted to making the story up. Eventually, the police got a break when they followed up a phone call from Robert Holmes, an acquaintance of John Muhammad from Tacoma, Washington. The police questioned Holmes on October 22, although he called five days earlier, saying he thought he knew who the sniper was.[15] This was unsurprising, considering Holmes was just one of 80,000 mostly erroneous leads. Besides, what could someone from Washington State possibly know about killings happening on the east coast? In retrospect, the groundwork for Muhammad and Malvo's capture was laid almost a year before. After all, it was Muhammad's previous criminal and violence-prone behavior witnessed by Holmes that led him to call the hotline.

The authorities quickly found out Holmes knew quite a bit about the snipers. This proved to be their demise. The two snipers were only able to operate under the noses of the people and police when they were anonymous. Once the police had two names, the game was up. These names led to social security numbers, pictures, and detailed records of both Muhammad and Malvo. Soon, the police also had the make, model, and description of the car the two were driving. In a little more than 24 hours after talking to Holmes, Muhammad and Malvo were spotted by a local citizen and captured by police in the early morning hours of October 24, 2002, at an isolated rest stop in Maryland.

Once Muhammad and Malvo's anonymity was stripped from them, they were sitting ducks. Then, it was relatively easy for the authorities to connect Muhammad and Malvo to most of the twenty-three people they shot. It was a simple task for the authorities to convict the two because Muhammad and Malvo were so forensically sloppy over the course of their killings. Part of this forensic sloppiness was a magazine Malvo left behind, with his fingerprints on it, at the scene of a killing in Alabama. Another crime scene had a map with both Muhammad's and Malvo's fingerprints on it. The police also found a small caliber pistol Malvo dropped at the scene of another shooting in Alabama. This pistol was then connected to a number of other shootings the two committed. At another shooting scene, the two left behind a duffle bag they used to conceal and transport their rifle in. This was an unintentional mistake because Muhammad was later seen buying a new duffle bag. The sloppiness continued. Muhammad left handwritten notes to the police on a tarot card and store-bought stationary and he was even caught on a surveillance camera entering the store to buy the stationary. Malvo also left behind DNA samples on a bag of raisons he ate at one of their sniper hides in the woods. At several locations Muhammad and Malvo left behind expended shell casings after the shootings.

To top it off, Muhammad and Malvo were caught with the Bushmaster rifle (lying in the trunk of their car) they used to shoot a majority of their victims with. The Bushmaster was then connected to the expended cartridges left behind and the actual bullets taken from the bodies of their victims. With all this evidence, it was an open and shut case. Muhammad and Malvo simply lacked the counter-forensic discipline to get away with their crimes. This is not really surprising, since it was their intent all along to keep killing until they were either caught or killed.

---

15 Horwitz & Ruane, p.175.

From South Armagh to Washington, DC to Baghdad

These killings show the kind of terror two trained and determined people can inflict on an unarmed community. The snipers' Caprice was the perfect urban sniper platform, allowing them to make repeated shots in broad daylight, in the presence of numerous potential witnesses and even police officers. As long as the snipers' identities remained unknown, they were impervious to law enforcement's efforts. They were impervious because they were swallowed up by a dense urban environment that forced police to try and find a single person and a single vehicle out of a pool of millions, which was the equivalent of finding a needle in a haystack. Malvo later claimed Muhammad got the idea of shooting from a car in a training manual written by the Irish Republican Army. (The author has been unable to locate such a manual). This may be true since we know years earlier, in the 1990's, an Irish Republican Army sniper team used a similar methodology – firing from the back of a car - to target British soldiers in Northern Ireland.

Ironically, while Muhammad and Malvo targeted American citizens, their urban sniping methodology was copied by insurgent snipers in Iraq and used against American soldiers. Instead of targeting and terrorizing unarmed civilians, these insurgent snipers targeted heavily armed soldiers positioned at check points and guard towers. These guerrilla snipers also shot from inside vehicles, in broad daylight, in dense urban areas, and got away with it. Every successful guerrilla sniping experience is subject to being learned by new generations of snipers. Muhammad and Malvo were just one link in a chain of sniper methodology started in Northern Ireland, imported to the United States, and then exported to Iraqi guerrillas.

General descriptions of the shootings.

• Victim #1- Feb 16, 2002, 7:00 pm, Tacoma, WA, 21 y.o. woman, shot in her house, hit in the head and died, from a .45 pistol. The shooter was on the porch, point blank.
• Victim #2- Mar 19, 2002, 12:30 am (est.), Tucson AZ, 60 y.o. man, shot on a golf course, hit in the back and died, from a rifle. The shooter was in the nearby woods, 100 m away. (All distances are estimated in meters.)
• Victim #3- Sep 5, 2002, 10:30 pm, Clinton, Maryland, 55 y.o. man, shot in a parking lot, hit in the upper body and lived, from a .22 pistol. The shooter was outside, firing point blank.
• Victim #4- Sep 14, 2002, 10:10 pm, Silver Spring, MD, 22 y.o. man, shot in a parking lot, hit in the lower back and lived, by a .223 rifle. The sniper was in a car, 50 m away.
• Victim #5- Sep 15, 2002, 10:00 pm, Brandywine, MD, 32 y.o. man, shot in front of liquor store, hit in the abdomen, by a .22 pistol. The shooter was outside, point blank range.
• Victim #6- Sep 21, 2002, 12:16 pm, Atlanta, GA, 41 y.o. man, shot in front of liquor store, hit in the back of head and killed, by a .22 pistol. The shooter was outside, at point blank range.
• Victim #7- Sep 21, 2002, 7:20 pm, Montgomery, AL, 52 y.o. woman, shot in front of a liquor store, hit in the spinal cord and killed, by a .223 rifle. The shooter was in a car, 50 m away.

• Victim #8- Sep 21, 2002, 7:20 pm, Montgomery, AL, 24 y.o. woman, shot in front of liquor store, hit in back of neck and lived, by a .223 rifle. The shooter was in a car, 50 m away.

• Victim #9- Sep 23, 2002, 6:40 pm, Baton Rouge, LA, 45 y.o. woman, shot in a parking lot, hit in the head and killed, by a .223 rifle. The sniper was in a car, 50 m away.

• Victim #10- Oct 2, 2002, 5:20 pm, Aspen Hill, MD, store window shot out, no one hit. The shooter was in a car (probably a botched hit).

• Victim #11- Oct 2, 2002, 6:02 pm, Wheaton, MD, 55 y.o. man, shot in a parking lot, hit in the spinal cord and died, by a .223 rifle. The sniper was in a car, 50 m away.

• Victim #12- Oct 3, 2002, 7:41 am, White Flint, MD, 39 y.o., shot mowing the lawn, hit in the back and died, from a .223 rifle. The sniper was in a car, 75 m away.

• Victim #13- Oct 3, 2002, 8:12 am, Aspen Hill, MD, 54 y.o. man, shot while pumping gas, hit in the chest and died, from a .223 rifle. The sniper was in a car, 75 m away.

• Victim #14- Oct 3, 2002, 8:37 am, Silver Springs, MD, 34 y.o. woman, shot sitting on bench, hit in head and died, from a .223 rifle. The sniper was in a car, 50 m away.

• Victim #15- Oct 3, 2002, 9:58 am, Kensington, MD, 25 y.o. woman, at a gas station, hit in the chest and died, by a .223 rifle. The sniper was in a car, 50 m away.

• Victim #16- Oct 3, 2002, 9:20 am, Washington, DC, 72 y.o. man, shot crossing a street, hit in the upper chest and died. The sniper was in a car, 75 m away.

• Victim #17- Oct 4, 2002, 2:27 pm, Fredericksburg, VA, 43 y.o. woman, shot in a parking lot, hit in the lower back and lived, by a .223 rifle. The sniper was in a car, 50 m away.

• Victim #18- Oct 7, 2002, 8:09 am, Bowie, MD, 13 y.o. boy, in front of a school, hit in the abdomen and lived, from a .223 rifle. The sniper was in the woods, 100 m away.

• Victim #19- Oct 9, 2002, 8:10 pm, Manassas, VA, 53 y.o. man, shot at a gas station, hit in the head and died, from a .223 rifle. The sniper was in a car, 50 m away.

• Victim #20- Oct 11, 2002, 9:28 am, Massaponax, VA, 53 y.o. man, shot at a gas station, hit in the chest and died, by a .223 rifle. The sniper was in a car, 50 m away.

• Victim #21- Oct 14, 2002, 9:15 pm, Falls Church VA, 47 y.o. woman, shot in a parking lot, hit in the head and died, by a .223 rifle. The sniper was in a car, 50 m away.

• Victim #22- Oct 19, 2002, 7:59 pm, Ashland VA, 37 y.o., man, shot in a parking lot, hit in the stomach and lived, from a .223 rifle. The sniper was in a car, 50 m away.

• Victim #23- Oct 22, 2002, 5:56 am, Aspen Hill, MD, 35 y.o. man, shot inside a bus, hit in the stomach and died, from a .223 rifle, by a sniper in the woods, 75 m away.

Chapter 16

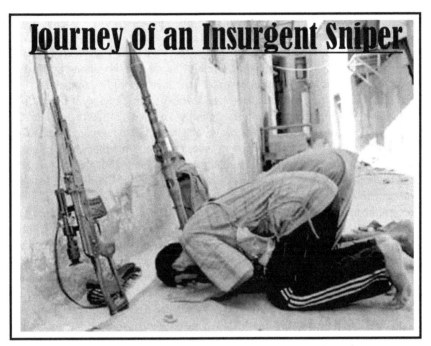

Journey of an Insurgent Sniper

Increase God's Mercy By Sniping Americans. – Abu Othman

Iraq: A History of Guerrilla Warfare

Guerrilla warfare is nothing new to the people of Iraq. From 1980-1988, Iraq fought a brutal campaign against Iran reminiscent of World War I, replete with trench warfare, human wave attacks, and poisonous gas. During this horrific bloodletting, both sides used resistance movements to advance their cause. Saddam Hussein gave sanctuary to the Mujahedin e-Khalq (MEK), an Iranian dissident group, which waged a low-grade insurgency against the Iranian regime since the 1970s. From their safe-havens in Iraq, the MEK made cross-border raids, collected intelligence, and conducted assassinations and acts of terror against the Iranian government. Along with the MEK, Saddam promoted insurgencies with Iran's Kurdish and Arab populations, but with little success.

Iran fought back with its own campaign of unconventional warfare. A central element of this guerrilla campaign included supporting opposition groups in Iraq, like the Supreme Council for Islamic Revolution in Iraq (SCIRI), which became a powerful Shiite political party. The SCIRI was more than just a political movement, it had real teeth in the form of the Badr Corps, the armed wing of the SCIRI. From the founding of SCIRI in the early 1980's until the fall of Saddam Hussein, the Iranian regime, through its SCIRI surrogate, waged a decades-long guerrilla war against the Iraq government.

The Saddam Hussein regime faced even more problems with its northern Kurd-

301

ish population, which tried for decades to secure their own independent state. From the 1960's until 2003, the Iraqi Kurds fought an ongoing guerrilla war against the Iraqi government with limited success. Saddam Hussein's counter-insurgency efforts against the Kurds involved the mass detention of Kurdish rebels, the bombardment of Kurdish villages with chemical weapons, and the smothering of rebellious Kurdish areas with loyal regime troops.

After the U.S. invasion and defeat of Iraq in the 1991 Gulf War, Saddam Hussein waged his own guerrilla war against the United Nations and the United States as the victors of the Gulf War tried to enforce various sanctions and no-fly zones against him. Saddam undermined the economic sanctions leveled against Iraq by bribing UN officials and funneling into his own coffers the limited amounts of international aid that did come in. He flouted the no-fly zone laws and played cat and mouse with UN air patrols, targeting them with anti-aircraft missiles and 'painting' them with Iraqi radar systems. To top it off, Saddam played a shell game with international arms inspectors, refusing to cooperate with them fully and creating the impression he had hidden stocks of Nuclear, Biological, and Chemical weapons.

To complicate the situation, in 2001, the Iraqi Kurds were themselves confronted with an insurgency when the Ansar al-Islam movement began to carve out a slice of territory in eastern Iraqi Kurdistan, along the mountainous Iranian border. In this hard-won sanctuary, Ansar al-Islam constructed a religious society where a strict interpretation of the Koran was enforced. Anyone who did not agree with the Ansar al-Islam agenda was shot, beheaded, blown up, or run out of town. As Ansar al-Islam dug in and consolidated its power base, it spread its influence deeper into Kurdistan, assassinating Kurdish political and military leaders whenever possible with sniper attacks, car bombs, and martyr operations. Consequently, the Iraqi Kurds, who were fighting a guerrilla war against the Saddam regime, now faced their own guerrilla movement.

As a result, it is no exaggeration to say every strata of Iraqi society had some level of experience in either promoting or combating an insurgency, even if this experience was forced on them.

The Iraqi Insurgency: 2003-2008

When the U.S. military invaded Iraq on March 20, 2003, they promised to bring with them 'Shock and Awe'. In short, the Iraqi military would be so overwhelmed with America's superior military technology they would be paralyzed and simply collapse. This is exactly what happened. Only nineteen days into the war, the Iraqi military imploded, Saddam Hussein was on the run, and the U.S. had virtual control of the country. Iraq's regime was unprepared for the kind of war the U.S. was trained to fight and they quickly disintegrated under the onslaught of precision cruise missiles, Abrams main battle tanks, and lumbering B-52's disgorging satellite guided bombs.

While the Iraqi military was completely unprepared for the American tidal wave, the same could be said of American forces who found themselves confronted by a rapidly growing resistance movement grounded among a people adept at living in a state of perpetual guerrilla war. In contrast, the U.S. military had virtually no modern experience in unconventional warfare and it showed. The five million Sunnis who supported Saddam Hussein for decades and fought a vicious counter-insurgency war against their Kurdish and Shia brothers now experienced a stark role reversal. The

An Iranian Child-Sniper Takes Aim From the Trenches

Because Iranian forces suffered such huge losses from unsophisticated tactics like human-wave attacks, they were forced to recruit and employ children as soldiers. This same drain on their manpower encouraged them to try guerrilla warfare as a means to pressure the Saddam Hussein regime.

Sunni people were no longer the enforcers of the status quo, they were now committed to toppling the new American-backed, Shia-dominated government. Over night, the oppressors became the oppressed, the counter-guerrillas became the guerrillas. It soon became apparent the Sunni resistance was more prepared for this kind of warfare than most experts thought.

Compounding the complexity of the situation was not all of the Iraqi Shia were on the same sheet of political music. Some, like Muqtada al-Sadr and his powerful Mehdi Army, waged their own guerrilla war against the American occupation forces and against the newly elected government. The Kurds in the north resisted any central control of their increasingly independent chunk of the country, which slowly developed into a safehaven for Kurdish guerrillas fighting for independence from Turkey. The situation in Iraq became similar to the various anti-Israel factions in Gaza and the West Bank. So many different factions were fighting for so many different reasons it was hard to keep track of them all. It was like trying to fight a headless monster whose many tentacles did whatever they wanted. There was no central brain to kill, no single head to decapitate.

Amidst this swirling morass of contradictory political ambitions, a sophisticated new form of guerrilla warfare developed. This new war was largely an urban one, fought in major population centers like Irbil and Mosul in the north, Ramadi and Fallujah in the west, Najaf and Basrah in the south, and of course in Baghdad, which alone had a population of six million people. In Iraq, car bomb attacks were used on a scale never seen before. As many as 800 car bombs a year were detonated, collapsing buildings and slaughtering crowds of people in a single blast. Improved Explosive Devices (IEDs) were also used on a massive scale; as many as 25,000 IED ambushes a year were set, causing the majority of American deaths in the country. Suicide bombers were used in vast numbers, where single individuals wearing explosive vests infiltrated crowded cafes and blew themselves up, shredding the surrounding people with ball bearings and nails.

Amidst this cacophony of spectacular car bomb attacks and deadly IED ambushes, a little talked about threat seeped into the battlefield: the urban sniper. Sniping attacks did not grab headlines, they did not create carnage on a massive scale, and they did not grab the imagination like mass casualties did. Getting killed by a rather boring bullet did not even rate being covered by the Brookings Institution's Iraq Index, a comprehensive report which continuously tracked how U.S. soldiers were killed in the war. The Iraq Index did tell how many soldiers were killed by IEDs, car bombs, Rocket Propelled Grenades, mortar/rocket fire, helicopter accidents/shoot downs, and non-hostile fatalities, but not snipers. By September 2007, the Iraq Index recorded 1,176 U.S. soldiers being killed by hostile fire, but we do not know how many of those were from guerrilla snipers. If one had to make a rough estimate, to date, there have probably been 2000 soldiers killed and wounded by snipers (with the understanding in Iraq there has been an 8 to 1 ratio of wounded to dead).

The sniper problem in Iraq was bigger than most people thought. Just as the insurgents took car bomb, IED, and suicide attacks to new heights, they also fully embraced the art of urban sniping. In Iraq, sniping was a widespread phenomenon, not just isolated to a specific city or region. U.S. and Iraqi government forces all over the country came under the crosshairs in the nation's major cities, especially in the capital of Baghdad. The sniper problem grew bad enough by October of 2006, U.S. military commanders met in Baghdad for a conference on the subject. They were prompted to hold the meeting in part from the fact thirty-six U.S. soldiers were shot by snipers in Baghdad alone that month, up from twenty-three recorded sniper attacks in September.[1]

By the fall of 2007, only four and a half years into the war, the insurgent snipers learned their profession at a rate faster than any other previous guerrilla movement. Many of these snipers fired from inside cars and vans, a method only used sporadically by the IRA a decade earlier. Some snipers used sound suppressors, just like the best PLO shooters did in the occupied territories of Israel. Others fired from within the bowels of the cities, using the complex three-dimensional urban terrain to confuse and overwhelm their targets, like the Chechens did. The Iraqi snipers also conducted home invasions, cut loopholes in the walls from abandoned buildings, toyed with the idea of remote sniping, and used deceit at all times, intentionally blending in with the population from start to finish. As we read in the earlier chapter on the psychology of sniping, the insurgents took the media war to new levels, filming sniper attacks and distributing them worldwide. To make sure other snipers learned from these lessons, the insurgents posted on-line sniping manuals and distributed them on compact discs to the public. No other guerrilla war witnessed such a sophisticated sniper campaign.

Genesis of an Urban Guerrilla Sniper

One of the guerrilla snipers fighting this sniper campaign was Abu Othman (not his real name). Abu Othman was from Fallujah, a calligrapher by trade. Despite no formal training, Abu Othman shot his way from being an inexperienced craftsman to an accomplished sniper who was sought out by various insurgent groups to ply his deadly trade. According to his own tally, he had twenty-nine kills to his credit.[2] Abu Othman

1 Jervis, Rick, *More Troops Mean More Targets for Snipers in Iraq*, USA Today, 24 Oct 06.
2 Jaber, *The Chilling Toll Of Allah's Sniper.*

Fallujah: Abu Othman's Urban Jungle

was also known simply as 'The Sniper' in insurgent circles and reportedly killed his prey out to distances as far as one thousand meters. How was it Abu Othman, the son of an Iraqi police officer and a deserter from Saddam Hussein's army, achieved such skill in such a dangerous environment and lived to tell about it?

Abu Othman's first step in becoming a guerrilla sniper came with the American invasion of Iraq. After the collapse of Saddam Hussein's regime, Abu Othman returned to Fallujah with his wife and four children and found themselves living under the occupation of U.S. forces. One day, American forces fired on a crowd of angry demonstrators in Fallujah and killed thirteen people.[3] This killing of Iraqis by American soldiers was the end of Abu Othman The Calligrapher and the beginning of Abu Othman The Sniper. Abu Othman, enraged by this atrocity, felt a sense of nationalism and religious fervor grow in him. He decided to do something about the American occupation.

With no one to teach him, Abu Othman set off on a self-designed sniper training program to become the best marksman and sniper he could be. He had some appreciation for shooting since he hunted birds for pleasure and he thought he was disciplined enough to be a sniper because the art of calligraphy demanded attention to detail and patience. To start, Abu Othman read manuals on the subject of sniping as well as material on mathematics and physics to learn the basics of ballistics and the capabilities of his weapon. All he needed to know about sniping was readily found on the internet to include personal accounts of soldiers in combat and their assessment of various rifles.

Besides reading these materials, Abu Othman showed some real ingenuity and studied films like *JFK*, *The Deer Hunter* and *Enemy at the Gates* to understand the tactics and art of sniping. He even used PlayStation shooting games as a means to better understand his new profession and 'sharpen his senses'. With these preparations under his belt, Abu Othman shot at homemade wooden targets on an improvised des-

3 Jaber, *The Chilling Toll Of Allah's Sniper.*

ert range with a borrowed rifle until he could hit targets at one thousand meters.

Now, his training complete and his skills up to the task, Abu Othman contacted an insurgent group operating in Fallujah and offered them his services as a sniper. His commitment was soon tested when the insurgents asked him to kill an American officer negotiating a cease-fire with Fallujan officials. To accomplish this mission, Abu Othman climbed to the top of a mosque minaret with a borrowed sniper rifle. From this vantage point, Abu Othman shot and killed the American officer who was standing among a group of U.S. soldiers. As a token of their appreciation for his successful attack, the insurgents gave Abu Othman a gift – his own Russian-made SVD sniper rifle.

With this first experience under his belt, Abu Othman was called on again to shoot an American sniper who had a group of insurgents pinned down somewhere in the dirty, sprawling streets of Fallujah. He was led to a roof overlooking the American sniper's position. Abu Othman then made a single shot, hitting the American sniper in the head, killing him instantly. Abu Othman recovered the fallen sniper's weapon and added it to his inventory. Later that week, Abu Othman killed two additional American snipers, quickly building up his reputation among his fellow insurgents.

The Guerrilla Sniper 'Virus' Spreads

Because of his proven success, Abu Othman was asked to train other guerrilla snipers in Fallujah. He soon developed a training curriculum for his students entitled *Increase God's Mercy By Sniping Americans* and produced an instructional CD-ROM displaying all the techniques he learned during his self-taught training regimen. Now, with his new group of thirty-five sniper students, Abu Othman could spread his skills to new recruits. Abu Othman and his crew were in big demand and they traveled across increasingly war-torn Iraq, conducting sniper attacks in the infamous Sunni Triangle - in Fallujah, Ramadi, and Baghdad.

During one mission, Abu Othman managed to secure $6,000 from an angry Iraqi citizen who paid him this sum to kill an American soldier who damaged local property and showed disrespect to the Iraqi community by urinating in public.[4] Abu Othman ended up shooting this American as he stood on top of a Bradley Fighting Vehicle. This much-needed money was invested back into the movement, used to buy new weapons and more ammunition for Abu Othman and his group of snipers. After these initial trials by fire, Abu Othman became a sniper for hire who plied his trade to whatever insurgent group needed someone killed. Once he got a mission, Abu Othman drove to his new assignment with a bag holding the tools of his trade: water, an inflatable mattress, a prayer mat, tapes of Koranic verses, maintenance tools for his rifle, and a few hand grenades.

When American forces pounded Fallujah in November 2004, retaking the city after weeks of bloody, close-in fighting, Abu Othman was out of town with his family. Even though Abu Othman did not take part in the fighting, members of his sniper group did, resulting in the death of nine of them. As of February 2005, Abu Othman was unable to conduct any more sniping attacks because his equipment was still trapped in Fallujah and he ran the risk of getting captured trying to recover it. So, Abu Othman waited to receive an Italian sniper rifle, which an insurgent cell was getting

4 Jaber, *The Chilling Toll Of Allah's Sniper.*

Abu Othman fired from a mosque minaret like the one pictured here. This was the perfect shooting platform to target unsuspecting American soldiers below.

Photo by DoD

him. As soon as he got this rifle, he would begin killing Americans again.

Analysis of Abu Othman as an Urban Guerrilla Sniper

The account of Abu Othman, written by the well known Journalist Hala Jaber, allows us inside the head of an urban guerrilla sniper, and is thus important for understanding his tactics, techniques, and procedures. We get to see how Abu Othman actually became a sniper, what his motivation was, how he trained, and how he grew in his profession. The reader also gets some insight to Abu Othman's successful methodology. While Abu Othman was apparently successful, he did make mistakes during the course of his operations, which may lead to his eventual death or capture.

The most interesting aspect of Abu Othman was his ability to train himself into an accomplished sniper. This shows a guerrilla with the right motivation can transform themselves into a credible threat using unconventional means. No one taught Abu Othman how to shoot – he made himself learn how to shoot. Abu Othman did not attend any expensive shooting schools, he did not pay an experienced sniper to instruct him in the art, and he never received any military or law-enforcement training to prepare him for the role of urban guerrilla sniper. Who would have thought playing video games and watching war movies would produce someone skilled enough to kill a platoon's worth of men?

Abu Othman shows the urban guerrilla can train themselves, despite the presence of security forces who seek to stop such training. This is because all the tools for learning urban guerrilla sniping are out there: the internet, movies, books and manuals, and self-made ranges. One just has to apply themselves to learn the trade. After Abu Othman became experienced and skilled in his craft, the insurgent organization he worked with was smart enough to make him an instructor of future guerrilla snipers. This type of knowledge transfer is exactly what the successful guerrilla organization must facilitate and what security forces must prevent at all costs. If someone like Abu Othman does develop into an experienced guerrilla sniper, there is nothing to stop him from producing his own manuals and instructional CDs. Anyone can type up a sniper manual on a home computer and burn as many copies of it as they want onto CDs - and security forces cannot stop them. Now, in modern times, with the ability to make and distribute cheap and untraceable media, a single urban guerrilla sniper can become a source of learning, spreading like a virus.

The Virgin Shooter

Abu Othman was difficult for security forces to defeat because they did not know who he was. He was not an Olympic shooter or a former military marksman. There were no official records anywhere indicating Abu Othman possessed the skills he had. From a security perspective, this is the exact kind of sniper the guerrilla organization looks for - a faceless, nameless nobody who security forces are completely oblivious to. It was equally advantageous to the Iraqi guerrilla organizations to recruit other novice shooters with clean records so Abu Othman could train them in the same anonymous manner. The more anonymous shooters there were out there, the more difficult it was for security forces to track them down through good police work.

Remaining anonymous would become more and more difficult for Abu Othman

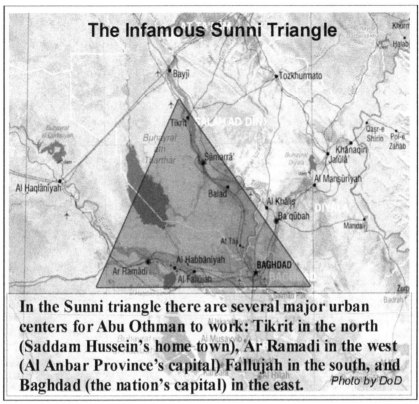

In the Sunni triangle there are several major urban centers for Abu Othman to work: Tikrit in the north (Saddam Hussein's home town), Ar Ramadi in the west (Al Anbar Province's capital) Fallujah in the south, and Baghdad (the nation's capital) in the east. *Photo by DoD*

the more successful he became. Abu Othman's skills already brought him notoriety among his fellow insurgents and you are reading about him now. Abu Othman no longer flew under the radar like some other less glamorous insurgent who did nothing so risky, like collecting information on the government. Being a successful sniper is a high-profile job and brings a lot of admiration from fellow insurgents, while also bringing potentially life-ending interest from enemy security forces. The fact that Abu Othman was popular enough to warrant an interview by someone as well known as Hala Jaber shows how vulnerable he became to discovery by government informants. This process is an inescapable spiral: the more people Abu Othman killed, the more well known he became, and thus the more vulnerable he became to exposure.

The Minaret Shot

We learn a lot by studying Abu Othman's first mission, when he shoots the American officer negotiating with the Fallujah officials. During this operation, Abu Othman was just one piece of a larger effort to conduct the attack. The insurgents already had the officer under surveillance and were planning his demise. Obviously, the insurgents had dedicated clandestine surveillance operators to determine the target's schedule and already picked out a place to shoot from - the minaret. All they needed was a skilled shooter.

Even though the minaret dominated the urban landscape, it was also the most obvious one. As soon as Abu Othman made the shot, he and the surveillance operative who identified the American officer to Abu Othman, had to run down the stairs of the minaret to escape. As they made their mad dash to safety, American forces opened fire on the minaret, instantly recognizing where the shot came from. If Abu Othman shot from obvious positions like that too many times, he was liable to wind up with a severely shortened career. Shooting from the mosque provoked American forces into a violent response that damaged the mosque in their counterattack. The damage to the mosque served to further incense the local populace who did not care the Americans were defending themselves. From this perspective, shooting from the mosque was a good move because it placed Americans forces in a lose-lose situation.

The Roof Shot

Abu Othman's second attack against the American sniper on the roof is also revealing. With the minaret shot, Abu Othman was just the shooter; one piece of a larger organization. It is important to note Abu Othman did not collect his own intelligence and was not a lone-wolf sniper. He was fed his targets from insurgent groups who had intelligence collection cells specializing in developing targets for insurgent shooters like Abu Othman. While stalking the American sniper, Abu Othman showed some sniper tradecraft usually reserved for more experienced snipers. In order to distract the enemy sniper, Abu Othman employed an assistant who held up a dummy silhouette with a scarf wrapped around its 'head'. All while the America sniper was pinning down another insurgent group with well-aimed fire. Abu Othman held all the cards by using deception and flanking the sniper from a better position, while his enemy was focused on another threat. Overall, this was a competent job of sniping for a novice engaged against the best army on earth.

The Bradley Shot

By the time Abu Othman targeted the soldier standing on the Bradley Fighting Vehicle, he was an experienced shooter. Again, Abu Othman was given this target by a surveillance cell who knew the target's pattern, where they would be going, and when they would be going there. Just before the target approached Abu Othman's position, he got a call on his cell phone warning him of his approaching prey. This reveals they had unseen surveillance assets at the place of attack who could watch the target and warn the shooter, all while remaining undetected by American forces.

On the other hand, this sniper attack reveals some areas that could be exploited by security forces. If the guerrillas are dependent on cell phones to warn the shooter, these calls are susceptible to interception by security forces. In the future, a similar phone call might warn local security forces of an imminent attack. Also, as Abu Othman was waiting for the call from his rooftop position he said he listened to Koranic verses to relax him and clear his mind. This may be an indication Abu Othman is becoming confident in his work - maybe too confident. Overconfidence can lead to sloppiness, which will get the urban guerrilla killed.

One should keep in mind using a rooftop position can be a life ending decision as it exposes the sniper to the security forces' aerial assets like airplanes, helicopters, unmanned drones, and satellites that can look specifically for a sniper on a roof. Abu Othman also mentioned he put padding on his elbows and knees to protect them while

Abu Othman is effective as long as he remains faceless, anonymous.

Photo by DoD

crawling on the hard surface of the roof. This is a smart move that made Abu Othman's movement into position less painful, so he could focus on making his shot and not worry about the pain of his joints.

However, this is a good tidbit for security forces when looking for incriminating evidence against him. If security forces find elbow or knee pads when searching a suspected insurgent residence or safehouse, they will probably look a little harder after making this discovery. Additionally, scraped knees and elbows may be an indication of someone conducting sniper attacks. In Vietnam, American forces looked at the shoulders of suspected Vietnamese guerillas to see if they were carrying rucksacks. In Chechnya, Russian forces checked suspected Chechen guerrillas for bruised shoulders from firing rifles. Today, security forces can check Iraqis' elbows and knees.

Have Sniper Rifle, Will Travel

The fact Abu Othman worked in several different large cities had its advantages and disadvantages. This travel was an advantage from a security perspective in that Abu Othman divided his operations against different security units located tens of miles away from each other. This made it difficult for the separate units to develop a single, comprehensive profile of him. Security forces probably thought they had several different snipers on their hand instead of just one. The more time and distance Abu Othman placed between his separate attacks, the less of a signature he created and the harder it was for local informers to get a read on him. The fact Abu Othman had a three-month lull after narrowly escaping the meat-grinder of Fallujah was advantageous to him because it lowered his profile. This absence also might have led security forces to think they killed Abu Othman just like his nine sniper students.

If Abu Othman actually traveled with a bag with his rifle in it and all of his sniping tools, then he was sloppy from a counter-forensics perspective. What if he got pulled over at a checkpoint? What if his car was broken into? What if his car got stolen?

What if he got in a car accident? Also, after studying Abu Othman's equipment, security forces could now look at inflatable mattresses as being associated with comfort for a long-term sniper position.

An End to the Killing?

It is important to note Abu Othman was a religiously motivated and devout Muslim. Perhaps one way to get Abu Othman to lay down his arms was to contact his Imam (religious leader). If his Imam knew about his activities, the Imam could be pressured to give up information about Abu Othman such as where he lived and what his name was. Furthermore, Abu Othman stated he felt comfortable killing Iraqi soldiers because religious leaders issued fatwas (religious edicts carrying the force of religious law) saying these Iraqis were collaborators and thus justly targeted. If Abu Othman's religious motivations could be influenced through his Imam, then so might his guerrilla activities. Perhaps a fatwa reversing the previous decision would put an end to Abu Othman's killing.

On the other hand, Abu Othman made it clear he would fight the American occupation forces until they left his country. While it might be possible to get Abu Othman to stop killing his fellow countrymen, he was unlikely to stop killing American soldiers. In this case, Abu Othman's killing might only end when U.S. forces withdraw from Iraq or when the bullet from an American sniper finds its own mark.

(Author's note: This article by Hala Jaber has been criticized by some as being fraudulent, a piece of insurgent propaganda. Part of their reasoning is they doubt a sniper could become self-taught, in part, from video games and movies. Skeptics believe the article is really a tall tale, yet offering very real ways to train potential homegrown snipers so they can better hunt U.S. forces. In essence, they argue, this story was put out by the insurgents as a training tool, which the leading media services distributed to a worldwide audience as a news article. If true, this was a clever, unconventional manner to inspire, educate, and train other potential guerrilla snipers. The reader should review this article for themselves and form their own opinions.)

Chapter 17

What has been taken in blood cannot be regained except by blood.
-A note left behind for security forces in
Iraq after every Juba shooting.

Deadly Sniper or Insurgent Propaganda?

'Juba' is the name of an alleged insurgent sniper who worked the Baghdad area in Iraq, conducting a string of successful sniper attacks against American forces from the start of the American invasion until the writing of this book. Supposedly, after each of Juba's attacks, security forces found a single bullet casing left behind with a note in Arabic stating, "What has been taken in blood cannot be regained except by blood. Baghdad Sniper."[1] Despite these accounts, some people claim Juba never existed and was really just a fictitious character created by Iraqi insurgents who turned the myth of Juba into an insurgent hero.

Regardless if Juba was fact or fiction, in November 2005, the Islamic Army in Iraq released a fifteen-minute compilation video of Juba's alleged sniper attacks, which was available on several web sites. While this propaganda video was meant to instill fear in American forces and raise the morale of the insurgents, it was also revealing of the sniper's tactics. This video shows, from the shooter's perspective, twenty-three separate attacks. The viewer can see Juba's target for a short time before the shot, during the shot, and usually for a few seconds afterwards. There is only 30-45 seconds of film for each attack so our understanding of Juba comes from what one can glean from these various clips.

Juba's Shooting Platform

It appears Juba shot from inside a vehicle, not from a building. First, it is statisti-

1 Carroll, *Elusive Sniper Saps US Morale in Baghdad.*

cally unlikely Juba could gain entrance to an appropriate building in every one of the twenty-three attacks. Plus, there were no high-angle shots taken from upper level buildings and civilian pedestrians and cars were visible passing between the camera-man and the target in every single attack. One can only conclude the attacks were conducted at street level. And shooting from a vehicle would produce the camera angle seen in every attack and would also explain how Juba found a suitable - indeed a per-fect - sniping position every time. With a vehicle, Juba could park his mobile hide site in any place providing a good vantage point. A vehicle would also fit into the city and would be an effective means of urban camouflage.

We can guess Juba not only shot from a vehicle, but most likely from a van. The camera views and angles could not have come from the confinement of a trunk of a car because several times we see the camera panning the surrounding area after the attack. Also, a van fit in all over Iraq and vans of every model, shape, and color filled Iraqi streets by the thousands. It was equally common for Iraqis to cover the windows of their vans with stickers, window tinting, sun blinds, and curtains to keep out the oppressive sun and prying eyes. This urban camouflage would provide excellent con-cealment for a sniper sitting in the back of van.

Why did Juba Target Heavily Armed Checkpoints?

In most of the video clips, Juba attacked an alert checkpoint consisting of half a dozen armed soldiers. These were definitely not considered 'soft' targets as Juba was not picking off lone, careless soldiers. Quite the contrary, Juba targeted enemy forces when they were alert and prepared. Why? There may be several reasons for this. First, most checkpoints were set in the same place day after day and never moved. For in-stance, a permanent checkpoint may be placed at a busy intersection allowing a sniper to take days, weeks, or months to plan the perfect attack. This regularity created a distinct pattern, allowing Juba to analyze his targets, study the surrounding terrain, and develop a tailored-made plan to fit a specific checkpoint at a specific location.

Also, Juba's mobile sniper platform allowed him to get into the perfect position, no matter where the checkpoint was located. The checkpoint did not have to be located next to a building, it only had to be located in an area where civilian vehicles had ac-cess. Since all of the checkpoints in the film were located on or next to roads, Juba's sniper van had ready access to them. Because American and Iraqi forces had hundreds of checkpoints set up all over the country, Juba had many targets to choose from. He could afford to choose a target with the right terrain, the right roads, and the right in-tersections for a quick getaway. If a particular checkpoint was in a bad location, Juba had other, better choices to select.

One Sniper or More?

While the insurgents would like their enemies to think they developed an unstop-pable super-sniper, this was more propaganda than reality. The strongest evidence supporting there was no single super-sniper was an insurgent sniper in Fallujah who was killed after conducting a string of similar attacks against American forces. This Fallujah sniper also filmed his attacks and used similar positioning when making his shots. However, while this sniper died in action and was celebrated as a martyr to the

Juba Shoots from a Van like This One

resistance, the attacks continued. In fact, there were several different insurgent sniper films on the market, from different groups working in different areas, all filming their attacks and using similar methods.

While there were most likely several snipers conducting these attacks in the Juba film, they may have all received training from the same source. One reason to believe this is because of the common threads in the filmed attacks. In fact, each and every attack had the exact same Modus Operandi. It was unlikely several different, unconnected snipers developed this level of disciplined methodology independently.

Experts studying Juba theorized these insurgent snipers received detailed instruction from Chechen snipers blooded and experienced in Grozny. While Chechen snipers have fought in Iraq, this theory is unlikely as there are no recorded instances of Chechen snipers operating from civilian vehicles against the invading Russians. Only the IRA and the DC snipers have been known to fire from the confines of a vehicle. It is quite possible insurgent snipers researching the art of sniping on the internet discovered this urban sniping methodology from open media sources and then began employing these tactics on their own initiative. Just as the insurgents took martyr operations, IED and car bomb attacks to new heights, they may have improved on the art of sniping in the same manner.

Did Juba Use a Gun Mounted Camera?

A point of much debate is exactly how the insurgents filmed their attacks. On initial observation, it appears the sniper used a gun mounted camera. With the majority of the shots, the camera visibly shuddered when the sniper fired a shot and in one attack, the camera was actually filmed through the sniper's rifle scope. However, a gun mounted camera could not be used in all of the attacks for several reasons. To start, when one sees the footage, we never even get a glimpse of the gun barrel or the aperture the sniper must be firing through. Several times the camera pans the local area after the shot, which would not be possible if the camera was on the gun. Furthermore, on several occasions, it appeared the camera was not attached to the gun since the gun fired and the camera remained stable and unaffected. On top of this, at other times the camera was not aligned to the target - the sniper shoots, but the camera does not show a good picture of the shot.

If the camera was separate from the weapon, then why did the camera visibly shudder most of the time? One explanation is the cameraman was collocated with the sniper, with both the cameraman and sniper concealed in the back of a van. If the sniper concealed their muzzle blast by firing within the van, the inside of the van absorbed the muzzle blast. If the cameraman was close enough to the muzzle of the weapon, this contained muzzle blast would be enough to affect the camera's stability for a split second. If the physics of this theory is true, then it may look like the camera is gun mounted when the camera and gun are really just in close proximity to each other.

Did Juba Use a Suppressor?

Most of the time, Juba did something to conceal the muzzle flash and blast of his rifle. In many of the attacks, Juba shoots someone who is looking directly at the sniper's position. Even after the sniper fired, the victims never saw the muzzle flash and blast. In fact, the victims often looked in a direction *different* from where the shot came from. One would think the sniper used a suppressor, which made the muzzle flash and blast almost impossible to see. On top of this, many times, people in the area of the shootings did not hear the gunshot. Some times people looked around after the gunshot while others kept on walking as if nothing happened. Overall, this presents a strong case the sniper used a suppressor for some of the attacks.

On the other hand, one of the attacks was filmed through the sniper's rifle scope and the muzzle flash from the weapon was clearly visible, taking up the entire screen for a split second. And other attacks, even though the Islamic Army in Iraq superimposed its propaganda music over the sound of the video, one still heard the rifle's gunshot. If the sniper used a suppressor in these cases, there would be no muzzle flash like the one seen through the scope and the gunshot would not be so loud as to be heard over the music. So, how was it the sniper fired an unsuppressed weapon some of the time, the sniper's victims and bystanders never saw the muzzle flash and blast despite looking at the sniper's position, and sometimes the surrounding people fail to hear the gunshot at all?

One explanation is the sniper and cameraman used a mobile shooting range. Think of how commercial in-door shooting ranges dampen the sound of their customers' gunshots by using specially designed, foam-lined walls to absorb the sound. What if this sniper team did the same thing, except they lined the inside of a van with sound absorbing material, except for a small hole to shoot from and a port to film from? This type of set-up would explain a lot. People could not see the muzzle flash and blast of the weapon because the sniper kept the barrel of the gun inside the van and only the bullet traveled outside the small firing hole. Because the van was lined with sound absorbing material, like mattresses, people did not hear or recognize the gunshot and thus had no idea where the shot came from. Because the cameraman and sniper were sitting next to each other in the back of a padded van, the muzzle blast was constricted to an enclosed place, which rocked the camera for a split second after each shot.

Juba's Tabuk Sniper Rifle

This militiaman holds high a Tabuk sniper rifle, a semi-automatic weapon firing a 7.62 mm x 39 mm round. The Tabuk is a modified Iraqi copy of an original Yugoslavian design.

In another film version of one of the shootings, the cameraman or sniper is heard saying over and over again in Arabic, '*Allahu Akbar*' or 'God is great'. The speech is very clear and distinct with no background noise. There are no honking car horns, there are no people talking or yelling, despite being in the middle of a very busy city. This could because the cameraman was in the back of a padded van where everything inside this self-contained environment was heard clearly, like gunshots and their own voices, while everything outside was silenced.

In this situation, one should remember the experiences of John Muhammad and Lee Malvo in their killings. These two fired from the trunk of a car without a suppressor, in much closer proximity than the Juba sniper, and they were never detected during their shootings. It may be enough Juba fired from within the enclosed space of a vehicle and the sound of the gunshot then became distorted as it bounced off and broke up in the surrounding urban terrain, preventing anyone from locating them.

Juba's Technical Sniping Ability

The video revealed that Juba had an excellent grasp of guerrilla sniping tactics, but was not a consistent shooter or did not understand the limitations of his weapon and the capabilities of his enemies. For example, it was common knowledge all American soldiers (and Iraqi security forces for that matter) wore ceramic body armor plates protecting their chests and backs. All one had to do was look at a soldier and they could see they were wearing body armor. The capabilities of this ceramic body armor are wildly known, are posted on the internet, and considered public knowledge. American-issued ceramic body armor, like all Level IV armor, was designed to stop the 7.62 mm rifle round, the round used in weapons like the AK-47 assault rifle and Dragunov SVD sniper rifle.

Inexplicably, in at least eight of the attacks, Juba shot the soldiers in their body armor. In some of these attacks Juba actually saw the soldiers get up and run away or simply bend over like they had the wind knocked out of them. Most likely, all the soldiers targeted in these eight attacks lived, with nothing more than bruising and maybe broken ribs. These incidents beg the question, why would Juba continue to shoot soldiers in the chest when he saw these shots had no effect? Perhaps he was not confident in his shooting ability and was unable to hit a harder target like a head. Or, he might have preferred to take the high-percentage body shot rather than miss a low-percentage head shot.

But, this analysis does not hold up because in six of the attacks, Juba made difficult head shots. It appeared when shooting soldiers in vehicles, Juba took the head shot because that is all he had. When facing dismounted soldiers, he preferred to shoot them in the chest, even though on more than one occasion he had easy head shots available.

In two of the attacks, it appeared Juba shot his victims in the groin/pelvis region. Both of these soldiers were on foot and it appeared Juba intentionally avoided shooting them in their body armor. In these cases, Juba learned shooting his victims in the body armor was a failed strategy, so he shot where there was no armor. Shooting a person in the groin or pelvic region was still a life threatening shot because the bullet could hit the femoral arteries and cause fatal wounds to the intestines and lower spine. One report stated Juba intentionally aimed at gaps in the soldiers' body armor, at the lower spine, in the ribs, or above the chest in order to avoid the body armor.[2]

Juba may not have been an extremely accurate sniper due to his limited experience or his inability to get regular training and practice. In one attack, Juba fired at a group of soldiers and hit one in the lower arm. A trained sniper might wonder how a person could shoot at a range of 150 meters and miss. More importantly, how was it Juba could at times make difficult head shots but then blow relatively easy ones? Juba may simply have been an inconsistent shot who was hot sometimes and cold other times. He may have used open sights as opposed to a scope (although one attack was filmed through a rifle scope) and making a tough shot was more luck than skill, hence the pattern of taking easy chest shots. What is most plausible is the video is a compilation of several different snipers, all with different shooting abilities, different preferences, and different understandings of their enemy.

Juba's Weapon

Juba probably used a Soviet SVD sniper rifle, which was relatively common in Iraq and the rest of the Middle East. When listening to the recoil of the gunshot in the video, it sounds like a weapon with some sort of buffer/recoil spring system, like the semi-automatic SVD, as compared to a bolt action weapon which sounds differently.

2 Carroll, *Elusive Sniper Saps US Morale in Baghdad.*

Photo by DoD

Juba intentionally targeted alert security checkpoints.

The weapon used in the video was of 7.62 mm size or smaller based on its inability to penetrate body armor designed to stop 7.62 mm rounds. Other analysts have actually seen a quick snapshot of Juba's weapon in the film and determined it was a Tabuk rifle, which is a modified Iraqi version of a Yugoslavian variant of the AK-47. The Tabuk rifle is common in Iraq and the picture at the beginning of this chapter is one of an insurgent sniper aiming such a weapon.

Juba's Game Plan

Juba was not an opportunist who took chance shots and rolled the dice. He was a professional sniper who developed a specific, detailed methodology for conducting his attacks. Juba's guerrilla organization most likely had dedicated undercover intelligence agents who picked out targets for him. Juba then conducted a reconnaissance of the selected target before his attack, wearing civilian clothing, looking like everyone else. He might have first driven or walked by his targets to observe them. On these reconnaissance missions he not only collected information on his target, but he determined where he would shoot from.

Juba intentionally picked targets in heavily populated areas with high concentrations of cars, people, and buildings. He used this urban clutter to hide in plain sight. He felt more secure the more people there were around him and the closer he was to his target. He was so obvious he easily passed the casual scrutiny of the security forces and civilian bystanders. He was not afraid to attack targets that were heavily armed, alert, or large in number. In fact, Juba flaunted his ability to take his shots undetected, right under the noses of his enemies, even with them looking directly at him and pointing their guns at him.

Once Juba found the right place to take the shot, he parked his vehicle there. He ensured other vehicles were around him so he blended in. He waited for his vehicle to became part of the urban landscape so it did not look unusual. This meant Juba may have been parked for several hours in order to melt into the background. He stayed inside the vehicle if this looked normal and he may have left it to conduct further reconnaissance and then came back to it to take the shot. Most likely, the rear of the

319

vehicle faced the target so it had a smaller signature. The vehicle could not face the target because there was no concealment in the front of a van with a large windshield. The vehicle was probably not broadside to the target either as there was less room to maneuver a sniper rifle for a shot, plus the vehicle was more noticeable that way. With the rear of the vehicle facing the target, Juba could use the full length of the vehicle to maneuver his weapon and make the shot. After Juba made the shot, he drove away from his target and made his escape. When he could, Juba parked his vehicle at "T" intersections where he could take a shot on an exposed target, and then drive down a side street and quickly disappear.

Juba did not get overly excited after making his shot and might have stayed in the parked vehicle until it was safe to leave the area. He hid his gun in the vehicle, made preparations to leave the area, and may have actually walked away from the vehicle, mixing in with local crowds to separate himself from the shooting. He might go back to pick up the vehicle later on in the day or the driver took off without him and picked him up at a nearby location away from the immediate scene of the shooting.

Juba's methodology showed a striking similarity to John Muhammad and Lee Malvo's (The DC Snipers). They both intentionally flouted the security of their enemies and took great pride in their ability to operate under their very noses. They both wanted to cause terror, to strike fear in their enemies, and to show they could operate with impunity and could not be stopped. Juba, essentially, took the D.C. snipers' methodology and modified it to fit the environment in Iraq.

The Integration of Sniping and Propaganda

The video compilation of Juba's sniper attacks by the Islamic Army in Iraq was innovative in that it illustrated an integration of sniper attacks with media as part of an organized, pre-planned propaganda campaign. Juba's guerrilla organization understood sniping was more important than just a tool for military attrition. The organization saw the sniper as a means for showing the weakness and vulnerability of their enemy as well as raising the morale of the guerrilla organization. It did not matter what the reality of the attacks were and if all the soldiers who got shot in the chest armor walked away. What did matter is it looked like these soldiers were killed, thus giving the guerrillas and their supporters the perception their cause was on the winning side. In this manner, the insurgents took the very tactical act of shooting an enemy soldier and turned it into a strategic operation.

Juba's Mistakes

Juba's tactical methodology must be given credit as a successful standard for conducting urban guerrilla sniping. We must remember Juba conducted attacks in a country controlled by the Iraqi and American militaries. Juba was not shooting from a trench or a prepared sniper hide and he did not have a quick reaction force to rescue him if he got in trouble. Juba traveled in areas controlled by the government and he had to conduct each and every attack anonymously. While government security forces could afford to hit or miss in their efforts to get Juba, he could not slip up even once.

Juba made several mistakes conducting his operations. The biggest error was publishing the film of his operations on the internet - the price paid for using his at-

Baghdad, Iraq An American helicopter flies over a Baghdad neighborhood. Note the complexities of the urban terrain Juba manipulates for his sniper operations.

Photo by DoD

tacks for propaganda. The film allowed security forces to analyze his tactics in order to defeat them. It was obvious Juba was shooting from a vehicle and most likely a van (although other insurgent snipers had been caught firing from inside passenger sedans). It was equally obvious Juba had someone with him filming the attacks. This camera was a red flag and would become incriminating evidence when security forces searched his vehicle at a checkpoint.

Based on the perspective the attacks were filmed from, security forces could easily backtrack from the place of the attacks to find out where Juba actually fired from. This alone would reveal from what distance Juba fired from and if in fact he was in a vehicle or in a building. In several of the attacks there were enough structural and positional clues in the film that backtracking from the victim would lead to the exact location of the shooter. This analysis of the film would show what kind of positions Juba liked to habitually use. Juba might not even know he was setting a pattern, but he was. Just as the security forces he attacked set their patterns, Juba in turn grew comfortable using a certain process to stalk and target his prey.

As mentioned in the Abu Othman chapter, a guerrilla sniper has a difficult time balancing anonymity and spreading the word of their feats. They cannot have it both ways. The more the insurgents trumped Juba's exploits, the more security forces learned about him and his methodology. Even if security forces failed to get Juba himself, they might get to someone in Juba's organization who could incriminate him. Importantly, the more security forces knew about Juba, the more they knew about his parent organization. The guerrilla organization had to balance how much they were willing to exploit the Juba myth, because they might expose the organization itself.

Juba's Methodology Exposed

On June 2, 2005, Private First Class Stephen Tschiderer was on patrol in Western Baghdad. While outside his Humvee, Tschiderer was shot in the chest with a single bullet, knocking him to the ground. Since the bullet hit him in his ceramic body armor, Tschiderer was not seriously injured by the attack. After laying flat on the ground for a second, Tschiderer got up and ran back behind his Humvee for protection. Having just taken a bullet directly to the chest, Tschiderer knew which direction the shot came from, enabling him to narrow down the source of the shot to a silver van parked across from an intersection, 75 meters away. Tschiderer and his patrol then opened fire on the van, forcing the two men in the vehicle to take off on foot. During the shooting, the American patrol managed to wound the sniper in the foot. Because the sniper was bleeding from his foot, it was easy to follow and capture him. The Americans also captured the other insurgent and recovered a Soviet SVD sniper rifle and a camera with a recording of the preceding attack still on it. Upon close inspection, the silver van was found to be lined with mattresses in order to muffle the sound of the sniper's gunshot. Also, a small hole was discovered in the van, from which the sniper fired from.[3]

This certainly sounds like the same procedures Juba used and would explain the camera angle taken during the attacks. The padded van would also explain why so many times in the video a shot was taken, but no one seemed to know where the shot came from. The small hole in the van would explain why people in the videos looked directly at the sniper's position, but could not see the sniper himself. The two captured men also supported the theory that one man was the driver/cameraman and the second person was the sniper. The fact that additional, similar sniping attacks occurred after the capture of this sniper/cameraman team, proved there was no single Juba, but several well-trained sniper teams using an identical methodology.

While Juba and his fellow snipers displayed some excellent urban snipercraft, they revealed enough of their methodology that a thoughtful person could see a pattern and take countermeasures. Specifically, security forces could set up a sting operation, using a patrol or a vehicle with a lifelike dummy as bait. They could then place their own undercover counter-sniper teams in the surrounding urban terrain, blending in just like Juba. Once Juba took his shot, he could be detected and put in the crosshairs while he focused on the obvious target. In a following chapter on counter-sniper tactics, the reader will see exactly how one Marine sniper team pulled off such a feat. A disciplined, talented shooter like Juba required an equally skilled response, which begins here, with studying your enemy.

---

3 Foster, *256th Brigade Soldier Survives Sniper Attack.*

Sniper Van Captured by U.S. Army

Sniper Vehicle Patterned After
Washington D.C. Snipers

Here is an inside view of the back of
the van that the snipers fired from.

Photos by DoD

Possible Firing Port or Camerman Viewport

This is a summary of Juba's 23 attacks viewed on the composite film released by the Islamic Army in Iraq - distances are educated guesses.

Target Description	Shot Placement.	Distance
1- Humvee checkpoint.	Shot in back armor.	100 meters.
2- Dismounted Checkpoint.	Shot in chest armor.	125 meters.
3- Humvee checkpoint.	Shot in the head.	125 meters.
4- Humvee checkpoint.	Unknown.	100 meters.
5- Humvee checkpoint.	Shot in chest armor.	100 meters.
6- Humvee checkpoint.	Shot in the arm.	125 meters.
7- Dismounted soldier.	Unknown (side of chest?).	125 meters.
8- Dismounted checkpoint.	Shot in chest armor.	75 meters.
9- Bradley checkpoint.	Shot in the head.	200 meters.
10- Humvee checkpoint.	Shot in the head (most likely).	200 meters.
11- Dismounted checkpoint.	Shot in chest armor.	125 meters.
12- Bradley checkpoint.	Shot in the head.	200 meters.
13- Humvee checkpoint.	Shot in leg/pelvis.	125 meters.
14- Humvee checkpoint.	Shot in chest armor.	125 meters.
15- Bradley checkpoint.	Unknown (probably in chest).	200 meters.
16- Bradley checkpoint.	Shot in the head.	200 meters.
17- Soldiers on roof.	Unknown.	200 meters.
18- Humvee checkpoint.	Shot in chest armor.	200 meters.
19- Humvee checkpoint.	Shot in the pelvis.	125 meters.
20- Bradley checkpoint.	Shot in the head.	200 meters.
21- Humvee checkpoint.	Shot in the head (most likely).	150 meters.
22- Bradley checkpoint.	Shot in chest armor.	125 meters.
23- Humvee checkpoint.	Shot in the chest armor.	75 meters.

Juba Sniper Attack # 1

The target is an American temporary checkpoint on a road consisting of several Humvees and dismounted soldiers. It is daylight and the insurgent cameraman is on the same elevation as the American soldiers. The sniper's target is a soldier standing adjacent to a Humvee with their back turned to the sniper. The soldier turns towards and looks directly at the sniper's position, does not see anything suspicious, and then turns away from the sniper's position. As soon as the soldier turns away, he is shot in the back. The camera jumps when the shot is fired. The soldier is then seen on his knees, but alive (he was probably shot in his ceramic body armor). Adjacent soldiers then come to the wounded soldier's assistance and other soldiers start looking for where the shot came from, but none of them look towards the sniper's position – they do not know where the shot came from. One of the Humvees is seen driving away from the sniper's position, perhaps to take the wounded soldier to get medical treatment. Judging from the camera angle, the sniper is relatively close to the soldiers' position and shot at an angle almost parallel to the road the soldiers' Humvees were parked on. During the video, several Iraqi civilians are seen walking in front of the cameraman and they are equally oblivious to the sniper's position. The camera cuts.

Juba Sniper Attack # 2

Two American soldiers are seen standing at what appears to be a checkpoint on a road, facing in the direction of the sniper. There are rolls of concertina wire visible in the background. Civilian vehicles are observed passing on a road in between the cameraman and the soldiers. The soldier standing on the right is then hit in the chest - judging from the dirt jumping from the shot - and falls to the ground. The camera jumps when the shot is fired. It also looks like the wounded shoulder sits up before being dragged off, so he was probably hit in his body armor and was only wounded. After the shot, a soldier does look in the direction of the sniper. It is daylight and the cameraman appears to be at the same level as the soldiers, for when a vehicle stops in front of the two soldiers, the cameraman's field of view is entirely blocked. The camera cuts.

Juba Sniper Attack # 3

Two American Humvees are parked next to each other and two soldiers with their heads visible from the roof turrets are talking to each other. The closest soldier has his head turned away from the sniper and is talking to the other soldier who is facing the sniper's position. It is daylight and the cameraman is at the same elevation as the soldiers and does not show the ground, just the upper part of the Humvees. The sniper shoots the closest soldier who had his head turned away from the sniper's position. From the film, the viewer cannot tell if the soldier was actually hit or not from the shot, as both soldiers immediately duck into their vehicles. The camera jumps when the shot is fired. The farthest soldier pokes his head up again, but the first soldier does not. The top of a car is observed driving between the cameraman and the soldiers. The camera cuts.

Juba Sniper Attack # 4

An American soldier is seen leaning against the hood of his Humvee, apparently at a checkpoint. It is daylight and the soldier is looking towards the sniper's position. The cameraman is at the same level of the soldiers as pedestrians often walk in between the cameraman and the soldiers. The people do not notice the sniper's position prior to the attack. A soldier walks several feet away from the Humvee and is then shot, falling to the ground. The camera jumps with the shot, but only part of the soldier can be seen when the shot is fired, as if the cameraman failed to follow the soldier as the sniper was tracking him. People are seen walking by after the shot, oblivious to the soldier being shot. Then, other people are seen running and some walking – some people heard the shot and others did not. The camera cuts.

Juba Sniper Attack # 5

Half a dozen dismounted American soldiers are observed congregating in a circle, talking to each other, apparently at a roadside checkpoint. The cameraman is at the same level as the soldiers. Civilian cars are seen driving in front of the cameraman and the soldiers. It is daylight and the camera film quality is hazy. A soldier walks directly towards the sniper's position, next to his Humvee, and is then shot in the chest. The soldier leans over, towards the sniper, as if he had the wind knocked out of him. The soldier most likely took the round straight in the ceramic body armor and is only wounded. The camera cuts.

Juba Sniper Attack # 6

There are several dismounted American soldiers standing near two Humvees - apparently a daylight, roadside checkpoint. The cameraman is at the same level as the soldiers. An Iraqi male on a motorcycle stops and talks to the soldiers (perhaps having his ID card inspected). Another civilian walks up to talk to the soldier. The sniper shoots and apparently hits a soldier in the arm since one of soldier grabs his left arm after the shot. The camera jumps with the shot. The soldiers run out of the camera's view. Several soldiers look towards the sniper's position but do not shoot. The camera cuts. (Note: The sniper is using the unsuspecting Iraqi civilians as bait to distract the soldiers and to make them expose themselves.)

Juba Sniper Attack # 7

An American soldier is seen kneeling, next to a car, looking away from the sniper. It is daylight. The cameraman is level with the soldier and civilians are seen walking in between the cameraman and the soldier. The sniper shoots and the soldier falls backward. The viewer cannot determine where the soldier was shot, or if he was shot. The camera jumps when the shot is fired. The camera cuts.

Juba Sniper Attack # 8

An American soldier is observed standing, facing the sniper's position. It is daylight. The cameraman is level with the soldier as passing cars travel in between the cameraman and the soldier. The camera appears to be shooting film through a telescopic sight as numbers, like those on a sniper's scope, are visible at the bottom of the film. The sniper shoots, apparently hitting the soldier in the chest as the soldier doubles over towards the camera. The camera did not appear to jump during the shot but the muzzle blast from the rifle is seen, blurring the camera for a split second. The camera cuts. This was a close shot, maybe as close as 75 meters.

Juba Sniper Attack # 9

There is an American Bradley Fighting Vehicle (BFV) with its turret and main gun oriented towards the sniper's position. It is daylight and cars are seen driving in between the cameraman and the BFV and behind the BFV. It appears as if the BFV is parked on a median in between two roads. The head of an American soldier is visible, sticking out of an open hatch on the top of the BFV turret. The sniper shoots, apparently hitting the soldier in the head. The camera jumps when the gun is fired. The BFV then drives off. The camera cuts. This was a longer shot, maybe 200 meters.

Juba Sniper Attack # 10

There is an American soldier sitting in the turret of a Humvee, which is parked in front of a military base. It is daylight. The soldier is facing away from the sniper. The cameraman is level with the soldier and Humvee. The sniper shoots and the soldier falls down into the turret. The camera jumps when the shot is fired. The impact from the bullet is seen impacting on the wall behind the soldier, either passing through the soldier, ricocheting off the soldier's helmet, or missing altogether. The camera cuts.

Juba Sniper Attack # 11

There are several dismounted American soldiers manning a temporary checkpoint alongside a busy road with various cars driving by. The cameraman is level with the soldiers and cars drive in between the cameraman and the soldiers. It is daylight. A soldier is walking along the road towards the sniper's position. The sniper fires and hits the soldier who then falls to the pavement. The camera does not jump, but some smoke from the weapon's muzzle blast is seen. Also, the camera was not centered on the soldier when he was shot. The soldier was towards the extreme left of the screen. the camera cuts.

Juba Sniper Attack # 12

There is an American soldier with his head sticking out of the top of the turret of a BFV. It is daylight and the cameraman is level with the BFV and the tops of cars can be seen passing between the cameraman and the BFV. The soldier is not looking toward the sniper, exposing the right side of his head and face to the sniper. The soldier then stands up in the turret, exposing his upper body and looks towards the sniper's position. The sniper shoots, apparently hitting the soldier in the head, as the bullet impact is seen on the turret hatch behind the soldier. The camera jumps when the gun fires. The BFV with the shot soldier then turns their turret towards the sniper's position but continues on past it. Another BFV sitting next to the targeted BFV does not show any indication that it saw the shot or the sniper's position. The camera cuts.

Juba Sniper Attack # 13

There are several dismounted American soldiers standing around two Humvees, apparently manning a temporary checkpoint on a road. It is daylight. The cameraman is level with the Humvees and civilians can be seen walking near the checkpoint. The sniper shoots a soldier walking on the road towards the sniper's position. The camera jumps. The soldier grabs his left leg and his body stiffens. Two Humvees then drive between the cameraman and the checkpoint, very close to the sniper's position, probably within 150 meters, but show no indication they heard or saw the shot. The camera cuts. (Note: The sniper in this clip recognizes the soldier is wearing body armor and intentionally avoids it by aiming for his leg/lower back.)

Juba Sniper Attack # 14

There are two dismounted American soldiers standing along a busy road as if manning a temporary check point. It is daylight and the cameraman is level with the soldiers. Cars can be seen driving in between the cameraman and the soldiers. One soldier is looking directly at the sniper's position and is shot in the chest. The targeted soldier immediately runs away after being hit, back towards several other soldiers and Humvees. The other soldiers show no indication they saw where the shot came from. The camera cuts.

Juba Sniper Attack # 15

There are three American soldiers sitting on the turret of a BFV with the turret and main gun facing towards the sniper's position. It is daylight and the cameraman is at the same level as the BFV. The BFV is adjacent to a road, as if part of a checkpoint. Cars can be seen driving in between the cameraman and the BFV. The camera screen is hazy and may indicate a longer shot – maybe 200 meters away. The sniper takes a shot, hitting the soldier in the middle, causing him to fall backwards on the turret.

The camera jumps when the shot is taken and there is a split second delay before the soldier is actually hit. The camera cuts.

Juba Sniper Attack # 16

There is an American soldier with his torso sticking out of the top turret of a BFV and he is facing the general direction of the sniper. It is daylight and the cameraman is level with the soldier. Cars are observed driving in between the cameraman and the BFV. The soldier begins eating a sandwich and is facing directly at the sniper's position. The sniper shoots the soldier in the head. The camera jumps. The soldier falls down the hatch and the camera cuts. (A truck is seen passing by the cameraman and then turns left, showing the sniper is situated at a "T" intersection.)

Juba Sniper Attack # 17

There are two American soldiers standing on a roof, silhouetted against the skyline and talking to each other. It is daylight and the cameraman appears to be at a level lower than the soldiers, as if he is looking up at them. The camera screen is not clear as the soldiers are further away, probably 200 meters. The sniper shoots the soldier on the left, who is looking at the sniper's position, and then falls over after being hit. The camera jumps when the shot is made. There is a second between when the shot is fired and the soldier is hit, indicating a longer shot. The camera cuts. (Note: On all the shots made from a distance of at least 200 meters or more, there is a second delay between when the shot is fired and when the target is hit, indicating it is taking some time for the bullet to travel the further distance.)

Juba Sniper Attack # 18

There are several dismounted American soldiers near a Humvee, besides a road, apparently manning a checkpoint. It is daylight, the cameraman is level with the soldiers and the screen is hazy, indicating the cameraman is about 200 meters away. The sniper shoots, the camera jumps, and hits the soldier in the chest. The soldier falls backwards into a Humvee after being hit. The camera cuts.

Juba Sniper attack # 19

There are several American dismounted soldiers standing besides a Humvee, apparently manning a roadside checkpoint. One soldier is facing the sniper's position. It is daylight and the cameraman is level with the soldier. A car is seen driving in between the cameraman and the soldiers. There is a tree branch that obscures the cameraman's view of the soldier's head. The sniper shoots and the camera jumps. The way the soldier falls, it appears the soldier was hit in the pelvic region, below his body armor. Two other soldiers immediately grab the fallen soldier and begin to drag him behind the Humvee. One of the soldiers looks for where the shot came from, but looks away from the sniper's position. The sniper fires again but it looks like he hits a tree that is in front of the fallen soldier. The camera cuts. (Note: The sniper loses their cool from all the activity and probably jerks the trigger, missing the group of soldiers entirely, even though they are an easy target.)

Juba Sniper Attack # 20

There is an American soldier with his upper torso sticking out of the top hatch of a BFV turret. The soldier is facing the sniper's position and the BFV's turret and main gun is pointing towards the sniper. It is daylight and the cameraman is level with the BFV. The sniper takes a shot, hitting the soldier in the head. The camera jumps when the shot is fired. The camera cuts.

Juba Sniper Attack # 21

There are several dismounted Americans standing near a Humvee, apparently manning a roadside checkpoint. One soldier is at the rear of vehicle facing towards the sniper's position. It is daylight and the cameraman is level with the soldier. There are civilians visible walking nearby the checkpoint. The sniper shoots, apparently hitting the soldier in the head, and the soldier falls to the ground. The soldier on the Humvee's turret mounted machine-gun looks around, but never looks towards the sniper's position. Another soldier is standing on the side of the Humvee and is apparently unaware the other soldier was shot. Some civilians walking by show they have heard the gunshot. Others walk by as if they did not hear the gunshot. None of them look towards the sniper's position. The camera cuts. (Note: In some of these film clips the sniper must be using a sound suppressor as people who are right near the shooting never hear the gunshot.)

Juba Sniper Attack # 22

There is a dismounted American soldier standing next to a BFV, apparently manning a roadside checkpoint. It is daylight and the cameraman is level with the soldier. Cars can be seen driving between the cameraman and the soldier. The sniper shoots, and the camera jumps. Judging from the way the soldier doubled over and fell, he was hit in the chest. A civilian runs away after the shot is fired. The camera cuts. (Note: Now that we are into the 22nd attack, it is difficult to understand why the sniper is still shooting their targets square in the body armor, especially after so many other soldiers who were previously shot in the same place simply ran away, unharmed.)

Juba Sniper Attack #23 (PFC Stephen Tschiderer Attack)

PFC Tschiderer is dismounted and standing next to a Humvee, apparently manning a checkpoint. It is daylight and the cameraman is level with the soldiers. PFC Tschiderer is standing and looking towards the sniper's position. The sniper shoots, hitting the PFC Tschiderer in the chest. The camera jumps. PFC Tschiderer falls backwards onto the pavement. The camera cuts.

(Author's note: I encourage the reader to go on-line and view this video for themselves so they can make their own assessments. I made my conclusions after studying the video which told a great deal about Juba's tactics, patterns, and overall methodology. You might see something I missed as a different perspective often reveals new details hidden to someone else. The reader should also view the other Iraqi insurgent videos out there - there are several - so you can compare and contrast the different techniques the shooters employed.)

Chapter 18

Asymmetric Sniping

Asymmetric warfare originally referred to war between two or more actors, or groups of actors, whose relative power differed by a significant amount. Contemporary military thinkers tend to broaden this original meaning to include asymmetry of strategy or tactics so today, "asymmetric warfare" describes a military situation in which two belligerents of unequal power interact and attempt to take advantage of their opponents' weaknesses.... The core idea is that "weaker" combatants will attempt to use strategy to offset deficiencies in quantity or quality.
- Wikipedia definition of Asymmetric Warfare

Guerrilla Tactics + Heavy Caliber Rifles = Asymmetric Sniping

While close-in sniper shots like that of Juba are the hallmark of urban warfare, longer distance ones are possible. For instance, during the siege of Sarajevo, the Serbians dug into the surrounding hills could take shots into the city from a mile away. Also, sometimes the urban terrain lends itself to a long shot. Every city, with their deliberately planned layout, has straightaways of varying distances that can be used to make a long shot. We must remember that using an elevated firing position allows the sniper to shoot over urban obstacles to make long distance shots. Think of the German and Russian snipers firing from the smokestacks of Stalingrad's factory district, giving them a mile of observation in all directions.

Along with extreme range, a heavy caliber sniper rifle will penetrate urban mediums like steel, concrete, glass, and wood. This means normal sniper counter-measures like staying behind 'bulletproof' glass and traveling in armored vehicles no longer provides protection. In fact, when a large caliber rifle's penetrating power is combined with its long range, most counter-sniper measures are rendered ineffective. The ability

Allied soldiers display a captured Mauser anti-tank rifle.

to penetrate and accurately hit intended targets at distance also means a heavy sniper rifle can be used to attack just about anything like planes, helicopters, boats, armored cars, tanks, and fuel farms. Consequently, the lone gunman using a heavy caliber sniper rifle against ill-protected targets is truly an example of asymmetric warfare. How else could a single person immobilize a warship, destroy a Stealth bomber, or render ineffective a nuclear submarine?

A Brief History of Heavy Sniping

Modern heavy caliber sniper rifles are the product of several historical influences. One of the first heavy caliber rifles used in modern warfare was the Germans' 13.2 mm anti-tank rifle made by Mauser. The drive to develop this large weapon originated with the German army's frustration in dealing with the French and British tanks, which deflected normal-size bullets. In response, Mauser developed their bolt-action anti-tank rifle in early 1918. However, the Germans used their 13.2 mm behemoths for more than just anti-armor operations, they also targeted enemy snipers. (Interestingly enough, after the war was over, the American military used captured Mauser 13.2 mm rifles to test .50 caliber cartridges in their efforts to develop a new .50 caliber heavy machine gun.)

The British World War I snipers also used heavy caliber rifles from their trenches against their German foes, but for different reasons. The British had a problem with German snipers because the Germans began firing from behind pre-fabricated steel plates impervious to the British's regular .303 caliber rounds. In order to defeat the Germans' steel sniper shields, the British brought into country large caliber hunting rifles, called 'elephant guns' because they were originally used to hunt large game – like elephants - on the African plains.

While heavy caliber rifles were in their infancy in The Great War, World War II saw a veritable explosion of anti-tank guns. The Germans produced their Panzerbusche 38 and 39 models, fielding tens of thousands of them against the Polish army in 1939, against the British in North Africa, and against the Russians on the Eastern Front. The

British developed their Boys .55 caliber anti-tank rifle in the late 1930's, which could penetrate about 20 mm of armor when fired perpendicular to the target. The Russians had their PRTD-41 bolt-action, anti-tank rifle, which they used in large numbers on the Eastern Front. The PTRD-41 fired a 14.5 x 114 mm tungsten steel core round that could punch through 40 mm of vertical armor at a 90-degree angle (meaning it could penetrate the side armor of most German tanks at close range). A variety of other countries fielded anti-tank rifles as well like Switzerland, Poland, Finland, and Japan. Ultimately, as tank armor grew in thickness, the man-portable anti-tank rifle became almost useless. However, by pure chance and sheer necessity, both the German and Russian sides on occasion tried using anti-tank guns for sniping. This was not widespread at the time because these anti-tank rifles were relatively crude, inaccurate, and not deigned for use with a scope.

Although the United States in World War I and II did not field anti-tank rifles, American soldiers did experiment with firing their M2 .50 caliber machine-guns on single shot with a scope. Perhaps the first .50 caliber rifle intended specifically for sniping was fabricated in 1946 by Frank Conway, an ordnance officer stationed at the Aberdeen Proving Grounds in Maryland. Conway took a German Panzerbusche 39, replaced the existing barrel with a .50 caliber machine-gun barrel, added a muzzle break, attached a bipod near the muzzle, and added a scope. With this custom sniper system, Conway could hit targets at 1400 yards and place rounds through a building's window at 2800 yards.[1] Despite these successes, little official interest was generated in the .50 caliber sniper rifle concept. The weapon seemed too large, crude, and unorthodox for the Army's conventionally minded military leaders.

During the Korean War, the Marine Corps recognized the usefulness of large caliber sniping and the First Marine Division included sniping with a .50 caliber M2 machine-gun in their curriculum. Major Hicks, USMC, stated, "Each student trained not only with the .30 caliber M1 rifle (or the 03 Springfield, depending on his preference) but also with the .50 caliber machine-gun, fired single shot. Scopes were mounted on the machine guns and they proved to be effective for ranges up to and beyond 1200 yards."[2]

Once again, just like during World War II, some snipers were dissatisfied with the effectiveness of their current sniper weapons at long range. As a result, an enterprising young captain by the name of William S. Brophy fabricated his own long-range sniper rifle. Brophy, who was an Army ordnance officer, took a .50 caliber aircraft machine-gun barrel and attached it to the frame of a Russian PTRD-41 anti-tank gun (which was captured from the Korean and Chinese forces), and added a bipod and a 20 x power Unertl scope. While field testing this new rifle in Korea, Brophy and his students made kills out to a range of 2000 yards.[3] Even after further testing and evaluation, the heavy caliber sniper rifle never caught on with the U.S. military and American soldiers fighting in Vietnam in the 1960's and 70's had to make due with firing single shots from their M2 heavy barreled machine-guns.

Breaking the Mold: The Barrett .50 Caliber Sniper Rifle

While the U.S. military showed no interest in designing a long range, heavy caliber,

1 Senich, *The German Sniper*, p. 152.
2 Senich, *The Complete Book of U.S. Sniping*, p. 134.
3 Senich, *The Complete Book of U.S. Sniping*, p. 134.

In this staged photo, Red Army men destroy a German panzer with a PTRD-41 anti-tank rifle.

sniping rifle, a private businessman named Ronnie Barrett did. Barrett saw the need for a mobile, accurate, large caliber sniper rifle and was intent on designing and manufacturing one. In 1982, after working on a design in his garage workshop, Barrett fabricated his own .50 caliber sniper rifle. This ground-breaking design would later become the Model 82A1. The M82 proved to be a break through, and even though the weapon was big, it had very low recoil, was easy to use, and could hit targets accurately at a mile and more. Barrett finally proved you could fabricate a purpose-built .50 caliber sniper rifle with the desired results in accuracy and range. After refining his original product, Barrett garnered some interest from the U.S. military as well as private shooting enthusiasts. The Marines employed .50 caliber rifles while deployed to Beirut in 1983 and a Navy SEAL unit used .50 caliber rifles during the invasion of Grenada in the same year.

After the M82 proved itself over the ensuing years, especially during the First Gulf War, manufacturers all over the world began to produce their own versions of the .50 caliber sniping rifle. While Barrett had the market cornered for the first years after his initial design, today, there is a veritable flood of similar weapons. Russia now has a heavy caliber sniper rifle, as does South Africa, Austria, Britain, and Germany just to name few. Also, a whole new crop of American arms companies has bloomed, all producing their own versions of the heavy caliber sniping rifle. In 2005, the U.S. Army officially designated Barrett's XM107 (a slightly modified version of the original M82) as its long range sniping rifle. After nearly sixty years of innovation, field testing, and varying degrees of official apathy going as far back as 1946, the U.S. military finally recognized the value of a heavy caliber sniping rifle.

20 mm & 25 mm Rifles

While anti-tank guns like the German's Panzerbusche 39 were of relatively small caliber and the PTRD-41 was 'only' 14.5 mm in size, some countries went even bigger. For instance, the Finnish military produced the Lahti 20 mm anti-tank rifle in 1939. The Lahti proved to be successful against Russia's light tanks out to a distance of 400 meters and, due to its accuracy, it was also used for smaller targets like machine-gun nests and enemy bunkers. The Lahti was a large weapon weighing over 100 pounds and was pulled on a sled in snowy conditions. The Japanese of World War II also produced a 20 mm anti-tank rifle, the Type 97, which weighed in at over 130 pounds and could penetrate more than an inch of steel at 300 meters. The Japanese Imperial Army only fielded several hundred of these enormous weapons which required at least two men to manhandle them.

The 20 mm anti-tank rifle died a quick death after the war, but saw a comeback in recent times where modern manufacturing methods have produced lightweight, man portable weapons that can be carried and employed by a single person. In the early 1990's, South Africa developed the NTW-20 anti-material rifle and in 1998 the South African National Defense Force began fielding it in numbers. The NTW-20 has a range of over 1500 meters and at a weight of about 57 pounds - the rifle can be broken down into two equal-size loads - it is truly man portable. At about the same time, Croatia, which was engaged in an ugly war with neighboring Serbia, developed its RT-20 anti-material/anti-tank rifle. The RT-20 fires a high-velocity 2000-grain 20 mm round at speeds of 2500 feet per second. This high-powered round, which can reach out to 1800 meters, produces a great deal of recoil which is dampened by a special recoil tube fitted above the receiver. This single shot, bolt-action rifle is considerably lighter than the NT-20 and weighs in at only 45 pounds.

Perhaps the best 20 mm rifle out there is Anzio Ironworks's 20 mm takedown rifle which only weighs 39 pounds! The Anzio takedown fires a 20 mm Vulcan round that weighs 1600 grains and travels at a velocity of 3300 feet per second. Believe it or not, when the Anzio takedown is fitted with a sound suppressor, it has relatively little recoil or muzzle flash. Especially important for the sniper who needs to conceal their activities, the Anzio 20 mm rifle comes with a custom carrying case which the weapon fits in when disassembled.

With the growth in popularity of the .50 caliber and 20 mm models, there was enough interest to produce an even larger anti-material rifle of the 25 mm size. The 25 mm rifle is an elite category because few such models are available for retail. When one talks about 25 mm rifles, they are really talking about Ronnie Barrett's XM109 which is a modification of the original M82. Essentially, the XM109 is an M82 with a different upper receiver. The XM109 is truly in a class of its own, weighing in at a slim 33 pounds, it fires a 25 mm HEDP round (High Explosive Dual Purpose), has a range of 2500 meters and can penetrate 40 mm of armor out to 500 meters. The modern heavy caliber sniper rifle has come a long way since Mauser's original 13.2 mm design in World War II.

Anti-Material Sniping

Modern heavy caliber sniper rifles began as anti-tank weapons. However, as the

An American sniper in Fallujah takes aim behind a Barrett .50 rifle.

Photo by DoD

armor of tanks and other armored vehicles improved during World War II, the anti-tank rifle grew out of favor and was not effective considering its weight and relative inaccuracy. Now, with the design of modern heavy caliber rifles that have excellent range, good penetrating power, and can be disassembled and carried by a single person, the old anti-tank gun is back in vogue. With these new lightweight models, the modern urban sniper has a whole range of targets they can disable or eliminate with accurate aimed fire. One of the primary targets for the modern heavy caliber sniper is the armored vehicle, for which it was first created. At first, one might not think a main battle tank would be vulnerable to the humble sniper, but through study and intelligent shot placement, the urban sniper can immobilize a heavy tank.

First, a tank can only protect its crew if they are actually inside the vehicle. Since a tank can get extremely hot inside, tank crew members often ride on top of their vehicles or open up their access hatches to let air in the vehicle in order to cool off. And because armored vehicles offer their crews such poor visibility of the surrounding urban terrain, tank drivers and tank commanders often stick their heads out of their hatches in order to see better. On other occasions, crew members open their hatches and expose themselves when talking to other ground soldiers.

For whatever reason crew members expose themselves, they become targets. During the battle for Stalingrad, Russian snipers intentionally waited for panzer crew members to expose themselves so they could be picked off. This practice hurt the Germans because trained panzer crews were extremely valuable and hard to replace because of the large numbers of casualties suffered in the Stalingrad slaughterhouse. Sixty years later, American tank crewmen in Iraq found themselves prime targets for insurgent snipers as they stuck their heads out of their hatches to watch for the enemy. The urban sniper taking careful aim at a main battle tank is a true example of asymmetric warfare where the tank, which is designed for high intensity warfare, is incapable of detecting and surgically eliminating a carefully hidden sniper who takes advantage of the city's urban clutter.

I had the chance to talk to members of an Abrams tank unit in Iraq who were victim of an insurgent sniper attack. When the incident happened, the tank unit was patrolling an area. As they drove slowly down a road, the driver had his head out of the hatch so he could see the narrow road better. Unknown to the unit, a small insurgent element set up an ambush site in a cluster of buildings near the road. As the tank approached the buildings, the sniper opened fire and shot the driver of the tank, killing him. The insurgents then ran out of the buildings, swam a nearby canal, jumped in a waiting car, and drove off. The tank unit was unable to detect the hidden sniper before the attack, they never saw the shooter make the shot, and they were unable to pursue their attackers because the cluster of buildings provided the insurgents with visual screening until they were safely across the water and in their car. What was the tank unit supposed to do now? There was nobody to blow up with their 120 mm cannons. Also, the unit had to treat their wounded man, which meant they had to immediately leave the area and go to a nearby aid station.

Shooting an armored vehicle crew member is pretty easy. If the sniper sees a person they shoot them. On the other hand, learning to physically disable a main battle tank takes homework and the sniper must know the vulnerable points of the vehicle. The sniper can learn this any number of ways like buying books about their targets or reading articles on the internet. One way to get an intimate understanding of an armored vehicle is to build a plastic model of it, like the ones at a hobby shop. Often times these model kits offer the builder more detailed knowledge of the vehicle than reading any book.

Common vulnerable points on armored vehicles include vision ports, thermal imaging sights, engine compartments, and the vehicle's roof, especially where the access hatches are. If a sniper shoots out the vision ports, driving becomes difficult for the crew and they may have to stick their heads out to see, making them even more vulnerable to follow on shots. Shooting out thermal imagers and other weapon targeting systems will immobilize the vehicle's main gun, making them less of a threat. If a sniper has the chance, they can also shoot the vehicle from the rear, because that is traditionally where armored vehicles have the thinnest armor and is usually where the engine is located. So, by hitting the engine compartment at the weak spot, a sniper can get a mobility kill on the vehicle. Finally, a sniper can try to get a top-down shot on a vehicle from an elevated position because the armor is thinner on top. Also, the armor on the vehicle is weakest at the hatches and wherever there is a hatch, there is usually a person. Consequently, the hatches make a convenient aiming point for the shooter.

It is useful to understand the majority of the world's armored personnel carriers and armored trucks are designed only to stop shell fragments and 7.62 mm rounds and smaller. These armored personnel carriers cannot withstand .50 caliber sniper fire. Vehicles like Russia's BTR-60/70/80 series only stop small arms fire and a 20 mm rifle with armor piercing ammunition will smoke right through the thin armor of a BTR like it was butter. With the advent of the lightweight, portable 20/25 mm rifle, a single shooter can hide in a building, shoot through a small loophole, and defeat any armored vehicle out there short of a main battle tank. The takedown 20/25 mm rifle combined with an urban setting gives the shooter a definite advantage over the light armored vehicles most of the world's armies use today.

But, let us be clear what we are talking about here. There are many exaggerated claims of what anti-material sniping can accomplish and we must be realistic about a heavy rifle's capabilities. Only the informed, surgical targeting of an armored vehicle will work. If a sniper shoots out a tank's thermal imaging system, the tank can still drive and fire its weapons; it just may not be able to fire accurately. A sniper may shoot and kill a tank commander, but the rest of the crew will still be able to maneuver their

Targeting Armor

Exposed Crew

Thin Armor

Vision Ports

These SS Sturmgeschutz assault guns are driving in a populated urban area as a show of force. Armored vehicles are most vulnerable in this close terrain as a sniper could pick off their crew members and anti-tank guns could strike them in their least armored areas.

vehicle and fire their weapons systems. Most likely, an anti-tank sniper will inconvenience a tank or make the vehicle retreat for repairs or to help a wounded crew member. The sniper will probably not permanently disable the tank. In Stalingrad, Russian anti-tank riflemen shot up plenty of German panzers, but the Germans recovered the majority of them, repaired them, and sent them back in action. Some of these Russian anti-tank gunners were not so lucky the second and third times around and were eventually gunned down by the panzers they already shot up and disabled multiple times before.

Targeting Airports and Aircraft

Airports are a prominent feature of the world's modern major cities. Many airports are located close enough to urban areas a sniper can target the runway and its aircraft without ever entering the airport property itself. A study of the vulnerability of U.S. military air bases by the Rand Corporation noted, "A clever adversary, faced with the insurmountable dominance of U.S. airpower in the air, could employ what we call an 'asymmetric strategy' , and, "A successful attack on a U.S. airbase may have a strategic effect out of proportion to the resources expended".[4] Sarajevo International Airport, for one, was within easy reach of the city's western-most neighborhoods and their high-rise buildings. On more than one occasion the United Nations-run airport had to be shut down due to incoming fire by Serbian shooters. In other instances,

4 Shlapak, David & Alan Vick, *Check Six Begins on the Ground*, p.13.

civilian airports are isolated to some degree from major urban areas to limit the inconvenience caused by the noise of continually landing aircraft. Even with these airports, there are many buildings on the airport property itself and many spots to park a car that can be used as a sniper hide.

Once a sniper gets within range of the airport, they can destroy an entire air force in just minutes because most aircraft are fragile machines that are unable to take punishment. The same Rand report identified this issue, "Indeed, the complexity and sophistication of modern aircraft may make them more vulnerable. For example, superficial shrapnel damage to a stealthy aircraft's aerodynamic surfaces would do more than just affect flight characteristics: It would increase its radar cross section (RCS), making it more vulnerable to detection and, hence, impairing its operational effectiveness even if no vital components were damaged. Further, repairing the composite skin to restore the original RCS would not be a trivial undertaking. Alternatively, consider the effect of .50 caliber sniper rifle rounds fired through an AWACS radome, struts, or fuselage: Regardless of precisely where the bullets struck, substantial damage to the delicate electronics packed into this aircraft would probably ensue – in contrast to the P-51's and F-86's of the 1940s and 1950s, which were largely aluminum skins wrapped around empty space, making these aircraft much less vulnerable to one or two rifle bullets passing through the airframe."[5]

As the Rand report shows, all it takes is a single .50 caliber bullet through the skin of a domestic airliner to make it un-flyable. Or, a single round through the windshield of a cockpit will ground that aircraft until they replace the glass. More importantly, in the cockpit area of an aircraft are sensitive avionics like radar and weapons control systems, which will be rendered useless with a direct hit and may cost millions to replace. A direct hit to the engines or the internal fuel tanks will ground the aircraft until the engine is replaced or the fuel leak is patched. If the sniper is using incendiary ammunition and is aiming for a plane's fuel tank, they may even set a fire from the extremely flammable, high-octane jet fuel. And let us remember a plane needs its wheels to taxi and take off, so blowing off the forward wheel at the nose of the aircraft will ground the aircraft, although a tire change is a pretty easy repair to make. Perhaps the best shot a sniper could make is shooting the pilot while they are in the cockpit – no pilot, no flying.

Helicopters are less fragile than aircraft, but they too have their weak spots. Aiming for a helicopter's landing gear is useless since they do not taxi to take off or land. Punching a hole in the cockpit windshield is a waste of time since helicopters do not have pressurized cockpits or interiors like jet aircraft do. Helicopters do have advanced avionics in the cockpit. A good location to place a shot is at the main rotor shaft, which will ground a helicopter until repairs are made. Because helicopters are low, slow flying aircraft that also hover, they are prime targets even in flight. Flying helicopters are especially vulnerable in urban areas because there are so many places a sniper can hide. Even Russia's Mi-24 HIND-D close attack helicopter, which is armored to withstand small arms fire, cannot survive carefully placed rounds from a .50 caliber rifle.

Air bases and airports offer more targets than just airplanes and helicopters, as Rand observed, "An air base is a classic "target-rich environment." Besides the aircraft themselves, air bases offer fuel storage facilities, munitions bunkers, the control

5 Shlapak, David & Alan Vick, *Check Six Begins on the Ground*, p.14.

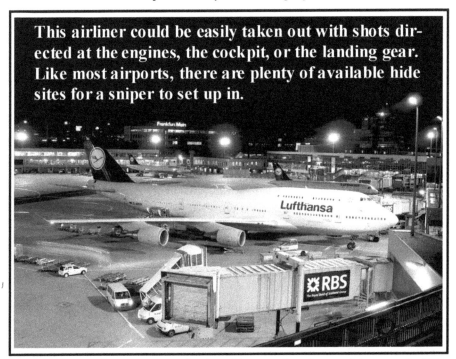

This airliner could be easily taken out with shots directed at the engines, the cockpit, or the landing gear. Like most airports, there are plenty of available hide sites for a sniper to set up in.

tower and operations center, navigation aids, crew housing, maintenance facilities, and aerospace ground equipment."[6] We cannot forget a civilian airport is a juicy target because it is a major source of revenue for the state. A separate Rand study about the vulnerability of Los Angeles International Airport (LAX) revealed, "Los Angeles International Airport (LAX) is vital to Southern California. It is the airport of choice for over 50 million passengers every year. According to Los Angeles World Airports (LAWA), it provides the Southern California economy with over $70 billion in revenue each year. It is vital to Southern California that LAX is a safe and secure airport." The report found LAX could be victimized in a scenario where, "A sniper set up on airport-adjacent property with a .50-caliber sniper rifle shoots at loaded planes, firing approximately 50 shots over five minutes," and, "From a roof of a high-rise building on the airport perimeter, a sniper using a .50-caliber rifle fires at parked and taxiing aircraft."[7]

Targeting Ships

If we think about it, most of the world's major cities are built on the water. This is because waterways are a major source for trade, commerce, and transportation. Where is Beirut? On the coast of the Mediterranean Sea. Where is Baghdad? Astride the Tigris River. Where is Stalingrad? Along the banks of the Volga River. Just as airports are located next to major urban areas, so are waterways and ports. These ports are often even closer to urban areas because there are no concerns about sound

---

6 Shlapak, David & Alan Vick, *Check Six Begins on the Ground*, p.54.
7 Stevens, *Near-Term Options for Improving Security at Los Angeles International Airport.*

restrictions or flight paths as with aircraft. Major naval installations have some sort of security perimeter protecting them, but these perimeters can be infiltrated and there is most likely a building within a mile of the port that can be used to target a seafaring vessel as it enters or exits the relative safety of the docks.

Are we a little crazy thinking we can actually take out a battleship or a nuclear submarine with a sniper? Actually, if one studies the characteristics and weaknesses of a seafaring vessel just like they would study a tank or armored car, they will find vulnerable areas that can disable a large sea craft. Case in point: on June 7, 2006 the U.S. Navy held what they call a 'sink exercise', off the coast of North Carolina. The targets of the exercise were two Spruance-class guided missile destroyers, the USS Stump and the USS Comte de Grasse. At 563-feet long, 7800 tons, and a crew of 350 men, these sister ships were the biggest destroyers ever built. During the exercise, the navy opened fire on these ships with a variety of weapons systems to determine their effectiveness.

In Jack Dorsey's article for the Virginian-Pilot he noted, "The Comte de Grass was targeted initially by .50-caliber machine guns to demonstrate disabling fire, then 40 mm grenade launchers and 5-inch guns. The Mason (a U.S. Navy destroyer), using a 20 mm cannon for close-in protection, demonstrated how it could disable a ship without sinking it. "Part of the test was to see how good it was for taking off various parts of the ship, say the rudder post," Franken said. "We do it to slow the ships," Weeldreyer said. "It was extremely accurate." The U.S. Navy already knows accurate .50 caliber and 20 mm fire can disable a ship on the open seas. This means the urban sniper, positioned near a harbor, port, or waterway can also disable ships similar in size as the two sister ships sunk off the coast of North Carolina. The sniper may not be able to get to a ship on the open seas, but they can certainly target it when it is docked for refueling, or for repairs, or for shore leave for its crew.

The real advantage of firing from an urban area at a naval vessel is the David versus Goliath aspect of it. A lone sniper pitted against a massive armored and armed ship is perhaps the distinctive example of asymmetric warfare. For example, let us say a sniper looking to take out a ship is armed with a 20 mm sniper rifle and is hidden in the upper floors of an occupied apartment building. Let us also say the sniper is using good tradecraft, has a sound suppressor on the weapon, and is hidden deep in a room. Most likely, the ship and its crew will be unable to determine from what location the firing is coming from. If the ship and crew did detect the general area or building the fire was coming from, what are they going to do about it? Open fire with a 5-inch naval gun? Launch a cruise missile? Pound the surrounding city with its 20 mm Phalanx gatling gun?

A sea vessel is not a counter-sniper weapon and is not equipped for the surgical removal of a lone gunman in a populated urban area. If the ship and crew responded to the sniper with their high-powered weapons, they would butcher the surrounding populace and destroy the surrounding infrastructure. If the ship is doing a layover at its home port, then the crew would be killing their own citizens and destroying their own real estate - a win-win situation for the guerrilla sniper. With just a dozen well-aimed shots, the sniper, armed with intimate knowledge of their target, could shoot out the ship's various radar systems, antennas, exposed munitions like anti-ship missiles or depth charges, and various anti-missile countermeasure systems. In the space of 60 seconds, the shooter could render the vessel incapable of conducting seaborne

Below, a picture of the Thames River running through London. Any of these vessels below could be effectively targeted with a sniper hidden somewhere in the surrounding buildings. Obvious targets would be the boat cockpits and engine compartments.

operations, cause millions of dollars of damage, delay launching of the ship until repairs were made, and cause secondary explosions further damaging the vessel.

To effectively cripple an enormous target like a ship, the sniper has to do some target analysis. For the purpose of learning, we will use the HMS Nottingham, which is a British naval vessel. First, if we type the name 'HMS Nottingham' into Google, we get a bunch of links and images back. Then, we select an article from *www.wikipedia. com* and we get some basic information about the ship. Wikipedia says, "The HMS Nottingham (D91), is a batch two Type 42 Destroyer of the Royal Navy, named after the city of Nottingham, England. She was launched on February 18, 1980, and commissioned on 8 April 1983 and is the sixth ship to bear the name." We also get basic information like the ship weight (4820 tons) and crew size (271 total - 27 Officers, 71 Senior Rates, 173 Junior Rates).

Now we have some background information, we need something better. Further web surfing reveals an article from *www.bbc.co.uk* offering a virtual video tour of the ship including the bow, the stern, the hangar, the engine room, and the bridge. Then, from that site we find a link to *www.royal-navy.mod.uk* where we can surf the Nottingham's official website. On that site, we learn more about the history of the ship to include a picture and biography of the current ship commander. While that information is good as background, we still need the specific components of the ship to target. After some more web surfing, we hit the mother load: *www.steelnavy.com,* which has a complete model of a type 42 destroyer in pictures, to include the directions and ship components! Of course, studying a big ship like a Type 42 Destroyer could take weeks to find the exact components and the weakest part of those components, but the point is the information is out there and readily available.

Targeting Submarines

Submarines are even more vulnerable to the urban sniper than are surface ships. Most submarines do not even have weapons capable of returning fire at a sniper, unlike a surface vessel. If the sniper targets a nuclear powered submarine armed with intercontinental ballistic missiles, what is the submarine's crew going to do? Launch a nuclear missile at the sniper? In this case, the nuclear powered and nuclear armed submarine, perhaps the most destructive weapon on the planet, is completely helpless as its weapons systems are utterly inappropriate for the threat. The submarine might be able to turn Moscow into a radiated parking lot, but it cannot touch the lone gunman with a bolt-action rifle.

More importantly to the sniper, because a submarine operates underwater, its hull must remain intact in order to submerge. A ship can sustain quit a bit of damage before it sinks, but a submarine, in comparison, is relatively fragile. Just a single armor piercing round shot through the hull of a submarine will make it unseaworthy. Different parts of a submarine are vulnerable to the sniper depending on what the sub is doing and where it is. A submarine setting out from or heading to the docks will most likely have little exposed except for its sail. However, the sail is an important part of the vessel because, depending on the model of submarine, it may house a conning tower (which has communications equipment), a periscope, and radar and antenna masts. Also, the submarine's commander or senior staff may occupy the sail and expose themselves in order to observe the surrounding terrain. Consequently, several carefully placed rounds from a sniper could result in the death of the vessel's captain and the disabling of its long range communications equipment.

If a submarine can be targeted while it is docked, then more of the vessel is visible. Not only can the sail be targeted, but shots can be directed against the entire upper half of the submarine. If a sub is in dry-dock and completely out of the water, then an informed shooter can target every part of the submarine to include its propulsion system and sensitive sonar equipment. For about $50 worth of 20 mm armor piercing incendiary rounds, a lone gunman can easily disable a $2 billion Virginia-class attack submarine, forcing it to stay off the high seas until repaired.

Other Uses of the Heavy Caliber Sniper Rifle

We have discussed briefly some of the major targets a sniper armed with a heavy caliber rifle could effectively target like tanks, armored vehicles, aircraft, ships, and submarines. But the list does not stop there as there are an almost endless number of objects or structures that could be targeted by a thoughtful sniper. For example, *Time Magazine* carried an article in the June 20, 2005 edition by Mark Thompson, detailing how .50 caliber rifles could be used to target and penetrate the armored security towers that protect nuclear power plants. Once terrorist marksmen used the big rifles to take out the security guards sitting in their guard towers - or iron coffins as they are cynically termed - other members of the assault force would be free to breach the protective walls of the nuclear facility with explosively rigged 'platter' charges. Once inside the reactor control room, the terrorists' goal would be to cause a nuclear meltdown. Engineers in the nuclear power industry agree it would not be terribly difficult to manipulate the controls to shut off the various pumps and valves that supply

This nuclear submarine off the coast of France could be hit from the surrounding shoreline, targeting the sail and exposed crew.

the water that keeps the reactor cool. The result - nuclear meltdown.

True, nuclear power plants are one possible target for gun-toting terrorists. However, various security analysts, gun control advocates, and sniping experts have determined there are an endless number of targets for the large caliber rifle like:

- Large gatherings of people at sporting events, such as at open football or baseball stadiums, where a sniper could shoot into the crowds from a mile away and kill dozens of people in order to spread terror.

- Above ground liquefied natural gas (LNG) storage containers, to include the ships and trucks transporting the LNG from large processing centers to local distributors, could be targeted, resulting in a large explosion.

- Bulk fuel tanks located at oil refineries and ports, fuel trucks and fuel transportation ships could all be set on fire

- Chemical manufactures could be fired on in hopes of creating a Bhopal, India-like catastrophe, where a Union Carbide container overheated in 1984 and released 27 tons of the pesticide methyl isocyanate (MIC) into the surrounding densely populated urban area, killing over 20,000 people and injuring a further 120,000; also trucks or trains transporting chlorine and propane gas could be likewise targeted and blown up.

- Armored cars transporting money for banks can be taken out to facilitate robbing them.

In short, a large array of targets are available in any society that, when hit with a large caliber, armor piercing, incendiary bullet could cause major explosions, the release of deadly chemical and gases into the surrounding population, or large scale fires. These resulting secondary effects can shut down major transportation arteries, result in the evacuation of tens of thousands of people, may cause death and injuries to hundreds of thousands of people in the right conditions, can cost a government millions – if not billions of dollars – in repairs, clean up costs, insurance pay outs, medical care, and can paralyze a population with fear of another catastrophe. Thus, any insurgent or terrorist organization could wreak varying degrees of havoc on an unprotected and unprepared urban center and population.

While I agree an educated sniper firing the proper ammunition at a defined target can wreak damage on the urban infrastructure, we should not overestimate the heavy caliber sniper rifle and think a gunman armed with a .50 caliber sniper rifle can shut down an entire city. That is pure nonsense. For instance, one of the most commonly recognized targets for a terrorist armed with a .50 caliber rifle is a fuel facility. For sure, a few well placed armor piercing incendiary rounds will penetrate the thin metal of a fuel container and then catch on fire but, will this fire result in an apocalyptic disaster where multiple fuel containers explode and spread burning fuel for miles in all directions? Some experts think not.

In the first part of June 2007, the Associated Press ran an article stating: "Federal authorities announced Saturday they had broken up a suspected Muslim terrorist cell planning a "chilling" attack to destroy John F. Kennedy International Airport, kill thousands of people and trigger an economic catastrophe by blowing up a jet fuel artery that runs through populous residential neighborhoods." According to authorities, these terrorists intended to blow up the airport fuel tanks with explosives, but they could just have easily – and probably with more success – had set them alight with a heavy caliber sniper rifle firing incendiary ammunition.

While a fuel tank or two might catch on fire, some people knowledgeable in the field thought the damage would be limited. "Richard Kuprewicz, a pipeline expert and president of Accufacts Inc., an energy consulting firm that focuses on pipelines and tank farms, said the force of explosion would depend on the amount of fuel under pressure, but it would not travel up and down the line. 'That doesn't mean wackos out there can't do damage and cause a fire, but those explosions and fires are going to be fairly restricted,' he said." In this situation, the company that manages JFK Airport's fuel network felt a simplistic attack, like starting a fire at their fuel farm with a sniper rifle, would be contained rather quickly.[8]

Protective Security Details

Another area of concern for security professionals is less horrific than the awful death of thousands caused by chemical poisoning or an uncontrollable gasoline fire. What they fear is their inability to protect a high value personality, like a head of state, from a sniper armed with a heavy caliber rifle. Don Edwards, a career Secret Service officer, wrote a National Defense University thesis about such a threat. In his thesis Edwards laconically summarizes, "There is an historical precedent for the use of large caliber weapons against individual personnel targets. Technology has greatly enhanced the range and lethality of man portable large caliber weapons. The author feels this coupled with widespread availability could result in the use of these weapons against U.S. National Command Authority (NCA) figures." Edwards also recognized, "These weapons could be employed effectively from places of conceal- ment outside the scope of normal security measures against personnel, aircraft, lightly armored vehicles, and buildings. They are more accurate than shoulder fired rockets and immune to electronic counter measures. They thus pose a threat in environments generally thought secure."[9]

8 Goldman, *Feds foil JFK Terror Plot, Arrest 3*, Associated Press.
9 Edwards, *Large Caliber Sniper Threat To U.S. National Command Authority Fig- ures*, p. ix.

This Blackwater security detail, protecting a State Department member, would be unable to stop a sniper firing a large caliber rifle, which would penetrate their body armor and their armored vehicle.

In other words, the job of security details have gotten harder. Security measures that would normally work for the person they are trying to protect will not work against a heavy caliber rifle fired at extreme ranges. For instance, an armored car or limousine will not stop a 20 mm armor piercing round. A shooter will be able to fire through an armored car door or bulletproof window, penetrate the vehicle, and continue on to strike the target. Furthermore, a sniper can hit and disable the vehicle's engine, making it a sitting duck for follow on shots.

With big sniper rifles, body armor becomes irrelevant. A .50 caliber sniper rifle firing armor piercing ammunition will go through the front ceramic plate of body armor, go through the person wearing it, go out through the back plate of ceramic armor, and then drill the person being protected. So, a bodyguard placing themselves in front of a sniper's bullet will not protect the target. Also, a shooter can penetrate other protective mediums found in structures like windows, doors, walls (concrete and plaster), and roofs. Not only will a large bullet penetrate these mediums, there may be little or no deflection to throw the shot off the intended target.

A shooter firing from an extremely far distance will most likely be able to get a shot off before they are detected by even alert counter-sniper teams. Since an urban area allows for a concealed sniper to fire from a thousand possible locations, security details are easily overcome by so much urban clutter and information overload. It could take hundreds of men to truly protect a dignitary from the threat of a sniper in a densely populated urban area. This massive effort would require security personnel to identify, observe, and be able to counter every potential sniper hide within a one-mile radius of a particular location. Additionally, the extreme range a .50 caliber sniper rifle could be fired from would negate most counter-sniper technology, which is only effective at relatively close distances of 500 meters or less.

Guerillas and Heavy Caliber Sniper Rifles

Since we know heavy caliber sniper rifles have been commercially available at least from the early 1980's, have any guerrilla organization used them in combat operations? The Violence Policy Center (VPC) reported that several people admitted at least twenty-five Barrett .50 caliber sniper rifles made their way into the hands of the mujahideen fighting against the Russians in Afghanistan. In the VPC's report, *Voting from the Rooftops,* they state, "Associated Press wire service also described the transaction as follows, quoting the president of Barrett Firearms, Ronnie G. Barrett: Ronnie Barrett, president of Murfreesboro, Tenn.-Barrett Firearms, likened sale of the .50-caliber armor-piercing rifles to the supply of the Stinger surface-to-air missiles given to anti-Soviet guerrillas in Afghanistan. "Barrett rifles were picked up by U.S. government trucks, shipped to U.S. government bases and shipped to those Afghan freedom fighters," Barrett said. There is a kernel of truth in these well-parsed representations. The U.S. government did in fact supply some Barrett .50 caliber sniper rifles to the Afghan resistance. It just did not supply or authorize the ones bought by Bin Laden's Al Qaeda. "We never sold anything to, or bought anything, or otherwise transferred anything to bin Laden in the 80s," according to the man who ran the program on the ground—the former CIA station chief in Pakistan." While Al-Qaeda might very well have U.S. produced .50 caliber sniper rifles, they could just as easily have bought similar weapons from a dozen other countries through illegal arms dealers and their own clandestine intermediaries.

The Irish Republican Army (IRA)

The IRA received several .50 caliber Barrett rifles in the early 1990s from the United States. It is believed these rifles were purchased legally through private gun sales by Americans, who were IRA sympathizers, who in turn smuggled these rifles into Northern Ireland through IRA intermediaries. The IRA published videos of them training with their newly acquired guns, which did not bode well for the British military. Eventually, an IRA sniper team working out of South Armagh targeted British checkpoints with one of their Barrett 90 .50 caliber sniper rifles. As stated elsewhere in this book, this sniper team fired the rifle while concealed in the back of a Mazda 626 hatchback. The IRA is not known to have targeted British armored vehicles or aircraft with these .50 caliber weapons. However, the IRA did conduct an operation where they mounted a .50 machine gun in the back of a truck and maneuvered this truck in front of a British police car. At point blank range, the IRA team opened the back of the truck and fired on the police, shredding the car in the process. The IRA could just have easily used (with a lot less trouble) a .50 caliber rifle for this operation and had the same results. In another incident, IRA snipers did engage a British vessel, the HMS Cygnet, off the Irish coast, but failed to significantly damage the craft.

Steyr HS .50

These were bought by Iran and smuggled into Iraq.

The Kosovo Liberation Army (KLA)

The Kosovo Liberation Army (KLA) received several hundred .50 caliber rifles in the late 1990s for their war against Serbia. The man instrumental in getting the KLA their weapons was a gunrunner by the name of Florin Krasniqi. Krasniqi, an Albanian by birth, entered the United States illegally in 1989, smuggled across the Mexican border in the trunk of a car. When war came to Kosovo in 1998, Krasniqi was ready and willing to help the KLA by shipping them weapons. It was easy. Krasniqi, who lives in Brooklyn, New York, noted, "Anything you need to run a small guerrilla army, you can buy here in America. You have all the guns you need here to fight a war. M-16s. That's what the U.S. soldiers carry in Iraq. All the rifles which U.S. soldiers use in every war, you can buy them in a gun store or a gun show. By far, the weapon of choice was a .50-caliber rifle. You could kill a man from over a mile away. You can dismantle a vehicle from a mile away."[10]

It was easy for Krasniqi to go out and buy any weapon he needed from private arms dealers at local gun shows. All he needed was a credit card and a clean criminal record and he could buy as many guns as he wanted, no questions asked. Krasniqi eventually had several other people, who lived in different parts of the country, buy guns for him, thus reducing his 'signature'. Then, they flew the guns to his native Albania on commercial flights. All they did was officially declare the weapons as hunting rifles and the airlines allowed them to ship the weapons with the rest of the regular baggage.

Krasniqi's team of gunrunners never had a problem getting the guns out of the United States. But, they often had to switch flights in Switzerland and the authorities there wanted to know what they were doing with such powerful weapons. So, Krasniqi told them they were going elephant hunting. The Swiss officials were skeptical because there were no elephants in Albania. Krasniqi told them they belonged to a hunting club

10 *Buying Big Guns? No Big Deal, Gunrunner Buys Rifles In U.S. To Equip Guerrilla Army,* 60 Minutes.

in Albania which organized trips to Tanzania. Eventually, Krasniqi actually bought an elephant in Tanzania for $10,000.00 - which he never saw - in order to prove they were elephant hunters. The ruse worked because they continued to fly their weapons from the United States, through Switzerland, and onto Albania.[11]

The KLA had a voracious appetite for .50 caliber rifles, so sending out the big guns in two's and three's was too slow a process. Former Newsweek correspondent Stacy Sullivan, author of *Be Not Afraid, For You Have Sons in America,* a book about Krasniqi, described how Krasniqi clandestinely increased the flow of rifles without getting caught by American authorities. The trickle of rifles became a flood with one hundred being flown out at once. All Krasniqi did was move the rifles by truck to John F. Kennedy airport in New York City and conceal the weapons with legitimate humanitarian goods like food and clothes. The pallets filled with the rifles were never inspected or x-rayed. The airport simply did not have the manpower to check every thing being shipped overseas, and unless there was some indication of impropriety, anything could get shipped out, to include anti-tank guns.

The KLA got their .50 caliber rifles in standard guerrilla fashion. They had a front man (Krasniqi) with a clean record buy the weapons legally in a country with liberal gun laws (the United States). The organization then shipped these weapons via commercial air, used a simple cover story to explain why they were shipping the big guns (for a hunting club), and then off-loaded the weapons in Albania. Then, the KLA moved the guns from Albania into Kosovo through illegal border crossings. Since Kosovo was populated mainly by ethnic Albanians, the Albanian government never looked too closely at their border and the activities of possible gunrunners.

Iraqi Insurgents

In 2005, the National Iranian Police legally purchased eight hundred HS50 .50 caliber sniper rifles from the Austrian weapons manufacturer Steyr-Mannlicher. Iran's given reason for buying these weapons was for use against drug smugglers on the dangerous Iran-Afghanistan-Pakistan border, where a bloody drug war raged for several years. Steyr-Mannlicher did nothing illegal since the Austrian government approved the transaction. The Iranians even provided an end-user certificate, proving they would not export these weapons to another country. The rifles were subsequently shipped to Iran in 2006.

The Steyr Arms web page describes their precision crafted sniper rifle, "The STEYR HS .50 is a long range, high precision rifle, with an effective range of up to 1,640 yards (1,500 m). It was designed as a single shot bolt action rifle, and is available in the caliber .50 BMG. The STEYR HS .50 features a cold hammer forged fluted barrel, adjustable bi-pod, and a highly efficient muzzle brake, which reduces recoil substantially to increase shooting comfort. The top mounted Picatinny rail (Mil. Std. 1913 rail) allows quick and easy installation of various optics, or night vision devices. The STEYR HS .50 is designed to field strip easily for transportation or maintenance purposes."

If Steyr sold these sniper rifles to any other country, the transaction would have been quickly forgotten. However, since Iran supported various insurgent groups in

11 *Buying Big Guns? No Big Deal, Gunrunner Buys Rifles In U.S. To Equip Guerrilla Army,* 60 Minutes.

by Ronnie Barrett

This is the .50 caliber prototype Ronnie Barrett built in his own garage. Just as Barrett was a guerrilla manufacturer in the American arms industry, actual guerrillas could fabricate their own large caliber sniper rifles.

Iraq, American and British observers of this transaction thought it was unwise to give Iran such powerful weapons. America and Britain raised the most opposition to the arms sale because it was their soldiers on the ground fighting the Iranian-equipped insurgents. Soon, these fears came true because, according to the Britain's Telegraph, just forty-five days after the arms transfer, an American officer was shot dead while in an up-armored Humvee. A .50 caliber round punched through the two-inch thick bulletproof windshield and then struck the unlucky soldier. Since the Steyr-Iran transaction, more than a hundred HS50s were found by U.S. forces during raids of insurgent arms caches.[12]

Of course, Iran denied giving the weapons to the Iraqi insurgents. Most likely, Iran removed the serial numbers from the HS50s so they could not be traced and so Iran could at least have a thin veil of plausible deniability. This 'sanitizing' would take some work since Steyr places the weapon's serial number on the bolt, the barrel, and the frame (in order to ensure these precision crafted pieces are kept together). Even if it could be proven the rifles came from the 2005 transaction with Steyr, Iran could still deny any official involvement. Tehran could claim the weapons were stolen from their National Police or corrupt members of the National Police sold them to Iraqi insurgents without any approval from the Iranian government. Because Iran had a sophisticated covert warfare ability and much experience secretly aiding Iraq's insurgents with Explosively Formed Penetrators (EFPs), one seriously doubts Iran would have supplied these HS50 sniper rifles in such a manner that they could be traced back to Tehran. To date no one has been able to provide a serial number trace of the captured weapons to Steyr-Mannlicher. Steyr-Mannlicher noted their HS50 licensing rights have expired so the rifle can also be built elsewhere, like Canada.

Revolutionary Armed Forces of Colombia (FARC)

In January 2006, ten foreign nationals – nine Colombians and one Palestinian - were

12 Harding, *Iraqi Insurgents Using Austrian Rifles from Iran.*

indicted in a Miami federal court for a variety of crimes. All ten were captured in Bogota, Colombia as the culmination of a sophisticated sting operation. The ten were planning to smuggle people and drugs into the United States and intended, in turn, to transfer fifty .50 caliber sniper rifles and two helicopters to the FARC. While the ten thought they were dealing with representatives of Colombia's deadliest insurgency movement, they were in fact set up by under cover agents. If the would-be arms dealers did not get busted when they did, they could have easily acquired 50 heavy caliber rifles, legally, just like the KLA did. While the FARC did not receive any of the .50 caliber rifles from this criminal crew, the FARC, with their almost endless coffers of cocaine millions, could easily buy such weapons from any number of countries in the future.

Heavy Caliber Rifles in Action

Even though the destructive potential for heavy caliber rifles in an urban guerrilla war is immense, how come they are not being used? Al-Qaeda has more than a couple Barrett .50 caliber rifles in Afghanistan, so where are the NATO armored cars being shot up in Kabul and elsewhere? Only one IRA team successfully used a .50 caliber sniping rifle in their operations against the British. The KLA had several hundred .50 caliber sniper rifles, but where were the reports of Serbian helicopters, fuel dumps, and vehicles being shot up? The Iraqi insurgents had at least one hundred HS50 sniper rifles, but only managed to shoot a single soldier with them.

What about the juicy, lucrative targets all over the world from naval bases to commercial airports? A Rand study of attacks on military airfields from 1940-1992 failed to reveal a single attack by heavy caliber sniper rifles. Although small, unconventional forces using unsophisticated weapons have successfully destroyed or damaged over 2000 aircraft, the much-hyped sniper rifle has resulted in zero destroyed aircraft.[13] The Rand study on LAX noted, "since 1980, there have been over 8,000 terrorist attacks against aviation targets worldwide, killing over 5,000 people. Since 1974, LAX has been the target of two bombings, two attempted bombings, and one gun attack."[14] The only example of anyone having used a heavy caliber rifle to destroy aircraft was the American Marine Second Raider Battalion in World War II, which managed to shoot up two Japanese sea planes moored in the water off Makin Island with a Boys .55 caliber anti-tank rifle.

So, that is the total sum of heavy caliber sniper operations conducted by the world's collective guerrilla, insurgent, and terrorist organizations? The heavy caliber sniper rifle may be the most under-utilized weapon in the guerrilla inventory. Why? There are several reasons. First, most guerrilla organizations are as ignorant of the capabilities of a heavy caliber sniper rifle as their conventional counterparts. It took the world's major militaries decades to recognize the usefulness of the .50 caliber sniper rifle and they have been commercially available only since 1983. It may take awhile for the trend to catch on in guerrilla circles. Importantly, acquiring .50 caliber weapons and larger is not as easy as getting smaller-size weapons. Would anyone have noticed if Iran purchased .243 caliber varmint guns? I doubt it. Because .50 caliber size rifles and larger are relatively exotic, the purchase and sales of these big guns raise eyebrows.

13 Shlapak, David & Alan Vick, *Check Six Begins on the Ground*, p.36.
14 Stevens, *Near-Term Options for Improving Security at Los Angeles International Airport*.

Barrett XM-109 25 mm Rifle

This 25 mm anti-material rifle is relatively light in weight and has a range of 3000 meters. The XM -109 can take out the full spectrum of targets: planes, helicopters, ships, tanks, armored cars, and anything in between.

Finally, heavy caliber sniper rifles make the life of the guerrilla difficult. Despite the modern advancements in rifle design, a .50 caliber rifle is still cumbersome compared to something like a .44 magnum revolver. It is harder to transport a large rifle clandestinely, it is harder to set one up for firing while remaining undetected, it is harder to fire a .50 caliber beast and conceal its gunshot and muzzle flash, and it is harder to flee the scene of shooting with a thirty pound hunk of steel. I am not saying a guerrilla organization cannot use a large rifle covertly, it is just much more difficult. It takes a sophisticated, disciplined, well organized organization to acquire, transport, set up, fire, and then escape with a large weapon. Sloppy, immature organizations will fail at such a task. Only top-notch organizations can pull off such a feat repeatedly, professionally, and securely - like the IRA - and they were eventually caught.

Heavy caliber sniper rifles have great potential as an anti-material tool. They can take out enormous weapon systems like battleships and submarines, planes and helicopters, they can cause severe damage to civilian infrastructure like fuel farms, chemical plants, tankers, airports, and naval facilities, and they can render most security details for dignitaries irrelevant. However, an organization, be it a conventional military unit or a guerrilla movement, must educate themselves about the limitations and strengths of the big rifles before they can have any success with them. To date, most guerrilla movements have failed to appreciate the heavy caliber sniper rifle and have thus failed to develop the organizational infrastructure required to clandestinely and securely employ these weapons.

Chapter 19

Countering the
Urban Sniper

The third general type of sniper is the armed irregular. He may have little or no formal military training but may have much experience in urban combat. He may or may not wear any distinguishing uniform and may even strive to appear to be merely another of thousands of noncombatants found in a large urban area. He may or may not carry his weapon openly and may go to great lengths to avoid identification as a sniper.

- FM-91-10-1, An Infantry Guide to Combat in
Built-Up Areas, Appendix J, Countering Urban Snipers.

No Easy Answer

There is no simple solution for the problem presented by the urban guerrilla sniper. What works in one situation, environment, or time period may not work in another. Importantly, a security force or population will remain vulnerable to attack – no matter what they do – if they are ignorant of guerrilla sniper methodology. Ultimately, the only way to defeat or limit the guerrilla sniper is to study and understand them.

Checkpoints and Guard Towers

Any uniformed soldier or police officer is a potential target for a guerrilla sniper. Security personnel are a target by the mere fact they wear a uniform identifying who they are. And due to the very activities uniformed police and soldiers have to perform, such as walking patrols and manning checkpoints, they are doubly vulnerable. The urban environment is so complex, security forces have no hope of eliminating all potential threats. However, the probability of effective sniper attacks can be significantly reduced.

First, let us tackle the problem of static security positions like checkpoints and guard towers. Any uniformed person who stands in the same spot, in the open, day after day, is vulnerable to sniper attack. The Juba sniper video, as we studied in a previous chapter, reveals that static security positions are quite vulnerable. It does not matter if the soldier is sticking their head out of the hatch of a tank or standing in an open guard tower – they are victims waiting to happen. If a uniformed soldier has to

Sniper-Proof Tower

This Israeli watchtower is sniper-proof, protected by heavy gauge steel, concrete, and bullet-proof glass.

man a static position, they must protect themselves using either cover or concealment. To defeat the threat of PLO snipers, the Israelis built sniper-proof surveillance towers which they used to monitor the surrounding terrain. These towers were completely enclosed with bullet-proof glass and other bullet proof materials like steel and concrete. From these towers, Israeli soldiers could look out, but no bullets could get in. A completely bullet-proof structure is one way to protect a static guard post.

Another technique is to construct a guard post that completely conceals anyone inside. For example, a guard tower can be covered with heavy camouflage netting so the people inside can see and shoot out, but snipers cannot see in. Urban counter-snipers used a similar technique for years. When a counter-sniper team is required to fire from inside a building, they hang sheer netting from the ceiling to the floor, covering a window or open area they want to shoot from. From a distance, this netting looks like a solid wall. The snipers, who are close to the netting, can see and shoot through it.

A variation of the netting method is using a solid material, like sheets, to conceal oneself from a sniper. After John Mohammad and Lee Malvo began killing people in the DC area, local gas stations hung bed sheets around their gas pumps. This way, customers could drive up to a gas station, pass through a wall of bed sheets, and then stop next to a gas pump, while they were surrounded by the sheets. Of course, these sheets would not stop a bullet, but they did not have to since they concealed everything behind them. Hitting anyone behind the wall of sheets would be a matter of pure luck.

Security forces establishing temporary checkpoints on roads can use this same methodology. These checkpoint teams can bring with them, on each patrol, camouflage netting and the material necessary for hanging them. When they get to their location, they hang the netting around their position. In this manner, the cars and people to be searched enter a completely enclosed and camouflaged position, effectively isolating them from observation from a sniper. After the cars and people are searched or questioned, they exit the enclosed checkpoint, and go back into the open and on their way.

Body Armor

Body armor is another defensive measure that saves lives and makes a sniper's job harder. However, the capabilities and limitations of the body armor worn must be taken into consideration. For example, soft body armor, commonly worn by police officers, only stops bullets fired from pistols. Level IIIA soft body armor, which is standard issue for most police departments, will stop up to a .44 magnum pistol round, but nothing larger. In order for a person to be protected from a rifle round, they must wear hard armor made either of a steel or ceramic plate. Level IV hard body armor is designed to stop six 7.62 mm rifle rounds and still protect the wearer.

A soldier can also wear a protective helmet, but even the most modern Kevlar helmets will only stop a 9 mm pistol round because they only provide Level IIIA, not Level IV protection. Consequently, a 5.56 mm rifle round will go clean through a Kevlar helmet. A soldier wearing a protective helmet can only hope it will deflect an imperfectly aimed incoming rifle round because the helmet will not stop a dead on shot. Even Level IV body armor can be defeated with armor piercing ammunition or weapons like the big .50 caliber guns, so they should not be relied on to stop a sniper. To be sure, body armor makes a sniper's job more difficult because they will most likely be forced to shoot around the armor, at a much smaller body part, like the pelvis or head.

Foot Patrols

Soldiers conducting foot patrols in the open are less vulnerable than those conducting static checkpoints because they are moving. A checkpoint can be studied for days on end to engineer the perfect attack. In contrast, a foot patrol is a dynamic element able to take different routes every day and change their course at any moment to thwart ambush. However, foot patrols are still targeted by urban snipers simply because they are in the open. If a patrol takes the same route every day, they too are setting a pattern that can be studied and exploited by a patient shooter. The sniper's job may be more difficult and require a more flexible plan of attack, but some snipers prefer a moving target when the urban terrain works in their favor.

As discussed previously, British foot patrols in Northern Ireland were favorite targets for IRA snipers. IRA sniper teams would observe an approaching British patrol with a system of lookouts that included school-age children and housewives. From the information received from the lookouts, the sniper team could predict the patrol's route. The sniper team would set up in a location to ambush the patrol at an intersection. Patrols were at a disadvantage when crossing an intersection because a shot could come from any direction.

In response, British patrols routinely ran through intersections so a waiting sniper would have a fleeting target. They also developed techniques where they covered all avenues of approach leading into an intersection so if a sniper took a shot, someone was bound to see it. The British also used multiple patrols, working together, to thwart snipers. The idea was one element would move while another element provided cover from an elevated position like the roof of a building. Then, the teams switched duties and the first element provided cover while the other team moved. These sniper-savvy tactics were designed to defeat a sniper attack before it even happened because, if an

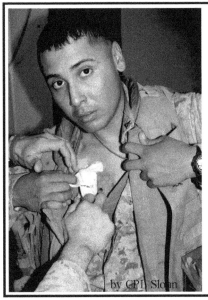

Body Armor

This Marine was shot in the chest by an insurgent sniper in Ramadi, Iraq. However, the Marine's Level IV, ceramic plate body armor stopped the bullet from penetrating and all he suffered was some bad bruising. Body armor makes a sniper's job much harder because they have a smaller target to hit in order to make a killing shot.

by CPL Sloan

IRA sniper saw a patrol employing effective counter-sniper tactics, they preferred to target a different, less vigilant patrol.

Preventative Measures

People who operate in the open can limit their exposure in other ways. Since we know snipers key in on lucrative targets like officers, radio operators, forward observers, close air support controllers, and other snipers, these people must conceal their identities from potential snipers. For instance, officers should not wear rank visible from a distance, superiors should not be saluted in the open (this is what soldiers call a 'sniper check'), and people should not give deference to their leaders in any manner detectable from a distance. Because, as a sniper searches for potential targets, they will look at body language – like standing at attention for a superior – to identify a person of rank.

Other key people, like radio operators, must conceal their radios and their duties. A communicator walking in the open with a radio on their back and an antenna sticking into the air is a dead man if a sniper sees him. Radio operators should conceal their radios in daypacks and use non-traditional modes of communication as opposed to their long-whip antennas. Communicators should consider weaving flexible whip or coax cable antennas into their gear, or consider using more concealable means of communications like walkie-talkies, cell, and satellite phones. Or, while on patrol, a communicator can move into a structure or an alley during a security halt, pull out their gear, and then make their communication in a covert manner.

The goal for soldiers operating in the open is concealment of information: to hide their rank, specific duties, and any special equipment or weapons to deny potential snipers an easy time of picking their targets. Ideally, everyone in a patrol should look as uniform as possible so no single person sticks out as more important than another. The patrol should start to act more like the guerrillas they are fighting, so the waiting sniper has a difficult time identifying who is who and who does what. There are many commercially available undercover equipment rigs for sale designed to be worn under a jacket to conceal ammunition, weapons, and equipment like radios. A unit can still conceal their equipment and weapons on their person, yet adhere to the laws of land warfare. This is a difficult thing to do for conventional military and police units because they are used to operating overtly, in either rural terrain (like the military) or in permissive, relatively peaceful environments (like the police). Units should consider training their men to change their rank oriented, overt cultures to deny snipers a unit-paralyzing shot.

Warnings for Soldiers and the Populace

In the chaotic world of the modern battlefield, nothing can be taken for granted. It only makes sense military units, policemen, and concerned citizens make an effort to warn others of the threat of enemy snipers. In World War II, all sides posted sniper warning signs, cautioning their own soldiers of the presence of enemy snipers as if they were warning people of 'Falling Rocks' or 'Bridge Ices Before Road'. This is because soldiers working a specific trench or neighborhood knew the threats in their area but, soldiers from rear supply units or from other organizations were oblivious to the threat of enemy snipers unless someone told them. In a business where ignorance can be a death sentence, it paid to inform your comrades. In Stalingrad, for example, both Germans and Russians put up warning signs, informing their men of particularly dangerous areas of the city.

While the IRA put up their infamous *Sniper At Work* signs in Northern Ireland to intimidate British patrols, the signs also served to warn both the enemy and fellow citizens a guerrilla sniper team was working in the area. In Beirut, during the civil war from 1975-1990, local radio stations announced the latest sniper activity to the city residents, cautioning them on where to go and not to go, like they were passing along a traffic report. This public courtesy allowed the various people living in the war torn city to buy their groceries, get gas, and visit relatives without taking a bullet along the way. The same was true of the besieged city of Sarajevo where the locals posted *Pazi! Snajper!* signs in order to warn uninformed citizens they were approaching Sniper's Alley or some other hazardous killing zone.

Vehicles

People traveling in vehicles may be less vulnerable to a sniper attack because of the protection provided by the vehicle and the fact they are moving. Conversely, in some cases, people in a vehicle may actually be more vulnerable to a sniper because they are a bigger target. Certainly, a regular, unarmored vehicle creates problems for a shooter. A car's windshield is thick and may deflect a bullet. Also, shooting through a car door may deflect and fragment a bullet, depending on the type of round fired and the weapon used. As a result, precision shooting through a car adds difficulties for the sniper.

However, a trained sniper can still shoot through a vehicle and hit their target. For instance, President Kennedy was shot in the throat by a high-velocity bullet that first went through the front windshield, was deflected downwards due to the angle of

With some irony, this SS shooter takes aim next to a sign warning of enemy snipers (*Scharfschutzen* in German).

the glass, and then found its mark. Snipers can also anticipate the negative effects of shooting through a vehicle by employing large caliber weapons that will go through a car door or windshield with little deflection. For example, a .50 caliber sniper rifle will penetrate a car door, a windshield, and even a car seat.

If a person is concerned with using a vehicle for protection from sniper attacks, they need an armored car with bulletproof glass and armor-plated doors. An armored vehicle can take many forms such as a regular car, like a Mercedes or BMW, modified to protect its occupants while appearing to be normal from the outside. Or, overtly armored cars can be used. The British police in Northern Ireland routinely drove armored Land Rovers for protection. In other wars, like those in Iraq and Chechnya, the conventional military forces employed heavily armored fighting vehicles like armored trucks, armored personnel carriers, and tanks. We should remember guerrilla snipers in Iraq, on one occasion, shot through the two-inch thick armored windshield of an American armored truck with a .50 caliber sniper rifle, hitting a soldier inside.

A person who rides in an armored vehicle, but exposes themselves outside the vehicle, are still vulnerable to attack. As mentioned previously, during the battle for Stalingrad, one of the greatest threats to German panzers was Russian snipers. Targeting an armored vehicle is an inherently effective technique for a sniper because the only person in the crew who has a chance to see where the shot came from is already dead. Consequently, despite a tank's massive firepower, they are relatively toothless when a careless crew member exposes themselves to a sniper.

Military organizations thus face the challenge of manufacturing armored vehicles that allow crew members to observe their surroundings without exposing themselves to snipers. Civilian armored cars, with a normal complement of windows, allow observation in all directions giving the occupants good situational awareness. One armored vehicle, produced by South Africa, the RG-31 Cougar, has a balance between good armor and good observation because the vehicle has bullet-proof windows and gun ports allowing observation in all directions.

Another dilemma faced by soldiers traveling in vehicles is they need to defend themselves against more than just snipers. They have to defend themselves against RPG attacks, roadside bombs, complex ambushes, and the like. Vehicles like the American Humvee employ a roof-mounted gunner as protection, but this leaves the gunner exposed to snipers. Newer versions of the Humvee have remotely controlled gun systems on the roof enabling the crew to return fire in all directions without anyone exposing themselves to enemy fire. A down side to this new Humvee is the occupants are crammed inside their claustrophobic truck so they have less situational awareness. A vehicle like this may be more secure from sniper attack, but is more vulnerable to other threats like IEDs and RPGs. An effective vehicle must balance protection from both snipers and other more lethal threats.

Get Out of the Kill Zone

When a person comes under fire by a sniper, they must take immediate action to reduce their vulnerability. The first thing a person under fire should do is take cover. For instance, a single individual can get off the street and into an armored vehicle. A squad of soldiers can seek cover in a nearby building. It is of the utmost importance the targeted person or persons leave the immediate area and get out of the sniper's line of fire. Since a sniper usually establishes a position allowing them to focus on a specific location, moving out of the sniper's kill zone may be all it takes. Of course, there are exceptions to every rule and we must remember Charles Whitman was able to shoot people in all directions from atop the Texas Tower. In that case, some of Whitman's victims thought they were moving to a safer area when in fact they were only exposing themselves more.

Immediate action drills must take into account a member of a patrol may be shot with the sniper's first bullet. So, as a group of men react to the sniper's first shot and find cover, a member of the team may be caught in the open because they are dead or wounded. In fact, a sniper may intentionally wound a patrol member to lure other members out and into the open who are in turn shot. A common method of dealing with this problem is the use of hand thrown smoke grenades to block a sniper's view of their target. If a member of a patrol is shot by a sniper, their teammates take cover, throw smoke grenades to obscure the sniper's field of vision, and then rescue their wounded mate while under the cover of smoke. The smoke is not bullet-proof, but it is the equivalent of hanging bed sheets around a gas pump – a sniper would have to get lucky to make a shot through the smoke in order to hit someone.

Battlefield Detectives

Once the targeted persons react to the initial sniper attack, they must become battlefield detectives. The first thing battlefield detectives do is determine from what direction the sniper fired from. The direction may be determined from a combination of things to include: the sound of the gunshot, observable muzzle blast/flash, and the impact of the bullet itself. Once the direction is determined, the distance to the sniper is estimated. This can also be deduced from a variety of clues like the time between hearing the supersonic crack of the bullet and hearing the actual gunshot, the force of

Bullet Proof Turret

After an airman was shot and killed by an Iraqi insurgent sniper, the deceased airman's unit built this protective gun turret out of bullet-proof glass.
by DoD

impact of the bullet, and likely places the sniper could be hiding in.

If a person sees the bullet's impact and hears the gunshot simultaneously, then the sniper is probably 300 meters or closer. If a person sees the bullet impact first (or hears the supersonic crack first) and then the gunshot, the shooter is further away, maybe 500 meters or more. Trying to determine the sniper's distance from sound alone creates problems because so many variations come into play. What speed is the bullet traveling? What is the speed of sound at your location and elevation? Is the sniper using a suppressor or subsonic ammunition?

Another important element for determining the sniper's direction and distance is the angle of the bullet. A bullet striking at a severe angle must have been fired from a tall structure, while a bullet striking the target at a perpendicular angle must have been fired from a street level position. A common method of backtracking the azimuth of a shot is to stick a weapon cleaning rod in a hole made by the bullet and see where the rod points. In Stalingrad, Vassili Zaitsev would hold up a helmet or mitten with a board to get enemy snipers to shoot through it. Once they shot the board, Vassili held the board up and looked back through the hole and directly at where the shot came from.

After evaluating the probable direction, distance, and angle the shot was made from, the battlefield detective makes an educated guess where the sniper is located. Once a location is determined, the targeted persons evaluate the assets available to them and choose a course of action based on the environment they are operating in. If the security forces are operating in an environment of extreme restraint, such as the British in Northern Ireland or American law-enforcement in the United States, then the targeted persons have limited options. An acceptable response would be surrounding the suspected sniper to capture them as they flee or to kill the gunman up close to limit collateral damage. If security forces succeed in surrounding the sniper, they still must identify the suspected shooter. This requires them to separate the guilty party from the surrounding innocent people. The responding security forces can only do this if they have the proper tools like gunshot residue detection kits, dogs trained in detecting gunpowder, and the ability to effectively question potential eyewitnesses to gather incriminating testimony.

The Importance of Restraint

Soldiers and police fighting a guerrilla war must understand restraint and thorough investigations are the best ways to defeat the urban guerrilla sniper. This is especially true when a sniper fires from a populated area to get an overreaction from security forces. The sniper wants the security forces to respond with artillery barrages, air strikes, and tank shells so they kill innocent civilians and destroy their own city. Every time security forces overreact with massive firepower, they provide prime propaganda for the guerrillas' cause, alienate the people from the government, and increase the costs of repairing their own city.

What the guerrilla sniper fears most is an educated response backed up with a relentless investigation into the shooting. A guerrilla wants their victims to shoot at everything around them that moves. This kind of emotional, knee-jerk reaction makes their job easier. In contrast, a trained, disciplined, educated patrol will quickly take cover and analyze the impact of the bullet to determine its back azimuth. Once a rough azimuth is determined, the patrol sets up counter-snipers and scans for the enemy. The patrol sets up a video camera and films the surrounding area for later use as evidence and to closely study the terrain, like people coming to and from the sniper's suspected location. The patrol then moves from cover to cover towards the suspected shooter's location, questions people, and searches for incriminating evidence. The guerrilla sniper does not want to encounter this kind of patrol.

If the targeted security forces are not operating under restraint, they may be able to kill the sniper using other methods. For example, if a patrol determines a sniper is in a particular building, security forces may want to destroy the entire building using heavy artillery, rocket launchers, attack helicopters, or precision aerial bombs. Always, security forces must understand the use of unrestrained firepower to take out a single sniper will result in significant structural damage and possibly civilian deaths.

In many wars – like Israel fighting in Lebanon in the 1980's and Germany fighting in Russia in World War II – the forces responding to an enemy sniper may not care about collateral damage. In fact, they may prefer to inflict disproportionate damage on the surrounding population in an attempt to deter future attacks. One must remember, when the Germans in Stalingrad pounded the city into ruins, they did not make the place any safer from Russian snipers. Just the opposite was true. The same could be said of the Russian destruction of Grozny and the American devastation of Fallujah. The rubbling of any urban area creates more sniper hides. In every situation, the responding forces must balance the destruction of infrastructure and the danger to the populace with the need to eliminate the sniper threat.

Counter-Sniper Teams

If massive force is ineffective or counter-productive or a skilled sniper shows a superior tactical ability thwarting all attempts to locate and surround them, security forces may need to employ their own counter-snipers to combat their unseen foe. A

Get Out of the Kill Zone

In this picture, a Marine is shot by an insurgent sniper in Fallujah, Iraq. The other two Marines in the photo were also shot as they tried to save their comrade.

by DoD

sniper team has some advantages as a counter-sniper weapon because they understand the art of sniping, how the enemy operates, what their mindset is, and they know the tricks of the trade. Often, it takes a sniper to catch a sniper.

In Stalingrad, Vassili Zaitsev and his specially trained snipers became a counter-sniper fire brigade. Whenever the hard-pressed Russians found themselves under the gun of an effective German sniper, they called in their own snipers to deal with the problem. Zaitsev and his fellow snipers were particularly effective in counter-sniper duties because they were skilled battlefield investigators and knew how to reverse engineer the scene of a shooting to determine the enemy snipers' locations. In most cases, a sniper team has a basic understanding of sniper forensics and can readily apply this knowledge on the battlefield.

Once a sniper team is brought in to track down an enemy sniper, it becomes a battle of wits and tactical ability. Standard counter-sniper methodology begins with determining the general area the enemy is operating in. Once this is known, the counter-snipers use their own experience to narrow down where they think their enemy is positioned. Then, the team sets up a clandestine hide site where they can view the terrain. In short, the counter-sniper team tries to out-sniper their opponent who is using the same techniques against them.

After the counter-sniper team moves into position undetected, they observe the terrain and search for the enemy. The counter-sniper team may catch their opponent moving to or from their sniper position. Or, the team may observe their opponent already set up in their position, unaware they are being stalked. Additionally, the enemy may reveal their position by exhibiting unnatural behavior. They might be seen with incriminating physical evidence (like holding a gun in their hands), or be exposed by a flash of light off their scope. If the team cannot find the sniper through observation alone, they might give their enemy bait and lure them into revealing their location.

A classic baiting technique is showing the enemy sniper something to get them to fire a shot, such as the top of a helmet or a stuffed dummy that looks like a human. The effort a counter-sniper team makes to coax a shot from their enemy is limited only by their imaginations. During World War II, German snipers were taught to construct elaborate life-like dummies with paper mache heads and moving arms. They even placed a burning cigarette in the dummy's hand, moved the cigarette to the dummy's head by a string as if smoking, and then blew smoke through a straw attached to the dummy's head. From a distance, the dummy looked like a careless German sentry having a smoke.

Once the sniper is coaxed into making a shot, the counter-sniper team observes their enemy's muzzle flash/blast and responds in kind. This duel is truly a chess game because the sniper and counter-sniper both try to reveal each other's positions through tricks, baits, and ruses. The superior thinker and tactician wins.

In an urban environment, it is helpful for the counter-sniper team to secure a dominant position, which in the city means an elevated one. From an elevated position, the counter-sniper team can see more of the surrounding terrain and may be protected from enemy fire from a lower elevation. In Stalingrad, some of the best sniper positions were in the towering smokestacks in the northern factory district. The snipers positioned atop these chimneys did not have to worry about being outflanked by a sniper in a superior position. In Israel, the Israelis perfected the art of creating their own elevated positions by raising encased shooting platforms into the air, high above the surrounding buildings, dangling from the ends of heavy cranes. From these metal and glass boxes, the Israeli snipers had dominant bird's eye views of the urban terrain, helping them to better target their enemies. Law enforcement counter-sniper teams all over the world routinely set up their positions atop the highest structures in the area so they have the best fields of observations. In the cities, a dominant sniper position may be atop an apartment building, a skyscraper, a radio tower, some scaffolding, or even a crane.

Minimize the Target

An important counter-sniper tactic is simply limiting one's exposure to potential snipers. Do not stand in the middle of an intersection if you can stand behind a wall or car. Do not silhouette yourself by standing on the roof of a building when you can lie down behind an object like a water tank or a generator. Do not stand outside if you can be inside an armored vehicle or inside a building. Do not stand in front of window or a doorway if you can stand to the side and still see outside. Do not stand in the light if you can stand in the shadows. In short, use all of the possible protection available in an urban environment to limit a sniper's view of their potential target.

An effective counter-sniper tool used extensively in World War II on the Eastern Front was the unsung scissors periscope. The scissors periscope was used widely by artillery observers to call in fire and commanders to survey the battlefield in safety. As the war went on, both sides discovered the periscope was an excellent tool to observe the surrounding terrain, free from the fire of enemy snipers. On the German side, in Stalingrad, panzer commanders used periscopes to look outside their tanks, and artillery observers, snipers, guard posts, and various leaders all used the periscope to observe the urban terrain while avoiding death at the hands of the omnipresent Rus-

Elevation

In an urban environment, elevation gives a counter-sniper team an advantage over their enemy.

sian snipers.

The simple periscope can still be used today to achieve the same effects and limit exposure of soldiers in sniper-plagued areas. Soldiers in guard towers, vehicles, and sniper hides, as well as those on patrol, can all benefit from the trusty periscope. The periscope allows them to search for enemy snipers, conduct post-shooting assessments, and perform a myriad of battlefield duties in complete safety from a sniper's gaze. Today, there are good tactical periscopes available that are lightweight, affordable, and durable. Believe it or not, the excellent Russian trench periscope from World War II is still available today through surplus stores for as little as $100.00.

Long-Term Investigations

It is quite possible security forces will encounter an urban guerrilla sniper who is superior to them in tactics and methodology and consistently avoids battlefield detection and the best efforts of counter-sniper teams. In these cases, firepower and battlefield measures are ineffective and possibly irrelevant. The next step is conducting a long-term investigation by a dedicated team of professional detectives. Security forces will have to discover the identity of the shooter through the analysis of forensic evidence and good police work to capture the sniper when the sniper is not 'on the job'.

One idea is to place a bounty on the head of the sniper to get the public involved in the search for the shooter. Security forces must then establish the means for the public to contact them like establishing dedicated hot lines, email addresses, and distributing the addresses and phone numbers of local police stations where people can come in to deliver relevant tips. The government can also marshal other resources and show pictures or a description of the suspected shooter on television, air this information on the radio, and place notices in newspapers, on flyers, billboards, and web sites. The battle thus becomes one of information flow. As an example, the police never did solve John Muhammad and Lee Malvo's urban sniper tactics. But by engaging the public to help find the snipers terrorizing them, the police got a call on their hotline by a person who revealed the shooters' identities. The police did not capture the DC snipers in the act, they caught them sleeping at a rest stop.

In other environments, law enforcement officials may be incompetent, corrupt, or terrorized into inaction, and incapable of conducting effective long-term investigations. In countries like modern Afghanistan, Iraq, Somalia, and Chechnya, the government may suffer from weak institutions and face a largely hostile population uninterested in helping the government solve their sniper problem. Traditional investigations may therefore be impossible through the local police. In these situations, the guerrilla organization sponsoring the sniper has to be infiltrated either through human agents or technical means of penetration like radio and cellular phone intercepts.

Infiltration and Deception

In order to capture some guerrilla snipers, security forces will have to infiltrate the guerrilla organization with an agent. An infiltrator can get into an organization in several ways. An infiltrator can volunteer or be selected into an organization through the group's established recruiting mechanism. Under cover police use this method to infiltrate crime organizations like the Mafia, motorcycle gangs, and other organized criminal groups. Once inside the organization, the infiltrator builds trust with the group and covertly collects information leading to the identity of the sniper.

Or, an existing member of the guerrilla organization may be recruited by the government to become an agent. There are several reasons a guerrilla may do this. First, a member may be disillusioned with the cause or reject the methods the group is using on moral, religious, or personal grounds. Eamon Collins, a one-time intelligence officer for the IRA, eventually left that organization and provided an avalanche of information to the British authorities because he grew weary of the war and no longer had the personal commitment to live such an extremely stressful double-life (he was later executed by the IRA). A member may also choose to help the government out of simple greed. In one infamous case in the United States, the FBI's counterintelligence agent Robert Hanssen voluntarily sold information to the Russian KGB for years and received $1.4 million in cash and precious stones. Many insurgents in Iraq have given up information on a sniper for a lot less.

Another means for getting information about the sniper may come through the questioning/interrogation of a captured member of the sniper's guerrilla organization. The German Gestapo of World War II frequently gathered critical information on resistance groups through the brutal beating and torture of captured partisans. The French in Algeria, from 1954-1962, also used torture to extract key information from captured Algerian insurgents (favorite French methods included electrocution, burning with blow torches, and drowning). The French methods were credited by some for their ability to crack the guerrilla network operating out of the capital of Algiers. However, an interrogation does not have to be brutal to be effective. Captured members of illegal organizations all over the world - from common prison gangs to the Taliban – have all provided information of some sort to security forces through persistent, skilled questioning by trained interrogators.

Battlefield Detectives

American soldiers in Germany search for hidden snipers.

National Archives

If the human element fails to work for security forces, they may find success with technical means of infiltration. To start, security forces can covertly install electronic listening devices in guerrilla safehouses, residences, or places of work. Security forces can tap the phone lines of suspected guerrillas and intercept their cell phone conversations or radio transmissions. Through these collection methods, security forces may learn of specific information leading to the identity of the sniper. A good example of both human and technical means of infiltration was when British forces got inside the Goldfinger sniper crew with an informant and (most likely) technical equipment. Despite repeated sniper attacks against British soldiers, the Goldfinger crew was never caught in the act. The crew was only busted wide open when a member on the inside gave up his own people.

If security forces cannot penetrate a guerrilla organization through human or technical means, they can make the guerrillas falsely believe they are compromised. For example, Paddy Flood was one of the IRA's top bomb makers and an accomplished sniper who worked out of Derry, Northern Ireland. Since the British were unable to kill him because of the political fall out, they had their informants inside the IRA finger Paddy as a double agent working for the Special Branch. The IRA swallowed the bait because one day in 1990, when Paddy went out to deliver a message for the IRA, he never came back. Only weeks later did his badly mutilated body show up gagged, hands bound behind his back, and shot in the head. The IRA thought he was a stool pigeon, so they killed him. Years later, well after the Good Friday peace agreement in 1998, the IRA realized they were deceived – Paddy was never an informant, but they were led to believe so.[1]

A Counter-Sniper Story: The Ramadi Rooftop Executions

Ramadi, Iraq - the capital of Al-Anbar Province and the heart of the Sunni led

---

1 Harkin, *How FRU got IRA to Murder Top Sniper*, June 23, 2002, Sunday People.

insurgency - was a dangerous place. Ever since American troops occupied Ramadi in the spring of 2003, they were locked in a vicious contest of wills with determined insurgents. In Ramadi, American and Iraqi security forces experienced the full gamut of guerrilla warfare: car bombings, IEDs, kidnappings and the inevitable torture and executions that followed, ambushes, drive-bys, mortar attacks, and everything in between. On any given day, one was likely to hear the sharp crack of a rifle and then the whiz of a bullet as opposing snipers tried to eliminate each other with a single, well-aimed shot. The situation in Ramadi got so bad that in 2005, a senior American intelligence officer reported that American forces did not control anything past the range of their guns and they had lost all of Al Anbar to the insurgents.

One piece of the Americans' security plan in Ramadi involved the establishment of sniper posts at key locations in the city. At these outposts, U.S. snipers quietly observed the urban terrain, reported to higher any relevant information about the enemy, and placed discriminating fire into insurgent gunmen so foolish as to expose themselves. Many American snipers in Ramadi – feared by the insurgents for their skill - had multiple kills to their credit as survival of the fittest led to careless enemy gunmen getting picked off one by one. In turn, the insurgents looked for any chance to rid themselves of those deadly shooters.

In June 2004, the 2nd Battalion, 4th Marine Regiment established three sniper posts overlooking 'Route Michigan', the main highway running through Ramadi. One of the sniper posts was located less than a kilometer from the main American base called 'Combat Outpost'. This particular sniper post was located in a two-story house, owned by a local Iraqi family, which was only partially built and still under construction. This made for a good location because the Marines did not have to dislocate an Iraqi family to use the building. Every couple of days the four-man sniper team positioned on the roof of the half-built structure was relieved and rotated out with a different team. This system gave the teams time to rest and recover as constant vigilance, 24-hours a day, was mentally and physically fatiguing. Just staring through a sniper scope in the oppressive heat for more than a few minutes, watching the heat waves and mirages dance off the burning pavement, wore you out.

In the early morning hours of June 24, at about one a.m., it was time for a new team to rotate into the outpost. The new team consisted of four Marines: Corporal Tommy Parker Jr., Lance Corporal Deshon Otey, Lance Corporal Juan Lopez, and Lance Corporal Pedro Contreras. Corporal Parker was the team leader and the only school-trained sniper in the group. Initially, everything went as planned. Parker's team left the base under the cover off darkness, drove to their outpost in Humvees, and took up positions in the house as the other team went back to the base to recover.

When the sun came up over Al Anbar Province and drenched Ramadi with its unmerciful rays, something was amiss. Parker's team was supposed to report in every thirty minutes to the main base, Combat Outpost. They did so for most of the morning, but then the reports stopped. This in itself was nothing to be alarmed about, because radios had problems all the time and it might take a little while to get them working again. Combat Outpost knew this and their policy was to send a Quick Reaction Force (QRF) to a sniper post only after two hours had gone by. According to official reports, a passing Marine patrol decided to check in with the outpost, just to be sure, less than an hour after the last check by Parker's team.

When the patrol made it to the outpost at around 11:30 there were no greetings by

Counter-Sniper Tactics

Iraq: One Marine holds up a helmet, hoping to bait a guerrilla sniper. The other Marine is looking for the enemy's muzzle flash so he can zero in on it and shoot the enemy through the loop hole in the wall.

photo by CPL Chavem

Parker's team, there was no guard standing alertly at the entrance, and, in fact, there was no sound at all. The patrol walked up the stairs to the roof to see what was going on and was horrified at what they saw – all four soldiers were dead and now laid in pools of their own blood. Three of them were shot in the head at point blank range and another one suffered multiple gunshot wounds to the body. One Marine even had his throat slit. How did this happen? How did four experienced Marines get killed in broad daylight and never even get off a single shot, all without any sounds being heard? It took a thorough investigation by the Naval Criminal Investigative Service (NCIS) to piece together the killings, but they came up with a likely scenario.

It was no secret the Marines were using the outpost. In fact, the Marines used the same building so often the Iraqis living in the area knew it was a sniper post. Some of the Marines thought this was a bad idea because they were setting a pattern the enemy could study and then make a plan for. Parker himself knew they were setting themselves up for an ambush and sooner or later they would get hit. Before that fateful June morning, Parker told his wife, Carla, "No wonder people are dying. They're sending us to the same place, by the same route at the same time of day." Also, before the killings, other Marines on patrol saw Iraqis entering the building, holding conversations as if they were discussing how to finish up construction on the house the Marines were using as an outpost. These Iraqis knew the house intimately and knew the exact location and procedures of the Marines using the house. This access to and knowledge of the house proved fatal.

The NCIS investigators later determined the Iraqi 'Carbede' family put out a 'hit' on the sniper team. Investigators know this because an intercepted cell phone conversation between Carbede family members revealed they authorized the hit and, "they were going to 'do these Marines.'" Then, a four-man hit team was assembled to take them out. Since the Marines' patterns were already known, as was the exact layout of the house, the hit team was able to study their objective and come up with a plan to take out the Marines. Instead of fighting the Marines one on one, the hit team decided to use deception and pose as construction workers. Some time in the morning this hit team arrived at the house.

No one knows what happened exactly, except the hit team. But here is a possible scenario: The hit team drove up near the outpost and got out of their car. They walked to the house dressed as laborers with accompanying paraphernalia like toolboxes and paint buckets. The hit team was cautious, but they did not try and hide their presence either. They walked right up to the house, went inside, and started to work on the house with their tools. One of the Marines probably went downstairs and investigated, gun at the ready. However, the cautious Marine was met with a wave of a hand, a friendly smile, and a jovial, "Hello, mister!" Since the Iraqis were obviously working on the house, were not trying to hide anything, and worked on the house in the past, the Marine thought nothing of it and went back to the roof.

The sniper team continued to call in their reports every half an hour, but failed to mention anything about the Iraqis in the house because the men worked there in the past, the outpost never reported the workers before, and the four men looked like harmless construction workers. The hit team worked in the house as they observed the Marines. They worked their way up to the second floor so they were near the stairwell leading to the roof. One of the hit men began working on or near the stairs so he had a good view of the Marines on the roof. As the Iraqi worked diligently on his project, he stole glances at the roof, pinpointing exactly where the Marines were and what they were doing. He could see two of the Americans were lying down asleep and the other two were focused on watching Route Michigan.

The hit team kept one man near the roof as a lookout as the other three went down to the first floor, made a plan, and got out their weapons. The time was 10:40 a.m. They went back up to the second floor and their lookout nodded to them – the Marines were completely vulnerable and not worried about them at all. It was now or never. The shooters walked calmly past their lookout and up onto the roof with their folding-stock AK-47's silenced with sound suppressors. The two Marines who were on sniper duty, Otey and Lopez, were shot first. Parker and Contreras, who were lying asleep on the roof, never heard a thing and were shot next since they were no immediate threat to the killers.

As soon as the shooting was over, one of the killers left the building to get the car. Another man went to the bottom floor to act as a lookout. The other two stripped the dead Marines of all their equipment to include two sniper rifles (one of which was Corporal Parker's rifle), four M16A4s, twenty-four magazines for the M16s, eight hand grenades, the Marines' PRC-119F radio, and an excellent AN/PAS-13 thermal weapon sight for shooting at night. As soon as their car was ready, the team loaded the stolen equipment into the trunk. It took a couple minutes to get it all, but they had plenty of time. They knew exactly what Combat Outpost's patrol schedule was. It was less than ten minutes from the time the first shots were fired to the time all four men were in their car driving off. By 10:50 a.m., the hit team was gone, on their way to a safehouse somewhere in the city. Only at 11:30 did the Marine patrol arrive and find out why the outpost was not returning their calls.[2]

Analysis of the Rooftop Killings

---

2 Lowe, *Rooftop Execution: NCIS report provides details of sniper deaths.* (Information and quotes about this story came from the article by Mr. Lowe.)

photo by DoD **Sniper Bait**

The Marines killed in the outpost were taken by complete surprise by the insurgents' unconventional methods. The Marines were ready to defend themselves from the most likely threat - an opposing sniper - and the insurgents knew this. While the Marines were well prepared for the obvious attack, they left their back door wide open, quite literally. The Marines' biggest error was using a half-built house for an outpost and continuing to let the laborers work on it. Since the house was still under construction, the insurgents knew they could use a ruse and pose as workers to gain access into the building. The Marines in the outpost got sloppy, never searched the workers, and failed to place a guard on them as they worked.

Since the Marines in Ramadi interacted with and worked in close proximity to Iraqi civilians all the time, day after day, they were overwhelmed by the sheer number of people. They were unable to distinguish an insurgent from innocent people as the insurgents blended in with the population. As long as the insurgents looked and acted like everyone else when the Americans were watching them, they were invisible. The insurgents who took out the outpost were able to do so because they mimicked the dress, body language, and actions of a regular work crew. There was nothing to indicate they were anything other than poor workers trying to make a living. In short, the insurgents took advantage of the complex, uncertain environment that is modern urban guerrilla warfare.

Not only did the insurgents exploit the urban and human terrain, they developed and executed a well-thought out plan of action. Obviously, they studied the Marine outpost in depth, knew the Marines' procedures, understood the quick reaction force's limitations, and were able to pull off, in broad daylight, an utterly silent hit (most likely with suppressed weapons, after all how did no one hear all the shooting when the outpost was on a roof only 800 meters from Combat Outpost, which housed thousands of soldiers?). No matter how one looks at it, this was a successful operation due to accurate intelligence, detailed planning, and maximum use of use of deception and surprise.

The insurgents benefited from this counter-sniper operation in many ways. First, they captured two excellent sniper rifles that could not be traced to them in any way. Even the M16A4s were accurate enough to be urban sniper weapons. Second, the capture of the AN/PAS-13 thermal sight allowed some guerrilla sniper in the future to target American soldiers at night, when it was pitch-black out, because thermal sights do not require any light source whatsoever to be effective. Third, the killing of the Marines provided great material for insurgent propaganda that was distributed on the internet for the world to see and given away on CD's in Iraq's streets for the average Iraqi to watch. Finally, the killings contributed greatly to a Marine Corps reaction requiring more Marines to go out on a sniper mission, making these sniper operations less effective and more vulnerable to detection because of their increased signature.

Two Years Later: Payback in Habbaniyah

In the sweltering heat of the Iraqi summer, a United States Marine Corps scout sniper team from the 3rd Battalion, 5th Marine Regiment lay in wait in a concealed sniper hide near Habbaniyah, Iraq. The date was June 16, 2006. As the team surveyed the urban terrain, they noticed something out of the ordinary. A military-age Iraqi male was sitting in the back seat of a parked passenger car, filming a passing American Marine patrol consisting of amphibious assault vehicles. The team also observed a rifle in the back seat. The Marine sniper team radioed down to the patrol that they were being watched by a sniper and to take caution. After warning the patrol, the guerrilla sniper reached for his rifle in preparations for making a shot.

The Marine sniper observed this and drew a bead on the insurgent's head. One well-placed round was enough to kill the would-be sniper. The heavy 7.62 mm bullet struck the rear passenger window, shattered the glass, deflected very little off its flight path, and punched straight into the sniper's head. There was very little bullet deflection because the rear glass of the window was thin and weak and the target's head was close to the window, only about a foot away. Then, the Marine snipers saw another young Iraqi male approach the passenger side door of the vehicle. He was surprised to find his companion dead in the back seat of their car. This second male then ran to the other side of the car and tried to drive off. He never had a chance. The Marine snipers shot him with three rounds from an M-4 carbine firing 5.56 mm rounds. The driver died on the scene. As the Marines searched the car, they discovered the rifle in the back seat was one of their own: a camouflaged, Marine-issue, 7.62 mm, M-40A1 sniper rifle.

After searching the vehicle, the Marines found some tools of the trade the Iraqi snipers had with them. The insurgents had several different license plates so they could change the identity of the car. License plates were important for deceiving the local police since different provinces used different plates and there were different levels of plates, like the much sought after official government plates. There were also several dozen of rounds of 7.62 mm ammo for the M40A1 rifle, a pistol, a camcorder,

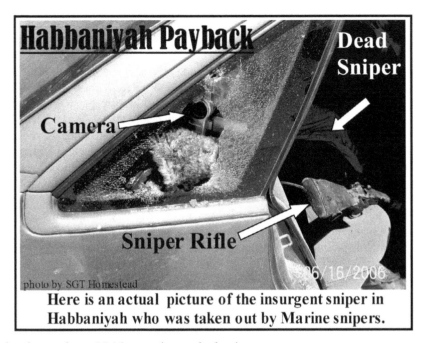

Here is an actual picture of the insurgent sniper in Habbaniyah who was taken out by Marine snipers.

a hand grenade, an M-16 magazine, and other items.

What intrigued the Marines most was that the insurgent sniper team used one of their very own sniper rifles against them. Over the course of the previous three years of guerrilla warfare in Iraq, the Marines lost several of their sniper rifles to the insurgents after Marine sniper teams were killed by the guerrillas and stripped of their equipment. So where did this rifle come from? Who owned it last? Since the rifle still had a serial number, it was an easy task to check the number with the Marines' own records. The serial number trace revealed this was the same rifle issued to Corporal Parker several years ago and stripped from his body on that Ramadi rooftop. The rifle had come full circle.

The Insurgent Sniper Team's Methodology

What can we determine about this guerrilla sniper team? First, they were probably an experienced team and conducted similar attacks in the past. They were professionals as can be seen by their choice of a car as their firing platform. Since a car is a mobile platform, the sniper can shoot, drive off, and disappear in seconds. Also, they chose a car, not a van, as a van would be a more obvious choice as a sniping platform. Also, the team understood the importance of information warfare and used every sniper attack as a propaganda victory over the American occupiers. The sniper intended to film the American patrol as it approached, set the camcorder on the rear seat with the patrol still in its view, take a shot so it was all captured on film, and then drive away.

This team had different jobs during their attack. The driver's job was to find a good location to park the car. His second was to get out, walk around, and conduct a reconnaissance of the are to make sure there were no threats to the sniper. In this case, the driver failed to detect the Marine sniper team hidden in a nearby building. One can guess when the Marine sniper fired his shot and killed the guerrilla sniper, the driver of the car thought the gunshot was from his companion. Hence, when the driver got back to the car to take off, he was surprised to see his dead friend sprawled across the back seat.

The insurgent sniper team was good, but made several crucial mistakes. First, the driver did not study the urban terrain sufficiently and failed to detect the opposing Marine snipers. Regardless, every guerrilla sniper must prepare for their shot as if they were under direct observation, regardless if they detect a threat or not. The insurgent sniper team failed to employ any urban camouflage like tinted windows, stickers, curtains, or sun shades even though they were readily available in the local Iraqi markets and would raise no suspicion. Because the insurgent sniper failed to effectively conceal himself within the car, he was observed by an American sniper with a clear view of his activities through the unobstructed glass of the vehicle. Another mistake the sniper made was letting himself be observed while openly filming an American convoy with a camcorder. In the wartime environment of Iraq, anyone seen filming security forces is presumed to be gathering information for a future attack. A guerrilla must conceal everything they do and the camcorder could have easily been concealed in a plastic bag with a hole cut out for the camera lens.

The final mistake the insurgent sniper made was reaching for his sniper rifle, in the open, without camouflaging the weapon in any way. For unknown reasons, the rifle was not concealed in urban camouflage like a newspaper, a jacket, or a simple scarf. Importantly, the American sniper knew he could take a shot because he saw the insurgent sniper reach for his rifle. In this case, the insurgent sniper team made numerous mistakes which ultimately contributed to their deaths.[3]

The Limits of Counter-Sniper Tactics

Ultimately, none of these counter-sniper methods work and even collectively they will not solve the threat of snipers. What do I mean by this? These methods may work against a lone sniper like Charles Whitman in the Texas Tower or the DC snipers. A determined, entrenched, mature guerrilla movement using snipers on a large scale is a different beast altogether. A covert organization designed to survive security force scrutiny is so resilient and has so many potential targets to choose from they can never be stopped altogether. Their effects can only be limited. The only way to stop the threat of guerrilla snipers is to defeat the movement spawning these shooters.

History supports this rather sober assessment. If we look back some sixty-plus years to the Battle of Stalingrad, the sniper war there only ceased when the Red Army surrounded and crushed the defeated German Sixth Army. Israel, considered by many to be one of the best militaries in the world, has failed to stop PLO snipers from killing their soldiers and people for the last forty years. The British and their counter-insurgency machine in Northern Ireland also never stopped the threat of IRA snipers from 1969 to1998. The IRA only stopped shooting people after they signed the Good Friday peace agreement in 1998 and voluntarily put down their arms. The urban sniper-terror in Sarajevo, perpetrated by Serbian shooters, came to conclusion in 1996 when both sides agreed to end the war. Today, Russian troops still suffer from sniper attacks by a

---

3 Sixbey, *Darkhorse snipers kill insurgent sniper, recover stolen Marine sniper rifle.* (All information about this event came from an article written by Mr. Sixbey.)

bloodied and bruised Chechen resistance movement whose elements have continued to fight on since 1994. In a final example, American forces only stopped taking large numbers of sniper casualties after 2007 when they came to an agreement with Sunni tribal leaders.

Widespread education and training in counter-sniper tactics will reduce the vulnerability of a populace and security forces to guerrilla snipers. It is better to have only one hundred sniper victims a year, as opposed to a thousand. But, as history has repeatedly shown, only a death blow to the guerrilla organization sponsoring a sniper campaign will lower the crosshairs from their targets permanently.

Chapter 20

Sniper Forensics

Just as we find it necessary to understand the enemy's interrogation techniques or surveillance and to train to overcome such obstacles, so too we must tackle the problem of Forensic Science.

- IRA Counter-Forensics Manual

Many of the shots were from the back of a specially converted car which was immediately driven away to avoid leaving any forensic traces.

- From the British report on Operation Banner, referencing the PIRA's Goldfinger sniper crew in South Armagh

The Foundation for Successful Counter-Sniping

Effective counter-insurgency forces have at their foundation a forensic mindset. This forensic approach enables security forces to take a discriminatory approach to counter-sniper operations. This discrimination minimizes civilian casualties, reduces infrastructure damage, and therefore limits a guerrilla organization's most potent weapon – bad press which shows government security forces as incompetent at best and murderous at worst. Importantly, forensic investigation is a way for security forces to pick the lone guerrilla out of the sea of people. Plus, forensic investigation increases the guerrilla sniper's problems. Even if the shooter escapes the government's massive firepower or immediate dragnet of security forces, a competent team of investigators may still run them to ground. These investigators may not get the sniper right away, but they will collect evidence over the course of days, weeks, months, and even years, leading to eventual exposure of the sniper. However, every war is different and guerrilla snipers face varying levels of forensic scrutiny depending on their own unique operational environment. We will briefly look at the forensic situations in Northern Ireland, Chechnya, and Iraq as they are some of the most recent experiences and were fought by the most advanced militaries in the world.

The IRA in Northern Ireland, 1969-1998

In Northern Ireland, the British's 20,000 soldiers and the 8,000 man Royal Ulster Constabulary (RUC) possessed an excellent forensic capability. As a result, IRA snipers were extremely thorough in their counter-forensic approach. Even the slightest clue, like a fingerprint or a drop of blood, could incriminate and expose an IRA shooter. Importantly, the war in Northern Ireland was small, almost microscopic, when compared to other wars. For example, some estimates placed the IRA's average op-

374

Suspected Chechen rebels being transported to a Russian filtration camp

erational strength at about three hundred active fighters, operating in a country with a population of only 1.5 million people. British investigators faced relatively few guerrilla fighters and perhaps a dozen dedicated snipers at any one time.

The IRA had to practice extreme forensic discipline to survive under such scrutiny. Because the British army and Northern Ireland security forces, like the RUC, had to operate with restraint (blowing up Irish family residences to get an IRA sniper was politically unacceptable) IRA gunmen worried little about being killed during their attack. However, the gunmen were very concerned with the British's investigative dragnet that would produce mind-bending interrogation sessions, suffocating surveillance, and unrelenting harassment of IRA suspects. The greatest threat to the IRA sniper was not the immediate reaction by their victims, it was the government's long-term investigation backed up by an aggressive team of forensic detectives and specialists.

Chechen Rebels, 1994-2006

Chechnya, like Northern Ireland, also had a small population of only 1.1 million people. The resistance movement there was estimated at its peak at 10,000 fighters with an undetermined amount of supporters. It is likely a majority of the population, which hated the Russians, undermined the Russian occupation in some form. In Chechnya, the Russians faced the same problem every foreign occupier does - they did not speak the language and they did not fit in with the population.

The Russians' 100,000-man army occupying Chechnya was a conscript force with a low degree of overall professionalism and counter-insurgency competence. As a result, the Russians' ability to conduct battlefield investigations was poor and their indigenous surrogates - the Chechen government - corrupt, infiltrated, and inept. Because of these problems, the Russian military and Chechen government were unable to conduct the investigations required to track down all the snipers they faced.

Unlike the British security forces, the Russian military policy towards Chechen guerrilla snipers was one of massive force and overwhelming response, even if this resulted in debilitating structural damage and widespread civilian deaths. All suspected guerrillas were captured and tortured in 'filtration camps' as a matter of policy and suspected guerrilla snipers were tortured then killed. Therefore, the Chechen guerrilla sniper was most concerned with escaping immediate Russia firepower after a shooting (the Russians would bomb an entire city block to get one sniper) and then avoid the suspicion of being a guerrilla. The Russians were not overly concerned with forensic evidence. A suspected Chechen who fit the Russian profile for a guerrilla sniper was simply killed just to be on the safe side.

The Iraqi Insurgents, 2003-2008

Consider the situation the American military faced in Iraq. Iraq had a population estimated at 27 million people and Baghdad alone, with a population estimated at six million people, had more people than all of Northern Ireland and Chechnya combined. High-end estimates of the Iraqi insurgency topped out at 20,000 active fighters with 250,000 dedicated supporters. Among all these fighters, America's 140,000-man army may have faced a hundred individual snipers. In a conflict of such magnitude, where close to 40,000 individual insurgent attacks were recorded in 2005 alone, the American and Iraqi government battlefield investigative ability was simply overwhelmed.

As with any conventional army, the American army was not designed to conduct widespread battlefield investigations and thus found itself unable to successfully and thoroughly follow up most sniper attacks. If an insurgent sniper was not immediately detected and captured after a shooting, they would most likely get away with their attack. As a result, the Iraqi insurgent sniper was worried most about making an immediate escape as opposed to withstanding the scrutiny of a prolonged investigation.

Furthermore, because American soldiers did not speak the language and did not blend into Iraqi society, their ability to conduct investigations was limited. Compounding the problem was their indigenous surrogates, the Iraqi police, suffered from widespread corruption, professional ineptness, and insurgent infiltration. As a result, an Iraqi insurgent had a much better chance to get away with repeated sniper attacks than did IRA snipers operating in Northern Ireland. And since the U.S. military was more restrained and disciplined than the Russians in Chechnya, they rarely used massive firepower to kill a lone shooter.

The IRA's Forensic Discipline

While all guerrillas make an effort to get away with their activities, the IRA took their operations to a higher level of counter-forensic discipline. The IRA had to achieve a new forensic plateau because they faced (arguably) the best counter-insurgency forces in the world. The British Special Air Service (SAS), the 14th Military Intelligence Security Company, and the Royal Ulster Constabulary combined to make a formidable collection of counter-insurgency specialists. Through sheer survival of the fittest, the IRA had to either adapt to their enemy or collapse as an organization. The IRA adapted. In fact, the IRA displayed some of the most sophisticated urban guerrilla warfare methodology seen in any conflict to date.

As part of this adaptive process, the IRA studied the British authorities' forensic capabilities. After fighting for decades and having hundreds of its members incarcerated, investigated, and questioned, the IRA as a whole formed a large pool of counter-forensic knowledge. Consequently, the IRA leadership tapped into this pool and created a

This Iraqi insurgent has little to fear from forensic investigations by the generally inept Iraqi police.

counter-forensics manual, which it published and distributed to IRA members. Author Tony Geraghty managed to gain access to the IRA's counter-forensics manual in his work *The Irish War* and revealed the IRA's level of counter-forensics instruction.

The IRA leadership understood the seriousness of the forensic threat and the manual clearly relays this: "Just as we find it absolutely necessary to understand the enemy's interrogation techniques or surveillance and to train to overcome such obstacles, so to we must tackle the problem of Forensic Science. We cannot afford to lose Oglaigh [volunteers] at any time, much less through sloppy preparation or execution of any operation. Not only can it cause us major problems in our operational capacity but the political mileage we achieve from a successful operation can be lost, or at the very least reduced, due to arrests."

The manual recognizes the tactics and thoroughness of the RUC, explaining their investigative procedures: "They will seek out witnesses not solely for identification but to establish the sequence of events: who came from where, who did what, was a vehicle used, what time did it happen, etc... It allows them with their Forensic Scientists to search for the type of evidence they would expect to find associated with the type of operation. It may be useful to employ a delaying tactic (such as a hoax bomb or booby trap) which apart from having obvious military advantages, also allows for time to lapse during which forensic evidence may be dispersed or destroyed."

The manual also specifically addressed the kinds of incriminating evidence the IRA guerrilla must avoid during an operation. The guerrilla should be aware that their hair (or wigs used for disguises) collects traces of explosive and chemical residue. Also, hair products, like gels and sprays, can be collected from their hair and then matched with the actual hair products kept at their homes.

Additionally, the manual covered in detail the problem created by firing a weapon and the resulting gunshot residue. When a weapon is fired, the shooter is covered in an invisible cloud of residue – consisting mainly of lead, antimony, and barium- which may deposit itself on the firer's clothing, hair, hands, face, and even in their nasal passage. The manual suggests the firer wear protective outer garments, including a mask that is washed as soon as the operation is over: "All clothes used during the operation should be washed immediately. It is now standard practice for the RUC when searching a house for trace evidence to take the filters from washing machines, or waste water from pipes, in order to analyze them for fibers, residues, etc... Always wash clothes by hand and dispose of the water into an outside drain, back garden or yard."

Clothes are a subject of concern for the IRA guerrilla, not just because of gunshot residue, but as a forensic link: "Fibers are the major forensic danger. They are links in a chain and can cross transfer in a number of ways... For example, if a fiber from an Oglach's [volunteer] sleeve could be found on a glove and a fiber from the glove found on a weapon, a link between weapon and Volunteer could be established. As we go about our daily business we are constantly shedding and picking up fibers of no significance. If we make such contacts as republican activists while engaged on active service we should understand a very basic crucial lesson – applicable to the forensic threat in general – "Every contact leaves a trace" and therefore also a potential link."

The IRA guerrilla is advised to wear clothes that do not easily provide this kind of incriminating trace fiber. For example, clothes made of wool, which shed fibers everywhere, should never be worn. Nylon and denim clothing are the safest to wear since they shed such few fibers. Washed blue denim jeans are the clothing of choice because they are made from a fiber that "is so common that it is microscopically indistinguishable from all other denim. It is of no use to the forensic scientist."

When using masks, there are procedures to be followed: "We do suggest, however, that the Oglaigh use ladies' nylon stockings as masks. If the Oglach is not fully happy with this disguise another mask can be worn over the top of the nylon stocking. The stocking would be a forensic barrier...Nylons can be easily burnt, destroying any possible trace evidence. This should be done after every operation."

DNA is another area of concern for the IRA guerrilla: "Taking suitable material for DNA testing from a captured Oglach is no simple task. Under their law they only have the power to carry out non-intimate searches on any 'suspect'...Even doctors cannot carry out blood tests. The only so-called non-intimate search they can do is the 'mouth swab'. There is however dispute among scientists as to the reliability of the tests. [But] if an Oglach has been wounded they will take his or her clothing or bandages and use them to make a forensic link".

As the reader can see, preventing or eliminating every one of the potentially incriminating links is difficult to say the least. The greater the government's forensic ability, the more counter-forensic hurdles the guerrilla sniper has to jump. With an effective forensic effort, security forces anticipate the urban guerrilla sniper will eventually slip up in one area or more, even if the sniper is aware of potentially incriminating evidence. While the IRA took its counter-forensic efforts seriously, even their manual was not thorough enough to protect the guerrilla sniper from eventual forensic compromise. The guerrilla sniper has far more to be concerned with if they are to remain anonymous.

Forensic Ballistics: Investigating the Scene of a Shooting

Security forces involved in fighting an organized guerrilla movement must have the ability to conduct multiple effective crime-scene investigations simultaneously. This is a particular problem for conventional military forces with no training in this area.

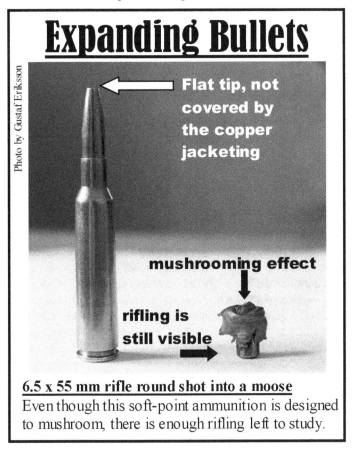

Expanding Bullets

Photo by: Gustaf Eriksson

Flat tip, not covered by the copper jacketing

mushrooming effect

rifling is still visible

6.5 x 55 mm rifle round shot into a moose
Even though this soft-point ammunition is designed to mushroom, there is enough rifling left to study.

However, this is no excuse as basic skills such as protecting a crime scene, preserving, identifying, collecting, and logging evidence, and interviewing witnesses can be readily learned. Most security forces think they do not need these skills, which is the most serious problem. One must understand in a guerrilla war, soldiers are not only soldiers, they are also policeman, investigators, detectives, researches, students, and historians all rolled into one.

Analyzing Recovered Bullets

If basic crime scene investigation is easy to learn, where do we start? Let us begin with the one piece of incriminating evidence that remains after every single shooting in the world: the bullet. When a person is shot somewhere in their body, the bullet itself remains as a link to the shooter. Or, if the bullet misses its mark and lodges in something else, like a door frame, this incriminating link can be recovered and analyzed. The bullet is important because it speaks volumes about the shooter. Even casual observation by the naked eye will reveal the caliber of the bullet. A 5.56 mm bullet is quickly distinguished from a 7.62 mm bullet just as a 9 mm slug is readily discerned from a .45 caliber one. A quick study of the retrieved bullet will determine the caliber of the weapon, what kind of weapon fired the bullet (rifle or pistol), which together can lead to the origin of the rifle, such as Soviet, American, or German.

Casual study of the bullet offers some conclusions, but closer investigation reveals even more. When a bullet is fired from a rifled barrel it no longer looks pristine as when it comes fresh out of the box. In contrast, the grooves from the barrel's rifling are forced into the sides of the bullet, leaving impressions visible to the human eye. While the human eye is not capable of detecting the unique characteristics left by the rifling, a microscope is.

Rifling marks are important because they can be matched to a specific weapon as every weapon leaves its own unique impressions on each and every bullet. For example, two separate Russian-made SVD sniper rifles each leave their own unique rifling impressions on their respective bullets despite the rifles being mass-produced copies of the same original design. In this sense, the rifling impressions left on a bullet are the weapon's fingerprint, as unique as the ridges found on a person's own hand. Because the rifling impressions on each bullet are unique, a bullet can be matched to the exact weapon that fired it. All an investigator has to do is compare a bullet recovered from the scene of a shooting with a comparison bullet fired from the suspected weapon to positively confirm or deny if the weapon fired the bullet.

Most likely, the bullets the battlefield detective encounters will be similar because of the Hague Convention of 1899 which determined what type of bullets the world's militaries use today. To quote: "The Contracting Parties agree to abstain from the use of bullets which expand or flatten easily in the human body, such as bullets with a hard envelope which does not entirely cover the core, or is pierced with incisions."

That one sentence guided the evolution of military bullet production ever since. As a direct result of this agreement, the most commonly fired bullets in a war zone are fully metal jacketed (FMJ) rifle rounds. NATO countries, like the United States, Germany and Britain, all fire 5.56 mm and 7.62 mm FMJ rounds from their battle rifles. Former Soviet Block countries, like Russia, Poland, and Romania, fire 5.45 mm and 7.62 mm FMJ rounds from their battle rifles. Since the U.S./NATO and Soviet Union/Warsaw Pact superpowers ruled the Cold War for more than four decades, the majority of the weapons in the world, from the Middle East to Southeast Asia, fire 5.54/5.56 mm and 7.62 mm FMJ rounds. What does this mean to us? When one examines a wound and the corresponding bullet, we know what kind of bullet we are likely to find.

Importantly, these FMJ bullets exhibit similar characteristics. All FMJ rounds are of durable construction and designed to penetrate their targets while traveling at high velocities. Consequently, the bullet itself deforms little when hitting bone and flesh, because the bullet's copper jacketing is designed to maintain the integrity of the bullet, even when impacting something hard. When we find a sniper's FMJ bullet lodged in a victim, the chances are the bullet will be intact, allowing us to analyze and match the rifling on the bullet with the gun that fired it. On the other hand, because these FMJ rounds travel at such high-velocities, they often leave through-and-through wounds of the body, meaning the bullet goes into and out of the person's body. With these types of wounds, the incriminating bullet is lost somewhere in the surrounding terrain.

Even with a through-and-through wound, FMJ bullets exhibit certain wound characteristics. For example, high velocity FMJ rifle rounds often cause large temporary wound cavities, injure surrounding organs and tissue due to bullet shock waves, and leave smaller permanent wound cavities. The Russian 5.54 mm and the American 5.56 mm rounds have a tendency to yaw upon hitting the human body, causing the rounds

7.62 mm Wound Ballistics

Photos and testing by brassfetcher.com

7.62 x 54 mm, 148-grain, FMJ bullet, 2676 fps

The bullet entered the gelatin block, traveled 5.6 inches, turned sideways, traveled 4.4 inches, righted itself and continued another 6 inches until it exited the gelatin. Notice the large permanent wound cavity, which was 8 inches wide. After the bullet entered the gelatin it yawed, tumbled, and traveled off its initial axis, creating torque on the gelatin block. While this round was fired from a Mosin-Nagant carbine, expect similar performance from SVDs and other Russian sniper rifles.

to tumble and create much larger wounds than if they continued straight ahead.

Ironically, the signatories of the Hague Convention intended FMJ bullets to be a more humane way of killing and wounding each other. I am not sure what the several million people who have since been shot and killed by these bullets, would think of such an assertion. From a forensics perspective, a FMJ bullet is more likely to retain its integrity, allowing for successful analysis and matching to the weapon that fired it. The disadvantage of a FMJ bullet is it tends to travel completely through the human body, so an investigator may have a gunshot wound victim with no bullet to analyze.

Civilian Bullets

In the hunting, personal defense, and law enforcement arenas, the goal is to kill your target, be it human or animal, as quickly as possible. In the hunting world, there are no constraints on the shooters to wound their prey in a more humane manner. In fact, hunters in America who stalk deer and other large game are prohibited by law from using FMJ bullets because they are not sufficiently lethal. Hunting laws demand hunters use soft-point rounds that mushroom on impact. The resulting mushroom creates a larger permanent wound cavity and ensures the bullet will stay in the animal – not pass cleanly through it like a FMJ round. Soft-point rifle ammunition not only mushrooms, but is designed to still penetrate into the target. This combination results in a highly deformed bullet, where the first two-thirds of the bullet are deformed beyond all recognition. However, the remaining one-third of the bullet retains its integrity, allowing forensic investigators to analyze and match the bullet based on the rifling marks left on the base of the bullet. With soft-points, there is less chance of a through-and-through wound.

Law-enforcement officers also prefer soft-point ammunition, but because of legal liability issues. A police department does not want its officers firing hyper-velocity FMJ rounds that will streak through a criminal and then hit an innocent bystander like a woman or child. From a liability standpoint, the police want their bullets to hit a criminal and stay inside them.

People using weapons for personal defense often shoot hollow-point rounds to inflict as much damage on an attacker as possible. Hollow-point rounds are designed to mushroom immediately upon impact, sacrificing penetration for a larger wound cavity. These gun owners, who need to protect their families from criminals armed with anything from knives to handguns, want to hit their assailant and put them down for good. They do not want the assailant to get off a dying shot or get to their loved ones in a final, adrenaline-fueled frenzy. Hollow-point rounds, when hitting flesh and bone, mushroom and often fragment. Since these types of rounds have relatively poor penetration ability, these rounds tend to stay in the body so investigators will have something to study. On the other hand, because these bullets suffer from such deformity, it may be difficult, if not impossible, to match the bullet with the weapon that fired it.

While these are the most common rounds used, there are some less popular ones that make forensic analysis of the round difficult, if not impossible. For example, a shooter may fire a sabot round out of their weapon, a bullet encased in a plastic shoe (*sabot* is French for the word shoe). As the bullet is fired, the plastic shoe is engaged by the rifling and is launched out of the weapon. During flight, the plastic shoe falls away while the bullet continues down range and into the target. Because the plastic shoe engages the rifling, not the bullet, there is much less friction and the bullet travels at greater velocities – as fast as 4000 feet per second.

As a result, there are rifling marks on the plastic shoe, but none on the bullet. This situation would definitely make a forensic investigator scratch their head when they recovered a bullet, smooth as a baby's bottom, with no rifle scoring whatsoever on it. The investigator would have problems since they would be unable to match the bullet to the rifle. They would have to first find the expended sabot, then match that to the rifle, and then match the bullet to the plastic shoe. This rifle-sabot-bullet connection would be no easy task since the plastic shoe does not hold marks on it like metal does. More importantly, a sabot round would enable a shooter to fire a bullet with rifle scoring on it from a *different* rifle. This way, a shooter could introduce misleading evidence into a shooting scene in order to frame someone else and throw detectives of the shooter's trail.

Another type of ammunition commonly used on ranges, because it is environmentally friendly, is frangible ammunition. Frangible ammunition, or 'exploding' bullets, consists of loosely bonded material that fragments upon impact with the target. They are used on indoor shooting ranges because they have poor penetrating power and will not ricochet upon impact, so they are safer to use in close proximity to people. From a forensic view, frangible bullets fragment so much upon impact that there are no rifling impressions left to be analyzed.

A final round we will mention is the Glaser Safety Slug. This round consists of a thin copper shell, filled with bird shot, and covered with a plastic nose. The round is billed as 'a favorite of air marshals' since it is designed specifically for low penetra-

Forensic Problems

Frangible Bullets

Photo by DOE

Above are examples of various frangible bullets made of bonded steel powder. When these bullets strike a hard object, they disintegrate into a pile of dust so that there is no rifling left on the bullet to be analyzed.

Sabot

⬅ **Actual bullet**

⬅ **Plastic shroud**

To the left we have an example of a rifle cartridge sabot round. The bullet is slightly smaller than the inside bore of the rifle so that it never touches the barrel of the weapon and thus has no rifling marks. The bullet sits snugly in a plastic sabot (which is French for the word 'shoe'). When the round is fired, the plastic shroud engages the rifling in the barrel so it's spinning when it exits the rifle. However, after traveling a short distance, the plastic sabot falls away while the bullet continues on its way to the target. Thus, there is never any rifling marks forced into the side of the bullet....it is completely smooth just as it came out of the factory.

tion (the air marshals do not want to shoot a terrorist and then have the bullet pierce the skin of the airplane while in fight). Upon impact, the thin copper shell peels back, launching the bird shot into the target. The Glaser causes enormous, relatively shallow, soft-tissue injuries. As a forensic investigator, the Glaser does not maintain its integrity well (as designed) and the thin copper shell is prone to fragmentation (as designed) so there is little metal remaining to analyze for rifling.

A separate problem for battlefield detectives are polygonal barrels, which do not use traditional rifling with lands and grooves and leave relatively faint marks on the bullet. Since there are no defined grooves forced into the bullet, it is difficult for someone to match a bullet fired from a weapon with a polygonal barrel (Glock, Steyr, and Heckler and Koch make weapons with polygonal barrels because it increases both barrel life and bullet velocity). The challenges for the forensic examiner multiply if a fragmenting/frangible bullet is fired from a polygonal barrel because even if a readable fragment was recovered, the rifling will be too faint to match.

Polygonal barrels are a problem and so are smoothbore barrels like those of a shotgun. Smoothbore barrels have no rifling and thus leave no marks on an exiting bullet. Michael A. Stone, a professional killer who worked for the Protestant Loyalist paramilitary groups in Northern Ireland, often preferred to commit his sectarian murders with a shotgun because he knew the authorities would be unable to trace the shootings to his weapon. Stone was eventually caught after a particularly audacious assault at an IRA funeral, but he was never connected to his shotgun killings through forensic evidence.

All the time a forensic examiner spends sweating over a microscope, carefully matching one bullet with another, is for naught if the shooter changes/discards their barrel after firing the round. For example, the barrels in automatic pistols from Glock and Sig Saur are designed to be changed out it mere seconds so they can be easily replaced. This means after firing a bullet, the barrel can be taken out and destroyed, thus removing the connection between the weapon and the bullet. Someone may be able to connect the bullet to the barrel, but not the barrel to the weapon. Or, after a period of use, a barrel can be drilled out so there are no more lands left so a bullet cannot be matched to it.

IRA shooters were acutely aware of this forensic problem because British authorities took exhaustive measures to recover, analyze, and catalogue each and every bullet left behind after an IRA shooting. Consequently, when British forces recovered a suspected IRA weapon, they compared test bullets from captured weapons with their collection of recovered bullets. This thorough forensic work connected many a suspected IRA member with a particular weapon to a specific shooting, resulting in prison sentences for those implicated in these crimes. In one particular breach of forensic security, an IRA member was captured with a rifle used in over a dozen shootings. Even if this person was not responsible for all of the shootings, he certainly took the fall for them. This prisoner now became especially vulnerable to pressure to reveal the real shooters' identities if he ever wanted to see life outside of prison again.

Shell Casings

Shell casings are as incriminating as the bullets themselves, although the link to the shooter is harder to establish. Cartridges fired in a weapon become unique for several reasons. First, a weapon leaves scrape marks along the outer walls of the casing as it is forced into the chamber (remember, most shell casings are made out of soft brass). Even if the bullet is not fired, the mere act of chambering a round leaves microscopic, identifiable marks on the casing. Then, when the firing pin hits the primer face, it leaves a unique, microscopically identifiable indentation that can be detected by a microscope and then matched to a specific weapon.

Next, as the round is fired, the shell is forced back against the breech face due to the recoil. This impact on the breech face leaves unique, microscopically identifiable marks on the bottom of the cartridge. Then, once again, as the shell is ejected (either automatically or by manipulation of the bolt action) the bolt extractors leave more marks on the shell casing, connecting the cartridge to that exact weapon. The only weapons free from extractor marks are those that do not have an extractor, like a re-volver or a weapon with a break-open action. While the cartridges from these weapons are free of extractor marks, they still have the other unique, identifiable marks.

With shell casings, the incriminating link to the shooter takes more effort because after investigators connect a spent bullet with a specific weapon, they have to compare the casings to that same weapon in order to make a definite bullet-weapon-casing link. In this case, the weapon is the common element connecting the bullet and casing. If the casing from a weapon is found on a suspected guerrilla's person or property, the link from the shooting to the person is complete. However, investigators still cannot prove a specific bullet was fired from a specific shell casing.

Shell casings are informative in other ways. Finding an expended casing reveals the caliber of the weapon and if it is a pistol or a rifle. This information can lead to the country of origin and the manufacturer of the weapon (and the origin of the ammuni-tion). Hence, finding an expended .308 caliber casing made by the Federal Cartridge Company suggests the weapon that fired it was an American rifle and the person firing it may be American as well.

Where a casing is found is equally illuminating for the investigator. The physical location of a casing shows where the firer was when they made their shot, thus reveal-ing the shooter's tactics and their technical ability. For example, a casing found in a building 800 meters from the target indicates a shooter with unusual technical shoot-ing ability. A casing found in a car indicates the shooter prefers to use a vehicle for a shooting platform as opposed to a building.

In sum, shell casings are another incriminating link in the chain of evidence that can lead to the capture and conviction of the sniper. Most common criminals know this as do guerrillas who cannot afford to be captured with casings in their possession or on their property. Experienced shooters never leave casings behind after a shooting and dispose of them immediately after an operation. To tie this subject in with an his-torical example, a lack of shell casing discipline revealed many things about the JFK assassination, to include the location of certain sniper teams and evidence Lee Harvey Oswald did not fire from the Texas School Book Depository.

Magazines

Magazines left behind at the scene of a shooting are as revealing as leaving shell casings behind. A quick look at a magazine indicates the exact kind of weapon that was fired from a particular location, revealing if the weapon fired was an AK-47 or an

M-16. Microscopic inspection of the magazine can match the markings on the magazine with the magazine well and release mechanism of the particular weapon used. However, this matching works best if the magazine was only inserted into a single weapon. If the magazine was loaded into multiple weapons, now leaving multiple marks, positive identification to a single weapon becomes difficult.

Fingerprints

While a weapon's unique extraction system, firing pin, and rifling is the weapon's fingerprint, actual fingerprints from the firer are also incriminating. (Remember, investigators eventually 'discovered' Lee Harvey Oswald's palm print on the barrel of the supposed murder weapon, underneath the actual stock of the weapon.) The shooter's fingerprints can be left not only on the weapon itself, but on the above mentioned magazines and shell casings. This incriminating identification makes the use of gloves a necessity for the shooter to break the link of their unseen fingerprints left on a physical item used in the shooting. This basic understanding of incriminating evidence through fingerprints is understood by most professional criminals in the world and is solved by simply wearing gloves.

IRA shooters habitually wore gloves, some even using surgical gloves, to prevent their fingerprints showing up on their weapons. As mentioned in the IRA's counter-forensics manual, microscopic fibers from the gloves used in a shooting may be left on the weapon, requiring the gloves to be destroyed after the operation. Fingerprints can be found elsewhere too. Did the person loading the bullets into the magazine of the weapon wear gloves? Did they inadvertently leave fingerprints on the unexpended cartridges in the magazine or on the magazine itself? The shooter themselves may be clean of fingerprints, but someone else in the shooting process may have exposed themselves.

DNA

DNA collected from any number of means is a particularly damning link in the chain of evidence because it positively identifies a particular human being. Items like hair follicles, skin particles, saliva, ear wax, and blood can irrefutably connect an individual to a shooting. These repositories of DNA can be transferred to a crime scene any number of ways. For example, a person's hair and skin is left on almost everything they physically touch or brush up against in an unprotected manner. Also, a person waiting in a sniper position for extended periods may urinate on the ground, leaving an incriminating link through their body waste. Or, a person may spit chewing tobacco on the ground at a sniper hide, leaving a DNA link to them.

One Iraqi insurgent sniper, firing from a van (we read about this in the Juba chapter), shot an American soldier at a vehicle checkpoint and was hit with accurate return fire, wounding the sniper in the foot. Even though the wounded sniper fled the scene and hid in a nearby building, it was easy for the American soldiers to follow the blood stains left from his foot and then capture the sniper. In this case, blood stains were not used in forensic analyses, but as simple spoor to track down the wounded sniper.

Physical Clues

Captured Viet Cong

This captured guerrilla is a forensic windfall for government security forces who can now take his fingerprints and DNA samples and thus positively link him to a crime committted against the state. In response, savvy guerrillas conduct their operations in such a manner as to avoid forensic compromise.

Physical damage to a shooter's body offers more clues for the investigator. For example, a high-powered rifle may leave a bruise or a mark on the firer's shoulder. Russian forces in Chechnya understood this and routinely checked the shoulders of suspected insurgents to see if they fired a weapon recently. A bruise on the shoulder is only a clue, but it will get the suspected Chechen guerrilla an all-expense paid trip to a filtration camp just to be sure. Also, a novice shooter (and even some veteran shooters) may fire a rifle with their head too close to their scope. When the rifle fires and jerks back from the recoil, the scope can hit the shooter above the eye, leaving a nasty, semi-circular cut in the eyebrow area. Anyone who has been around sniper rifles for a while will instantly recognize this unique wound for what it is.

Another relatively common type of injury is having a shooter's hand 'get bit' when working the action on their weapon. This is a more common occurrence when handling pistols. When the pistol's action slides forward, the slide may catch a small piece of skin at the webbing of the hand or even on one of the fingers, making a small cut. People that handle and shoot weapons frequently may have these small cuts on their hands. Again, this does not prove one's guilt, but it is an indicator which may place a shooter under unwanted scrutiny. These cuts become a real problem if skin and blood samples are left on the action of the weapon, providing an incriminating DNA link from the weapon to the shooter. Or, if a shooter does get a cut above their eye from their scope, their blood will be left on the scope itself, providing an irrefutable DNA link from the shooter to their weapon.

Gunshot Residue (GSR)

As discussed in depth by the IRA's counter-forensic manual, gunshot residue (GSR) produces a serious forensic problem. Imagine a person firing a rifle, with their head next to the action of the weapon; their entire head and face will be covered in a cloud of GSR. The GSR will settle on a person's clothes, in their hair, in their ears, nostrils, eyebrows, under their nails, and all over the weapon itself. Dogs can be trained to sniff out and detect GSR and a variety of companies manufacture portable GSR wipe kits that change colors when they are rubbed up against GSR. Only an immediate, thorough, post-operation clean-up will remove this GSR from the shooter's clothing and body. Burning a shooter's clothing is common after an operation as is taking a long bath where every inch of a person is cleaned with soap and water. The IRA was very GSR conscious and trained their shooters to clean themselves after an operation. One should also remember using a sound suppressor helps to contain the majority of the GSR propelled out of the barrel of the weapon. A person using a suppressed weapon is likely to have little or any GSR left on their person after a shooting. *(Author's note: since GSR can be found in common household items like paint, false positive reads are common and thus these tests often carry little weight in the court of law. For example, GSR tests carried little weight in the Iraqi legal system.)*

Auditory Evidence

An often overlooked aspect of sniper forensics is the auditory evidence that can be used to identify a specific weapon. This capability is becoming more common in such places as American cities where civilian law enforcement agencies use a series of remote audio systems to detect gunshots in crime-infested areas. Armies are also starting to use acoustical devices on their vehicles to detect gunshots so enemy snipers can be rapidly found and taken out. These acoustical detection devices are a threat to the sniper because they can determine the location of the sniper by analyzing the sound of the gunshot and coming up with a back azimuth of the incoming bullet. Audio recording devices are also capable of capturing a specific gun's audio signature whose graphic representation can then be examined by an auditory specialist in order to match a recorded gunshot to a specific weapon. (This auditory problem is discussed further in the chapters on sound suppressors and counter-sniper methods.)

A Counter-Forensic Perspective

A guerrilla sniper will try to defeat or delay an investigation by using good sniper tactics and will in fact choose their firing position based on counter-forensic principles, not traditional ideas of immediate survival. With a counter-forensic mindset, the sniper uses the urban terrain in such a way making it difficult or impossible for crime scene investigators to find out exactly where they fired from. This is why so many Chechen, IRA, PLO, and Iraqi snipers fired from urbanized areas so security forces were overwhelmed by the number of possible sniper positions and gave up on finding them. If security forces cannot find the sniper's nest, then they have nothing to investigate. At worst, experienced snipers use the urban terrain in such a manner investigators are delayed in finding their firing position so the shooter has time to forensically sterilize their position.

From a counter-forensic perspective, the more distance a shooter places between themselves and the target, the harder it is to catch them. For one, it is harder for security forces and bystanders to identify the source of the fire. At extreme distances it is

Anonymous Shooters

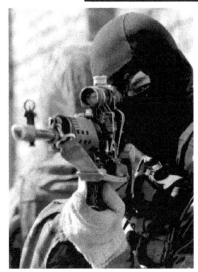

One of the oldest tricks in the book is wearing a mask. IRA snipers regularly concealed their identity from those around them, as did Chechen guerrillas and Iraqi insurgents. Interestingly, Russian troops operating in Chechnya often concealed their identities with ski masks. This did help protect them from threats to their families, but it also enabled them to commit war crimes.

difficult to see the muzzle flash and hear the gunshot from the weapon. Distance helps in other ways, by eliminating the association between the target and the sniper. If the sniper is so far away from their victim the people near the sniper cannot even see the target and do not even know someone was shot, they will not be alert to suspicious activity in their area – in other words, the shooter will remain invisible. From the investigator's side, the increased distance means they have to consider a staggering variety of options: which one of the hundreds of buildings, thousands of doors and windows, and thousands of cars did the shot come from? And which one of these thousands of hostile people actually know something about the shooting?

Identity Security

It is true effectively concealing the muzzle flash, muzzle blast, the sound of the gunshot, and the angle of the shot will prevent identification of the sniper's position, thus buying the sniper time. These are not the only considerations. The skilled sniper is also concerned with eyewitnesses or security cameras that can identify them during their sniping operation. A sniper cannot remain anonymous if their face is plastered across the evening news and on rewards posters at the local market. Once a sniper's physical identity is revealed, government security forces have the advantage and can use their resources to track down their now-exposed target.

To limit this possibility of exposure, guerrilla snipers intentionally move into and out of their firing sites in a natural manner that raises no suspicion. This means the sniper tries to look and act like everyone else in the area. Ruses such as dressing like a police officer, a soldier, or other kind of public employee provide a good cover for a sniper's movement before and after their operation. Furthermore, experienced guerrillas have a credible cover story already prepared so if they talk to anyone, the sniper's story appears uninteresting and is quickly forgotten (like the DC snipers telling inquisitive police officers they were just in the area visiting family). The sniper understands they cannot allow themselves be seen actually pulling the trigger. To do this, the sniper achieves relative isolation. That means the sniper shoots from inside a room, or inside a vehicle, so they may still have people near them but, inside that protective space, there is no one who can physically see the sniper pull the trigger. The sniper protects their physical identity and actions in other ways such as firing from an area where there are no people, like a bombed out building, or by operating at night where the shooter cannot be seen because of the darkness or because people are inside for the night because of a government enforced curfew.

Other measures include wearing a disguise, like a wig, or using commonly worn items to hide their features like a hat, scarf, and sunglasses. IRA shooters wore balaclavas, ski masks, and full-face motorcycle helmets to cover their faces. Guerrillas across the Middle East cover their faces with their head scarves and Chechen guerrillas often mimicked their Russian foe, wearing a variety of head nets and balaclavas. Guerrillas also intentionally employ their snipers in areas the sniper is not from, so if the sniper's face is seen, eye-witnesses will not know who they are.

If the guerrilla sniper conducts their attack from an area that supports them, then concealing their identity may not be an issue. A Chechen rebel shooting a Russian soldier in Grozny, an insurgent shooting an American in Fallujah, an IRA sniper targeting a British soldier in Belfast, or a Hamas gunman targeting an Israeli in the Gaza Strip, may not have to worry about the local population exposing them because the people support their actions.

Operational Signature

One thing investigators can study about a sniper in the absence of any incriminating physical evidence is their operational pattern. Humans are creatures of habit and often conduct repetitive activities because it is easier to do something they know than to repeatedly operate in the unknown. No matter how good a guerrilla sniper is technically and tactically, they often set a predictable pattern. A sniper who is comfortable working a specific neighborhood is setting a pattern. A sniper who only fires from a van is setting a pattern. Security forces use these established patterns to build a profile so they can set a trap or at least be conscious of the sniper's habits and favorite shooting platforms.

A smart sniper develops several different profiles with several different sets of habits so not to create an easily recognized pattern. For instance, the sniper can develop a methodology used for firing from vehicles, a methodology for firing from occupied buildings, and a methodology for firing at night from wooded areas. The sniper then mixes theses methodologies at random so as not to create a pattern. Even in Stalingrad, Vassili Zaitsev and his snipers were conscious about setting a pattern and intentionally changed their tactics to deceive the Germans to survive another day.

Forensics Investigation as a Counter-Insurgency Tool

In a guerrilla war, a competent team of forensic investigators who can read a crime scene and reverse-engineer a shooting is the sniper's greatest foe. An experienced sniper detective is in fact more effective than an entire battalion of heavy artillery or a

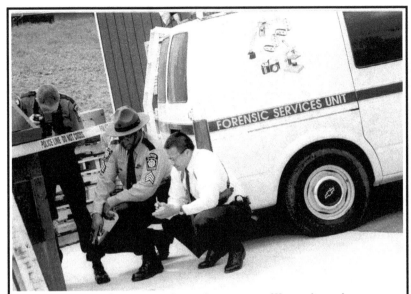

The greatest threat to the urban guerrilla sniper is a competent, motivated, trained team of crime scene investigators and forensic experts. *photo by PSP*

squadron of helicopter gunships. The battlefield detective is dangerous to the guerrilla because they are discriminating and have the tools and know-how to pluck a single guerrilla fish from the ocean of people without destroying the urban infrastructure or killing innocent people. Of even more importance is in the way an investigative team captures a sniper. Burning up an entire city block with napalm to get a sniper is a quick,s atisfyinga ct,but i ss elf-defeatingf roma c ounter-insurgencype rspective.

However, if investigators identify and capture a sniper through incriminating evidence, they can successfully prosecute the shooter through the legal system. Prosecuting a sniper through the courts reinforces a sense of due process, justice, and respect for individual rights. In fact, it is important for security forces to make a deliberate show of due process to gain legitimacy with the people. As we know, governments rule a nation because the people give their consent to do so. The more legitimate a government is in the eyes of its people, the less resistance it meets from them. Of course, on occasion, security forces may have to use superior firepower to eliminate a sniper, but this should be a rarity, not the rule. Taking all of this into consideration, a well-trained forensic investigative team is not only effective for counter-sniping, they are a good counter-insurgency tool.

Chapter 21
Counter-Sniper Technology

Rise of the Machines

Counter-sniper technology is a relatively new phenomenon. While snipers have existed since the invention of the long musket in 14th Century China, counter-sniper technology is in its infancy, only having been around since the early 1990's. One of the events driving the creation of modern counter-sniper technology was the protracted sniper war in Sarajevo. The UN and NATO forces attempting to enforce various cease fires in the city found they could not detect and counter snipers with any measure of effectiveness. Most of the time, no one knew where an incoming bullet originated from. Other times, the perpetrators were long gone by the time a patrol showed up to investigate. Humans were just too easy to deceive. What was needed was a mechanical device that could not be fooled and would immediately recognize a gunshot and determine where it came from.

Over recent years, various companies have developed technological solutions to the problem posed by urban snipers. We must keep in mind that none of the current counter-sniper systems we are going to review can actually stop a sniper before they shoot. These systems are designed to quickly and accurately locate a sniper after they have fired a shot. Thus, the information acquired by the machines enables the persons targeted by the sniper to react quickly enough to kill or capture the shooter after the shot is already made.

Acoustic Counter-Sniper Technology

The most commonly used counter-sniper systems are those based on acoustical technology. The basic premise of these systems is several acoustic sensors, arrayed in

392

BBN's Boomerang

This is a close up of a microphone cluster whose job is to detect a gunshot and then relay data back to a computer.

different locations in the same general area, will detect supersonic bullet shock waves and a weapon's muzzle blast. The acoustic sensors immediately record the sound data from the weapon and feed this information to a computer that determines the trajectory of the bullet and tells the operator from what direction and distance the weapon was fired from. Some systems, based on the variations in the sound waves detected, can even determine the caliber of the round fired. Acoustic counter-sniper systems are designed in several formats: ground mounted, vehicle mounted, or even mounted on a soldier's kit.

In field testing, acoustic systems have detected a gunshot from the waves of the muzzle blast and the shock waves of the supersonic bullet and have accurately determined the caliber of the bullets fired. Furthermore, in the majority of shots made during said testing, acoustic systems did accurately determine the correct azimuth of the shot, the correct trajectory and elevation of the shot, and the distance to the shot, all within several degrees of error. Testing revealed it was harder to determine the location of the shooter from muzzle blast alone, especially from a great distance. In contrast, the shock waves emitted along the trajectory of the bullet itself were more reliable.

One of the most popular acoustic systems is the Boomerang, created by BBN Technologies. BBN has a contract with the U.S. government and the U.S. military currently uses Boomerang counter-sniper systems in Iraq and Afghanistan. BBN said this about their Boomerang system: "Boomerang uses passive acoustic detection and computer-based signal processing to locate the shooter. When mounted on a vehicle, the system operates when the vehicle is stationary or moving. Boomerang uses a single mast-mounted, compact array of microphones to detect incoming fire. And Boomerang is the only shooter detector shown to operate successfully in urban terrain (MOUT) on moving vehicles. Boomerang detects incoming supersonic small arms fire for bullet trajectories passing the mast, and for shooters firing at maximum effective weapons' ranges. It detects and reports incoming fire and the relative shooter position (including elevation) quickly. Boomerang indicates the azimuth of incoming small-arms fire by actuating a light to show the clock direction, and Boomerang announces that direction using a recorded voice. Boomerang indicates the range and elevation on an LED screen display. The lighted displays can be dimmed. [Boomerang] worked great for the Marines on post when they received fire from multiple directions [and] when just a few rounds are fired. [Without Boomerang] it is difficult to pinpoint where you're getting shot at from in an urban environment because of the echoes from the buildings and within the post."

ShotSpotter Gunshot Location System (GLS)

Another acoustic gunshot detection system popular with U.S. police forces is the ShotSpotter Gun Location System. ShotSpotter uses acoustic detection like BBN's Boomerang, but ShotSpotter is set up with multiple, stationary sensor collectors in order to blanket an urban area. When these remote, acoustic devices hear what they have identified as a gunshot, they instantly collect the data and send it to a central command center, like a police station. Because the time between the collection of the acoustic data and the notification to the user is so short, police know the exact location a gunshot was fired from in seconds.

According to ShotSpotter: "ShotSpotter Gunshot Location System utilizes patented technology to detect weapons-fire events over large, complex environments. ShotSpotter products range from systems for public safety agencies and 911 dispatch centers (which instantly identify, locate and give a visual of the location of a gunshot event in an urban area) to fully mobile, inter-networked wireless systems for the military that are capable of detecting and locating many types of weapon events in various challenging environments.

All ShotSpotter products are built on the same proven ShotSpotter Gunshot Location System technology. ShotSpotter uses either wired or wireless sensors deployed over areas from one-half square mile up to tens of square miles or hundreds of linear miles. For example, 90 miles of Interstate were covered in central Ohio during the Columbus, OH sniper investigation. *(Author's Note: There has been no evidence presented to date that the Ohio sniper was actually apprehended due to information provided by ShotSpotter. The Ohio Sniper was captured when family members provided information to the police about the shootings and provided guns for forensic analysis.)* The technology can also be used in airports, stadiums or other public ventures.

ShotSpotter utilizes the principle of acoustic triangulation to locate gunfire across wide areas. Because of its patented spatial filter technology, ShotSpotter systems are not fooled by noises which sound like gunfire but are misleading (like car backfires, firecrackers, etc.). Similarly, the technology filters out echoes and other acoustical anomalies. Using a continuous feedback loop which constantly adjusts sensor trigger and other parameters, ShotSpotter is able to deliver instantaneous system reports to dispatchers within seconds of a weapon being fired.

The unique spatial filter technology makes for a very cost-effective solution: ShotSpotter systems deploy with only 8-12 sensors per square mile—far fewer than the number required by any other systems. ShotSpotter sensors detect gunfire at a

Shotspotter Gunshot Location System

A gun is fired

Microphone & radio transmitter

BANG

This drawing shows how ShotSpotter works. A person fires a gun, a nearby microphone on the roof of a building hears the gunshot and then relays this information to the local police station.

range of one to two miles away from the sensors, and ShotSpotter systems have been shown to be accurate to within 25 meters over one to two mile ranges.

In addition, ShotSpotter performs real-time spooling of all signals captured at a sensor, to support later detailed forensic and intelligence analysis of events. Such information can include other non-weapons events, weapon type and direction of fire analysis, and even information related to the direction and speed of shooters on the move."

The biggest drawback with the ShotSpotter when deployed in stationary locations and wired to a central command center is the delay in reaction time by security forces. ShotSpotter may detect a gunshot in a certain part of the city, but if it takes the police ten minutes to arrive on the scene, the shooter is long gone. What security forces need is the ability to have an instant presence at the sight of the gunshot. But the police cannot be everywhere at once, can they?

Again, from ShotSpotter: "Joint Forces Command announced in December 2005 that they had conducted a test of unmanned aerial vehicle, gunshot detection and interoperation capabilities in urban environments as part of a U.S. Marine Corps exercise in Louisiana. "One of the primary goals for the experiment involved the testing of the ShotSpotter system, an acoustic locating system that cues a UAV (unmanned aerial vehicle) sensor to locate an enemy when he fires a weapon, whether on a battlefield or in an urban environment," said Cdr. James Joyner, US JFCOM.

In field-testing, the ShotSpotter wireless systems "provided improved awareness of the intelligence, surveillance, and reconnaissance (ISR) data – in near real-time with less than a ten-second delay," according to Joyner. In addition, the integration of "ground-based sensors with UAV sensors made it possible to visualize the shooter's location within seconds."

With this method, the ShotSpotter acoustic detection system was paired with UAVs. When ShotSpotter detected a gunshot, the location of the gunshot was transmitted immediately to a UAV loitering somewhere overhead. The UAV then looked down on the reported location with its cameras to 'see' what was there, all within the space of a few seconds. If ShotSpotter detected a gunshot at a certain location and a UAV looked at the spot and saw a car speeding away, then the UAV could key in on and follow the car. If the UAV was armed with guided Hellfire missiles, the UAV could target and destroy the car when commanded to do so. While the ShotSpotter/ UAV team does not allow for instant coverage, it does allow for near- instant coverage and provides a far faster reaction than any roving police patrol could provide.

Acoustic Counter-Sniper Applications

The implications of an effective acoustic counter-sniper system like BBN's Boomerang or ShotSpotter are significant. Acoustic sensors determining exactly where a shot was fired from allow security forces to react quickly to a sniper, compensating for their own human failings. The computer does all the work. All the reacting security forces have to do is go where the computer tells them to. In this case, the acoustic system is the battlefield detective, taking the imperfect human response out of the equation.

Locating the sniper is important, but so is the forensic evidence collected by the acoustic system. To start, the computer recording of the bullet trajectory and shooter location will help recreate the scene of the shooting. The recorded acoustic signatures of the shock wave and muzzle blast could then be used to determine the type of weapon used and the kind of bullet fired. If the suspected sniper's weapon was captured at a later time, the weapon could be test fired in a controlled environment and its acoustical signature recorded and compared to the existing data. Thus, each weapon would have an acoustic 'fingerprint'. The acoustic fingerprint could then be used as evidence in a court of law to convict suspected snipers.

The Sniper's Response to Acoustic Systems

Is there any way to defeat these machines, or is the modern day shooter going to be acoustically detected out of existence? While acoustic counter-sniper systems are the most common, they are also the easiest to defeat. All a sniper has to do to defeat a system dependent on 'hearing' a gunshot is to employ a sound suppressor. With a suppressor, there is no muzzle blast to detect. A system like the ShotSpotter, which is deployed in various positions throughout a city, detects gunshots, not the bullet's invisible shock waves. Consequently, a common sound suppressor purchased on the black market for a hundred dollars (or a homemade one built for half the price) will defeat a multi-million dollar system like the ShotSpotter.

What about systems that detect bullet shock waves? Defeating these systems is just as easy. All the shooter has to do is use subsonic ammunition that does not break the sound barrier and thus does not emit shock waves. We discussed before, the Russians' excellent VSS Vintorez suppressed, sub-sonic sniper rifle that fires such a heavy bullet it is lethal out to 400 meters, despite the bullet never breaking the sound barrier. Subsonic ammunition can be bought legally from scores of manufacturers or hand loaded by the shooter themselves.

The shooter can exploit counter-sniper machines in other ways to take advantage of the fact acoustic detection systems are susceptible to changes in the weather, tempera-

Shock Waves & Suppressors

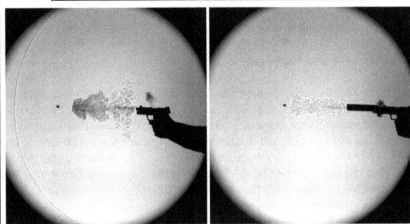

The picture at left shows the shock waves from a pistol. The one at right shows the pistol suppressed. Notice how the shock waves are greatly reduced with the suppressed weapon, making them difficult to detect with acoustic technology. (Photo courtesy of Greg Settles, from the article 'High-speed Imaging of Shock Waves, Explosions and Gunshots' at American scientist Online).

tures, and humidity. For instance, a sniper firing a shot in extremely hot weather (like that found in the Middle East) with heat waves rising off of the urban environment's oven-hot pavement, parking lots, roads, and sidewalks, may remain undetected. This is because the super-hot environment affects the sound and shock waves of the bullet in such a way that increases the acoustic system's margin of error. The system may detect a gunshot and its supersonic bullet, but it may not be able to pinpoint the exact location the shot was made from.

A sniper can defeat attempts to acoustically 'fingerprint' their weapon by deceiving the acoustic system's established templates. Acoustic systems recognize the caliber of weapon fired based on previously recorded noise and shock wave data. In order to throw off the acoustic system, a sniper can hand-load their own rounds in order to change the ballistic characteristics of their bullets. The sniper could also fire a sabot round. In this case, a sniper would fire a 5.56 mm bullet from a 7.62 mm rifle, thus altering the sound and shock wave template already programmed into the acoustic system's computer.

Importantly, systems like the ShotSpotter's citywide system only work in a permissive environment where the government and security forces are in control of day to day life. The ShotSpotter is ideal in places like America where the police control the city, not the gangs doing the shootings. However, imagine American security forces setting up a citywide ShotSpotter system in Fallujah or the British in the IRA stronghold of South Armagh, or the Russians Grozny. As soon as the insurgents located a ShotSpotter device (which must be camouflaged or hidden to survive) they would destroy them. The last gunshots the devices would pick up would be the guerrillas shooting them to pieces. And if the ShotSpotters all report to a central command post like a police station, what happens when the guerrillas detonate a car bomb in front of the station and collapse the entire structure, destroying the ShotSpotter command center with it? Having a certain counter-sniper technology is not enough. This technology must also be practical and be able to survive in the environments they will be used in.

Optics Laser Reflection Technology

Acoustic technology may be the most common counter-sniper system, but optics laser reflection technology is much less expensive and even strives to be pro-active by detecting a sniper before they ever make a shot. With this technology, a hand held device emits an eye-safe laser out to a range of a kilometer and more. When the laser strikes a layered optics, like a telescopic sight, it sends a reflection of the diffused laser back to the user, pinpointing the location of the enemy. Just like a traditional laser range finder, the device tells the user what the distance is between them and their target. The more sophisticated optics laser reflection devices are even advertised as being able to discriminate between common objects like eyeglasses and can see through smoked glass windows.

The Sniper's Response to Optics Laser Reflection Technology

The sniper has several options for dealing with this threat. First, if the sniper can manipulate the urban terrain so they can make a close shot - around two hundred meters or less – then the sniper can defeat laser detection by simply not using a scope. No scope equals no reflection. At absolutely no cost to the shooter, the multi-thousand dollar optics detection devices can be rendered useless before they can even be used. Or, the sniper can take a 'snap' shot. With a snap shot, once the sniper sees a target with their naked eye, they raise their weapon from hiding, take aim, acquire the target, make the shot, and lower their weapon...all in the space of several seconds. In this manner, the optics detection team only has a split second to find and locate the exposed optics – an unlikely prospect in a cluttered urban environment.

Other options include the employment of anti-reflection filters on the sniper's scope that effectively block the wavelength of the laser. That way, a laser can hit the scope and never make a reflection, keeping the sniper invisible. If this anti-reflection filter is not available, the sniper can put an extended hood over the end of their scope or attach a honey-combed anti-reflection piece on the glass of the scope. The hooded cover will ensure a laser, or any light, does not strike the face of the scope from an angle. Unless the detection team is directly opposite of the sniper, they will not detect the sniper's scope. This technique does not make the sniper invisible; it just makes the counter-sniper team's job more difficult.

Other options for the sniper include the use of light reflecting or light absorbing materials for concealment. While optics laser reflection devices can 'see' through smoked glass, can they see through extremely dark, heavy window tinting? Can the device see through the mirrored reflective coatings often placed on the windows of office buildings in sun-drenched areas of the world? If not, the sniper can use these coatings as a concealment device from laser threats. For example, a sniper could crack open a window covered with a reflective mirrored coating. The sniper would then slide the

Mirage 1200 by TP Logic

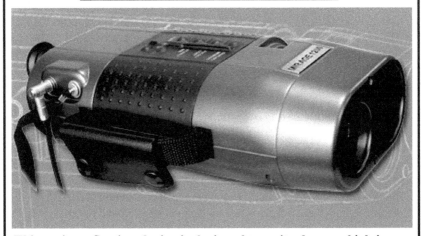

This optics reflection device is designed to emit a laser, which in turn reflects off of a glass lens, like a telescopic sight on a rifle, giving away a sniper's position before they actually take a shot.

barrel of their weapon under the window frame so just the muzzle was visible. While the sniper looks through the one-way, mirrored window with their scope, the detection team's laser would bounce off the window, never picking up or identifying the sniper's scope. In another instance, a sniper could cut a small opening in the rear window of a car so only the muzzle of their rifle protruded. Then, they could hide behind a heavily tinted rear window, invisible to the laser, while they prepared to take their shot.

Since the laser device will pick out all layered optics, it will home in on rifle scopes, binoculars, telescopes, video cameras, still cameras, glasses and sunglasses. A sniper can use this knowledge to their advantage by setting up decoy optics in their operational area to saturate it with false alarms. What would a counter-sniper team do when their optics laser reflection device picks up a dozen separate hits? Would they send a reaction force to a dozen different locations to check out all the possible threats? By doing this, a sniper could 'smoke out' a counter-sniper team by getting them to react to a false alarm. A sniper could use these decoy optics as bait to ambush the counter-sniper team when they go forward to investigate the suspicious optics. To take this a step further, an enemy sniper could set up a stuffed dummy with a scope to get the laser-armed counter-sniper team to take a shot and reveal their location. The tactical options for exploiting the optics laser reflection device are many.

Millimeter-Wave Radar Technology

A step up from the relatively simple acoustic and optics detection systems is millimeter-wave radar systems using portable radar units to detect bullets as they fly through the air and then collect data on the bullet's trajectory, enabling the system to backtrack the bullet to its original source. There are already radar systems in existence that can accurately detect incoming mortar and artillery rounds and then provide a back azimuth to the point of origin. However, the projectiles this radar detects are much larger than a bullet and have a much longer hang time, giving the radar system more time to track the projectile. Attempting to track a bullet, which is an extremely small object with a traveling time to the target of a second or two at most, is difficult with current technology. Testing shows the average 7.62 mm bullet, if fired from 500 meters away or less, can be tracked with a high-probability of locating the sniper. To date, millimeter-wave radar systems are expensive, complicated, and fragile as compared to other systems. Practical counter-sniper radar systems are still years away from production, although several companies are pursuing them.

The Sniper's Response to Radar Systems

It is difficult to counter a radar system, but certain weaknesses can be exploited. For instance, bullet detecting radar works best when aimed skyward to avoid ground clutter. In response, a sniper could fire at ground level, amongst a busy area filled with cars and people, so the radar would be overwhelmed with clutter and unable to detect and identify a single bullet. Natural clutter that can be exploited includes rain, snow, and sandstorms. Or, a sniper could intentionally fire a small-size bullet, like a 5.56 mm round, which has a smaller radar cross section, making it more difficult for the radar system to pick it up. To cause even more difficulties for a radar system, a sniper could fire a radar absorbing/deflecting round so their bullet would be effectively invisible (I am not aware of any such bullets on the market today).

LIDAR (Laser Radar) Technology

The proper term for this technology is really LIDAR (Laser Imaging Detection And Ranging) as opposed to radar (radio detection and ranging), but many people refer to the technology as laser radar. LIDAR works much the same as radar bullet detection technology except LIDAR does not use radio waves to detect a bullet, it uses light. When a laser hits an object like a bullet, it creates backscatter that is reflected back to and detected by the LIDAR receiver. In this way, the laser radar detects a bullet in flight and then backtracks the azimuth to its point of origin.

The Sniper's Response to Laser Radar Systems

LIDAR systems suffer from the same basic limitations as a radar system, but to a lesser degree. LIDAR is more reliable because the system uses light reflections as opposed to radio reflections to detect a bullet. Laser systems still suffer from urban and environmental clutter, but less so. And while radar systems can be jammed, LIDAR systems cannot. A LIDAR detection system too can be fooled with a small bullet, made from material that does not easily reflect light (a sniper would not want to use a shiny, copper jacketed bullet for instance), and if intentionally fired amid the clutter of a busy city during rain, snow, or sandstorms.

Infrared (IR) and Thermal Imaging Counter-Sniper Technology

Some counter-sniper technology employs infrared (IR) cameras to observes and record the muzzle flash from a weapon. Frequently, the IR camera system is inte-

Infrared Technology

This infrared picture shows heat as white and cold as black. Notice that a sniper firing from deep in a room is invisible to IR cameras.

grated with a visible light camera system to help eliminate false alarms. Companies have even emplaced these IR systems in UAVs (Unmanned Aerial Vehicles) which proved successful in identifying ground muzzle flashes from their lofty perches. Like LIDAR and acoustic technology systems, muzzle flash identification technology has the ability to determine the azimuth and elevation of a gunshot, but not the distance. However, the distance to the shooter could be determined by simply analyzing the terrain.

IR technology can also detect the thermal signature of a bullet in flight. This is possible because as a bullet flies through the air, it creates friction, and the bullet and the air around the bullet become hotter than the surrounding air. Consequently, as the heated bullet passes through the relatively cooler air, IR sensors looking in the direction of a gunshot can 'see' the heated path of the bullet. By looking at the path of the bullet, the infrared system can backtrack the bullet to the source. IR systems can be used to not only track the bullet's path, but to detect the firer themselves through their body heat. If a sniper's position can be positively identified, then the sniper can be tracked through their body heat signature alone. An IR system gives the operator an advantage because it can see through darkness, smoke, clouds of dust, and even walls (depending on the capabilities of the IR system and the characteristics of the walls). IR technology can even see a sniper's gun barrel as it heats up from firing the bullet and the friction caused by the bullet traveling down the weapon's rifled barrel.

The Sniper's Response to Infrared Technology

A sniper can defeat infrared detectors in a variety of ways, but it is difficult. Let us look at the problem of IR muzzle flash technology since this is the easiest type of system to defeat. Muzzle flash detection systems are inherently limited because they must see a muzzle flash to work. However, from the reading we have done so far, it is easy to hide a weapon's muzzle flash by using a suppressor, or firing from within an enclosed space like the trunk of a car, or from a small hole cut out of a wall. Also, muzzle flash technology can be overwhelmed with false alarms in dense urban areas with thousands of random lights flashing on and off in any given area of a city.

When it comes to IR systems designed to detect body heat signatures, most systems are incapable of producing pictures of sufficient quality to identify more than an outline of a person. Thus, the thermal imager is unable to determine if a person is reaching for their wallet or grabbing a pistol. It falls upon the sniper to fool the thermal imaging operator by displaying non-threatening body language. Therefore, a sniper would not want to lie down on a deserted roof (a dead give away) when they could sit on a balcony, in a chair, with several people nearby, thus creating a natural and non-hostile posture.

IR imaging can be made less effective if there is some sort of screening between the shooter and the IR sensor. A person sitting behind a thick, concrete wall will be harder to detect by an IR sensor than a person in an open field. The person behind the concrete wall will appear to the IR operator as an indistinguishable blob and not as an identifiable threat. When it comes to their weapon, a sniper can reduce its thermal image by cooling it (keeping the weapon in a freezer, refrigerator, cooler, cold room, a bag of ice, or by placing cold packs on it) before they use it. Since thermal imagers only pick up heat, a cold object is invisible. While a sniper may be able to defeat IR technology searching for their body or weapon heat signature, there is no way for the sniper to fire a cold bullet that does not create friction (and therefore heat) while it flies through the air. (The Discovery Channel's *Mythbusters* show tried firing an ice bullet and found it to be impractical except at point-blank ranges.)

One thing to consider when confronted with LIDAR, radar, and IR systems is these counter-sniper systems are most likely not up and running twenty-four hours a day. Because these systems may be man portable and thus battery powered and are expensive and maintenance intensive, many have to be triggered by a specific event to turn them on. A common means of triggering these more sophisticated systems is with acoustic sensors. With these acoustically triggered systems, only when a gunshot is 'heard' do the other LIDAR, radar, or IR systems switch on. Thus, the sniper comes full circle, back to beating an acoustic system, to avoid turning on the other more sophisticated counter-sniper systems.

Closed Circuit Television Systems (CCTV)

A common form of technical surveillance used to target criminals is CCTV. CCTV is a system of visible light cameras (IR cameras are also available, but less common) networked together that record specific areas of interest. The cameras transfer what they view to a central location where the operators view real-time activity or review the unseen film at a later time. Visible light cameras have their limitations in that they cannot detect a flying bullet because it is too small and is moving too fast for the camera to pick it up. Be this as it may, CCTV is useful for a variety of other tasks like recording the faces, license plates, and movement of criminals as they conduct their operations. As a result, CCTV is generally more useful in post-shooting investigations than as a preventative system.

CCTV Camera

This picture shows a CCTV camera at Heathrow Airport in London. England has become the most surveilled country in the world, a trend that began with their efforts to provide security against the Irish Republican Army.

One nation using CCTV on a large scale is Britain, due in part as a reaction to the IRA's bombing campaigns during The Troubles. Law enforcement in Britain use CCTV to deter criminal activity, to view real-time events, and to record actions where the film may be used at a later date for criminal investigations and prosecutions. An informal study estimated Britain had approximately 400,000 surveillance cameras positioned throughout the country, with the majority of them focused on public urban areas. This extensive use of surveillance cameras proved useful during the July 7, 2005 London suicide bombings when four men blew themselves up, killing fifty-two people and wounding another seven hundred. CCTV captured pictures of the suicide bombers before the attack, which then aided British authorities in identifying the men during the post-bombing investigation.

CCTV used on a massive scale, as in Britain, causes problems for any organization conducting illegal activities. In CCTV monitored areas, a sniper will have to observe the surrounding camera systems and determine the areas the cameras cover. Consequently, the sniper's first strategy is camera avoidance. If a sniper cannot avoid surveillance, then they will try to avoid being filmed in the act. It is far better to be filmed from afar, walking through a crowded area, than is to get caught pulling the trigger.

While extensive CCTV systems make a guerrilla's activities difficult, successful operations are still possible. For example, the IRA still conducted effective operations in London despite the presence of cameras. IRA members hid their identity from cameras by using simple ruses like wearing motorcycle helmets, wigs, ball caps, and sunglasses (so facial recognition software programs would not get them). IRA vehicles used for operations either had fake license plates or the cars were stolen (so cameras taking pictures of a car's license plate for running red lights were rendered useless). While under the surveillance of cameras, IRA men mimicked the 'normal' body language of the people around them so they did not trigger a reaction from screen watch-

403

ers. CCTV definitely made the IRA work harder, but they still exploited the reactive nature of the CCTV system to carry out their operations. CCTV systems have other weaknesses: they can be put of action by cutting their power sources, spray painting their lenses, shooting them out, or blowing up the control room where the cameras are monitored.

Automated/Robotic Counter-Sniper Systems

When discussing counter-sniper technology, the subject of automated response systems is often brought up. Some have suggested a good counter-sniper system would be one that automatically detects an enemy sniper and then returns fire at the sniper - all in a matter of seconds and all based on a computer's artificial intelligence. This is not a good idea for several reasons, but mainly because it removes the human element of judgment from the equation, something a computer has yet been able to replicate. An automated sniper system is a flawed one because its automated response would be easy to fool. Just imagine a guerrilla remotely firing a rifle from a crowded apartment building. Would you want an automated system returning fire into a building filled with innocent people? The goal in this situation is not to return fire at a weapon, the goal is to catch or kill the sniper. But, an automated counter-sniper system would equate the firing of a weapon to the presence of a sniper when they may be two separate things.

Also, the margin of error inherent in any automated system could be easily manipulated by the guerilla sniper. Since the determination of the location of the sniper is an educated guess, even for a computer, there is no guarantee the automated system would direct its return fire at the right target. A sniper manipulating this margin of error could get a computer to return fire at a location, filled with people, that is not the sniper's true position.

Also of concern is the ease in which a guerrilla sniper could overload an automated system with false alarms. How does an acoustically triggered computer differentiate between the noise of a gunshot, a firecracker, and a backfiring car? How does an infrared triggered computer differentiate between a muzzle flash, a light bulb being flashed, and an exploding cherry bomb? How does an optics laser triggered computer differentiate between a rifle scope, a magnifying glass, and a cell-phone camera? How does a radar or LIDAR-triggered computer differentiate between the bullet fired from a sniper, a marble launched by a ten-year old girl with a sling-shot, and a pellet fired by a young boy wielding an air-rifle? Computers are unable to distinguish between friend and foe, are unable to make judgments based on nuance, and could be tricked into committing automated mass murder.

Sniper Detection Technology

Without doubt, counter-sniper technology can make life difficult, or very short, for an unwary sniper. A skilled sniper may be able to defeat one or two of the available counter-sniper systems, but they probably cannot defeat an integrated system employing all of these systems used in combination. A specific area of a city, scoured constantly by acoustic, LIDAR, and infrared counter-sniper systems, will most likely detect a sniper's shot. Significantly, this counter-sniper technology will only be useful

This carbine with a $500 sound suppressor will beat million dollar systems like ShotSpotter and BBN's Boomerang counter-sniper systems.

in an area where a sniper is expected to operate so the system users know where to direct their machines. After all, a city like Baghdad is a huge area to cover and finding the right place to employ a counter-sniper system may be akin to finding a needle in a haystack.

Of course, the operators of this counter-sniper technology must be aware of the limitations of their equipment. All things mechanical and electrical require regular maintenance and will eventually break down. Also, the equipment is only as good as the people operating it. A human must monitor this equipment every second while it is running. One must keep in mind extreme weather – either very hot or very cold - has a way of degrading the effectiveness of everything mechanical. While companies are striving to make this counter-sniper technology omni-directional, today's operators still have to point their sensors in the right direction for them to work. The system operators must be concerned if they use electronic jamming equipment - to counter cell phones and radio waves used to initiate remote attacks like IEDs - because they may jam their own equipment. In turn, these electronically dependent counter-sniper systems are themselves vulnerable to jamming.

The Sniper's Response to Sniper Detection Technology

The most salient limitation of sniper detection technology is its reactive nature. The systems only detect a sniper after they have taken their shot (except for the optical laser reflection systems and they cannot ensure the optics they detect are being used by a sniper). However, there are several situations where detecting the location of a sniper is irrelevant. For example, Chechen snipers in Grozny routinely fought it out with Russian soldiers even after their positions were revealed. These sniper-martyrs did not care the Russians knew where they were since they were going to kill as many Russians as they could until they were killed themselves. Locating a sniper only works if the sniper cares about being located.

On a variation of the above tactic, a sniper can intentionally fire a shot, with the understanding a counter-sniper system will detect them, to lure security forces into an ambush. If security forces are fond of using helicopters to react to and destroy a suspected sniper position, guerrillas can be waiting with shoulder launched anti-aircraft missiles for the express purpose of shooting down the responding aircraft. Or, guerrillas can rig a building with explosives and wait for security forces to surround and enter the building to search for the sniper. Once the security forces begin their search of the building, the guerrillas blow up the entire structure and collapse it with everyone inside.

If the sniper exploits the basic fundamentals of urban guerrilla warfare and fires from amidst a crowded area, then security forces may be incapable of responding with force because they will kill innocent people in the process. Security forces will then have to surround and search the area in hopes of finding the culprit. However, all the sniper then has to do is get rid of their rifle before security forces arrive so there is no physically incriminating evidence linking them to the shooting. Once again, detecting where the shot came from becomes irrelevant.

A sniper can also make detection irrelevant by employing a remotely fired weapon. In this case, a sniper sets up a rifle fired any number of remote ways (via cell phone, pager, garage door opener, etc...). After the sniper fires the weapon, security forces respond to the scene of the shooting only to find an empty car or a deserted room and no actual person. We should keep in mind if the weapon can be fired remotely, an explosive device, placed on or near the weapon, can also be remotely triggered when security forces arrive on the scene.

If the sniper wants to make a clean getaway after detection, all they have to do is apply the fundamentals of urban guerrilla sniping. Since all counter-sniper systems have a certain margin of error, the sniper can exploit these 'seams' in the systems. For instance, a sniper could select a firing position in line with several other firing positions. Consequently, when the counter-sniper system backtracks the bullet's trajectory, the system operator realizes the shot could have come any number of positions because of their machine's margin of error.

If the sniper cannot defeat the counter-sniper system, then, perhaps, they can defeat their enemy's ability to react. If a sniper fires from the trunk of a car and a counter-sniper system detects the exact location of the car, this information can be made irrelevant. As soon as the sniper fires, the car drives off with the sniper in it. When the reaction force arrives, only minutes later, at the exact location where the machine told them to go, the sniper is long gone. In a scenario such as this, a good escape plan trumps the counter-sniper system's ability to detect where the shot came from.

If a sniper is aware their enemy is using counter-sniper systems, they can use this knowledge to their advantage and incorporate it into their reconnaissance of their target. Since the sniper is on the alert for possible counter-sniper technology, they can scan the terrain for acoustic sensors and infrared cameras just as they search for police checkpoints and other security measures before they make their shot. If a sniper detects a counter-sniper system, they can make the decision to work somewhere else. In such a situation, the counter-sniper system would have worked because it made the sniper move to an area less secure. Or, if the sniper wants to be a little more aggressive, they can locate and shoot the system itself. Along this same line, the sniper can target the operator manning the counter-sniper system. Just as snipers intentionally target officers and radiomen, they can now put counter-sniper operators at the top of their lists.

Counter-Sniper Story: The Limitations of Technology

Aerial Counter-Sniper System

Above, pictures of the blimp outfitted with the Viper system. At the upper and lower right are the visible light and IR cameras that were supposed to detect a gunshot fired from below.

During John Muhammad's and Lee Malvo's October 2002 sniping spree in the Washington D.C. area, law enforcement officials attempted to use counter-sniper technology to find the two killers. More specifically, police tried to use the Viper Muzzle Flash Detection and Location System, employed from a both a helicopter and an airship, to find the shooters. The overall experience revealed some of the limitations of current counter-sniper technology.

The Viper system consisted of a midwave infrared camera intended to pick up the muzzle flash of a weapon. Once the IR camera detected a muzzle flash, it cued a visible light camera that then focused on and recorded the area where the muzzle flash was detected. When the Viper detection system was tested from a helicopter at the Fort Meade, Maryland rifle range, it reliably detected muzzle flashes down below. However, this was unrealistic testing as the DC snipers were firing in dense urban areas while the rifle range was open, rural terrain.

The Viper system was fundamentally flawed because it was based solely on detecting the muzzle flash of a weapon. To be fair, the Viper's IR system was equipped with various filters to limit the number of false alarms and to distinguish a true muzzle flash from other infrared clutter. The problem was, the DC snipers fired the majority of their shots from the trunk of their car so there was no visible muzzle flash. So, if the Viper system was deployed in a manner where it could operate within its capabilities, Viper would have detected absolutely nothing. In this case, the street savvy tactics of the two shooters outwitted millions of dollars of technology and machinery.

Because the visible light camera on the Viper was cued by the detection of a muzzle flash, this part of the system was also eliminated as a useful tool. It would have been great if the visible light camera, set up to automatically slew towards an identified muzzle flash, filmed the shooters in the act or as they tried to get away. This footage could be used in court as evidence to prosecute the killers. However, since there were no muzzle flashes, there would be no infrared detection, and there would be no visible light recording of the events. With the Viper, one flawed system was tied to the other, rendering both of them useless.

Part of the difficulty of employing the Viper system was finding the right platform for it. Using the system in a ground configuration was quickly ruled out because the area to be covered was huge (an area roughly from Frederick, MD, to Baltimore, MD to Richmond, VA). For the Viper to work, the operators needed the exact location of the shooters and they had to be within line of sight of their muzzle flash. Since the shooters struck at random with no predictable pattern, a ground based strategy had a zero percent chance for success.

Consequently, the Viper operators decided to cover a much larger area and to guarantee a better chance for line of sight detection of a sniper's muzzle flash, they set up the Viper system in a JetRanger helicopter. To accommodate the system, the left door of the JetRanger was removed and the Viper, powered by two car batteries, was ready to go. Testing of the Viper/JetRanger system revealed that flying below one hundred feet caused an unacceptable number of false alarms due to random objects being blown around from the rotor downwash. However, FAA restrictions mandated the JetRanger fly at or above one thousand feet. At that height, during testing, muzzle flashes were reliably detected.

While helicopter operations were feasible, the JetRanger suffered from relatively short air endurance and had to return frequently to base to refuel. Therefore, it was decided to mount the Viper system on a U.S. Navy leased Airship 600. The airship had several advantages such as its relatively slow speed and long air endurance. On the other hand, operating the airship in the relatively limited Washington, DC Temporary Flight Restriction Area was a challenge. In the end, the aerial Viper system was never employed, because the DC snipers were caught the day before the airship was finally ready to be used.[1]

Another Attempt at Sniper Detection: The RC-7

As the DC snipers continued to spread terror despite a massive police presence, a decision was made to employ military assets to try and detect the shooters. Secretary of Defense Don Rumsfeld authorized the military to use their RC-7 Airborne Reconnaissance Low (ARL) aircraft. There were some legal concerns using the military's RC-7 to help in a domestic criminal case because of possible violation of the 1878 Posse Comitatus Act, which prevents the U.S. military from performing civilian law enforcement. The military got around the law by agreeing the military personnel operating the plane would only work the surveillance equipment and the police would conduct the analysis and investigative follow up.

Defense officials thought the RC-7 could help with the sniper problem because of its sophisticated infrared sensors that could perform surveillance of large areas, both day and night, and then transmit what its cameras saw to operators on the ground. The military even considered using Predator Unmanned Aerial Vehicles (UAV) and Navy P-3 Orion surveillance planes to help in the search, but because they were in such

---

1 by M. C. Ertem, E. Heidhausen, M. Pauli in a paper presented at 32nd AIPR, 2003. (Most of the information on this subject is from this article.)

RC-7 ARL

The multi-million dollar ARL was unable to detect a sniper firing from the trunk of a car in an urban environment.

heavy use against the Taliban in Afghanistan, the option was cancelled.

What exactly were the capabilities of this plane which was supposed to succeed where earth-based law enforcement failed? GlobalSecurity.Org describes the plane's capabilities in depth: "The Airborne Reconnaissance Low (ARL) is a multifunction, day/night, all weather reconnaissance intelligence asset developed and fielded by the Army in support of an urgent requirement for a low profile intelligence aircraft. It consists of a modified DeHavilland DHC-7 fixed-wing aircraft equipped with communications intelligence (COMINT), imagery intelligence (IMINT), and Moving Target Indicator/Synthetic Aperture Radar (MTI/SAR) mission payloads. The payloads are controlled and operated via onboard open-architecture, multi-function workstations. Intelligence collected on the ARL can be analyzed and recorded on the aircraft workstations in real-time or stored on-board for post-mission processing. During multi-aircraft missions, data can be shared between cooperating aircraft via ultra high frequency (UHF) air-to-air datalink to allow multi-platform COMINT geolocation operations. The ARL system includes a variety of communications subsystems to support near-real-time dissemination of intelligence and dynamic retasking of the aircraft.

The ARL system was developed to accommodate diverse mission requirements through the implementation of an open architecture, modular, reconfigurable mission sensors. These systems can be operated separately or can be used to cue each other for examining targets using different sectors of the electromagnetic spectrum. The systems are controlled from four workstations within the aircraft by the mission analysts.

The DeHavilland of Canada Dash-7, a four-engine, turboprop, commuter airplane was chosen as the platform for SIGINT and IMINT collection. The Dash-7 aircraft's ability to operate out of austere runways, its ability to carry the mission payload and its endurance led to the Dash-7's selection. It is an extensively modified aircraft that has a higher maximum gross weight and extended range capability added in the ARL conversions. The Dash-7 is a medium sized, four engine, passenger and cargo transport. It is pressurized and can operate at up to 20,400 feet with a full mission crew. Mission duration can be up to eight hours with a range of 1,400 nautical miles at a cruising speed of 230 knots. Proposed future engines and "wet wing" fuel tanks may extend the range to 2,800 nautical miles. The cockpit has been upgraded to Airspace 2000 standards.

The system developed from a Commander in Chief U.S. Southern Command (SOUTHCOM) requirement for a manned aviation platform that could provide an IMINT and SIGINT collection capability in SOUTHCOM. The design requirements submitted stated that Airborne Reconnaissance Low should support nation-building, counter-narcotics, and promote-democracy missions (now classified as stability and support operations or operations other than war) in SOUTHCOM's area of responsibility. The RC-7s were initially deployed with US Southern Command (SOUTH-COM) in 1993 to assist in counter-drug surveillance operations and later deployed to Haiti in support of US peacekeeping operations. In 1996 an RC-7 was deployed to Bosnia-Herzegovina to support NATO's IFOR peacekeeping force."

So, how did this all-weather, $10 million-plus, superplane perform as a counter-sniper system? The RC-7 never did detect the snipers in the act. This is because the RC-7 suffered from the same limitations as the Viper system. The RC-7 relied primarily on IR imaging to detect a muzzle blast from a weapon and therefore had no better chance of detecting the needle in the haystack than did the Viper. And the fact the RC-7 had powerful cameras capable of reading a license plate from its orbit and then transmit this detailed imagery to users on the ground also was of no use. If the RC-7 did not know where to look and point its sensors, then it was out of luck. Once again, because the DC snipers fired a single shot, at random, throughout a large geographic area made up of a dense urban environment, the military's multi-million dollar surveillance plane, which worked great in the open waters against drug runners in cigarette boats, was useless against a lone shooter firing from the trunk of an old, beat up Caprice Classic.

Into The Future

We are truly in the computer age and the trend towards technical means of counter-sniper detection is not going to fade away. Quite the opposite is true. We can expect a growth in counter-sniper technology as it becomes more reliable, accurate, and rugged. Some day, every soldier or police officer may be a counter-sniper system, each armed with a small, hand-held or vehicle mounted device able to detect a gunshot through a variety of means such as acoustics, radar, and thermal imaging. As of the writing of this book, the trained, educated sniper still holds the edge over the counter-sniper machines when working in the complex urban environment. Someday, one can expect more sophisticated counter-sniper machines will eventually take the edge away from the sniper and the lone shooter, no matter how skilled they are, will be at a disadvantage.

However, all is not lost for the sniper. The sniper will not be wiped out by the machines if they adapt to their new environment. What kind of adaptation are we talking about? Are we talking about better camouflage? Better rifles? Exploiting the urban terrain more cleverly? No. For the modern sniper to adapt into the future they must accept the fact technology is growing and it must be embraced, not avoided. In turn, the sniper can also use technology to their advantage. Use a machine to defeat a machine. The following chapter will explore how snipers can exploit modern technology to defeat the growing threat from counter-sniper technology.

Chapter 22

The Genesis of Remote Sniping: The Periscope Trench Rifle

The need for a remote sniping capability was recognized as far back as World War I. During the Great War, deadly German snipers, working from the cover of their muddy trench systems, made daily life in the Allied trenches hazardous. Even if an allied sniper carefully poked their rifle and part of their head over the parapet of their dugouts to observe the German lines, they still ran the risk of taking a bullet in the face from a waiting German marksman. No matter what the allied snipers did, they still had to expose themselves to some degree just to look down the sights of their weapon. What was the answer to this problem, where the very act of aiming your rifle was a death sentence?

As early as 1915, Allied troops developed a system to protect themselves from the always-scanning German snipers. This invention was the periscope rifle. Specifically, one Sergeant William Beech, an Australian soldier who fought in the gruesome trenches of Gallipoli, developed a version of the periscope rifle. In the same year, the French also created a version of the periscope rifle. There were different models of the periscope rifle, but they all had the same basic design, which included a frame to hold a rifle above the trenches, a periscope so the shooter could remain in the trenches, but still look over the rifle's sights through the periscope's mirrors, and a method of remotely pulling the rifle's trigger. Some historians credit two Americans with developing the periscope rifle, although it is more accurate to say they developed a version of the periscope rifle.

Even though the United States did not enter World War I until 1917, many Americans believed they would eventually be dragged into the horrible conflict and some were actively preparing for such an eventuality. Such men included James L. Cameron and Lawrence E. Yaggi, two avid riflemen from Ohio. They were following the events of the Great War and understood what a deadly menace enemy snipers presented. Their answer to this problem was the periscope rifle. The two created a metal frame a rifle sat in, there was a periscope attached to it, and levers for working the bolt-action of the rifle and the trigger. With this system, the rifle and frame sat on the shoulders of the shooter, above their head, so the weapon could be fired without any exposure to the enemy.

Once they had a working model of their invention, they traveled across the Atlantic

Sergeant William Beech aims his periscope rifle, which he created in May 1915. This photo is from the trenches of Gallipoli.

in order to present their design to the British and French soldiers locked in combat with the Germans. At the time, the Allied response to the German sniper threat was to observe the enemy lines with traditional box periscopes. Once they had a target, they would put down the periscope, pick up their rifle, and take their shot. However, the Germans recognized this tactic and could see the sun glint off the box periscopes. In response, the German shooters patiently waited for the Allied sharpshooters to stick their head over the trench with their rifle and then promptly shot them.

The two inventors took advice from these combat veterans and further refined their system. Following guidance from the United States Ordnance Department, the two inventors had to create a device that did not require any 'significant or permanent' alterations to the standard U.S. service rifle - the Springfield M1903 bolt-action rifle. In the end, Cameron and Yaggi produced a lightweight metal frame weighing only six pounds. The weight of the frame was actually advantageous since it dampened the recoil of the rifle and made follow on shots easier.

The most important piece of the entire design was the periscope sight, which was called a 'sightascope'. The sightascope was a stable device as it was securely attached by screws to the left side of the rifle's stock. Different from the earlier French and Australian designs, the sightascope was its own aiming device and did not require the shooter to look over the rifle's sights - it was an independent scope. During testing, this system was able to fire ten bullets in a 1.3 inch group at two hundred yards. Importantly, after hearing from the French and British veterans, the visible lenses of the sightascope were recessed so light would not reflect off them. While this system performed admirably during America's short experience in the war, as soon as the conflict ended, interest for the Cameron-Yaggi design quickly disappeared and the invention was all but forgotten[1].

---

1 Canfield, Bruce, *Man At Arms,* September/October 1993. (Information about the Cameron-Yaggi device is from Mr. Canfield's interesting article.)

Cameron-Yaggi Periscope Rifle

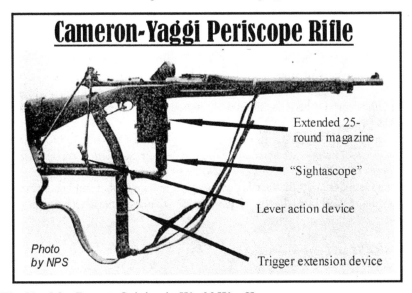

Extended 25-round magazine

"Sightascope"

Lever action device

Photo by NPS

Trigger extension device

The Need for Remote Sniping in World War II

The need for a remote sniping capability was very real in the trench warfare of the Great War, but as so often is the case, a weapon important in wartime suddenly loses its appeal in peacetime. By the time World War II came in the fall of 1939, the ghosts of World War I were laid to rest. This new war was one of movement, of slashing panzer formations, screaming dive bombers, and mobile artillery. The paradigm of World War I, where the world's great nations bled themselves white in the god-awful trenches, was discarded as a failed model. Discarded along with the idea of static, attrition warfare was the trench periscope rifle. Plus, World War II began a full twenty years after the Great War ended. There were probably few soldiers left in the militaries of the participating countries who even remembered what a trench periscope rifle was. They were not fighting a trench war any ways, so who cared?

It was in the fall of 1942, when the Germans' doomed Sixth Army was trapped in the blood soaked streets of Stalingrad, that the German army wished they developed the trench periscope rifle into a modern, useable weapon system. During the ferocious urban warfare in the bombed out ruins of Stalin's city, the German army realized they needed the ability to fire around corners without being seen. As it was, whenever a German solider peered around a corner with their weapon, they were met with a hail of gunfire or fell victim to an invisible Russian sniper concealed somewhere in the maze of rubbled buildings.

A few Russian soldiers, who were also fighting for their lives in Stalingrad and suffering tremendous casualties, also realized they needed the ability to fire their weapons at the Germans while remaining concealed. Vassili Zaitsev mentions in his book *Notes of a Sniper* that he met a Russian infantryman who rigged several PPSH-41 submachine guns to fire remotely when the Germans assaulted the building he was defending. Vassili described exactly what the hard pressed soldiers devised in order to defend the Metalworking Factory, "Inside the boiler room were six of our Tommygunners and one machine gunner, the sailor Plaskin. Since their group was cut off from our battalion, they had turned the boiler room into a fortress, from which they had been able to repel one German attack after another. Misha and I were amazed by their cunning and ingenuity. They had taken several of their Tommy-guns and aimed their barrels through breaches in the wall. The Tommy-guns had been bracketed in place by twisted pieces of water pipe. They had run wires from the triggers back to Plaskin who at this stage was the only soldier left with injuries minor enough to be able to fire anything. I asked Plaskin how it worked, and he demonstrated by jerking on the wires."

The Germans did not know it, but they already had a ideal weapon for remote sniping in the pockmarked wasteland of Stalingrad: their excellent, general purpose machine-gun - the MG-34. The MG-34 could be fired single-shot like a regular rifle and both the Germans and Allies used machine-guns for single-shot sniping during the trench warfare of World War I. But, by the time of Stalingrad, these techniques were forgotten.

German MG-34 Medium Machine-Gun

The MG-34 came with a scope, so the weapon could be precisely aimed, and with an excellent tripod that was standard issue to all German MG-34 teams. Consequently, any German MG-34 team could aim their machine-gun at a specific target, like a doorway, window, or bunker, and left the weapon sitting on its tripod. They could have connected a wire to the trigger, like the Russians did, and moved a couple of meters away from their remote sniping system, staying hidden in a bunker or building. When a Russian appeared in their sights they could remotely pull the trigger, all while remaining safe from the Russians' own sniper teams. While a few individual machine-gun teams may have cracked the code on remote sniping, it never became formal instruction at the German infantry schools.

While the German infantry could have jury-rigged their MG-34s into remote sniping platforms, the German military did create a remote controlled MG-34 towards the end of the war called the Rundumsfeuer (Remote Control Mount). However, this remote machine-gun was mounted on armored vehicles like the Sturmgeschutz and Hetzer tank destroyers. It was designed to be controlled from inside the safety of the vehicle so the crew could fire the machine-gun in urban environments and against enemy anti-tank teams. The Rundumsfeuer was a relatively simple design and allowed the operator to remotely fire their MG-34 on single shot as a sniper weapon.

The Krummer Lauf (Bent Barrel)

By the fall of 1943, after the Sixth Army's resounding defeat in Stalingrad, the German military requested a weapon be designed that could fire around corners. As fate would have it, a German officer by the name of Colonel Hans-Joachim Schaede was already working on such a device, except it was being designed to help armor crews defend themselves from enemy anti-tank teams. Schaede was designing a bent barreled weapon specifically for the German assault guns - the Sturmgeschutz - which suffered from not having a bow mounted machine-gun and were thus extremely vulnerable from enemy anti-tank teams during street fighting in Russia. After fabricating a workable design, Schaede received approval from Der Fuhrer in December 1943 to

MG-34

The MG-34 was a general purpose machine-gun that could be fired single shot from a tripod and aimed with a telescopic sight. All one had to do was pull the trigger with a wire or string and you had a remote sniping system.

move forward with his Krummer Lauf - or bent barrel.

With official backing from Hitler himself, the device went into full production. However, the Krummer Lauf suffered from excessive recoil and was best when fired from an armored vehicle in order to stabilize it. An initial production of ten thousand units went forward in August 1944 and soon saw service in combat. The German panzer crews, who had to fight off determined Russian tank-hunting teams, had great praise for the Krummer Lauf design, which ensured the bent barrel weapons would see continued use.

While the vehicle-mounted model proved successful, Schaede was determined to design a bent barrel for infantry use. His idea was to create a barrel with a lesser bend, of only thirty degrees. He eventually designed a model that was eleven inches long, .787 inches in diameter, and rifled. This infantry model could also be used as a grenade launcher if so desired. However, firing around a corner was not enough. The German soldier had to aim and accurately hit a target. Consequently, Schaede went to the famed Zeiss optical firm and requested their assistance in producing a prismatic visor/sight with a set of mirrors positioned near the muzzle so soldiers could see a target, aim through the sight, and accurately engage the enemy. Because the infantry version was only bent thirty degrees, it had manageable recoil. The final infantry version was successfully completed and began production in early 1945.

The Krummer Lauf did not change the outcome of the Germans' losing war, but it was an important leap forward in the evolution of remote firing weapons designed for urban combat. During the fighting on the Western front, American forces captured many of these Krummer Lauf systems. These captured systems were sent to the U.S. Army's ordnance corps where they were studied and their performance analyzed. Captain Philip B. Sharpe of the U.S. Army Ordnance Corps tested the 90-degree models designed for use in armored vehicles and noted, "Over two-thirds of the bullets were torn into two or three pieces--but at very short range it would have been deadly." This was because the bullets fired through the barrel bent at ninety degrees suffered from yaw - tumbling off their axis - and thus became unstable. Sharpe noted the recoil on these ninety-degree models was severe and simply impractical for infantry soldiers to use. However, he made the observation when fired from a tank - as designed - the Krummer Lauf, "shot excellently."

Then, Sharpe tested the thirty-degree model which the Germans intended to equip their machine-pistol armed infantrymen with. Captain Sharpe saw the infantry model, "shot perfectly. At 100 meters this author could place four out of five shots in a letter-head size target....Had these [Krummer Lauf devices] ever gotten into full production and distribution, they would have cost us many thousands of casualties."[2]

As with the trench periscope rifle of World War I, the Krummer Lauf was quickly forgotten. The German, Russian, and American militaries - who all had first-hand experience with these innovative weapon systems – discarded the Krummer Lauf as an exotic piece of equipment, which had a limited application at best. It would be exactly sixty years from the Krummer Lauf's birth when a modern, more sophisticated version of the bent barrel finally came to light. This new device was called simply the 'Corner Shot' and was created by Israeli soldiers who discovered the need for such a weapon after decades of urban guerrilla warfare against Hezbollah, the PLO, and Hamas. Ironically, it was the survivors of Hitler's Holocaust who perfected the original German design and created a weapon system heralded by many as the major evolution in dismounted urban warfare and close quarters battle. What was born in the streets of Stalingrad and died in the smoking ruins of Berlin was resurrected in the Gaza Strip and the West Bank.

The Corner Shot

In December 2003, the Corner Shot was officially released, the result of five years of product development and a cost of $2 million. The Corner Shot is similar to its father, the Krummer Lauf, but with some important distinctions. First, the system is designed to accept a variety of pistols that are inserted into a synthetic, lightweight frame. The frame is hinged so when the Corner Shot is fired around a corner, the pistol itself is placed around the corner. Unlike the Krummer Lauf, there is no bent barrel as the entire weapon moves on the hinged frame. Also, the Corner Shot uses a small camera, which is attached to the frame and is connected to a small LCD screen that enables the shooter to see what their pistol sees, all without exposing themselves to enemy fire. The Corner Shot also comes in versions that can fire assault rifles and grenade launchers.

A former Israeli soldier involved in the Corner Shot's design had high praise for the system, "I believe that the Corner Shot weapon system can be extremely beneficial in the global war on terror. It protects soldiers' lives and increases their chances of survival, while drastically improving their ability to gather information and transmit the combat scenario as well as pinpoint and engage targets out of their line of sight. Today's combat situations, especially in low intensity conflicts, involve fighting in urban terrain, and inside inhabited buildings, forced entry into airplanes, buses or trains. This unnecessarily exposes security forces to the enemy and presents an immediate risk to their lives. Corner Shot removes the need for this initial exposure."[3]

2 Czech, Kenneth P., *Weaponry: Krummer Lauf*, www.historynet.com. (All the quotes in this chapter concerning the Krummer Lauf is from an article by Mr. Czech.)
3 Shuman, *New Weapon System Helps Engage Targets Lurking "Around the Corner"*, December 16, 2003, www.IsraelInsider.com

Krummer Lauf

Here is a picture of a Krummer lauf 90-degree bent barrel attached to the end of a Stg 44 assault rifle. This picture simulates the weapon being fired from inside of an armored vehicle. The original intent was for tank crews to fight off enemy anti-tank teams.

One of Corner Shot's creators, Asaf Nadel, a veteran of Israel's military, agrees with the importance of such a weapon system in an urban environment, "The Corner Shot system is designed in a way that enables security forces to engage targets from the left, and right, from the front, up or down, and to move to each of these shooting positions very rapidly without the removal of hands from the weapon. This shortens reaction time and increases accuracy in sudden engagement situations. The weapon system can be triggered completely from behind cover."[4]

Urban Sniping Implications

The use of remote sniper systems like the trench periscope rifle, Krummer Lauf, and Corner Shot give the urban sniper a lot of options. A benefit of using such a device is it reduces a sniper's physical profile. When using one of these devices, the sniper does not expose their head, their face, or any other part of their body when making their shot. As long as the shooter stays behind cover, they do not even have to camouflage themselves. All they have to do is camouflage their weapon, which is a much easier task. Consequently, enemy forces will have a difficult time observing the sniper and their unobtrusive weapon.

Even more important for the sniper is their new found immunity to counter-sniper efforts. The best an opposing counter-sniper team could do against a weapon like the Corner Shot is to shoot the weapon itself, which is a very small object. But the shooter has nothing to fear. Because the shooter is protected by remaining behind cover like the corner of a building, a sniper can aim their weapon at a target, while under direct fire from opposing counter-sniper teams, and still make their shot undisturbed. Opposing counter-sniper teams armed with high-powered rifles are a nuisance at best.

Let us compare the three designs and see how they measure up. The grandfather of remote sniping, the original trench periscope rifle, is still a valid concept. Gun enthusi-

---

4 Shuman, *New Weapon System Helps Engage Targets Lurking "Around the Corner".*

asts have made modern reproductions of the original design (all the necessary materials are readily available and cheap) and have proven they can hit man-size targets at 300 meters and beyond. But, the system's limitations have to be taken into consideration. The trench periscope rifle frame is bulky, not very concealable, and accuracy suffers at distance. A shooter firing the same rifle the conventional way, without the trench periscope frame, can hit targets at two and three times the distance because the weapon is more stable, easier to control, and the shooter has a better sight picture when they look through their scope with the naked eye. However, if the shooter is in an urban environment with close ranges, the system works fine.

The Krummer Lauf design does not have to die either as a gunsmith could engineer a similar one. We can guess a modern version Krummer Lauf would only be good for close range, a hundred meters or less, because of the inherent limitations of firing a bullet through a curved barrel. Any bullet propelled at high velocities through other than a straight barrel suffers from bullet instability and yaw. On the positive side, a Krummer Lauf device is small, may only weigh a pound or two, and is therefore concealable.

The Corner Shot is by far the device of choice among the three. The sighting mechanism, which is used in conjunction with the LCD screen on the Corner Shot, is far superior to other two, making sight alignment and a good sight picture easier to attain. Also, since the Corner Shot frame mimics a traditional rifle with its shoulder stock, the shooter can hold the weapon more securely and make more accurate shots at distance. Accuracy will still suffer because there is some slop in the weapon that is created between the weapon and the Corner Shot frame itself. A shooter will still get a better sight picture and sight alignment if they can sight their weapon with the naked eye. And one must always consider price and availability. The average person is unable to afford the Corner Shot that is priced up to $5,000.00 a model. Plus, it is a controlled item and not easy to get a hold of. In contrast, an old-school trench periscope can be built in a day in your garage and costs almost nothing.

Rise of the Robots

Are the trench periscope rifle, Krummer Lauf, and Corner Shot really remote weapon systems? After all, the firer is still physically connected to the weapon system and must control it in some manner. However, modern man has produced truly remote weapon systems requiring no human contact with the weapon system (we mentioned the MG-34 Rundumsfeuer previously, but that was vehicle mounted). The origins of these weapons are diverse and can be traced in some form to military explosive ordnance disposal (EOD) research, competitive bench rest shooters, and first person shooter video games.

An EOD technician's primary goal is to deal with explosives as remotely as possible. One of the leaders in modern EOD methodology has been the British due in part to their experience in dealing with unexploded ordnance (UXO) when they were bombed by Germany in World War II. Then, following the war, the British dealt with increasingly clever and deadly improvised explosive devices (IEDs) set by the Irish Republican Army (IRA) in their decades-long guerrilla war spanning from the 1960s to the 1990s. It was during Britain's counter-insurgency campaign in Northern Ireland that the first remote control vehicles (RCVs) were used to assist in the removal of IEDs

Corner Shot

Israeli commandos practice vehicle entry techniques using the corner shot to look inside, which would otherwise be impossible.

set by the IRA.

Since then, several countries, to include the United States and Israel, have developed RCVs used by both police and military forces to combat IEDs. For decades, security forces all over the world have used sniper rifles to target UXO and IEDs with long range accurate fire in order to detonate them from a safe distance. Why try and defuse a 250-pound aerial bomb up close when you can shoot it with a .50 caliber sniper from a hundred meters away? With the advent of modern technology, various manufacturers have created RCVs with rifles and shotguns mounted to them so EOD personnel can fire at UXO and IEDs from the safety of a remote location. This combination of RCV and weapon resulted in the ability to remotely control and fire a weapon system without any physical contact with the weapon. In this case, the shooter uses a joystick and a computer to maneuver the RCV and fire the weapon.

Precision Remotes T-2

One of the more popular and effective modern remote sniping systems to evolve from these rather humble roots is the The TRAP (Telepresent Rapid Aiming Platform) T-2 made by Precision Remotes, Inc. The T-2 is a lightweight (23 pounds) weapons platform, with tilt and pan capabilities, that can accommodate a variety of 7.62 mm semi-automatic sniper weapon systems. This remote weapons platform can accommodate both traditional visible light and thermal imaging cameras for employment day and night. Once a sniper weapon is fitted to the T-2, it is remotely controlled from a separate control station. Therefore, a person can control and fire the weapon from a location physically separate from the sniper weapon itself.

A robotic weapons platform like the T-2 has advantages over a human sniper. First, the weapon is not adversely affected by human contact like poor breath control, eye fatigue, trigger jerk, or a poor cheek-stock weld. With the absence of human contact, the robot sniper can shoot more accurately at distance since the biggest element of poor shot placement at long ranges is human error. From a tactical perspective, the use of an automated sniper platform can make most counter-sniper efforts irrelevant. With a robot, one does not have to worry about the shooter getting hurt, wounded, blown up, or knocked unconscious from an artillery barrage, an air strike, or an enemy sniper team. All one has to worry about is the cost of replacing the platform if it gets destroyed or captured.

There are disadvantages with an automated platform, like expense. Additionally, a robot is a large, heavy device, and although it may be smaller than a human, it cannot crawl under a car on its belly, it cannot stealthily climb a flight of stairs, and it cannot jump out of a window. The T-2 is only appropriate for overt military operations because of its price, limited availability (sales are tightly controlled, it is available to law enforcement and government organizations only), and its inherent limitations as a machine. A machine cannot judge the wind, it cannot read a mirage, and it cannot instantly make all the fine motor adjustments a human shooter can in order to adapt to a changing environment. To date, the human being is still the most sophisticated and versatile weapons platform on the planet.

Internet Sniping

The 1997 film *The Jackal*, a takeoff of the original movie *The Day of the Jackal*, shows how one would produce their own remote control weapon system without the help of a large corporation or funding by a government. In this movie, Bruce Willis is the Jackal and he has been hired to kill the First Lady. Willis in turn hires a techno-geek (played by Jack Black) to produce a weapons platform for him. Black designs a system armed with a modified Barrett .50 caliber rifle, which is controlled remotely from a laptop. After Willis is satisfied the remote weapon system works properly, he kills Black to cover his tracks and keep Black from talking about the Jackal or his creation.

When the day comes to kill the First Lady, Willis has his weapon system set up in the back of a minivan, legally parked along the street and hidden in a sea of cars. Since the minivan blends into the urban environment and its tinted windows conceal the weapon, it proves to be the perfect firing platform. When it is time for Willis to make his shot, he shoots through the window of the minivan. Since the .50 caliber rifle rounds are so big and heavy, they shoot through the thin glass with very little deviation off their flight path. Also, the first bullet shatters the glass and the subsequent bullets fly through the air with no deviation at all. While Willis' assassination attempt fails, he is able to make a clean getaway because his remote system enables him to be positioned away from the minivan, which draws everybody's attention.

Clearly, the technology for remote sniping is out there, but is it so sophisticated only a large company with an equally large budget can afford to produce one? Does a more affordable, more concealable system only exist in Hollywood movies? The answer is no. In fact, John Lockwood, a Texas entrepreneur, created his own internet hunting company in 2004. Lockwood's idea was to build an inexpensive weapon platform with off-the-shelf technology, which could be controlled via the internet. Then, Lockwood sold hunting trips on his game preserve to people who were either handicapped or lived in a different country and were unable to go hunting. Basically,

Precision Remotes' T-2

photo by Precision Remotes, Inc

a person would log onto Lockwood's internet site, *www.live-shot.com*, get control of a remote weapon platform equipped with a rifle, locate a wild boar on the screen, press a button, and shoot the animal. Then, Lockwood would ensure the animal was dead, mount the head, and send it to the 'hunter' who made the kill.

Lockwood has since faced fierce criticism from the anti-gun and hunting lobby for creating a 'pay-per-kill' system that removes all the traditional qualities that make hunting a sport. Others fear this internet killing creates a moral slippery slope where, one day, people will be killing other people over the internet, as if they were playing just another first-person shooter game. There was enough of an outrage over Lockwood's new business that to date more than a dozen states have passed legislation banning internet hunting to include Virginia (the first state to do so), Pennsylvania, and Lockwood's home state of Texas. There is also pressure to pass federal legislation, making internet hunting illegal, nationwide.

How was it Lockwood could build a remotely controlled weapon platform without spending millions of dollars as with the T-2? Actually, it was easy. First, he constructed a simple frame to hold the rifle. Then, he mounted a webcam on the rifle so the internet hunter could see what they were shooting at. Next, he connected a car door actuator to the trigger so when a button on the computer was pushed, the trigger was pulled by the actuator. Lockwood also constructed a motorized tilt pan unit so the rifle could be directed at its prey. Overall, Lockwood spent an estimated $20,000 designing this system. The only problem - a minor one - was the camera only showed fifteen frames per second, causing some lag time for the shooter at the other end of the connection.

The implications of remote sniping through the internet are enormous. This type of methodology enables an organization to covertly emplace a weapon system and then control and fire it from a separate location. The shooter could be down the street in the back of a van, they could be across town in a rented apartment, or they could be in an entirely different country, thousands of miles away. In order to ensure operational security, a team could be designated just to set the weapon up so they had no idea who they were setting the system up for. Or, in another scenario, a shooter could set up the system in an apartment and then fly out of the country and conduct the actual sniping attack days or weeks later. Anyone can get pan/tilt units, webcams, actuators, and laptops and they can be purchased anonymously over the internet or in pawn shops.

Imagine if security forces discovered and captured a remote sniper system, what are they going to do? Who are they going to arrest? Who are they going to interrogate? Remote sniping not only makes the shooter safe from enemy counter-sniper measures, it creates an enormous forensic gulf, which security forces would have to try and bridge. A drawback to a remote sniping system is it is not very concealable and the organization using them must be prepared to lose the weapon system in the course of their operations. Another consideration is such a sniper system is exotic and would raise eyebrows. Any illegal movement using such a system would quickly get a reputation and would be placed high on the security forces' list, receiving extra scrutiny.

Back to Benchresters and 'Dumb' Sniping

Perhaps what the guerrilla sniper really needs is the ability to remotely fire a weapon, not the ability to control it from afar, which entails too large of a compromising signature. Where do we look for a remotely fired weapon that does not require software patches, computer servers, and wireless connections? One place to start is with the simple gun rest (slightly different versions are referred to as a gun vise). Gun rests are used for a variety of reasons, like holding a weapon steady so it can be cleaned or gunsmithed and for holding a weapon steady as it is fired to test its inherent accuracy. Scores of companies produce a wide variety of rests and vises selling as cheaply as fifty dollars depending on the model.

The beauty of a gun rest is it holds the weapon absolutely steady so there is no human interference. Companies even manufacturer remote devices intended to be used in conjunction with the gun rest and that pull the weapon's trigger so there is no human error introduced into the process. This way, a person checking out the inherent accuracy of the weapon can be sure their weapon is shooting true. Some gun rests are even manufactured with a built in recoil system so subsequent shots can be fired with continued accuracy. Importantly, it is quite simple to rig the trigger to fire electrically, meaning a cell phone or a car door opener could be used to initiate the trigger pull.

Since a weapon secured in a gun rest can be fired remotely, a weapon could be sighted in on a target or an object and then fired by an observer when a target moves in front of the weapon. Guerrilla organizations all over the world use this simple aiming principle to detonate IEDs. If an organization wants to detonate a buried mortar shell against a moving car, they bury the shell in front of a telephone pole and arm it with an electric firing device connected to a receiver from an automatic garage door opening system. When a car passes in front of the pole, they press the garage door opener which in turn makes an electric connection and detonates the mortar shell. The same principle can be used with a remote weapon system where a gun is sighted on a target like a mail box. When an enemy soldier walks in front of the mailbox, the gun is fired remotely, striking the soldier. Since a rifle or pistol and the corresponding gun rest is such a small object, they can be hidden in the trunk of a car, in a closet, or any number of small enclosed spaces found in a city.

Rifle on a Hyskore Gun Rest

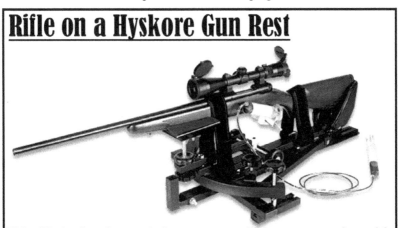

This rifle is placed securely in a gun rest which comes complete with a hydraulic device for pulling the trigger. A remote trigger system could be easily affixed, allowing this rifle to be fired remotely from a distance with a cell phone, pager, or car door opener.

Does one need to use a complete rifle or pistol to get the job done? Could one scale the system down even smaller so it is more concealable and has a smaller signature? Yes. All one needs to do is look to the sport of competitive bench rest shooting and its 'unlimited class'. In the unlimited class, shooters can use any type of weapon system they want to make the most accurate shot. Shooters discovered that by bolting the gun to a small platform, they can remove any 'play' in their weapon system. Since the gun is bolted to a platform, they do not need the stock anymore so they remove it. The resulting weapon is nothing more than a barrel, receiver, and trigger and is referred to as a 'rail gun'. Since these rail guns do not have a stock, they are small, about half the size of a normal gun. Also, they are the most accurate guns in existence because of the lack of human contact when fired.

From the perspective of the guerrilla sniper, a rail gun is the perfect design for remote sniping. It is small, easy to make, cheap, and does not raise any eyebrows when acquiring parts for the system. A pistol rail gun is so small it could fit in something like a tissue box or a purse and could then be fired from within these concealment devices. A rifle rail gun is small enough it could fit under the hood of a car or fired from a concealment device like a gym bag. We are talking guerrilla sniping theory here, but could this actually be done and has anyone already done this?

The Iraqi Insurgent Sniper Juba

The German magazine *Spiegel* aired a televised documentary in 2006 on Juba revealing a new Iraqi insurgent urban guerrilla sniper methodology. In this documentary, an insurgent propaganda video is shown, detailing Juba's tactics. The first thing the viewer saw was an immaculate, well-oiled AK-47 rifle. On the end of the rifle was a suppressor. The insurgent in the video - you never saw their face - demonstrated the effectiveness of the suppressor by firing it at a target in their backyard. The suppressor was quiet and one could hardly hear the weapon firing at all. In fact, the moving of the action of the weapon itself was as loud as the suppressed gunshots.

A closer look at the rifle revealed a short stock, which protruded only about six inches from the rear of the rifle's receiver. This specially designed stock reduced the overall length of the rifle, making it easier to maneuver in confined spaces, like inside a vehicle. Mounted on the rifle was a civilian scope, not the usual mass-produced Soviet variety. With this configuration, the insurgent sniper had the ability to fire a quiet shot, at a target several hundred meters away, from a relatively enclosed space. While these modifications revealed an experienced, savvy sniper, it showed nothing new. However, the insurgent video did not stop there. The video then showed the weapon being placed in a small, lightweight metal frame. The weapon sat perfectly secure in this frame which could be moved to point the rifle in any desired direction. Then, a small metal piece was attached to the trigger so the weapon could be fired mechanically.

This fabrication had several implications. First, this meant the shooter could set up this weapon in the trunk of a car or the back of the van, or even in a building. The shooter could sight in the weapon on their target, but did not actually have to get down behind the weapon to fire it. As a result, a sniper could sit in the front of a car facing forward and pull the trigger mechanically, firing the rifle at a target located to the rear of the vehicle. Furthermore, the rifle in the frame could be easily hidden in a specially designed box of some sort.

If we take this one step further, the weapon could also be fired remotely, by radio control from a separate location. A shooter could set the weapon up in the trunk of a car, with a small hole cut in the back of it, and line the weapon up with a soldier or police officer standing at a checkpoint. The actual firer could be located hundreds of meters from the car, press a button, and remotely fire the weapon, hitting their target. The counter-forensic implications of this remote methodology are enormous. In this manner, the person remotely firing the weapon would have no gunshot residue on them and would thus be physically and forensically separated from the attack, making investigative efforts difficult. The Iraqi insurgents have taken a nearly century-old idea, modified it using modern accessories like a good suppressor, a modern scope, and an after-market stock, and have created a modern, remotely fired sniping weapon.

Sniping Evolution

The art of remote sniping is still in its infancy. The world's militaries have yet to take the idea of remote sniping seriously and most guerrilla movements are not sophisticated enough or educated in the field to make it a common tactic. In fact, the only movement we have seen attempt the art of remote sniping is the Iraqi insurgency. However, John Lockwood and his internet hunting venture show us just how easy it is to create an effective, truly remote sniping system. It is possible a movement like the Iraqi insurgency will seize on sniper tactics like the ones presented by Lockwood and Juba to protect themselves forensically and to defeat increasingly effective counter-sniper methods and technologies. Just as other resistance movements in Afghanistan and Lebanon seized on the Iraqi insurgents' innovative use of IEDs and car bombs, they too may copy more suitable guerrilla sniping tactics.

The battle between sniper and counter-sniper has a long history and is always changing. There has truly been an evolution in the art of sniping and the responses to it – sniper Darwinism if you will. Both sides of the same coin have continued to

A Bench Rest "Rail Gun"

Note how this gun is nothing more than a barrel, an action, and a scope bolted to a moveable platform.

evolve since the sniper is always trying to learn new and effective tactics and, in turn, the counter-sniper is continually coming up with creative ways to thwart the threat of the lone gunman. This deadly game is never stagnant and is always changing. The sniper/counter-sniper methods described in this chapter and this book may be outdated in ten years or even next month. However, the unrelenting drive to learn new tactics and exploit new technologies will keep the sniper and counter-sniper evolving far into the future.

Chapter 23

Martyr's Square

Kataeb Party Offices, Beirut, Lebanon – November 23, Early Morning

The men sat stone-faced around the circumference of a beautiful maple table. The room was a 'whose who' of security officials for the Kataeb Party. Two days earlier, Pierre Amine Gemayel - the Minister of Industry and a leading member of the Party – was assassinated in broad daylight in downtown Beirut. Now, the assembled security leadership waited for Camille, the head of the Kataeb Security Council. After ten minutes, the door swung open and Camille walked in. He had on his trademark light-gray suit with a white, open-collared shirt.

"Thank you for waiting, Gentlemen, I was delayed in traffic."

Two large men in cheap suits shut the door behind Camille. This was a closed-door conference and Camille's bodyguards would remain in the hallway. Camille sat down at the only open leather chair and drank deeply from the cold glass of water set in front of him.

"Okay, Fuad, tell us what happened," Camille started. Men in their profession got right to the point.

"As you know, Pierre and his driver were assassinated as they drove to work. They were in the Jdeideh neighborhood. According to reports, their car was run off the road by a group of men in ski-masks driving a Honda CRV. The windows of the car were tinted so no one could see in." Fuad was responsible for the security of Pierre Gemayel and his immediate family. Right now his head was throbbing from the bottle of Kentucky Bourbon he had downed the night before.

"Has anyone found the car?" Camille asked.

"Nothing yet. We questioned some local vendors and got a general description of the assassins. They said that they looked about the same height and weight because they all wore black ski-masks and dark clothes. I'm guessing this was intentional so that they all looked the same. We're scrubbing the local car dealers and rental agencies to see who might have that type and model of Honda, but they're pretty common. If they're smart they'll burn it and dump it somewhere in the south."

"I'm not asking if their smart, Fuad, I'm asking what we know." Fuad's face turned red at Camille's barb. Camille was more than a little annoyed. It was Fuad's job to keep Pierre alive and he obviously didn't do that. Plus, Camille knew that Fuad, with his jet black hair, athletic build, and striking good looks, spent as much time chasing women as he did doing his job. Even though Pierre refused to travel with a large contingent of bodyguards, Fuad knew no one else could take the blame for his death. After all, it was no mystery any number of people wanted to kill someone in the Gemayel family. Pierre's uncle, Bachir Gemayal, was murdered back in 1982, soon after he was elected president of Lebanon. Fuad cleared his throat and continued.

"There were about a hundred 9 mm shell casings at the scene of the shooting. The killers most likely used suppressed Heckler and Koch MP5's for the attack. They're plentiful with the arms dealers and hard to trace. We'll canvas the usual arms dealers and see what we find."

"Fuad, I want you to put a team of your men with the police and focus on the evidence that we do have to figure out who actually pulled the triggers. If anyone at police headquarters has a problem with that, have the chief give me a call and I'll clear it up for them." They had enough contacts and family members on the force that it shouldn't be a problem. But, Camille wanted to make it clear he wasn't playing games. Maybe Fuad could at least get this assignment right. "The next question: who was behind this?"

"Someone wants us to think it's Syria," William noted. William was head of intelligence for the Gemayel family. "The people who supposedly did this called in to a newspaper and said that they were the 'Fighters for the Unity and Liberty of Greater Syria.' But I think that's bullshit."

"Well there's one group who benefits....Hezbollah." A low murmur broke out around the table. Camille just named the one group on everyone's mind. Hezbollah - the Party of God - was formed after Israel's 1982 invasion of Southern Lebanon. Hezbollah grew into a major power player since its birth only two decades prior and the party was influential down south. Hell, Hezbollah owned southern Lebanon. Everyone knew that. The Gemayel family and their men never went too far south.

"Well," William interjected, "they're a likely candidate. We all know Hezbollah's status skyrocketed with the Israeli withdrawal in 2000. They have solidified their political influence since then by joining the parliament. They control ten percent of the seats now and one-fifth of the municipalities."

"This summer certainly didn't help us any," Dori noted. Dori was special advisor to Camille and handled 'special projects'. "Hassan Nasrallah thinks he can get away with anything now."

"Hmmm." Camille nodded his head in agreement. Just that summer, only months before Pierre's assassination, Hezbollah fought a short but vicious war with Israel. This now-famous 'July War', fought from July 12 until August 14, brought Hezbollah even more notoriety when Israel agreed to a cease-fire and withdrew its troops.

"Hezbollah would like us under their boot as much as Syria would," Dori spit out, "Are we supposed to sit here and let our families get killed, one by one, and do nothing as the Christians get squeezed out of our own country? We'll be swimming across the goddamned Mediterranean in ten years. Maybe we can all live on Crete. Or Malta."

"No, Dori, we will not do 'nothing', but we will be smart about whatever we do." Camille assured him. "Gentlemen if you would excuse us, I need to speak with William and Dori." The others stood up and filed out into the hallway. "Okay, what we're about to talk about stays in this room with us three."

"Yes," William agreed.

"Of course," Dori echoed.

"The family has made a decision to take action. The decision has been made to get rid of Nasrallah."

"You can't be serious!" William exclaimed in disbelief, "Do you want another civil war? One we can't win?"

"No we don't, but we won't have the leading members of the Kataeb Party killed in broad daylight. The other parties, the Sunnis and Shiites, can smell weakness. They can smell it like a sickness. Weakness is death. Either we show them we're not weak or we get pushed to the side politically, socially, religiously, and militarily."

"Well, what do you want from me?" William might disagree, but it wasn't his decision to make. He got paid to take orders.

"I want you to start collecting information on Nasrallah. Dori, you'll execute the action. Make it deniable. Make it untraceable to the Gemayels and the Kataeb Party. If you need outside help, get it. Money is no object. Spare no expense. You have the backing of the family, at the highest levels, to get anything you need."

"Yes, alright. What's the time window for action?"

"As soon as feasible. As long as it's untraceable. If it takes months, it takes months. Are we clear with everything here?"

William and Dori looked at each other and then at Camille and nodded in unison.

Hezbollah Headquarters, Beirut, Lebanon – January 7, Afternoon

Hassan Nasrallah sat with his legs crossed on an ornate silk carpet, sipping hot tea. Around him were the other members of the Shura Council. They were discussing the current situation: the Christians and Sunnis didn't want to give up their traditional status in Lebanese politics, while Hezbollah was determined to rewrite Lebanon's political map. Hezbollah intended to continue their pressure on the government until the Party of God had a political stranglehold on Southern Lebanon and the eastern Bekaa Valley. Hezbollah didn't want a civil war, but the threat of civil war could be very useful.

"We must keep up the pressure on the government using all available means. Every avenue should be pursued and looked into," Nasrallah said after finishing off his tea. "It would be wise to use our latest victory as a show of strength. A public demonstration would do much for the organization."

"Yes, a display of Hezbollah's popularity and numbers would indicate to the government our political strength." Sheik Amin agreed whole-heartedly. Sheik Amin was long a vocal supporter of popular means to extract concessions from their political opponents.

"What better date to show our political unity than a celebration on the first anniversary of our great victory." Nasrallah, as Secretary General of Hezbollah, always had a sense for combining public spectacle with political expediency.

"A large gathering of our supporters would show not only Lebanon, but the entire region, our vitality as a movement," Sheik al-Mussawi stated matter of factly. Al-Mussawi, with his gray beard and receding hairline, was the eldest member of the council. "It is important to show the world that we have recovered from the July War and that we are spiritually unbroken."

Nasrallah stared thoughtfully at the wall, squinting through his prescription glasses. "What do you think, Imad?"

"Anytime we organize a large public rally, our enemies will have a chance to exploit the confusion. Absolute security cannot be guaranteed in such a situation." Imad had been a member of Hezbollah from the very beginning and had worked his way up the ranks until he was now head of security for the organization. Imad had masterminded such prominent operations like the car bombing of the Americans' Beirut barracks in 1983, the attack on the U.S. Embassy in 1984, the kidnapping of four Soviet officials in 1985, and scores of other operations of every description from plane-jackings and hostage-taking to assassinations and high-risk raids. Imad was wanted by every Western government on the planet and therefore had impeccable credentials with the Shura Council.

"It is worth the risks. Hezbollah will not hide from its enemies like a milk snake hiding from the gardener. I will speak to the gathered followers of Hezbollah on August 14 and show them our will power just as they show us their commitment. We will hold our rally at the Martyr's Square in the very heart of the capital. Lebanon and Israel will see our strength and see our fearlessness."

Imad nodded his head in agreement. He had a large task ahead of him, but he would have the help of the security battalion he personally trained. Allah would look over Hezbollah and so would Imad's gun-toting security guards.

A Cafe, Marseille, France – March 24, Lunch Time

Jacques and Dori sat at a busy sidewalk cafe with a wide view of the water. The temperature was a comfortable sixty degrees as a mild breeze blew in from the perennially warm waters of the Mediterranean. They just finished a satisfying meal of scrambled eggs, warm croissants, and reasonably priced wine. Dori leaned closer to Jacques.

"Well, I must say you come highly recommended in the circles that we travel."

Jacques smiled pleasantly as he eyed the surrounding terrain. Jacques wasn't going to show his cards until he knew what the Lebanese was going to put on the table. He was sure the Lebanese was legitimate because not just anyone knew what Jacques did for a living or knew how to find him. Nonetheless, Jacques searched the Lebanese in the men's room to ensure he wasn't wearing a wire. Jacques then whispered quietly in his ear, "we will refer to Lebanon as 'the park', to the intended target as 'the traffic' and to one hundred thousand Euros as 'apples'."

The Lebanese seemed reassured Jacques was so security conscious. Once they got to the table, Jacques made the Lebanese take the battery out of his cell phone, asked him to put his watch in his pocket, and then placed a small pocket radio on the table and turned it on for background noise.

. "Well, going to the park won't be easy or cheap," Jacques began. If the Lebanese couldn't afford his services, it was best to figure this out first.

"Yes, I know. That won't be a problem."

"How bad is the traffic at the park?"

"It's a real problem."

"Well, I can think of several traffic problems that are bigger than others." Jacques knew about Lebanese politics and knew Dori was representing the Christian Kataeb. The target could be from several problem groups: Syria, Hezbollah, the Amal Shiite Group, or even a rival Christian party.

"The traffic is worse at the southern entrance to the park," Dori advised.

"Hmmmm. A very big problem indeed." The Lebanese was definitely talking about Hezbollah. But who in Hezbollah? "Who's causing this traffic problem? I can think of one in particular who can redirect all this traffic at will."

"Yes, that's the problem." Dori knew exactly who the Frenchman was referring to. Jacques thought the Lebanese must be out of his mind.

"There will have to be quite a few apples at the park to make all the traffic worth while," Jacques grinned. The Lebanese had to know hiring someone to kill the head of Hezbollah wouldn't come cheap. Suicide missions never came for free.

"Would three apples be worth it?" Dori threw out a ballpark figure.

"Three apples up front to get the ball rolling. And three apples after the park."

"That's a lot of apples my friend."

"Yes, but if you think the traffic is worth anything less, good luck to you."

"Hmmmm." Dori thought aloud for a second. 600,000 euros was nothing to laugh at. Dori could hire an entire battalion of militia for that much money...for ten years.

"If you want to get some wet-behind-the-ears amateur, go ahead. There are plenty of clowns in your neighborhood to screw it up for you." If the Lebanese thought he could kill Nasrallah by pinching pennies, he was mistaken. But, Jacques knew the Lebanese wouldn't be here if they could do the job themselves. The Christian militias were as ineffective as the rest of the ragtag Sunni and Shiite mobs plaguing Lebanon. Jacques worked in Beirut before when he was in the military and he knew first hand the unsophisticated antics of the various militias.

"No, no. You are right. Six apples is good."

"Okay, we'll meet in three days, at the same time, at the main entrance of Fort Saint Nicholas at the Old Port. Do you know where that is?"

"I heard of it. I can find it." Dori went to school in Paris for four years and spoke French fluently. He could find anything in the country.

"We'll arrange the specifics of my consulting fee then. Be prepared to transfer the apples at that time."

"Until then." Jacques left a twenty Euro note on the table, grabbed his pocket radio, and walked away from the docks, towards the heart of the old city.

Kataeb Party Offices, Beirut, Lebanon – April 4, Late Afternoon

Camille was still on the phone, wearing his ubiquitous gray suit, when William knocked on the door, then entered. Camille motioned him to sit down. William rarely wore a full suit like Camille because he thought it attracted too much attention. William preferred to wear an inexpensive sports coat, a fifty dollar watch, a polo shirt, and either slacks or jeans, depending on the company. In the world of intelligence, it paid to blend with one's surroundings. At five feet eight inches tall and a healthy 180 pounds, William certainly didn't attract any undue attention. He could either be a Taxi driver or a store owner. Only the Walther P99 pistol, secured in a leather holster in the small of his back, gave any indication to his real trade.

"Well, William, what do we have?' Camille asked as he hung up the phone.

"Hezbollah is planning a rally this summer in Beirut to show their strength. We don't know the exact date yet or the exact location. But as the rally gets closer, we'll get it. They can't keep the lid on something that big for long."

"Agreed. Imad is nothing if not careful." Camille and William both knew who Imad was because they tried to kill him before. Not many people were in the game as long as Imad. This longevity was no small feat seeing as how Israel would love to find out where Imad was at any given time. Jerusalem had a GPS-guided bomb with Imad's name on it if they could just find the right address to send it to.

"Dori made contact with the Frenchman. He's a contract killer, a professional shooter. He did that job in Algeria and..."

"Oh really?" Camille interrupted, "that was a high-risk job if there ever was one."

They were referring to the recent guerrilla war in Algeria. Fighting flared up in 1991 after the Algerian government cancelled elections when it looked like the Islamic Salvation Front would win handily. A bitter war ensued for the next fifteen years. Jacques was hired to deal with a splinter group called the Salafist Group for Preaching and Combat, which publicly endorsed Al-Qaeda in 2003. Jacques dealt a severe blow to the group when he took out their charismatic leader, getting him with a shot to the head from six hundred meters while the target stood in front of his family at a friend's funeral.

"Yes. He's also done some 'work' for the Afghan government since 9/11. He's costing us a pretty penny."

"I know." Camille looked at it as a long-term investment. All investments carried some sort of risk.

"Dori says he's a real tight-ass about security."

"Well, that's nice for a change," Camille said dryly. "Make sure security is our priority throughout the operation."

"Of course."

Hezbollah's Security Office, Beirut, Lebanon – May 27, Late Morning

Imad had the entire leadership from his security battalion present. The rally was still months away, but it would take that long to prepare for it. The security battalion protected the members of the Shura Council, the Secretary General himself, and defended Hezbollah's headquarters in times of war.

Imad started the discussion. "This is a most serious event, not only for the image of Hezbollah, but because Sayyid Nasrallah will be speaking to the people."

Everyone nodded their heads.

"Mohammad, your section will be responsible for the outer ring of security. You'll establish checkpoints at all the major intersections. Block off whatever roads you can't man effectively. You are the shield against car bombs. Better for them to be stopped at the checkpoints than let them get to the heart of the people."

"I'll come up with a security plan this week and show you the layout. I'll need some equipment like the under-the-car mirrors and barriers." Muhammad had fifty men in his section. He would have to look carefully at the city's roads to control the most crucial intersections.

"Ragheb, your platoons will man the rooftop positions, near Muhammad's check-points, depending on the buildings." Ragheb had five fifteen-man platoons, each with an SA-14 anti-aircraft team, an RPG team, and a machine-gun team.

"Yes. Once I see Muhammad's plan, I'll make my own, so they overlap with each other." SA-14's were always needed because the Israelis preferred to take out lucrative Hezbollah targets with their helicopters armed with anti-tank missiles. The RPG teams could take out armored vehicles down on the streets or a helicopter flying overhead. The machine-gun teams could deal with any civilian vehicles and also target enemy helicopters. Ragheb's positions would be out far enough to provide early warning for the checkpoints.

"Very good, Ragheb. Hassan, you have the close-in security positions, down at the podium and the special seating. Have you gotten the new equipment yet?" Hassan had a forty-man section providing physical security for the speakers and special guests. They acted as a physical barrier to any over-enthusiastic supporters or visible threats from the crowd. Most of them were chosen for their size. Physical intimidation was a valuable trait in a large crowd.

"Yes, sir. I received most of the new equipment last week and will get the rest before August. We'll be ready." Hassan and his men just received fifty new sets of Level IIIA soft body armor vests. Each man was also issued a Glock 17 pistol. Now they were just waiting on the arrival of the ear-piece communication sets. Imad insisted they use the most up-to-date tools.

"Assad, you know your task."

"We just need to make sure we can talk to you during the rally." Assad led a group of twenty men who would dress and act like the rest of the crowd of Hezbollah sup-porters. As they intermingled with the crowd in two-man teams, they would look for any enemy agents and either deal with them on the spot, or call Imad so he could take action and get the Shura out of the danger zone.

"Assad, make sure your cell phones are in working order. We may have to react fast in an emergency." Cell-phones were the quickest, most reliable way to communicate and they were so common they didn't raise any suspicion.

"And Ibrahim, you have the counter-sniper duty with your men." Since Imad had started his career helping the PLO as a sniper, he took a special interest in making sure Ibrahim's section was well-trained and ready for their duties. Imad personally trained Ibrahim and Imad knew he could handle any task.

"We have completed the testing on the new system and will be ready to use it at the celebration." Ibrahim was referring to the acoustic counter-sniper system they just purchased through a contact in Saudi Arabia. Ibrahim would have one group monitor-ing the acoustic sensors and computer, but he would also have three teams of snipers located on the roofs nearest the speaker's podium. These men, armed with Dragunov sniper rifles, binoculars, and radios would keep a sharp eye out for other snipers and threats in the crowd.

Imad would personally command a twenty-man section that would be stationed in a near-by building, out of view of the people. This section was a heavily armed reaction force, ready to take on any unforeseen threats.

"Take this assignment seriously, as Allah is watching you and so is Sayyid Nasral-lah. Allah Akbar!"

"Allah Akbar!" they returned in unison. *God is great.* There was nothing else to say.

Central Airport, Iraklion, Crete – June 8, Early Afternoon

The plane trip from Marseille to the capital of Crete, the largest of the Greek islands, was uneventful. It was easy to get aboard Dori's private plane in France, unnoticed by the airport officials. All Jacques had to do was lie down in the back of Dori's blacked-out limousine and then get on the plane while it was still parked in the hangar. Since no one saw Jacques get on the plane, when they were asked to supply a manifest of those on board, Dori listed himself, the crew chief, and the pilot. Just in case the plane was boarded by French officials, Dori had a smuggler's compartment built into the private bathroom where Jacques could hide if needed.

After four hours of smooth flying, Dori and Jacques were on the ancient island of Crete. When they arrived at Dori's hangar, they got off the plane and into a waiting vehicle. They didn't have to worry about nosy customs officials because the officials at the airport were paid to look the other way. As long as there were no embarrassing incidents associated with Dori while he stayed on the island, he could discretely move one or two people in and out of the airport with no questions asked.

Crete was a major European tourist attraction, with millions of people a year traveling to the beautiful, mountainous island. There was a constant flow of planes flying in and out of the island and privately chartered aircraft, like Dori's, were common. The island also boasted a booming recreational and pleasure boating community. In addition to the legal means of getting in and out of Crete, there were the extralegal ones. Due to Crete's ideal location in the Mediterranean, the island was a minor hub for trafficking illegal drugs and people. All in all, Crete provided the perfect locale for a person to discretely arrive and then depart without anyone from officialdom taking notice.

The next leg of the journey would take a little longer. Dori and Jacques would depart Crete on a private yacht, cross the remainder of the eastern Mediterranean over the course of several days, and arrive at a private dock on the coast of Lebanon. Jacques could have flown commercially to Lebanon with much less hassle. However, an incriminating trail of credit card transactions and receipts could be connected to him. Also, Jacques didn't want to 'burn' one of his assumed identities when he didn't have to. It was a hassle acquiring professional-grade forgeries. This way, Jacques could deny he was ever in the country.

At worst, while in Lebanon, Jacques could be charged with illegal immigration. After all, he didn't carry anything incriminating on his person: no weapons, no plans, nothing. He did have a fake French identification card with him and Dori had prepared for him forged Lebanese papers as well. While in Lebanon, Jacques would be referred to as his Lebanese nom de guerre of 'Abbas'. All the tools Jacques needed for the operation would be acquired in-country. Dori had most of the tools ready from the list Jacques gave him back in March. Soon, they would be in Lebanon and the next phase would begin.

A Safehouse, Jbail, Lebanon – June 10, Late Morning

Jacques and Dori arrived at Jbail as planned. Dori's men were waiting to help dock the yacht. A car was waiting to take them to the safehouse. While they had a secure house to work in, they also had access to a secluded farm just north of the town they could use as needed. Security wasn't an issue this far north because it was a Christian dominated area.

After settling in, Jacques took inventory of the equipment he ordered. First, he looked at the rifle, an Israeli-made Galil AR 7.62 mm assault rifle.

"Dori, where'd the rifle come from?"

"We got it off the body of a Shiite in southern Beirut a year ago."

"Okay, we need to make sure it's 'clean' and can't be connected to your group in any way."

"Yeah, it's clean. Hezbollah probably got it off an Israeli soldier and we took it from them. There's nothing tracing it to us. Weapons get stolen or captured in this country all the time. We couldn't trace them if we wanted to. We got the scope from our own stocks. Untraceable of course."

"Good. We'll have to test fire it at the farm and make sure it's reliable. It looks relatively unused and in good condition."

"Just like you asked for, Abbas," Dori grinned, finding it slightly amusing Jacques was using an Arab name.

"And this suppressor?" Jacques was looking at a BR-Tuote reflex suppressor. He preferred this model of suppressor because it snapped on the Galil with ease and only lengthened the weapon by a couple of inches. It was a quiet, reliable suppressor.

"Brand new. Out of the box. Got if from one of our regular contacts in Europe. No connections to us."

"How about this tilt-pan unit?"

"That was easy. We got it off the black market, paid in cash, with no questions asked. My guy who bought it said he needed it for his camera so he could make home movies with his girlfriend." Dori smiled again. He thought that was pretty funny.

"And the web-cam?" Jacques inspected the camera as he talked.

"Yep, that's an easy one too. From a local vendor in a cash transaction. Latest model. Good optics. Came with the software and everything. Everyone is buying those things around here. We got it near the university. "

"The laptops?" Jacques looked at two Compaq Toughbook laptop computers.

"Bought those two used, but in good shape, from a consignment shop in the capital. About a year old. Cash. No questions asked."

"How's internet service in the capital?"

"It depends on where you're at. All the major hotels have the latest and most of the lines have been repaired since the Israelis bombed them in the summer. You can just plug your laptop in once you're in your room and you're connected. In other areas, people go with satellite service. You may have some lag time, but it's pretty reliable. Or, we can use any one of the coffee shops that specialize in by-the-minute internet service. If we go by satellite, we pay for the service on-line, with a credit card. Totally anonymous."

"I'm guessing these car batteries, power inverter, and automatic car door lock actuator were easy."

"Yup. Our family owns an automobile import-export businesses. We can get any part from any car you need. What's all this stuff for? I mean, I understand the rifle, scope, and silencer, but I don't get the rest."

"Well, Dori, I'm assuming that Hezbollah's security is going to be really tight and that they'll be prepared for a traditional sniper."

"Yes, of course."

"You and I aren't going to be a traditional sniper. We're going to build a remotely controlled sniper rifle that we can control via the internet either from a hundred meters away or a mile away or an entire country away."

Dori looked dumbfounded as he tried to put all the pieces together in his mind.

"Let me help you out, Dori. We're going to mount the rifle, after we modify it, onto a frame and then onto the tilt-pan unit. We're going to sight the web-cam through the scope. We're going to attach the automatic car door actuator to the trigger. We're going to wire the tilt-pan unit, web-cam, and actuator to the laptop. We're going to power all this with the car batteries, if we have to. Then, we're going to network the second laptop to the first one so we can control the rifle remotely. When we have it all connected, we'll be able to sit at the laptop and see what the rifle sees through its scope. We'll be able to tilt and pan the rifle in any direction we want with the arrow keys. And we'll be able to pull the trigger by hitting a specific key on the keyboard."

"Ohhhhh! I see!" It all made sense now to Dori, "Just like a video game."

"Yeah, pretty close to it. Now, we can control the rifle using the remote-control that came with the tilt-pan unit. However, we would have to be about a hundred meters from the unit. It would also be susceptible to jamming and normal city interferences. So, it would be best to have one of your people, with programming skills, come up with a software patch so we can all do it through the computers."

"No problem. I have someone ready from our family waiting to help us. She's completely trustworthy and has her degree in computer science from the American University of Beirut. Pierre Gemayel was her cousin."

"Okay, we'll get started tomorrow. We'll zero the rifle at the farm and then modify it by removing its stock, taking off the pistol grip, and shortening the magazine. Then we can construct the frame. It'll take us a week just to get the system set up. Then, we're going to have to start working in the capital and study the terrain and pick the right spot." Jacques couldn't finalize the plan until he actually walked the streets where the operation would take place.

"Well, let's get a good night night's sleep and get to work in the morning."

"Yeah, see you then, Abbas."

Jacques was glad Dori didn't offer up the usual night of women and booze. *If you're here to kill someone, then spend every iota of mental and physical energy killing that person.*

Safehouse, Beirut, Lebanon - July 17, In the Evening

Jacques and Dori arrived at their safehouse, an apartment located in the south central part of the city where the old Green Line was. It was called the 'Green Line' because of all the trees and bushes that thrived in the no man's land between the warring factions. The safehouse was on the very fringe of the Christian controlled area that was patrolled by the Kataeb militia. The apartment was only a ten minute drive and a twenty-five minute walk from the heart of the Shiite area.

"Well, Dori, this looks like a good place for us."

"The man who owns this building is a Christian and I have two of my undercover men living next door to us for security." Jacques was the shooter, but Dori's family ran this part of town.

"We need to get a feel for the city and see what kind of security Hezbollah has set up here." Jacques walked through the apartment as he talked, inspecting the kitchen and the refrigerator.

"Bring! Bring!" Dori's cell phone rang from inside his jacket.

"Yes. Okay – got it." Dori hung up the phone. "That was William. We got a location for August – Martyr's Square. No exact date yet. One of our other safehouses has a view of the square. We knew such a location would come in handy eventually. It's a popular area for the Shiites to gather."

"Perfect. We'll set up the system in that location. Is it an apartment?"

"Yes. We put one of Pierre's second cousins by marriage there six months ago. He uses a Shiite name, prays at a Shiite mosque, and goes to the university to study for religion. The day we do our operation, he'll go back north and disappear like he was never there." Dori had already called the cousin so that he knew to expect visitors. Jacques wondered to himself how many family members Dori had. They were like the Corsican mob. They had their hands in everything.

"Okay, we'll have to check it out and then start moving the equipment up their piece by piece so no one notices. We can bring it up in food bags, appliance boxes, coolers, or anything else that fits in. We're going to have to hide it in there too."

"Yeah, we're prepared for that. The couch in there is hollowed out, so we can lift up the cushions and store it in there, completely hidden from view."

"First thing we have to do is check out the window we'll be shooting from. What kind of windows are in the apartment?" Jacques wanted to know what kind of tools they would need to modify the window.

"Just the normal windows with panes." Dori's eyes were shut tight as he searched his memory, trying to conjure up an image of the windows in the building.

"So, just like the ones in this apartment?" Jacques knew from experience that no matter where you were in the world, a specific area usually exhibited the same kind of architecture. If a building in one neighborhood had a certain design, a building in another part of the city probably had the same architectural features: the same doors, the same windows, the same roof, etc.

"Yes. Now that I think of it, exactly the same. Are we going to shoot with the window open just a crack?"

"No, standard counter-sniper procedure throughout the world, either here, in Europe, or wherever, is to ensure all windows in the area are closed shut. Because, if a sniper shoots through a plane of glass, the first round will deflect and probably miss the target. Also, the shattered glass will not only be heard, but can be seen from a distance."

"So, if you're saying the window will be shut, but we're not shooting through it, what are we going to do?" Dori didn't understand.

"Here's what we do. We replace the bottom panes of glass with thin, clear plastic. So, from a distance, it looks like normal clear glass. However, when we shoot through it, the rounds punch straight through with no deflection. And, the plastic doesn't shatter – there are just small holes in it from where the bullets go through."

"Ohhhhhh. I see...very clever...I never would have thought of that." Dori was impressed.

"We could do other techniques if we had to, like cut a small hole in the glass and cover it with plastic or even make a gunport by knocking out a small hole in the wall so we don't even have to go through the window. But, since the windows have panes like the ones here in our apartment, that's the best way to go. We can change out the panes of glass with plastic ones quickly and quietly at night. But first, let's go drive by Martyr's Square and the apartment so we can come up with a plan."

"Okay, I'll let my men know that we're leaving."

The Apartment Overlooking Martyr's Square - August 10, After Breakfast

Jacques peered through the side window of the corner apartment. If he looked at an angle, he could see a large part of Martyr's Square. The apartment's location was perfect – it was on the third, top level of the building and its location on the corner gave an excellent view of the surrounding neighborhood.

"This looks good," Jacques commented as he tapped his knuckles on the plastic window panes.

"And we know for sure that the big gathering is on the 14th." Dori had just gotten that from William a day earlier.

"I bet they use that administration building to conduct their preparations for the rally." Jacques was thinking aloud as he surveyed the buildings. "They'll need power for their speakers and microphones, toilets and water, and a place for the party leadership to loiter before the actual speech."

"That one to the south is a Hezbollah party building." Dori agreed with Jacques' educated guess.

"I bet they'll set up the speaker's stand in front of that building. This window gives us a good angle. Even if they set up somewhere near by, we have them covered. It'll be a three-hundred meter shot at least. Maybe three-twenty-five. We'll check the map again to be sure." They had a good aerial map of the city, so estimating distance was no longer an art, but a matter of accurately measuring the distance with a ruler.

"Yeah," Dori nodded in agreement as he looked out the window and guessed the distance on his own.

"Let's get this room set up so we can do a test run when it gets darker." Jacques wanted to make sure all the components of the system were in working order, even though they had tested it in Jbail several times.

"What do we need to do?"

"We're going to move that wardrobe in front of the door so if someone looks in they don't see our system. Also, we're going to attach the drapes on the window to the tip of the suppressor."

"Why's that?" Dori wondered.

"Well, we'll put a piece of wire around the suppressor and secure the drapes there. The drapes will conceal the system from anyone looking in the window from the outside, like counter-sniper teams with binoculars. As we pan the system right or left, the drapes will move with the weapon, keeping it concealed. But, if we pan the system more than a foot to the right or left, the drapes will pull free."

"Why would we pan the system any more than that...we would be shooting the wall."

"You'll see. We're going to have a few surprises set up like a counter-assault package and a counter-forensics package. That's why we brought the explosives. But we won't set up the packages until the night before in case they sweep the rooms before the rally. Tonight, we'll make the stuff we need to conceal our packages."

"Oh, that's why we bought the flag and the five-gallon cooler." Dori was starting to put it all together.

"Let's get to work."

Martyr's Square - August 14, 10:05 a.m.

Jacques and Dori sat in front of the Toughbook. Even though their hotel room was air-conditioned, both were sweating as they peered intently at the screen. They could clearly see the reticles of the scope and the front of the administration building. Outside their fifth-story hotel window, six hundred meters away, they could just see the east end of the square and the crowds of people mobbing it. The apartment where their system was set up was hidden from their view.

The square itself was packed with thousands of Hezbollah supporters dressed in black with bright green headbands. Hundreds of yellow Hezbollah flags hung from the surrounding buildings. Scores of tents were in place, serving refreshments and protecting the crowd from the blistering sun. The air in the square was hot and stale. There was no wind blowing at all. The crowd had begun to gather hours earlier, even though the Secretary General of the party wasn't scheduled to speak until ten.

Imad surveyed the sea of people. He called his lieutenants on his hand-held Motorola radio, verifying that they were in position. All was clear. Imad called inside the administration building and signaled that it was okay for the Secretary General to come outside.

Nasrallah walked through the front door in his flowing robes. As soon as the crowd saw him they began a thunderous chant: *'Hezbollah! Hezbollah! Hezbollah!'* The sound was absolutely deafening as ten thousand voices reverberated off the surrounding buildings. Hassan's burly, armored bodyguards leaned into the crowd, keeping them back from the Secretary General and the members of the Shura Council seated behind him on a modest wooden platform.

Nasrallah strode confidently to the podium and held both arms up in the air, silencing the crowd with a stern look. Nasrallah slowly looked around the square and then called out in a deep voice, *"Allaaaaaaaah Akbar!"* He dragged out the last part of *'Allah'* for dramatic effect. The crowd - hot, sweating, agitated - roared back as one, *"Allaaaaaaaaaah Akbar!"* Then, they chanted with renewed vigor, *"Hezbollah! Hezbollah! Hezbollah!"*

The first 7.62 mm, fully-jacketed, armor-piercing round entered Nasrallah's mouth and blew out the back of his head in a bright red spray that included tiny pieces of his skull and globs of gray brain matter. It was as if he had a watermelon sitting on his shoulders instead of a skull with muscles and sinew and hair. The Secretary General slumped to the pavement like a puppet with his strings cut. The next round struck one of Hassan's bodyguards directly in the chest, piercing his soft body armor, punching through his left lung. Blood oozed out of his chest and mouth. His eyes stared wide open, uncomprehending. The entire square broke into pandemonium. As if on command, the crowd instantly split into a hundred separate mobs as they rushed the

Hezbollah Rally
Beirut, Lebanon

checkpoints in search of cover.

Imad instinctively crouched below a barrier near the podium and called Ibrahim on the radio, "What do you have?"

"Nothing...absolutely nothing! We're looking!" Ibrahim listened to Imad in one ear as he listened to his other radio, which his sniper team leaders were calling.

"What about the counter-sniper system?!"

"I'm checking it...nothing!"

By now, Hassan's men were physically grabbing the members of the Shura Council and manhandling them into the cover of the administration building.

Jacques and Dori watched the chaos through their web-cam. The crowd looked like some giant organism trying to fight its way out of an enclosed space, looking for any opening it could find to squirt out of.

"Goddamned internet lag! It's throwing my shots off!" Jacques wasn't too upset seeing as how his first shot was dead on.

"They're going in the building, through the door, right there!" Dori excitedly jabbed a finger at the screen.

"I'm tracking." Jacques pushed the button and sent another bullet down range, hitting a bodyguard in his lower spine, just below his armor. Jacques was trying to get the council members before they got inside, but the bodyguards were shielding them with their bodies. "I'm going to target the checkpoints and then the crowd." There were only twenty rounds in the magazine, so Jacques had to choose his targets carefully to inflict as much terror as possible with judicially selected targets.

"We got something! The computer says the shooting is coming from one of those corner apartments on the right side, but I can't tell from what floor!" Ibrahim screamed into his walkie-talkie. He knew someone was using a suppressed rifle, because he couldn't hear any gunshots, even as the bodies were dropping. He was still in mental shock. He couldn't believe what he had seen before his eyes. The great leader's head had exploded right in front of Allah and everyone else.

"I heard you! Have your sniper teams cover that part of the building. I'm sending the assault teams in. We'll search each floor until we get the right one." Imad would have his men in the building in a minute...maybe two at the most, depending on how hard it was to fight through the panic-stricken crowd.

"We only have one round left." Jacques panned the gun away from the window, breaking free of the drapes, and towards the doorway inside the room. "When we see the first guy come through the door, we'll start the sequence."

Imad's assault team reached the bottom apartment in a frenzy. They kicked in the door, their AK-47's at the ready. An old lady stood across the room, by the window, scared to death. The assault team swarmed through her two-room apartment.

"We got nothing on the first floor!" Imad announced on the radio to anyone who was listening.

Thirty seconds later they had torn the second apartment apart and were onto the third floor. The first assault team member kicked the door in with his boot and eyed the room wildly, his assault rifle at the ready. Four more gunmen poured in behind him, sweat pouring off their brows. All they saw was well-used furniture and a Hezbollah party flag hanging in the corner of the room. One man kicked in the door to the adjacent bedroom, but fell after running into a wardrobe positioned two feet from the door. The second man stepped over the first and rounded the corner. Just as he cleared the wardrobe, he took a bullet square in the chest, knocking him flat on his back. Two other assaulters blindly fired their assault rifles on full auto, shredding the wardrobe and hammering the room with 7.62 mm bullets.

Jacques and Dori only saw a blur as the first man came around the wardrobe. The assaulter had filled the entire web-cam and scope because he was so close.

"That's it, they found the gun. Here goes the mine." Jacques pushed a button on the Toughbook. This sent a signal to the laptop in the apartment, completing a circuit. The circuit ran from the laptop, through a wire that went under the rug, up along the wall, through a small hole drilled in the adjacent wall, and into a blasting cap secured firmly in a Soviet MON-100 anti-personnel mine. The MON-100 was hanging from a nail in the top left corner of the adjacent room. However, no one in the room could see it because of the Hezbollah flag hanging in front of it. The electric blasting cap detonated the mine's four and a half pounds of explosives in a deafening explosion that hurled four hundred pieces of shrapnel throughout the close confines of the living room, shredding five members of the Hezbollah assault team.

"Now, for the counter-forensics charge." Jacques pressed another key on the Toughbook. A five pound charge of Semtex plastic explosives obliterated the pan-tilt unit, the other laptop, and blew the Galil and its aluminum frame mount to pieces. Simultaneously, a tandem charge ignited and blew a cheap plastic, ten-gallon cooler filled with a mixture of high-octane gasoline and liquid soap - homemade napalm. The entire room burst into a ball of flame, burning alive two men from the assault team, and charring to a blackened crisp the one who had been shot in the chest.

"Okay, we're done here. We'll sit tight for a couple of hours while we erase the hard drive on the laptop. Once we get back to the safehouse, we'll remove the hard drive and destroy it. We might stay here for the night if the streets are still crazy."

"Yeah, we'll stay here until it clears up." Dori, too, didn't want to risk getting stopped and questioned by a Hezbollah patrol.

"They're going to find parts of the Galil, the pan-tilt unit, and the computer, but there won't be much left. Any witnesses from the assault team who saw the complete system are dead. Depending on how long the apartment burns for, they probably won't figure out how the attack took place. Once they count all the bodies, they'll think the shooter got away." Jacques was sure there wouldn't be any incriminating evidence left behind.

Hezbollah Headquarters – August 14, 5:30 p.m.

Imad sat in the headquarters aid station, holding his right arm that was bandaged and in a sling. He was in the hallway when the anti-personnel mine blew. The shrapnel from the blast had gone through the wall of the apartment and into the man standing in front of him. Only Allah had spared him from death. Even though he had a dozen pieces of shrapnel in his arm, he was alive.

The door to the medical room swung open. Ibrahim walked in.

"Are you okay?"

Imad grunted.

"We searched the apartment after the explosion but didn't find much. Part of the third floor collapsed. It'll take a week to sift through the wreckage." Ibrahim looked at Imad's arm. Red stains of blood seeped through the stark white bandages.

"Well, thanks be to Allah, we went through with all of our security precautions," Imad croaked with some satisfaction.

Ibrahim took this as a sarcastic rebuke of not just him, but of all the security sections. Ibrahim tried to understand what happened. "We couldn't see anything, Imad. Even when the shooting started, we didn't hear or see anything. How was this possible? The acoustic system said it might have been that apartment, but it could have been from the other ones further down the same street. Now the General Secretary is dead and we helped cause it."

"Not to worry, Ibrahim, Allah watches over Hezbollah and you and me. You did your job very well and I am proud of you and our fallen comrades."

"What are you talking about, Imad? Are you hallucinating from loss of blood? The Secretary General is dead, fifteen of our men have gone to paradise, and scores of our people were trampled to death in the streets. Are you mad?" Ibrahim couldn't believe what he was hearing.

Imad looked up at Ibrahim, "Are you so sure our great leader is dead, old friend?"

Kataeb Party Offices, Beirut, Lebanon – August 15, 10:00 a.m.

Camille and William sat smugly at the small conference table in Camille's office, sipping hot, sweet tea as they watched the news by the Lebanese Broadcasting Corporation. Yesterday, they had seen live footage of the shooting of Hassan Nasrallah. This footage had been broadcast all over the world. It was on the internet and the major television stations. Over and over again the world saw Nasrallah's head split open like an overripe melon. Several people had actually taken footage of different stages of the mayhem with their cell phone cameras and were posting them everywhere. Of course, the Kataeb Party was one of the first to denounce the assassination as a 'despicable act of murder that had a destabilizing effect on Lebanon and the region.' Hezbollah remained strangely silent since the attack. As Camille and William watched the television, a 'breaking story' flashed.

"What could be any more 'breaking' than the death of Nasrallah?" Camille wondered aloud. Hassan Nasrallah appeared on the screen, surrounded by a ring of reporters and armed guards. Camille's and William's jaws dropped.

"Yesterday, unknown killers tried to assassinate me and silence the Party of God. As you can see, they did not succeed and the representative of Allah is still here. Hezbollah will find the jackals who murdered scores of our people and we will not rest until justice is served. This I can promise you. This is a perfect example of how the current government in Lebanon is incapable of protecting its people, incapable of providing law and order, and incapable of governing this country." Nasrallah stared icily into the camera until the image was cut and the LBC newsman returned.

Camille and William stared at each other in disbelief.

"Are you kidding me?" William managed to get out first.

"Didn't we get him?" Camille exclaimed. "I saw his fat head explode on the TV screen myself!"

"I don't know. Maybe the person we just saw wasn't Nasrallah, maybe someone who looked like him." William's mind worked in overdrive as he analyzed the possibilities.

"Or, maybe that wasn't Nasrallah yesterday, only someone who looked like him!" Camille didn't want to believe it.

"You mean a body double? A goddamned look alike!?!" William was incredulous.

"Why not? That bastard Saddam used a double all the time. And I know Khomeini did too. They duped us!" Camille was incredulous. They had executed a flawless, forensically secure assassination of the wrong person. Hezbollah's counter-sniper measures had bought their Secretary General a new lease on life.

Bibliography
Books

An Infantry Guide to Combat in Built-Up Areas, FM-91-10-1, Appendix J, Counter-ing Urban Snipers.

A Study of Assassination. (No author or date of publication given.)

Chuikov, Vasili I., *The Battle For Stalingrad*, Ballantine Books, New York, 1963.

Cohen, Roger, *Hearts Grown Brutal*, Random House, New York, 1998.

Collins, Aukai, *My Jihad*, Pocket Star Books, New York, 2002.

Collins, Eamon, *Killing Rage*, London: Granta Publications, 1998.

Corrigan, Peter, *Soldier U: SAS, Bandit Country*, Kent: 22 Books, 1995.

Dillon, Martin, *Stone Cold*, London: Hutchinson, 1992.

Dillon, Martin, *The Trigger Men*, Great Britain: Mainstream Publishing Company, 2003.

Dominick, Joseph T., et al, *Crime Scene Investigation*, London: The Reader's Digest Association, Inc., 2004.

Edwards, Don A., *Large Caliber Sniper Threat To U.S. National Command Author ity Figures*, Washington, D.C.: The National War College, 1985.

Falk, John, *Hello To All That*, Picador, New York, 2005.

Fetzer, James H., *Murder in Dealey Plaza: What We Know Now that We Didn't Know Then about the Death of JFK*, Chicago: Catfeet Press, 2000.

Furiati, Claudia, *ZR Rifle: The Plot To Kill Kennedy And Castro*, Melbourne: Ocean Press, 1994.

Geberth, Vernon J., *Practical Homicide Investigation:Tactics, Procedures, and Fo-rensic Techniques, Second Edition*, Boca Raton: CRC Press, 1993.

Geraghty, Tony, *The Irish War-The Hidden Conflict between the IRA and British In-telligence*, Baltimore: The Johns Hopkins University Press, 2000.

Gilbert, Adrian, *Sniper*, St. Martin's Press, New York, 1994.

Glenn, Russell W. (editor), *Capital Preservation: Preparing for Urban Operations in the Twenty-First Century: Proceedings of the RAND Arroyo-TRAQDOC-MCWL-OSD Urban Operations Conference, March 22-23, 2000*, RAND, Santa Monica, CA, 2001.

Grodon, Robert J, *The Killing Of A President: the Complete Photographic Record Of The JSK Assassination, the Conspiracy, And The Cover-Up*, New York: Vi-king Studio Books, 1993.

Harnden, Toby, *Bandit Country: The IRA & South Armagh*, London: Hodder and Stoughton, 1999.

Herman, Douglas, *The Guns of Dallas*, San Diego: Aventine Press, 2005.

Horwitz, Sari, & Ruane, Michael E., *Sniper: Inside the Hunt for the Killers Who Terrorized the Nation*, Ballantine Books, New York, 2003.

Image Of An Assassination: A New Look At The Zapruder Film, MPI Media Group, 1998.

Kapic, Suada, *Guide to Siege of Sarajevo*, FAMA, 1996.

Lavergne, Gary M., *A Sniper in the Tower, The Charles Whitman Murders*, Univer-sity of North Texas Press, Denton, Tx, 1997.

Lonsdale, Mark V., *Sniper Counter-Sniper*, Specialized Tactical Training Unit, Los

Angeles, CA, 2005.

Maass, Peter, *Love Thy Neighbor,* Vintage Books, New York, 1996.

MacStiofain, Sean, *Memoirs of a Revolutionary*, Gordon Cremonisi, 1975.

Mark, Jason, *Death of the Leaping Horseman*, Leaping Horseman Books, Australia, 2003.

Mark, Jason, *Island of Fire*, Leaping Horseman Books, Australia, 2006.

Marighella, Carlos, *Minimanual of the Urban Guerrilla ,* Paladin Press, Boulder, CO 80301, 1985.

McLean, French L., *The Ghetto Men*, Schiffer Publishing, Ltd, Atglen, PA, 2001.

Moloney, Ed, *A Secret History of the IRA,* New York: W. W. Norton & Company, Inc., 2002.

Murphy, Paul J., *The Wolves of Islam, Russia And The Faces Of Chechen Terror*, Brassey's, Inc., Dulles,Virginia, 2004.

Operation Banner: An Analysis of Military Operations in Northern Ireland, England, Ministry of Defense, 2006.

Ottoway, Susan, *She Who Dared: Covert Operations in Northern Ireland with the SAS,* South Yorkshire: LEO COOPER, 1999.

Paulson, Alan C, et. Al, *Silencer History and Performance, Volume One, Sporting and Tactical Silencers*, Boulder: Paladin Press, 1996.

Paulson, Alan C, et. Al, *Silencer History and Performance, Volume Two, CQB, Assault Rifle, and Sniper Technology*, Boulder: Paladin Press, 2002.

Rennie, James, *The Operators: On The Streets With Britain's Most Secret Service*, South Yorkshire: Pen and Swords Book Limited, 2004.

Roberts, Craig, *Kill Zone: A Sniper Looks At Dealey Plaza,* Tulsa: Consolidated Press International, 1994.

Roffman, Howard, *Presumed Guilty,* Associated University Presses, Inc, 1975.

Senich, Peter R., *The Complete Book of U.S. Sniping*, Boulder: Paladin Press, 1988.

Senich, Peter R., *The German Sniper 1914-1945*, Boulder: Paladin Press, 1982.

Shlapak, David & Alan Vick, *Check Six Begins on the Ground*, Monterrey: Rand, 1995.

Simon, Scott, *Pretty Birds*, Random House, 2005.

Stevens, Donald , et all, *Near-Term Options for Improving Security at Los Angeles International Airport,* Rand, Monterrey, 2004.

Wacker, Albrecht, *Sniper on the Eastern Front,* Pen & Sword Military, England, 2005.

Zaitsev, Vassili, *Notes Of A Sniper*, 2826 Press Inc, Los Angles & Las Vegas, 2003.

Articles

Ackerman, Robert K., *Echoes of Chechnya Warfare Resound in Moscow*, Quantico, SIGNAL Magazine, May 2000.

Anastasijevic, Dejan, *The End of The Sniper War, Death In The Eye*, Vreme News Digest Agency No 152, August 22, 1994.

Associated Press, *Bosnian Serb General Goes on Trial at Yugoslav War Crimes Tribunal for Sarajevo Siege*, Published: January 11, 2007

Associated Press, *NATO Forces Seize Terrorist Training Camp in Bosnia*, February 17, 1996.

Backgrounder on Russian Fuel Air Explosives ("Vacuum Bombs"), Human Rights

Watch, February 2000.

Bagrov, Yuri, *Chechen Snipers Halt Russian Troops*, Associated Press, January 20, 2000.

Blandy, C.W., *Chechnya: Two Federal Interventions An Interim Comparison and Assessment*, Conflict Studies Research Center, January 2000.

Bochkayev. S., *White Pantyhose...Black Widows...What's Next?* The Chechen Times, September 14, 2003.

Bogati, Vjera, *Counsel for Bosnian Serb commander describes Sarajevo sniper victims as "accidental victims".* TU No. 253, February 4 - February 9, 2002

Buying Big Guns? No Big Deal, Gunrunner Buys Rifles In U.S. To Equip Guerrilla Army, www.cbsnews.com, March 20, 2005.

Carroll, Rory, *Elusive Sniper Saps US Morale in Baghdad,* www.guardian.co.uk, August 5, 2005.

Colucci, Frank, *Explosive Ordnance Disposal Robots Outfitted With Weapons,* www. nationaldefensemagazine.org, August 2003

Committee or the Collection of Data on Crimes Committed against Humanity and International Law, *Decapitation as a Means of Genocide Over the Serbs in the Former Bosnia and Herzegovina,* No.471/95, August 23,1995, Belgrade.

Czech, Kenneth P., *Weaponry: Krummer Lauf,* www.historynet.com

Foster, Chris, *256th BCT Soldier Survives Sniper Attack,* Media release, 256th Brigade Combat Team, Camp Tigerland, Baghdad, Iraq, APO AE 09326, Release 20050705-1, dated July 5, 2005.

Goldman, Adam, *Feds foil JFK Terror Plot,* Arrest 3, Associated Press.

Gordon, Michael R., *Bold Chechen Rebels Fight the Russian Army on Two Fronts,* New York Times, January 3, 2000.

Gordon, Michael R., *Chechen Rebels Fiercely Attack Russian Forces,* January 6, 2000.

Grau, Lester W. & Charles Q. Cutshaw, *Russian Snipers In the Mountains and Cities of Chechnya,* Infantry Magazine, pages 7-11, Summer 2002.

Harding, Thomas, *Iraqi Insurgents Using Austrian Rifles from Iran,* www.telegraph. co.uk, February 13, 2007.

Human Rights Watch, October 1994, Vol. 6, No. 15, Bosnia-Hercegovina Sarajevo International Criminal Tribunal Indictment, *The Prosecutor of the Tribunal against Stanislav Galic, Dragomir Milosevic,* Case IT-98-29-I.

Jaber, Hala, *The Chilling Toll of Allah's Sniper,* The Sunday Times-World, February 20, 2005, www.timesonline.co.uk.

Jervis, Rick, *More Troops Mean More Targets for Snipers in Iraq,* USA Today, 24 Oct 06.

Koopman, John, *Traveling Through the Lunar Landscape - Poor People Line the Road Asking for a Handout,* The Chronicle, March 25, 2003.

Lichtblau, Eric and Eric Schmitt, *Secret Military Spy Planes Enlisted in Hunt for Sniper,* October 16, 2002, www.nytimes.com.

Lowe, Christian, *Rooftop Execution: NCIS report provides details of sniper deaths,* Marine Corps Times, August 5, 2006.

Montgomery, Michael, *Face of Mercy, Face of Hate,* Minnesota Public Radio.

Mottram, Linda, *Russian Casualties Under-Reported,* The World Today, January 27,

2000.

NATO Forces Kill Sarajevo Sniper, CNN, February 1, 1996.

Novichkov, N.N., Snegovskiy V.Y., Sokolov A.G., Shvarev V.U. *Psycho-physiological Support of Combat Activities of Military Personnel*

Quilty, Jim, '*White Ravens': Speaking Through the Silence*, www.dailystar.com September 27, 2005.

Reynolds, Maura, *Russian Atrocities in Chechnya*, Los Angeles Times, Moscow, September 17, 2000

Russian Armed Forces in the Chechen Conflict: Analysis, Results, Conclusions, Moscow 1995, pg. 42.

Russian General's Body Found, BBC News, January 23, 2000.

Russia Pays Heavily for Gains, The Telegraph, www.viexpo.com

Safrunchek, Ivan, *Russia's Experience of Asymmetrical Warfare*, Updated November 19, 2002, Center For Defense Information.

Russian Troops' Tales of War, BBC News, January 26, 2000.

Sixbey, Mark, *Darkhorse snipers kill insurgent sniper, recover stolen Marine sniper rifle*, Marine Corps Times, June 20, 2006.

Snipers Keep Russians Out of Grozny, The Associated Press, Lkhan-Kala, Russia, January 28, 2000.

Speyer, Arthur L., Appendix C: *The Two Sides of Grozny*, Marine Corps Intelligence Activity, Chechnya: Urban Warfare Lessons Learned.

Suljak, Ante, *Seve Practiced by Shooting Civilians in Sarajevo*,F oreign Affairs,S eptember 12, 2000.

Thomas, Timothy L, & Charles P. O'Hara, *Combat Stress in Chechnya*: "The Equal Opportunity Disorder", first published in Army Medical Department Journal Jan-Mar 2000, fmso.leavenwort.army.mil

Traynor, Ian, *Fighting Phantoms: The Toll Mounts, Russian Hospitals Bear Witness to the Price Moscow's Army is Paying in Chechnya*, The Guardian, December 11, 2001.

United Nations Report, *Study of the Battle and Siege of Sarajevo*, S/1994/674/Add.2 (Vol. II), 27 May 1994)

Vasic, Milos, *The Spiritual State of Siege*, September 26, 1994 Vreme News Digest Agency No 157.

Vickland, Bill, *Fred Cuny: The Lost American*

Vladmirov, Kit, *Valor Medal for Dead OMON Sergeant*, Saint Petersburg Press #101.

Vogel, Steve, *Military Aircraft With Detection Gear To Augment Police*, October 16, 2002, www.washingtonpost.com

War in Chechnya - 1999, news archive, www.aeronautics.ru, January 20, 2000.

Wines, Michael, *Colonel's Trial Puts Russian Justice to Test*, March 8, 2001, www.criminology.fsu.edu

Other Sources

1943: Germans Surrender at Stalingrad, news.bbc.co.uk

www.aarclibrary.org

www.archives.gov/research/jfk/search

www.assassinationresearch.com

The author is a career Special Forces soldier who has served 22 years in the United States Army. He served three tours in Iraq in 2003, 2004, and 2005 where he and his team conducted urban counter-insurgency operations. He also served as an instructor teaching guerrilla warfare tactics at the John F. Kennedy Special Warfare Center and School at Fort Bragg, North Carolina. One of the many subjects he taught Green Beret students was guerrilla sniping. The author holds a Bachelor of Arts in Political Science and History and a Master of Arts in International Relations. He is currently working on another project about modern urban guerrilla warfare.

For any questions, comments, or advice on this work please contact: administration@spartansubmissions.com

CPSIA information can be obtained
at www.ICGtesting.com
Printed in the USA
BVHW081629180521
607638BV00013B/2431